World Communications

A 200-country survey of press, radio, television and film

Gower Press/Unipub/The Unesco Press

First published 1975 by
The Unesco Press,
7 Place de Fontenoy, 75700 Paris, France,
Gower Press Limited,
Epping, Essex, England, and
Unipub, Box 433, New York, NY 10016, USA.

© Unesco 1975

ISBN Gower Press   0 7161 0261 7
ISBN Unipub   0 89059 001 X
ISBN The Unesco Press   92 3 101180 4

LC 74 83488

Set in IBM Press Roman by Preface Ltd., Salisbury, Wilts
and printed in Great Britain by
The University Printing House, Cambridge

CONTENTS

Preface

Compiled after an interval of ten years since the last edition of *World Communications*, this fifth edition contains new or completely revised texts for over 200 countries and territories covering practically every inhabited area of the globe.

In almost all of them during the ten-year lapse, communication coverage has been significantly extended by the technical growth of at least one of the principal media; in many, political, economic and social developments have demanded or dictated changes in the pattern of communication; in certain cases (though a few exceptions remain), information not previously available has come to hand. For these reasons alone, Unesco has considered this new edition warranted.

Public demand in many countries has been a further encouragement. Students, researchers and teachers in institutions of communications studies, journalists, broadcasters and other media professionals, workers in libraries and information centres, offices and administrations have all expressed appreciation of it as a compact source of reference.

The purpose of this, as of previous editions, is to describe the situation of the four principal media (press, radio, television, film) in the various countries and territories of the world, indicating, with statistical support, the general structure, facilities, output, distribution and coverage of each in individual local and national contexts. The chapter structure of earlier editions has therefore been maintained, although technical, economic and organizational developments are beginning to make this categorization a little arbitrary in certain respects. Two additional categories of information newly introduced in this edition are 'Space communications' and 'Professional training and associations'.

SOURCES

This book is based mainly on information supplied regularly to Unesco by governments of member states in reply to the Organization's annual statistical questionnaire on mass media facilities* and to a special supplementary *World Communications* questionnaire. Official reports and publications, technical journals and standard reference works have also been used to supplement these sources.

*This questionnaire elicits official information on newspapers and other periodicals, film and cinema, radio and television broadcasting, to be published annually (along with other data relating to population, education, science and culture) in the *Unesco Statistical Yearbook* which is thus a logical companion and supplement to the present publication.

Information thus obtained is naturally not always complete or up to date, nor is it always expressed in terms or based on criteria that are strictly comparable. Notwithstanding these difficulties, and working on the assumption that a well-founded approximation is better than an over-prudent silence, figures have been given wherever there were fair guarantees of reliability. Less precise or less well authenticated data are, however, qualified in the text by the use of the terms 'approximate', 'estimated', 'reported', etc.

The data cited may generally be considered valid for 1971–2, unless otherwise indicated. Population figures apply to mid-1972 and are estimates published by the Statistical Office of the United Nations

NOMENCLATURE

Grouping and nomenclature of geographical areas have been adopted for convenience of presentation and apply to early 1973. The designations employed and the presentation of the material in this publication do not imply the expression of any opinion whatsoever on the part of the Unesco Secretariat concerning the legal status of any country or territory, or of its authorities, or concerning the delimitations of the frontiers of any country or territory.

DEFINITIONS

Newspapers of general interest are publications which are devoted primarily to recording current events. Specialized papers, such as trade and technical journals, are not regarded as newspapers of general interest.

Daily newspapers are defined as newspapers of general interest published at least four times a week. They may include printed or roneotyped bulletins.

Non-daily newspapers are newspapers of general interest published three times a week or less. Sunday or week-end editions of daily newspapers are included in this category.

Periodicals are publications of general issue, other than general interest newspapers, containing either general or specialized information. Weekly news magazines are included in this category.

Circulation figures are given with the reservation that they may sometimes represent certified circulation, reported circulation, copies printed, copies distributed, copies sold, etc.

Copies per 1000 people, as is sometimes noted in the text, may not always represent real readership since group or family reading, reading aloud, hiring or lending copies, may greatly multiply the actual number of persons exposed to the medium, just as, conversely, partial and cursory reading may reduce the exposure coefficient.

Radio and television receivers are shown where possible as the actual numbers in use, otherwise as the number of receivers licensed or receiver licences, it being understood that one licence may in fact represent more than one receiver.

Television transmitters are usually shown as the total number of transmitters in operation, the numbers of main and auxiliary transmitters being noted separately in the text.

Fixed cinemas (including 16mm, 35mm and larger format) have been used as the basis for calculation of total cinema seating capacities and annual visits per 1000 people, unless otherwise noted in the text.

Introduction

Far more people and a greater percentage of the populations of all countries are receiving information and ideas and being entertained through the mass media – and particularly through radio and television – than ten years ago. There have been marked increases in the numbers of transmitters and receivers in all countries. The figures and the trends indicate that radio and television are reaching larger numbers of people, and in more languages than have been, or ever will be, reached by the daily press which in most countries is developing hardly at all. There has been a notable decrease in most countries in the number of cinema attendances.

Marked progress has been made in the use of electronic transmission of facsimiles and offset printing, communication satellites, simpler lightweight production equipment, video cassettes and distribution of television programmes by multichannel earth cables. These offer technical possibilities for diversifying production and diffusion to serve the interests of differing groups, for providing individuals with greater freedom of choice in what they receive and for improving exchanges between countries. They could be of particular value to many countries in expanding and speeding-up the use of mass communication for social and economic development.

TRENDS AND CONTRASTS

In terms of numbers of titles and circulation per 1000 of the population, it will be seen that the daily press stands more or less where it did ten years ago; it still hardly exists in the countries of Africa. There are, however, in most countries a large number of papers and periodicals appearing several times a week, weekly or monthly which have large, and often increased, circulations. In spite of greatly accelerated means of news transmission by press agencies, and in spite of developments in composition and production, the press is now often outstripped by radio and television as the reporter of current news. Economically, because of increasing costs, particularly of newsprint which is in short supply, loss of advertising revenue to radio and television and the reluctance of the public to pay for a newspaper what it costs, daily newspapers in many countries are constantly in financial difficulties. In more and more countries, they seek to protect themselves by acquiring interests in commercial radio and television organizations. In some countries, notably in Europe, the State gives assistance in various forms to the press. The film shown in public cinemas has lost its place to television as the first medium of mass entertainment in most developed countries, but films are seen by very large audiences through television.

Statistics, however, are not all. There is evidence to suggest that what people read makes a more lasting impression on them than what they hear by radio or see on television, that they still rely on newspapers and periodicals to confirm news and to present views and that millions find a film seen with an audience more satisfying than one seen on a television screen.

The expansion of radio transmission services, the general reduction in the cost of receivers and, above all, the production of cheap transistor receivers which do not depend on mains-supply electricity have introduced new audiences to radio broadcasting. In most countries, including those where television is highly developed, radio broadcasts, mainly of music but with frequent news bulletins, are on the air for most and sometimes all hours of the day and night. The ratio of receivers to population in many countries indicates that numerous families have several receivers so that parents and children, for example, can listen to different programmes. In addition, the installation of receivers in cars has greatly increased radio-listening, particularly of morning and evening news broadcasts. In most developing countries, while transmission services now cover the whole population, audiences are still small, even allowing for spontaneous or organized listening by groups, and they are often largely limited to urban areas.

Television services now exist in many more countries than ten years ago but in most the number of receivers is still small, except for those countries where the services were already highly developed and where the number of receivers per 1000 people is constantly increasing. In around 30 countries of Asia and Africa there are no television services. The difficulties and expense of setting up transmission services over large geographically difficult areas, the lack of mains-supply electricity in rural areas and the high cost of receivers are among factors preventing expansion. In some developing countries, television was introduced and still mainly operates for educational purposes.

If one assumes an average household to consist of four or five persons, the rates of over 200 to 250 per 1000 of the population for daily newspaper circulation and for radio and television receivers would indicate that, in general terms, the whole population of a country is being reached by the medium concerned. On this basis, it seems that such a saturation point has been or is about to be reached for daily newspapers in 30 countries (19 in Europe), for radio in 48 (26 in Europe) and for television in 22 (15 in Europe). Twenty-one countries, 14 in Europe plus Australia, Canada, Cuba, Japan, New Zealand, the USA and the USSR, seem to be at this point for all three media. It is noted that three of these countries – Japan, the USA and the USSR – are among the largest producers of feature films shown in public cinemas. It will also be seen that the five world news agencies are based in four of these countries (France, the UK, the USA and the USSR). The same four countries are the major suppliers of television programmes to other countries.

The contrasts between these countries and the rest of the world are striking. In Africa nine countries and territories have no daily newspapers, only 15 of the others have a daily circulation of more than 10 per 1000 of the population and in none does it exceed 100. In 40 African countries the number of radio receivers is less than 100 per 1000. There are still no television services in 20 countries and in those with television the number of receivers does not exceed 30 per 1000. In Asia, daily newspaper circulation is less than 10 per 1000 in 12 countries, and in only six is it more than 100. The ratio of radio receivers in 17 countries is much less than 100 per 1000, and in only eight is it more than 200. In eight of the countries there are no television services; in 19 the number of receivers is less than 100 per 1000; only in Japan is it more than 200. In seven only of the Spanish-speaking countries of North and South America is daily newspaper circulation more than 100 per 1000. While the number of radio receivers in eight of them is more than 100 per 1000, and in another five more than 300, the number of television receivers is less than 100 per 1000 in 10 countries and in only two is it more than 200. There is no national news agency in 15 countries of Africa, 11 Spanish-speaking countries of North and South America and six Asian countries.

COMMUNICATION SATELLITES

Today, only ten years after the first experimental television transmissions between North America and Europe by means of communication satellite, it is accepted as normal that events like the Olympic Games in Tokyo, a United Nations meeting in New York or men in space are seen as they happen, simultaneously, by hundreds of millions of people in all parts of the world. Daily coverage of the Egypt—Israel war in 1973 was transmitted by both sides via satellites over the Atlantic and Indian Oceans to earth stations which passed it on to television transmitters in North America, Europe and the USSR. In June 1972, cardiologists in Montreal and Lyons conferred for two hours in the first university television discussion by means of satellite channels leased by the Canadian and French television services.

Multinational transmissions and bilateral exchanges are possible on a global scale thanks to the Intelsat and Intersputnik communication satellite systems which exist for the transmission of all types of messages — telephone, telegraph, telex, facsimile and data transfer between computers — as well as radio and television programmes. Intelsat, started by the USA in 1965 and now operated by a consortium of more than 80 countries, comprises satellites in synchronous orbit over the Atlantic, Indian and Pacific Oceans — thus covering the whole globe — and 80 nationally owned earth stations in 60 countries, to and from which signals can be transmitted and which are linked with terrestrial telecommunication networks. Intersputnik, created in 1971 by an agreement between the USSR, the countries of Eastern Europe, Cuba and Mongolia, and open to all countries, is being developed from the Soviet Union's elliptical orbit system, consisting of satellites orbiting the earth every twelve hours with a high arc over the northern hemisphere and 40 earth stations. The system was established to extend radio and television services to vast areas of Siberia and central Asia which could only be reached by terrestrial means with great difficulty and expense. It is likely that the Intersputnik system will eventually comprise synchronous orbit satellites. Simultaneous global diffusion of messages originated by Intelsat or Intersputnik can be achieved by linking national and regional terrestrial networks.

In 1973, Canada started to operate the world's first domestic synchronous orbit satellite system for telecommunication purposes and for the distribution and reception of television programmes, through low-cost earth stations and low-powered transmitters, over vast distant areas of the country. The system is to be developed to cover all but central Canada. Australia, Brazil, India, Indonesia, Japan and the USA are considering the establishment of similar domestic systems as a means of achieving, more quickly and/or at less expense, full and efficient telecommunication services and of expanding education. The countries falling within the European Broadcasting Zone have also, for some years, been studying the establishment of a satellite system to complement the present terrestrial Eurovision network.

In 1974, the first of a new generation of broadcasting satellites was put into orbit. These can transmit television programmes directly to community reception points within a defined area equipped with special antennae. They do not require the very sensitive and expensive receiving terminals on earth needed to pick up and retransmit weak signals from point-to-point communication satellites, nor must the signals pass by terrestrial links to television transmitters for diffusion to receivers in their coverage areas. This development makes it possible to broadcast educational and cultural programmes to rural and remote populations long before this could be achieved by the gradual and slow expansion of terrestrial networks.

The first of these broadcasting satellites was launched by the United States National Aeronautics and Space Administration, to broadcast to four large and remote target areas in the USA. In 1975, it is to be moved to a point over the east coast of Africa to beam programmes for a year to 5000 villages in India, 3000 of which will be reached through terrestrial links and 2000 directly through village community receivers. The Indian authorities will be responsible for the programmes and the reception arrangements. They are planning to implement an operational system to follow the experiment, which would provide direct satellite broadcasting to more than 500 000 villages as well as telecommunication facilities throughout the country. In Brazil, experiments already begun may lead in 1975–6 to the launching of a Brazilian satellite to provide educational television broadcasts directly to schools. Few individual countries have the population and the means that would justify and support the installation of such domestic satellite systems, but studies made for the Arab States, Africa and South America show that technologically it would be possible to develop regional systems in which the participating countries shared the use, the control and the costs.

Looking some, but probably not many, years ahead it is possible to envisage systems using satellites that could broadcast to community receivers throughout the world and later directly to home receivers, first in one or a group of countries, then to any country. It would be possible for the same messages to be transmitted and received instantaneously in all parts of the world. As the technological and economic conditions for this global free flow of information – with all its potentialities – are achieved, even greater responsibility will be required of those who control the services and produce the material diffused. The United Nations, the International Telecommunication Union and Unesco, governments and broadcasting organizations are studying the situation with the object of establishing principles and arriving at international agreements that will permit the fullest use of satellite broadcasting in the service of the free flow of ideas, the expansion of education, and the promotion of mutual understanding of peoples, with proper respect for sovereignty of nations and diversity of cultures.

TELEVISION BY CABLE

The extent to which television broadcasting organizations can serve at the same hours a variety of national and local publics, audiences with special interests, schools and educational institutions is limited, apart from all other circumstances and conditions, by the small number of channels available. The distribution of visual images, as well as sound, by earth-laid cables offers technical possibilities, already being exploited in a few countries, for the development of cable teledistribution systems which can provide simultaneously, within the area covered, a variety of programmes for general audiences or designed for special groups; individuals linked with or subscribing to the system may thus have a wide choice of programmes. Operators of such systems can bring in by relays and redistribute national, or even foreign, programmes. They can also originate and feed into the cables locally produced programmes, recorded programmes or films of their choice. Cables carrying 50 channels are already in service and it is expected that there will be cables carrying hundreds. Thus channels could be made available for the use of local communities and for the use of schools either following courses given in one of them or requiring the projection of recorded programmes on days and at times best suited to them. There can be two-way channels allowing for questions and discussion.

Teledistribution, together with simpler and less expensive methods of production and the use of video cassettes by individuals, could revolutionize the nature and the structure of the means of communication and give new dimensions to the freedom to diffuse and receive information and to exchanges between peoples.

Teledistribution has reached different stages in Canada and the USA (where it started), a dozen countries of Europe and Japan. Installation of the systems involves heavy financial investments and raises both legal and political problems in countries were both television and the laying and maintenance of cables are a monopoly of the State or bodies operating under licences granted by it. Undertaken originally and, for many years, developed merely as a means of overcoming geographical and physical obstacles to good reception of programmes from local television transmitters, teledistribution is now realizing its full possibilities as a new means of communication.

There are in the USA more than 2500 cable networks with more than 6 million households as paying subscribers and it is expected that within ten years there will be 4000 networks serving 28 million households. Most of the networks each serve about 1000 households with an average of 15 programmes but the largest, with 35 000 subscribers, offers a choice of 40. Like the radio and television organizations, they are run by commercial and private companies but subject to the general control of the Federal Communications Commission. The FCC has set limits to programme retransmission and requires the 300 networks with more than 3000 subscribers also to offer programmes which they themselves acquire or produce. It also requires the 100 with more than 10 000 subscribers to provide free-access channels in the cable for return communication between subscribers and the teledistribution centre. The policy is to promote teledistribution as a new and supplementary means of providing information, entertainment and education and to facilitate local participation in programme formulation and production. In Canada more than 25% of households are served by teledistribution networks providing a wide choice of national and external programmes some of which are served by Canada's domestic telecommunication satellite. Equipment is made available to local communities so that they can produce their own programmes for distribution on their local network. In both countries, commercial and public service groups are producing programmes in video cassettes to be sold, hired out or lent to teledistribution systems.

In the European countries and in Japan, networks are being developed slowly compared with Canada and the USA. In Belgium, 200 000 subscribers can choose from a range of programmes which includes 2 national and 2 Dutch, 2 French, 3 German and 1 Luxembourg, all of them brought via relays to Brussels by the teledistribution company; but local origination or production is not yet permitted. Similar provision of French, German and Austrian programmes is being developed in Switzerland. In France, Holland and the UK, experiments in local production in a number of selected towns have been authorized or begun.

FLOWS AND EXCHANGES

While the use of communication satellites makes possible the very rapid, even instantaneous, flow of news to, and between, news agencies, the press and broadcasting services in all parts of the world, not all of them benefit to the same extent from the new facilities available. There are national news agencies in 90 countries but they are unequally distributed, and there are great differences in the scope and effectiveness of their operations. Most national news agencies depend on the five world agencies to carry news about their countries to other countries.

The majority of countries operate external broadcasting services as a means of communicating, directly or through the intermediary of national radio services, with people in other countries. The number of languages used, of hours on the air and of countries reached varies greatly between countries.

All television services give time to foreign news and show considerable quantities of television programmes and films obtained from other countries. Many of them, from time to time cooperate in covering events of common interest and in producing programmes for each others' audiences. Television in the home has taken the place of films shown in public cinemas as the means by which most people get knowledge and form ideas about other peoples and countries which influence their attitudes.

Given the numbers of people who buy newspapers and have radio and television receivers, a far larger part of the population in most countries is receiving more information and ideas about other countries than in the past. But the facts and figures also show imbalances in the flow and exchanges between countries and in the content of what flows. The greater quantity of the flow is from a small number of countries to the rest and from technically developed countries to others. There is a much greater flow between countries with the same or similar languages and cultures, with long historical and political ties and similar economic and social systems, than between countries with diverse pasts and presents. Much the largest part of the material for television transmissions received by most countries from others covers sports events and popular music — which show little of the country concerned except people in a stadium or a theatre — fictional serial stories and old films, most of them presenting limited views of the life and cultures of the countries in which they are set and offering little more than passing entertainment. News reports on other countries in the popular newspapers and programmes of most countries tend to show a similar imbalance of sensational and bad news, and eccentric and unrepresentative aspects of life.

There is room for more two-way flow in place of the present dominant flow from a few countries to the rest and for news programmes presenting, more regularly, more aspects of what the countries of the world are like and what is going on in them. All peoples should be able to speak as well as be spoken to, and to present themselves to others as they see themselves. Mass media organizations and governments in many countries are seeking to increase the amount and to improve the quality of information material and programmes flowing between countries. Regional associations of national press agencies and radio and television organizations exist to facilitate exchanges between their members and with the rest of the world.

EDUCATION FOR MASS COMMUNICATION

More institutions in more countries are providing mass communication education and training than ten years ago. More universities offer two- or three-year academic and professional courses leading to a degree and offer the facilities for research. Courses cover the history, theory, practice and technology of mass communication, its role in society and in economic and social development, and the use of the various media in education, science and culture. This approach, which is being followed in more and more universities. marks an important advance on journalistic training as it has been long practised in some countries. The object is to produce qualified communications experts capable of planning, directing and administering technical or programme services. Technological advances and changes in the role of mass communication within and between countries demand such people. Shorter courses designed to lead to more specific professions such as journalism, or to provide training in particular production, techniques and skills in the various media, are given by some universities, in technological institutes, polytechnics and other higher education schools. Such courses often provide basic education which cannot be acquired simply through on-the-job training. on which many countries still largely rely. Some of them send people to work in newspapers, radio and television organizations in other countries.

The world map of these institutions indicates that mass media organizations and governments in all countries – the technically developed as well as the underdeveloped – are coming to recognize the need to educate and train people to make best use of the increasingly sophisticated technology and to exercise the responsibilities attached to the conduct of mass communication.

In many countries, problems arise through the lack of well-trained teachers and through the cost of the buildings and equipment needed to provide practical training for relatively small numbers of students. A number of regional training projects have been developed with the assistance of Unesco in the last ten years. The film and television schools set up to support India's education via the satellite project are open to students from other Asian countries. The radio and television training institute for Asia, based on a Malaysian national centre, is designed to produce 300 specialists a year. Four African universities have schools of mass communication studies which are also regional centres, and Ecuador's

International Centre for Advanced Studies in Journalism for Latin America organized annual ten-week seminars for directors of university schools of journalism.

PROFESSIONAL ASSOCIATIONS

Associations of professionals working in the mass media exist in all countries. The situation varies according to the structure of the different media. In some, there are associations of those owning, financing and operating newspapers, radio, television and film companies, which exist to promote common attitudes and serve common interests in relation to governments and the public. In some countries, they have set up common services such as news agencies and — together with associations of journalists writers and producers — professional standards or codes of ethics. In almost all countries, there are associations of newspaper editors, journalists, producers of radio and television programmes and films, and in many also, different associations of technicians: printers, cameramen, sound engineers, etc. While most of these have as a first aim the protection of their conditions of work, many are also concerned with maintaining professional and technical standards. Some organize training courses for newcomers and in-service training. When functioning well, such organizations of those who operate or who work in the mass media fulfil an essential role in improving technical efficiency and in cultivating among their members a recognition of the role of the mass media and of their own responsibilities.

There is also an international federation of national associations of professional and technical workers in the mass media; this is intended to assist the member associations and to promote cooperation between them.

PATTERNS OF CONTROL

Responsibility for the policies, operations and output of the mass media is assigned, assumed and exercised in different ways in different countries. In some countries, all or some of the media are operated as organs of the State. In others, private commercial companies, or independent public corporations created by the State, operate this or that medium. Thus in 50 countries, news agencies are operated as organs of the State, while in 40 others, they are cooperative organizations owned and operated by national newspapers and sometimes radio and television organizations. While in most countries, newspapers — the oldest means of mass communications — are produced and published by private commercial companies, in 10 African and eight Asian countries, Cuba, the USSR and the Eastern European countries they are published by, or under the control of, State organs. The pattern is more complicated for radio and television. In all but six African and five Asian countries, 15 European countries, the USSR and Cuba, these services are run under direct control of the State. In some South American countries, there are State services but the major services are operated by private commercial companies. In six African, five Asian, four North American and 11 European countries, the services are operated independently by corporations created by the State. In Australia, Canada, New Zealand and the UK, there are independent public corporations created by the State, also licensed commercial companies which, unlike the public corporations, finance their operations solely by revenue from advertising. In three European countries, there are single commercial companies. In the USA, domestic radio and television services are run by a large number of private companies. The majority are commercial companies financed from advertising revenue; the others, which broadcast only educational programmes, are non-profit-making organizations financed by grants and contributions. In contrast, the production, distribution and exhibition of films − until the coming of television − the dominant world mass medium in terms of audiences are conducted solely by private commercial companies except in the Asian Communist countries, Cuba, the countries of Eastern Europe and the USSR.

PART ONE

THE MEDIA

CHAPTER 1

THE PRESS

Regarded statistically over the past ten years, the press in most countries seems just to be holding its position; in some, there are now more newspapers and/or more readers; in others, there is no progress. Thus, while in many countries of Europe, there are fewer daily newspapers, the majority maintain high circulations ranging from 200 to over 500 copies per 1000 of the population. In the three most populous countries of South America, which also have the largest number of dailies, the number of titles has decreased, and in two, the circulation ratio is well below 100 per 1000. In 20 countries of Asia dailies and circulations have increased, but in 10, circulation remains below 20 per 1000. In Africa, there are nine countries with no dailies, and in only 10 is the circulation more than 20 per 1000. However, it should be noted that many countries have considerable numbers of newspapers appearing once or several times a week, and even larger numbers of periodicals – both general and specialized – which may have quite sizable readerships. Perhaps the main role of the press will come to be one of analysis and in-depth coverage of the news events which radio and television can now report almost instantaneously.

As a medium of mass communication of news, the press in almost all countries reaches a much smaller public than radio broadcasting or even, in many, than television does. Outside the highly industrialized and largely literate countries, it hardly reaches rural people, whereas radio, and increasingly television, transmissions may cover the whole country. In most countries where several or many languages are spoken besides the official one, there are no newspapers in these other languages and it seems unlikely that the press will ever be able to compete with radio and television in reaching a multiplicity of language groups of relatively small size spread over large areas. The economics of newspaper production would seem to make it impossible. Newspapers, like periodicals and books, have become increasingly expensive to produce (and hence to buy) because of rises in production and, especially, newsprint costs and the loss of advertising revenue to other media.

In spite of a world increase of some 50% in the rate of production over ten years. newsprint is in short supply. It is produced in only 36 countries, and of these only six – Canada, Finland, Sweden, Norway, the USSR and New Zealand (in order of importance) – produce enough to be able to export considerable quantities. The USA which is, after Canada, the second largest producer consumes more than three times its own annual production of 3 million metric tons. Practically no newsprint is produced in Africa. Of 11 Asian producing countries, only four can supply enough for their own needs. In Europe another nine countries besides the three mentioned above produce enough for their needs, and a further six produce some. In South America, only two countries produce any, one of them enough for its needs.

AFRICA

The countries of Africa, as a whole, have fewer daily newspapers and lower circulations than the countries of any other region and the figures show little development over the past ten years. In five countries – Algeria, Kenya, Madagascar, Morocco and Nigeria – there are now fewer dailies and no increase in circulation. In Egypt, the number of papers has fallen from 37 to 15 while the circulation has risen to 23 per 1000 people, the third highest rate in Africa. In nine countries, there is no daily newspaper. In 13 countries, there is 1, if government daily news-sheets are included, sometimes 2, but circulations are very small. In 17 countries, there are from 3 to 11 newspapers but the circulation in all of them, with the exception of Botswana, Ghana, Libya, Mauritius (78 per 1000, the highest in the African region), is less than 20 per 1000. In the Republic of South Africa, 21 dailies are published, 15 in English and 6 in Afrikaans, with a circulation of 53 per 1000; no dailies are published in any other of the languages spoken in the country, although a few weeklies appear. In some of the countries, weekly newspapers are published (with larger circulations per 1000 than for dailies) and in most of them, some periodicals. But generally, there are no signs that the press will develop as an information medium as it has done in most other countries in the world. The late start of a national press in most of the countries, the high rates of illiteracy, the number of languages spoken, the lack of printing-presses, the high cost of imported newsprint, poor telecommunication facilities for transmission of news, and slow and poor rural communication between the few cities and towns and the large rural areas all militate against the development of the press. Radio broadcasting may soon come to play the role of diffusion of news and ideas which, historically, the press played alone for centuries in other countries.

Full courses in journalism for press and radio are now established at 17 universities in 10 African countries – Algeria, Cameroon, Egypt, Kenya, Madagascar, Nigeria, Senegal, South Africa, Tunisia and Zaïre – as compared with 3 in 1965. Short courses are offered by some other universities and higher education institutes. Four of the university schools – Nairobi, Yaoundé, Lagos and Dakar – are also regional centres which accept students from other African countries. They resulted from experience gained at training courses organized during the sixties by the International Press Institute and by Unesco.

NORTH AMERICA

More newspapers and periodicals are published in the USA than in any other country in the world. A few of the major-city dailies have also some country-wide and international readerships; the rest, while dealing with national and international affairs, are essentially local in editorial character and in distribution. There are now 1761 daily newspapers as compared with 1763 in 1961. The number of individual towns with a daily newspaper has increased from 1460 to 1500, but in 85% of these, only a single daily is published; only in some cities of more than 650 000 population are there any longer 2 or more competing dailies. In 1971, more than 900 dailies were owned by 155 groups as compared with 560 owned by 109 groups in 1961. Groups and individual papers and magazines between them also own some 500 radio and some 200 television stations. Each of the six largest groups controls between 18 and 33 dailies, but none controls more than 6% of the total national daily circulation. While overall circulation figures have increased by over 3 million to more than 65 million during the last ten years, circulation per 1000 has dropped from 326 to around 300. There are 590 Sunday newspapers with a total circulation of almost 50 million. In addition, there are more than 9000 weekly and other non-daily newspapers, including 177 black papers, 68 American Indian papers and 250 newspapers published in more than 30 foreign languages.

Canada has 116 daily newspapers (compared with 103 ten years ago), some 220 non-dailies and some 900 periodicals. Circulation of dailies rests at around 220 per 1000 people. Dailies appear in some 90 cities and towns; only 13 are published in French, the mother tongue of about 30% of the population and (with English) an official language. Group ownership of dailies, often linked with ownership of radio and television stations, has increased and, by 1971, 68 dailies were controlled by 10 groups, the largest of which, besides owning 28 smaller-city English-language papers, owned papers in the UK, USA and southern Africa. A French-language consortium owned 4 Quebec dailies, 6 important weeklies, 4 radio and 2 television stations.

The USA is the world's largest consumer of newsprint, at around 10 million metric tons a year, of which it produces less than a third. Canada is the world's largest producer of newsprint, around 9 million metric tons, but its own consumption is only around 800 000 metric tons.

Among the Spanish-speaking countries of Central America, Nicaragua – with a population only 2 million less than Canada – has only 4 daily newspapers, with a circulation of 40 per 1000, compared with 8 dailies and 60 per 1000 ten years ago. In Cuba, on the other hand, the number of dailies has increased from 10 to 16 and circulation from 80 to over 200. In Mexico, 200 dailies are published (in 1967 the number had risen to 228), total circulation has almost doubled and circulation per 1000 has increased from 80 to 100. While 26 dailies are published in Mexico City alone, more than 80 other cities and towns have their own daily press, the larger state capitals having 4 to 6 papers each.

SOUTH AMERICA

In South America, a large number of daily newspapers and also non-dailies and periodicals are published in all countries except Paraguay. Almost all are owned and controlled by private companies, some of which own many newspapers and sometimes radio and television stations. Many newspapers have affiliations with political parties. Dailies are published in many provincial towns, as well as in capital cities, but all in Spanish; there are none published in Indian languages. Circulations are largely confined to the cities and towns because of a lack of cheap, rapid transport between urban and rural areas.

Brazil, Argentina and Colombia, with the largest populations, have the largest numbers of dailies but their number and their circulation continue to decrease. In Brazil, 257 dailies (30 less than ten years ago) are published in some 95 towns, and the circulation ratio has dropped from 50 to 40 per 1000. In Argentina, the number of dailies has dropped from 230 to 179, but circulation is maintained at around 150 per 1000. In all the other countries, the number of dailies has increased, but circulations are below 100 per 1000, except in Peru where the figure has increased from 45 to over 130. In Uruguay, which now has 29 instead of 26 dailies, most of them nation-wide papers with political affiliations, circulation is 265 per 1000, one of the highest in the world.

Newsprint presents problems; only Chile has the facilities to produce more than it needs, while Brazil produces about half its needs, and Argentina a small amount.

Almost all countries in South America have at least one institution providing education and training in journalism or mass communication, most of them associated with universities. Of some 80 institutes, more than half were started in the sixties when the development of radio and television led to the recognition of the value of training not only for the newer media but also for the press. Large numbers of students enrol for courses, more than are likely to find jobs. CIESPAL (the International Centre for Advanced Studies in Journalism for Latin America), established by the Government of Ecuador and the University of Quito, with the assistance of Unesco, has done much since 1960 to improve education and training in Latin American universities. Through annual ten-week seminars, some 700 journalists and university schools of journalism from 21 countries have been given training by visiting professors from 18 countries in North and South America, Europe and Asia. As a result, concepts of education and training have been broadened, new subjects introduced into curricula and academic criteria laid down. Most recently, CIESPAL has begun sending itinerant experts to give short courses in universities and schools.

ASIA

The state of the press in Asian countries presents great contrasts. In some 20 countries, the number of daily newspapers, the number of copies circulated per 1000 of the population, or both, have increased over the past ten years although in 10, circulation is still below 20 per 1000. In Iraq, Jordan and Syria, the press has seriously declined, and in Israel the number of dailies has dropped from 28 to 24 and circulation from 210 to 160 per 1000. Newspapers are published by private companies (some affiliated to and subsidized by political parties) in all countries except Afghanistan, Burma, the People's Republic of China, Iraq, and the Democratic People's Republics of Korea, Mongolia, Vietnam and Yemen.

Newsprint is produced in 11 countries but in only four of them in sufficient quantities to meet needs.

In Japan, side by side with great developments in radio and television, the number of daily newspapers has risen from 157 to 168 and the circulation per 1000 to 511, the second largest in the world after Sweden (566). While dailies are published in some 60 cities, 3 large Tokyo-based newspapers (in all, 23 are published in Tokyo) dominate the scene, with satellite papers in five other cities and, between them, a daily circulation of almost 17 million. Facsimile pages are transmitted by radio to satellite papers and increasing use is being made of offset printing. Equipment is being developed for the transmission of facsimile pages to home television sets. Some 90% of Japanese newspapers are sold by subscription and home-delivered through more than 200 000 distribution agencies. With a newsprint production of 2 270 000 metric tons in 1972 (the third largest in the world), Japan met its consumption needs.

The Indian press publishes 721 daily newspapers (the fourth largest number in the world after the People's Republic of China, the USA and the Federal Republic of Germany) in more than 20 languages; but circulation, largely limited to cities and big towns, is only around 17 per 1000, an increase of over 11 per 1000 compared with ten years ago. While a few papers are widely distributed, there is really no national press to span the country's vast geographical areas and its linguistic and cultural diversity. Over 4000 non-dailies and around 11 000 periodicals are published in 52 different languages. Financial and technical difficulties (eg besides English, only Bengali, Hindi and Tamil can be adapted for linotype machines and no type face has yet been developed for Urdu) make the existence of many newspapers and periodicals precarious. More and more papers are associated in ownership groups which between them now account for 57% of the total daily circulation.

Newsprint, the bulk of which must be imported against much-needed foreign currency, is a great problem and plans are in hand to increase production from the present 40 000 metric tons to 195 000 which might then match consumption.

For the People's Republic of China, the latest figures available showed a total of 1908 daily newspapers in 1966 (circulation figures for 1455 dailies around 1960 were 21 million copies or about 27 copies per 1000 people). It is likely that in 1973 the number of dailies is as large as in 1966 and that circulation figures are higher; it can also be assumed that readership figures are much higher than circulation figures. The pattern of the daily press is probably the same, ie a small number of papers with national circulation published in Peking, with editions using facsimiles or stereotyped mats being published in a number of large cities, and large numbers of provincial and local papers, particularly in rural areas.

Annual newsprint production is reported to have risen in ten years to 2.5 million metric tons which is presumably equal to national consumption.

EUROPE

Europe as a whole continues to have more newspapers, dailies and non-dailies, and more periodicals than any other region of the world and, in most of the countries, the circulation of dailies per 1000 is among the highest. In 11 countries, circulation ratios stand at over 300 copies per 1000 persons (in five of them at over 400, indicating an average of more than 1 daily newspaper per household), in six countries at between 200 and 300, in six at 100 to 200 and in five at less than 100.

In the countries of Western Europe, most newspapers are owned by private enterprises, some by political parties. In those of Eastern Europe, the important newspapers are directed by political party and public organizations.

In 14 out of 28 countries, the number of dailies and the circulation per 1000 people are about the same as ten years ago, and in six, there are more newspapers and somewhat higher circulations. In six countries, all with long newspaper histories, the number of newspapers has decreased although circulation per 1000 people has been maintained or even increased. However, in France, dailies decreased from 136 to 106 and circulation from 270 to 238 per 1000, and in the UK, dailies decreased from 123 to 100 and circulation from

506 per 1000 (the highest in the world ten years ago) to 435. In Sweden, where newspapers have decreased from 123 to 108, circulation has risen to 566 per 1000 (now the highest in the world).

In some countries, there are a large number of non-daily newspapers, usually weeklies, with large total circulations. Hungary, Ireland, Italy and Spain are striking examples. In the UK, where more than 1000 local weeklies are published and 7 nationally published Sunday newspapers circulate around 24 million copies per week, the circulation per 1000 of non-dailies is 672.

Newsprint is produced in 18 countries. Three, Finland, Norway and Sweden, export the larger part of their production and in nine, Austria, Czechoslovakia, the German Democratic Republic, Italy, Poland, Romania, Spain, Switzerland and Yugoslavia, production is equal to national consumption.

OCEANIA

In Australia and New Zealand, the number of newspapers is about the same as ten years ago, and even if the number of copies per 1000 has dropped, it still stands at over 300 which is more than 1 daily newspaper per household. While in New Zealand most of the dailies are independently owned, in Australia, ownership is becoming increasingly concentrated, 3 major groups and 2 smaller groups owning most of the metropolitan dailies as well as other newspapers, periodicals, and radio and television companies. Australia has more than 40 papers for immigrants published in 17 foreign languages.

In Australia, newsprint production has doubled to 173 000 metric tons a year compared with a consumption rate of some 450 000 metric tons, while in New Zealand, 50% of an annual production of 200 000 metric tons is exported.

USSR

The number of daily newspapers in the USSR increased in ten years, from 457 to 639 in 1970, when total circulation stood at over 81 million and circulation at 336 copies per 1000 people. The 3 largest dailies, with a combined daily circulation of over 25 million copies, are the official organs of the Central Committee of the Communist Party, of the Supreme Soviet, and of the Central Committee of the Young Communist League. There were also more than 8000 non-dailies, half appearing two or three times a week with a total circulation of 60 million. Newspapers, daily and non-daily, appear in Russian and in 57 other languages of the USSR. There were some 6000 periodicals of which 5000 were published in Russian, over 900 in other languages of the USSR and 140 in 23 foreign languages.

Newsprint production in 1970 amounted to 1 150 000 metric tons, of which almost 250 000 metric tons were exported.

CHAPTER 2

NEWS AGENCIES

There are now national news agencies in 90 sovereign countries, an increase since ten years ago, but some 40 countries have none; these include 25 countries with populations of more than 1 million. All agencies serve not only the press but also radio and television broadcasting organizations with domestic and foreign news. In 50 of the countries, these agencies are directly controlled or operated by the State; in the other 40 countries, one or more of the agencies are organizations cooperatively controlled and financed by the newspapers (and sometimes radio and television organizations) or autonomous public corporations, in some cases created by the State. There are great differences between the news agencies of different regions in the scale, scope and effectiveness of their operations; many are hardly more than government information offices.

Among the national agencies there are five — Agence France-Presse (France), Associated Press (USA), Reuters (UK), TASS (USSR) and United Press International (USA) — which dominate the world scene by the size and technological strength of their systems of collecting news and distributing it in many languages throughout the world. Most national agencies subscribe to or have exchange arrangements with two, and sometimes more, of the world agencies to receive foreign news and provide domestic news. Apart from the world agencies, few national agencies (and few national newspapers and other mass media organizations) maintain their own offices or correspondents abroad to collect or distribute news. Most agencies are the only channel for foreign news in their respective countries, and they receive it from the world agencies on which they also depend for the distribution of their domestic news abroad. There are, however, national agencies of particular importance, eg in Egypt and Morocco, India and Japan, the two German Republics, Italy, Poland and Spain. Exchange of news between agencies usually takes place within familiar political, cultural and linguistic groups. Regular world-wide collection and distribution of news is largely effected by and through the five world agencies.

Each of these has offices in between 100 and 200 countries, and large numbers of full-time staff and part-time correspondents (Reuters does not itself gather or distribute news in the UK; this is done by the press-owned Press Association which is a part-owner of Reuters). They collect hundreds of thousands of words a day and, including domestic distribution, transmit millions of words. Each issues news 24 hours a day, to thousands of national agencies, subscribing newspapers, radio and television organizations in upwards of 100 countries. All have regular services, usually daily, in Arabic. English, French, German, Portuguese, Russian and Spanish; some also issue in other European languages.

In some countries, eg France, India, the UK, the USA and USSR, there are agencies or services run by newspapers or professional groups which supply finished articles giving background to and comment on the news and current events to subscribing newspapers in many parts of the world. While, at present, the scale of such services is small compared with that of the long-established news agencies, this development may have significant effects on the exchange and internationalization of views.

The past ten years have seen spectacular technical developments in methods of collecting, editing and transmitting increasingly large quantities of news more and more rapidly. But, in general, only the world agencies and a few other large national agencies directly benefit from these developments. It is possible now, by use of the cathode ray, to write, correct and edit for immediate automatic transmission. Computerized systems are in use for the storage, retrieval, editing and automatic transmission of news and economic, financial and other data. The capacity, range, speed and quality of transmission of news, messages, photos and facsimiles have all been increased. Improved and extended cable systems, telephone and teleprinter services and radio circuits within and between countries and continents are now supplemented and, in some situations, have come to be replaced by transmission via satellites. Technically, news and reports in verbal and visual form can be transmitted simultaneously via the different satellite systems to earth stations throughout the world which, in turn, can pass on the messages instantaneously by land-based systems to the news agencies.

AFRICA

Not surprisingly, in view of the small numbers and recent establishment of newspapers, radio and television stations in most of the countries of Africa, news agencies are developing slowly. In addition, poor, although improved, telecommunication facilities within and between African countries and with the outside world are still a serious obstacle. Nevertheless, there are now agencies in 27 countries as compared with 21 ten years ago; in 22, they are directly run by the respective governments. In 13 countries, there is no agency. The two large territories administered by Portugal are serviced by the Portuguese agencies. The agencies are of more importance for radio and television organizations and government services than for the few newspapers. While they have correspondents at home, most have none abroad. They are the channel for foreign news received usually from one English-language and one French-language world agency and sometimes from a third. All of the world agencies have a correspondent in most of the countries, and in some a few other foreign agencies are represented. Few of the African agencies have arrangements for exchange of news and rely mainly on the world agencies for news about other African countries. The Union of African News Agencies founded at Tunis in 1963 with a membership of 20 agencies to develop regional assistance and cooperation failed to survive its first ten years.

In north Africa, there are two agencies of special importance to Arabic-speaking countries. The Middle East News Agency, in Cairo, has offices in nine other Arab countries and in Belgrade, East Berlin, London and Paris. It subscribes to two of the world agencies and exchanges news with another and with a number of European national agencies. It provides 400 subscribers daily with 20 000 words in Arabic and 6500 in English. The Mahgreb Arabe Presse, a private Moroccan company, has a similar organization and arrangements and issues daily 210 000 words in Arabic and 180 000 words in French to 70 subscribers in Morocco and to 60 foreign subscribers.

In Ghana, which has three dailies with a circulation of 30 per 1000 and radio and television services covering a large part of the country and operating extensive external broadcasts, the government news agency has nine regional and 17 district offices with over 340 permanent staff and 380 part-time correspondents. It has permanent offices in London, New York and Nairobi and exchange arrangements with three world agencies. Similarly, Agence Zaïre Presse has some 50 reporters and editorial staff and a European office in Brussels. It receives foreign news from two world agencies and several national ones. A second agency in Zaïre is Documentation and Information for and about Africa, founded in 1956 by three Catholic bishops but, since 1965, an independent private company. It issues daily bulletins totalling 20 000 words in French, English, Dutch and, occasionally, in African vernaculars in Zaïre and to branches in Rwanda and Burundi and to its Brussels office for communication to agencies and subscribers outside Africa. Some 50% of the material is religious news and 35% socio-economic.

The oldest agency is the South African Press Association. a newspaper-owned cooperative founded in 1938, which supplies domestic and foreign news to domestic subscribers and to Rhodesia and Zambia. Four world agencies with offices in South Africa subscribe to its services. It receives its foreign news from AP and Reuters with which it has exchange arrangements. Reuters, which has offices in 16 cities in southern Africa, provides a special southern African news service for the republic and neighbouring countries while AFP sends 30 000 words daily in English and French to Paris and issues daily French and twice-weekly English bulletins for African countries.

NORTH AMERICA

In the North American area, there are news agencies in only two of the eight Spanish-speaking countries, Cuba and Mexico, and in Canada and the USA. The English-speaking Caribbean islands are served by the Caribbean Press Association situated in Grenada, Windward Islands. It seems likely that plans under study for some years will shortly result in the establishment of a cooperatively run Caribbean news agency to serve press, radio and television concerns in the whole area.

The Cuban agency, PRELA, which is a State organization, has some subscribers in South American countries, while Mexico's largest agency, Informex, and two other privately run agencies, seem to serve only Mexican subscribers.

Canada's CP, which is cooperatively owned and operated by 103 newspapers and serves some 400 subscribers in all the media, has branches or staff correspondents in 13 cities and 650 part-time correspondents throughout Canada and 25 abroad. CP carries world news from AP, AFP and Reuters, all of which receive CP news on a reciprocal basis. UPI of Canada, serving some 40 subscribers in Canada, is an affiliate of UPI (USA) and, through it, is another outlet for Canadian news to the world.

In the USA, the two world agencies, AP, a cooperative venture owned by its American newspaper members, and UPI, a chartered corporation, supply domestic subscribers in all the media with both national and foreign news. Each has subscribers to both its American and world news services in over 100 countries including the Spanish-speaking countries of North and South America, in many of which – for lack of national agencies – newspapers use the world agencies as sources for their own domestic as well as foreign news. There are also in the USA several hundred other privately run services and agencies. some of them operated by leading newspapers, which provide subscribers with edited news stories, feature articles or photos, or specialized news services in many fields of national and international life.

SOUTH AMERICA

In South America, only four of the Spanish-speaking countries – Argentina, Colombia, Chile, Venezuela – and Brazil have news agencies. Buenos Aires is the headquarters of the Latin American Information Agency established in 1969 to serve the Latin American countries. The agencies are private enterprises but Brazil has also one government agency. With the exception of one Chilean agency, they depend entirely for foreign news on the world agencies, all of which have offices in most of the countries, and other outside agencies or newspapers, notably the Spanish agency Efe. One Brazilian agency has a daily domestic news service in Spanish which is received by Efe.

In the countries which have no agency (including Uruguay which had one until 1967), with populations ranging from 2 to 13 million, all but two have large numbers of newspapers and hundreds of radio and television broadcasting stations; in two of them, government radio stations run important external radio broadcasts. The mass media in these countries depend for their domestic news, on their own reporters, government bulletins and sometimes the local offices of the world agencies from which they also receive their foreign news. In Argentina, in 1973, the Government decreed that the world agencies were not to gather or distribute domestic news for transmission to Argentine mass media. This decision led to the establishment of a new domestic news agency by a consortium of 57 newspapers.

ASIA

Of the countries in Asia – from the eastern Mediterranean to the Pacific Ocean and southward through India to Indonesia – all have a national agency except Cyprus, Kuwait, Saudi Arabia, Singapore and Thailand. In Thailand, with 35 dailies and many radio and television stations, the Government provides a free daily bulletin of domestic news and a subscription-paid summary of Reuter's foreign news. From Singapore, where the media depend on their own reporters for domestic news and on four world agencies for foreign news, some 60 foreign correspondents send out news of Singapore and south-east Asian countries. In 20 out of 28 countries, the news agency is operated by the government or is under its direct control. The activities of most of the agencies, both government and private, are limited to collection and distribution of news within their own countries although some distribute international news coming from the world agencies.

In India, where more than 700 daily newspapers are published in more than 20 Indian languages (the largest number of newspapers in Asia and the third largest in the world), there are some 30 domestic news and feature agencies, all privately owned and independently operated. The largest, the Press Trust of India, founded in 1949 to take over the outlets of Reuters and the Associated Press of India, is a cooperative enterprise owned by Indian newspapers. It sells its domestic services to Reuters and holds the distribution rights in India for Reuters, AFP and UPI. Japan — which in all media is one of the most highly developed countries in the world — has two agencies, both established in 1945 and both cooperatively owned by newspapers, which rank among the most important in the world. Kyodo has 51 offices in Japan and 24 abroad and has exchange arrangements with four world agencies and 28 national agencies. It distributes daily some 220 000 letters in Japanese and 35 000 words in English. The Jiji Press has 62 offices in Japan and 31 abroad and exchanges news with Reuters, UPI and AFP. It has a daily output of 400 000 Japanese letters on national news for domestic use, the equivalent of 12 000 words for overseas Chinese use and 30 000 English words for domestic and overseas use.

The small circulation of most newspapers, difficulties in teletype transmission of characters, multilingualism and inadequacy of telecommunication facilities continue to hamper agency development at home and exchanges within the area and with the rest of the world.

The Organization of Asian News Agencies, founded in 1961 to promote regional cooperation, has still only 12 member agencies from eight countries. Its plans to establish radio transmission links for news with all members through Djakarta will increase its usefulness and this may lead to increased membership.

EUROPE

Europe is the seat of two of the five world agencies — AFP (France) and Reuters (UK) — or three if the USSR's TASS is included. It is also the region with the largest number of long-established and highly developed national agencies. Only four smaller States have no agency. In 16 countries, the agencies are owned and run by newspaper and mass media cooperatives or by autonomous public or private corporations. In nine, they are operated directly or indirectly by the State.

All of the national agencies subscribe to or have agreements with at least one of the world agencies (and most with several) for the reception of foreign news and the distribution abroad of their domestic news. The majority have similar bilateral agreements with many national agencies. Many, in addition, maintain offices and permanent correspondents abroad to collect news and distribute domestic news in several foreign languages. They include ANSA (Italy), PAP (Poland), ADN (German Democratic Republic), DPA (Federal Republic of Germany) and Efe (Spain). This last agency sends 190 000 words (including 50 000 on foreign news) daily in Spanish to 200 daily newspapers and broadcasting stations in Latin America, where most countries have no national agency.

In 1972, the European Alliance of News Agencies founded in 1957 to promote technical cooperation in means and rates of transmission, expanded its one agency/country membership to 23 with the inclusion of six Eastern European countries. Working relations exist between the two associations of photo agencies set up in 1965, one by the Western European and the other by the Eastern European countries.

OCEANIA

In Australia, as in New Zealand, the major national agency is a cooperative enterprise owned by the press. Both these agencies are part-owners of Reuters, from which they receive world news and through which they distribute domestic news abroad. Both agencies also receive overseas news from AP and UPI and in both countries a number of agencies have representatives. However, most Australian newspapers rely on their own large reporting staffs for national and local news (as does the Australian Broadcasting Commission) and several of the larger ones have overseas correspondents.

USSR

The national news agency, TASS, which comes under the direction of the Council of Ministers of the USSR, collects and distributes news and photos in the USSR and throughout the world. There are associated agencies in each of the 14 Union republics. A second agency, Novosti, was founded in 1961 by the Unions of Journalists and Writers and other societies. It is the channel through which articles, essays, etc. by eminent Soviet writers and public figures are made available to subscribing newspapers and periodicals and throughout the world.

CHAPTER 3

BROADCASTING

Broadcasting, both sound and visual, in all countries is subject to State legislation. States find themselves obliged for technical reasons, notably allocation of frequencies, and (given the impact of broadcasting) for reasons of both internal public order and external international relations, to exercise a degree of control over broadcasting services to which press and film are much less frequently subject. The majority of States operate or directly control radio and television services usually financed by State funds or licence revenue. In many countries in Western Europe and in many English-speaking countries, the services are operated by autonomous corporations established by the State and ultimately responsible to it but not subject to its control in day-to-day operations. Most of these services are financed by revenue from licence fees, the amount of which is fixed by the State, but in some countries this revenue is supplemented by advertising revenue. In many States, notably in the Americas and Asia, the services are operated by private commercial companies and financed from advertising revenue. In some countries in almost all parts of the world except Eastern Europe, there exist private commercial companies operating services side by side, and usually in competition with, State or autonomous public services.

In all States, direct external broadcasting services are operated under the responsibility of the State and financed exclusively by it, although here and there, private organizations, most of them of a religious character, broadcast to other countries with the consent, but not under the responsibility, of the State in which the transmitters are situated. However, public corporation and commercial broadcasting services in countries where they exist are free to, and in fact do, sell recorded radio and television programmes to other countries or exchange programmes with them.

In each of the large geographical and cultural regions of the world, there is now an international union of broadcasting organizations designed to promote cooperation and mutal assistance, especially in technical matters, and exchange of programmes among the member organizations and between unions. They are the Union of National Radio and Television Organizations of Africa (URTNA), the Arab States Broadcasting Union (ASBU), the Inter-American Association of Broadcasters (AIR), the Caribbean Broadcasting Union (CBU), the Ibero-American Television Organization (OTI), the European Broadcasting Union (EBU) and the International Radio and Television Organization (OIRT). Of these, the two oldest and the most active are EBU and OIRT, both based in Europe, the countries of which have long-established and highly developed radio and television services. Each has associate members outside Europe and each collaborates with other regional unions. It is to be expected that the other more recently established unions will develop comprehensive activities along the lines of EBU and OIRT and that, with the advent of satellites, cooperation in the exchange of programmes will be greatly developed.

There is little cooperation in the production, transmission or exchange of radio programmes either within or between regions, except for occasional sports or musical events, and most radio services produce all their own programmes although many consist of, or are based on, recordings of popular and classical music imported from other countries. In television, the situation is different. By means of satellites, there are considerable links for transmission and exchanges between some countries, and increasingly between continents, of live television programmes, most dealing with sports, wars, disasters and dramatic political events. Television services in almost all countries import a considerable percentage of their entertainment programmes from a very limited number of other countries in order, mainly, to compensate for lack of production capacity. Only a small part of cooperative transmissions or imports are broadcast with the express purpose of promoting mutual understanding, and then, usually between countries with long-standing cultural or political links.

Both radio and television are being more widely used for broadcasts to schools, universities and adults seeking further education but full potentialities in these fields are far from being realized in most countries.

SECTION 1 RADIO

AFRICA

Radio broadcasting services are run directly by the State in all the countries of Africa except Ghana, Kenya, Malawi, Nigeria, Rhodesia and South Africa where they are run by autonomous public corporations created by the State. While in most African countries, services are financed from licence revenue, in many they are also assisted by government subsidies and in some by revenue from commercial advertising.

In Liberia, besides the State service, there is a non-commercial station, ELWA, operated by the Sudan Interior Mission, a religious body, which broadcasts home services in English and Liberian languages for 280 hours a week and foreign services beamed to all parts of Africa in 35 African languages and to the Middle East. In Angola, besides the Portuguese Government services, broadcasting in Portuguese, English and French, there are a religious station, 12 radio clubs, and 3 commercial stations, one of which broadcasts in six local dialects. In Mozambique, broadcasting is run by four private organizations, the most important of which is financed by government subsidy, licence fees and advertising, while another is run by Franciscan monks; they broadcast in vernacular languages as well as Portuguese. The Lutheran World Federation operates its Radio Voice of the Gospel from Addis Ababa; it is on the air for 180 hours a week in 13 languages; its programmes are beamed to areas in West and southern Africa and the Middle and Far East; it also broadcasts local programmes on medium wave.

In the majority of the countries, the number of transmitters has considerably increased over the past ten years so that most of the populations could be reached if there were receivers in sufficient numbers. In the whole of Africa, there are 340 long- and medium-wave transmitters, 420 short-wave and 60 FM (apart from the 78 FM stations of the special Bantu service in South Africa).

The number of receivers has greatly increased in almost all countries, but the numbers per 1000 people, although much higher, are still so low that, even allowing that one receiver often serves many people or a listening group and that there may be more receivers than are declared, the actual population coverage of the radio broadcasting services is still a minority. In 26 countries, there are less than 50 receivers per 1000; in Ethiopia and Zaïre, two of the most populated countries, there are less than 10. In 14, including South Africa, there are between 50 and 100. In Egypt, Gabon, Gambia, Mauritania and Mauritius, there are up to 150 per 1000 people.

The particular importance of radio broadcasting lies in the fact that, unlike the press, it can be easily and economically used for communication in the many vernacular and oral languages of the peoples of Africa. All countries broadcast in several vernaculars, some of which are common to neighbouring countries, and most of them also in English or French, according to the colonial history of the country; Cameroon broadcasts in both. The South African Broadcasting Corporation in addition to its English and Afrikaans national services operates a special Radio Bantu service in seven African vernacular languages through a network of 78 FM transmitters.

By comparison with countries in other parts of the world, most African broadcasting services are on the air for few hours, less than 12 a day usually. More time proportionately is given to news, information and general educational programmes than in most countries outside Africa. Systematic broadcasts for schools are organized in a minority of the countries, among them Algeria, Botswana, Ethiopia, Ghana, the Ivory Coast, Madagascar, Niger, Sierra Leone, Tanzania, Tunisia, Uganda and Zambia.

About half the countries run external radio broadcasting services, usually in English, French and Arabic. Most are directed at other parts of Africa, a few to countries in the Middle East and Europe. Ghana broadcasts in English, French, Arabic, Portuguese and Hausa to all these and to North America and the Caribbean. South Africa beams programmes totalling 180 hours a week in nine languages to 23 areas in Africa, the Middle East, Europe, Australia and New Zealand. Egypt broadcasts in 36 languages to all parts of the world.

Africa is the seat of two regional radio and television unions. URTNA, with its headquarters in Senegal, has members from 25 African countries. ASBU, with headquarters in Cairo, has members from 16 countries including five — Algeria, Egypt, Libya, Morocco and the Sudan — which are also members of URTNA. Both are particularly concerned to develop the exchange of news between their members and with other unions.

NORTH AMERICA

The United States of America has a larger number of radio broadcasting organizations (commercial and private non-profit-making), stations, transmitters and receivers than any other country, both absolutely and in relation to territorial size and population. It probably also affords the greatest variety of uses — national and local — and of choice of programmes. There are more than 6600 transmitters as compared with 4500 ten years ago, of which 2350 are FM. Approximately 93% of all stations are privately owned and obtain their revenue from advertising. More than 2300 stations are affiliated to one or other of four national networks and there are 135 regional groups of from 3 to 70 stations. Some 500 stations are owned by newspaper and magazine publishers. Besides these, there are 550 FM stations operated for educational purposes by universities and public authorities and financed from public and private funds, subscriptions and some permitted advertising revenue. The number of radio receivers, now at 354 million, has doubled in ten years. Over 250 million are in 64 million homes, 90 million in cars and 10 million in public places.

All broadcasting activities inside the USA are regulated by the Federal Communications Commission whose functions include assignment of frequencies, granting of station licences, classification, location and operation of stations, and the formulation of regulations 'as public convenience, interest or necessity requires'. The FCC is responsible for limiting ownership or control by any one individual or organization to no more than 7 AM, 6 FM, or 5 television stations and no more than 1 commercial radio and 1 commercial television station in the same city.

Foreign short-wave broadcasting is conducted by the US Government's Voice of America. It operates 33 transmitters in the United States and 60 overseas relay transmitters in nine countries. It broadcasts in 35 regularly scheduled languages throughout the world and is on the air for over 800 hours a week. International broadcasting to Europe and Central and South America is also conducted by a private company, Radio New York Worldwide, and to South America and parts of Asia, in five languages, by a station operated by the Far East Broadcasting Company, a non-commercial Christian organization.

In Canada, where radio broadcasting is also highly developed, there are parallel systems of broadcasting by the government-financed public corporation, Canadian Broadcasting Corporation, one-third of whose income is advertising revenue, and by private enterprises, wholly dependent on advertising revenue. Both systems are regulated and supervised by the Canadian Radio—Television Commission, a public authority set up by Parliament in 1968. Both the systems cover about 98% of the population. CBC runs both English and French programmes and some in other languages including Indian languages. As from 1973, one audio circuit of the domestic communication satellite, Anik, has been available for distribution of news and programmes to regional and remote stations. Of the commercial stations, 80% broadcast principally in English, some in both English and French and in some other European languages. It is estimated that 5.8 million households have radio receivers, which means almost all.

External broadcasting is conducted by CBC in 11 European languages to Europe, Africa, the south Pacific, the Caribbean, the USA and South America, for 90 hours a week.

In Central America, radio broadcasting is highly developed in Cuba, Jamaica, Mexico, Panama and Trinidad and Tobago, and the ratio of receivers ranges from 250 to 360 per 1000. In the other countries, the ratio is below 150 per 1000; in Haiti, it is below 20. In Cuba, broadcasting is run directly by the State; in Barbados, Jamaica and Trinidad and Tobago, by public corporations, and in the others by commercial and private companies financed by advertising revenue or donations. There are Christian mission radio stations in a number of the countries. In Mexico, besides 330 commercial stations, there are some cultural stations owned by the Government and operated by government services or educational institutions. All stations in Mexico must make up to 12.5% of their time available to the Government for educational and civic programmes. Broadcasting is conducted in Indian languages as well as in Spanish. Educational radio broadcasting has been significantly developed only in Cuba, Guatemala, Mexico and Panama.

Only Cuba and Mexico operate external services, Cuba to six areas in Europe and the Americas for about 300 hours a week.

SOUTH AMERICA

While in all the countries of South America, the State operates radio broadcasting services, the situation is dominated in all but Peru by commercial stations, of which there are many with large numbers of transmitters of all categories on the air for up to 24 hours a day. In several countries, there are also important services run by universities, public foundations and religious missions of various denominations. All services are largely financed by revenue from advertising which in some countries occupies a large part of time on the air. The situation is highly competitive.

Brazil, with an area of 8.5 million square kilometres and a population of over 95 million has 860 long- and medium-wave, 80 short-wave and 50 FM transmitters. Fifty of these transmitters are operated by the State, and the rest by 390 private and commercial organizations; 140 transmitters are operated by Catholic organizations. In Ecuador, with an area of only 283 000 square kilometres and a population of some 6 million, there are some 350 transmitters operated by 336 stations, of which 16 are State owned. The most powerful network is La Voz de Los Andes operated by the World Radio Missionary Fellowship, a US-based organization, which transmits religious and cultural programmes to Ecuador for 20 hours a day and international services to all parts of the world, in a dozen languages, for 60 hours a day. In Uruguay, which by South American standards has a modest number of transmitters (less than 100) and of stations, the State service broadcasts school, educational and cultural programmes for 15 hours a day and the 22 commercial stations broadcast between them 11 000 hours a week, of which 20% is news and information and 16% advertising.

The number of receivers, which may be higher than estimated since no licences are required, has increased in ten years in all countries except Brazil where it seems there are less than 100 per 1000 people. In Argentina, the ratio per 1000 has doubled to 380; in Bolivia, quadrupled to 300; and in Ecuador, increased from 40 to 280.

In all the larger countries (except Portuguese-speaking Brazil), stations broadcast mainly in Spanish and the programmes are received more in the cities and towns than in rural areas, but many also broadcast for some hours in Indian languages and for rural audiences. In most South American countries, radio is the major, and often the sole, source of news and entertainment. A special feature of services in almost all the countries is educational broadcasting at all levels from literacy classes to the universities. Most of this broadcasting is conducted by State, university and religious stations. There are outstanding educational radio services in Bolivia, Colombia, Ecuador and Uruguay.

Brazil is the headquarters of AIR, of which membership is open to radio and television organizations in all countries of South and North America. Organizations from South America, Spanish-speaking countries of North America, Portugal and Spain are members of OTI, headquarters in Mexico, the most recently established international regional television union.

ASIA

In almost all Asian countries, radio broadcasting services are run directly by the State and financed from licence fees, sometimes supplemented by revenue from advertising. In the Republic of Korea, there are also 3 commercial networks and some non-commercial Christian organizations, and in the Philippines, more than 100 commercial stations and 25 religious stations. In Cyprus, Iran, Israel and Sri Lanka, the services are run by autonomous bodies established by the State. In Japan, NHK, the public corporation financed by licence revenue, operates three national networks through some 300 medium-wave and 300 FM transmitters while commercial stations owned by 50 companies operate through some 150 medium-wave, 2 short-wave and 5 FM transmitters.

The number of transmitters has greatly increased in ten years almost everywhere so that in most countries the larger part of the population is covered. In Israel, with an area of 20 000 square kilometres and a population of 3 million, there are 20 medium-wave, 12 short-wave and 15 FM transmitters. Indonesia, spread over nearly 2 million square kilometres of islands, with a population of 121 million, has 140 short- and tropical-wavelength transmitters and studios in 45 towns, all operated by the State service; there are also more than 500 small commercial and amateur broadcasting stations over very small, densely populated areas. All-India Radio's 105 medium-wave transmitters cover 78% of the population of 550 million and its 32 short-wave transmitters practically the whole country.

But in spite of the large increase in receivers — which has been enormous in 14 countries — in more than half, the larger part of the population is still not reached, even allowing for communal receivers. In 19 countries, the ratio is between 10 per 1000, as in Afghanistan, and 80 per 1000, as in Thailand; in India, it is only around 25. In the People's Republic of China, the number of receivers, including loudspeakers linked to rediffusion networks, has increased to 15 million, tens of thousands of them in community receiving centres. In nine countries, the number of receivers per 1000 people runs from around 120 in Indonesia, Mongolia and the Republic of Korea, to 180 in Iran and 200 in Lebanon. In Israel, it is 215, in Japan 255, Cyprus 260, Syria 270 and Hong Kong 370, which means that in these countries virtually all households are reached.

The content pattern of programmes in most countries is the one familiar throughout most of the world, with light entertainment and music taking up the larger part of broadcasting time. In Japan, NHK on two networks devotes more than 60% of hours to news, information and cultural subjects, while the commercial stations devote more than 60% to light entertainment and music; a similar pattern exists in the Philippines. In India, the four regional services give as much time to news and information as to light entertainment while a distinct national service broadcasts only popular entertainment and advertising. Almost all the countries rely entirely on nationally produced programmes. There is little exchange of programmes except that the People's Democratic Republic of Korea exchanges programmes with the People's Republic of China, the USSR and Eastern European countries.

In a number of countries, broadcasting is conducted in several widely spoken languages and in local languages. In Singapore, regular services are in English, Chinese, Malay and Tamil as is also the case in neighbouring Malaysia which broadcasts in eight other languages as well. All-India Radio broadcasts in nine major Indian languages, 50 local languages and 80 tribal dialects.

Organized systematic use of radio broadcasting for schools and adult education is found in only a dozen countries. In Japan, one NHK chain devotes 80% of hours to educational broadcasts for schools, universities, etc.; practically every school and university is equipped with receivers. In India, more than 20 000 schools regularly receive educational broadcasts and there are 28 500 radio rural forums. In Indonesia and the Philippines also, there are programmes for organized rural and farmers' groups. In the Philippines, 22 broadcasts a week are for the use of 48 000 primary-school classes, and the University of the Philippines broadcasts extramural courses.

Almost all the countries operate external broadcasting services but most are directed to neighbouring countries in Asia or only to one or two other parts of the world. Those broadcasting for a large number of hours in more than six languages to areas in most parts of the world include: the People's Republic of China, India, Indonesia, Israel, Japan, the Republic of Korea, Lebanon, Saudi Arabia and Thailand. Programmes from the People's Republic of China, which sends out 1500 hours a week to all parts of the world, are relayed by Albania in five European languages. The Voice of America transmits from the Philippines in English and Asian languages throughout Asia as does the BBC from Malaysia. Also from the Philippines, several Christian stations broadcast to continental Asia, including the Far East Broadcasting Company which transmits to seven target areas in Asia, the Pacific and the USSR in 46 languages.

The headquarters of the Asian Broadcasting Union is in Tokyo, and the Secretary-General's office is in Australia. There are 20 full members from Asian countries and Oceania, and associate members from 20 countries in Africa, Europe and North America, as well as Asia.

EUROPE

Radio broadcasting in 15 countries of Europe is run directly by the State; in two, Portugal and Spain, private commercial companies conduct domestic broadcasting services. In 11 countries, it is run by single autonomous public corporations set up by the State which are financed by revenue from licence fees fixed by the State; a few also obtain revenue from advertising. In the United Kingdom, the autonomous BBC is responsible for national and local broadcasting services financed from licence fees and for external services financed by an annual parliamentary grant, while the Independent Broadcasting Authority, an organization of private commercial companies, also established by Parliament, operates local broadcasting services financed by advertising revenue. In three countries – Andorra, Luxembourg and Monaco – and in the Federal Republic of Germany, there are commercial organizations financed from advertising revenue which exist to transmit programmes to neighbouring countries in Western Europe.

The number of all transmitters and of FM transmitters has increased in all countries over the past ten years. All parts of all the countries are effectively covered for reception of more than one programme.

The number of licences and receivers per 1000 people has increased in all but a few countries (in which the numbers were already among the highest); in nine countries, there have been large increases including 300% increases in Spain, Turkey and Yugoslavia. In 13 countries, there are between 150 and 300 receivers per 1000 people, and in another 13, the range is from 300 to 400, which means that in almost all of them virtually all households are reached.

The number of hours devoted to different types of programmes — news and reporting, light entertainment, music, drama and education — varies considerably between countries. Broadcasting services for individual cities and towns and their immediate localities, as distinct from large regional areas, are being developed in some countries and introduce further variety of programmes. In all countries where services are run by the State or by public corporations, there are school broadcasting services, and in many, educational courses for adults with, in some cases, formal enrolment of listeners as students seeking diplomas and degrees.

Exchange of programmes is common, either direct or by recordings, bilateral between pairs of countries or multilateral, in particular through the two European broadcasting unions, but apart from light entertainment programmes, exchanges tend to be confined to familiar language and ideological groupings.

All countries, with the exception of Andorra, Iceland, Ireland, Luxembourg and Monaco, operate government-sponsored external broadcasting services in their own and other languages as a means of making known their culture and policies and, in some cases, of maintaining contact with nationals or former nationals in other countries. Most of them broadcast to all parts of the world and in many languages, from 10 to as many as 40, and some of them for hundreds of hours a week. In the Federal Republic of Germany, there are two privately operated stations, Radio Liberty and Radio Free Europe, subsidized by the US Government which broadcast to Eastern Europe and the USSR. Trans World Radio, a privately financed Christian organization, transmits programmes from Monaco in 35 languages to all parts of the world.

Europe is the seat of the two oldest and most important international regional unions of national sound and visual broadcasting organizations — the European Broadcasting Union, EBU (headquarters Geneva) and the International Radio and Television Organization, OIRT (headquarters Prague). A third union, Nordvision, covers organizations in the five Scandinavian countries, which are also members of EBU, but is only concerned with television. These organizations cooperate with one another and with other regional organizations — the Asian Broadcasting Union (ABU), the Union of National Radio and Television Organizations of Africa (URTNA) and other multinational groups.

The active membership of EBU, created in 1950 to succeed the International Broadcasting Union founded in 1925, consists of one or more broadcasting organizations in 30 countries within the European Broadcasting Area as defined by the International Telecommunication Union, which includes the eastern Mediterranean and north Africa. There are also associate (non-voting) members in 34 countries outside the Area; they have the same basic rights as active members except the right to vote. The Union is non-governmental, non-political and non-commercial. It exists to promote the study of common problems and the exchange of information, to assist the development of broadcasting and to facilitate multilateral and bilateral exchanges and coproductions of radio and television programmes. By means of microwave links and cables, it maintains a permanent rented network of sound, vision and control circuits. The network can be linked, via earth stations, with satellites. It can also be linked with a similar network maintained by OIRT. Regular television news exchanges between the two organizations started in 1965 through EBU's Eurovision system (set up in 1954) and OIRT's Intervision system (set up in 1960).

OIRT, founded in 1946, has a member organization in 25 countries, 15 of them in Europe and the USSR, one of which, Finland, is also a member of EBU; the other countries are Algeria, the People's Republic of China, Cuba, Egypt, Iraq, the Democratic People's Republic of Korea, Mali, Mongolia, the Sudan and the People's Republic of Vietnam. Members of OIRT must be either State-owned and operated organizations or public corporations under the control of the State. Its purposes are the same as those of EBU and it maintains similar technical services to facilitate exchanges.

The activities and services of EBU and OIRT have greatly increased multilateral exchanges and general cooperation between their respective members and between the countries of Eastern and Western Europe and the USSR. Their services also facilitate bilateral exchanges and single-country to single-country broadcasts.

OCEANIA

Radio broadcasting services are highly developed in Australia and New Zealand and cover practically the whole population; in both, there are around 700 receivers per 1000 people. In both countries also, there is a government authority responsible for supervising the operation of services provided by a public corporation and by private commercial companies. In Australia, many of the 118 stations run by private companies are linked with newspapers or publishing concerns; in New Zealand, where the public corporation operates stations which carry commercial advertising, there are only 5 private commercial stations broadcasting for some 800 hours a week, compared with nearly 6000 hours by the public corporation.

While Australia beams programmes for more than 100 hours a week to eight areas throughout the world in English, French and six Asian languages, New Zealand beams programmes for 36 hours a week to Pacific Islands, Australia and south-east Asia, almost entirely in English.

An important place is given by the public corporations to educational broadcasts to schools and for adults. In Australia, 90% of the schools use daily broadcasts; in New Zealand, 70 hours a week are devoted to school broadcasts, and more than 100 to adult education.

USSR

All radio broadcasting comes under the Radio and Television Committee of the USSR Council of Ministers and is financed, for the larger part, from the State budget. Radio programmes and broadcasts are initiated from Moscow and the capitals of the Union and autonomous republics. Local responsibility is vested in some 150 radio and television committees. There are now more than 3000 transmitters covering virtually the whole of the USSR as compared with some 400 ten years ago. There are almost 95 million receivers, as compared with 44 million ten years ago, 40 million of which are linked to wired redistribution networks; this is a ratio of 390 receivers per 1000 people, ie virtually all households.

The Central Radio Service for Moscow broadcasts seven programmes in Russian for 990 hours a week. Each programme has a distinct character by content or by audience envisaged. These programmes are relayed in whole or in part in the republics and districts and are supplemented with locally originated programmes in one or other of the 67 national languages. A considerable amount of time is devoted to school broadcasts and to the Lenin University of the Millions.

Broadcasts to foreign countries throughout the world are carried out by Radio Moscow and the stations of ten Union republics in 60 languages for a total of more than 1500 hours a week. Another station, Peace and Progress, operated by Soviet professional organizations, broadcasts to all areas of the world, except North America, in 14 languages.

SECTION 2 TELEVISION

AFRICA

Television has still hardly touched Africa. In the past ten years, 14 countries have started television services, making 24 in all. All these services are run or controlled by the State; in a few countries, there are also commercial stations. There is still no television in 20 countries including Angola, Mozambique and Namibia. South Africa is preparing to start services in 1975 with, first, one channel in English and Afrikaans covering the highly populated urban areas, and later, a channel for Africans.

The potential geographical coverage and audiences are very low in most of the countries and the number of hours on the air is small. The ratio of receivers per 1000 people is between 10 and 30 in the Ivory Coast, Kenya, Mauritius, Morocco, Tunisia and Egypt; in the rest, it is below 10, and − in most − well below. Egypt has the largest television broadcasting services although the number of receivers is only around 20 per 1000 people. Egypt exports some 1200 hours of programmes a year to other Arabic-speaking countries in Africa and Asia; it imports some 1800 hours a year from the USA, 300 hours from France and 400 from Eastern European countries; in all, about 40% of total programmes. In other countries where the number of hours on the air is much less, the percentage of imported programmes is smaller.

In several countries, television was specifically introduced as a means of promoting education and economic and social development, and it is notably used for these purposes in Ghana, the Ivory Coast, Niger and Senegal. In the Ivory Coast, an important experiment, assisted by the United Nations Development Fund and Unesco, is being carried out in the use of television for school education: in 1971–2, over 450 classes with some 20 000 pupils were receiving 8 hours a week of televised instruction and the intention is to expand this service to cover all schools. In Ghana, school programmes take about a third of the hours on the air. In Senegal, the first television programmes were a series of programmes on health and nutrition for women's teleclubs around Dakar and the major part of the small number of hours on the air is still devoted to adult education.

NORTH AMERICA

Television services exist in all the countries of English-speaking and Spanish-speaking North America, and the number of transmitters and receivers has greatly increased in most of them. But only in Canada, Cuba and the USA is a large part of the population reached. Thus in Mexico, where there are over 70 stations covering more than 70% of the population, and the number of receivers has increased from around 1 million to over 3 million, the ratio is below 100 per 1000 people, and most of the receivers are in the towns. In the Spanish-speaking countries, except Cuba, the major services are run by private companies; in two of these countries, El Salvador and Mexico, there are also government stations. In the English-speaking Caribbean countries, the services are run by autonomous public corporations. In Cuba, the services are State operated; educational broadcasts, of which there are more than 70 a week, include morning and afternoon programmes for secondary schools, 10 000 of which have receivers. In Mexico, educational and cultural programmes only are broadcast by two government networks and educational programmes for secondary schools produced by the Government are broadcast by the commercial stations under a law which requires them to make 12.5% of their air-time available for this purpose.

In the Spanish-speaking countries, Cuba apart, the amount of advertising time and the pattern of programmes are much the same as in the South American countries. For foreign news and information, the stations depend on one or more of the world agencies. The percentage of imported programmes shown, most of them serials and feature films, ranges from 40 to 80%, and of this, 50 to 60% comes from the USA, 30 to 40% from Spanish-speaking countries, mainly Mexico and Argentina, and an average of 10% from Western Europe – Spain, Italy and France. Mexico is a very large exporter of programmes, but many of them are dubbed versions of US programmes. In Cuba, where the programme structure is markedly different (80% education, culture and news and 20% entertainment), practically all programmes are nationally produced.

In the English-speaking Caribbean countries, a large proportion of programmes are imported from the USA and the UK, and occassionally from Canada and Western European countries.

The USA has the largest number of television companies, transmitters and receivers in the world. It is also the largest programme exporter. In all countries of the world outside China, Cuba, Eastern Europe and the USSR, American programmes exported by television companies and films distributed by film companies compose the major part of all imported programmes and, in many countries, a large part of total programmes. On the other hand, the USA – commercial and non-commercial stations alike – imports less than 2% of total programmes whereas the total hours broadcast are greater than in any other country. The largest part of the imported programmes are British; some come from Canada, Japan and the Federal Republic of Germany; some films are imported from Western and Eastern Europe and the USSR.

There are 915 stations and 2780 transmitters covering the country, and almost 99 million sets in use in 65 million homes (over 95%); some 37 million have colour receivers, a higher proportion than in any country in the world. Some 700 stations are commercially owned and operated (178 being owned by newspapers and magazines) and almost all are affiliated to one of the three large networks which also dominate radio broadcasting. There are 220 non-commercial educational stations in 47 of the 50 states, operated by universities, public schools systems and cooperative educational television organizations and covering more than 80% of the population. Cable or community-antenna television has expanded greatly; there are now some 4900 CATV systems serving about 6 million homes, the majority serving around 1000 subscribers with an average of 15 different programmes, and the largest, with 35 000 subscribers, offering a choice of 44 programmes. Systems with over 10 000 subscribers (100 of them in 1972) are required by the FCC to install feedback equipment for audience participation.

In Canada, the public corporation, CBC, broadcasts through 19 originating stations and over 300 relay and rebroadcasting stations organized in two networks, one English and the other French. As from April 1973, CBC began to distribute its full television services via the domestic geostationary satellite, Anik, and will eventually cover the whole country, except the central area, in this way. Some 250 privately owned stations operated by more than 70 companies provide local services but also have network facilities through affiliation with the CBC or with CTV, a cable distribution network owned by 12 stations which serves a million subscribers and distributes programmes originating in both Canada and the USA. Some 5.8 million households (in a population of 22 million) have receivers, and 18% has colour receivers. General educational programmes and school programmes are broadcast by the CBC and by some commercial stations. One CBC station in Toronto broadcasts educational programmes for 15 hours a day for both schools and adults.

CBC imports some 40% of its programmes, of which 50% comes from the USA, 20% from France and the rest from the UK and a wider than usual range of other European countries.

SOUTH AMERICA

Television now exists in all the countries of South America. The number of transmitters, geographical coverage and the number of receivers have greatly increased over the past ten years in all countries except Bolivia, where the State-run service initiated and still largely operated for educational purposes began only in 1969. But in only two countries, Argentina and Uruguay, is the number of receivers per 1000 people over 100. The majority of receivers are in urban areas because of lack of electricity and purchasing power in the rural areas.

The pattern of ownership and operation of television services is different from that of radio broadcasting. The State owns and operates television services of varying importance in all the countries except Ecuador where there are only private commercial stations, the most powerful of which is operated by the North America-based World Radio Missionary Fellowship. Argentina, Brazil, Uruguay and Venezuela, where the services are predominantly private and commercial, also have State services, notably Brazil, which are of particular importance in the fields of information and education. In most countries, State services – like the private stations – are largely financed by advertising revenue. On average, as much as 25% of transmission hours are taken by advertising and commercially sponsored programmes.

In Colombia, one of three government channels is devoted exclusively to education. In Chile, besides the State service, there are services run by universities; these are financed by the State and by advertising. In Peru, the State operates educational television centres.

Around 70% of programme time (ie excluding advertising) seems to be devoted to entertainment and, in most countries, the larger part of that time is devoted to serials and feature films, most of them imported. The amount of imported programmes ranges from around 30 to 70% and most come from the USA. Some programmes are imported from Argentina and Mexico, but few from elsewhere.

ASIA

Television services have been started in 12 Asian countries in the past ten years, and now exist in all except Afghanistan, Bahrain, Burma, Laos, Nepal, Sri Lanka and the Yemen Arab Republic. In many of the countries, coverage in terms of transmitters and the audience reached in terms of receivers per 1000 people are low. In 17, the ratio of receivers is less than 50 per 1000 people; in five, it is between 100 and 200, and in Japan, more than 200. The size and physical configuration of many of the countries, lack of electricity outside the towns, and low incomes are factors impeding development.

In most of the countries, television services – like radio services – are run by the State directly or sometimes through arrangements with commercial companies, and in a few, by commercial companies alone. In Lebanon, where radio broadcasting is run by the State, television services are run by two private commercial companies. In Cyprus and Israel, the services are run by public corporations set up by the State. In Japan, the public corporation, NHK, broadcasts on two networks through 1000 transmitters, and there are also some 80 commercial companies broadcasting through more than 1200 transmitters. Both systems cover practically the whole country and, although the number of receivers per 1000 people is low compared with industrialized countries in Europe and North America, it is probable that most of the population view television programmes. Cable television systems now exist in Tokyo and Osaka.

The People's Republic of China, India, Israel, Japan and Singapore, make great use of television for strictly educational purposes. In China, the Peking TV University broadcasts study courses at the secondary and university levels. In Israel, some 30 hours a week are received by 1100 schools with over 500 000 pupils. In Japan, 90% of pre-primary and primary schools and over 30% of secondary schools have receivers, and 90% of the time on one of the two NHK networks is used for school broadcasts. In Singapore, all primary and secondary schools have receivers, and lessons are broadcast every day in the country's four official languages. In India, school broadcasts reach some 400 schools around

Delhi, and there are broadcasts for farmers' teleclubs; in 1975, educational programmes will be transmitted from a ground station to a geosynchronous satellite and retransmitted by various means to 5000 villages, for a one-year experiment.

At the Film Institute of India at Poona, which provides a three-year course to some 150 students including many from other Asian countries, a television training institute was set up in 1972 by the Government of India, with assistance from the United Nations and Unesco, to train staff that will be needed to produce programmes for this satellite community reception project. In Malaysia, the first steps have been taken towards the establishment of an Asian Broadcasting Training Institute, based on the existing national centre, to provide professional, technical and administrative training for television and radio personnel for Asian countries.

With the exception of a few countries, notably the People's Republic of China, and India, the countries of Asia rely for a large part of their television programmes on programmes and films imported from other countries, in particular from the USA. The percentage of imported programmes ranges from 30% to as much as 70%. Within these percentages, more than half the programmes come from the USA. Imports from other countries vary, although the UK usually comes second, well below the USA. Exceptions are the Arabic-speaking countries, which exchange programmes between themselves and import programmes from Egypt. Language problems limit exports from Japan, which otherwise leads in the television field, but a number of features originally produced for exhibition in cinemas are shown on television in many countries of the world.

The Asian Broadcasting Union, from 1968 to 1971, produced a fortnightly news magazine – *Asian Vision* – to promote the exchange of television news and information but the operation was abandoned because of uncertain delivery of the programmes by aeroplane. The union is now working on a plan to exchange material by television transmission via Indonesia, on the lines of Eurovision and Intervision.

EUROPE

Highly developed television services have existed for a long time in almost all the countries of Europe, and the number of channels and transmitters (now in colour as well as black and white in almost all) has increased over the last ten years. The number of receivers has increased two to five times in most countries, and in some, by even more. The number of receivers per 1000 people is below 100 in six countries, up to 200 in nine, over 200 in 12, and over 300 in the UK and Sweden.

The television services are controlled and operated by the same State organizations, public corporations and commercial services as run the radio broadcasting services. In the Netherlands, the system of operation entitles certain religious and social organizations to a number of hours of transmission time per week, the programmes for which are not controlled in advance, by the Netherlands Broadcasting Foundation. In more and more countries, whatever the type of operation, commercial advertising – even if very limited compared with many countries in the Americas, for example – is now allowed and supplements State funds and revenue from licence fees.

Television distribution by cable exists in a few countries at different stages of development and others seem to be preparing for it. In Belgium, some 200 000 subscribers have a choice of 11 programmes originating in Belgium and three adjacent countries; in Switzerland, the number of subscribers is smaller and for some there is a choice between 7 or 8 programmes. In the UK, where only national programmes are distributed to subscribers, local production has been authorized in selected towns as an experiment. In France, where distribution by cable has yet to begin, experiments are being carried out in six towns.

In many parts of Europe, it is possible for viewers to receive programmes originating in neighbouring countries, which can result in political and commercial problems and competition for viewers, besides cultural exchanges across frontiers.

Educational television broadcasts are highly developed throughout most of Europe. In many countries, the morning and, often, afternoon hours are taken up by broadcasts to schools and universities organized in cooperation with, or by, Ministries of Education. In some countries, there are also organized evening programmes for adult education. In a few of these, notably the Federal Republic of Germany, France, Poland, Switzerland and the UK, recognized higher education courses are broadcast in the evenings for adults who may register and take examinations leading to diplomas and degrees.

The countries of Western Europe broadcast from 2000 to 7000 hours of programmes a year, and they take between 10 and 30% of their programmes from other countries, except for Finland which takes 40%, Ireland 50% and Iceland 60%. Apart from news and sports, the largest part of the programmes taken are serials and films. For the Western European countries, the USA is the largest source, accounting on average for probably 50%, followed by the UK. Few take much from many other countries; exceptions are Finland – receiving from 20 countries including 10% from Eastern Europe and the USSR – and Sweden, receiving 75% from European countries, including 7% from Eastern Europe and the USSR and 25% from other countries, including the USA. The UK, and then the Federal Republic of Germany, France, Italy and Spain are large exporters to countries outside Europe.

The countries of Eastern Europe broadcast from 2000 to 6000 hours a year, and receive between 30 and 40% of their programmes from other countries, the larger part from the USSR and other Eastern European countries. A few acquire up to 40% of their programmes from Western European countries, and occasional programmes and films from the USA.

Through Eurovision (EBU) and Intervision (OIRT) (see Radio, Europe), the countries of Europe regularly exchange, in increasing quantity, news items and programmes within their respective organization and with the other one. Exchanges are also organized between the five Scandinavian countries which are members of EBU through Nordvision.

Under bilateral arrangements the countries also exchange and sell programmes, by direct transmission via EBU and OIRT networks or in video-tape form; they also arrange coproductions. An increasing number of exchanges are being effected via space satellite links.

Of Eurovision's total volume of exchanges, consisting of some 2000 programmes and news items a year (totalling about 1200 hours' transmission time), around 90% are either news or sports. Almost half (45%) of all the news items of Eurovision originate in the UK, London being the film distribution centre for the major newsfilm agencies – Visnews (UK), UPITN (UK and USA) and CBS-Newsfilm (USA) – to which all television services in Europe and nearly all television stations in the world subscribe. Other major originating countries of news items are France (10%), Italy (10%), the Federal Republic of Germany (7%) and the Intervision countries (7%).

The major originators of Eurovision news, however, are only minor receivers. The BBC in 1970 took only 12% of the total supply of news items, whereas Yugoslavia and Austria, the major receivers, took nearly three-quarters. Of all Eurovision programme exchanges (as distinct from news items) in 1970, the UK originated 14% and the Intervision countries another 14%, the Federal Republic of Germany 10% and Yugoslavia 9%. Ten Western European countries took more than 20% of programmes offered and Intervision took one-third.

In 1970, the Intervision countries originated around 1400 hours of news items and programmes and took approximately 3500 hours (including Eurovision exchanges). In the 1971 news exchange alone, Eurovision accepted 4300 news items which were taken on an average by 12 organizations while Intervision accepted 3400 items which were taken by 2 or 3 organizations.

Of the total hours of Intervision exchanges in 1971, news and sports formed 70%. The USSR originated one-third of all the Intervision news items. Other major originators were Czechoslovakia (20%) and Poland (19%). Bulgaria and the USSR took more than a half the total supply, Czechoslovakia a third, and the others around 20%.

As for the programmes accepted by Intervision in 1970, Eurovision countries originated 28% (mainly sports), the USSR 23% and other socialist countries 4 to 12%. The main receivers of Intervision programmes were the USSR and the German Democratic Republic, each taking almost half the total supply. About a third of the Intervision programmes taken by each Intervision country originated in the USSR and another third in Eurovision countries.

In the exchange of news items between Eurovision and Intervision in 1971, Intervision took almost 3000 items from Eurovision while the Eurovision countries took 300 from Intervision. Intervision takes approximately 65% of all the news items offered to it by Eurovision while Eurovision takes only 10% of the items offered by Intervision.

In the exchange of programmes (other than news items), Eurovision stations in 1970 used 640 hours of 214 programmes transmitted by Intervision, and Intervision used 945 hours of 374 programmes transmitted by Eurovision. More than half the Eurovision programmes originated in three countries because of big sports events. Of the Intervision programmes a third originated in the USSR, 20% in Czechoslovakia, 18% in Romania and 15% in the German Democratic Republic. These three also took about half the Eurovision programmes offered while the remaining Intervision members took around 25%.

It has been estimated that the total number of hours of all television material taken by the countries of Eastern Europe and the USSR via Eurovision, and through bilateral arrangements and purchases, runs at about 3000 hours a year. The countries of Western Europe take around 1000 hours. The total transmission time of all television services in the countries of Western Europe amounts to some 60 000 hours, which is about double that in the Intervision countries. This would suggest that the countries of Western Europe as a whole devote around

2% of their transmission time to material from Eastern European countries and the USSR while the latter devote 10% of their time to material from Western Europe.

OCEANIA

Television services have developed greatly over the last ten years in both Australia and New Zealand and it is estimated that over 80% of households have a receiver. In Australia, there are parallel public corporation and private commercial services as for radio whereas, in New Zealand, television services are run only by the public corporation, and the programmes include commercial advertising four days a week, in a total of 40 minutes.

In Australia, educational programmes are broadcast for almost the whole school day to primary and secondary schools, some 6000 of which (out of some 11 000) have television receivers. In New Zealand, a pilot project for educational television services to schools, beginning with primary schools, is under consideration.

Both countries import about 50% of their programmes of all kinds but, as elsewhere, particularly serials and films, and of the imported programmes, about 60% come from the USA and 30% from the UK.

USSR

The television services, which are operated by the State, have greatly developed, and the number of receivers has increased from 7 to 35 million, which is around 150 per 1000. There are 285 transmitters covering practically the whole country. In addition, programmes are relayed from Moscow via satellite to ground stations in 37 towns in Siberia, and in the Far Eastern and central Asian regions. Educational broadcasts directly related to secondary education and university curricula are broadcast on one channel morning and afternoon, five days a week, and on another, there are broadcasts in the afternoon and early evening by the Lenin University of the Millions.

Little programme material is imported from outside and most of it comes from the countries of Eastern Europe. Soviet television is a major supplier of programmes to Eastern European countries through Intervision and bilateral arrangements.

CHAPTER 4

FILM

The world film pattern in the seventies is markedly different from the pattern for the other media. Some 50 countries are regularly producing feature-length entertainment films (in all, around 4000 a year) and the rest of the world depends on them for supply. Eight countries in Africa have recently produced their first feature-length films. Other countries are regularly producing documentary and educational films only. In all countries except those of Eastern Europe, the USSR, Cuba, the People's Republic of China and the Democratic People's Republic of Korea, film production, distribution and exhibition are run by private commercial enterprises. In a dozen or so countries (nine in Western Europe), the State, for cultural and economic reasons, gives financial and other concrete assistance to private commercial production.

The two largest producing countries, each making around 400 feature films a year, are Asian – India and Japan (in 1965, Japan produced nearly 900 and was by far the largest producer ever of feature films). Four Asian countries (the Republic of Korea, the Democratic People's Republic of Korea, the Philippines and Hong Kong) produce between 100 and 200, three others more than 50, and seven from 5 to 30 each. No figures are available for the People's Republic of China later than 1964 when the number of feature films produced was reported to have been well over 400. Asian feature films are produced essentially for domestic exhibition; most Asian countries have large numbers of cinemas and high cinema attendances, although attendances, as in almost all countries in the world, are small in relation to the total population and are predominantly urban. Only a small number of films produced in Asia reach audiences outside the continent – these are shown in Europe and North America, usually in a limited number of cinemas specializing in foreign films.

The three largest feature-film producing countries outside Asia, producing between 200 and 300 films a year, are Italy, the USA and the USSR; in the USA production which had dropped from 400 to 140 in 1961 had risen to 280 in 1971. Next in output, producing between 100 and 200, come France, the Federal Republic of Germany, Greece, Spain and Turkey in Europe and, in Central America, Mexico. Then come the UK (90), Egypt (60), Brazil (50) and Czechoslovakia (50). Besides the countries in Asia already referred to, 12 countries – including Argentina – produce between 10 and 30, while another ten, including two Spanish-speaking countries, produce around 5. Half of the 28 countries producing less than 30 films have languages peculiar to themselves, which means that, except for occasional outstanding ones, their films are rarely shown in other countries.

In all, 17 Asian countries produce more than half the world's feature-length entertainment films. Twenty-four European countries and the USSR produce about a third. The rest are produced by ten countries, notably the USA, Mexico, Egypt and Brazil.

The numbers of cinemas, cinema seats and annual cinema attendances in Asia are increasing whereas in most of the rest of the world they now seem to be more or less stable at much lower figures than ten years ago. Even so, in seven Western European countries, the number of cinemas ranges from 1000 in Greece to over 10 000 in Italy, and in five Eastern European countries from 2800 in Poland to over 6000 in Romania. In the USSR, the number of cinemas and halls in which films are regularly shown has increased by 50% to 147 000, and attendances by 30%.

The world distribution pattern is largely determined by language (and has been since the coming of sound). Dubbing or subtitling is expensive and is now obligatory in a number of countries for films which are widely released. Cultural affinities, as well as political and commercial ties, also affect the pattern. Thus, Chinese-language films are distributed in many Asian countries which have large Chinese populations, but other Asian-language films are largely confined to their country of origin. American films are the most widely distributed foreign films in most Asian countries. Indeed, English-language films, and predominantly those of American origin, occupy a very large part of screen time in almost all countries except the USSR, the countries of Eastern Europe, the People's Republic of China, India and a few others. The distribution of the great majority of Russian-language films is limited to the USSR and other countries with similar economic, social and cultural systems. The USSR imports around 100 films a year from a wide range of countries. The 20 or so Spanish-language countries receive Spanish-language films from the three countries regularly producing them – Mexico, Spain and Argentina. Arabic-speaking countries are almost entirely dependent on Egypt, although in the coming years Algeria, Morocco and Tunisia, together with Lebanon, may increase the supply. The Spanish- and Arabic-speaking countries, because of Latin cultural affinities and other ties and contacts, import a number of French and Italian films. Similar considerations of language and colonial history affect the import of films in the different countries of Africa. The USA imports films from many countries, notably the UK, France, and Italy, but often only for distribution to the increasing number of small, specialized cinemas. To enhance the possibilities of wider international distribution and hence to offset costs, and occasionally for artistic reasons also, producers in several larger film-making countries are increasingly resorting to coproduction with enterprises in other countries; the major coproducers, in some cases to the extent of almost half their total production, are France, Italy, Spain and the UK, particularly with the USA.

The vast majority of feature-length films produced in almost all countries are dramatized fictional films designed for showing in public cinemas where people pay to be entertained. Other kinds of films – newsreels, documentaries, and even short entertainment films such as animated cartoons – have almost disappeared from the public screens in most countries. But thousands of documentary and educational films are produced every year, not only in countries where feature films are produced but in many others as well. They are produced for television or for showing in schools and other educational institutions. In many countries where there is commercial feature-film production by private enterprise, and also in some countries where there is none, there are government film services and autonomous public film boards producing and distributing such films and even exhibiting them by means of mobile units in schools, community halls, libraries, museums, etc. These films are seen by tens of thousands of small audiences of schoolchildren and students of all kinds, industrial workers and farmers, scientists, doctors and other professional workers and by general community audiences seeking information and instruction. Many of the films are diffused by television organizations during hours devoted to educational programmes. It seems likely that it will be via television in different forms rather than by means of film projectors installed in schools, etc. that the use of films for educational and instructional purposes will be extended and developed to its full potential. Exchanges and coproduction of educational films are developing. In these various ways, the film continues to be used deliberately to spread information, education and culture and to promote understanding between peoples. Films made to entertain people will continue to have powerful influences on how they think and feel, and on their knowledge of and attitudes towards other peoples.

PART TWO

AFRICA

Algeria
Angola
Botswana
Burundi
Cameroon
Cape Verde Islands
Central African Republic
Chad
Comoro Islands
Congo (People's Republic of)
Dahomey
Egypt (Arab Republic of)
Equatorial Guinea
Ethiopia
French Territory of the Afars
 and the Issars
Gabon
Ghana
Guinea
Ivory Coast
Kenya
Lesotho
Liberia
Libyan Arab Republic
Madagascar
Malawi
Mali
Mauritania

Mauritius and Dependencies
Morocco
Mozambique
Namibia
Niger
Nigeria
Portuguese Guinea
Reunion
Rhodesia
Rwanda
St Helena and Dependencies
São Tomé and Principe
Senegal
Seychelles
Sierra Leone
Somali
South Africa (Republic of)
Spanish Sahara
Sudan
Swaziland
Tanzania
Togo
Tunisia
Uganda
Upper Volta
Zaïre
Zambia

ALGERIA

Population	15 270 000
Area	2 381 741 sq. km.

PRESS
Newspapers	Dailies 4, Non-dailies 8
Total circulation	Dailies 275 000, Non-dailies 160 000
Copies per 1000 people	Dailies 18, Non-dailies 10

RADIO
Transmitters	Long/medium-wave 20, Short-wave 5
Total receivers	700 000 estimated in use
Receivers per 1000 people	46

TELEVISION
Transmitters	13
Receivers	150 000 estimated in use
Receivers per 1000 people	10

FILM
Cinemas	Fixed 640
Total seating capacity	218 758
Seats per 1000 people	14
Total annual attendance	89 323 000*
Annual visits per capita	6

*Including attendance at mobile cinemas.

PRESS

Of the four major dailies, two appear in the capital, Algiers, the largest being published in French by the government party organization and the other published in Arabic, also under official auspices. Constantine and Oran also each have one daily published in French. Among the main current affairs weeklies, one is published in Arabic, the rest in French. One monthly has separate French and Arabic editions.

Over 100 periodicals are published with an aggregate circulation of 238 000 copies, the main subject categories being legal and administrative (18 titles circulating 47 000 copies per issue), general interest (14 titles, 36 000 copies), trade and industry (9 titles, 15 000 copies), education, politics, agriculture, sports, etc. Five sports papers together circulate 43 000 copies per issue.

All imports, exports and distribution of periodicals and books are carried out by a single national publishing and distributing agency.

NEWS AGENCIES

The national agency is the State-owned Algérie Presse Service (APS), founded in Tunis in 1961 and now established in Algiers. It issues, in Arabic, French and English, international news received through AFP, UPI and Reuters and national news received from its own home correspondents. News transmission from the latter to the central office is effected by permanently leased cable-teleprinter circuit and by radio teleprinter, telex and telephone. Special APS services include features, photos and economic news bulletins and an audio-radio service.

Foreign agencies repesented in Algeria include ANSA, AP, BTA, CTK, MENA and Novosti (with bureaux in Algiers), and AFP, DPA, MAP, PRELA, Reuters, TASS and UPI.

RADIO

All broadcasting, both radio and television, is carried out by Radiodiffusion-Télévision Algérienne (RTA), a State-owned and operated, but financially autonomous public, corporation. Its revenue is derived from radio (or combined radio—TV) receiver licence fees and also, since January 1971, from advertising.

RTA sound-radio services consist of three networks broadcasting respectively in Arabic and French (each up to 18 hours a day) and Kabyle (up to 12½ hours a day) on both medium and short wave. The 16 medium-wave transmitters (located in eight cities) include two of 600kW and two of 120kW, and the 8 short-wave transmitters consist of two of 120kW, two of 100kW and four of 50kW. The entire country is thus covered by radio services.

Weekly programmes, totalling over 300 hours, include light entertainment (121 hours), arts, letters and science (75 hours), broadcasts for special audiences (35 hours), news and information (34 hours), school and adult education including literacy (34 hours), and broadcasts for ethnic minorities (4 hours). Over 95% is of national production.

Arabic-language broadcasts are also relayed on short wave for 18 hours a day for listeners in Morocco and the Middle East, while some French-language relays (12 hours a day) are beamed to Europe.

TELEVISION

RTA's television service, which began in 1956, is potentially available to 80% of the population living in the northern parts of the country through a network of seven main transmitters and six auxiliaries (625 lines). The national programme, in Arabic, French and Kabyle, is on the air for 40 hours a week broadcasting news and information (9½ hours), cultural and scientific programmes (8½ hours), light entertainment (8 hours), programmes for special audiences (8 hours), educational programmes (5½ hours) and broadcasts for ethnic minorities (30 minutes). Educational programmes include two 30-minute periods a day for schools, four times a week, during school terms. About 36% of the programmes broadcast are of national origin; some others are the result of exchanges with Morocco and Tunisia through the joint Mahgreb-vision organization.

FILM

The Office National pour le Commerce et l'Industrie Cinématographiques, established in 1967, is the government body, within the Ministry of Information, responsible for the import and distribution of films, the granting of production permits and the general regulation and production of the industry. It may also produce films itself. Under the same ministry, the functions of the Centre Algérien de la Cinématographie include the programming of cinemas, censorship, film education (by means of clubs, itinerant cinemas, and film libraries) and various administrative responsibilities.

Though scantily equipped technically, the Algerian film industry, both nationalized and privately financed, maintains a steady level of production, averaging between three and four full-length features annually in recent years, plus one or two coproductions (with Italy and France in 1971) as well as a number of documentaries (about 12 in 1971).

Feature films imported totalled 104 a year in 1971 coming mainly from France, the USA, Italy, India, the UK, Egypt, Lebanon and the USSR. In the same year, 40 documentaries were imported.

Cinemas (which include 290 35mm and 150 16mm units) operating all the year round are managed by local communal authorities. In addition, there are 200 16mm cinemas open for only six months of the year and 16 mobile units operated both by government services and by private enterprise.

SPACE COMMUNICATIONS
An Atlantic Intelsat earth station near Algiers is to come into operation in 1974.

PROFESSIONAL TRAINING
Journalists are trained at the École Nationale Supérieure de Journalisme in Algiers.

ANGOLA

Population	5 430 000
Area	1 246 700 sq. km.

PRESS

Newspapers	Dailies 4, Non-dailies 15
Total circulation	Dailies 66 000
Copies per 1000 people	Dailies 12

RADIO

Transmitters	Long/medium-wave 24, Short-wave 40, VHF–FM 13
Total receivers	110 000 estimated in use
Receivers per 1000 people	20

FILM

Cinemas	Fixed 35
Total seating capacity	28 000
Seats per 1000 people	5
Total annual attendance	2 900 000
Annual visits per capita	0.5

PRESS

Four daily newspapers, all in Portuguese, are published in the capital, Luanda. The 15 non-dailies, which are mostly weeklies and include one official bulletin, appear in Luanda, Lobito, Benguela and eight other centres.

Periodicals cater for religious, cultural, technical, sports and youth readerships, and again are mostly published in Portuguese.

National newsprint production amounts to some 600 metric tons a year as against an annual consumption of 2100 metric tons.

NEWS AGENCIES

The Government Information and Tourist Centre, which receives ANI, AFP, Reuters and UPI services, is the main source of international and national news.

RADIO

The government-owned network Emissora Oficial de Angola operates 4 medium-wave transmitters, 5 short-wave transmitters (including two of 100kW) and 2 FM transmitters in Luanda, as well as 2 medium-wave regional stations in Saurimo and Menongue. Its three programmes are broadcast, respectively, in Portuguese for 19 hours a day, in Portuguese, French and English for 13 hours a day, and in Portuguese for 6 hours every evening.

The other 17 organizations broadcasting on medium and short wave and FM are privately owned and commercially operated. They include the Catholic station, Radio Ecclesia, with 2 medium-wave and 2 short-wave transmitters, which is on the air for 24 hours a day; 12 radio clubs, some with several programmes, broadcasting in Portuguese and also in French and English; and 3 other commercial stations, all in Luanda, one of which broadcasts in nine local dialects as well as in Portuguese. A diamond-mining enterprise operates a private station broadcasting programmes of music intended for its employees working near Luanda.

FILM

There is no local film production. Of the films exhibited, 40% are imported from Portugal and 50% from the USA. Public cinemas are located in Luanda (11), Lobito (4) and 15 smaller towns.

SPACE COMMUNICATIONS

An Atlantic Intelsat earth station, near Luanda, is to come into operation in 1974.

BOTSWANA

Population	690 000
Area	600 372 sq. km.

PRESS

Newspapers	Dailies 2, Non-dailies 2
Total circulation	Dailies 13 500, Non-dailies 9000
Copies per 1000 people	Dailies 20, Non-dailies 13

RADIO

Transmitters	Long/medium-wave 1, Short-wave 2, VHF--FM 1
Total receivers	11 744 licences
Licences per 1000 people	17

FILM

Cinemas	Fixed 11
Total seating capacity	3000
Seats per 1000 people	4
Total annual attendance	75 000
Annual visits per capita	0.1

PRESS

The government information department sponsors daily newspapers in each of the country's two official languages, English and Setswana. These are published in the capital, Gaborone, as are two non-dailies, one in English and one in Setswana. A third non-daily, which is bilingual, is actually printed across the South African border in Mafeking.

Some 50 periodicals (including 33 yearly publications) are reported as circulating in the country. Almost all are in English and the majority deal with political science, law and economics.

RADIO

The government station, Radio Botswana, broadcasts in English and Setswana, potentially reaching 90% of the population.

Programmes, totalling 102 hours a week, include news and information (38 hours, including relays of BBC news), educational (31 hours, including 16 hours specially for schools), light entertainment (26 hours), broadcasts for special audiences (3 hours) and cultural and scientific (2 hours). Almost all programmes are of national origin.

A licence fee is payable for radio receivers.

FILMS

Gaborone has two cinemas with seating capacities of 754 and 400. Films are also exhibited in the larger towns in the south of the country.

BURUNDI

Population	3 620 000
Area	27 834 sq. km.

PRESS

Newspapers	Dailies 1*, Non-dailies 3
Total circulation	Dailies 300, Non-dailies 47 000
Copies per 1000 people	Dailies 0.08, Non-dailies 13

RADIO

Transmitters	Long/medium-wave 4, Short-wave 2, VHF–FM 1
Total receivers	100 000 estimated in use
Receivers per 1000 people	28

FILM

Cinemas	Fixed 2
Total seating capacity	600
Seats per 1000 people	0.17
Total annual attendance	151 500
Annual visits per capita	0.04

*A bulletin.

PRESS

A government information bulletin is the country's only daily newspaper.

Three fortnightly journals, all carrying current news, features and letters from readers, are published in the capital, Bujumbura. Two of these, which together have a circulation of over 45 000, are in Kirundi, the national language. The other, with a circulation of about 1500, is published in French. The widespread practice of group reading, however, makes the effective readership of these papers much higher than the figures given. After its neighbour Rwanda, Burundi has the highest population density in continental Africa.

A dozen other periodical publications, all in French, have a total circulation of 7600.

NEWS AGENCIES

Though there is as yet no national agency, the Government operates a daily news service which could be the nucleus of a State-owned press agency. A daily bulletin is issued, carrying about 1600 words of local news, 1200 words of news from other African countries, 2000 words on overseas affairs, and miscellaneous items. It is served by local adminstrative offices acting as correspondents for domestic news and by the foreign agencies AFP, CTK and TASS.

Among the local press, AP has three subscribers and CTK and TASS one each. The State radio and one government department subscribe to AFP.

RADIO

Owned and completely financed by the Government, the station La Voix de la Révolution broadcasts two programmes, both covering the whole country. The first, consisting mainly of entertainment, adult education and medical and agricultural broadcasts carried by the 25kW short-wave transmitter at Bujumbura, is on the air daily for a total of 122 hours a week. The second, on the air for 2½ hours, five evenings a week, includes both light entertainment and educational programmes. About 80% of programmes are of national origin. Broadcasts are in Kirundi, French and Swahili.

A privately supported Christian missionary station, Radio Cordac, with one medium-wave (0.25kW) and two short-wave (3kW) transmitters broadcasts for 30 hours a week from the capital in Kirundi, Swahili, French and English.

Radio licences numbered 50 000 in 1971, but the number of receivers in use is considerably higher.

FILM

Two documentaries on Burundi have recently been produced at the Government's request, one by a film unit from the USSR and the other by an oil company. There is no national film production.

Films are imported mainly from France, the USA, Italy and the USSR. In 1971, 76 features and 80 documentaries were imported. The government censor's requirements, especially for the protection of children and young people, must be met for films exhibited.

PROFESSIONAL TRAINING

The Ministry of Information has plans for the establishment of a school for the training of broadcasters.

CAMEROON

Population	5 840 000
Area	475 442 sq. km.

PRESS

Newspapers	Dailies 2, Non-dailies 4
Total circulation	Dailies 17 000, Non-dailies 19 000
Copies per 1000 people	Dailies 3, Non-dailies 3

RADIO

Transmitters	Long/medium wave 4, Short-wave 8
Total receivers	1 700 000 estimated in use
Receivers per 1000 people	291

FILM

Cinemas	Fixed 38
Total seating capacity	20 000
Seats per 1000 people	3

PRESS

In Cameroon, one of the most linguistically and ethnically complex countries in Africa, official policy encourages bilingualism, ie use of either French or English with African vernaculars.

Daily newspapers are published in French in Douala, the main port and largest city, and in English in Victoria, part of the triple-town area of Tiko–Victoria–Buéa. Non-dailies appear in French (the weekly *Journal officiel*), English, Ewondo and Bulu.

Periodicals, which include a fair number of Christian mission journals, are published in English, French and various vernaculars. Journals from neighbouring countries also circulate in Cameroon (which shares frontiers with six other states).

NEWS AGENCIES

The national agency is ACAP, Agence Camerounaise de Presse, with head-quarters in Yaoundé. Founded in 1960, it now has four permanent bureaux with a national staff of 46 permanent members including correspondents and 102 part-time correspondents. ACAP is the country's sole distributor of foreign news which it receives from AFP, DPA, UPI, AP and TASS. It exchanges bulletins with ATP, AZAP (Kinshasa) and ACI (Brazzaville). Its subscribers, which include the national broadcasting service and various government departments, receive a daily 40-page bulletin in French, of which 1500 copies are printed. A weekly summary bulletin is issued in English.

RADIO

Government-owned stations operated by Radio Cameroon are situated at Yaoundé, which has 2 medium-wave (10 and 1kW) and 3 short-wave (30, 10 and 4kW) transmitters; at Douala, which has 1 medium-wave (10kW) and 1 short-wave (1kW) transmitters; at Garoua, which has 1 medium-wave (1kW) and 2 short-wave (30 and 4kW) transmitters; and at Buéa, which has 2 short-wave transmitters (each 4kW).

Total programme transmission hours are 220 a week, of which about 50% are light entertainment, 18% news and information, 17% for special audiences, 12% cultural and educational and 10% advertising. The main services are in French and English, with early morning and late afternoon broadcasts in vernacular languages, principally Bassa, Ewondo, Bamiléké, Douala, Foulfouldé and Hausa. Radio Garoua also broadcasts in Arabic.

No licence fees are charged for receivers. Broadcasting funds come from the federal budget and from advertising revenue.

FILM
Short films are produced occasionally by the cinema service of the Ministry of Information.

Feature films and documentaries (about 500 in 1970) are imported mainly from France, the USA, Italy, the Federal Republic of Germany, the UK, the USSR, Canada, Japan and the Netherlands.

The Ministry of Information encourages the establishment of both commercial and non-commercial cinemas, and over the last ten years the number of fixed and mobile establishments has more than doubled. There were 20 mobile units in 1970.

SPACE COMMUNICATIONS
Responsibility for space communication rests with the Ministry of Post and Telecommunications. An Atlantic Intelsat earth station at Zamengoe, near Yaoundé, came into operation in 1972.

PROFESSIONAL TRAINING AND ASSOCIATIONS
Training in journalism is offered at the newly founded École Supérieure Internationale de Journalisme at Yaoundé, academic prerequisites for which are completion of full secondary education (baccalaureate) or equivalent qualifications. Thirty students from Cameroon and neighbouring countries are enrolled (1970) in the current three-year course leading to a higher diploma in journalism. The first two years of the course consist of general training at the school while the third year of professional specialization (in press, radio or television) is spent in France.

Scholarships are offered by the governments of each of the States sponsoring the École Supérieure Internationale (Cameroon, Central African Republic, Chad, Gabon and Rwanda) to their own nationals passing the competitive entrance examination.

The Syndicat National des Journalistes Professionnels Camerounais has its office in Yaoundé. Its members subscribe to a professional code of ethics.

CAPE VERDE ISLANDS

Population	246 000
Area	4033 sq. km.

PRESS
Newspapers   Non-dailies 2

RADIO

Transmitters	Short-wave 3, VHF–FM 1
Total receivers	5000 licences
Receivers per 1000 people	20

FILM

Cinemas	Fixed 6
Total seating capacity	2700
Seats per 1000 people	11
Total annual attendance	300 000
Annual visits per capita	1

PRESS

A weekly journal put out by the official information and tourist centre circulates throughout the ten inhabited islands of the archipelago. Another fortnightly newspaper is also published. Both are in Portuguese.

RADIO

A government-operated short-wave station, Radio Barlavento, on the island of São Vicente is on the air for 4 hours daily (6 hours on Saturdays and 8 hours on Sundays). There are also two privately owned radio clubs. One in the capital, Praia, on São Tiago, with one 5kW short-wave and one FM transmitter, broadcasts for 3 hours nightly and the other at Mindelo on São Vicente broadcasts on short wave for 6 hours a day. Broadcasts are in Portuguese. Some 5000 radio licences are issued (a ratio of 20 receivers for every 1000 inhabitants).

FILM

Films exhibited in commercial cinemas are imported through Portugal.

CENTRAL AFRICAN REPUBLIC

Population	1 640 000
Area	622 984 sq. km.

PRESS

Newspapers	Dailies 1
Total circulation	Dailies 500
Copies per 1000 people	Dailies 0.3

RADIO

Transmitters	Long/medium-wave 2, Short-wave 3, VHF–FM 1
Total receivers	60 000 estimated in use
Receivers per 1000 people	37

FILM

Cinemas	Fixed 8
Total seating capacity	2000
Seats per 1000 people	1
Total annual attendance	500 000
Annual visits per capita	0.3

PRESS

One mimeographed French-language bulletin is published daily in the capital, Bangui, by the Ministry of Information.

Periodicals include information bulletins published by the Ministries of Public Works and Education (250 and 100 copies per issue respectively), an agricultural quarterly (150 copies per issue) and a monthly Chamber of Commerce journal (250 copies).

NEWS AGENCIES

AFP, Reuters and TASS maintain correspondents in the republic.

RADIO

The Radiodiffusion Nationale Centrafricaine is the government body responsible for radio broadcasting. It broadcasts a home service with two medium-wave transmitters totalling 1.5kW, three short-wave transmitters of 4, 30 and 100kW, and one FM transmitter. Programmes, mainly in French and Sango and almost all of local origin, total over 130 hours a week including news and information (58 hours), light entertainment (40 hours), broadcasts for special audiences (20 hours), broadcasts for ethnic minorities (7 hours), cultural (5 hours), advertising (4 hours) and education (3 hours).

An annual receiver licence fee is payable.

FILM

Features, documentaries and newsreels are imported from France and other countries. There are six cinemas equipped for 35mm film and two for 16mm, plus one mobile projection unit.

CHAD

Population	3 800 000
Area	1 284 000 sq. km.

RADIO	
Transmitters	Medium-wave 2, Short-wave 3, VHF—FM 1
Total receivers	60 000 estimated in use
Receivers per 1000 people	16

FILM	
Cinemas	Fixed 9
Total seating capacity	6000
Seats per 1000 people	2
Total annual attendance	1 300 000
Annual visits per capita	0.3

PRESS

There is no daily press apart from the bulletin published (in French) by the national news agency. Foreign newspapers are received by air. The country's six other periodicals, totalling 9000 copies per issue and all published in Fort-Lamy, the capital, include an official bulletin (agriculture and commerce).

NEWS AGENCIES

The Agence Tchadienne de Presse (ATP) in Fort-Lamy — founded in 1964 — publishes a daily news bulletin circulating between 600 and 1000 copies. UPI, TASS, Reuters and AFP all have bureaux in Chad.

RADIO

The government broadcasting service is Radiodiffusion Nationale Tchadienne, financed from the State budget, and operating two medium-wave transmitters (1 and 20kW), one experimental FM transmitter and three short-wave transmitters (100, 30 and 4kW). Its home service, on the air for 96 hours a week, broadcasts light entertainment (46 hours), news and information (28 hours), educational programmes (12½ hours), broadcasts for special groups and ethnic minorities (4½ hours) and cultural programmes (4 hours).

Some 45% of programmes are in French and the rest in Arabic and seven vernaculars (Sara, Gorane, Kanembou, Toupouré, Moundang, Foulbé and Massa).

FILM

The government service responsible for films is the Secretariat of State for Information. Local film production consists of a small number of documentaries and educational films made by the film and photo section of the Department of Documentation. These, along with weekly newsreels, are supplied to the commercial cinemas and the five mobile units which show imported feature films. Feature films shown in the fixed cinemas and by the mobile projection units are all imported.

COMORO ISLANDS

Population	271 000
Area	2171 sq. km.

RADIO

Transmitters	Short-wave 1, VHF—FM 1
Total receivers	24 000 estimated in use
Receivers per 1000 people	89

FILM

Cinemas	Fixed 4
Total seating capacity	1300
Seats per 1000 people	5
Total annual attendance	100 000
Annual visits per capita	0.4

PRESS
In the absence of a local press, newspapers from Madagascar circulate throughout the four main islands of the archipelago.

Three periodicals are published: one legal and administrative, one of general interest, and one school bulletin, with an aggregate circulation figure of 1100.

RADIO
One short-wave station (4kW) and one FM station (0.05kW) are operated by the Office de Radiodiffusion Télévision Française at Moroni, the capital. Programmes are broadcast for 56 hours a week in French and Comorian.

FILM
Films shown are all imported; 1892 were imported in 1969, mainly from France, India and Arab countries.

CONGO (People's Republic of)

Population	980 000
Area	342 000 sq. km.

PRESS	
Newspapers	Dailies 3, Non-dailies 12
Total circulation	Non-dailies 12 000
Copies per 1000 people	Non-dailies 12

RADIO	
Transmitters	Long/medium-wave 1, Short-wave 4, VHF−FM 5
Total receivers	65 000 estimated in use
Receivers per 1000 people	66

TELEVISION	
Transmitters	1
Receivers	2500 estimated in use
Receivers per 1000 people	3

FILM	
Cinemas	Fixed 24
Total seating capacity	6500
Seats per 1000 people	7

PRESS

Two dailies are published in the capital Brazzaville (one with a circulation of 45 000) and one in Pointe-Noiré, all three being in French.

A number of weekly newspapers, mainly published by political or religious organizations, circulate throughout the country and, in one case, in neighbouring countries as well.

Periodicals include an official government publication and a monthly Chamber of Commerce bulletin.

NEWS AGENCIES

The national agency, owned by the Government, is the Agence Congolaise d'Information (ACI), founded in 1962, with its head office in Brazzaville, and a national staff of 46 persons. In addition to the daily information bulletin issued to its 700 subscribers, ACI supplies news to the national radio and television networks.

Foreign news services with representatives in Brazzaville are AFP and TASS.

RADIO

The government-owned Radiodiffusion Télévision Congolaise operates 1 medium-wave, 4 short-wave and 5 FM transmitters with a total power of 133.95kW. Its Brazzaville station, La Voix de la Révolution Congolaise, with a relay station at Pointe-Noire, broadcasts in French, Lingala and Kikongo for 93 hours a week. Programmes include news and information (31 hours), cultural broadcasts (19½ hours), light entertainment (19 hours), educational broadcasts (10½ hours, including 7 hours to schools), broadcasts to special audiences (9¼ hours, 7 hours of which are political) and advertising (3½ hours). Programmes are almost entirely of national origin.

Radio Brazzaville, with 6 short-wave transmitters (total power 162kW), operated by the Office de Radiodiffusion Télévision Française, is on the air for 115 hours a week. The three area programmes of its international service in French, English and Portuguese are relayed from Paris and beamed to Africa, Madagascar and the Far East.

TELEVISION
Radiodiffusion Télévision Congolaise has one transmitter in Brazzaville, which broadcasts for 25 hours a week. Programmes include 16 hours of news and information, 5½ hours of cultural programmes and 2 hours of light entertainment. The principal countries from which television programmes are imported are the People's Republic of China, France, the Federal Republic of Germany, the UK and (less frequently) Canada.

FILM
National film production in 1969 consisted of a dozen short films made by the national television service. But it is hoped that the national cinema agency now being set up will stimulate local film-making initiative.

PROFESSIONAL TRAINING AND ASSOCIATIONS
A three-year diploma course in journalism was instituted in 1970 at the École Nationale d'Administration in Brazzaville, with an initial intake of 12 students. Candidates must have passed the baccalaureate examination to qualify for admission.

The Union des Journalistes Congolais de Brazzaville has its own statutes and a code of ethics to which members subscribe.

Analyses and surveys of national information services will be undertaken by the Government's Service d'Études de l'Information founded in 1970.

DAHOMEY

| Population | 2 760 000 |
| Area | 112 622 sq. km. |

PRESS	
Newspapers	Dailies 1, Non-dailies 2
Total circulation	Dailies 1500, Non-dailies 1700
Copies per 1000 people	Dailies 0.5, Non-dailies 0.6

RADIO	
Transmitters	Medium-wave 2, Short-wave 2
Total receivers	97 000 estimated in use
Receivers per 1000 people	35

FILM	
Cinemas	Fixed 6
Total seating capacity	9000
Seats per 1000 people	3
Total annual attendance	1 211 000
Annual visits per capita	0.4

PRESS

The national daily, founded in 1969, is published in French by the government printing and publishing establishment at Cotonou. Two other general interest newspapers appear fortnightly.

Fifteen periodicals with a total circulation of over 4000 deal principally with ethnology, fine arts, religion and sociology. All are in French and have editorial offices in Cotonou or Porto Novo.

NEWS AGENCIES

The Agence Dahoméenne de Presse (ADP) founded in 1961 is the official national agency. The permanent staff of ADP's head office in Cotonou and its regional information centres consists of 6 journalists, 5 technicians and 14 administrative personnel. No representation is maintained abroad.

Utilizing dispatches received through its exchange agreement with AFP, and features supplied by the information services of governments represented in Dahomey, ADP issues a daily foreign news bulletin in French to some 1000 subscribers including newspapers and the national radio.

AFP and TASS have regional bureaux in Dahomey. Reuters, UPI, DPA and AP are represented by correspondents in Cotonou.

RADIO

Radiodiffusion du Dahomey, with two medium-wave transmitters (1 and 0.1kW) and two short-wave transmitters (30 and 4kW) situated near the inland town of Parakou, broadcasts for 70 hours a week in French and six of the country's many vernaculars: Fon, Yoruba, Bariba, Mina, Peuhl and Dendi. About 10 hours a week are filled by imported programmes.

Programmes are mainly news and information (39%), cultural and scientific (35%), educational (11%), light entertainment (5%) and religious (4%). A small percentage (14%) of programmes are imported.

FILM

In 1971, six long films were produced. Short films are produced by a government-sponsored company (SODACI) and also by an adult education audio-visual centre.

Films exhibited are all imported. Figures for 1969 were 456 long and 124 short feature films and 325 long and 72 short documentaries imported from France, the USA, the Federal Republic of Germany, Italy and the USSR.

EGYPT (Arab Republic of)

Population	34 840 000
Area	1 001 449 sq. km.

PRESS
Newspapers	Dailies 14, Non-dailies 20
Total circulation	Dailies 712 231, Non-dailies 703 661
Copies per 1000 people	Dailies 20, Non-dailies 20

RADIO
Transmitters	Long/medium-wave 27, Short-wave 16
Total receivers	5 000 000 estimated in use
Receivers per 1000 people	144

TELEVISION
Transmitters	28
Receivers	529 264 estimated in use
Receivers per 1000 people	15

FILM
Cinemas	Fixed 246*
Total seating capacity	219 626
Seats per 1000 people	6
Total annual attendance	62 444 000
Annual visits per capita	2

*Including 93 open for only six months of the year.

PRESS

Newspaper publishing is concentrated in Cairo and, to a lesser extent, in Alexandria. Languages of publication, besides Arabic, include French, English, Greek and Armenian.

Three major Cairo morning editions, dispatched early in the day to other parts of the country and abroad, account for over half the country's total daily circulation. But circulation figures far from represent the actual number of persons reached by newspapers, since individual copies are read aloud and may pass through many hands in families, coffee houses and local communities.

Periodicals number 181, with an overall circulation of 1.3 million per issue, the largest single category being those devoted to religious matters (about 50 titles).

Following legislation introduced in 1960 which nationalized the press, the major publishing houses and their newspapers became public authorities within the State, run by boards of directors with provision for workers' representation and profit-sharing. They operate under the general oversight of the Public Organization for News Publishing, Distributing and Printing, set up in 1961.

Under the constitution of 1964, freedom of the press, printing and publication is guaranteed within the limits of the law.

NEWS AGENCIES

The Middle East News Agency (MENA), founded in 1955, is constituted as a company within the public sector, affiliated to the public organization responsible for general supervision of the press. In addition to its head office in Cairo, it has bureaux within the Republic in Alexandria and Aswan, and abroad in Beirut, Damascus, Baghdad, Kuwait, Amman, Sanaa, Abu-Dhabi, Khartoum, Tripoli, Algiers, Paris, London, Belgrade and East Berlin. Its permanent staff numbers 330, including permanent correspondents.

MENA provides its 400 subscribers with 20 000 words of news daily in Arabic and 6500 words in English. Services offered include features, photographs, a special audio service and an economic-news service. Transmission is effected by cable-teleprinter circuit, telex, telephone and air mailers.

MENA subscribes to three overseas news services: Reuters, AFP and DPA and exchanges news with ADN, Agerpress, CTK, PAP, Tanjug and TASS.

Foreign agencies distributing news in the country are UPI, AP, Reuters, AFP and TASS.

RADIO

The State-owned Broadcasting Corporation of the Arab Republic of Egypt operates 27 medium-wave transmitters, including Cairo I (500kW), and 16 short-wave transmitters, including the 100kW station at Abu Zaabal, with a total transmission power of 4806kW, reaching 99.6% of the country's population in addition to large audiences in the rest of the Arab world and overseas. Services include Radio Cairo's general and second programmes, the Alexandria regional programme, the Voice of the Arabs, the Holy Koran, the overseas programmes, With the People and Middle East Radio, the two latter, and the Alexandria programme, broadcasting commercial advertising. Of the total broadcasting time of about 1200 hours a week, light entertainment accounts for 46%, religious broadcasting 15%, information programmes 14%, cultural programmes 14%, drama 4%, services 5% and education 1%.

The corporation's foreign-language programmes are now broadcast in 36 languages.

The estimated ratio of receivers to population is among the highest in the continent. No licence fee is charged.

TELEVISION

Since the introduction of television in 1960, potential coverage of the population is now almost complete. The government-owned Television Corporation operates 28 transmitters with a total power of 54kW, broadcasting over two channels. Channel I reaches all the populated areas of the country, while Channel II covers the delta and an area extending to about 100km south of Cairo. It is intended in the next few years to give this channel the same coverage as the first and to use it for educational purposes. Overall programme time is 115 hours a week, of which entertainment and advertising account for 53 hours (47%), educational and cultural broadcasts 43 hours (38%), information programmes 13 hours (12%) and religious broadcasts 7 hours (6%). Around 40% of programmes are imported, two-thirds of imports coming from the USA.

Television broadcasting is financed from annual licence fees, State subsidies, income from advertising and the sale of programmes abroad, principally to Arabic-speaking countries. The corporation has its own well-equipped studios and facilities, and is therefore able to produce most of its programmes locally. Receivers in use are mainly assembled in the country .

FILM

The principal centre of the film industry in the Middle East, Egypt has a number of well-equipped studios and film-processing laboratories situated in and near Cairo. In 1971, 64 features, including 6 coproductions with Turkey (3), Lebanon and France, and 144 short films were produced; of the latter, 3 were entertainment films, 52 documentaries and 89 instructional. The main producers of short films, apart from the private sector, are the Arab Agency for Cinemas, the National Centre for Informative Films, and the State Information Department – all of which service government departments – and the Cairo Company for Cinema Production.

A large number of feature films are exported, the Government insisting on minimum artistic standards. Imports for 1971 totalled 357 feature films, principally from the USA (163), Italy (71), France (29), the USSR, the UK and India. Of around 120 documentaries imported, 84 were from the USA and others from Czechoslovakia, France and the UK. The import of films is subject to government technical, customs and monetary controls.

In recent years, the Government has founded a cinema institute and a motion-picture centre and sponsored the publication of a magazine dealing with cinema techniques. It also encourages the establishment of local film clubs.

In addition to the fixed cinemas, most of which are to be found in Cairo and Alexandria, government-operated mobile units reach large audiences in towns and villages. Annual attendance figures have dropped by 8 million over the last ten years.

SPACE COMMUNICATIONS

The republic is a member of Intelsat. Construction of an earth station is planned near Cairo.

PROFESSIONAL TRAINING

The national Radio Broadcasting Training Institute, established to raise standards in the profession, has already trained over 1100 broadcasting staff including some 200 trainees from other countries.

An information-media training institute within the University of Cairo offers full-time undergraduate and post-graduate courses for prospective journalists and broadcasters.

EQUATORIAL GUINEA

Population	290 000
Area	28 051 sq. km.

PRESS

Newspapers	Dailies 1, Non-dailies 1
Total circulation	Dailies 1000
Copies per 1000 people	Dailies 3

RADIO

Transmitters	Short-wave 2
Total receivers	7500 estimated in use
Receivers per 1000 people	26

FILM

Cinemas	Fixed 11
Total seating capacity	6300
Seats per 1000 people	22
Total annual attendance	500 000
Annual visits per capita	2

PRESS

One Spanish-language daily is published in Santa Isabel, the capital, on Fernando Po. Other publications include one weekly paper published in Bata, the administrative and economic capital in Rio Muni, and several religious and official journals. Newspapers are also imported from Spain.

RADIO

La Voz de Guinea Ecuatorial is the government radio station at Santa Isabel with one short-wave transmitter (10kW) broadcasting a home service for 18 hours a day, mainly in Spanish but with periods of 30 to 90 minutes in various vernaculars (Fang or Pamués, Bubi, Annobonés, Combe) and a 2-hour period in English.

Radio Bata in Rio Muni is a government-sponsored commercial station with one short-wave transmitter (5kW) which is on the air for 17½ hours a day in Spanish.

FILM

Over 100 documentary and other short films were produced in 1971. All films exhibited in public cinemas are imported.

ETHIOPIA

Population	25 250 000
Area	1 221 900 sq. km.

PRESS

Newspapers	Dailies 3, Non-dailies 2
Total circulation	Dailies 39 000
Copies per 1000 people	Dailies 2

RADIO

Transmitters	Long/medium-wave 5, Short-wave 4
Total receivers	500 000 estimated in use
Receivers per 1000 people	20

TELEVISION

Transmitters	6
Receivers	25 000 estimated in use
Receivers per 1000 people	1

FILM

Cinemas	Fixed 30
Total seating capacity	26 138
Seats per 1000 people	1
Total annual attendance	9 540 370
Annual visits per capita	0.4

PRESS

The daily newspapers are published in Addis Ababa, two in Amharic and one in English. While circulation figures have changed little, the number of dailies has dropped from 10 to 3 over the last ten years. Amharic is the principal language used by non-dailies and other periodicals, along with English, French, Italian, Tigrigna and Arabic. In 1973, there were 177 periodicals published, the main subject categories being general readership (41 titles), education (39 titles), religion (23 titles), law and administration (18 titles), agriculture, etc. (18 titles), military (8 titles), medicine (7 titles), natural sciences (6 titles), recreation (5 titles), and trade, sociology, political sciences and geography.

NEWS AGENCIES

The Ethiopian News Agency (ENA), established in 1941, is government owned. It has a head office in Addis Ababa and 28 permanent bureaux in the country and issues a continuous 24-hour service of national, local and foreign news in Amharic, English and French to 5 newspapers, 3 radio and 1 television stations and other subscribers. It also issues a daily news bulletin in English and French. Dispatches are received from Reuters, AP, AFP and CTK, all of which have correspondents in Addis Ababa. News transmission is carried out by leased teleprinter and point-to-point radio networks.

RADIO

The Ethiopian Broadcasting Service, comprising both radio and television, was established in 1968 as an autonomous public authority operating under the direction and supervision of the Minster of Information.

The radio service, founded in 1941, now operates three 100kW short-wave transmitters in Addis Ababa and 3 medium-wave transmitters totalling 250kW and located in Addis Ababa, Asmara and Harrar. Its home service is on the air for 121 hours a week broadcasting a national programme in Amharic to an estimated 10 million listeners, as well as programmes in Somali, Tigrigna, Tigre, Afar, English, Arabic and French, 98% of which are of national origin. Programmes consist of entertainment (62 hours), news and information (26 hours), education (25 hours) and advertising (11 hours). No licence fee is payable for radio receivers, the radio service's revenue being derived from government subventions and advertising.

The Lutheran World Federation operates its station, Radio Voice of the Gospel, with one 100kW short-wave transmitter located at Addis Ababa. It is on the air for 182 hours a week in 13 languages, broadcasting religious programmes (30% of the total) and cultural, educational and entertainment programmes beamed to areas in the Middle and Far East and west and southern Africa, as well as to local audiences. It also has a local medium-wave programme for Addis Ababa transmitted 6 hours a day. At Asmara, the United States Armed Forces operate a 250kW medium-wave transmitter. Programmes relayed from United States stations and United States transcriptions are broadcast daily in English.

TELEVISION

The television service, inaugurated in 1964, now operates three main and two auxiliary transmitters in Addis Ababa and at Nazret about 100 miles south of the capital, together covering areas with a population of about 1 million people. Programmes are broadcast 61 hours a week, consisting of educational broadcasts (36 hours, including 30 to schools), cultural and films (9 hours), news and information (7½ hours), entertainment (3½ hours), broadcasts for special audiences (3½ hours) and advertising (30 minutes). Principal languages of transmission are Amharic and English. Imported programmes, representing about 35% of total programme time, come mainly from the USA, the UK, Federal Republic of Germany and France.

The United States Armed Forces operate a low-power television station at Asmara which transmits daily for local viewers.

FILM

Local film production totalled about 50 short films in 1972–3. Newsreels and documentaries are made locally by the Ministry of Information, and the Ethiopian Broadcasting Service produces some educational films.

Of the 463 feature films imported in 1972–3, 182 came from the USA and others from Italy (81), India (71), the UK (64), France (25), the USSR (25) and elsewhere (15). In the same year, 276 documentaries were imported from the UK (14), the USA (75), India (56), Canada (14), Italy (10) and Japan (7).

SPACE COMMUNICATIONS

Construction of an Atlantic Intelsat earth station at Sululta, near the capital, is planned for 1976.

PROFESSIONAL TRAINING AND ASSOCIATIONS

Some film training is offered at the Educational Mass Media Centre in Addis Ababa.

Professional associations include the Ethiopian Press Club and the Foreign Press Association in Addis Ababa.

FRENCH TERRITORY OF THE AFARS AND THE ISSAS

Population	97 000
Area	22 000 sq. km.

PRESS

Newspapers	Non-dailies 1
Total circulation	Non-dailies 2300
Copies per 1000 people	Non-dailies 24

RADIO

Transmitters	Long/medium-wave 2, Short-wave 1
Total receivers	8000 estimated in use
Receivers per 1000 people	82

TELEVISION

Transmitters	1
Receivers	1000 estimated in use
Receivers per 1000 people	10

FILM

Cinemas	Fixed 8
Total seating capacity	6700
Seats per 1000 people	69
Total annual attendance	216 000
Annual visits per capita	2

PRESS

An official weekly newspaper in French is published in the capital, Djibouti.

The territory's three other periodicals – the fortnightly official gazette, a trade journal and a journal of ethnography – have a combined circulation of 1550 copies. All are in French.

NEWS AGENCIES

There is no local news agency.

RADIO

All broadcasting is conducted by the Office de Radiodiffusion Télévision Française (ORTF) in Djibouti, which is financed by local receiver licence fees and a subvention from the French Government.

Radio programmes are broadcast in French (63½ hours a week), Afar (35½ hours), Issa (35½ hours) and Arabic (28 hours), totalling 162½ hours a week. Of this time, almost 50% consists of light entertainment, 25% of cultural and scientific broadcasts, 16% of educational programmes, 10% of news and information and 3% of broadcasts to ethnic minorities. A considerable amount of programme material is supplied by ORTF.

The station's short-wave and two medium-wave transmitters (each 4kW) cover the entire territory.

TELEVISION

ORTF's television station in Djibouti, with one 50kW transmitter (625 lines), potentially reaches 80% of the population. The weekly programme time of 19½ hours (every evening except Monday) consists of news and information (6 hours), broadcasts to special audiences (5½ hours), light entertainment (5 hours), cultural programmes (2 hours), and broadcasts for ethnic minorities (1 hour). French-language programmes, largely supplied by ORTF from France, account for 10½ hours a week, the remainder being in the three local languages.

GABON

| Population | 500 000 |
| Area | 267 667 sq. km. |

PRESS
Newspapers	Dailies 1, Non-dailies 1
Total circulation	Dailies 700, Non-dailies 5000
Copies per 1000 people	Dailies 1, Non-dailies 10

RADIO
Transmitters	Medium-wave 6, Short-wave 4
Total receivers	65 000 estimated in use
Receivers per 1000 people	130

TELEVISION
Transmitters	3
Receivers	1300 estimated in use
Receivers per 1000 people	3

FILM
Cinemas	Fixed 2
Total seating capacity	1700
Seats per 1000 people	3
Total annual attendance	385 000
Annual visits per capita	0.8

PRESS
An information bulletin in French issued daily by the Ministry of Information in Libreville circulates about 700 copies, and a weekly produced by the same Ministry circulates about 5000 copies. Other periodicals include five monthlies dealing with religion, commerce, statistics, and public health.

NEWS AGENCIES
The national news agency, the Agence Gabonaise de Presse, founded in 1961, issues a daily bulletin in French. Foreign news is received by subscription from AFP and Reuters.

RADIO
The Radiodiffusion Télévision Gabonaise (RTG) is a government service with stations in Libreville, Franceville, Oyem and Port Gentil. It operates 10 transmitters (six medium-wave of up to 20kW and four short-wave of up to 100kW). Its home service is on the air for 18½ hours daily and includes 16 week-day and 18 week-end daily news bulletins. The regional network is on the air for 3 or 4 hours every evening.

TELEVISION

The television service of RTG began operating in 1963 and now has two main transmitters (625 lines) in Libreville and Port Gentil, plus one auxiliary. Programmes are broadcast for 3 hours daily.

FILM

There is no national film production. Features and documentaries are imported mainly from France, Italy, the USA, India, Egypt, the UK and Federal Republic of Germany.

SPACE COMMUNICATIONS

An Atlantic Intelsat earth station at Nkoltang, near Libreville, came into operation in 1972.

GAMBIA

Population	375 000
Area	11 295 sq. km.

PRESS	
Newspapers	Non-dailies 11
Total circulation	Non-dailies 7500
Copies per 1000 people	Non-dailies 20

RADIO	
Transmitters	Medium-wave 1, Short-wave 1, VHF–FM 1
Total receivers	50 000 estimated in use
Receivers per 1000 people	133

FILM	
Cinemas	Fixed 15

PRESS

Gambia, the smallest country in the African continent, has no daily newspaper. The government information office in Bathurst, the capital, issues an English-language bulletin carrying international and some local news three times a week. Ten other news-sheets of local interest appear twice-weekly, weekly or less frequently.

Six periodicals have a total circulation of 4000; in addition to these there are four parish and school journals.

NEWS AGENCIES
There is no national agency. Reuters, AFP and the Agence de Presse Sénégalaise have correspondents in Bathurst.

RADIO
Radio Gambia, with one 3.5kW short-wave transmitter and one FM transmitter owned and operated by the Department of Information and Broadcasting, is on the air for 77 hours a week. Its programmes are principally in English (including relays of world and African news from the BBC) and in two vernaculars, Woloff and Mandinka.

The breakdown of broadcasting time in hours per week is: light entertainment (25), news and information (22), commercial programmes and advertising (15), broadcasts for special audiences (8), broadcasts for ethnic minorities (5), educational (2). Of these programmes, 60 hours a week are of local origin.

A commercial station operating a 5kW medium-wave transmitter broadcasts for 20 hours a day in English, French and the two main vernaculars, with a periodic information service in Swedish, for Swedish tourists.

FILM
The film unit of the information and broadcasting service produced two short documentaries and seven short instructional films in 1970.

Feature and other films exhibited in the country's 15 public cinemas are imported, mainly from the UK, France, India and Italy. The two main cinemas in Bathurst exhibit films distributed through a circuit based in Senegal. A mobile 16mm unit reaches about 100 000 persons a year. Film showings are also organized by cultural and information agencies.

GHANA

Population	8 858 000
Area	238 537 sq. km.

PRESS

Newspapers	Dailies 3, Non-dailies 39
Total circulation	Dailies 270 000, Non-dailies 680 000
Copies per 1000 people	Dailies 30, Non-dailies 77

RADIO

Transmitters	Short-wave 16, VHF–FM 7
Total receivers	750 000 estimated in use
Receivers per 1000 people	85

TELEVISION

Transmitters	4
Receivers	16 000 estimated in use
Receivers per 1000 people	2

FILM

Cinemas	Fixed 13
Total seating capacity	14 400
Seats per 1000 people	2
Total annual attendance	1 027 796
Annual visits per capita	0.1

PRESS

Two of the daily newpapers, each circulating over 100 000 copies, are published in the capital, Accra. The third is published in the large inland town of Kumasi. All three are in English.

The majority of the non-dailies, which include 12 twice-weekly or weekly papers ranging from 5000 to 100 000 in circulation, are published in English from Accra. Local papers are based in Cape Coast, Legon and Tamale. The Bureau of Ghana Languages sponsors monthly papers in eight vernaculars (Ashanti, Fante, Akwapim, Ewe, Ga, Nzema, Dagbani and Kasem), with an aggregate circulation of over 150 000 copies, while one religious journal appears in English, Twi, Ga and Fante.

National and local news occupies 46% of space in the country's newspapers, advertising 45%, foreign news 6.25% and editorial matter 2.6%.

Periodicals also are almost entirely English-language. A reported total of 34 titles includes several mass circulation illustrated magazines (one of which is the Ghana edition of a regional monthly), three current affairs quarterlies, yearbooks, trade journals, etc. A number of business firms have their own house journals.

Of the total population, about 60% are exposed to newspapers and periodicals, and of this readership 87% live in towns and 13% in rural areas.

Newsprint imports are regulated through the Government's three-monthly quota system.

NEWS AGENCIES

The Ghana News Agency (GNA) was founded by the Government in 1957. It has permanent regional bureaux in Accra, Koforidua, Kumasi, Sunyani, Tamale, Bolgatanga, Cape Coast, Sekondi and Ho, and 17 offices in district centres, with an overall total of 341 permanent staff and 380 part-time correspondents. Permanent bureaux abroad are in New York, London and Nairobi.

GNA issues, in addition to its daily news summary and its weekly news feature bulletins, a daily service of 26 000 words of local news and 35 000 words of foreign news, in English, these services being received by the three national dailies, one broadcasting station, and a number of government establishments. The regional printed news service is subscribed to by 140 organizations and diplomatic posts.

GNA has exchange agreements with Reuters, AFP, CTK, TASS, ANSA and Tanjug, which have offices in the capital. DPA is also represented in Ghana.

RADIO

All broadcasting is carried out by the Ghana Broadcasting Corporation which is financed by government subsidies, advertising revenue and subscriptions to the corporation's relay service. It operates 16 short-wave transmitters of 10, 20, 100 and 250kW and seven VHF–FM transmitters with a total power of 22.5kW. These transmitters, operating from Accra, Ejura and Tema, cover 99% of the national territory.

Broadcasting hours total 221 hours a week, of which 38% is light entertainment, 20% news and information, 20% cultural and scientific programmes, 10% broadcasts for special audiences, 7% education and 3% advertising and announcements.

Of the three national networks, GBC1, which is on the air for 13½ hours a day, carries general programmes, news and all important ministerial announcements in local languages (Akan, Owe, Dagbani, Ga, Hausa and Nzema); GBC2 broadcasts light music, commercials and news in English; while GBC3, which is on the air every day from 17.00 to 23.00 hours, broadcasts rather more serious programmes (health information, citizen's advice, national affairs, etc.).

In addition, there is an external service which broadcasts in English, French, Swahili, Arabic, Portuguese and Hausa to the whole of Africa and to North America, the Caribbean, Europe and the Middle East.

TELEVISION

The Ghana Broadcasting Corporation broadcasts from four transmitters at Kissi, Jamasi, Adjankote and Jawale, relayed by transmitters at Ho, Oda, Tarkwa and Sunyani, thus covering most of the country's densely populated centres.

Apart from the 2-hour morning programme for schools, broadcasting hours are from 17.55 to 22.50 hours, totalling 45 hours a week: light entertainment (12½ hours), educational (11½ hours), broadcasts for special audiences (10¾ hours, including 9 hours for children and youth), news and information (9 hours), science and culture (45 minutes) and 30 minutes' commercial advertising.

Locally produced programmes are exchanged with other member countries of the Union of National Radio and Television Organizations of Africa (URTNA), while imported programmes come mainly from the USA, the UK, the Federal Republic of Germany, and German Democratic Republic.

FILM

In 1971, the State Film Industry Corporation produced, for the Government, 3 long films and 15 short documentaries and instructional films, all 35mm, in addition to its annual series of 26 magazines. Local production activities are encouraged by the Ministry of Information which seeks to promote sponsorship of films by organizations and other users.

Of a total of 61 35mm features imported in 1971 (under government import licence), 29 came from Italy, 12 from the USA, 11 from the UK, 5 from India and 4 from the USSR.

PROFESSIONAL TRAINING AND ASSOCIATIONS

The Ghana Institute of Journalism at Accra offers a two-year post-secondary diploma course in journalism. Since the institute's foundation in 1958, 260 students have graduated (including 60 women). Present enrolment is 29 male and 11 female students.

National associations exist for journalists, editors and public relations practitioners, all of which are working out professional codes of ethics.

GUINEA

Population	4 010 000
Area	245 857 sq. km.

PRESS

Newspapers	Dailies 1, Non-dailies 1
Total circulation	Dailies 5000
Copies per 1000 people	Dailies 1

RADIO

Transmitters	Medium-wave 1, Short-wave 4
Total receivers	85 000 estimated in use
Receivers per 1000 people	21

FILM

Cinemas	Fixed 28
Total seating capacity	10 000
Seats per 1000 people	2

PRESS

There is one daily newspaper published in French by the government press service in Conakry, with a circulation of 5000 copies, the same paper also has a week-end edition. Other periodical publications include one weekly paper, an official gazette, and a trade union journal.

NEWS AGENCIES

There is now no national news agency. Foreign agencies represented in Conakry include Novosti and TASS.

RADIO

The government broadcasting service, Radiodiffusion Nationale, with one medium-wave transmitter of 100kW and four short-wave transmitters of up to

100kW, is on the air for 11 hours a day, broadcasting in French, English, Portuguese, Arabic and local dialects.

FILM

National film production is being developed. A laboratory for 35mm films in black, white and colour has been installed and equipped for the local production of feature and short films. Since 1968, 2 full-length and 2 medium-length feature films and 5 documentaries have been produced. Imported films are shown in the fixed cinemas, 14 of which are controlled by a State enterprise. The distribution of nationally produced films is now largely taken over by a State distribution company limiting foreign distribution.

IVORY COAST

Population	4 420 000
Area	322 463 sq. km.

PRESS
Newspapers	Dailies 2, Non-dailies 2
Total circulation	Dailies 26 000, Non-dailies 38 000
Copies per 1000 people	Dailies 6, Non-dailies 9

RADIO
Transmitters	Long/medium-wave 3, Short-wave 4, VHF–FM 4
Total receivers	86 000 estimated in use
Receivers per 1000 people	19

TELEVISION
Transmitters	4
Receivers	40 000 estimated in use
Receivers per 1000 people	9

FILM
Cinemas	Fixed 88*
Total seating capacity	80 000*
Seats per 1000 people	18
Total annual attendance	11 500 000*
Annual visits per capita	3

*Including outdoor and mobile cinemas.

PRESS

A government-sponsored morning newspaper published in French in the capital, Abidjan, and circulating over 30 000 copies is the country's main daily. There is also a daily bulletin issued by the national news agency (800 copies).

A weekly paper, belonging to the main daily, and an official government gazette are also published in the capital. All are in French. Other periodicals, a number of which are produced by the Government, total 37 titles, the principal subjects being religion (6 titles), agriculture (4 titles), sociology, political science and education (3 titles each). Newspapers and magazines imported by air from France command a considerable readership in Abidjan.

NEWS AGENCIES

The Agence Ivoirienne de Presse (AIP), founded in 1961 under the Ministry of Information, is the national news agency. National and local news is gathered by reporters in the capital and some 45 correspondents in various parts of the country, while foreign news is received through the daily services of AFP, Reuters, UPI and DPA. AIP supplies all information media in the country; in addition to the daily French-language bulletin referred to above, it also issues a fortnightly bulletin in English.

AFP maintains a permanent representative in Abidjan.

RADIO

The government-owned Radiodiffusion Télévision Ivoirienne (RTI), established as a public corporation in 1962 and deriving its income from government subsidies and receiver licence fees, is responsible for all broadcasting in the country.

Radio broadcasting covers 80% of the country. The national network, with medium-wave transmitters in Abidjan (4kW) and Bouaké (5kW) and short-wave transmitters (25 and 100kW) in Abidjan, is on the air for 144 hours a week broadcasting in French and 10 vernaculars. News bulletins are frequent, and there are educational broadcasts for schools not reached by television; also teacher training courses. The 'international' service, with one medium-wave (1kW) and two short-wave transmitters (10 and 100kW), all in Abidjan, broadcasts in French and vernaculars for about 48 hours a week, including broadcasts for ethnic minorities (29 hours), cultural and scientific (6 hours), education (5 hours), news and information (3 hours), broadcasts for special audiences (2 hours) and advertising (2 hours).

Experimental FM broadcasts are carried out from stations at Abidjan, Bouaflé, Man and Koun-Abroussou.

TELEVISION

Television broadcasting began in August 1963. RTI now has four stations located in Abidjan, Bouaflé, Man and Koun-Abroussou which are on the air daily for 1 hour at midday and 3 hours in the evening with information and entertainment programmes. Programmes totalling 58 hours a week include education (24 hours), light entertainment (16 hours), news and information (13 hours), cultural programmes (3 hours) and broadcasts for special audiences (2½ hours). Over 60% of programmes are nationally produced.

Daytime broadcasting hours are largely occupied by a pilot project of unique importance in educational television, designed to renovate the country's entire primary education system. Established with international assistance, the project became operational in 1971. During the school year 1971–2, over 450 classes with some 20 500 pupils throughout the country were receiving about 8 hours a week of televised instruction, in 20-minute periods interspersed with breaks for practical exercises, recreation, etc. A teacher briefing session is also broadcast at the end of each schoolday.

Planning and production of programmes and of printed support material are carried out in a new well-equipped studio centre at Bouaké. French is the language of instruction. The number of programmes and of schools and classes served will be stepped up from year to year until the whole school system is fully served. Receivers are supplied to schools by the Government and include special battery sets for non-electrified areas.

About 60% of the national territory is effectively covered by the existing television network but present extension work will give good reception to 80% within a few years. The definition system used is 625 lines.

FILM

One feature film was produced in 1972. In addition, documentary and news films are produced by the Société Ivoirienne de Cinéma for the Ministry of Information's film department, and there have been a few films made abroad by Ivory Coast producers.

Imported feature films, totalling 420 in 1971, are shown in the country's 48 indoor cinemas (mostly in the Abidjan area and the larger towns) and some 25 outdoor cinemas and projection points visited by government mobile units. Imports in 1971 came from France (60%), Italy (15%), the Federal Republic of Germany (10%), the USA (10%) and elsewhere (5%).

SPACE COMMUNICATIONS

An earth station near Abidjan, linked with the Atlantic Intelsat network, came into service in 1972.

PROFESSIONAL TRAINING

Broadcasting personnel working within RTI receive some on-the-job training, and special courses for teachers of school television classes are provided by the teacher training college in Bouaké.

KENYA

Population	12 070 000
Area	582 644 sq. km.

PRESS

Newspapers	Dailies 3, Non-dailies 12
Total circulation	Dailies 119 000
Copies per 1000 people	Dailies 10

RADIO

Transmitters	Long/medium-wave 6, Short-wave 11, VHF—FM 1
Total receivers	774 000 estimated in use
Receivers per 1000 people	64

TELEVISION

Transmitters	4
Receivers	22 850 estimated in use
Receivers per 1000 people	2

FILM

Cinemas	Fixed 32
Total seating capacity	18 800
Seats per 1000 people	2
Total annual attendance	7 300 000
Annual visits per capita	0.6

PRESS

The largest daily, circulating a reported 60 000 copies on week-days and more at week-ends, is an English-language paper established in 1902. It also publishes a weekly in Swahili (58 000 copies). Another firm established in 1959 publishes an English-language daily (with a combined circulation of over 35 000 for its Nairobi and Mombasa editions), as well as an associated Sunday paper (40 000 copies), a Swahili daily (24 000 copies) and a Swahili weekly. Both groups have correspondents in the main towns but experience difficulty in obtaining news from rural areas. All their publishing operations are based in the capital, Nairobi, but have readerships in most parts of the country and, in some cases, in neighbouring countries as well.

There are 12 weeklies: 6 in English, 3 in Swahili, 2 in Gujarati and 1 in Dholuo, the latter produced by a government-sponsored vernacular publishing house. With the exception of English-language papers published in Kitale (2 titles) and Thika, the non-daily press is also based in Nairobi.

Other periodicals include an English/Swahili fortnightly published by the East African Railways Corporation, 3 monthlies appearing in English and Swahili, about 10 English-language monthlies, 7 quarterlies and various annual directories. Subjects covered include agriculture, education, trade, medicine, pharmacy, films and general information.

NEWS AGENCIES

The national agency, Kenya News Agency (KNA), founded in 1963, with headquarters in Nairobi, is part of the information department of the Ministry of Information, Broadcasting and Tourism and receives local news through the Government's regional information officers. KNA also has its own reporting staff and a number of part-time correspondents throughout the country. Foreign news is received from Reuters, TASS, AFP and UPI. The agency supplies both national and local news to the national press, radio and television.

Foreign agencies represented in Nairobi include Reuters, AFP, AP, TASS, Ghana News Agency, CTK and Novosti.

RADIO

The Voice of Kenya (VOK), so named in 1964, is an independent public service body responsible to the Ministry of Information and Broadcasting for both radio and television broadcasting throughout the country, succeeding the former Kenya Broadcasting Corporation (established in 1961) and the earlier Kenya Broadcasting Service. Its revenue is derived from radio and television licence fees, broadcasting advertising and direct government subvention.

VOK radio has three home services, the first of which, the national service, is broadcast, in Swahili, from 3 medium-wave transmitters (5, 20 and 100kW) and 4 short-wave transmitters (three of 100kW and one of 10kW) located in Nairobi, Mombasa and Kisuma and serving the central Kenya, coastal and rift valley areas in particular, but providing reasonable coverage for most of the country. It is on the air for about 17 hours a day, broadcasting either the central programme from Nairobi or programmes originating in the regional studios. The general service, which uses English, is broadcast for up to 17 hours a day from 4 transmitters in Nairobi: 1 medium-wave (100kW), 2 short-wave (10kW each) and 1 FM. The third home service is the vernacular network broadcast from 1 medium-wave (20kW) and 2 short-wave (10kW) transmitters in Nairobi, 1 medium-wave and 2 short-wave transmitters (all 5kW) in Kisumu and a 20kW medium-wave transmitter in Mombasa. In all, the vernacular services use 18 languages which include Hindustani, Kikuyu, Kikamba, Kimeru, Masai, Somali, Borana, Luluyia, Kalenjin, Kisii, Kuria, Teso and Swahili in addition to relays of national programmes in Swahili. Their overall broadcasting time adds up to over 330 hours a week.

Programmes include fairly frequent newscasts in all languages, along with health and hygiene information, etc.

Of the total numbers of receivers in use, some 6000 are installed in public places for community listening.

TELEVISION

Voice of Kenya Television began broadcasting in October 1962 with a transmitter at Hillcrest near Nairobi. Boosters were added at Timboroa in 1963 and at Nyeri and 1964. Both the Hillcrest and Timboroa transmitters have since been increased in power and, in 1971, a new station broadcasting its own programmes for 3 hours a day was opened at Mazeras to serve the Mombasa area.

The Nairobi transmitter's programmes are on the air for about 7 hours a day and consist of about 40% local production. Broadcasting languages are English, Swahili and Hindustani. The definition system used is 625 lines.

Some 850 receivers are installed in public places for community viewing. An annual licence fee is payable.

FILM

The government Kenya Film Corporation produces documentary and tourist films. Other films are produced by foreign companies using local technical services.

Practically all films exhibited in the commercial circuits are imported, mainly from the USA, UK and India. The fixed cinemas are located in 13 towns (Nairobi has 12 and Mombasa 7) while a mobile cinema company with two 35mm and one 16mm projection units holds monthly showings in 23 towns (usually in football stadiums) with average audiences of about 5000 persons. In addition, an east African touring-circuit enterprise, based in Nairobi but also operating in Tanzania and Uganda, provides over 300 towns and villages in 11 regional circuits in Kenya with regular monthly showings attracting audiences of around 2000. Drive-in cinemas in Nairobi (2) and Mombasa (1) have a total capacity of 1800 cars.

SPACE COMMUNICATIONS

An Indian Ocean Intelsat earth station at Longonot Peak, north of Nairobi, came into operation in August 1970.

PROFESSIONAL TRAINING AND ASSOCIATIONS

The University of Nairobi's School of Journalism, opened in 1970 following the International Press Institute's successful African training scheme (1964–8), offers a two-year diploma course in newspaper journalism to both Kenyan students and others from east and central Africa. It has some emphasis, additionally, on radio and television. A post-graduate course is also planned. Twenty-eight scholarships are awarded annually to candidates sponsored by media organizations.

The Kenyan Union of Journalists was founded in 1962.

LESOTHO

Population	950 000
Area	30 355 sq. km.

PRESS
Newspapers　　　　　　　　Non-dailies 2

RADIO

Transmitters	Medium-wave 1, Short-wave 1
Total receivers	10 000 estimated in use
Receivers per 1000 people	11

FILM

Cinemas	Fixed 1

PRESS

There is no national daily press, but three or four South African daily newspapers are circulated regularly.

Two bilingual newspapers (in Lesotho and English) are published by the Government Information Department in Maseru, one weekly and the other less frequently, and another bilingual weekly is published by a Catholic mission in Mazenod.

Four other periodicals include a general interest digest which appears two or three times a year.

NEWS AGENCIES

There is no national news agency; Reuters maintains a correspondent in Maseru. Radio Lesotho receives Reuters' news service.

RADIO

The government-owned Lesotho National Broadcasting Service (LNBS), opened in 1966 (earlier broadcasts were carried out by a Catholic Community Centre transmitter), now has sole responsibility for sound broadcasting, under the direct jurisdiction of the Prime Minister. It derives its income from government assistance, advertising and radio licence fees.

Now equipped with two 10kW transmitters (medium- and short-wave respectively) Radio Lesotho broadcasts mainly in English and Lesotho, but also in four other local languages for about 115 hours a week. Programmes include eight news bulletins daily (one relayed from the BBC), music (both indigenous and Western), educational, religious, health and hygiene and agricultural broadcasts, children's sessions, etc. as well as imported documentary and entertainment material. Educational programmes (since 1973) are broadcast for two hours a day, five days a week, both in school terms and during vacations.

One licence covers all sets in a household (including a car radio).

TELEVISION

Apart from closed-circuit systems installed in two hotels, there is no public television service.

FILM

Feature and documentary films are imported from the UK. Maseru, the capital, has a commercial cinema and there are two government mobile projection units.

LIBERIA

Population	1 571 000
Area	111 370 sq. km.

PRESS
Newspapers	Dailies 1, Non-dailies 4
Total circulation	Dailies 7000, Non-dailies 7100
Copies per 1000 people	Dailies 5, Non-dailies 5

RADIO
Transmitters	Long/medium-wave 8, Short-wave 8*
Total receivers	400 000 estimated in use
Receivers per 1000 people	255

TELEVISION
Transmitters	3
Receivers	6000 estimated in use
Receivers per 1000 people	4

FILM
Cinemas	Fixed 8
Total annual attendance	825 266
Annual visits per capita	0.5

*In addition, the Voice of America (USA) operates 6 relay transmitters.

PRESS
The country's only daily is a government-sponsored newspaper published in the capital, Monrovia.

The non-daily press includes two English-language papers, also published in Monrovia and circulating 5000 and 400 copies respectively, and two rural mimeographed weeklies published by the government information service in the vernacular languages, Kpelle (900 copies) and Loma (840 copies). There are about 30 other periodicals, 11 of which are general interest, historical and literary publications; other subject categories are religious, sociological, educational and technological (4 titles each), medical sciences (2 titles) and ethnography, entertainment and law.

NEWS AGENCIES
There is no national news agency, though the possibility of establishing one is being studied. The Department of Information, Cultural Affairs and Tourism receives news through its five regional centres and from its information officers. World news is received through AFP, TASS, Reuters and DPA, while UPI provides world news photos.

Foreign news agencies represented in Monrovia are Reuters, UPI and TASS.

RADIO

The Liberian Broadcasting Corporation (ELBC) is owned and operated by the Government of Liberia. Its revenues come from government subsidy and advertising. No receiver licence fee is payable.

ELBC operates one medium-wave and two short-wave transmitters of 10kW each in Monrovia, and a 5kW medium-wave transmitter at Harper. Programmes are broadcast for about 125 hours a week in English and Liberian languages (Gio, Mano, Kpelle, Bassa, Vai, Kru, Greboh, Loma and Mandingo).

A second radio station in Monrovia is ELWA, a non-commercial station operated by the Sudan Interior Mission. ELWA broadcasts on one medium-wave transmitter (10kW) and four short-wave transmitters (two 50kW and two 10kW). Programmes consist of a home service of 280 hours a week, in English and Liberian languages, including light entertainment (108 hours), news bulletins, etc. (92 hours), broadcasts for special audiences (55 hours, including 45 hours religious), advertising (12½ hours), cultural programmes (7 hours), local-language broadcasts (5 hours) and adult education (2½ hours), and a foreign service beamed to east, west, north and central Africa and the Middle East, in Arabic, French, English and 35 African languages.

Another privately owned station operated by a mining company in Nimba with two 0.1kW medium-wave transmitters, relays ELBC programmes and BBC World News (UK) and also broadcasts its own educational and news programmes in English and African languages (Mono and Gio) for the company's employees.

The Voice of America (USA) has a short-wave relay station in Monrovia with six 250kW and two 50kW transmitters broadcasting in English, French and Swahili.

TELEVISION

The Liberian Broadcasting Corporation began television broadcasting in 1964. With a main transmitter at Monrovia and translators at Bomi Hills and Buchanan, it now potentially serves 20% of the population. Weekly broadcasting time in English and Liberian languages (see under Radio) now totals almost 40 hours a week, including light entertainment (19½ hours), broadcasts for special audiences (10½ hours), news and information (5 hours), educational programmes (3 hours) and advertising (2 hours).

FILM

The Ministry of Information, Cultural Affairs and Tourism produces documentaries (by 1972 some 75 titles had been produced).

In 1972, about 1132 imported feature films were being shown by commercial firms throughout the country, the main sources being the USA, the UK, Japan, China, India, Italy, Saudi Arabia, France and the Federal Republic of Germany. During the same year, 334 documentary films were imported from the USA, France and the UK.

In addition to the 35mm and 16mm fixed cinemas, there are two mobile (16mm) units with a total annual attendance of 120 540 persons.

Diplomatic missions in and around the capital also show educational and documentary films.

PROFESSIONAL TRAINING AND ASSOCIATIONS

Radio and television personnel are trained by the Ministry of Information. There is a press association in Monrovia.

LIBYAN ARAB REPUBLIC

Population	2 080 000
Area	1 759 540 sq. km.

PRESS

Newspapers	Dailies 7, Non-dailies 10
Total circulation	Dailies 35 000, Non-dailies 50 000
Copies per 1000 people	Dailies 17, Non-dailies 24

RADIO

Transmitters	Long/medium-wave 8, Short-wave 4
Total receivers	85 000 licences
Licences per 1000 people	41

TELEVISION

Transmitters	2
Receivers	1000 licences
Receivers per 1000 people	0.5

FILM

Cinemas	Fixed 28
Total seating capacity	19 100
Seats per 1000 people	9
Total annual attendance	3 400 000
Annual visits per capita	2

PRESS

Daily newspapers are published in the joint capitals Tripoli and Benghazi. Non-daily papers — mostly in Arabic, several in English and one in Italian — appear weekly in these and other centres.

Periodicals include 11 monthly magazines, two of which are bilingual Arabic and English.

NEWS AGENCIES

The Libyan News Agency (LNA), with headquarters in Tripoli, was founded in 1965 as the national agency in association with the Ministry of Information. It supplies news to the national press and broadcasting media and to government departments.

DPA, Reuters and TASS have offices in Tripoli and MENA has one in Benghazi.

RADIO

All broadcasting is conducted by the State-owned Libyan Broadcasting and Television Service.

With medium-wave transmitters located in seven cities, including two 1000kW transmitters at El Beida and Tripoli, and short-wave transmitters in Tripoli (all 100kW), the radio service is on the air in Arabic for 17½ hours a day. In addition, the station at Benghazi broadcasts in English, Italian and French on medium wave.

TELEVISION

The television service, with transmitters in Tripoli and Benghazi (625 lines) broadcasts a single programme for six hours daily. A network of six repeater stations is planned.

FILM

Feature films and newsreels shown in public cinemas are imported from Egypt, the USA and European countries. Films are also shown by foreign cultural missions.

MADAGASCAR

Population	6 750 000
Area	587 041 sq. km.

PRESS

Newspapers	Dailies 13, Non-dailies 19
Total circulation	Dailies 103 300, Non-dailies 111 500
Copies per 1000 people	Dailies 15, Non-dailies 17

RADIO

Transmitters	Long/medium-wave 9, Short-wave 9
Total receivers	600 000 estimated in use
Receivers per 1000 people	89

TELEVISION

Transmitters	5
Receivers	6000 estimated in use
Receivers per 1000 people	0.8

FILM

Cinemas	Fixed 43
Total seating capacity	15 000
Seats per 1000 people	2
Total annual attendance	4 500 000
Annual visits per capita	0.6

PRESS

The daily newspapers are all published in the capital, Tananarive, 7 in Malagasy, 3 in French and 3 in both Malagasy and French, one of the latter having the highest circulation. Of the non-dailies, 16 appear in Malagasy and 3 in French.

The content of general interest newspapers includes an average of 16% of space devoted to local news, 10% to national news, 9.5% to foreign news, 11% to official texts and announcements, 12% to background articles, 9% to literary pages, 8% to sports, 7% to women's interests, etc. Some 44 periodicals other than newspapers (26 in Malagasy, 17 in French and 1 bilingual) circulate 154 000 copies, with a wide range of subjects including religion and theology (4 titles circulating 6800 copies) and education (13 titles with 6000 copies). The two general interest periodicals circulate 6200 copies.

The production of newsprint (300 metric tons in 1970) is approximately equal to the national requirements.

NEWS AGENCIES

The national agency is the Agence Madagascar Presse (AMP) located in Tananarive with six permanent offices and a staff of 33 people on the island as well as seven other, part-time correspondents. It was founded in 1962 as a public corporation. AMP receives the world news services of AFP and Reuters, and distributes a 10-page bulletin and teletype service of foreign news in French. National and local news is distributed through a daily 30-page news bulletin, also in French. Its subscribers include the national press, radio and television, private companies, embassies, government services and individuals.

The Office de Radiodiffusion Télévision Française (ORTF) supplies news for radio and television broadcasting, and Visnews of London also supplies television newsfilm.

AFP, Reuters and UPI maintain bureaux in Madagascar.

RADIO

Radio and television broadcasting comes under the general control of the Ministry of Information.

The two radio stations, Radio Madagasikara and Radio Université are public services of the Government, deriving their financial resources from government subventions and advertising revenue.

Radio Madagasikara, with medium-wave transmitters (each 4kW) and short-wave transmitters (of up to 100kW), operates two home-service networks broadcasting in Malagasy for 18½ hours daily on Network I and in French for 20 hours daily on Network II, and, under normal atmospheric conditions, reaching 90% of the population. The weekly total of 102 broadcasting hours consists of light entertainment (63 hours), educational programmes (9 hours), news and information (19 hours), broadcasts for special audiences (6 hours), cultural and scientific programmes (4 hours) and advertising (30 minutes). All programmes are of national origin.

In addition, Radio Université, with one medium-wave and one short-wave transmitter, broadcasts educational courses and related programmes for 35½ hours weekly during the academic year.

The international short-wave service, Network III, broadcasts programmes in English and French beamed to east and central Africa for 1 hour per day.

The Netherlands overseas broadcasting service has two 300kW short-wave relay transmitters at Talata and Volonondry.

TELEVISION

Malagasy television is a public service financed by State subsidy, advertising revenue and, to a small extent, the sale of programmes. It first began broadcasting in December 1967. Its two main and three auxiliary transmitters are now on the air for 16 hours a week with cultural programmes (7 hours), news and information (5 hours), light entertainment (2 hours), programmes for special audiences (30 minutes) and educational programmes (15 minutes). About 70% of programmes are imported, from France, the Federal Republic of Germany, the USA, UK, Japan, Italy and the United Nations, or received under exchange agreements with the French ORTF and the Mauritius Broadcasting System. About 10% of the population are covered by the television service. No receiver licence fee is payable.

FILM

There is no local feature-film production, but the government photographic and film service produces some news and short films. In 1969, 19 educational films were made by the government centre for the production of educational films. In 1972, 168 features were imported from France (61), the USA (53), Italy (32), the UK (11), Spain (6), the Federal Republic of Germany (3) and Japan and Yugoslavia (1 each). A total of 29 documentaries in 1969 came from the USA (23) and France (6).

In addition to the fixed cinemas, there are four mobile units with a total annual attendance of 100 000.

PROFESSIONAL TRAINING

A professional training centre for journalists, financed by the Government, was established in 1965 within the University of Madagascar, offering professional training for journalists in press, radio and television (three-year course).

MALAWI

Population	4 670 000
Area	118 484 sq. km.

PRESS

Newspapers	Non-dailies 3
Total circulation	Non-dailies 23 000
Copies per 1000 people	Non-dailies 5

RADIO

Transmitters	Medium-wave 7, Short-wave 3, VHF—FM 3
Total receivers	110 000 estimated in use
Receivers per 1000 people	24

FILM

Cinemas	Fixed 13
Total seating capacity	5335
Seats per 1000 people	1

PRESS

There are no daily newspapers. Two papers appear twice weekly, one published in Blantyre in English and circulating 8500 copies, and the other, an official organ of the Malawi Congress Party, published in Limbe in both English and Chichewa, circulating 15 000 copies.

Periodicals include a weekly official gazette in English published in Zomba, the administrative capital, and circulating about 1500 copies, and two government-sponsored weekly magazines published in Blantyre, one in English and Chichewa and the other in Chichewa and Chitumbuka. A fortnightly Catholic magazine, published in English, Chichewa and Chitumbuka, is issued in Lilongwe and circulates approx. 8000 copies.

NEWS AGENCIES

The Malawi News Agency (MANA) was founded in 1966 and is located in Blantyre. Reuters maintains a permanent correspondent, while AFP, IANA and AP have part-time correspondents in the country.

RADIO

The Malawi Broadcasting Corporation (MBC) is an independent statutory organization set up by the Government and responsible for all radio broadcasting. It is controlled by a government-appointed board headed by a Director-General.

With one medium-wave (10kW) and three short-wave (10, 20 and 100kW) transmitters in Blantyre, six regional medium-wave transmitters and three FM transmitters (at Chichiri, Dedza and Limbe), MBC broadcasts a home service in

Chichewa and English for over 127 hours a week, consisting of light entertainment (61 hours), educational programmes (27½ hours), news and information (26 hours), cultural and scientific broadcasts (6 hours), programmes for special audiences (4 hours), advertising (2 hours) and language courses (30 minutes). The majority of the programmes are of national origin and are presented in Chichewa (known also as Nyanja), which is understood by all the local African population, and in English which is understood by 35 to 40% of the people of Malawi.

An external service designed for both domestic and foreign listeners, with programmes in Chichewa and English, is broadcast daily on short wave. There is no licence system.

FILM

There is no local film production. All films exhibited are imported. There are five 35mm cinemas (in Limbe, Blantyre and Lilongwe) with a combined seating of 2335, and eight 16mm cinemas in community centres, missions and one factory together seating 3000 (six of these cinemas are in Zomba, and one each in Blantyre and Lilongwe).

MALI

Population	5 260 000
Area	1 240 000 sq. km.

PRESS

Newspapers	Dailies 2
Total circulation	Dailies 3350
Copies per 1000 people	Dailies 0.6

RADIO

Transmitters	Medium-wave 2, Short-wave 6
Total receivers	60 000 estimated in use
Receivers per 1000 people	11

FILM

Cinemas	Fixed 19
Total seating capacity	17 100
Seats per 1000 people	3
Total annual attendance	2 500 000
Annual visits per capita	0.5

PRESS

The daily press consists of a government-sponsored newspaper circulating 3000 copies per issue, which also has a separate weekly edition, and a general information bulletin published by the Chamber of Commerce, Agriculture and Industry (350 copies). Other periodicals include a government tourist publication, an official gazette, a statistical bulletin and, since early 1972, a monthly journal carrying some news along with educational and general reading matter, for new literates in rural areas (circulation 8000 copies). French is the official language and the language of all the publications mentioned, except the last mentioned, which is in Bambara, the most widely used vernacular.

NEWS AGENCIES

The national agency is the Agence Nationale d'Information du Mali (ANIM), which has headquarters in Bamako and was established with government assistance in 1961. It issues a daily information bulletin. AFP maintains a permanent correspondent in Bamako, while CTK, Novosti and TASS are also represented in Mali.

RADIO

The government-owned Radio Mali, broadcasts a home service with two medium-wave transmitters at Bamako (60kW) and Mopti (4kW) and six short-wave transmitters of up to 50kW. Its home service, in French and eight vernacular languages, is on the air for about 100 hours a week.

FILM

The Office Cinématographique du Mali produces documentary and instructional films, and also exercises some control over film distribution and exhibition. All feature films shown in commercial cinemas are imported. There are also two mobile units.

MAURITANIA

Population	1 200 000
Area	1 030 700 sq. km.

PRESS

Newspapers	Dailies 1, Non-dailies 2
Total circulation	Dailies 300
Copies per 1000 people	0.2

RADIO

Transmitters	Medium-wave 2, Short-wave 2
Total receivers	150 000 estimated in use
Receivers per 1000 people	125

PRESS

A daily news bulletin is issued in Arabic and French versions with a combined circulation of 300 copies by the government information service in the capital, Nouakchott. A government-sponsored weekly in both Arabic and French versions, and a fortnightly official gazette, are also published. Specialized periodicals include educational, agricultural, trade and industrial and economic and statistical journals.

NEWS AGENCIES

There is no national press agency, the main source of national and local news being the information service's daily bulletin. AFP, Reuters and TASS news services are received by Radio Mauritania. AFP maintains a bureau in Nouakchott.

RADIO

The Radiodiffusion Nationale de Mauritanie is the official broadcasting organization, financed by a government subsidy, receiver-licence fees and advertising. With two medium-wave transmitters of 20 and 1kW and two short-wave transmitters of 30 and 4kW, Radio Mauritanie broadcasts in Arabic and French and in three vernacular languages (Toucouleur, Sarakolé and Wolof) for 61 hours a week, and reaches 90% of the population. News and information account for almost 40% of broadcasting time. Other programmes include cultural and scientific (17½ hours), school broadcasts (1 hour), other educational programmes (1½ hours), programmes for special audiences (2 hours), language courses (1 hour) and advertising (35 minutes). The programmes are almost entirely of national origin.

The number of radio receivers in use in 1971 was 150 000, a ratio of 128 receivers per 1000 of the population.

FILM

The first Mauritanian feature film was produced around 1970. All the main towns have one or more cinemas, and there are also six mobile projection units.

MAURITIUS AND DEPENDENCIES

Population	836 000
Area	2045 sq. km.

PRESS

Newspapers	Dailies 12, Non-dailies 14
Total circulation	Dailies 14 500, Non-dailies 6000
Copies per 1000 people	Dailies 17, Non-dailies 7

RADIO

Transmitters	Long/medium-wave 1, Short-wave 2
Total receivers	107 474 licences
Licences per 1000 people	129

TELEVISION

Transmitters	6
Receivers	28 700 estimated in use
Receivers per 1000 people	34

FILM

Cinemas	Fixed 53
Total seating capacity	52 000
Seats per 1000 people	62
Total annual attendance	8 275 000
Annual visits per capita	10

PRESS

All the daily newspapers are published in Port Louis, the capital; 9 are in French and 3 in Chinese, with casual use of English. The non-daily press includes a twice-weekly paper in Hindi (1500 copies), 7 weeklies in French only or bilingual English and French and 6 others published less frequently.

Periodicals include a Muslim monthly in French and English and 2 other religious journals, 3 trade journals, 2 medical, 2 literary, 1 sociological and 1 art.

NEWS AGENCIES

There is no local news agency. Reuters and AFP maintain permanent bureaux in Port Louis and together have 258 local subscribers.

RADIO

The government-controlled Mauritius Broadcasting Corporation operates both radio and television broadcasting and is directed by a board of governors. Its revenue is derived from government subsidies, licence fees and advertising.

The home and dependencies service, with one medium-wave transmitter (10kW) and two short-wave transmitters, is on the air for 116 hours a week, broadcasting in French, English, certain Indian languages (mainly Hindustani) and Chinese, with programmes consisting of light entertainment (52 hours), cultural programmes (19½ hours), news and information (16½ hours), programmes for special audiences (13 hours), educational programmes (7½ hours), language courses (5½ hours) and advertising (2½ hours). Over 90% of the programmes are nationally produced. Potential coverage of the population is 100%.

TELEVISION

The Mauritius Broadcasting Corporation operates a commercial television service inaugurated in February 1965, with five main stations and one auxiliary station in Port Louis, Malherbes, Souillac and Flacq (also 35 experimental transmitters in various localities) broadcasting, for over 50 hours a week, a programme consisting of light entertainment (13 hours), news and information (13 hours), educational programmes (5 hours), programmes for special audiences (10 hours), cultural programmes (4 hours) and advertising (about 3 hours).

Television programmes are imported from the UK, USA, France, the Federal Republic of Germany, India and the USSR, and are exchanged with the UK and France. About 35% of the programmes are nationally produced. The definition system used is 625 lines. Broadcasts cover the whole of the territory.

FILM

The Ministry of Information and Broadcasting produces documentary films and newsreels. These are shown by the Government's mobile units. The Government also encourages the production of tourist films by private companies.

All feature films exhibited are imported, mainly from the USA, France, the UK, India and Italy. Of the fixed establishments, six are outdoor cinemas. In addition, there are 10 mobile projection units with an annual attendance of 775 000 in 1972.

MOROCCO

Population	15 830 000
Area	446 550 sq. km.

PRESS

Newspapers	Dailies 6, Non-dailies 52
Total circulation	Non-dailies 251 000
Copies per 1000 people	Non-dailies 16

RADIO

Transmitters	Long/medium-wave 22, Short-wave 7, VHF–FM 6
Total receivers	1 500 000 licences
Licences per 1000 people	95

TELEVISION	
Transmitters	14
Receivers	225 000 estimated in use
Receivers per 1000 people	14

FILM	
Cinemas	Fixed 260
Total seating capacity	150 000
Seats per 1000 people	9
Total annual attendance	18 200 000
Annual visits per capita	1

PRESS

Daily newspapers are published in the capital, Rabat (3 in Arabic and 1 in French), with a combined circulation of about 95 000 copies, and Casablanca (3 in French). The year 1971 saw the merger of 2 Arabic-language titles in Rabat and the disappearance, in November, of 4 other daily titles (3 French-language in Casablanca and 1 Spanish-language in Tangier). In place of 2 of the Casablanca papers, new morning and evening newspapers were created. Non-dailies include 6 weekly papers mostly in Arabic, and several French-language monthlies.

NEWS AGENCIES

The national agency is the private company, Mahgreb Arabe Presse (MAP), founded in 1959, with headquarters in Rabat and branches in Casablanca and Tangier, and offices in Paris and Madrid. Permanent staff number 90 in Morocco and 27 abroad. MAP receives the foreign services of AFP, UPI, Reuters, ACP, Efe, APS, and TAP, and has exchange agreements with TASS, CTK, ADN, DPA, Tanjug, PAP, ANSA, Agerpress and Antara. Its national and international news services, including press and stock-exchange reviews and sports news, amounting to 210 000 words daily in Arabic and 150 000 words in French, are received by 71 subscribers in Morocco, including 7 newspapers, 5 radio stations, 1 television station, and 58 diplomatic and official and commercial organizations and individuals, and by 60 foreign subscribers. Transmissions are effected by telegraph (24 hours a day) and radio teleprinter (6 hours a day).

RADIO

All broadcasting is conducted by the Radiodiffusion Télévision Marocaine (RTM), a public service under the Ministry of Information, financed from receiver licence fees, State subsidies and advertising receipts. While television licence fees will be maintained, it is proposed to discontinue licences for radio receivers in order to increase the number of listeners.

With a powerful long-wave transmitter (400kW) at Azilal in the centre of the country, 22 medium-wave transmitters (of up to 140kW) covering the main populated areas from the Mediterranean coast to Agadir, and six FM transmitters at Rabat, Casablanca and Sebaa-Aioun (serving the urban communities of Meknès, Fes and Azrou), RTM broadcasts three separate home-service programmes: the national programme in Arabic, the 'international' programme in

French, English and Spanish (12 hours a day), and the Berber programme (8 hours a day). These, with their networks of regional stations, are on the air for well over 400 hours a week. With the 400kW transmitter at Azilal now functioning and the present development of the medium-wave network, it is expected that the whole national territory will have radio coverage in the next few years.

TELEVISION

Television broadcasting dates from 1962 (apart from a private company's short period of operation in 1954). RTM's network of nine main transmitters and five low-power repeaters (625 lines) now covers the most densely populated areas of the country and is expected to expand even more in the current five-year plan. A microwave relay system connects all these transmitters, and links the national network with Spain (via Tangier) and thence with Eurovision. Production studios are located at Rabat (2) and Casablanca.

Daily programmes in Arabic and French are on the air for 4½ hours, consisting of religious, educational and children's programmes (45 minutes), news in French (15 minutes), imported programmes in French (1 hour), news in Arabic (30 minutes), entertainment (2 hours), with 3½ hours of sports on Sunday afternoons.

Programmes are imported from Europe, the USA and the Middle East and are exchanged with other African countries and with Eurovision member countries.

FILM

The Centre Cinématographique Marocain at Rabat is the government body concerned with the film industry. It also has well-equipped studios and is the main producer of feature films. Since 1968, there has been one feature film produced yearly and a number of documentary and educational short films.

Feature films imported number around 900 a year, mainly from the USA, France, Egypt and Italy. These are shown in 214 35mm and around 50 16mm cinemas, all privately owned by about 30 companies, mostly Moroccan. Of these cinemas, 52 are in Casablanca.

SPACE COMMUNICATIONS

An Atlantic Intelsat earth station at Souk el Arba des Seouls was put into service in December 1969 under the technical direction of the Ministry of PTT.

PROFESSIONAL TRAINING AND ASSOCIATIONS

A Journalism Training Centre at Rabat, opened in April 1969, conducts seminars to which students with secondary education may be admitted after passing an entrance examination. The 1970 enrolment consisted of 82 male and 12 female students.

Professional associations include the Syndicat National de la Presse Marocaine and the Association Marocaine de la Presse Sportive.

MOZAMBIQUE

Population	7 376 000
Area	783 030 sq. km.

PRESS
Newspapers	Dailies 6, Non-dailies 7
Total circulation	Dailies 60 000
Copies per 1000 people	Dailies 8

RADIO
Transmitters	Long/medium-wave 15, Short-wave 19, VHF–FM 2
Total receivers	110 000 estimated in use
Receivers per 1000 people	15

TELEVISION
Transmitters	1
Receivers	1000 estimated in use
Receivers per 1000 people	0.1

FILM
Cinemas	Fixed 22
Total seating capacity	22 000
Seats per 1000 people	3
Total annual attendance	2 500 000
Annual visits per capita	0.3

PRESS

Four of the six dailies are published in the capital, Lourenço Marques, and the other two in Beira, with a reported combined circulation of some 60 000 copies per issue. All are in Portuguese. Some are published by private owners, some by the Church, but most are subject in some degree to the financial control of banking interests and to editorial control by the Government.

All the non-daily newspapers are in Portuguese. Of the larger journals, some 50% are sold by subscription while sales of smaller ones are almost entirely by subscription. Periodicals, dealing with cultural, technical and administrative subjects, include a number of government publications.

NEWS AGENCIES

There is no local news agency, the main sources of foreign news being Lusitania, ANI, AFP and Reuters.

RADIO

Radio broadcasting is conducted by four organizations, the most important being the Radio Clube de Moçambique, a private non-profit-making organization which derives its revenue from government subsidies, licence fees and commercial advertising. Located in Lourenço Marques, the Radio Clube operates 6 medium-wave, 16 short-wave and 1 FM transmitters, broadcasting four home-service programmes. The first, in Portuguese, is on the air for up to 18 hours a day; the second, in English and Afrikaans, for 24 hours a day; the third, including Radio Universidade, in Portuguese, for 12 hours a day; and the fourth, also in Portuguese, for 9½ hours a day. In addition, programmes in local vernaculars (Ronga, Shangane, Chissena, Chuabo, Chinungue and Macua), as well as Nyanja, Swahili and Alaua, are broadcast over a network of regional stations located at Beira, Quelimane, Nampula and Porto Amelia, which also relay the main Portuguese-language programmes.

Radio Pax, in Beira, which is owned by Franciscan monks, broadcasts a home service in Portuguese and vernaculars on short- and medium-wave and FM transmitters. Also in Beira is the Aero Clube de Beira, a private commercial station which broadcasts in Portuguese and vernaculars for 18 hours a day, while Radio Mocidade, in Lourenço Marques, is run by young people for young people, and broadcasts in Portuguese only. Two private firms in the capital produce programmes for the radio.

TELEVISION
Radio Clube de Moçambique is reported to have begun a commercial television service in 1972.

FILM
There is no local film production. All feature films are imported. Of the fixed cinemas, 11 are in Lourenço Marques, 4 in Beira and 1 in each of seven other towns. In addition, at least 10 mobile units circulate throughout the country.

NAMIBIA

Population	574 000
Area	824 292 sq. km.

PRESS
Newspapers	Dailies 3, Non-dailies 2
Total circulation	Dailies 7500
Copies per 1000 people	Dailies 13

RADIO
Transmitters	VHF—FM 4
Total receivers	47 000 licences
Licences per 1000 people	82

FILM

Cinemas	Fixed 17
Total seating capacity	6600
Seats per 1000 people	11

PRESS

The daily press consists of one morning paper in Afrikaans and two afternoon papers, one in German circulating over 5000 copies and one in English circulating 2500 copies. All are published in Windhoek, which is the seat of the administration.

Non-dailies include two papers published twice weekly, one published in Walvis Bay and one in Afrikaans published in Windhoek. The other periodicals are a monthly agricultural publication in Afrikaans, English and German and an annual, also trilingual.

RADIO

South African Broadcasting Corporation programmes in English and Afrikaans and in African vernaculars can be received throughout the territory. SABC has FM transmitters at Windhoek transmitting both home and Radio Bantu services, the latter in the Herero and Nama languages, while Radio Bantu programmes in Ovambo are broadcast from FM transmitters at Windhoek, Walvis Bay and Oshakati.

FILM

There is no local film production. Of the fixed cinemas, five are in Windhoek (in addition to two drive-ins accommodating 500 and 520 cars respectively) and three are in Walvis Bay.

NIGER

Population	4 210 000
Area	1 267 000 sq. km.

PRESS

Newspapers	Dailies 1, Non-dailies 1
Total circulation	Dailies 2000, Non-dailies 2000
Copies per 1000 people	Dailies 0.5, Non-dailies 0.5

RADIO

Transmitters	Long/medium-wave 10, Short-wave 3
Total receivers	100 000 estimated in use
Receivers per 1000 people	24

TELEVISION

Transmitters	1

FILM

Cinemas	Fixed 4
Total seating capacity	3800
Seats per 1000 people	0.9
Total annual attendance	828 000
Annual visits per capita	0.2

PRESS

One daily paper and one weekly, each printed in offset and each circulating 2000 copies, are published in French in the capital, Niamey. The largest of the country's six printed or roneoed periodicals is a general interest magazine circulating 4000 copies; others deal with education (1500 copies), trade and commerce (1000), agriculture (1000), local customs and folklore (1000), and entertainment and sports (500).

NEWS AGENCIES

There is no local news agency, but AFP. Reuters and UPI maintain bureaux in Niamey and supply news to the national press, the radio, the President's Office and foreign embassies.

RADIO

All broadcasting is conducted by the State-subsidized Office de Radiodiffusion-Télévision du Niger (ORTN), which operates 10 medium-wave and three short-wave transmitters (including one of 30kW), covering 90% of the population. Programmes on its four networks are in French and five vernacular languages (Djerma, Hausa, Peulh, Tamachek, and Béri-béri), with some news bulletins also in English. The total broadcasting time is over 158 hours a week, consisting of light entertainment (64 hours), programmes for special audiences (35½ hours), news and information (27½ hours), educational broadcasts (23 hours), advertising (23 hours), language courses (about 2 hours) and cultural programmes (nearly 4 hours). Programmes are mainly of national origin.

TELEVISION

The television service of ORTN exists exclusively for schools. It is run by the State and financed by the Governments of Niger and France, and all programmes are imported from France.

FILM

A national film industry is being developed with the assistance of the Government, which allotted the funds in 1970–71 for the purchase of production equipment. In 1969, the Centre Nigérien de Recherches en Sciences Humaines, at Niamey, produced 3 long and 10 short films, 5 of which were educational, 2 documentaries and 3 for entertainment; 13 coproductions were made with France.

NIGERIA

Population	55 074 000
Area	923 768 sq. km.

PRESS
Newspapers	Dailies 11

RADIO
Transmitters	Long/medium-wave 16, Short-wave 21
Total receivers	1 275 000 licences
Licences per 1000 people	23

TELEVISION
Transmitters	7*
Receivers	75 000 licences
Receivers per 1000 people	1

FILM
Cinemas	Fixed 183
Total seating capacity	36 800
Seats per 1000 people	0.7
Total annual attendance	68 750 000
Annual visits per capita	1

*Including 2 auxiliary transmitters.

PRESS

At least 11 dailies are published, six appearing in Lagos, the capital city, one of which circulates 114 400 copies per issue, another 47 300 copies. Several Lagos papers enjoy nation-wide readerships. Other dailies appear in regional centres (Ibadan, Kaduna, Benin City and Kano). With the exception of one Lagos paper in the Yoruba language and one bilingual in English and Hausa, published in Kano, the daily press is in English.

The non-daily press is also mainly concentrated in Lagos, where there are 10 weeklies, including Sunday editions of dailies. Two of the weeklies are in Yoruba and one bilingual weekly is in English and Yoruba. Other non-dailies are published in Ibadan, Kaduna, Kano, Port Harcourt and Owerri. Periodicals include several women's journals, a broadcasting magazine and some English-language magazines which circulate in a number of African countries.

NEWS AGENCIES

Plans for the foundation of a national news agency have been submitted to government authorities. The foreign press agencies represented in the country are AP, GNA, Novosti, Reuters, DPA, Jiji and TASS.

RADIO

Radio and television broadcasting are carried out by the Nigerian Broadcasting Corporation (NBC), a statutory corporation set up in 1958 and financed by government subvention, licence fees and commercial advertising revenue.

The NBC, with 12 medium-wave transmitters of up to 10kW and 12 short-wave transmitters of up to 100kW, broadcasts a national programme, from Lagos, and six state programmes, including national programme relays, from Ibadan, Benin City, Kaduna, Maiduguri, Enugu and Calabar; each programme is on the air for 19 hours a day. The principal languages used are English, Yoruba, Hausa and Igbo with some programmes also in other vernaculars (Efik, Ijaw, Fulani, Kanuri, Tiv, Edo, Urhoho).

Western and northern Nigeria both have commercially operated broadcasting services for radio and television. Radio Television Kaduna (northern Nigeria), with two medium-wave transmitters (150 and 10kW) and three short-wave transmitters (10kW each), broadcasts in English and Hausa for about 18 hours per day. Western Nigeria Radiovision Service, with two medium-wave and one short-wave transmitters (all of 10kW) located in Abafon (Lagos) and Ibadan, broadcasts in English, Yoruba and Hausa, also for 18 hours a day; its 18 daily news bulletins in English include three relayed from the BBC.

The NBC's external service, the Voice of Nigeria, with five short-wave transmitters of 100kW at Ikorodu, broadcasts programmes in French, English, Arabic and Hausa for about 9 hours a day, beamed to four areas in west Africa, east Africa and the Middle East, central and south Africa, and north Africa, Europe and the Mediterranean.

TELEVISION

Television in Nigeria is both a federal and an individual state responsibility, attempting to express both the national unity and its cultural diversity. It uses not only the main languages (English, Yoruba, Hausa and Igbo) but also a number of other vernaculars.

The Nigerian Broadcasting Corporation (NBC) operates the Federal Government's television service, which began broadcasting as the Nigerian Television Service in 1962. NBC Television (integrated with the NBC in 1967) is financed by a government subsidy and commercial advertising revenue. Based in Lagos, NBC–TV is on the air for about 37 hours a week, broadcasting light entertainment (33% of total time), broadcasts for special audiences (17%), news and information (12%), education (11%) and commercial advertising (10%). About 25% of programmes are nationally produced. Daily programmes for schools are produced by the Lagos State Ministry of Education. News film is received from Visnews (UK). NBC–TV has a relay station at Ibadan.

The state-owned services are based in Ibadan (west), Kaduna (north) and Benin (mid-west). These are commercially run stations which cooperate among themselves and with the NBC for programme exchanges, joint programme purchasing, etc. They are each on the air for 35 hours a week. Some have relay stations in addition to their main transmitters.

The line definition system used is 625 lines.

FILM

Three feature films were produced in 1970, the first in the history of the Nigerian cinema. These films were coproduced with American, Swedish, Lebanese and German companies. Newsreels and documentaries are produced by the federal film unit, mostly used by the Ministry of Information and often sent abroad to Nigerian embassies. Several private companies also produce publicity films, both for the cinema and for television. Adequate studio and laboratory facilities are available. There are about 100 cinemas and 83 outdoor projection points, largely supplied by three distribution circuits, which show imported films, mainly from the USA, the UK and India.

SPACE COMMUNICATIONS

Nigeria has two earth stations located at Lanlate, 170km north of Lagos: one for Atlantic Intelsat transmission, opened in 1971, and the other for Indian Ocean Intelsat, opened in 1972.

PROFESSIONAL TRAINING AND ASSOCIATIONS

The Institute of Mass Communication, University of Lagos, offers three-year degree programmes and one-year diploma courses in mass communication (press, radio–television and government information services), with a total enrolment of 115 students in 1971–2. It also organizes in-service training courses and workshops for employed media personnel.

Training in journalism is being resumed at the University of Nigeria in Nsukka, where there is a department of journalism. Other training and research facilities in mass communication are available at the universities of Zaria (Communication Section, Department of Administration) and Ibadan (Institute of African Adult Education).

There are two professional associations for the press – one for newspaper publishers and one for journalists.

PORTUGUESE GUINEA

Population	563 000
Area	36 125 sq. km.

PRESS

Newspapers	Dailies 1, Non-dailies 1
Total circulation	Dailies 500, Non-dailies 500
Copies per 1000 people	Dailies 1, Non-dailies 1

RADIO

Transmitters	Medium-wave 1, Short-wave 1
Total receivers	8000 estimated in use
Receivers per 1000 people	14

FILM

Cinemas	Fixed 4
Total seating capacity	1500
Seats per 1000 people	3
Total annual attendance	300 000
Annual visits per capita	0.5

PRESS

One newspaper, published daily in the capital, Bissau, circulates 500 copies per issue, and a weekly published in Bolama also circulates 500 copies; both are in Portuguese. Other periodical publications include an official gazette, a cultural quarterly and an agricultural and commercial bulletin.

NEWS AGENCIES

The Portuguese news agency Lusitania is represented in Bissau and provides an information service for the local administration and the press.

RADIO

An official government station, operating one medium-wave transmitter (1kW) and one short-wave transmitter (10kW), broadcasts a home service for about 15 hours a day in Portuguese.

FILM

Feature films obtained through Portugal are mainly from the USA.

REUNION

Population	470 000
Area	2510 sq. km.

PRESS

Newspapers	Dailies 2, Non-dailies 11
Total circulation	Dailies 28 000, Non-dailies 63 000
Copies per 1000 people	Dailies 60, Non-dailies 134

RADIO

Transmitters	Medium-wave 2, Short-wave 3
Total receivers	80 897 licences
Licences per 1000 people	172

TELEVISION

Transmitters	14
Receivers	25 000 estimated in use
Receivers per 1000 people	53

FILM

Cinemas	Fixed 20
Total seating capacity	7000
Seats per 1000 people	15
Total annual attendance	1 200 000
Annual visits per capita	3

PRESS

The daily newspapers are published in the capital, St Denis. The non-dailies, like the dailies, are in French.

NEWS AGENCIES

AFP, which maintains a bureau in St Denis, is the main source of world news.

RADIO

Radio broadcasting is operated as a local service of the Office de Radiodiffusion-Télévision Française (ORTF) and is financed by licence fees, a government subvention and advertising. Radio Réunion broadcasts on medium and short wave for nearly 128 hours per week, including light entertainment (69 hours), cultural programmes (22 hours), news and information (18 hours), advertising (4 hours), and programmes for special audiences (10 hours), mainly of local origin.

TELEVISION

Television broadcasting is also operated by ORTF and financed by licence fees and a government subvention.

The main transmitter at St Denis, with 13 satellite transmitters, potentially covers the whole population, broadcasting mainly imported ORTF programmes from Paris. The total programme time of 33 hours weekly includes light entertainment (almost 13 hours), news and information (6 hours), cultural programmes (3 hours), programmes for special audiences (3 hours) and educational programmes (1½ hours).

FILM
All films exhibited are imported. Apart from the fixed cinemas there is one mobile unit.

RHODESIA

Population	5 690 000
Area	389 361 sq. km.

PRESS
Newspapers	Dailies 4, Non-dailies 10
Total circulation	Dailies 83 000
Copies per 1000 people	Dailies 15

RADIO
Transmitters	Long/medium-wave 12, Short-wave 10
Total receivers	215 000 estimated in use
Receivers per 1000 people	38

TELEVISION
Transmitters	3
Receivers	115 000 estimated in use
Receivers per 1000 people	20

FILM
Cinemas	Fixed 90
Total seating capacity	51 443*
Seats per 1000 people	9*

*For 80 cinemas only.

PRESS
There are two daily newspapers both owned by a group which also controls a chain of newspapers in South Africa; one appears in Salisbury, the capital, and circulates 56 000 copies both inside and outside Rhodesia, and the other in

Bulawayo, circulating 5250 copies. Both are published in English. Since 1960 two dailies have ceased publication.

Non-daily papers, all in English, consist of one published in Umtali three times a week, one Sunday paper in Salisbury and one in Bulawayo, and seven other weeklies.

Over 50 periodicals appear, mostly in English but a few in Afrikaans, Shona and Ndebele. Main subject categories are general interest (18 titles), trade, technical and financial (10 titles), travel and transport (5 titles) and agriculture (4 titles).

Newsprint production (10 000 metric tons annually) is approximately equivalent to the country's needs.

NEWS AGENCIES

The Inter-African News Agency (IANA), founded in 1964, a subsidiary of the South African Press Association, has its headquarters in Salisbury and serves the local newspapers and broadcasting stations. UPI and Reuters maintain bureaux in Salisbury.

RADIO

The Rhodesia Broadcasting Corporation (RBC) is an independent statutory body which controls radio and television broadcasting. The RBC operates four radio services, a general service, an African service and three regional commercial services.

The general service, with seven medium-wave transmitters (1, 2 or 100kW) and five short-wave transmitters (up to 100kW), is on the air for 17 hours a day broadcasting in English. The African service, broadcasting in vernacular languages (Shona and Ndebele) and in English, with three medium-wave transmitters (2kW each) and five short-wave transmitters (up to 100kW), is also on the air for 17 hours a day. The regional commercial services, Radio Jacaranda, serving Salisbury and districts, and Radio Matopos serving Bulawayo and districts, broadcast light entertainment, both with medium-wave trans-mitters of 1kW each, for 6 hours daily. Another commercial service, Radio Manica, serves the Umtali region with its own programmes for 1 hour a day, and otherwise relays the general-service programmes.

TELEVISION

Rhodesia Television, under contract to the Rhodesia Broadcasting Corporation, operates a television service with three transmitters serving Salisbury and the midlands area, the Bulawayo area, and the midlands (from Gwelo). Programmes are broadcast for 42 hours a week.

FILM

Of the total number of indoor and outdoor cinemas, 46 are reserved for non-European audiences; 20 are located in the capital city, 12 in Bulawayo, 6 in Gwelo, 4 each in Umtali, Gatooma and Que Que and the remainder in 28 other towns. There are also 5 drive-ins (in Salisbury, Bulawayo, Gwelo, Umtali and Gatooma) with a combined capacity of 3367 cars. Mobile 16mm units cover government circuits in seven provinces.

RWANDA

| Population | 3 827 000 |
| Area | 26 338 sq. km. |

PRESS

Newspapers	Non-dailies 1
Total circulation	Non-dailies 8000
Copies per 1000 people	Non-dailies 2

RADIO

Transmitters	Short-wave 1
Total receivers	50 000 estimated in use
Receivers per 1000 people	13

FILM

Cinemas	Fixed 4
Total seating capacity	800
Seats per 1000 people	0.2

PRESS

The most frequently published newspaper, with 8000 copies issued, is a weekly in the national language, Kinyarwanda, published by the Archdiocese of Kabagyi. Three other general interest news journals, also in Kinyarwanda with a total circulation of 45 000, are published in the capital, Kigali. One of these, which appears fortnightly under government sponsorship, has a circulation of 40 000. But if the current practice of group reading is taken into account the content of these journals reaches some 400 000 people. Though predominantly rural, with few towns of any size, Rwanda is the most densely populated country in Africa.

Official news and announcements appear in a French-language monthly (circulation 3000) published by the Ministry of Information. Other periodicals, the majority dealing with religious, educational or sociological affairs, total 34, with an aggregate circulation figure of 35 500. Of these, 20 are in French and 14 in Kinyarwanda.

NEWS AGENCIES

There is no national news agency, the main news source being the Ministry of Information.

AFP and Reuters are represented in the capital.

RADIO

From Kigali, the 50kW government short-wave station operated by Radiodiffusion de la République Rwandaise, known as Radio Kigali, broadcasts 95 programme hours a week in French, Kinyarwanda and Swahili from its transmitter built in 1965. Programmes constitute approximately 50% light entertainment, 17% news and information, 17% educational and cultural broadcasts, 7% broadcasts for special audiences and 5% commercial advertising.

Also at Kigali, Deutsche Welle (Federal Republic of Germany) has two relay stations (250kW each), from which programmes in German, English, French, Hausa, Kiswahili and Amharic are directed to the whole of the African continent.

A factor which increased the availability of radio receivers in the country, by drastically reducing domestic purchase prices, was the establishment in Kigali, in 1965, of a cooperative assembly plant for electronic equipment including radios. Capacity production of radio receivers is said to be about 1000 sets a month.

FILM

Films shown in the four 16mm cinemas are imported at the rate of about 20 features and 120 short films a year, mainly from Belgium, France, and the USA.

ST HELENA AND DEPENDENCIES

Population	5000
Area	314 sq. km.

PRESS	
Newspapers	Non-dailies 2
Total circulation	Non-dailies 1800
Copies per 1000 people	Non-dailies 360

RADIO	
Transmitters	Medium-wave 1
Total receivers	750 estimated in use
Receivers per 1000 people	150

FILM	
Cinemas	Fixed 1
Total seating capacity	650
Seats per 1000 people	130
Total annual attendance	25 500
Annual visits per capita	5

PRESS

The local press consists of two government-sponsored newspapers, one weekly and one monthly. Two periodicals also appear, including an official gazette. All are published in English.

RADIO

The St Helena Government Broadcasting Station operates one medium-wave transmitter of 0.5kW, which broadcasts for 16 hours a week. Programmes consist of light entertainment (6½ hours), school broadcasts (4 hours), adult education (2 hours), information on public affairs (1 hour) and advertising (15 minutes).

FILM

There is no local film production. Feature films exhibited are supplied through South Africa, while news films are supplied by the UK information services. The one cinema is used twice weekly. There are also two non-commercial mobile units.

SÃO TOMÉ AND PRINCIPE

Population	70 000
Area	964 sq. km.

PRESS
Newspapers	Non-dailies 2

RADIO
Transmitters	Medium-wave 1, Short-wave 1, VHF–FM 1
Total receivers	7000 estimated in use
Receivers per 1000 people	100

FILM
Cinemas	Fixed 1
Total seating capacity	1000
Seats per 1000 people	14
Total annual attendance	105 000
Annual visits per capita	1

PRESS

One weekly general interest newspaper and a weekly official bulletin are published in São Tomé. Other periodicals include a statistical monthly and a mission journal.

RADIO

The government-owned Emissora Regional de São Tomé e Principe operates three transmitters: one medium-wave (5kW), one short-wave (1kW) and one FM, broadcasting in Portuguese for over 18 hours a day.

FILM

Of the 241 films imported in 1969, 13 came from Portugal and 228 from other countries, mainly the USA.

SENEGAL

Population	4 022 000
Area	196 192 sq. km.

PRESS

Newspapers	Dailies 1, Non-dailies 4
Toal circulation	Dailies 20 000, Non-dailies 40 000
Copies per 1000 people	Dailies 5, Non-dailies 10

RADIO

Transmitters	Medium-wave 5, Short-wave 7
Total receivers	268 000 estimated in use
Receivers per 1000 people	67

TELEVISION

Transmitters	1
Receivers	1600 estimated in use
Receivers per 1000 people	0.4

FILM

Cinemas	Fixed 87
Total seating capacity	50 415
Seats per 1000 people	13
Total annual attendance	5 200 000
Annual visits per capita	1

PRESS

In addition to the government-sponsored French-language daily published in the capital, Dakar, since 1970, there is also a daily bulletin issued to subscribers by the Chamber of Commerce.

The non-daily general interest newspapers include four weeklies (two of which are published by the government information service) and several monthlies. All are in French, two also having associated editions in Arabic. A wall newspaper (monthly), consisting of news photos with captions in French and Wolof, the most widely used vernacular, is also distributed throughout the country by the government information service.

NEWS AGENCIES

The Agence de Presse Sénégalaise (APS), set up by the Government in 1959 and working in conjunction with the Government's regional information offices, is the national press agency, with headquarters in Dakar. It is commercially operated and receives a government subsidy. Its subscribers, which include newspapers, radio stations, government ministries, foreign embassies and private companies throughout the country, receive two news bulletins daily.

Foreign agencies represented in Dakar include AFP, Reuters, UPI, AP, TASS, Novosti, ANSA and DPA.

The Radiodiffusion Télévision du Sénégal (RTS), set up in 1960 as an autonomous public corporation, is financed by government subsidy and advertising revenue.

Its national and international networks, with 2 medium-wave transmitters (10 and 200kW) and 5 short-wave transmitters (one 4kW, two 25kW and two 100kW) in Dakar, are each on the air for 18 hours a day in French. Network II also carries daily 20-minute broadcasts in Portuguese, Arabic and English.

There are four regional stations, at St Louis, Tambacounda and Kaolack (each with a medium-wave transmitter of 1 to 5kW) and Ziguinchor (with two short-wave transmitters), each of which originates programmes of its own and is on the air for 8 to 9 hours daily. These stations broadcast mainly in six local languages: Wolof, Toucouleur, Sarakolé, Serere, Diola and Mandingue. Programmes include rural education broadcasts specially designed for group listening in village radio clubs.

TELEVISION

The first telecasts, made under government and Unesco auspices in 1965, were a series of experimental health and nutrition programmes in the Wolof language, intended for women's teleclubs in and around the capital. Other experimental programmes followed but were discontinued in 1969. In 1972, television services were resumed to receive the Olympic Games broadcasts from Munich via the satellite earth station at Gandoul, and are to be extended, with transmitters at Thiès and Zuiginchor, to cover the Diourbel and Siné-Saloun areas as well as the original Cap Vert/Dakar area. Programmes, many of which are imported from France, now consist mainly of entertainment, information and general cultural material.

FILM

In recent years, annual production has consisted of one or two features and several short films and documentaries, including some coproductions (three features were produced in 1971). There is no official film production agency. Film processing is done abroad, in the absence of local laboratory facilities.

Cinemas, found in most population centres throughout the country (there are 25 in Dakar), show locally produced and imported films, including a number from other African countries. These are distributed by two companies also operating in other African countries.

SPACE COMMUNICATIONS

An Atlantic Intelsat earth station was opened at Gandoul, 50km from Dakar, in March 1972.

PROFESSIONAL TRAINING AND ASSOCIATIONS

A mass communication centre within the University of Dakar, set up in 1967, offers a three-year diploma course mainly for journalists.

There is an association of printers in Dakar.

SEYCHELLES

Population	53 000
Area	376 sq. km.

PRESS
Newspapers	Dailies 2, Non-dailies 3
Total circulation	Dailies 2550, Non-dailies 2675
Copies per 1000 people	Dailies 48, Non-dailies 50

RADIO
Transmitters	Long/medium-wave 2, Short-wave 2
Total receivers	7500 estimated in use
Receivers per 1000 people	142

FILM
Cinemas	Fixed 2
Total seating capacity	546
Seats per 1000 people	10
Total annual attendance	150 000
Annual visits per capita	3

PRESS

Newspapers are published in Victoria, the capital, on Mahé, the largest of the 84 Seychelles Islands and home of 80% of the population. The two dailies (both evening papers) are respectively English-language (2000 copies per issue) and bilingual English/French, the former being an official government production. Two weeklies and another paper published less frequently appear in English.

There are three periodicals: one religious (2000 copies per issue), one literary (400 copies) and one school magazine (400 copies).

Since a new international airport was opened in 1972, the world's newspapers are now received frequently.

NEWS AGENCIES

Seychelles has no agency of its own. News is received by radio from Reuters and the BBC, for both printing and broadcasting. The Government, through its information department, supplies news for use by its own newspaper and radio.

RADIO

The government-owned station, Radio Seychelles, has two medium-wave transmitters, with a total power of 11kW, broadcasting – for 60 hours a week – an output of light entertainment (40%), educational and cultural programmes (31%), news and information (15%), broadcasts for special audiences (6%) and advertising (1½ hours per week). Languages used are English, French and Creole. About 75% of programmes are of local origin.

The Far East Broadcasting Association, a Christian missionary organization, operates the station FEBA Seychelles with a short-wave transmitting power of 30kW. Its programmes in 12 languages, on nine frequencies, are beamed to southern Asia, the Middle East, and eastern, central and southern Africa.

Broadcasting revenue is derived from government funds, advertising and (for the private station) from subscriptions and donations. No receiver licence fee is payable.

FILM

There is no film production at present but finance is being sought for tourist information documentaries about Seychelles.

Imported films, passed by a film censorship board, totalled 141 in 1972, mainly from the UK, France, the USA and India. In the same year, 30 documentaries were imported from the same countries.

In addition to the fixed cinemas, one non-commercial mobile unit recorded 7500 visits during the year.

SIERRA LEONE

Population	2 600 000
Area	71 740 sq. km.

PRESS

Newspapers	Dailies 2, Non-dailies 13
Total circulation	Dailies 15 000*
Copies per 1000 people	Dailies 6*

RADIO

Transmitters	Long/medium-wave 1, Short-wave 2
Total receivers	50 000 estimated in use
Receivers per 1000 people	19

TELEVISION	
Transmitters	1
Receivers	5000 estimated in use
Receivers per 1000 people	2

FILM	
Cinemas	Fixed 10
Total seating capacity	5500
Seats per 1000 people	2
Total annual attendance	122 000
Annual visits per capita	0.04

*For the larger daily only.

PRESS

Both dailies, published in English in the capital, Freetown, are government owned. Non-dailies, which include 5 twice-weekly and 6 weekly English-language papers, are all published in Freetown with the exception of 2 government-sponsored vernacular monthlies (in the Mende and Temne languages) published in the provincial town of Be. Periodicals number 26, including 15 school magazines with a total circulation of 7500 copies, 8 sociological journals (total 12 000 copies), and 1 title each for education, linguistics and history.

NEWS AGENCIES

There is no national news agency. Reuters and several other foreign agencies are represented in Freetown.

RADIO

The Sierra Leone Broadcasting Service (SLBS), which deals with radio, television and film under one management, was formed in 1972 to incorporate the former Sierra Leone Radio and Television and the film unit of the government information service. It is a government service, under a director of broadcasting.

A radio home service, reaching 90% of the population, is broadcast on one medium-wave transmitter (10kW) and two short-wave transmitters (0.5 and 5–10kW) in English and four African languages (Mende, Temne, Krio and Limba) for 108 hours a week, 88 hours of which are of domestic origin. Main programme categories are news and information (36 hours), light entertainment (31½ hours), broadcasts for special audiences (17½ hours), arts, letters and science (9 hours), advertising (7 hours), education (6 hours), and broadcasts for ethnic minorities (1 hour). A new 250kW short-wave station with four studios is to be constructed at Waterloo, near Freetown.

Over the last ten years, radio licence figures have increased from 9700 (of which 3600 were for wired receivers) to 35 000 (all wireless, the wired system having been superseded by transistor sets). The actual number of receivers in use far exceeds the number of licences.

TELEVISION

Begun in 1963 by a government-controlled company operated by private contractors, television broadcasting is now part of the commercially operated, government-owned Sierra Leone Broadcasting Service. Revenue is derived from receiver licence fees and commercial advertising.

Broadcasting for about 33 hours a week with one transmitter (625 lines) covering the Freetown area, SLBS carries light entertainment programmes (14 hours), news and information (9 hours), programmes for special audiences (3 hours), educational programmes (2 hours) and cultural programmes and advertising (over 1 hour each). Of these programmes, about a third are of domestic origin.

FILM

Documentaries are produced by the film service of SLBS and by private producers (two long and seven short films in 1970).

Approximately 600 films are imported annually from the USA, Italy, Lebanon, Egypt, India and the UK, through three main commercial importer-distributor-exhibitor organizations, and are shown in fixed indoor and outdooor cinemas in the main towns, as well as by some 14 mobile units.

PROFESSIONAL TRAINING

Mass communication is included in Njala University College's degree course in education.

SOMALIA

Population	2 940 000
Area	637 657 sq. km.

PRESS

Newspapers	Dailies 1, Non-dailies 2
Total circulation	Dailies 4450, Non-dailies 2500
Copies per 1000 people	Dailies 2, Non-dailies 0.8

RADIO

Transmitters	Short-wave 5
Total receivers	50 000 estimated in use
Receivers per 1000 people	17

FILM

Cinemas	Fixed 26
Total seating capacity	23 000
Seats per 1000 people	8
Total annual attendance	4 700 000
Annual visits per capita	2

PRESS

The newspaper press consists of one daily, with Arabic and Italian-language editions, and two general interest weeklies in English and Arabic – all published under government auspices – and one Arabic-language weekly published by a political party.

The Ministry of Information also publishes a monthly information journal and an illustrated quarterly magazine. Three other periodicals appear in English (3500 copies), Arabic (3000 copies) and Italian (3500 copies).

NEWS AGENCIES

The government-owned Somalia National News Agency (SONNA), founded in 1964 in Mogadishu, has a total headquarters staff of 12 reporters, subeditors and feature writers. Stringers, usually public servants in various government offices, also supply local and regional news. SONNA has no foreign staff or representatives. It receives the overseas services of Reuters, AFP, ANSA, TASS and ADN and has exchange agreements with Tanjug and CTK. The daily output is 1000 words of national and local news and 1000 words of foreign news, all in English. Domestic subscribers include three newspapers and one radio station.

RADIO

The national broadcasting service, a division of the Ministry of Information and National Guidance, operates a main government station, Radio Mogadishu, in the capital, broadcasting in Somali, English, Arabic, Swahili, Amharic and Qoti, and a northern regional station, Radio Somali, located in Hargeisa, broadcasting its own programmes in Somali and also relaying Radio Mogadishu's Somali and Amharic programmes. The service has five well-equipped studios and two mobile vans. The five transmitters in use, all short-wave, have a total power of 71kW.

The two stations are on the air for about 52 hours a week with programmes consisting of news and information (19 hours), arts, letters, science (18½ hours), education (4½ hours), light entertainment (4 hours), programmes for special audiences (3½ hours) and advertising (2½ hours). These figures include daily programmes prepared for children by the Ministry of Education. All programmes are of national origin.

The estimated number of radio receivers in use includes public receivers in government Orientation Centres (13 in Mogadishu and others in each of the 48 districts of the Somali Democratic Republic).

FILM

The film and visual services of the Ministry of Information and National Guidance produced 13 short films for instructional purposes in 1969. The feature films imported for that year totalled 400: from Italy (200), India (120), the USA (60) and other countries (20). Documentary films imported totalled 358: from the USSR (144), Italy (72), India (36), the Democratic People's Republic of Korea (36), France (18), the UK (18), People's Republic of China (18) and USA (18).

Apart from the fixed cinemas there are two mobile units.

PROFESSIONAL TRAINING AND ASSOCIATIONS

All media personnel are trained either abroad or on the job. A Somali journalists' association exists, within the Ministry of Information and National Guidance.

SOUTH AFRICA (Republic of)

Population	22 990 000
Area	1 221 037 sq. km.

PRESS
Newspapers	Dailies 21, Non-dailies 130
Total circulation	Dailies 1 075 000
Copies per 1000 people	Dailies 47

RADIO
Transmitters	Long/medium-wave 70, Short-wave 12, VHF–FM 95
Total receivers	2 350 000 estimated in use
Receivers per 1000 people	102

FILM
Cinemas	Fixed 685
Total seating capacity	498 000
Seats per 1000 people	22

PRESS

The most highly developed and commercially prosperous news-gathering and disseminating system in the continent, the South African press is characterized by its division into the two constituent language groups of the white population: English and Afrikaans. Despite increasing bilingualism, these separate traditions are maintained by well-established ownership links among the papers themselves and by the distinctive opinions and interests of their readers.

Although users of Afrikaans as their first or 'home' language among the white population clearly outnumber users of English, only 6 dailies are published in Afrikaans, as against 15 in English (including the 7 largest), the respective circulation totals for the two languages being 210 000 and 865 000. The third-largest daily, an English-language paper published in Johannesburg, with a circulation of 103 000, is specifically designed for non-white readers.

Johannesburg, the republic's largest city and most important publishing centre, has 3 English-language dailies and 1 in Afrikaans. Cape Town, which is the legislative capital, has 2 English dailies and 1 in Afrikaans. Durban has 2, both in English, as has Port Elizabeth; the administrative capital, Pretoria, and Bloemfontein, chief city of the Orange Free State, each have 1 in Afrikaans and 1 in English.

Some 130 non-daily general interest newspapers appear once, twice or three times a week. Of these, 16 Sunday or week-end papers together sell almost 2.5 million copies per issue. Published in the same large towns, and with a similar language pattern, a number of the weeklies are linked with leading dailies and have nation-wide readerships. The top circulation figure of 444 000 copies is recorded for a Johannesburg English-language Sunday paper, though this position may be challenged as a result of impending mergers in the Afrikaans

One large Johannesburg weekly paper (circulation 218 000) is published in English especially for non-whites, with three editions on different days of the week for Africans, Asians and coloureds.

Other weeklies for non-white communities include two in English (one for coloureds in the Cape area and the other for Indians in Durban), two bilingual Zulu/English papers in Natal, two in Xhosa for the Transkei and one in Sesotho.

The Government sponsors, through its official South African Information Service, a range of monthly publications in the main African vernaculars; these are distributed free to schools and other organizations. Other magazines and periodicals are chiefly in English and Afrikaans, and their ownership, as with newspapers, is almost entirely white. Two illustrated monthlies for non-white readers have proved commercially successful, one appearing in four separate language editions within South Africa, and the other, in English only, circulating in east, central and west Africa as well. In all, over 425 periodical titles, including 30 annuals and a wide range of popular and specialized journals, are currently published.

An interesting technical innovation is the adoption by five leading publishers of a standard format (320 x 240mm) for all their periodicals in English and Afrikaans.

NEWS AGENCIES

The South African Press Association (SAPA), a cooperative founded by newspaper owners in 1938, supplies domestic and foreign news to all daily and Sunday newspapers and to the national broadcasting services within South Africa; through its subsidiary the Inter-African News Agency (IANA) in Salisbury, it also serves daily and Sunday papers in Rhodesia and Zambia and the Rhodesian Broadcasting Corporation. It has its own teleprinter network linking its headquarters in Johannesburg with eight other South African cities and with Salisbury. Branch offices are in Cape Town, Durban, Pretoria, Bloemfontein and Umtata, with an overseas office in London (UK). Reuters, AP, AFP and UPI subscribe to its domestic news service.

SAPA receives its foreign news from Reuters and AP, with which it has exchange agreements, by radio teleprinter from London and New York.

There are several local agencies and press services in the main cities, handling syndicated material, features and pictures.

Four world agencies have bureaux in South Africa. Reuters provides a special South African news service for the republic and neighbouring countries and has offices in 16 cities in southern Africa. AFP in Johannesburg has a permanent radio-teletype link with Paris and distributes 30 000 words daily in English and French in addition to its African bulletins issued bi-weekly in English and daily in French. Both AP and UPI have bureaux in Johannesburg.

RADIO

All radio broadcasting in the republic is entrusted to the South African Broadcasting Corporation (SABC), a public-utility organization established in 1936 and later empowered by Act of Parliament to broadcast to South West Africa and foreign countries. Its policies are directed by a control board appointed by the President of the republic, and its income is derived from licence fees and from advertising revenues from the corporation's commercial services. Total SABC staff in 1969 was 2342 persons.

The English and Afrikaans-language national services are on the air for 17 hours a day, broadcasting information, cultural and entertainment programmes. The third national programme, Radio Springbok, is commercial and broadcasts sponsored programmes, news and advertising for 18 hours a day. These services cover the whole of the national territory and South West Africa.

Three regional commercial services, Radio Highveld, Radio Good Hope and Radio Port Natal, give additional coverage to the main areas of population concentration, broadcasting light music, news and advertising for 18 hours a day. When they close down, the all-night commercial station Radio South Africa takes over till morning.

For its national and commercial services, SABC operates 70 medium-wave transmitters (ranging in power from 0.5 to 10kW), 17 FM transmitters and 12 short-wave stations (four of 20kW and eight of 100kW each).

Radio Bantu is SABC's special service in the seven main African vernaculars (Zulu, Xhosa, South and North Sotho, Tswana, Venda and Chonga), broadcast almost entirely by a network of 78 FM transmitters grouped in nine areas.

The seven language programmes of Radio Bantu together total 592 hours a week and include news, talks, religious programmes, school broadcasts, drama, sports, programmes for old people, etc. They reach an estimated audience of about 4 million, including the 700 000 children who hear the special broadcasts to schools, for which 4400 FM receivers were recently provided by the Government.

The number of radio receivers in use in the republic has almost doubled over the last ten years.

External broadcasting services are operated by the Voice of South Africa with four 250kW and two 100kW short-wave transmitters at Bloemendal in the Transvaal. Programmes totalling 182 hours a week in nine languages (French, English, Afrikaans, Swahili, Chichewa, Dutch, Portuguese, Tsonga and German) are beamed to 23 different areas in Africa, Europe, the Middle East, north Africa, Australia and New Zealand.

TELEVISION

While closed-circuit television installations have been used in South Africa for some time, it is only recently that the Government has announced plans for the introduction of a public television broadcasting service which should be functioning for both colour and black and white reception by 1975. SABC is to effect the operation in two stages: first, one channel broadcasting for 37 hours a week in English and Afrikaans, covering the most densely populated areas, to be followed later by a second channel for Africans. The service will be non-commercial but with time made available for advertising.

FILM

A small number of feature films are produced annually, usually with Afrikaans soundtracks. In addition, there are many 16mm production units making short films for home and foreign (mainly television) consumption. The principal association of motion-picture producers has 30 member companies.

The National Film Board, founded in 1964, is responsible for all government functions relating to films. It also has its own well-equipped studios and makes a large number of newsreels and information films.

Film archives are kept by the South African Film Institute which also seeks to arouse interest in South Africa by promoting the showing of tourist and information films overseas.

Films are imported free of import duties but must pass the government censor before being exhibited publicly. Of the total number of indoor and outdoor cinemas, including 95 16mm establishments, 328 are reserved for non-whites, 17 admit white and non-white audiences and the remainder are for whites only. Many viewing places are provided for their employees by mining companies, sugar estates and other large concerns. There are 120 drive-ins with a combined capacity of 65 000 cars.

PROFESSIONAL TRAINING AND ASSOCIATIONS

The University of Potchefstroom has had a degree course in communications and press since 1960, while the University of South Africa and the Rand Afrikaans University have recently set up departments of communications. Degree courses in journalism (three years) and visual communications and a diploma course in photography (one year) have been offered by Rhodes University since 1970.

The Newspaper Press Union, grouping together owners and employees, was responsible for the setting up of a press council and has formulated a code of professional conduct for the press in South Africa.

Periodical circulation figures are certified by an Audit Bureau of Circulations with a membership of about 400 publishing and advertising concerns.

Other professional associations exist for journalists, publishers, printers, typographical workers, motion-picture producers, film laboratories, etc.

SPANISH SAHARA

Population	50 000
Area	266 000 sq. km.

PRESS

Newspapers	Non-dailies 1
Total circulation	Non-dailies 3000
Copies per 1000 people	Non-dailies 60

RADIO

Transmitters	Long/medium-wave 4, Short-wave 1
Total receivers	17 000 estimated in use
Receivers per 1000 people	340

TELEVISION

Transmitters	2*
Receivers	2500 estimated in use
Receivers per 1000 people	50

FILM

Cinemas	Fixed 4
Total seating capacity	1768
Seats per 1000 people	35
Total annual attendance	455 000
Annual visits per capita	9

*Including 1 auxiliary transmitter.

PRESS

There is no local daily press, the only newspapers circulated being a bilingual (Spanish/Hasania) weekly bulletin (3000 copies per issue) and various Spanish and Arabic newspapers received by private subscription from Spain and Morocco. Other periodicals are two bilingual monthlies each circulating 800 copies per issue and a bilingual annual publication circulating 1000 copies.

RADIO

The two government stations, in the capital El Aaiún and in Villa Cisneros, with medium-wave transmitters of 50 and 5kW and one short-wave transmitter of 10kW, broadcast both locally originated programmes (40% of the total) and relays of Radio Nacional de España (RNE) for 120 hours a week. Programmes for one station include light entertainment (35 hours), news and information (18½ hours), arts, letters and science (1½ hours), advertising (1 hour 10 minutes) and other programmes (13 hours, including a regular evening educational broadcast relayed from RNE). Languages used are Spanish, Hasania and other vernaculars. Radio coverage extends to 50% of the population by day and 80% by night.

TELEVISION
One main television transmitter is in operation, with one auxiliary transmitter, potentially covering 28% of the population.
No radio or television licence fee is payable.

FILM
In 1971, the territory imported 363 feature films, as well as documentaries, for showing in the fixed cinemas or by the one mobile unit.

SUDAN

Population	16 490 000
Area	2 505 813 sq. km.

PRESS
Newspapers	Dailies 4, Non-dailies 12

RADIO
Transmitters	Long/medium-wave 3, Short-wave 6
Total receivers	1 600 000 estimated in use
Receivers per 1000 people	97

TELEVISION
Transmitters	2
Receivers	100 000 estimated in use
Receivers per 1000 people	6

FILM
Cinemas	Fixed 52
Total seating capacity	84 000
Seats per 1000 people	5
Total annual attendance	16 000 000
Annual visits per capita	1

PRESS
Following the establishment of a nationalized General Press and Publishing Corporation in 1970, several Khartoum dailies became weeklies and a number of

others ceased publication. The largest daily circulated 90 000 copies per issue in 1973. It is also the publisher of a weekly magazine (20 000). Other non-dailies, including a number of government publications, appear weekly and monthly. There were 20 periodicals reported in 1973.

NEWS AGENCIES
The government-owned Sudan National News Agency (SUNA), with head-quarters in Khartoum, was founded as the Sudan News Agency in 1955 and reorganized in 1970. It operates with a permanent staff of 60 and 14 part-time correspondents. Overseas news services received are Reuters, AP, TASS, MENA, AFP and SANA (Damascus).

Foreign news agencies distributing news to 100 subscribers in the Sudan include Reuters, TASS, MENA, AP and Hsinhua.

RADIO
The Broadcasting Service of the Democratic Republic of the Sudan, which is a government department within the Ministry of Infomation and Culture, operates three medium-wave transmitters of 50 and 100kW and five short-wave transmitters of 20, 50 and 120kW. Four other medium-wave relay transmitters scheduled for completion by 1974 should substantially increase radio coverage of the country's vast territory.

Total broadcasting time is 149½ hours weekly, of which 108 hours are devoted to the general programme in Arabic, 25 hours to programmes directed to the southern provinces in various tribal languages, 16 hours to the Koran and religious programmes in Arabic, and 30 minutes to programmes in Somali directed to Somalia. Included in these programmes are broadcasts to special audiences including women, children and youth (30% of total time), entertainment, principally music, (28%) and news and public affairs (19%). There are no regular educational broadcasts but some special end-of-year programmes are transmitted for higher secondary students.

Most programmes are nationally produced. Imported programmes come from the Federal Republic of Germany (30% of all imported material), Eastern Europe, the USA (Voice of America), the United Nations and its agencies, Egypt and other Arab countries, the African Broadcasting Union, China, India, Pakistan and other African countries.

TELEVISION
The government-sponsored television service, inaugurated in December 1962 and operating regularly since 1963, has one transmitter at Omdurman serving the three urban areas which form the Sudanese capital: Khartoum, Omdurman and Khartoum North. In addition, a new microwave link to the station at Wad Medani now provides coverage of the Gezira irrigated area, thus bringing the population within reach of television broadcasts to something over 1 million. Further plans are for stations at Atbara, 300km north of Khartoum and at Port Sudan on the Red Sea.

Total weekly programme time of 38 hours consists of light entertainment (28%), education and information (each 23%), cultural programmes (20%) and broadcasts for special and minority audiences (15%). School broadcasts at secondary level, organized in cooperation with the Ministry of Education, are transmitted on three days a week during school hours. All programmes are introduced in standard Arabic and most imported material is subtitled in Arabic.

Some 60% of programmes are produced locally, other material consisting mainly of European and United States serials and films, as well as cultural exchange programmes from Arab countries and programme releases from foreign diplomatic missions.

Broadcasting is financed from the State budget, and recently an annual licence has been introduced. Commercial advertising is accepted on both radio and television.

FILM

The film production section of the Ministry of Information and Culture provides the television service and government departments with newsreels and documentaries (two short entertainment films and two documentaries were produced in 1972). Processing and sound-recording facilities are available at the unit's new building in Omdurman, so that only colour films are now sent abroad for completion.

In 1972, 336 feature films were imported from Italy (90), Egypt (66), the USA (53), the UK (50), India (38), France (1) and the USSR (8). Ten documentaries were imported from Egypt and 10 from the UK in 1970.

Many commercial cinemas are open-air establishments. In addition to these, about 40 government-operated 16mm mobile units serve large audiences, mainly in rural areas.

SPACE COMMUNICATIONS

Construction of an Intelsat earth station near Khartoum is planned for 1975.

SWAZILAND

Population	430 000
Area	17 363 sq. km.

PRESS
Newspapers	Non-dailies 2

RADIO
Transmitters	Medium-wave 1, VHF—FM 1
Total receivers	13 000 estimated in use
Receivers per 1000 people	30

FILM

Cinemas	Fixed 2
Total seating capacity	800
Seats per 1000 people	2
Total annual attendance	100 000
Annual visits per capita	0.2

PRESS

There are no daily newspapers. One English-language weekly appears in the capital, Mbabane, circulating 6500 copies. The government information services issue a fortnightly news-sheet in the siSwati language and in English. South African newspapers are widely circulated.

Over 20 periodicals are published, the main subject categories being sociology (10 titles, circulating 5000 copies), law and public administration (4 titles, 1000 copies), town planning (4 titles, 200 copies) and agriculture (2 titles, 600 copies).

RADIO

The government-owned Swaziland Broadcasting Service operates on a semi-commercial basis with one medium-wave transmitter of 10kW and one FM transmitter, broadcasting mainly in siSwati with some programmes in English. The home service is on the air for over 62 hours a week and its programmes consist of light entertainment (27½ hours), educational broadcasts (18 hours), news and information (11½ hours), programmes for special audiences (about 4 hours), advertising (½ hour), language course (15 minutes) and cultural items (10 minutes). School programmes are broadcast for 5½ hours every school day, and include 1 hour of English. The BBC (UK) news is broadcast three times daily, local news in English once a day and there is one news bulletin a day in siSwati.

FILM

There is no local film production. The two fixed cinemas are in Mbabane and Manzini. There is also one drive-in equipped for 250 cars. Tourist hotels and social clubs have cinema shows which are open to the public.

TANZANIA

Population	14 000 000
Area	939 703 sq. km.

PRESS

Newspapers	Dailies 7, Non-dailies 23
Total circulation	Dailies 61 000*, Non-dailies 213 000
Copies per 1000 people	Dailies 4*, Non-dailies 15

RADIO

Transmitters	Long/medium-wave 4, Short-wave 5
Total receivers	150 000 estimated in use
Receivers per 1000 people	11

FILM

Cinemas	Fixed 36
Total seating capacity	14 500
Seats per 1000 people	1
Total annual attendance	5 000 000
Annual visits per capita	0.4

*For 4 Dar es Salaam dailies only.

PRESS

Four daily newspapers are published in the capital city, Dar es Salaam. Two appear in Swahili and two in English (one of the latter having a special Sunday edition). Three other dailies are published in Zanzibar, one in English, Gujerati and Swahili, one in Swahili and one in Swahili and English. In addition, Swahili and English-language newspapers published in neighbouring east African countries also circulate in Tanzania. Non-daily general interest papers using all the languages mentioned are published in Dar es Salaam, Arusha and Zanzibar.

Some 17 periodicals, among which are a weekly official gazette, four religious monthlies and several farming journals, appear in provincial centres, as well as in the capital.

NEWS AGENCIES

The Government's information division of the Ministry of Information and Broadcasting distributes press releases and periodical bulletins, as well as photographs which are widely used in the local press.

The following news agencies maintain permanent correspondents in Dar es Salaam: ADN, AFP, CTK, KCNA, Hsinhua, Novosti, Reuters and TASS, along with Radio Berlin and Radio Moscow.

RADIO

Radio Tanzania is government owned and fully financed by the State. The station at Dar es Salaam is equipped with five short-wave transmitters totalling 135kW and four medium-wave transmitters of 103.75kW each.

Three programmes are broadcast simultaneously, totalling 165 hours a week: the national programme in Swahili, the external programme in English; and the commercial programme, also in Swahili. During school terms, programmes for primary and secondary schools and teacher-training colleges are on the air for 28 hours a week.

From Zanzibar, Radio Tanzania Zanzibar broadcasts in Swahili for about 50 hours a week.

FILM

A number of documentary and newsreel films, mainly intended for public audiences, have been produced locally under government sponsorship. In 1969, 11 newsreel and documentary films were made by the Tanzania Film Unit. The information services division of the Ministry of Information and Broadcasting maintains a library of 1000 titles, from which informational, instructional and entertainment films are lent to schools and rural development centres.

Seven of the fixed cinemas are located in Dar es Salaam, and the remainder in other large towns. In addition, educational institutions and industrial concerns own projectors. The Government operates a number of mobile units.

PROFESSIONAL TRAINING AND ASSOCIATIONS

An 18-month course leading to a diploma in journalism is offered by the Publicity Media Institute, Nyegezi Social Training Centre. Completion of secondary education is a prerequisite for admission. In all, 20 students had graduated by 1970.

The Tanzania Press Club and a journalists' association are both based in Dar es Salaam.

TOGO

Population	2 022 000
Area	56 000 sq. km.

PRESS

Newspapers	Dailies 3, Non-dailies 4
Total circulation	Dailies 13 000
Copies per 1000 people	Dailies 6

RADIO

Transmitters	Long/medium-wave 2, Short-wave 3
Total receivers	40 000 estimated in use
Receivers per 1000 people	20

FILM

Cinemas	Fixed 4
Total seating capacity	2000
Seats per 1000 people	1
Total annual attendance	600 000
Annual visits per capita	0.3

PRESS

The national daily, founded in 1962 as a Unesco-assisted project, is produced in the Government's well-equipped printing and publishing house in Lomé. It is published in French with one page in Ewe and circulates about 6000 copies per issue. Both the other dailies are printed in French. A monthly rural newspaper is published in the Ewe language as part of the country's current literacy campaign.

Periodicals include a fortnightly religious journal (3000 copies), the monthly Chamber of Commerce bulletin, and three government monthlies: the *Journal officiel* (750 copies), the Education Office's bulletin (600 copies) and a statistical bulletin. All are in French.

NEWS AGENCIES

There is no national agency. AFP and DPA have offices in Lomé.

RADIO

Radiodiffusion du Togo, owned and operated by the Ministry of Information, broadcasts on two medium-wave transmitters of 1kW and 20kW and three short-wave transmitters with a combined power of 105kW.

Programmes totalling 89 hours a week, mostly of national origin, are broadcast in French and various vernaculars (Ewe, Hausa, Bassari, Moba, Cotocolis, and Cabrais). Maximum use is made of community receivers in rural areas. Light music and entertainment (31 hours a week), news and information (27½ hours), cultural and scientific programmes (16½ hours), broadcasts for special audiences (10 hours, including 4 hours for women) and education (3 hours) are the main programme categories.

FILM

The government information service produces a newsreel, of which one 35mm and four 16mm copies are made for foreign and local exhibition. In addition to the two cinemas situated in Lomé and the Government's two mobile projectors which show films nightly in different quarters in and around the capital, various foreign cultural agencies and information centres organize film showings and lend films to interested organizations.

TUNISIA

Population	5 137 000
Area	164 150 sq. km.

PRESS

Newspapers	Dailies 4, Non-dailies 7
Total circulation	Dailies 107 000, Non-dailies 59 000
Copies per 1000 people	Dailies 21, Non-dailies 11

RADIO

Transmitters	Long/medium-wave 3, Short-wave 3
Total receivers	250 000 estimated in use
Receivers per 1000 people	49

TELEVISION

Transmitters	11
Receivers	80 000 estimated in use
Receivers per 1000 people	16

FILM

Cinemas	Fixed 104
Total seating capacity	44 800
Seats per 1000 people	9
Total annual attendance	8 500 000
Annual visits per capita	2

PRESS

The daily press, consisting of 2 party-owned newspapers (1 Arabic and 1 French language), 1 French-language government paper and 1 privately owned paper in Arabic, is concentrated in the capital, Tunis. Circulation totals are almost equally divided between the Arabic and the French-language papers. Together they employ 40 full-time journalists and a large number of part-time correspondents. Three of the papers have their own printing-presses. One daily French-language newspaper ceased publication in 1967.

Non-dailies (mainly weekly) are published in Arabic (3 titles with a combined circulation of 3200 copies) and French (4 titles, totalling 2700 copies). The Tunisian press carries, on average, 35% national news, 15% local news, 27% foreign news, 5% editorial matter and 18% advertising.

Arabic-language newspapers have a considerably larger audience than circulation figures would suggest since in many villages, particularly where there is no cinema, the day's edition is read aloud in the evening to the assembled inhabitants.

Some 60 periodicals, with a total circulation of 283 000, almost all published in Tunis, deal with general topics (11 titles circulating 55 700 copies), education (9 titles, 35 000 copies), law, administration, etc. (6 titles, 19 700 copies), literature (6 titles, 13 800 copies), etc. One monthly magazine circulates throughout other Arab countries, and 2 current affairs monthlies intended largely for women are published by the national women's organization. None have their own printing-presses, and they are printed by daily newspaper or other jobbing presses.

Daily and weekly newspapers and periodicals imported from other countries in French, Arabic and other languages have considerable circulations in Tunisia.

All dailies and some periodicals operate their own distribution systems, while a central national enterprise handles other publications throughout the country – with the exception of journals from France and those from other foreign countries, distributed by two private firms.

Newsprint importation is unrestricted and is subsidized by the Government. The 1972 total consumption of 2600 metric tons, more than double that of ten years earlier, is due to the increased size of the daily papers (8–12 instead of 4–6 pages).

NEWS AGENCIES

The national agency, Tunis-Afrique-Presse (TAP) is a public corporation, founded in 1961. Apart from its headquarters in Tunis, it has 12 permanent correspondents in the main centres of the country, with a total home full-time staff of 175 persons, and 10 part-time correspondents. TAP's Paris office has 2 permanent staff members.

It receives the foreign services of AFP, UPI and Reuters, all of which in turn receive TAP's general service, and exchanges news with APS, MAP, LNA, MENA, DPA, ADN, Tanjug, CTK, TASS, Agerpress, ANSA, Efe and Visnews. Its national and local news service (10 000 words a day in Arabic and French) and foreign news service (13 000 words a day), plus features and photos, are received by 4 domestic newspapers, 1 radio and 1 television station, 6 foreign agencies and 30 administrative, diplomatic and commercial subscribers.

Transmissions are effected by direct telephone lines to Algiers, Paris, Rabat, Tripoli and Madrid, by 91 teleprinters and by 2 daily radio broadcasts in Arabic beamed to west and central Africa, central and Eastern Europe and the Middle East.

AFP, Reuters, UPI and TASS have bureaux in Tunis.

RADIO

The Radiodiffusion Télévision Tunisienne (RTT), under the Ministry of Information and Culture, is the national broadcasting organization, financed from the State budget. A licence fee is payable for radio receivers.

Virtually the whole country is covered by RTT's national programmes in literary and dialectal Arabic and French (18½ and 15 hours a day respectively), broadcast from two medium-wave stations at Djedeida, near Tunis (600kW), and Sidi Mansour, near Sfax (100kW), with an additional regional input of 8 hours a day. In addition, three short-wave services (with 50 and 100kW transmitters at the same localities) are beamed to north African and Middle East listeners respectively.

The international programme, broadcast from one 100kW medium-wave transmitter at Tunis for 108½ hours a week, includes French-language programmes (with 4 hours of university lectures a day for part of the year), 1 hour a day in Italian and relays in Arabic of the national programme.

Total programme time of 248½ hours a week includes light entertainment (93 hours), scientific and cultural broadcasts (61½ hours), news and information (54 hours), education (27 hours) and broadcasts for special audiences (13 hours). Of these programmes, about 70 hours a week are imported material.

TELEVISION

Practically the whole of the national territory is covered by RTT's seven main transmitters and four low-power repeaters which broadcast a national programme for 26½ hours a week in Arabic (including 5½ hours imported material), with a further 18 hours a week in French partly supplied by ORTF (France). Programmes include light entertainment (18½ hours), news and information (10 hours), cultural and scientific programmes (7½ hours), educational programmes (7½ hours) and programmes for special audiences (4 hours) and ethnic minorities (45 minutes). The news programmes in both Arabic and French include sequences filmed by the national newsfilm service or purchased from agencies, or recorded from Eurovision transmissions received via Italy. Permanent links with other Mahgreb countries are in the course of construction.

FILM

The Société Anonyme Tunisienne pour l'Expansion Cinématographique (SATPEC), founded in 1957, is the national film enterprise; it produces its own films, processes films in its laboratories at Gammarth and also owns projection centres.

Production in 1970 included 2 feature films, 1 long 16mm documentary and 6 short films (two entertainment and four documentary). Newsreels are produced by the government information department, which also has a film library holding 1100 titles.

Features imported in the same year totalled 346: from the USA (167), France (48), Egypt (35), Italy (17), the UK (15), India (7) and other countries. Documentaries (251 in 1970) mostly came from the same countries.

Some of the country's cinemas belong to SATPEC, others are privately owned. Of the total number, 79 are equipped for 35mm and 25 for 16mm film. About half the cinemas are in Tunis and Bizerta. Non-commercial exhibition includes: 23 government mobile units which give some 5000 free showings a year; 30 cultural and 20 youth centres with 16mm projection equipment (2500 showings a year); 250 cultural groups (5000 showings a year); and 26 rural circuits serving 156 villages (1250 showings a year).

Public and official encouragement of the film includes State aid for production and the establishment of film clubs.

PROFESSIONAL TRAINING AND ASSOCIATIONS

Tunis University's Institute of Press and Information Sciences has offered a four-year course in journalism since 1967–8, for candidates with university-entrance qualifications. Current enrolment is 113 male and 4 female. Of those proceeding to the diploma level, 8 graduated in 1971. State aid is available for the training of journalists and printing workers and for broadcasting personnel. RTT has its own training programmes. Film workers are trained abroad.

Professional associations include associations of journalists, newspaper publishers and foreign press correspondents, and organizations of film distributors and exhibitors. There is also a State-subsidized federation of amateur film-makers, with 24 clubs as members.

UGANDA

Population	10 460 000
Area	236 036 sq. km.

PRESS

Newspapers	Dailies 7, Non-dailies 26
Total circulation	Dailies 90 000, Non-dailies 133 000
Copies per 1000 people	Dailies 9, Non-dailies 13

RADIO

Transmitters	Long/medium-wave 6, Short-wave 1
Total receivers	509 000 estimated in use
Receivers per 1000 people	49

TELEVISION

Transmitters	6
Receivers	15 000 estimated in use
Receivers per 1000 people	1

FILM

Cinemas	Fixed 17
Total seating capacity	16 000
Seats per 1000 people	1
Total annual attendance	2 000 000
Annual visits per capita	0.2

PRESS

The majority of the daily newspapers are based in Kampala, the capital, and are published in the main Bantu language, Luganda, with the exception of one morning paper, circulating 20 000 copies, which is published in English (the official national language). The government information services issue two of the dailies, circulating 5000 and 8000 copies. Others include a popular morning paper, circulating 12 000 copies, and a Catholic mission society publication which circulates 18 000 copies.

The non-daily press, including a number of government and mission publications, uses not only the main languages (Luganda, English and Swahili) but also some of the country's 40 or so tribal languages including Lango, Ateso, Madi, Runyoro-Lutoro and Lwo. English-language papers from neighbouring African countries are also circulated.

NEWS AGENCIES
The Government has a project for the establishment of a national news agency, in addition to the service provided by the Ministry of Information on which the press relies along with wire services of AP, Novosti, Reuters and UPI.

RADIO
The national broadcasting organization, Radio Uganda, is government owned, and operated by the Ministry of Information and Broadcasting. With medium-wave transmitters of up to 100kW and a 7.5kW short-wave transmitter, the home service is on the air in English, Luganda and 17 vernaculars for 230 hours a week. Its two networks, known as the Red and Blue Channels, provide the national and northern programmes and the midland and west regional programmes respectively. These include health, sanitation and agricultural broadcasts, as well as those of the school broadcasting system which serves over 1000 schools and colleges.

TELEVISION
The Uganda Television Service, established in October 1963, is also operated by the Ministry of Information and Broadcasting.

Using the 625-line system, television programmes are broadcast from a main station in Kampala with a 55kW transmitter and from five relay stations located in Masaka, Mbale, Mbarara, Lira and Soroti.

Programmes, on the air for 9 hours a day, include 1½ hours, daily, of educational broadcasts. Most programme material is in English and is imported.

FILM
Documentary and short films are locally produced. Feature films are imported from India, the UK and the USA. There are four fixed cinemas in Kampala and a drive-in for 744 cars; this has 116 additional seats. There are also three cinemas in Jinja, two in Mbale and one each in seven other towns.

UPPER VOLTA

Population	5 491 000
Area	274 200 sq. km.

PRESS

Newspapers	Dailies 1, Non-dailies 3
Total circulation	Dailies 2000, Non-dailies 6000
Copies per 1000 people	Dailies 0.3, Non-dailies 1

RADIO

Transmitters	Long/medium-wave 1, Short-wave 3
Total receivers	87 000 estimated in use
Receivers per 1000 people	16

TELEVISION

Transmitters	1
Receivers	500 estimated in use
Receivers per 1000 people	0.09

FILM

Cinemas	Fixed 6
Total seating capacity	2000
Seats per 1000 people	0.3
Total annual attendance	1 000 000
Annual visits per capita	0.2

PRESS

A government information bulletin published simultaneously in the capital, Ouagadougou, and in Bobo-Dioulasso, with a circulation of 2000 copies, is the only daily general interest newspaper. Another, more specialized bulletin is issued by the Chamber of Commerce. Non-dailies consist of a general interest weekly circulating 3000 copies, a government-sponsored weekly and a monthly bulletin.

Other periodical publications number 13 with a total circulation of 10 900 copies, dealing with subjects of general interest (7 titles circulating 5880 copies), law, administration, etc. (2 titles, 1220 copies), education (2 titles, 2500 copies) and mathematics.

The press devotes 20% of its news content to national news, 40% to African news, 30% to international events and 10% to miscellaneous and sports news.

NEWS AGENCIES

A national press agency, Agence de Presse Voltaïque (APV), was set up in 1963 under the auspices of Unesco and is located in Ouagadougou.

AFP, Reuters, UPI and TASS maintain bureaux in the capital and supply news to eight subscribers in the country, including the press, broadcasting stations and the Government.

RADIO
The Radiodiffusion-Télévision Voltaïque (RTV) is a government-owned organization located in Ouagadougou, operating one medium-wave transmitter of 1kW and two short-wave transmitters of 4kW each. There is also a regional station in Bobo-Dioulasso.

Home-service programmes, in French and 13 vernacular languages, are on the air for 82 hours a week, consisting of cultural and scientific programmes (28½ hours), news and information (27¾ hours), language and other courses (8¼ hours), broadcasts for special audiences (6¾ hours), educational programmes (1¾ hours) and advertising (7 minutes). About 25% of the programmes are of national origin.

TELEVISION
Television broadcasting, like radio, is government owned and is financed by government subsidy, licence fees, advertising and French Government aid for equipment. Voltavision broadcasts from Ouagadougou for 4 hours a week, 1 hour of which consists of nationally produced material, the remaining material being imported from France, the Federal Republic of Germany and the USA. Daily transmissions are received by individual set owners and at collective viewing centres in the capital only.

FILM
In 1969, the Centre Cinématographique de l'Information produced three educational films and one other short film. A special fund, financed by taxes on box-office returns, has been set up to encourage national film production. All the cinemas, including one mobile unit, are run by the Société Nationale Voltaïque du Cinema (SONAVOCI).

PROFESSIONAL ASSOCIATION
There is one autonomous national union for the press.

ZAÏRE

Population	22 480 000
Area	2 345 409 sq. km.

PRESS
Newspapers   Dailies 6, Non-dailies 12

RADIO

Transmitters	Long/medium-wave 4, Short-wave 18, VHF—FM 5
Total receivers	20 000 estimated in use
Receivers per 1000 people	0.9

TELEVISION

Transmitters	2
Receivers	6500 estimated in use
Receivers per 1000 people	0.3

FILM

Cinemas	Fixed 57
Total seating capacity	17 000
Seats per 1000 people	0.8
Total annual attendance	1 100 000
Annual visits per capita	0.05

PRESS

Three daily newspapers, one with a circulation of 25 000, are published in the capital, Kinshasa, two more in Lubumbashi and one in Kisangani. All are in French. Of the 12 weekly and fortnightly journals, eight carry some current news. In all of these, French is used either as the sole language of publication or as the main language along with one or more of the 'intermediary' vernaculars in this large and linguistically varied country.

The majority of the republic's 100 or more periodicals are published in Kinshasa, with a wide range of emphasis, among which political affairs, sociology, religion and education are the most notable. Apart from a few publications in Lingala, Tshiluba and Kikongo, the periodical press appears in French.

The newsprint consumption in Zaïre for 1970 was 500 metric tons, giving a *per capita* consumption of 0.03kg.

NEWS AGENCIES

The official agency is the Agence Zaïre Presse (AZAP) founded (as Agence Congolaise de Presse) in 1960. At its headquarters in Kinshasa, the agency has an editorial staff of 30, plus 19 reporters and 13 telex operators. Regional news within the republic is gathered by 15 staff correspondents in the various provinces. In addition, AZAP has a European office in Brussels with 2 permanent staff correspondents. The total staff, at all locations, of the agency's editorial, administrative, technical and documentation services amounts to some 130 persons.

Foreign news is received direct by radio-teletype receiver from the Brussels office and from the following overseas agencies to which AZAP subscribes: AFP, Reuters, Belga, DPA, ANSA and AP. In turn, AZAP has special agreements with Reuters and AFP for reciprocal services. AZAP issues daily some 20 000 words of national news, sports information and foreign news summaries, in addition to special bulletins, features and monographs, as occasion demands. Subscribers, who receive either the agency's direct French-language telex service or its daily printed bulletin, include all the country's newspapers, radio and television networks, and various diplomatic missions, business firms and government services. Plans for the near future include the establishment of a photo service and the installation of additional radio facilities allowing AZAP to improve its reception of world news, including satellite transmissions, and also to broadcast to foreign countries.

A second agency established in Kinshasa is DIA (Documentation and Information for and about Africa), founded in 1956 by the Catholic Bishops of Congo, Rwanda and Burundi. Since 1965, it has been an independent private company, although still maintaining its links with its founders. With an editorial staff of about 10 and news desks for Zaïre and Congo, Rwanda and Burundi, Africa, Europe, the Third World, America and other countries, it issues daily bulletins totalling some 20 000 words in French, English, Dutch, and occasionally in African vernaculars to its branches in Rwanda and Burundi and to its Brussels office for communication to agencies and subscribers in Europe and other continents. On average, DIA material consists principally of religious news (50% of total) and socio-economic and development affairs (35%).

Foreign agencies represented in Kinshasa include AFP, AP, DPA, Reuters, Agerpress and TASS.

RADIO

The government-owned national broadcasting service, now one of the most powerfully equipped in Africa, operates 16 transmitters: 3 medium-wave, at Kinshasa (total 600kW), Kisangani and Lubumbashi (300kW each), 12 short-wave (including two of 100kW at Kinshasa and Lubumbashi) and 1 FM.

The national station at Kinshasa now broadcasts 23 hours a day in French, Swahili, Lingala, Tshiluba and Kikongo, while the six regional stations at Lubumbashi, Mbandaka, Bukavu, Kasai, Kisangani and Mbuji-Mayi each broadcast for 13 hours a day, using French and the main local vernaculars. Both national and regional stations broadcast half-hour programmes for schools once or twice a week under the direction of the Ministry of Education.

An international service is broadcast from Radio Lubumbashi in French (50%), Swahili, Portuguese and English for 42 hours a week.

TELEVISION

Two stations, one operated by the Government's broadcasting service in the capital and the other by a private missionary college in Lubumbashi, broadcast for a total of 46 hours a week. Of this, 21 hours is taken up by news and information programmes, 8 hours by cultural and scientific programmes, 6 hours by light entertainment and 5½ hours each by educational broadcasts and broadcasts to special audiences.

FILM

The Ministry of Information's national newsreel unit makes news films for both cinema and television, while another company produces news and documentary films.

Total imported length of film in 1970 was 20 297m, coming from the following countries: Belgium and Luxembourg, the Netherlands, Bulgaria, Burundi, the Federal Republic of Germany, Japan, Nigeria, the USA and the USSR.

The distribution circuits of three major import firms control most cinemas and projection points. There are 210 outdoor cinemas in addition to the fixed indoor establishments.

The Ministry of Information has a film library as, also, have four foreign diplomatic missions.

SPACE COMMUNICATIONS

A ground station for Atlantic Intelsat transmissions has been in operation at N'Sele, near Kinshasa, since 1971.

PROFESSIONAL TRAINING AND ASSOCIATIONS

The Université Nationale du Zaïre offers post-graduate training in communications in the Department of Social Communication (Kinshasa campus) and full-time studies for either a diploma in journalism or a diploma in information sciences in the Department of Information Sciences (Lubumbashi campus). Professional training for journalists is available, as from 1971, at the Centre d'Enseignement Supérieur de Journalisme, Kinshasa, while more intensive courses (six months' study plus six months on the job) are organized by the Maison de la Presse, also in the capital. Mass media studies are one of the options for students taking the four-year course for welfare officers at the Institut Social Africain at Bukavi.

Telecommunications and radio personnel are trained, respectively, at the École Nationale de Postes et Télécommunications, Kinshasa, and at the Institut Nationale Préparation Professionnelle, Kinshasa-Ngombe.

Associations for media professions group together newspaper publishers, national journalists, foreign correspondents, sports writers and film-makers.

ZAMBIA

Population	4 520 000
Area	752 614 sq. km.

PRESS

Newspapers	Dailies 2, Non-dailies 13
Total circulation	Dailies 60 000, Non-dailies 150 000
Copies per 1000 people	Dailies 13, Non-dailies 33

RADIO	
Transmitters	Long/medium-wave 8, Short-wave 10, VHF–FM 2
Total receivers	250 000 estimated in use
Receivers per 1000 people	55

TELEVISION	
Transmitters	3
Receivers	18 500 estimated in use
Receivers per 1000 people	4

FILM	
Cinemas	Fixed 29
Total seating capacity	13 359
Seats per 1000 people	3

PRESS

One daily, with a circulation of about 40 000, is published in the important copper-belt town of Ndola; associated with it is a Sunday newspaper with a circulation of 20 000. The other daily, circulating 20 000 copies, is government-owned and published in the capital, Lusaka. All are in English. Of the non-daily general interest newspapers produced in the provincial centres, 3 appear weekly and 10 fortnightly, either in English alone or in English plus the main local language. A number of fortnightlies, in the Bemba, Lozi, Nyanja and Tonga languages, are published by Zambia Information Services, a government department. Mining companies in the copper belt have newspaper-type house-organs with considerable readerships.

A dozen periodicals are also published, including Zambia Information Services' two magazines, and various church, trade, technical and professional journals. In addition, several journals from neighbouring countries designed for a regional readership circulate in Zambia.

The law in Zambia requires all publications to be licensed and registered with the Government Post Office. Freedom of expression for the mass media is guaranteed by the constitution.

NEWS AGENCIES

Zambia News Agency (ZANA) was founded in 1969 as a government department, distinct from Zambia Information Services but initially drawing on its network of provincial and district offices for the supply of domestic news. It now has its own network of reporters throughout the country. It distributes government news releases and fulfils the function of a national agency within the country, but has no foreign correspondents.

By agreement, dispatches from Reuters and an English-language service from AFP are received by the Government Post Office and relayed by private-wire teleprinter to subscribers consisting mainly of the government-owned and privately owned press and the national broadcasting services.

Other news services with offices in Zambia are AP, UPI, IANA and Argus African News Service.

RADIO

All broadcasting is carried out by Zambia Broadcasting Services, a government department under the Ministry of Information, Broadcasting and Tourism, which operates eight medium-wave radio stations ranging in power from 1 to 20kW at Lusaka Kitwe, Kabwe and Livingstone, ten short-wave stations of 10, 20, 50 and 120kW at Lusaka and two FM stations serving the immediate vicinity of Lusaka.

General and home-service programmes are broadcast for about 240 hours a week, general-service programmes principally in English with some in Bemba and Nyanja at off-peak hours, while the home service broadcasts are in the seven main vernaculars: Bemba, Nyanja, Lozi, Tonga, Kaoundé, Lunda and Luvale, generally programmed in blocks of about 2 hours per language in a rotating pattern to ensure some peak-hour listening for all audience groups.

Programmes include news, public affairs, music, drama and light entertainment, sports, religion and a range of broadcasts for schools, teachers, farmers and other groups, including 260 adult listening clubs. School broadcasts, on the general service, occupy three hours a day during school terms. The Ministry of Agriculture's broadcasts to farmers in both general and home services now cover almost all country areas, and listening is encouraged by free provision of receivers for farm radio forums, of which there are now some 600 in existence. More than half the population have access to a radio set and listen regularly. A large proportion of the domestic demand for radio receivers is met by a transistor-radio factory opened near Livingstone in 1966.

An annual licence fee is payable, but the great majority of sets are not licensed.

TELEVISION

The first television programmes in the territory were broadcast from Kitwe in the heavily populated copper-belt area in 1961. In 1965 and 1968, additional stations were opened at Lusaka and Kabwe, thus serving two of the country's other main areas of population concentration. (About 50 000 Africans over 15 years of age watch television daily.) With the completion of its new television centre and the establishment of a microwave link with the copper belt, Lusaka has become the headquarters of the national network, Television Zambia, which with Radio Zambia constitutes Zambia Broadcasting Services. Financial support comes from government subventions, licence fees and commercial advertising.

Programmes are broadcast daily from 15.00 to 21.00 hours on three channels, with an additional educational programme on the Kitwe channel from 09.45 to 11.00 hours on school days. An increasing proportion of programme material (in English) is locally produced by government information services, industrial enterprises, etc. Imported programmes come largely from the UK and USA.

To help offset the limitations imposed by the high cost of receivers, the Government has made provision in its development plans for group-viewing centres and, through the Ministry of Education, for the purchase of special equipment for schools. The definition system used is 625 lines.

A licence fee is payable.

FILM
Film production is carried out by Zambia Information Services which produces newsreels, educational films for schools and documentaries for tourism promotion and for use on the national television network. Commercial interests also produce film material for their own and for public use. Most imported films shown in public cinemas or through the Government's fleet of 75 mobile 16mm film vans are from the USA and UK. Most of the 35mm cinemas (total seating capacity 7937 persons) are in Lusaka, Kitwe and the copper belt. Mining companies provide 16mm film showings, either free or for a nominal charge, for their own workers. In addition to the fixed cinemas, there are 135 mobile units and one drive-in cinema.

SPACE COMMUNICATIONS
An earth station near Lusaka for Indian Ocean Intelsat transmissions was opened in 1972.

PROFESSIONAL TRAINING AND ASSOCIATIONS
The Department of Broadcasting has its own technical training school at the Lusaka Transmitter Centre. In addition, the Evelyn Hone College of Further Education in Lusaka offers advanced courses in communications and journalism. To these will shortly be added a professional training course for journalists at the University of Zambia and full-scale training courses for other media personnel at the Evelyn Hone College. Other training needs are met by the Mindolo Ecumenical Centre, Kitwe.

PART THREE

NORTH AMERICA

Antigua
Bahama Islands
Barbados
Belize
Bermuda
Canada
Canal Zone
Cayman Islands
Costa Rica
Cuba
Dominica
Dominican Republic
El Salvador
Greenland
Grenada
Guadeloupe
Guatemala
Haiti

Honduras
Jamaica
Martinique
Mexico
Montserrat
Netherlands Antilles
Nicaragua
Panama
Puerto Rico
St Kitts-Nevis and Anguilla
St Lucia
St Pierre and Miquelon
St Vincent
Trinidad and Tobago
Turks and Caicos Islands
United States of America
Virgin Islands (UK)
Virgin Islands (USA)

ANTIGUA

Population	60 000
Area	442 sq. km.

PRESS

Newspapers	Non-dailies 1
Total circulation	Non-dailies 4000
Copies per 1000 people	Non-dailies 66

RADIO

Transmitters	Medium-wave 2, VHF—FM 1

TELEVISION

Transmitters	1
Receivers	8800 licences*

FILM

Cinemas	Fixed 2
Total seating capacity	1700
Seats per 1000 people	28
Total annual attendance	130 000
Annual visits per capita	2

*Including those on Montserrat and Sint Maarten.

PRESS

The only daily paper and one twice-weekly ceased publication in 1972, leaving one other twice-weekly published in St John's (in English) as the island's only newspaper. Its readership includes a number of visitors (tourist visits per year total more than the permanent population of Antigua).

NEWS AGENCIES

News is received from Reuters' Caribbean service. A Caribbean news agency is in process of formation.

RADIO

The government-owned Antigua Broadcasting Service, established in 1956, now broadcasts for 16 hours a day. It has one 0.5kW medium-wave transmitter at St John's. Its programmes, totalling 114 hours a week, consist of light entertainment (70 hours), news and information (20 hours, including three BBC news bulletins daily from the UK), broadcasts for special audiences (14 hours), advertising (10 hours) and education (30 minutes).

Radio ZDK, a privately owned commercial station, with one 10kW medium-wave transmitter and one FM transmitter, is on the air for 18 hours daily. It also relays BBC news broadcasts.

A licence fee is payable for radio receivers.

TELEVISION

Leeward Island Television Services, a commercial station with government participation, has a main transmitter at St John's, Antigua (ZAL–TV) and relays on Montserrat and (in the Netherlands Antilles) on Sint Maarten, potentially reaching 95% of the population of these islands. Its 14-hour weekly programme time includes educational broadcasts (5 hours), news and information (4½ hours), broadcasts for special audiences (4 hours) and cultural programmes. The definition system used is 525 lines.

A licence fee is payable for television receivers.

FILM

Films shown in the commercial cinemas are imported, mainly from the USA and some from the UK.

BAHAMA ISLANDS

Population	190 000
Area	11 405 sq. km.

PRESS
Newspapers	Dailies 3, Non-dailies 5
Total circulation	Dailies 30 000, Non-dailies 50 000
Copies per 1000 people	Dailies 158, Non-dailies 262

RADIO
Transmitters	Long/medium-wave 4, VHF–FM 2
Total receivers	80 000 estimated in use
Receivers per 1000 people	421

FILM
Cinemas	Fixed 5
Total seating capacity	4100
Seats per 1000 people	22

PRESS

Both dailies, established in 1844 and 1903 respectively, are published in the capital, Nassau, New Providence, as are several twice-weekly and weekly general interest papers. Freeport, Grand Bahama, also has a twice-monthly newspaper. Periodicals include a monthly review and various tourist and geographical publications (1.4 million tourists visited the Bahamas in 1971), an industrial journal and a legal journal. All publications are in English.

NEWS AGENCIES

There is no local news agency. Reuters and AP services are received by the press in Nassau, by radio teleprinter. The official Bahamas Information Service provides information on matters of public interest and government policy, for internal use through its Office of Public Affairs and for external promotion through the Bahamas News Bureau, all under the general direction of the Ministry of Tourism.

RADIO

The government-owned Broadcasting Corporation of the Bahamas (BCB), formerly the Bahamas Broadcasting and Television Commission, with both medium-wave (of up to 20kW) and FM transmitters in Nassau, provides round-the-clock services totalling over 300 hours a week. Weekly programmes include light entertainment (180 hours), news and information (50 hours), cultural programmes (19 hours), advertising (27 hours), broadcasts for special audiences (27 hours), education (1¼ hours) and broadcasts for ethnic minorities (45 minutes).

No licence fee is payable for radio receivers.

TELEVISION

There is no local service yet but programmes can be received from stations in Florida (USA).

FILM

Films shown in the fixed cinemas and the four drive-ins (accommodating 1600 cars) are all imported. Annual film imports of 2 560 815m in 1971 included over 1500 features from the USA, around 30 features from the UK, some 5 380m from Surinam and 198m from Jamaica.

BARBADOS

Population	240 000
Area	430 sq. km.

PRESS
Newspapers	Dailies 1, Non-dailies 2
Total circulation	Dailies 24 000, Non-dailies 17 000
Copies per 1000 people	Dailies 100, Non-dailies 71

RADIO
Transmitters	Medium-wave 2, VHF–FM 1
Receivers	89 000* estimated in use
Receivers per 1000 people	371

TELEVISION	
Transmitters	1
Receivers	20 000 estimated in use
Receivers per 1000 people	83

FILM	
Cinemas	Fixed 6
Total seating capacity	4700
Seats per 1000 people	20
Total annual attendance	1 300 000
Annual visits per capita	5

*Including 26 000 wired receivers.

PRESS
The only daily newspaper, published in the capital, Bridgetown, also has a Sunday edition with a circulation of some 30 000 copies. Non-dailies are also published in Bridgetown as are most of Barbados' 130 periodicals, the main subject fields being law (19 titles), education (17 titles), political science (14 titles), commerce and industry (11 titles), sociology (10 titles), medicine and health (9 titles), religion, history, agriculture and fisheries (6 titles each), etc. as well as 24 school, house and parish magazines.

NEWS AGENCIES
Reuters' Caribbean service, through a block contract agreement with the Caribbean Publishers and Broadcasters Association (CPBA), which is based in Jamaica, is received by the daily press and by both broadcasting organizations. UPI news is also received by the daily press and the Caribbean Broadcasting Corporation. A Caribbean regional news agency is in process of formation.

Reuters' Caribbean desk, with a permanent correspondent and editorial and teleprinter staff, is located in Barbados.

RADIO
The Caribbean Broadcasting Corporation (CaBC), a statutory corporation financed by government subventions, receiver licences and advertising revenue, was licensed in 1963 and began operations the following year. With two medium-wave transmitters (1 and 10kW) and one FM transmitter, CaBC broadcasts a home service in English for over 135 hours a week. Programmes, which are received throughout the eastern Caribbean, consist of light entertainment (56 hours), news and information (27 hours, including seven relays daily of news bulletins from the BBC (UK)), broadcasts for special audiences (22 hours), advertising (12 hours), education (8½ hours), and cultural programmes (7½ hours).

Licensed by the Government in 1965, the privately owned commercial service, Barbados Rediffusion Service, operates under the same conditions as to general policy and programme content as CaBC. Its wired programmes are distributed for 120 hours weekly to 26 000 subscribers throughout the island.

TELEVISION
The Caribbean Broadcasting Corporation's television service, inaugurated in 1964, is now broadcasting for about 73 hours a week, of which 4½ hours are education programmes. About 75% of programmes are in colour (NSTC system). Imported programmes, accounting for about 65% of the total, come mainly from the UK, Canada and the USA. The definition system used is 625 lines.

A licence fee is payable for receivers.

FILM
Apart from occasional teaching films made by the government Audio-Visual Aids Department, there is no national film production. Provision has been made, however, for a film unit to be established within the government information service.

Films shown in commercial cinemas and the two drive-ins (accommodating 395 cars) are all imported. Total length of both features and documentaries imported in 1971 (33 024m) came mainly from the USA (18 893m) and UK (8295m) and from India (2752m), Canada (793m) and Trinidad (746m).

SPACE COMMUNICATIONS
An Atlantic Intelsat earth station at Barbados came into operation in 1972.

PROFESSIONAL TRAINING AND ASSOCIATIONS
Most press professionals are trained on the job. The Caribbean Christian Communications Network in Bridgetown is concerned with the training of both serving media personnel and potential recruits for the media.

The Barbados Press Association, Bridgetown, has a code of ethics to which its members subscribe.

BELIZE

Population	124 000
Area	22 965 sq. km.

PRESS
Newspapers	Dailies 1, Non-dailies 4
Total circulation	Dailies 3000, Non-dailies 11 500
Copies per 1000 people	Dailies 24, Non-dailies 93

RADIO
Transmitters	Medium-wave 3, Short-wave 1
Total receivers	57 000 estimated in use
Receivers per 1000 people	460

FILM

Cinemas	Fixed 8
Total seating capacity	4500
Seats per 1000 people	36
Total annual attendance	300 000
Annual visits per capita	2

PRESS

The daily newspaper is published by the governing political party in Belize City. It also appears on Sundays (but not Mondays). The non-daily press consists of four weeklies. An official gazette and a weekly government information service newsletter are also issued. All are based in Belize City except the last mentioned which is published in the new capital, Belmopan. It is estimated that the press reaches about 50% of the population. Apart from the daily and one of the weeklies which publish 10 and 5% respectively foreign news, all papers carry virtually 100% local news. The press is entirely in English, though Spanish is a widely spoken language.

Periodicals include two titles dealing with agriculture and one each dealing with general information, education, industry and literature.

NEWS AGENCIES

There is no national agency. AP, UPI and Reuters have stringers in Belize.

RADIO

The first public broadcasts were made in 1937 with a small short-wave transmitter. A medium-wave transmitter was added in 1952. Rebuilt after hurricane damage in the early sixties, Radio Belize now operates one short-wave (5kW) and three medium-wave (20 and 1kW) transmitters, broadcasting a home service for 119 hours a week in English (92 hours) and Spanish (27 hours) effectively covering the whole territory and the whole population. Programmes consist of cultural broadcasts (76 hours a week), news and information (22 hours), broadcasts for special audiences (12½ hours), educational broadcasts (3 hours) and light entertainment (2 hours). Over 80% of programmes are of national origin. Radio Belize is a government agency operated on a semicommercial basis. Commercial advertising now provides 80% of its budget.

An annual licence fee is payable for radio receivers.

FILM

Apart from some films on topical events shot by the government information services, there is no local film production.

Feature films are imported at the rate of around 190 a year, mainly from the USA through distributors in Panama. Similarly, about six documentaries are also imported. Apart from the fixed cinemas, there are also three mobile projection units operated by government services touring rural areas.

BERMUDA

Population	54 000
Area	53 sq. km.

PRESS
Newspapers	Dailies 1, Non-dailies 3
Total circulation	Dailies 13 600, Non-dailies 29 000
Copies per 1000 people	Dailies 252, Non-dailies 537

RADIO
Transmitters	Long/medium-wave 4, VHF—FM 2
Total receivers	38 000 estimated in use
Receivers per 1000 people	704

TELEVISION
Transmitters	2
Receivers	17 000 estimated in use
Receivers per 1000 people	315

FILM
Cinemas	Fixed 4
Total seating capacity	2215
Seats per 1000 people	41

PRESS
One daily newspaper, established in 1828, is published in the capital, Hamilton. There are also three weekly general interest papers (two of which have circulations in excess of 10 000) and some 30 specialized periodicals, including a large number designed for tourist visitors (who number over 350 000 annually); also other periodicals of religious, artistic, geographic, commercial, agricultural, historical and military interest.

NEWS AGENCIES
There is no local agency. The press, radio and television receive the news services of Reuters and UPI. The Government Information Office issues news releases, radio tapes and television film clips to the news media, all these being supplied by the Central Office of Information (UK).

RADIO
The Bermuda Broadcasting Company, a private corporation now sponsored by the Government but originally founded in 1943 under private ownership, is financed by subventions from public funds and advertising revenue. It operates medium-wave and FM (stereo) transmitters broadcasting two programmes in English for 24 hours a day. Weekly programme hours total around 100, consisting of broadcasts for special audiences (61 hours, including over 40 hours

religious programmes), news and information (53 hours), arts, letters and sciences (33 hours), advertising (27 hours), education (11 hours), light entertainment (10 hours), and broadcasts for ethnic minorities (5½ hours, in Portuguese). Over 60% of programmes are nationally produced.

The privately owned Capital Broadcasting Company, founded in 1961, operates a 24-hour daily service on medium wave and FM. Its programmes are divided into blocks intended for specific audiences at various times of the day, eg programmes for children and youth from 15.00 to 18.00 hours.

No licence fee is payable for radio receivers.

TELEVISION

The Bermuda Broadcasting Company, whose first television programmes were transmitted in January 1958, is now on the air for over 70 hours a week, including over 40 hours in colour (NSTC system). Weekly programmes include broadcasts for special audiences (22 hours, of which 17 are for women), light entertainment (21 hours), education (17 hours), news and information (8 hours), advertising (8 hours), and arts, letters and science (2 hours). Television programme exchanges are carried out regularly with the CBS (USA) and the BBC (UK) and programmes are also imported from both these countries.

The Capital Broadcasting Company, transmitting television programmes since August 1965, carries a larger proportion of imported recorded light music, drama and serials and is on the air for over 80 hours a week.

The definition system used is 525 lines.

FILM

There is no local film production. The chain of commercial cinemas in Hamilton (2), St Georges and Somerset, associated with a newspaper publishing firm, exhibits imported feature films. Of 142 features imported in 1971, 141 came from the USA and one from the UK. The Government Information Office releases a 35mm weekly newsreel supplied by the Central Office of Information (UK), for showing in local cinemas.

PROFESSIONAL ASSOCIATIONS

Broadcasting stations are members of the National Association of Broadcasters (USA).

CANADA

Population	21 850 000
Area	9 976 139 sq. km.

PRESS

Newspapers	Dailies 121, Non-dailies 1031
Total circulation	Dailies 5 117 700, Non-dailies 5 800 000
Copies per 1000 people	Dailies 234, Non-dailies 265

RADIO

Transmitters	Long/medium-wave 441, Short-wave 8, VHF–FM 280
Receivers	17 932 000 estimated in use
Receivers per 1000 people	821

TELEVISION

Transmitters	534
Receivers	7 296 000 estimated in use
Receivers per 1000 people	334

FILM

Cinemas	Fixed 1156
Total seating capacity	665 996
Seats per 1000 people	30
Total annual attendance	92 315 452*
Annual visits per capita	4

*Including drive-ins.

PRESS

Daily newspapers appear in about 90 towns, most of these being served by a single daily, a few by two dailies and four cities by more than two: Montreal with 6 (4 in French, 2 in English), Toronto with 4 (3 in English and 1 in Italian), Ottawa with 3 (2 in English and 1 in French) and Quebec City with 3 (all in French). Most dailies are in English, but 13 are published in French — which is the mother tongue of about 30% of the population and has equal status with English as an official language – and 6 are in other languages. Highest circulations are recorded by two Toronto dailies with respectively 374 000 and 263 000 copies per issue; the second of these (which also has a separate daily business edition circulating 286 000 copies) is the only Canadian daily with appreciable nation-wide and international readerships. A dozen other dailies throughout the country exceed the 100 000 circulation mark. The trend towards group ownership has accelerated in recent years and, by 1971, 68 dailies were controlled by ten groups, the largest (which also has newspapers in the UK, USA and southern Africa) owning 28 smaller-city English-language titles, and another two owning 10 and 8 main-city dailies respectively, while a French-language consortium controlled 4 Quebec dailies, along with 6 important weeklies and 4 radio and 2 television stations.

The non-daily general interest press consists mainly of papers published weekly or more frequently, serving metropolitan suburban areas and smaller local communities. The majority are in English, 147 in French and over 80 in 14 other languages, either alone or in combination with English.

Canadian periodicals published in 1972 totalled 1015 titles. Over 500 of these, circulating 4.4 million copies per issue, were of professional, industrial and commercial interest while a further 300, mostly monthlies, were concerned with recreation, education, religion, etc. English is the main language (813 titles), French has 118 titles, other languages 48, while 36 periodicals are bilingual.

Mass readership magazines are few, and their existence is increasingly precarious in view of the competition of imported publications from the USA far outnumbering domestic production.

The world's largest newsprint supplier, Canada produced 7 814 000 metric tons in 1970 (as compared with just over 6 million metric tons in 1960), of which over 85% is exported. Domestic newsprint consumption amounted to 474 700 metric tons in 1970 (as compared with 505 700 metric tons in 1960).

NEWS AGENCIES

The country's largest agency is Canadian Press (CP), founded in 1917, which has: its headquarters in Toronto; domestic branches in Halifax, Quebec City, Montreal, Ottawa, Toronto, Winnipeg, Edmonton and Vancouver; staff correspondents in five other Canadian cities, and 650 part-time correspondents throughout the country; branches abroad in London, New York, Washington and Paris; and 15 part-time correspondents in a number of Commonwealth and foreign countries. It is a cooperative, owned and operated by 103 Canadian daily newspapers, and employing a total permanent staff of 432 persons at home and 25 abroad. CP carries world news from AP, Reuters and AFP (French-language service), all of which receive CP news on a reciprocal basis. CP issues daily national and local news services of 144 000 words in English and 48 000 words in French, and foreign news services of 36 000 words in English and 24 000 words in French. Its other services include features (5200 words daily), photographs (70 a day) and audio-radio transmissions (65 a day).

Subscribers include 104 newspapers, 242 radio stations and 56 television stations; also 19 Canadian colleges and universities, 6 government agencies and 1 weekly news magazine. Transmissions are effected by leased teletype, wire-photo and telephone lines.

The private company, United Press International of Canada (formerly British United Press) with headquarters in Montreal, is an affiliate of UPI (USA). It supplies Canadian and international news and pictures to about 40 press and broadcasting subscribers in Canada and is an outlet for Canadian news through UPI facilities throughout the world.

Visnews (UK) supplies news film to television stations.

Major Toronto and Montreal dailies have their own news service, with correspondents abroad. Another operates a syndicated feature service. Various other syndicated agencies and wire services also supply the press and broadcasting stations.

Foreign agencies represented in Canada include UPI and APP (Paris), both with bureaux in Montreal, and DPA, Reuters and TASS.

RADIO

Alongside the Canadian Broadcasting Corporation (Société Radio Canada) (CBC), a public corporation established by Act of Parliament in 1936 to provide a national broadcasting service, Canada also has a highly developed private broadcasting industry. CBC is financed by government subventions and its advertising revenues (advertising accounting for about a third of the total), while private stations depend solely on their commercial activities. Both public and private broadcasting (radio and television) are regulated and supervised by the Canadian Radio–Television Commission, a public authority set up by the Broadcasting Act of 1968, which also provided a statutory statement of national broadcasting policy.

CBC's domestic radio services, in 1971, covered 98.6% of the total population. Its English-language services consist of a medium-wave network of 27 main stations throughout the country, with 200 low-power relay stations, plus antenna time of an average of 25 hours a week on 67 privately owned affiliated stations; and an FM service in five major cities (Vancouver, Toronto, Montreal, Ottawa and Winnipeg). Similarly, CBC has a French-language medium-wave network of 9 main stations with 55 low-power relays, and time on 35 privately owned affiliated stations; also 2 French-language FM stations (in Montreal and Vancouver). Both medium and short wave are used by the northern service broadcasting in English, French, Indian (Dogrib, Chipewyan, Loucheux, Slave and Cree) and Eskimo languages to northern areas of Canada.

As from 1973, one audio circuit of the domestic communications satellite, Anik, is available for distribution of national news and programmes from Montreal and Toronto to regional and remote stations.

Private enterprises operate some 196 medium-wave, 6 short-wave and 76 FM stations, over 80% of which broadcast principally in English, most of the remainder in French, some in both and a few in other languages as well (including Croatian, Dutch, German, Greek, Hungarian, Italian, Portuguese and Ukrainian). Population coverage is also around 98%. About 95% of these stations belong to the Canadian Association of Broadcasters. Many are linked in ownership with publishing and other interests.

Broadcasting time totals over 53 000 hours a week (on all medium- and short-wave stations), of which about 65% is light entertainment, 25% news and information, 4% broadcasts for special audiences, 4% music and other cultural programmes, and 0.5% broadcasts for ethnic minorities. Not included in these figures is advertising time, which must not exceed 25 hours a week. FM stations transmit for over 8000 hours a week, of which more than 90% consists of musical programmes.

No licence fee is payable for radio receivers. Over 5.6 million households have one or more receivers (including car radios).

External broadcasting is conducted by the CBC international service, Radio Canada International, which broadcasts from two 250kW short-wave transmitters at Sackville, New Brunswick, and is also relayed from Daventry (UK) and Sines (Portugal). Programmes, originated in Montreal, are transmitted by microwave to Sackville. Using 11 languages (English, French, Czech, German,

Hungarian, Polish, Portuguese, Russian, Slovak, Spanish and Ukrainian), Radio Canada International broadcasts to seven target areas (Europe, Africa, the south Pacific, Caribbean, USA, Latin America and the Canadian north) for 90 programme hours a week. It also distributes programmes abroad by means of transcriptions and special relays.

In cooperation with the Department of National Defence, the CBC Armed Forces Services provide recorded and short-wave radio programmes for Canadian military bases at home and abroad.

TELEVISION

Television services, like radio, are financed and operated under both public and private ownership and are regulated by the same authorities. Some 97% of the population is covered by television.

CBC first began television broadcasting in 1952. By 1971, it had 318 national outlets: 17 CBC-owned originating stations in English and French networks, with their 101 relay and broadcasting stations, 18 Frontier Coverage Packages (stations in northern areas programmed by film recordings) and 43 privately owned affiliates with their 156 rebroadcasting stations. One station, in Toronto, broadcasts educational programmes for 15 hours a day.

As from April 1973 CBC has begun to distribute its full television network schedule direct via the domestic geostationary satellite, Anik, first to remote northern stations and eventually to all Canada except the central area, which will still be served by terrestrial means.

There are some 250 privately owned stations operated by over 70 companies with 180 relays in addition to their main transmitters. Their services are primarily local but the majority also have network or cooperative facilities through affiliation with the CBC or with CTV (a cable distribution network owned by 12 independent stations and serving a million subscribers) and the Canadian Association of Broadcasters which conducts programme exchanges for its members. Cable television is increasing rapidly and, by 1971, 53.5% of homes in British Columbia, 33.4% of homes in Ontario, 21.8% of homes in Quebec, etc. were served by cable networks distributing programmes originating in Canada and the USA. Early in 1973, there were 365 cable television enterprises in Canada.

A sample of Canadian television programmes in late 1972 showed the following main categories: light entertainment (47%), news and information (32%), education (18%), arts, letters and science (2%) and religious broadcasts (2%). This breakdown does not include advertising programmes, which are broadcast on both publicly and privately owned stations.

The definition system used is 525 lines, and the colour system NTSC. About 20% of Canadian households had colour television in 1971.

No licence fee is payable for television receivers.

FILM

Approximately 135 private film companies, 10 government agencies, 72 television stations and 16 motion-picture laboratories were engaged in the making of films, video tapes and filmstrips in 1970.

The production of feature films is fostered by the Canadian Film Development Corporation, established by Act of Parliament in 1967, which invests in productions and offers grants, loans and various other awards to film-makers and technicians, and assistance in distribution and administrative matters. From a total of 3 features produced in 1960, production had risen to 19 in 1969 (8 by government and 11 by private producers) and 25 in 1970. In 1970 also, 60 theatrical shorts, 405 films for non-theatrical exhibition, 224 silent films and 600 other motion pictures were produced.

The National Film Board, founded in 1939 and reconstituted by the National Film Act of 1950 to 'initiate and promote the production and distribution of films in the national interest', is the main producer of documentary films (572 titles in 1969) and other visual aids. Its productions, including electronic video recording (EVR) cartridges, are distributed in the country through commercial channels and by loan to community groups, schools, etc. and abroad by its own offices (in London, Paris, New Delhi, Tokyo, Buenos Aires and New York).

Films released in 1970 for commercial exhibition included 733 imported features from the USA (291), the UK (131), Italy (113), France (90) and other countries (108). Commercial exhibition (in 1970) was carried on by 1156 fixed cinemas and 279 drive-ins (accommodating 115 512 cars), recording annual attendances respectively of 80.8 million and 11.5 million persons, a noticeable improvement on the previous year, although still well below the 1960 total of 117.5 million. The four largest circuits (with 334, 132, 66 and 31 houses respectively) operated more than 50% of the country's cinemas.

SPACE COMMUNICATIONS

Canada has two Atlantic Intelsat ground stations at Mill Village, Nova Scotia, opened in 1966 and 1969, and a Pacific Intelsat station at Lake Cowichan, Vancouver Island, opened in 1972.

Using its first geostationary satellite, Anik I, owned by Telesat Canada (a combination of Canadian telecommunications and electronics firms) and launched by the North American Space Agency in November 1972, the Canadian Domestic Satellite Communication Service began operating on 1 January 1973. The system will eventually use three satellites and is designed for telephone, telex, data and television and radio transmission.

CBC has a contract with Telesat providing initially for the use of three channels to distribute the corporation's French- and English-language television- and radio-network services throughout the country's five major time zones. The earth segment provides for CBC use of eight southern earth stations (the two main ones linked to the Montreal and Toronto production centres) and 25 Television-Receive-Only earth stations in remote and northern regions. When the second satellite is launched in 1973 it is expected that channels will be rented by broadcasting organizations in the USA.

PROFESSIONAL TRAINING AND ASSOCIATIONS

Carleton University and the University of Western Ontario have both offered (since 1945 and 1946 respectively) four-year honours courses for the Bachelor of Journalism degree. The Ryerson Institute of Technology has had a similar three-year course since 1949. Various community colleges provide training in printed and broadcast journalism of 1, 2 or 3 years' duration and many other colleges and universities offer courses in journalism, as part of their arts and social sciences curricula, some with growing emphasis on broadcasting, although much broadcasting training is received in service. CBC has a national training centre in Montreal for Canadian and overseas technical broadcasting staff. The Ryerson Institute of Technology also offers film training, as does Sheridan College.

Press organizations include national associations of community newspapers (400 members), daily newspapers (84 members), the periodical press (with constituent agricultural, business and magazine associations), a managing editors' conference, and a national and several provincial press clubs.

The Canadian Association of Broadcasters groups 95% of private broadcasting stations, and there are associations of broadcasting technicians, performers and journalists. Film professionals are grouped in associations of directors, producers, technicians, laboratories, performers, authors, distributors, exhibitors, etc. (some national, some provincial), and there is a Motion Picture Industry Council of Canada whose members represent all branches of the industry. Institutions such as the Canadian Film Institute, the Cinémathèque Canadienne, the National Science Film Library, the Canadian Society of Cinematographers, etc., as well as various film clubs and libraries, promote the film medium both professionally and among the public at large.

CANAL ZONE

Population	45 000
Area	1432 sq. km.

RADIO	
Transmitters	Long/medium-wave 1

TELEVISION	
Transmitters	2

FILM	
Cinemas	Fixed 9
Total seating capacity	4800
Seats per 1000 people	107
Total annual attendance	400 000
Annual visits per capita	9

PRESS

Daily and weekly papers from the Republic of Panama, in both English and Spanish, circulate throughout the Zone as do papers from the USA (80% of the population of the Canal Zone are US citizens).

RADIO

The United States Armed Forces operate a 5kW medium-wave transmitter at Fort Clayton, which is on the air 24 hours a day. Otherwise listeners tune to the stations of the Republic of Panama.

TELEVISION

The United States Armed Forces have a main transmitter at Fort Clayton serving the Pacific side of the isthmus and an auxiliary transmitter at Fort Davis on the Atlantic side. These are on the air for 10 hours a day. Most of the Zone is also covered by transmitters of the Republic of Panama.

FILM

Imported films, mainly from the USA, are shown in the Zone's fixed cinemas.

CAYMAN ISLANDS

Population	10 000
Area	259 sq. km.

PRESS
Newspapers	Non-dailies 1
Total circulation	Non-dailies 3750
Copies per 1000 people	Non-dailies 375

RADIO
Total receivers	6000 estimated in use
Receivers per 1000 people	600

FILM
Cinemas	Fixed 7*
Total annual attendance	115 000*
Annual visits per capita	12

*Including 1 drive-in.

PRESS

A privately owned weekly newspaper and a monthly Church journal (1450 copies), both based in Georgetown, Grand Cayman, are the only regular publications. They are in English. Press readership includes many tourist visitors who total some 20 000 every year.

RADIO

There is no local radio or television broadcasting station. Some 6000 radio sets are in use, receiving programmes from neighbouring islands.

FILM

There are six cinemas (all 16mm) in the islands and one drive-in with accommodation for 100 cars.

COSTA RICA

| Population | 1 840 000 |
| Area | 50 700 sq. km. |

PRESS
Newspapers	Dailies 5, Non-dailies 7
Total circulation	Dailies 130 000
Copies per 1000 people	Dailies 71

RADIO
Transmitters	Long/medium-wave 35*, Short-wave 4, VHF–FM 12
Total receivers	250 000 estimated in use
Receivers per 1000 people	136

TELEVISION
Transmitters	4†
Receivers	125 000 estimated in use
Receivers per 1000 people	68

FILM
| Cinemas | Fixed 132 |

*Plus 13 repeaters.
†Main transmitters only.

PRESS

All daily newspapers are published in the capital, San José, in Spanish – the national language. One, considerably larger than the others, has a circulation varying between 68 000 and 75 000 copies. Most dailies have Sunday editions with higher than week-day circulations. Several other weeklies also appear in San

José (the four largest totalling some 60 000 copies per issue), making the capital and the surrounding Meseta area – with about 55% of the national population – the consumers of almost 80% of the total newspaper circulation. San José papers are also distributed outside the Meseta; the largest San José daily has a weekly section devoted to the Caribbean coast city of Limon. Puntarenas on the Pacific coast has a twice- weekly paper and there are small weeklies in two other provincial towns.

Periodicals other than newspapers include a government gazette, a women's weekly (circulating 7000 copies per issue), an agricultural monthly, 3 medical journals, 3 social and cultural publications, 2 Catholic magazines and several political journals.

NEWS AGENCIES

There is no local agency. Papers receive local news from their own correspondents and mainly use the foreign services of AP and UPI. In addition, Reuters serves two papers, and AFP and Efe one each. United States Information Service material is also used, particularly for broadcasting.

RADIO

General supervision of broadcasting is exercised by a government department, but all stations, owned by 23 organizations, are commercially operated with the exception of one cultural and two religious and cultural. The majority have interlocking ownership links and are members of an association of station owners. The two largest networks each consist of nine medium-wave stations in various parts of the country and one of them also has FM transmitters in San José. Several broadcast for 24 hours a day on both medium and short wave, and a number – like the Christian mission station Faro del Caribe (which broadcasts in Spanish and English on medium and short wave and FM) – transmit to audiences in neighbouring countries, as well as Costa Rica.

The national broadcasting law requires all stations to devote at least 30 minutes a week of programme time to improving the nation's cultural level. The law also restricts the amount of certain types of imported programmes broadcast. Radio is certainly the main source of information for a large proportion of the population, almost all of which is covered by one or more programmes. From around 80 000 receivers in 1960, set ownership in homes has trebled in ten years, and some estimates would add a further 150 000 portable and car receivers.

TELEVISION

Television broadcasting began with one commercial station (Televisora de Costa Rica) established in 1960, and another in 1962. There are now four stations, all based in San José, though booster towers bring transmissions from the capital to most of the country's main population areas and to some parts of Nicaragua and Panama. Televisora has four relays, in Buena Vista, Palmira, Turrialba Volcano and Golfito. Set ownership, however, is mainly confined to San José and the Meseta. The law requires at least 20% of programmes to be domestically produced – in fact, imported programmes make up about 75% of the total. The definition system used is 525 lines. Some stations broadcast in colour.

FILM

A Department of Audio-Visual Communication under the Ministry of Culture, Youth and Sport produces, through two production units, a regular series of 16mm documentary films for screen and television on subjects of national interest related to social, economic and cultural development. This department services the film and audio-visual needs of all ministries and government institutions. It is planned to expand present production facilities in order to provide film training facilities for the Central American region and for production by video-tape recording (VTR).

One local production organization in the private sector produces short advertising films for television.

Theatrical feature films are all imported, with approximately 75% of the titles coming from the USA. The remainder are productions from Mexico, Spain, France, Italy and the USSR.

The Ministry of Agriculture, Health and Community Development has 17 mobile cinema units which screen films to local community audiences and to a number of schools and educational institutions which are equipped with 16mm projectors.

PROFESSIONAL TRAINING AND ASSOCIATIONS

The journalists' guild, which has its own professional charter, was responsible in 1968 for establishing a school of journalism, offering a four-year course, within the national university. Broadcasting stations belong to an owners' association. A film training scheme for the Central American region is being planned (see above).

CUBA

| Population | 8 660 000 |
| Area | 114 524 sq. km. |

PRESS
Newspapers	Dailies 16
Total circulation	Dailies 924 500*
Copies per 1000 people	Dailies 107*

RADIO
Transmitters	Long/medium-wave 94, Short-wave 16
Total receivers	1 330 000 estimated in use
Receivers per 1000 people	154

TELEVISION

Transmitters	19
Receivers	575 000 estimated in use
Receivers per 1000 people	66

FILM

Cinemas	Fixed 428

*For 8 titles only.

PRESS

With four daily newspapers (two evening and two morning), totalling 868 000 copies per issue, the capital, Havana, accounts for more than 80% of the country's total daily circulation. The largest of these (408 000 copies per issue) is a Spanish/English morning paper founded in 1965 and published by the Central Committee of the Communist Party. In addition to its urban readership, it reaches 75% of the village population and 80% of the urban population and all school teachers receive subscriptions to it. The second largest, an evening paper, also founded in 1965 and also with a nation-wide readership, is published by the Communist Youth League and circulates 260 000 copies per issue. Both Santiago de Cuba and Santa Clara have three dailies while other provincial towns have one each. All dailies publish educational television timetables and course subjects and other study aids particularly for the benefit of teachers.

Apart from daily newspapers and non-dailies (figures for which are not available), about 200 periodicals are published, 35 being of a general nature, 27 dealing with economics and political science, 27 with engineering and technology, 27 with agriculture, fisheries, etc., 15 with literature, etc. The largest circulations are recorded for a weekly illustrated (220 000 copies), a monthly women's magazine and a satirical weekly (each 150 000 copies), a monthly magazine for small farmers (90 000 copies) and a political monthly (60 000 copies). All are in Spanish, a few having sections in other languages or separate foreign-language editions (English, French, Russian).

NEWS AGENCIES

The national agency is Prensa Latina, Agencia Informativa Latinoamericana (PRELA), founded in 1959, with headquarters in Havana and branch offices in the six provinces. PRELA has branches abroad in Moscow, Prague, Sofia, Paris and Mexico, a correspondent in Hanoi and stringers in Latin American countries. Its news services in Spanish, French and English are transmitted by teleprinter and radio teletype to subscribers in Europe, Africa and Latin America. Special services include photo and economic services and a Spanish-language bulletin on Latin American economic affairs.

Foreign agencies represented in Havana include BTA, CTK and Novosti.

RADIO

Under the Ministry of Communications, the Cuban Radio Broadcasting Institute is responsible for all sound and television broadcasting throughout the country.

Medium-wave stations and networks cover the national territory. The three most powerful networks, Radio Liberación (with 8 transmitters including one of 50kW and one of 60kW), Radio Progreso (with 8 transmitters including two of 50kW each), and Radio Rebelde (with 11 transmitters including one of 150kW), are on the air for more than 1672 hours a week, broadcasting light entertainment (993 hours), news and information (414 hours) and educational programmes (264 hours). Apart from programmes received through exchange agreements with other national broadcasting organizations, broadcast material is mainly of national origin. One station is reserved exclusively for serious music and cultural programmes.

The national external broadcasting organization, Radio Havana (with short-wave transmitters of up to 100kW) is on the air for over 40 hours a day, broadcasting programmes in Spanish, English, French, Creole, Quechua, Portuguese, Arabic and Guarani, beamed to six areas in Europe, the Mediterranean and the Americas.

TELEVISION
The first television programmes were broadcast in early 1950. There are now two national networks with 19 stations operated by the Officina Televisión Nacional and the Cuban Radio Broadcasting Institute. On the air for 136 hours a week, the national networks broadcast educational and cultural programmes (78 hours), news and information (33 hours) and light entertainment (25 hours). Educational broadcasts, of which there are more than 70 a week, include adult-education and literacy courses, language classes and special 4-hour morning and afternoon programmes for schools, for which purpose 10 000 receivers have been installed in pre-university secondary establishments throughout the country. Most programmes are nationally produced.

FILM
The cinema, as both an art and an industry, is the responsibility of a government institute set up by law in 1959, the Instituto Cubano del Arte y la Industria Cinematográfica (ICAIC).

Films produced in 1969 included 1 long (documentary) and 24 short films (3 entertainment, 14 documentary and 7 educational). Over the period 1960–68, the total output was 44 feature and medium-length films, 204 documentaries, 77 educational films, 49 animated cartoons, 94 items of the *People's Encyclopedia*, and 435 numbers of the ICAIC's Latin American newsreel. The ICAIC also maintains the national film library and publishes a film review.

Imports for the year 1969 totalled 115 titles, coming from Japan (18), the USSR (17), USA (11), Italy (9), Romania (8), France and the UK (7 each), Hungary and Mexico (6 each), Czechoslovakia, Spain, Brazil and the German Democratic Republic (3 each), Poland, Bulgaria, Viet-Nam, Bolivia, Yugoslavia, Senegal and Sweden.

Management, maintenance, extension and programming of the nationalized fixed-cinema networks are the responsibility of the ICAIC, as also is the operation of the country's 75 mobile projection units which, in 1970, gave almost 70 000 shows to 7 280 000 spectators in rural communities and schools. One drive-in has space for 500 cars.

SPACE COMMUNICATIONS

A scientific and technical cooperation agreement signed in 1970 between Cuba and the USSR provided for the construction in Cuba, within the next few years, of an earth station which would permit the exchange of television programmes, as well as telephone and telegraph communications between the two countries by Molnya satellite.

PROFESSIONAL TRAINING AND ASSOCIATIONS

Training in journalism is provided at the University of Havana. The Cuban journalists' union (UPEC) is responsible for the general supervision of professional training for all media personnel.

DOMINICA

Population	72 000
Area	751 sq. km.

PRESS
Newspapers	Non-dailies 3
Total circulation	Non-dailies 6500
Copies per 1000 people	Non-dailies 90

RADIO
Transmitters	Medium-wave 2

FILM
Cinemas	Fixed 3
Total seating capacity	1500
Seats per 1000 people	21

PRESS

There are three weekly newspapers, a weekly government gazette and an educational monthly, all published in English in the capital, Roseau.

NEWS AGENCIES

Reuters' Caribbean service is received. A Caribbean news agency in process of formation is expected to serve the media in Dominica.

RADIO

At the end of 1971, on the dissolution of the Windward Islands Broadcasting Service, the government-owned and operated Radio Dominica was on the air for 39 hours weekly, broadcasting mainly light entertainment and news and information programmes.

FILM

The government Audio-Visual Centre has a film unit. Apart from the fixed cinemas, there are six mobile projection units.

DOMINICAN REPUBLIC

Population	4 300 000
Area	48 734 sq. km.

PRESS

Newspapers	Dailies 5, Non-dailies 30
Total circulation	Dailies 150 000
Copies per 1000 people	Dailies 35

RADIO

Transmitters	Long/medium-wave 100, Short-wave 13, VHF–FM 38
Total receivers	170 000 estimated in use
Receivers per 1000 people	40

TELEVISION

Transmitters	9
Receivers	150 000 estimated in use
Receivers per 1000 people	35

FILM

Cinemas	Fixed 73
Total seating capacity	43 000
Seats per 1000 people	10

PRESS

The capital, Santo Domingo, has four dailies with country-wide circulations ranging between 10 000 and 50 000 copies per issue, while a fifth (15 000 copies) appears in Santiago. All are in Spanish.

Non-dailies are published in Santo Domingo and in provincial centres. Periodicals, of which 17 titles are reported, appear in Santo Domingo principally and in Puerto Plata and San Pedro de Macorís.

NEWS AGENCIES

There is no national agency. The press receives domestic news from its own reporters and correspondents, and foreign news from AP and UPI and, in the case of one paper, from AFP and Efe as well.

RADIO

All broadcasting comes under the general supervision of the government telecommunications service.

Radio stations are commercially operated by over 90 companies and individuals. The majority have medium- and short-wave transmitters of 1kW or less and are on the air for about 18 hours a day; 38 also have FM transmitters, 23 of these in Santo Domingo. Several stations are operated by Radio Television Dominicana which is partly government owned. One private station, Radio Santa Maria de la Vega, with a 10kW medium-wave transmitter, broadcasts adult education and literacy courses to 'radio schools' throughout the country. More than 10 000 enrolled students pay a fee which remunerates both the local group instructors and the station. News broadcasts occupy up to 4 hours of programme time a day on certain stations.

TELEVISION

A private commercial station began television broadcasting in 1952. There are now three stations, one of which, Radio Television Dominicana, financed by both government funds and commercial advertising, potentially covers 90% of the population with its main transmitter in the capital and two relay stations. Some of this station's programmes are educational. Rahintel, based in Santo Domingo, with three repeaters, and a third station based in Santiago, with a relay in the capital, both potentially cover about 80% of the population.

Together, these three broadcast for about 217 hours a week, the majority of programmes being imported long films and series from the USA and Latin American countries. News and newsfilm are received from AP and UPI.

The definition system used is 525 lines.

FILM

There is no local production. Films are imported from the USA and Latin American and European countries.

PROFESSIONAL TRAINING AND ASSOCIATIONS

Santo Domingo has two schools of journalism. One, in the Universidad Autónoma, was established in 1953 and now offers a three-year course leading to a recognized professional qualification. The other is a private school with a two-year non-university-level course.

There is a national union of professional journalists, a press association, an association of broadcasters and a radio announcers' union.

EL SALVADOR

Population	3 534 000
Area	21 393 sq. km.

PRESS

Newspapers	Dailies 12, Non-dailies 12
Total circulation	Dailies 267 000
Copies per 1000 people	Dailies 76

RADIO

Transmitters	Long/medium-wave 61, Short-wave 3, VHF–FM 5
Total receivers	500 000 estimated in use
Receivers per 1000 people	141

TELEVISION

Transmitters	4
Receivers	125 000 estimated in use
Receivers per 1000 people	35

FILM

Cinemas	Fixed 57
Total seating capacity	57 000
Seats per 1000 people	16
Total annual attendance	10 400 000
Annual visits per capita	3

PRESS

The six dailies published in the capital, San Salvador, but also widely read in other parts of the country (which is the most densely populated in continental America), account for almost 80% of the national daily circulation. The two largest circulate over 65 000 copies on week-days (with Sunday circulations of around 85 000 copies); two others circulate over 35 000 copies each. Six other cities have dailies, mostly with circulations of only a few thousand copies. Non-dailies appear twice weekly (2 titles), weekly (7 titles) and less frequently (3 titles).

There are 48 periodicals, mostly published in the capital, the largest group of which deals with literary subjects (10 titles), general information (5 titles), arts (4 titles), religion, education and agriculture (3 titles each). Spanish is the language of the newspaper and periodical press.

NEWS AGENCIES

There is no national agency. Local and national news is supplied to the press through its own correspondents and the Government's daily information bulletin. Foreign news is received from AP, UPI and AFP.

RADIO

Overall control of broadcasting is exercised by a special department of the Ministry of the Interior.

There is one government-owned and operated station, Radio Nacional, with 1 medium-wave (10kW), 2 short-wave (5kW) and 1 FM transmitters, in San Salvador, broadcasting for 18 hours a day.

Apart from one religious station in Zacatecoluca, all other stations (about 50 in all) are commercial enterprises operating independently or in jointly owned services like those of Cadena YSU (three medium-wave stations of 5 and 10kW), Cadena Central (three medium-wave stations of up to 10kW and two FM transmitters), Circuito YSR and Cadena YSKL (both with five medium-wave transmitters of up to 10kW and two FM transmitters), etc. About 20 stations are located in San Salvador and the remainder in ten provincial cities.

Average transmission time per station, all in Spanish, is about 140 hours a week, consisting of light entertainment (42 hours), news and information (40 hours), commercial advertising (35 hours), sports (12 hours), broadcasts for special audiences (8 hours) and adult education (3 hours). Most of this is recorded material.

No licence fee is payable for radio receivers.

TELEVISION

Television broadcasting (525 lines) was introduced in 1956 by a commercial station. There are now two other commercial stations operating as well, thus giving television coverage to practically all of the population. Programmes of the two main stations, totalling 154 hours a week, consist of advertising (70 hours), news and information (38 hours), light entertainment (35 hours) and broadcasts for special audiences (8 hours).

No licence fee is payable for television receivers.

A government station, operated by the Ministry of Education on two channels, broadcasts only educational programmes for schools. Introduced in 1969, this scheme is being systematically extended to cover fourth to ninth grade classes by 1975. (In 1972, 1179 classes in 263 schools were regularly receiving two or three television classes a week in five subject fields.)

FILM

Occasional documentary and educational films are produced in the country, but virtually all films shown are imported. Features are imported mainly from the USA, Mexico, Argentina and European countries.

PROFESSIONAL TRAINING AND ASSOCIATIONS

A five-year professional training course in mass communication is offered by the Journalism School (founded in 1954) at the Universidad Nacional Autónoma, in San Salvador. In 1969, the private Universidad Centroamericana, also in the capital, introduced a two-year course in the media of social communication (for which 80 students were enrolled in 1970).

Professional associations include journalists and sports writers and broadcast associations. Radio and television announcers and technicians have their own association. Over 40 commercial radio station owners are members of the Asociación Salvadoreña de Empresarios de la Radiodifusión.

GREENLAND

Population	50 000
Area	2 175 600 sq. km.

PRESS

Newspapers	Non-dailies 22

RADIO

Transmitters	Long/medium-wave 5, Short-wave 6, VHF—FM 2
Total receivers	7000 estimated in use
Receivers per 1000 people	140

TELEVISION

Transmitters	2

FILM

Cinemas	Fixed 47
Total seating capacity	7000
Seats per 1000 people	140
Total annual attendance	400 000
Annual visits per capita	8

PRESS

There are no daily newspapers. Non-daily general interest papers appear in Greenlandic (2 titles) or are bilingual, Danish and Greenlandic (20 titles).

RADIO

The government-owned broadcasting service, Grønlands Radiofoni, operates 1 medium-wave transmitter (25kW), 6 short-wave transmitters (up to 10kW) and 1 FM transmitter, all located in Godthaab, 2 other medium-wave transmitters located in Godhavn (5kW) and Simiutaq (20kW) respectively and 1 FM transmitter in Frederikshaab. Grønlands Radiofoni is on the air for 73½ hours a week, in Danish and Greenlandic, broadcasting light entertainment (25½ hours), news and information (21 hours), programmes for special audiences (10 hours), educational programmes (7 hours), artistic and cultural programmes (7 hours) and language and other courses (3 hours). Of this total, 64 programme hours are locally produced.

The United States Armed Forces Radio and Television Service has two medium-wave stations (0.25 and 1kW) at Søndre Strømfjord and Thule, both of which are on the air for 24 hours a day.

TELEVISION

There is no national television service. The United States Armed Forces Radio and Television Service has television transmitters at its Søndre Strømfjord and Thule air bases.

FILM

Apart from the fixed cinemas (all 16mm), there are six mobile projection units.

GRENADA

Population	96 000
Area	344 sq. km.

PRESS

Newspapers	Dailies 1, Non-dailies 1
Total circulation	Dailies 3000, Non-dailies 1000
Copies per 1000 people	Dailies 31, Non-dailies 10

RADIO

Transmitters	Medium-wave 3, Short-wave 2
Total receivers	10 000 estimated in use
Receivers per 1000 people	104

FILM

Cinemas	Fixed 3
Total seating capacity	3000
Seats per 1000 people	31
Total annual attendance	200 000
Annual visits per capita	2

PRESS

The general interest press consists of the one daily newspaper and one published three times a week. A government gazette issued by the Premier's Office appears every Saturday. All are published in English, in the capital, St George's.

NEWS AGENCIES

News is received through Reuters' Caribbean service and UPI. A Caribbean news agency is being set up to serve local media.

RADIO

Radio Grenada (RGda) came into being at the end of 1971 on the dissolution of the Windward Islands Broadcasting Service. It is government owned and operated and broadcasts for 16 hours daily via three medium-wave transmitters (all 0.8kW), at Morne Rouge and Sauteurs on Grenada and at Carriacou, the largest of the Grenadine Islands, and via two short-wave transmitters (each of

5kW). Programmes include participation by local artists and community groups and some locally produced commercials.

FILM

Apart from the fixed cinemas, there are three mobile projection units.

PROFESSIONAL ASSOCIATIONS

The Caribbean Press Association has its headquarters in St George's.

GUADELOUPE

Population	332 000
Area	1779 sq. km.

PRESS	
Newspapers	Dailies 1
Total circulation	Dailies 4500
Copies per 1000 people	Dailies 14

RADIO	
Transmitters	Medium-wave 2
Total receivers	26 000 licences
Receivers per 1000 people	78

TELEVISION	
Transmitters	3
Receivers	8000 licences
Receivers per 1000 people	24

FILM	
Cinemas	Fixed 20

PRESS

The only daily newspaper, established in 1908, is published in Pointe-à-Pitre, while a thrice-weekly Guadeloupe edition of a Martinique daily has a reported local circulation of 20 000 copies per issue. Other non-dailies and periodicals include a widely circulated Catholic weekly journal published in the capital, Basse-Terre, an official administrative weekly, a thrice-monthly newspaper (circulating 7000 copies), a women's magazine (2000 copies) and several political and trade-union publications. All are in French.

NEWS AGENCIES
There is no local agency. The press receives overseas news through AFP, which has a permanent correspondent in Basse-Terre.

RADIO
Both radio and television broadcasting are conducted by the Office de Radiodiffusion-Télévision Française (ORTF) and are financed by French Government subventions, receiver licence fees and (in the case of radio) advertising revenue. With two medium-wave transmitters (20 and 4kW), giving full coverage to both main islands and the dependencies, the station is on the air for 132 hours a week, broadcasting light entertainment (71 hours), news and information (33 hours), broadcasts for special audiences (11 hours, including some in Creole), educational and cultural programmes (6 hours each) and advertising (5 hours). Programme material includes ORTF transcriptions and relays from Paris but over 50% of programmes are locally produced.

TELEVISION
The Guadeloupe station of ORTF, potentially reaching 80% of the population, is on the air for 23 hours weekly, broadcasting news and information (6 hours), light entertainment (12 hours), programmes for special audiences (2½ hours), etc. The majority of the programmes broadcast are supplied by ORTF in Paris. The definition system used is 625 lines.

An annual licence fee is payable for television receivers.

FILM
There is no local production. Cinemas in Pointe-à-Pitre, Basse-Terre and smaller centres show imported films.

GUATEMALA

Population	5 350 000
Area	108 889 sq. km.

PRESS
Newspapers	Dailies 8, Non-dailies 38
Total circulation	Dailies 143,000
Copies per 1000 people	Dailies 27

RADIO
Transmitters	Long/medium-wave 85, Short-wave 4, VHF—FM 2
Total receivers	559 000 estimated in use
Receivers per 1000 people	104

TELEVISION

Transmitters	3*
Receivers	80 000 estimated in use
Receivers per 1000 people	15

FILM

Cinemas	Fixed 105
Total seating capacity	75 400
Seats per 1000 people	14
Total annual attendance	4 600 000
Annual visits per capita	0.9

*Includes 1 auxiliary transmitter.

PRESS

The daily press is concentrated in Guatemala City, but one paper is published in the republic's second largest town, Quetzaltenango. All but one of the dailies (an English-language paper serving visitors and tourists) are published in Spanish, which is the official language of the country although it is only a trade or 'intermediary' language for the Indian communities which constitute 45% of the population. One daily is government owned and another has official backing; the largest circulations are those of two independent afternoon papers, both of which carry international and domestic news, as well as features, sports news, etc. Circulation is confined almost entirely to the larger towns.

Several other papers appear twice or three times weekly (28 titles) or weekly (10 titles).

Periodicals other than newspapers number 86, with an average total circulation of 67 500 copies per issue. They include a number of publications by government ministries, professional, industrial and commercial associations and university faculties.

NEWS AGENCIES

There is no official national news agency although some services are supplied by the privately owned Agencia Información Centroamericana in Guatemala City. Newspapers receive domestic news mainly from their own correspondents and from government information services. Foreign news is supplied by AFP, AP, UPI and Reuters. AGP and ANSA have correspondents in the capital.

RADIO

Government supervision of broadcasting is exercised through the Dirección General de Radiodifusión y Televisión Nacional. Of the country's 75 licensed stations, six are government-owned; they broadcast entertainment, official news, announcements and information programmes, as well as educational programmes.

Another five which also carry educational programmes in Spanish and Indian languages are owned by non-commercial cultural or Christian organizations. For example, the station Escuelas Radiofónicas Chortiz, financed by Belgian donations and subscriptions, is on the air for 84 hours a week on medium wave and 77 hours on short wave, in Spanish and Indian languages (Quiché, Cakchiquel, Mam and Kelchi), with adult-literacy and school programmes which are received by groups under the supervision of monitors in all parts of the country. The largest religious station is the Central American Mission's Radio Cultural with 5 and 10kW medium- and short-wave transmitters and one FM transmitter. It also carries news and educational programmes in several local languages in addition to its religious broadcasts.

There are 64 commercial stations, about half of which are based in Guatemala City and the rest in larger provincial centres, which broadcast on medium and short wave for daily periods ranging from 4 to 24 hours.

With the availability of transistor sets (numbers of which are distributed free as part of educational and community development programmes), receiver ownership has more than doubled over the past ten years.

TELEVISION
All three stations are commercially owned and operated. The oldest established, Radio-Televisión Guatemala, first began broadcasting in May 1956 and is now on the air 12 hours a day. The other two, Tele Once and Televicentro, both broadcast for 6 hours daily. All three have their transmitters in Guatemala City, where most of the viewing public live, but Radio-Televisión Guatemala also has relay installations in Quezaltenango by means of which, through an agreement with the Mexican authorities, transmissions can be fed into or received from the microwave network covering the whole territory of Mexico. All stations use 525-line definition.

Of the total weekly broadcasting time of about 175 hours, news and information occupy about 7 hours and advertising 11 hours. About 10 hours a week are of national origin, the remainder consisting of imported material from Spain, Mexico, the USA, Argentina and Italy.

Various experiments have been made with educational broadcasts ranging from primary education to teacher training and university levels and including literacy for adults, frequently with supervision and follow-up in local centres and listening groups.

FILM
All films shown commercially are imported — principally from the USA, Mexico, France, Italy, Spain, Argentina and the Federal Republic of Germany — but some documentary and instructional films are produced in the country by government departments for their own requirements. Of the six importing and distributing enterprises, three also supply films for television. About half the cinema attendance figures are for Guatemala City where, in addition to some well-equipped theatres, there is one drive-in cinema with space for 534 cars.

PROFESSIONAL TRAINING AND ASSOCIATIONS
Training in journalism is provided by the Escuela Centroamericana de Periodismo at the San Carlos University in Guatemala City which awards a diploma after three years' academic study and two years' professional training. Assistant teachers and technicians for 'radio schools' are trained at the centre run by the Federación de Escuelas Radiofónicas. Other short courses for

bilingual monitors (Spanish plus an Indian language) for listening groups and classes are organized for young Indians with full primary education. The centre also organizes and maintains educational listening groups in both town and country areas.

Professional associations include an association and a union of journalists, a sports writers' association and an association of private broadcasters, all with headquarters in Guatemala City.

HAITI

Population	5 070 000
Area	27 750 sq. km.

PRESS
Newspapers	Dailies 6, non-dailies 6
Total circulation	Dailies 35 000, Non-dailies 8000
Copies per 1000 people	Dailies 7, Non-dailies 2

RADIO
Transmitters	Long/medium-wave 25, Short-wave 27, VHF–FM 5
Total receivers	85 000 estimated in use
Receivers per 1000 people	17

TELEVISION
Transmitters	1
Receivers	11 000 estimated in use
Receivers per 1000 people	2

FILM
Cinemas	Fixed 20
Total seating capacity	12 300
Seats per 1000 people	2
Total annual attendance	1 500 000
Annual visits per capita	0.3

PRESS

All dailies are in French and are published in the capital, Port au Prince, as are several non-dailies including a thrice-weekly official gazette, a political weekly and an English-language fortnightly. Other non-dailies are published in Gonaïves, Les Cayes, Port de Paix and Cap Haïtien. Periodicals, mainly in French but also in English, Spanish and Creole (the only language of the majority of the population) include religious, historical and technical journals.

NEWS AGENCIES
There is no local agency. Haitian newspapers obtain local news through their own correspondents, and foreign news through AFP, which also has a correspondent in Port au Prince.

RADIO
General oversight of broadcasting is exercised by the Department of Public Works. There are 23 commercial and four non-commercial stations, all privately owned, broadcasting mainly in French and Creole, for periods of up to 18 hours a day. The two largest networks are the non-commercial Christian mission stations, the Evangelistic Voice of the West Indies and Radio Lumière, the former broadcasting over 30 programme hours daily in English, French, Creole and Spanish via its 2 medium-wave and 4 short-wave transmitters, and the latter broadcasting in French, Creole and English with 4 medium-wave (up to 20kW), 2 short-wave and 3 FM transmitters in the capital and other parts of the republic.

Many transmitters have only local coverage but the more powerful stations reach audiences in all parts of Haiti and in neighbouring Caribbean countries as well.

No licence fee is payable.

TELEVISION
A privately owned commercial television station, Télé-Haïti, which began operations in December 1959, now broadcasts from Port au Prince on two channels (525 lines), one in English and one in French, both of which are also linked to cable redistribution networks. The majority of the programmes carried are imported from the USA. Télé-Haïti has exclusive television transmission rights for the republic.

FILM
There is no local film production. Feature films, imported mainly from the USA and also from France and other countries, are shown in commercial cinemas in the main towns and in the three drive-ins in the capital.

HONDURAS

| Population | 2 582 000 |
| Area | 112 088 sq. km. |

PRESS

Newspapers	Dailies 8, Non-dailies 95*
Total circulation	Dailies 114 000
Copies per 1000 people	Dailies 44

RADIO

Transmitters	Long/medium-wave 104, Short-wave 37, VHF–FM 10
Total receivers	147 000 estimated in use
Receivers per 1000 people	57

TELEVISION

Transmitters	5*
Receivers	22 000 estimated in use
Receivers per 1000 people	9

FILM

| Cinemas | Fixed 60† |

*Data for 1968.
†Data for 1960.

PRESS

Of the four dailies published in the capital, Tegucigalpa, three have circulations between 10 000 and 25 000 while the fourth, established in 1830 and published by the Department of the Interior, circulates around 2500 copies. The provinces are served by dailies from the capital or from the country's second town, San Pedro Sula, where the largest daily circulation of 48 500 (60 000 for the Sunday edition) is recorded, or from the Atlantic port of La Ceiba, or by the widely read non-daily press.

Non-daily general interest newspapers include 24 titles issued weekly or more frequently, 28 fortnightly and a large number of monthlies. Many of these are published in the capital and the larger towns already mentioned, others in La Paz, Puerto Cortes, Santa Barbara, Tela and smaller centres.

The press is estimated to reach 75% of the national territory, including all the most populated areas. It is published in Spanish, in which language about 60% of the population is litrate, and its news coverage consists, on average, of 50% foreign news, 20% national and 30% local.

Periodicals, numbering about 175 titles, are published mainly in Tegucigalpa and deal with education (79 titles), sociology and statistics (15 titles), literature (14 titles), law and public administration (10 titles), political sciences, trade and transport, and ethnography (5 titles each), etc. Monthly and quarterly reviews cover current official, commercial, industrial and cultural affairs, the literary and political scenes, and an official guide to Central America is published periodically.

NEWS AGENCIES

Honduras has no national agency. Newspapers receive domestic news from their own correspondents, and foreign news mainly from AP and UPI services.

Agencies with permanent correspondents in Tegucigalpa are UPI, AP, AFP, Efe and Reuters.

RADIO

Although the overall control of broadcasting is the responsibility of the Government's Dirección Nacional de Comunicaciones Eléctricas, the Government itself has only a few transmitters, the majority being operated by the 84 licensed private broadcasting enterprises. These are mainly commercial stations, wholly financed by advertising and using medium wave and frequently short wave as well. A small number have FM transmitters serving the Tegucigalpa and San Pedro Sula areas. Cultural and educational programmes are broadcast by two religious stations, each of which has a powerful transmitter in the capital and several others in different parts of the country. Radio coverage thus extends to the whole of the national territory. Broadcasts are in Spanish and 10 stations carry some English-language programmes as well.

Time on the air varies from one station to another but, for most, is between 70 and 140 hours a week.

TELEVISION

A commercial station operated by the Companía Televisora Hondureña first began television broadcasting in September 1959. With transmitters at Tegucigalpa and San Pedro Sula and intermediate relays (on 525 lines), the station is now on the air for 72 hours a week, potentially reaching some 60% of the population. Some programmes are exchanged with the Panamanian station, Televisora Nacional.

FILM

Feature films are imported mainly from the USA, Canada, Mexico, Argentina, the UK, Italy, France, Spain and Japan. No recent figures are available for cinemas. In 1960, there were 60 with a total seating capacity of 42 000.

SPACE COMMUNICATIONS

Honduras is a member of Intelsat and has an earth station, opened in 1971, at Tegucigalpa.

PROFESSIONAL TRAINING AND ASSOCIATIONS

In 1969, the Universidad Nacional Autónoma, at Tegucigalpa, instituted a four-year post-secondary diploma course in journalism.

Professional associations include a national press association, an association of sports writers and announcers, and an association of licensed broadcasting stations.

JAMAICA

Population	1 900 000
Area	10 962 sq. km.

PRESS

Newspapers	Dailies 2, Non-dailies 14
Total circulation	Dailies 130 759, Non-dailies 363 500
Copies per 1000 people	Dailies 69, Non-dailies 191

RADIO

Transmitters	Medium-wave 8, VHF–FM 6
Total receivers	775 000 estimated in use
Receivers per 1000 people	408

TELEVISION

Transmitters	11
Receivers	105 000 estimated in use
Receivers per 1000 people	55

FILM

Cinemas	Fixed 42
Total seating capacity	39 400
Seats per 1000 people	21
Total annual attendance	6 400 000*
Annual visits per capita	3

*For 47 cinemas in 1971.

PRESS

The dailies and the bulk of the weekly press are concentrated in Kingston, the capital. Each daily has a week-end or Sunday edition, one with a special magazine section. Both dailies are under the same management. Two weeklies are published in Montego Bay and a bi-monthly in Spanish Town. There is also one Chinese-language weekly newspaper. English is, however, the main language of the country and of the press and, to a large extent, the 450 000 tourists who visit the island every year. A notable feature of the press is the large amount of space devoted to advertising which in the dailies can run as high as 60%.

Among the 40 or so periodicals with an overall circulation of some 300 000 copies per issue, the main subject categories are religion (7 titles, together circulating 20 440 copies per issue), agriculture, fisheries, etc. (6 titles, 15 949 copies), business management (4 titles, 95 250 copies), commerce and communications (4 titles, 38 500 copies), education (1 title, 11 500 copies), etc. In addition, a children's weekly circulates 98 500 copies.

NEWS AGENCIES

Jamaica is served by the Caribbean Press Association whose headquarters are at St George's (Grenada). The newspapers also draw on the USA, UK and Canadian news services and have their own correspondents on other islands of the West Indies. JBC television subscribes to the newsfilm service of Visnews (UK). A Caribbean news agency is in process of formation. Reuters maintains a bureau in Kingston.

RADIO

There are two broadcasting organizations, the Jamaica Broadcasting Corporation (JBC), publicly owned and operated by a statutory corporation on semi-commercial lines, and Radio Jamaica (RJR), a commercial company which is a subsidiary of Rediffusion (UK), deriving its revenue from advertising. Population coverage is 80%.

JBC, which began broadcasting activities in June 1959, has four medium-wave transmitters (5kW each) in Kingston, Montego Bay, Galina and Spur Tree, and three FM transmitters in Kingston, Half Way Tree and Christina. The station is on the air for 20 hours a day, broadcasting entertainment, news, advertisements, BBC (UK) and United Nations transcriptions, as well as 6 hours of school broadcasts throughout the week during school terms, under the supervision of the Ministry of Education. News and feature programmes are provided by the official Jamaica Information Service.

RJR, which has been operating in Jamaica since 1950, is equipped with four medium-wave transmitters of 5kW each at the same locations as the JBC transmitters, and three FM transmitters in Kingston (2) and Spur Tree. The wireless service is on the air for 19 hours a day. In addition, the station operates a continuous music service on a wired redistribution system serving the Kingston area. Both the wireless and wired networks of RJR also carry government news and feature programmes produced by the Jamaica Information Service, as well as broadcasts to schools and other educational institutions. Several hundred schools are equipped with receivers.

TELEVISION

Jamaica Broadcasting Corporation began television broadcasting in August 1963. It now operates, in addition to the main station in Kingston, relay stations at Coopers Hall, Port Antonio, Montego Bay, Oracabessa, Spur Tree, Yallahs and Morant Point, bringing potential coverage to 80% of the total population. Surveys show that in the course of an average day some 165 000 persons, or 16% of the total adult population, watch JBC television. JBC is an independent public corporation and its television network is commercially run and has links with commercial broadcasting enterprises in the UK and USA. Stations are on the air for 66 hours a week. Programmes include light entertainment (30 hours), news and information (22 hours), education (3½ hours), etc. Foreign newsfilm is received by subscription from Visnews (UK). The special schools broadcasts are prepared by the educational television service. The definition system used is 625 lines.

FILM

The government film unit, a section of the Jamaica Information Service, produces a number of 35mm and 16mm documentaries and newsreels. It maintains a library of approximately 450 films which are exhibited on television, as well as by mobile units. The Motion Picture Industry (Encouragement) Law, introduced in 1948, provides generous tax concessions to recognized film producers in order to stimulate the development of a local film industry. Feature films shown in 42 fixed cinemas in 1973 (there were 47 in 1971) and in Kingston's one drive-in (420 cars) were imported, mainly from the USA and UK.

SPACE COMMUNICATIONS

An earth station for Atlantic Intelsat transmissions was opened at Prospect Pen in the parish of St Thomas, about 30km west of Kingston, in February 1972. The station is owned and operated by Jamintel, a partnership between the Jamaican Government and Cable and Wireless.

PROFESSIONAL TRAINING AND ASSOCIATIONS

A diploma course in mass communication with emphasis on journalism was introduced as from late 1972 in the University of the West Indies, Kingston (Mona campus). The Jamaica College of Arts, Science and Technology offers a three-year course for telecommunications technicians.

The Press Association of Jamaica, founded in 1943, has a membership of some 150 press, radio and television journalists, information officers, etc.

MARTINIQUE

Population	341 000
Area	1102 sq. km.

PRESS
Newspapers	Dailies 2, Non-dailies 8
Total circulation	Dailies 28 000
Copies per 1000 people	Dailies 82

RADIO
Transmitters	Medium-wave 1, Short-wave 3, VHF–FM 1
Total receivers	33 000 licences
Receivers per 1000 people	97

TELEVISION
Transmitters	6
Receivers	9500 licences
Receivers per 1000 people	28

FILM

Cinemas	Fixed 38
Total seating capacity	15 300
Seats per 1000 people	45
Total annual attendance	2 100 000
Annual visits per capita	6

PRESS

Both dailies are published in Fort de France, the capital, where 30% of the population live. One, with a reported local circulation of some 25 000 copies, also has a special Guadeloupe edition. Non-dailies include twice-weekly and weekly Catholic information journals and six other weeklies. All are published in French.

NEWS AGENCIES

AFP's office in Fort de France supplies the press with overseas news.

RADIO

Both radio and television broadcasting are conducted by the Office de Radiodiffusion-Télévision Française (ORTF) and are financed by French Government subventions, receiver licence fees and (in the case of radio) advertising revenue.

With 1 medium-wave transmitter (50kW), 3 short-wave transmitters (4kW) and 1 FM transmitter, the radio station broadcasts a home service of 96 hours a week, covering the entire population. Typical weekly programmes include light entertainment (67 hours), news and information (9 hours), broadcasts for special audiences (7 hours), education (7 hours), advertising, etc. Of these, about 66 hours originate from ORTF in Paris.

An annual licence fee is payable for radio receivers.

TELEVISION

ORTF's Martinique station, with a main transmitter in Fort de France and five relays in various parts of the island, potentially reaches the whole population. It is on the air for 28 hours a week, broadcasting light entertainment (12 hours), cultural programmes (3 hours), news and information (6 hours) and broadcasts for special audiences (6 hours). The bulk of the programme material broadcast is received from ORTF in Paris. The definition system used is 625 lines.

FILM

There is no local production. Films shown in commercial cinemas are all imported.

MEXICO

Population	52 640 000
Area	1 972 546 sq. km.

PRESS

Newspapers	Dailies 200, Non-dailies 288

RADIO

Transmitters	Long/medium-wave 510, Short-wave 26, VHF–FM 54
Total receivers	14 005 000 estimated in use
Receivers per 1000 people	266

TELEVISION

Transmitters	78*
Receivers	2 978 000 estimated in use
Receivers per 1000 people	57

FILM

Cinemas	Fixed 1765
Total seating capacity	1 496 000
Seats per 1000 people	28
Total annual attendance	251 500 000
Annual visits per capita	5

*Including 4 auxiliary transmitters.

PRESS

From 173 titles in 1960, the number of daily newspapers rose to 199 in 1962 and 228 in 1967, dropping again to 200 in 1970 (179 morning and 21 evening papers). Over the same ten-year period the overall circulation total almost doubled.

Mexico City's 26 dailies together account for a circulation of 2.3 million copies representing almost half the national total; of these, the four largest have individual circulations of between 175 000 and 200 000 copies, a pictorial sports paper circulates 160 000 and several other dailies exceed the 100 000 mark. With the exception of three appearing in English, all papers are in Spanish. Several publishers have separate morning and evening newspapers.

Over 80 other cities and towns have daily newspapers, the larger state capitals having 4 to 6 titles (Monterrey and Guadalajara each have a daily circulation total of over 200 000). Although most of the press is independently owned, one chain publishes over 30 state and provincial dailies. Another chain owns six provincial dailies.

Non-dailies include 24 appearing twice or thrice weekly, 140 weekly and 124 less frequently.

The general interest press circulates throughout the country, with an average content of 40% local, 20% national and 10% international news, and 28% advertising.

Periodicals number 1485, about half of which appear monthly. The majority are published in the capital and are distributed throughout the country. The largest circulations are recorded for popular, general readership and women's magazines, but there are also many well-established specialized periodicals. Apart from imported periodicals there are 19 publications in English, one in German and one in Hebrew.

Mexico consumed 158 800 metric tons of newsprint in 1970 (3.1kg per person), 40 000 metric tons of which were nationally produced. Imports and distribution of newsprint are controlled by a joint government-private enterprise board.

NEWS AGENCIES

The largest agency is Informex, a private company founded in 1960 with headquarters employing 64 persons, in Mexico City, and 85 permanent offices throughout the country employing 150 persons full-time plus 86 part-time correspondents. It also uses the services of 17 part-time correspondents abroad. International news is received mainly from foreign agencies, including AFP, UPI and AP, and TASS, Tanjug, ADN and DPA, with which Informex has exchange agreements. Informex has some 200 subscribers (including 40% of the country's daily newspapers, 50% of radio stations and 10% of television stations) which it supplies with 23 500 words of national and local news daily and 3000 words of foreign news, in Spanish; it also supplies them with features. Special services are also issued for radio and television stations. Channels used for news distribution are radio, telegraph, telephone, microwave links and air mail, in addition to a teleprinter service for subscribers.

The other main news agency is Notimex, a private agency founded in 1968 with headquarters in Mexico City, employing 5 full-time and 8 part-time staff in the country and 4 full-time and 5 part-time correspondents abroad, from whom it receives its foreign news. It works principally for the broadcast media, supplying special audio-visual services, mainly domestic features and television films, to 30 radio and five television stations. News transmission is effected by telex, teleprinters and television networks.

The Agencia Mexicana de Noticias (AMEX), also founded in 1968, is a private agency with headquarters employing 250 persons, in Mexico City, and correspondents in the various Mexican states, the main Latin American capitals and the USA, Canada and Spain.

Foreign agencies with bureaux or correspondents in Mexico include AFP, UPI, CTK, AP, Kyodo, DPA, PRELA, Reuters and TASS.

RADIO

General operating conditions for broadcasting are set out in a federal government law on radio and television, updating previous legislation, which became effective in 1960. It divides responsibilities among the Ministry of Transport and Communications (allocation of frequencies, licensing, operation and location of stations, control of advertising rates), the Ministry of Internal Affairs (public order, rights of third parties, coordination of official programmes) and the Ministry of Education (educational broadcasting, programmes of cultural and civic interest, authors' rights, etc.).

Radio broadcasting stations are divided into two types, commercial and cultural, the former being by far the most numerous.

Commercial stations, numbering 330, operate 500 long- and medium-wave transmitters, 51 FM and 16 short-wave transmitters located around the capital (about 40 stations) and throughout all states of the country and ranging in power from 0.25kW up to the 150 and 250kW medium-wave transmitters of La Voz de América Latina which belongs to the 60-station network Radio Cadena Nacional (RCN).

Another large network, Radio Programas de México (RPM), has more than 70 affiliated stations but, apart from these large groupings, most provincial stations are independent. All these stations are financed by commercial advertising, and the bulk of their programmes consist mainly of brief news reports and recorded music with numerous commercial spots. There are occasional live programmes. In addition, all radio (and television) stations both commercial and cultural, must make up to 12.5% of their broadcasting time available to the Government, as required, for programmes of educational, cultural and civic interest which are prepared by a special government service.

Cultural stations are government owned and are operated either by government services or by educational institutions with government assistance. Together they operate 10 medium-wave, 10 short-wave and 3 FM transmitters. Their programmes may consist of specialized offerings for cultivated audiences, foreign-language courses, etc., or they may include fundamental education, literacy, technical, agricultural and general cultural broadcasts such as those of the short-wave 'radio schools' of the Universidad Ibero-americana.

No licence fee is payable for radio receivers, the number of which in use has more than quadrupled since 1960 (when there were 3.3 million).

External short-wave broadcasting is carried out by Radio México, a government station with two 100kW transmitters which are on the air for 12 hours a day.

TELEVISION

The first television programmes were broadcast in August 1950. There are now over 70 stations in operation potentially reaching 70% of the population. More than half of these are affiliated to one private corporation, Telesistema Mexicano, which operates three commercial networks, each with a main station in Mexico City, and microwave links bringing at least one-channel coverage to most of the main population centres. The main network is on the air for 24 hours a day, the others from 12 to 18 hours a day, with a large proportion of programmes in colour. Telesistema's stations carry government-sponsored secondary-education programmes from 08.00 to 14.00 hours daily. The corporation also has four stations in the USA – in Texas, California and New York State – which carry some direct retransmissions from its home networks. It has exchange and coproduction agreements with other Latin American broadcasting organizations and also exports more than 20 000 programmes a month. Another network, Televisión Independiente de México now operating under a joint arrangement with Telesistema, groups seven stations which are on the air for up to 12 hours a day, while some 20 independent stations (some with several relay stations) are found in the capital and in the larger towns; one of these is affiliated to a network in the USA.

A government-owned station, broadcasting only educational and cultural programmes, is operated by the Instituto Politécnico Nacional in Mexico City. A former privately owned network – Telecadena Mexicana – is now financed by the Government, and broadcasts mainly cultural programmes for more than 12 hours a day, mostly in colour, including one feature film and one theatrical classic daily. It serves the capital and the surrounding highland area. In addition, government-sponsored educational programmes are also broadcast by the commercial stations under the terms of a law requiring them to make up to 12.5% of their air-time available for this purpose. Educational programme material, supplied by the official secondary-school broadcasting service, originates in the Government's own audio-visual studios which are linked directly to the national microwave network. Students following such courses, individually or in organized viewing classes throughout the country, may take official examinations in all subjects and at various levels. Universities and other institutions also provide a certain number of programmes.

The definition system used is 525 lines. Colour television broadcasts (NTSC system) began in September 1968; by 1973, there were 300 000 colour receivers in use.

FILM

After a period of decline, largely due to the competition of television, Mexican film production rose to a total of 124 features in 1970 (from 64 in 1960 and 48 in 1967) and 557 short films (487 entertainment and 70 documentary). The increase in short-film production (totalling less than 100 titles in 1960) has been even more notable.

Since 1960, the Government has sought to encourage the industry by nationalizing the larger production studios and by forming a special fund to assist and coordinate film financing. Finance from the fund is dependent upon the quality of the films produced and on the maintenance of a steady rate of production (usually two films a year for each producer). Two marketing organizations for Mexican films have also been established, one for the Spanish-speaking countries, the other for the rest of the world. Feature films are imported, at the rate of over 400 a year, subject to quotas and exchange agreements with originating countries, except for the USA and Latin American countries. Features imported in 1970 came mainly from the USA (162), the UK (43), Spain (30), France (24), Italy (24), Japan (18), Argentina (14), and the Federal Republic of Germany (12). In the same year, 85 short films were imported from the USA (63), France (11), the UK (4), Spain (3), etc.

Cinemas are either independently operated or grouped in circuits of government-owned rented or affiliated establishments, the latter enjoying preferential conditions and showing mainly Mexican and some foreign films. Probably more than 400 cinemas operate under this government-sponsored scheme. Private cinemas show more foreign films (chiefly from the USA) than national productions. There are over 1000 16mm and several hundred 35mm houses, eight cinemas equipped for large-gauge exhibition and four drive-ins accommodating 2470 cars.

Over the last ten years, during which time the population has increased by more than 40%, the number of fixed cinemas in operation has dropped by about 12% and the total annual attendance by over 30% (1961 figures were 2000 fixed cinemas with 374 million annual attendance, or 10.4 visits per person per year).

SPACE COMMUNICATIONS
Radio and television programmes are received and transmitted via Atlantic Intelsat through the earth station opened in 1968 at Tulancingo (Hidalgo State) under the general control of the Ministry of Communications and Transport.

PROFESSIONAL TRAINING AND ASSOCIATIONS
Five-year degree courses in journalism and/or mass communications have been offered at the Universidad Nacional Autónoma de México (UNAM) since 1951 (with a total enrolment of 334 students in 1970), at the Universidad Ibero-americana since 1960 and the Universidad de Guadalajara since 1970. UNAM also has three-year technical courses for periodical-press and other editorial trainees. Schools of journalism have also been established in the Universidad Femenina de México since 1943, the Universidad de las Américas, the Universidad de Chihuahua since 1963 and the Universidad Veracruzana since 1954.

Non-university training is available in four schools of journalism requiring university-entrance qualifications in Mexico City (a private school and a correspondence college) and in Guadalajara and Monterrey.

Applied communications courses and research facilities are available at the National School of Agriculture and at various educational communications institutions including the Instituto Latinoamericano de Comunicación Educativa (ILCE), the Universidad Ibero-americana and higher technological institutes in Monterrey and Mexico City, as well as through the training programmes and seminars of the Organization of American States, which has a regional centre for educational television in Mexico. Telecommunications engineers are trained at the Politécnico Nacional in the capital.

Professional associations include: national journalists' associations, sports-writers' associations and a newspaper publishers' chamber; associations of radio and television announcers and of broadcasting personnel and a national radio industry chamber; and a National Film Chamber which groups together studios, laboratories, producers, distributors and exhibitors as well as a Mexican motion-picture producers' and distributors' association and several associations of film directors, technicians, authors, actors, independent cinema owners and other personnel in the industry.

MONTSERRAT

Population	12 000
Area	98 sq. km.

PRESS

Newspapers	Non-dailies 1

RADIO

Transmitters	Medium-wave 3
Total receivers	6000 estimated in use
Receivers per 1000 people	500

FILM

Cinemas	Fixed 1
Total seating capacity	200
Seats per 1000 people	17
Total annual attendance	10 000
Annual visits per capita	0.8

PRESS
One weekly newspaper is published in the capital, Plymouth.

RADIO
Radio Montserrat, begun as a private venture in 1952, then officially constituted as a government service in 1957, now operates a 1kW medium-wave transmitter at Plymouth, which is on the air for about 95 hours a week. Programmes include broadcasts to schools.

A privately owned commercial station, Radio Antilles, with two medium-wave transmitters (250 and 25kW), broadcasts for 19 hours a day in English, French and Spanish.

TELEVISION
Montserrat has no television service of its own but a relay station near Plymouth carries the programmes of station ZAL–TV, Antigua.

The number of television receivers in use is not available. Figures for Montserrat are included in those for Antigua.

FILM
The cinema at Plymouth is equipped for 16mm film only.

NETHERLANDS ANTILLES

Population	230 000
Area	961 sq. km.

PRESS

Newspapers	Dailies 5, Non-dailies 7
Total circulation	Dailies 33 000, Non-dailies 19 000
Copies per 1000 people	Dailies 143, Non-dailies 83

RADIO

Transmitters	Long/medium-wave 10, Short-wave 4
Total receivers	125 000 estimated in use
Receivers per 1000 people	543

TELEVISION

Transmitters	3
Receivers	33 000 estimated in use
Receivers per 1000 people	143

FILM

Cinemas	Fixed 11
Total seating capacity	7000
Seats per 1000 people	30

PRESS

Daily newspapers are published on the two largest of the islands off the Venezuelan coast; the capital, Willemstad, on Curaçao, has two in Dutch, circulating 8000 and 6000 copies respectively, and a third in Spanish and Papiamento (the local lingua franca) with 8700; while Oranjestad, on Aruba, has an almost identical edition (7000 copies) of a Curaçao daily, and another daily in English (3000 copies).

Non-dailies include: on Curaçao, Catholic, trade-union and political-party weeklies, all in Papiamento; on Aruba, Papiamento and English weeklies; on Bonaire, a monthly party organ in Papiamento; and on Sint Maarten, in the Leeward Islands, an English weekly. Circulations range between 1000 and 3500 copies.

Periodicals include: on Curaçao, the government information service's weekly and another irregular information publication (the latter distributed free to 44 000 readers), a weekly broadcasting magazine, all in Papiamento, and a legal quarterly in Dutch; on Aruba, several oil-company house organs in English and Papiamento, two Papiamento and English magazines appearing monthly and twice monthly and a Dutch legal quarterly. Bonaire, in the Leeward Islands, has a monthly party organ in Papiamento.

Some publications are oriented towards tourist visitors who number over 200 000 a year.

NEWS AGENCIES

ANP, which has a branch office in Curaçao, serves press and broadcasting organizations as does the government information service. Broadcasting stations also receive AP news (two stations) and CBS news (one station). Reuters, AFP, AP and UPI are also represented in Willemstad.

RADIO

All domestic radio broadcasting stations are privately owned and supported either by commercial advertising or by donations and subscriptions.

Curaçao has three stations: Radio Curom, owned by a foundation operating commercially but with some government support, broadcasting with one medium-wave (5kW) transmitter for 110 hours a week in Papiamento, Dutch, English and Spanish; Radio Hoyer, a commercial cultural station with two medium-wave transmitters on Curaçao and a third on Bonaire, broadcasting respectively in Spanish and Papiamento, Dutch and English, and in all four languages (the first and third of these services only carrying commercial advertising); and Radio Caribe, a commercial medium-wave (1kW) station, broadcasting for 114 hours a week, mainly in Spanish and Papiamento, but with 3 hours of religious programmes in English on Sundays.

Aruba has four medium-wave stations, three of which (Radio Kelkboom, Radio Antiliana and Voice of Aruba) are commercial stations each broadcasting in three of the four local languages for 97, 143 and 134 hours a week respectively, while the fourth is a Christian mission station, Radio Victoria, whose 10kW transmitter is on the air in all four languages for 104 hours weekly.

On Bonaire, in addition to the two 300kW short-wave transmitters of the Radio Nederland Wereldomroep (Netherlands) relay station and the third transmitter of Radio Hoyer (Curaçao), is the region's most powerful medium-wave transmitter (500kW), as well as the two short-wave transmitters (260 and 50kW), operated by the Christian organization Trans World Radio, which also has a station in Monaco. Trans World Radio is on the air for 110 hours a week on medium wave in English, Spanish, Portuguese, Dutch, Norwegian and French. Its short-wave service, beamed to five target areas in the Americas, the East and Far East and Europe, is on the air for 95 hours a week in Arabic, Armenian, Czech, English, French, German, Hungarian, Norwegian, Polish, Portuguese, Romanian, Russian, Serbo-Croat and Spanish.

Saba, in the Leeward Islands, is reported to have a commercial station, opened in 1972.

No licence fee is payable for radio receivers.

TELEVISION

Curaçao and Aruba both have a television station (525 lines): Tele-Curaçao, founded in 1960, which is on the air for 54 hours a week, and Tele-Aruba, founded in 1963, broadcasting for 51 hours a week. Both stations, while commercially operated corporations, are under government ownership and are partly financed by subsidies.

A Venezuelan station, Radio Caracas Televisión, also has a repeater station on Curaçao.

Islands in the Leeward group are within receiving range of transmitters from neighbouring islands. Over 70% of homes on Curaçao and Aruba have television receivers.

The majority of programmes are imported, mainly from the USA and the Netherlands. Languages used are Dutch, English, Papiamento and Spanish.

FILM

There is a Government Film Production Department based in Willemstad. Films shown in commercial cinemas are all imported. Aruba has a drive-in cinema.

NICARAGUA

| Population | 1 990 000 |
| Area | 130 000 sq. km. |

PRESS
Newspapers	Dailies 4
Total circulation	Dailies 76 600
Copies per 1000 people	Dailies 38

RADIO
Transmitters	Long/medium-wave 67, Short-wave 11, VHF–FM 59
Total receivers	115 000 estimated in use
Receivers per 1000 people	58

TELEVISION
Transmitters	7
Receivers	60 000 estimated in use
Receivers per 1000 people	30

FILM
Cinemas	Fixed 104
Total seating capacity	60 000
Seats per 1000 people	30
Total annual attendance	9 987 000
Annual visits per capita	5

PRESS

By March 1973, the country's two largest dailies, published in the capital, Managua, had resumed publication after the earthquake of 23 December 1972. One, an evening paper, circulates 30 000 copies, the other 20 000, rising to

35 000 and 29 000 respectively at week-ends. Other dailies appear in Leon and Granada. All are in Spanish and are privately owned. Non-dailies include three weeklies (one in Leon and two in Managua).

No figures are available for other periodicals.

NEWS AGENCIES

There is no national agency. The main dailies receive domestic news from their own correspondents and from government press services, and for foreign news subscribe to AP, UPI and AFP, all of which are represented in the capital.

RADIO

All broadcasting is supervised by the Government's Dirección General de Radio y Televisión.

All radio stations are commercially owned and operated, with the exception of: the government station, Radiodifusión Nacional, which broadcasts for 19 hours a day on medium-wave (40kW), short-wave (100kW) and FM transmitters located in Managua; the Christian mission station, Ondas de Luz, which is on the air almost continuously in Spanish and some English, with medium-wave, short-wave and FM transmitters; and one cultural station.

Most of the commercial stations are associated with one or other of two main networks and some also relay the programmes of networks in the USA. Spanish is the main language used but some English-language programmes are also broadcast.

TELEVISION

The first telecasts were made in 1956 by the commercial station, Televisión de Nicaragua, which is now on the air for 8 hours a day. Three other privately owned stations are also based in Managua, one with a translator in Chinandega. Apart from advertising (on which all stations depend for their financial resources), programmes consist, on average, of about 90% entertainment, 8% educational and cultural broadcasts and 2% news. Around 50% of programmes are imported from the USA.

The definition system used is 525 lines.

FILM

Apart from occasional short newsfilms, there is no local film production. Of the 500 feature films imported annually, about 75% come from the USA and others from Mexico, Argentina and European countries.

Foreign diplomatic missions organize public and school film showings. The United States Information Agency and the Alliance Française, in particular, maintain cultural and educational film libraries. Both the number of commercial cinemas and their overall annual attendance figures have increased by about 20% over the last ten years.

SPACE COMMUNICATIONS

An Atlantic Intelsat earth station at Managua was opened in October 1972.

PROFESSIONAL TRAINING AND ASSOCIATIONS

The Universidad Nacional Autónoma in Managua offers a four-year diploma course in press, radio and television journalism at its school of journalism, established in 1960. In 1970, 36 students graduated.

Media associations include two journalists' and writers' associations, associations of radio and television stations, and a broadcasting professionals' association.

PANAMA

Population	1 520 000
Area	75 650 sq. km.

PRESS
Newspapers	Dailies 7, Non-dailies 11
Total circulation	Dailies 130 000
Copies per 1000 people	Dailies 86

RADIO
Transmitters	Long/medium-wave 73, Short-wave 4, VHF—FM 37
Total receivers	500 000 estimated in use
Receivers per 1000 people	329

TELEVISION
Transmitters	13
Receivers	125 000 estimated in use
Receivers per 1000 people	82

FILM
Cinemas	Fixed 23
Total seating capacity	28 400
Seats per 1000 people	19
Total annual attendance	5 000 000
Annual visits per capita	3

PRESS

Daily newspapers published in Panama City include one with separate morning and afternoon editions and two (in Spanish) which have associated English-language editions. Circulations ranging from 8000 to 27 000 copies per issue include a number of readers outside the capital (and in the Canal Zone) since the larger papers are flown daily to the Atlantic port of Colon and to the main provincial cities.

Among non-daily newspapers are several Sunday editions of Panama City dailies. One weekly with a Spanish supplement caters for the large British West Indian community in Panama. Periodicals other than newspapers number 143, mostly published in Panama City. In addition to general information magazines (43 titles) the main subject fields covered are education (16 titles), trade and communications (15 titles), law and public administration (9 titles), the arts and sport (7 titles each), etc. Monthly surveys on various fields of interest are published by the Chamber of Commerce, and there are two literary periodicals, one of which (in Spanish and English) prints 7000 copies per issue.

NEWS AGENCIES

Panama has no news agency of its own, and newspapers obtain their domestic news from their own correspondents. Foreign news for press, radio and television is obtained from outside sources, including AP, Reuters, ANSA, UPI, DPA, AFP, *Toronto Telegram, Latin American Report*, AMEX, NBC, *Orbe latino-americano*, TASS, Efe, etc. Efe has its Central American office in Panama City.

RADIO

The government authority with overall responsibility for broadcasting is the Dirección Tecnica de Telecomunicaciones. All stations are affiliated to the Asociación Panameña de Radiodifusión. The only government station is operated by a subsidized but autonomous cultural institute. Of the privately owned stations, 53 are commercially operated, one belongs to a church in Santiago and one to the World Missionary Radio Fellowship which has other stations in Latin America. Two commercial stations are powered with 10kW medium-wave transmitters, the two religious stations with 5kW each and the remainder mostly with 1kW or less. In all, there are 72 medium-wave, 37 VHF–FM and 4 short-wave transmitters in Panama.

Total broadcasting time amounts to 2458 hours a week, consisting of light entertainment (1256 hours), advertising (547 hours), news and information (360 hours), arts, letters and science (132 hours), religious, women's and youth programmes (131 hours), education (28 hours) and broadcasts for ethnic minorities (4 hours). Many programmes are relayed or rebroadcast from USA and European broadcasting organizations. Since 1949, all schools have been provided with receivers enabling them to listen to government educational programmes broadcast on air-time provided free by some of the larger private stations. Some of these stations also broadcast to foreign countries.

No licence fee is payable for radio receivers.

TELEVISION

The country's two television networks are both privately owned commercial companies. The larger, Circuito RPC-Televisión, which also owns a number of radio stations, was the first to broadcast public television programmes in Panama, in 1959. It now operates seven television stations in Panama City and provincial centres. Televisora Nacional has a main station in Panama City and three repeaters in provincial centres. Both derive their income from advertising, their programmes being imported mainly from the USA, Mexico, Peru, Argentina, Spain, Italy, Puerto Rico and Japan. RPC exchanges programmes with stations in Mexico, Peru, Costa Rica, Nicaragua and Guatemala, while Televisora Nacional has exchanges with Ecuador, the Dominican Republic and Honduras. Together, the two networks are on the air for 180 hours a week, broadcasting on 525-line definition and covering practically all populated areas of the country. The number of receivers has increased more than tenfold since 1960.

FILM
Of the 13 films produced in 1969, 12 were short films commissioned by the Government, which also seeks to encourage production by subsidizing films made in the country. Of the country's 12 importer–distributors, six supply mainly television films. Feature films are imported mainly from the USA and also from Mexico, the UK and other Latin American and European countries.

SPACE COMMUNICATIONS
Panama has an Atlantic Intelsat earth station at Utive, which began operating in 1968.

PROFESSIONAL TRAINING AND ASSOCIATIONS
The Escuela de Communicación Social (originally Escuela de Periodismo) of the University of Panama, founded in 1960, awards a diploma in journalism after four years' post-baccalaureate study. In 1971–2 there were 46 students, of whom 17 graduated.

Media associations include a journalists' union (founded in 1949), an association of licensed broadcasting stations and (since 1957) an association of broadcasting announcers.

PUERTO RICO

Population	2 757 000
Area	8897 sq. km.

PRESS

Newspapers	Dailies 3, Non-dailies 10
Total circulation	Dailies 246 000
Copies per 1000 people	Dailies 89

RADIO

Transmitters	Medium-wave 60, VHF–FM 17
Total receivers	2 100 000 estimated in use
Receivers per 1000 people	762

TELEVISION

Transmitters	17
Receivers	600 000 estimated in use
Receivers per 1000 people	218

FILM

Cinemas	Fixed 168
Total annual attendance	9 000 000
Annual visits per capita	3

PRESS

The two largest dailies, together circulating 190 000 copies, are published in Spanish in the capital, San Juan, and in the city of Ponce, while a third (56 000 copies), also based in San Juan, is published in English. Spanish is the official and main language of Puerto Rico, but about 15% of the population also use English. Newspapers and periodicals from the USA have considerable readerships among both local residents and tourist visitors who total over 1 million annually.

Non-daily general interest newspapers include several weeklies, a fortnightly and two monthlies, all in Spanish, a weekly government newsletter in separate English and Spanish editions and an English-language weekly. Periodicals total about 60, many of them quarterlies, covering general interest, literary and cultural, educational, sociological, religious, legal and technical fields. In addition, there are a large number of parish, school and house magazines.

NEWS AGENCIES

There is no local news agency. The press and broadcasting stations depend almost entirely on AP and UPI services for domestic and overseas news.

RADIO

All stations are commercially run, with the exception of the educational station WIPR (with one 10kW medium-wave and one FM transmitter) which is operated by the Department of Education, and a Christian missionary station operated by the same mission as Radio Lumière in Haiti. Most stations are on the air for about 17 hours daily though a few broadcast for 24 hours using mainly Spanish but also English. Stations are located in all sizable towns, and radio coverage of the island is complete.

The United States Armed Forces Radio and Television Service operates medium-wave transmitters at Aguadilla and San Juan.

No licence fee is payable for receivers, the number in use having quadrupled over the last ten years.

TELEVISION

The first television broadcasts were made in 1954 when two commercial stations began operation in San Juan. Now there are 14 stations serving the main population centres, all commercial and all broadcasting in colour, except for two educational stations operated by the Department of Education at Hato Rey and Mayaguez. A number of stations are affiliated with other media interests in

Puerto Rico and the USA. Most are supplied with news by AP or UPI wire services and UPI or network newsfilm services. The definition system used is 525 lines.

No licence fee is payable for television receivers which have more than quadrupled in number over the last decade.

FILM

The Ministry of Community Development has a film unit which produces a number of documentaries principally for use in its own community-education programmes.

Feature films shown in commercial cinemas are imported, mainly from the USA and also from Mexico, Spain, Argentina, the UK and Italy, and are distributed by some 20 distribution organizations. A Film Board of Trade is the official body responsible for the oversight of the industry.

SPACE COMMUNICATIONS

An earth station for Atlantic Intelsat transmissions, at Cayey, was opened in January 1969.

PROFESSIONAL ASSOCIATIONS

There are professional associations of journalists, radio and television personnel and motion-picture operators. The Broadcasters' Association of Puerto Rico, grouping together radio- and television-station owners and operators, has about 50 members.

ST KITTS-NEVIS AND ANGUILLA

Population	62 000
Area	357 sq. km.

PRESS	
Newspapers	Dailies 1, Non-dailies 2
Total circulation	Dailies 1200
Copies per 1000 people	Dailies 19

RADIO	
Transmitters	Medium-wave 2

FILM

Cinemas	Fixed 2
Total seating capacity	1000
Seats per 1000 people	16
Total annual attendance	70 000
Annual visits per capita	1

PRESS

One daily newspaper, the official organ of a trade and labour union, circulating about 1200 copies per issue, and one weekly are published in Basseterre, capital of St Kitts. A weekly newsletter is printed in Anguilla.

RADIO

The government commercial station, Radio Ziz, at Basseterre, St Kitts, operates one 3kW medium-wave transmitter which broadcasts in English, for 17 hours daily. Also on St Kitts is Radio Paradise, a religious station transferred in 1972 from the Netherlands Antilles.

Anguilla has a British Government-operated station, Radio Anguilla (0.5kW), broadcasting in English on medium wave for nine hours daily.

ST LUCIA

Population	103 000
Area	616 sq. km.

PRESS

Newspapers	Non-dailies 3

RADIO

Transmitters	Medium-wave 3
Total receivers	40 000 estimated in use
Receivers per 1000 people	388

TELEVISION

Transmitters	1*
Receivers	2300 estimated in use
Receivers per 1000 people	22

FILM

Cinemas	Fixed 9
Total seating capacity	9500
Seats per 1000 people	92

*Experimental

PRESS
Three newspapers published in English in the capital, Castries, appear respectively twice-weekly (9000 copies per issue), weekly and fortnightly. There are also two periodicals (one religious, one agricultural).

NEWS AGENCIES
Reuters' Caribbean service is received by the television station. A Caribbean news agency now in the process of formation is expected to serve the press and broadcasting stations.

RADIO
Radio St Lucia, the government-sponsored station, autonomous since the dissolution of the Windward Islands Broadcasting Service at the end of 1972, operates two medium-wave transmitters (10 and 0.25kW) at Castries, broadcasting in English for 16 hours a day.

A commercial station, Radio Caribbean, with one 10kW medium-wave transmitter, broadcasts a home service in English (6½ hours a day) and French (10½ hours a day).

Programmes for both stations, totalling about 210 hours a week, consist of light entertainment (125 hours), news and information (67 hours), advertising (8 hours), cultural programmes (7 hours), broadcasts for special audiences (2 hours) and education (1½ hours). The majority of programmes are of local origin.

TELEVISION
An experimental privately owned station, St Lucia Television Service (SLTV), relaying CBC–TV Barbados and carrying some locally originated programmes, is on the air for 11 hours a week, some of the time in colour (NSTC system). Programmes are imported from the USA and the UK.

FILM
There is no film production. Imported films from the USA and UK principally are shown by the country's nine fixed and two mobile cinemas.

ST PIERRE AND MIQUELON

Population	5000
Area	242 sq. km.

RADIO

Transmitters	Medium-wave 1
Total receivers	2800 licences
Licences per 1000 people	560

TELEVISION

Transmitters	3
Receivers	1500 licences
Receivers per 1000 people	300

FILM

Cinemas	Fixed 3
Total seating capacity	900
Seats per 1000 people	180
Total annual attendance	10 000
Annual visits per capita	2

PRESS
An official gazette carrying some general news is published twice monthly in St Pierre. French and Canadian papers are also received.

NEWS AGENCIES
AFP and CP have part-time correspondents in St Pierre.

RADIO
The broadcasting service is provided by regional radio and television stations of the French Office de Radiodiffusion Télévision (ORTF).

The radio service based in St Pierre, with one 4kW medium-wave transmitter covering the entire population, is on the air for 64 hours a week, in French, broadcasting light entertainment (40 hours), news and information (12 hours), arts, letters and science (12 hours), broadcasts for special audiences (4 hours) and education (1½ hours). About 20 hours consist of imported programmes mainly from ORTF in Paris.

A receiver licence fee is payable.

TELEVISION
The ORTF station, opened in 1967, now operates one main transmitter (625 lines) in St Pierre, with two relay transmitters on other islands. Programmes, broadcast for 22 hours a week (daily except Monday), are largely supplied from Paris by ORTF and consist mainly of light entertainment (10 hours), news and

information (5½ hours), arts, letters and science (2 hours) and broadcasts for special audiences (2 hours).
About 1500 receivers are licensed.

FILM

The three cinemas show mainly French and American films imported from Canada at the rate of about 120 features and 100 documentaries a year.

ST VINCENT

Population	90 000
Area	388 sq. km.

PRESS	
Newspapers	Non-dailies 1
Total circulation	Non-dailies 15 000
Copies per 1000 people	Non-dailies 167

RADIO	
Transmitters	Medium-wave 2

PRESS

The one weekly newspaper is published in Kingstown, as is an occasional government information bulletin.

RADIO

Formerly part of the Windward Islands Broadcasting Service, Radio St Vincent now broadcasts for about 16 hours a day via medium-wave transmitters at Kingstown and Chateaubelair. Programmes include local and regional news, and relays of BBC (UK) and Radios Grenada, Dominica and St Lucia, as well as request and other recorded programmes, religious and children's programmes, etc.

TRINIDAD AND TOBAGO

Population	1 040 000
Area	5128 sq. km.

PRESS

Newspapers	Dailies 3, Non-dailies 7
Total circulation	Dailies 145 000
Copies per 1000 people	Dailies 139

RADIO

Transmitters	Long/medium-wave 2, VHF–FM 2
Total receivers	293 000* estimated in use
Receivers per 1000 people	282

TELEVISION

Transmitters	3
Receivers	82 000 estimated in use
Receivers per 1000 people	79

FILM

Cinemas	Fixed 66
Total seating capacity	42 100
Seats per 1000 people	40
Total annual attendance	8 400 000
Annual visits per capita	8

*Including wired receivers.

PRESS

Daily newspapers are published in the capital, Port of Spain. One morning and one evening paper, established in 1917 and 1936 and circulating 55 000 and 50 000 copies respectively, are under the same ownership and management. The third daily, more recently established (in 1967), is a morning paper. Both morning papers have Sunday editions, the larger of the two, which also circulates in other islands of the eastern Caribbean, exceeding 90 000 copies per issue. In addition to these Sunday papers, there are four other privately owned weeklies (with a combined circulation of around 50 000 copies) as well as a weekly government gazette. One of the weeklies is in Chinese but, otherwise, all papers are published in English, which is the official and generally used language. Newspapers are also imported from the USA, Canada and the UK.

About 24 other periodicals are published, mainly monthlies and quarterlies, dealing with social, religious, legal, commercial and cultural subjects, sports, medicine, agriculture, etc.

NEWS AGENCIES

The larger papers have their own correspondents supplying local news, but Reuters' Caribbean service (which has a resident part-time correspondent in Trinidad) is the principal news source. Other international sources are UPI and AP, as well as ADN and the official information services of the United Nations, the USA and UK. Broadcasting stations use CBS News (New York) and UPI Television News (London) services. A Caribbean regional news agency is in process of formation.

RADIO

Bought by the Government in 1969 and now operated by an officially appointed board of directors, the national (commercial) station, Radio 610 began broadcasting in October 1957 under private ownership. With a 10kW medium-wave transmitter and a 0.25kW FM transmitter, both in Port of Spain, it broadcasts a home service in English for 119 hours a week including 10½ hours of Government Public Relations Division programmes, and relays of seven BBC (UK) world-service news bulletins daily. It is financed from advertising revenue.

Radio Trinidad, which was the island's first wireless broadcasting service, established in 1947, is owned and operated by the Trinidad Broadcasting Company Ltd, a subsidiary of Rediffusion (Trinidad) Ltd, which is itself a subsidiary of Rediffusion Ltd (UK). Its revenue is derived from advertising. With a 20kW medium-wave transmitter covering the whole of Trinidad and Tobago, as well as the neighbouring Windward and Leeward Islands, and a 1kW FM transmitter serving the Port of Spain area, Radio Trinidad is on the air for 130 hours a week, in English. Its programmes include frequent news bulletins, Government Public Relations Division programmes (10½ hours weekly), school broadcasts (six 15-minute sessions weekly), in addition to entertainment, cultural broadcasts, etc.

Radio Trinidad is also relayed on one of Rediffusion (Trinidad) Ltd's two wired programmes with centres in Port of Spain, San Juan and San Fernando, the other programme consisting of a combination of locally originated programmes and relays. Both are transmitted for 17 hours a day, serving 6700 subscribers.

The number of radio receivers in use has more than trebled over the last ten years.

TELEVISION

In 1961, a licence was granted to the Trinidad and Tobago Television Service, owned by a consortium in which the Government and the Columbia Broadcasting System (USA) had minority interests, to operate a television station. The station began broadcasting in 1962. In 1969, it was purchased by the Government with CBS retaining a minority (10%) shareholding, and now operates as the Trinidad and Tobago Television Company Ltd (TTT) under the same board of directors as Radio 610.

Its transmitters serve Port of Spain and the surrounding areas and the island of Tobago. Programmes total over 73 hours a week and include feature films (37 hours), broadcasts for community groups, designed to contribute to the Government's adult education campaign (13½ hours), news and information (9 hours), programmes for special audiences (5 hours), other light entertainment (3½ hours), literature and arts (3 hours), in addition to commercial and sponsored programmes. Imported programmes, which represent 70% of total broadcasting time, come mainly from the USA, UK, Canada, Australia and the Federal Republic of Germany.

FILM

Documentary and educational short films are produced (at the rate of four or five a year) by the Public Relations Division's film unit, under the Prime Minister's Office.

All feature films shown in fixed cinemas and the country's four drive-ins are imported (mainly from the USA, India, the UK and Italy), as are the majority of the documentary and instructional films shown non-commercially by the Government's fleet of 13 mobile projection units.

SPACE COMMUNICATIONS

An Atlantic Intelsat earth station, jointly owned by the Government and Cable and Wireless (West Indies) Ltd, located at Matura Point on the east coast of Trinidad, has been in operation since November 1971.

PROFESSIONAL TRAINING AND ASSOCIATIONS

Most journalists are trained on the job. Graphic arts training (a four-year course) is available at the John Donaldson Technical Institute, Port of Spain. The University of the West Indies, which offers courses in electrical engineering at its St Augustine campus in Trinidad, also has a Unesco-sponsored project for training in the educational use of multimedia audio-visual aids.

Membership of the Caribbean Publishers and Broadcasters Association (CPBA), based in Port of Spain, includes most major and some smaller newspapers and radio and television stations of the region. CPBA promotes the interests of its members and the development of the media, facilitating exchanges, news supplies, training, etc.

TURKS AND CAICOS ISLANDS

Population	6000
Area	430 sq. km.

PRESS

Newspapers	Non-dailies 1
Total circulation	Non-dailies 1600
Copies per 1000 people	Non-dailies 267

RADIO

Transmitters	Short-wave 1
Total receivers	1350 estimated in use
Receivers per 1000 people	225

FILM

Cinemas	Fixed 1
Total seating capacity	200
Seats per 1000 people	33
Total annual attendance	5000
Annual visits per capita	0.8

PRESS

A privately owned weekly duplicated news-sheet has been published since late 1970.

RADIO

A privately owned station, VS18, with one 0.75kW short-wave transmitter on Grand Turk, is on the air for 1½ hours every evening. A daily government broadcast including official notices, paid announcements and Reuters press releases is carried by courtesy of the station owners.

UNITED STATES OF AMERICA

Population	208 840 000
Area	9 363 353 sq. km.

PRESS

Newspapers	Dailies 1761, Non-dailies 10 100*
Total circulation	Dailies 65 510 000, Non-dailies 79 834 000*
Copies per 1000 people	Dailies 314, Non-dailies 382

RADIO

Transmitters	Long/medium-wave 4306, Short-wave 61, VHF–FM 2352
Total receivers	354 000 000 estimated in use
Receivers per 1000 people	1695

TELEVISION

Transmitters	3695†
Receivers	98 600 000 estimated in use
Receivers per 1000 people	472

FILM

Cinemas	Fixed 14 300‡
Total seating capacity	10 000 000
Seats per 1000 people	48
Total annual attendance	920 600 000
Annual visits per capita	5

*Including 590 Sunday newspapers circulating 49 664 600 copies.
†Including 1915 VHF and 865 UHF television translators at 1 July 1972.
‡Including 4600 drive-ins.

PRESS

More newspapers and periodicals are published in the USA than in any other country in the world. Apart from the few major-city dailies which have influential (though restricted) country-wide and international readerships, there are no national dailies as the term is generally understood. In a country spanning as many as six time zones, and where the remotest newspaper can subscribe to one or more wire and news services, the press remains typically local in character.

The overall number of United States daily newspapers has varied little over the last decade (1761 titles in 1972 as compared with 1763 in 1961), though the number of towns served by dailies has increased from 1460 to over 1500 (or even 1600 if those served by the inter-city dailies which circulate in two or more adjacent non-metropolitan cities are counted). This extension of daily coverage has taken place very largely as a result of the disappearance of competitive titles in communities served by several dailies and through the establishment of new titles in communities previously without a local daily service.

The daily ownership pattern now shows around 85% of these 1500 cities and towns as having one daily only, a further 12% with one morning and one evening paper under the same ownership and a few others with dailies under separate ownership but pooling their production and/or business operations. Only in cities of over 650 000 population are two or more competing dailies now to be found. Over 900 dailies in 1971 were owned by 155 groups (a group being defined as two or more dailies in different cities under the same ownership or control) as compared with 560 dailies owned by 109 groups in 1961. The half-dozen largest groups control between 18 and 33 titles each (though none controls more than 6% of the total daily circulation or 10% of the Sunday circulation).

Overall daily circulation figures have increased by 3 million over the last ten years, though the increase has not kept pace with the growth in population, and there are now 24 fewer copies per 1000 persons than in 1961. It is estimated that 78% of the population aged 18 years or more read at least one daily paper.

Circulation growth has been slightly more marked for morning than for evening papers. The 337 morning dailies have a combined circulation of 26 million copies, and the 1441 evening dailies 36.4 million. (The difference between the total number of evening plus morning dailies and the total of all dailies is accounted for by the fact that some papers publish both morning and evening editions under the same name.) One New York City (morning) daily exceeds 2 million copies per issue, and others circulate 814 000, 606 000, 518 000 (a financial paper) and 429 000. Los Angeles has morning and evening dailies circulating 980 000 and 506 000 copies respectively. Chicago's two large morning papers circulate 745 000 and 546 000 copies, and its two main evening papers 452 000 and 439 000. Other cities with dailies circulating more than 400 000 copies are Detroit (650 000 and 574 000), Philadelphia (613 000 and 453 000), Washington DC (510 000), San Francisco (457 000) and Cleveland (409 000), while a further 20 cities have one or more dailies which exceed the 200 000 mark.

Of the nation's 590 Sunday newspapers, circulating around 49.6 million copies, there are some 40 with individual circulations of 300 000 or more, the four largest being published in New York City (2.9 million and 1.4 million), Los Angeles (1.1 million) and Chicago (993 000). In addition, there are over 9000 weekly, semi-weekly and bi-weekly general interest papers, including the 177 black newspapers (mostly weeklies), the 68 American Indian papers and the 250 newspapers published in over 30 foreign languages.

The content of morning, evening and Sunday newspapers averages about 36% news to 64% advertising while the average number of pages per issue for each of these categories is around 57, 55 and 176 respectively.

Of the country's 9573 periodicals published mainly in English but also in 34 foreign languages, 4314 are monthlies, mostly of specialized interest. The top dozen mass readership magazines with individual circulation totals of over 5 million copies per issue include a general interest publication circulating 17.9 million copies in the USA alone, a television weekly (15.4 million), six women's and home magazines and one geographical magazine, while a further 30 magazines circulate over 1 million copies each per issue. Rising costs and the competition of other media have caused the disappearance or reduced frequency of many mass readership magazines. Others have cut down on page size or increased their advertising volume. A number have moved into the field of the electronic media as well – there are now some 650 radio and 190 television stations throughout the country owned by newspapers and magazine publishers; in 72 metropolitan areas the only broadcasting stations are owned by the only local newspaper.

Newsprint consumption, totalling 6.6 million metric tons at the beginning of the sixties has risen in ten years to 8.9 million metric tons, of which 3 million metric tons are domestically produced (domestic production in 1960 was 1.8 million metric tons).

NEWS AGENCIES

Two of the world's largest news agencies, which provide national and international news reports at home and abroad, are headquartered in New York City: Associated Press (AP) and United Press International (UPI).

Founded in 1848, AP is a cooperative venture owned by its American newspaper members. Within the United States, costs are shared by the members under a fixed formula, and the members in turn contribute their news and photos to the agency. It currently has more than 10 000 subscribers in some 107 countries, more than half of them overseas. United States members include 1264 newspapers and 3285 broadcasting (radio and television) outlets. AP employs 3300 persons in 107 United States and 62 overseas bureaux. In addition, there are individual AP correspondents at many other overseas non-bureau points.

Arrangements with TASS and AFP supplement AP's own reporting in their areas. It also receives Canadian domestic news from CP to which it supplies its full service, and other agreements have been made with other agencies.

The London and Tokyo desks serve as relay centres for news and photos for the general headquarters in New York. London is connected with the capitals and major cities of Europe through AP's European circuit. London also serves as the relay station for news from the Middle East, the Indian subcontinent, Africa and Australia. New York and London communicate 24 hours a day. The Tokyo desk is the news-collection point for the Far East, and it relays to New York. Besides cables, the agency makes extensive use of satellites. Using the cathode-ray tube, AP bureaux can now report, edit and transmit automatically.

The other big agency, UPI, was formed when United Press (founded in 1907) and International News Service merged in 1958. UPI has 6417 subscribers including 3598 radio and television stations. It operates in 114 countries with more than 10 000 employees working from 238 bureaux. A new automatic communication system introduced in 1971 links Asia with the United States and European circuits, and since 1972, the agency has been operating its new information storage and retrieval system to handle news gathering, editing and transmitting automatically. Some 4½ million words of copy are transmitted every day, some of which is translated into various languages. In all, 48 languages are used.

UPI or its affiliates conduct a variety of communications operations including a world-wide news film service (UPITN, jointly owned with the British company Independent Television News), a wireless news bulletin for ships at sea, computerized stock-market lists for teletypesetter transmission, and a feature service which supplies comic strips, columns, cartoons and non-fiction series to newspapers throughout the world.

As distinct from a news agency which collects news for its clients, there are several hundred news services which distribute stories already written to subscribing publishers. A major news service is provided by the *New York Times* which sells its news and columns to 350 clients in 40 countries. Transmitting by cable exclusively, the Times News Service operates for 14 hours a day and moves an average of 35 000 words in that period. Since it is a service growing out of the newspaper's regular reporting, it lists no employees as such, its operations being handled by employees of the newspaper itself. Another newspaper-based news service links two dailies transcontinentally — the *Washington Post* and the *Los Angeles Times* — which joined forces in 1962. Starting with 34 clients, the Los Angeles Times–Washington Post News Service now has 225 clients, 100 of them outside the United States in 43 different countries. While the service makes use of the reporters of both newspapers, it also employs 30 others who operate bureaux in Washington, Los Angeles, London and Paris. Like the Times News Service, it transmits an average of 35 000 words every day.

In addition to these international-scale agencies, there are several hundred relatively smaller news, feature and photo agencies in the USA (though some are of considerable size), often with regional or specialized interests, serving all communications media; and a number of major newspapers also syndicate their own material.

Most of the larger foreign news agencies have bureaux in New York City (also covering United Nations affairs) or Washington, and nearly all agencies maintain one or more regular correspondents in the United States.

RADIO

Regular commercially licensed sound broadcasting in the United States began in 1920. With the rapid and competitive development of broadcasting, the Government was obliged to introduce regulatory legislation, the main enactments being the 1927 Radio Act and the 1934 Communications Act establishing the Federal Communications Commission (FCC) which now regulates all radio and television broadcasting activities in the country. The FCC's functions include the assignment of frequencies, the granting and renewal of station licences, the classification, location and operation of stations, and the formulation of regulations for network stations 'as public convenience, interest or necessity requires'. It is also responsible for limiting the number of stations which any single individual or organization may own or control (eg no more than 7 AM, 6 FM or 5 television stations, and no more than 1 commercial radio and 1 commercial television station in the same city).

Approximately 93% of all radio stations are privately owned and gain their revenue from advertising. These commercial stations, in 1972, numbered 6719 (4367 AM and 2352 FM) serving local communities throughout the entire national territory (the licensing and programming objectives of the FCC include the equitable distribution of radio service, the provision of opportunity for local self-expression and for the development of local talent, and the satisfaction of a variety of programme interests). Many of these stations, however, are also affiliated with one or other of the four national networks by means of contracts whereby (subject to FCC regulations) they are remunerated for carrying the network's programmes (including advertising for the sponsors of those programmes). Advertising time, which is not quantitatively limited by the FCC, is voluntarily restricted by members of the large National Association of Broadcasters to 16 or 10 minutes per prime or non-prime hour respectively.

Over 2300 commercial stations are affiliated to the big networks: over 1250 to the American Broadcasting Company (ABC)'s four programme networks, 246 to the Columbia Broadcasting System (CBS), 236 to the National Broadcasting Company (NBC) and 581 to the Mutual Broadcasting System (MBS). In addition, there are 135 regional radio networks or groups constituting from 3 to 70 or more stations. Some 325 AM and 170 FM radio stations are owned by newspaper and magazine publishers.

Non-commercial radio consists almost entirely of FM stations (549 in 1972), most of them operated by colleges, universities and public authorities for educational purposes and variously financed from public and private funds, subscriptions and some permitted advertising revenue. Over 100 of these stations are linked nationally by the National Public Radio Agency which receives funds from the Corporation for Public Broadcasting set up under the Public Broadcasting Act of 1967. The corporation is not a federal agency but it is financed by federal government and private funds. Its purpose is to provide leadership and finance for the development and improvement of a system of educational and cultural radio and television for the public as a whole.

During the last ten years, the number of radio receivers in use has almost doubled. Of the total number, over 250 million are in 64.1 million homes (95% of all households), around 90 million in cars and a further 10 million in public places.

International short-wave broadcasting is mainly conducted by the Voice of America (VOA), the broadcasting service of the United States Information Agency (USIA), reaching world audiences estimated to total up to 26 million persons on an average day. Its total transmitting power of 23 000kW includes 18 short-wave transmitters of 50, 250 and 500kW at Greenville (North Carolina), six of 175 and 250kW at Bethany (Ohio), eight of 50, 100, 200 and 250kW at Delano and Dixon (California) and one 50kW medium-wave transmitter at Marathon (Florida), as well as 60 overseas relay transmitters in the Federal Republic of Germany, Greece, Liberia, Morocco, Philippines, Ryukyu Islands, Sri Lanka, the UK and Republic of Vietnam. The VOA also has seven transportable transmitters all of 50kW (six medium- and one short-wave). The VOA is heard in 35 regularly scheduled languages (other languages are specially programmed) and is on the air for 805 hours a week, apart from programme material supplied, in the form of tapes or direct relays, to local stations overseas.

International broadcasting is also conducted by Radio New York Worldwide, a private company with a 100kW short-wave transmitter whose programmes in English and Spanish are beamed to Europe and the Americas; and by the International Broadcasting Station KGEI, a non-commercial Christian organization owned and operated by the Far East Broadcasting Company, which broadcasts programmes from Belmont (California), in English, German, Russian, Spanish and Portuguese, on 50 to 250kW beamed to Latin America and other areas and relayed by its stations in the Philippines, Okinawa, Japan, Indonesia and the Seychelles.

The Armed Forces Radio and Television Service broadcasts news and a variety of other programmes in English (from the commercial domestic networks) to the local transmitters operated by United States forces stationed abroad via its short-wave transmitters on the Atlantic and Pacific coasts and a relay transmitter in the Philippines.

The United Nations Office of Public Information in New York, leasing transmission time on the United States Government's short-wave transmitters at Greenville, Bethany and Dixon and also on its overseas relay transmitters in Morocco, Liberia and the Philippines, broadcasts regular 30- or 15-minute information programmes for five days a week in English, French, Spanish, Greek, Italian, Turkish, Arabic, Somali, Swahili, Chinese, Tagalog, Thai and Indonesian to 12 target areas throughout the world. Meetings of the Security Council are also broadcast in English, French and Spanish from the Greenville and Bethany transmitters during Council sessions. In addition, recorded programmes prepared and distributed by the United Nation's radio and visual services division, are broadcast by stations in more than 120 countries and territories, in 27 languages (Amharic, Arabic, Bengali, Chinese, Duri, English, French, Greek, Hebrew, Hindi, Hungarian, Italian, Malay, Malgache, Persian, Polish, Portuguese, Pushtu, Russian, Somali, Spanish, Swahili, Shqiptar, Tagalog, Thai, Turkish and Urdu).

The Organization of American States also broadcasts a 45-minute daily programme beamed to Central and South America, using VOA facilities at Greenville.

TELEVISION

Telecasting began on an experimental basis in the United States in the 1920s. By 1950, there were 97 stations on the air and 6 million receivers. By the end of 1962, stations had increased in number to 607 (including 59 educational) and the total number of receivers to 60 million. Ten years later, there were 915 stations (including 214 educational) plus 2780 translators and 98.6 million sets in use in 64.8 million (95%) of the nation's homes. Some 37 million of these homes have colour television, the system adopted being that proposed by a National Television System Committee (NTSC) and accepted by the FCC in 1953. Average viewing time for television-equipped homes is estimated at 6 hours 20 minutes per home per day.

The main functions of the Federal Communications Commission (FCC), which regulates all broadcasting activities in the United States, both radio and television, are as described under Radio (above).

About 76% (701) of all stations are commercially owned and operated, some (178) of these being owned by newspapers and/or magazines. In view of the high production costs in television, almost all commercial stations are affiliated to a network, of which the three main largest, the Columbia Broadcasting System (CBS), National Broadcasting Corporation (NBC) and American Broadcasting Company (ABC) – each with five fully owned and operated VHF stations (the maximum permitted number) in major cities – respectively served 192, 219 and 250 television affiliates in 1972. Affiliation is by (renewable) contract under FCC regulations as described under Radio (above).

In a typical week, around 66% of affiliated stations' programming is supplied by the networks. Network affiliates are on the air for an average of 122 hours weekly and non-network stations for 79 hours weekly, carrying 10% and 18% respectively of local live programming. There are also 23 regional television networks. Most network and commercial programmes are devoted to entertainment (drama, variety and films), which represents about 70% of total output. The remainder is extremely varied and, on average, may be classed as follows in descending order of broadcasting time: sport, broadcasts for children, news and public affairs, music, cultural programmes, religion and programmes for women.

The 220 non-commercial educational stations, located in 47 of the 50 states, cover more than 80% of the nation's population. Some are on the air for only a few hours a day, while one broadcasts 80 hours weekly. Some are operated by colleges and universities, some by public school systems, some by communities, and some by educational television authorities set up on a cooperative basis by a number of cultural and educational institutions. Certain stations receive the bulk of their income from schools and colleges and provide programmes primarily for them. Others rely on the support of foundations and local citizens, and their programmes are intended for a wider adult audience. While educational stations produce the greater part of their programmes locally, they are also linked together by the Public Broadcasting Service – founded by the Corporation for Public Broadcasting (see under Radio, above) – which provides each station with 13½ hours a week of programmes on film or kinescope. There are also a number of regional networks which are linked by live-relay facilities.

All stations use 525-line definition. Television-set owners do not pay a licence fee or a fee to receive programmes.

To overcome reception difficulties due to distance, terrain features, large-city interference, etc., the use of 'community antenna television' (CATV) systems has been greatly extended in recent years. There are now 4875 CATV systems serving a total of about 6 million homes with both regular broadcasts and additionally supplied programmes. The majority of systems serve about 1000 subscribers with an average of 15 programmes; the largest offers its 35 000 subscribers a choice of 44 programmes. Systems with over 10 000 subscribers (of which there were almost 100 in 1972) are required by the FCC to install feedback channels for audience participation. No system may relay more than the three national networks and three independent stations in the 50 highest television-density areas, or three networks and two independents in other areas. A monthly CATV subscription fee is payable in addition to the initial registration fee. A number of 'pay as you view' systems have made application for licences from the FCC. Under these systems, viewers would pay for the programmes they see and broadcasts would not be sponsored by advertisers.

FILM

Feature-film production in the United States has remained fairly stable at around 280 titles annually over the last few years. In 1971, of the 531 features approved by the code administration of the Motion Picture Association of America (MPAA) 284 were domestically produced as compared with 142 titles in 1961 when the industry was most heavily hit by the rise of television. This recovery (though still some way from the annual domestic production of around 380 features in the late forties) is attributable to various factors, including the new film markets opened up by television, the adaptation of cinema theatres for new viewing publics and the trend towards lower-budget production (some 90% of feature films are now said to be shot on location to offset high studio costs, often in foreign countries affording appreciable economic advantages). Over 55% of United States film earnings are regularly accounted for by remittances from abroad, mainly from the distribution of domestic productions, but also from coproductions with foreign film-making interests and from earnings from US-financed enterprises incorporated in other producing countries. In 1971, the main markets for United States film exports (for either cinema or television showing) were Canada (15% of US export total), the UK (9%), Japan and Brazil (each 7%), Australia and Mexico (each 5%), Argentina (4%) and South Africa (3%).

The production of short films for commercial exhibition is largely oriented towards television markets. This is particularly true in the field of magazine and current affairs films where practically all the once regularly exhibited newsreels have been superseded by television newsfilms. Newsfilm for cinema showing is, however, exported to countries with limited or no television coverage.

The total number of persons employed in the domestic film industry is around 200 000, of whom a third are engaged in production and distribution and two-thirds in cinema theatres and services. The principal exporters also employ around 10 000 persons in foreign countries.

Non-theatrical productions total over 14 000 a year, about two-thirds of which are accounted for by business and industry, and the remainder principally by government and education, as well as by medical groups, community agencies, religious groups and *avant garde* cinematographers.

Among government bodies producing documentary films are the Departments of Agriculture, Commerce, the Interior, the Atomic Energy Commission and the United States Information Agency. The USIA's motion picture and television service adapts or produces several hundred films annually for exhibition abroad. These films are frequently dubbed in the language of the country where they are shown.

Film imports have doubled over the last decade – 229 foreign features were approved by the MPAA code administration in 1971 as against 112 in 1961 – partly as a result of the greatly increased use of foreign productions, both features and short subjects, on television. The principal source of imported films is Europe, with the UK supplying by far the largest share.

The number of fixed cinemas, which totalled some 19 000 in 1953 (with a total annual attendance of over 2 300 million) and then dropped to fewer than 10 000 in 1965, has gradually risen to 14 300 in 1972, of which 4600 are drive-ins (with an average capacity of 562 cars each). Annual attendances, however, have dropped by more than 50% over the last ten years, though box-office receipts, thanks to increased admission prices, have shown a gradual rise from $989 million in 1967 to around $1 250 million in 1971. The pattern of cinema attendance is changing, the decline in admissions to large downtown cinemas being offset by the growing popularity of smaller suburban establishments many of which are being built in shopping centres. A large number of these small automated theatres are being planned and built by local enterprises and by larger franchise companies. Some of these 'mini-theatres', often with fewer than 300 seats, are grouped in 'multi-auditorium' establishments running two or more programmes simultaneously. About 53% of the country's cinemas are controlled by some 700 circuits operating four or more theatres, while the remainder are in the hands of 6800 individual distributors or companies.

SPACE COMMUNICATIONS

The world's first active communication satellite, Telstar I, developed by the American Telephone and Telegraph Company and Bell Telephone Laboratories, was launched on 10 July 1962, by the United States National Aeronautics and Space Administration. In addition to transmitting telephone messages, facsimile and telephotos, it carried the first live monochrome and colour television transmissions between the USA and Europe. It was followed by Telstar II and the Relay I and II programme, demonstrating the feasibility of two-way transmission of long-distance colour television, as well as other types of information, via satellite. Though the use of a non-synchronous orbit proved costly and allowed only for intermittent operation, these programmes provided impetus for the development of satellite communication earth terminals throughout the world. Then, in 1963–4, came the Syncom programme demonstrating the practicality of synchronous satellites.

The way was now open for the establishment of an international system and in 1964 the International Telecommunications Satellite Consortium (Intelsat) was founded, under the interim management of the Communications Satellite Corporation (Comsat) which represents the USA in Intelsat and has the largest ownership participation in the various earth stations utilized by the United States for international services. United States earth stations served by the Intelsat satellite series I to IV were opened at Andover, Maine (1966), Etam, West Virginia (1969) and Cayey, Puerto Rico (1969) for the Atlantic region, and Paumalu, Hawaii (1966), Brewster, Washington (1966), Jamesburg, California (1968), Pulantat, Guam (1969) and Bartlett, Alaska (1970) for the Pacific region. In addition, there are experimental earth stations in Antarctica (1972) which are owned by the National Science Foundation, and in Clarksburg, Maryland, and Washington DC, both wholly owned by Comsat.

Five major US communications corporations lease satellite circuits from Comsat and in turn rent them out to the wire services, newspapers, radio and television stations and networks. They are the American Telephone and Telegraph Company, the International Telephone and Telegraph Company, Western Union International, RCA Global Communications and the Hawaiian Telephone Company. In addition, some lease channels from the Canadian system, Telesat, which is already in operation, and applications have been received by the FCC from these and other interests for permission to operate domestic satellite broadcasting services.

Several officially sponsored satellite broadcasting projects are also in active preparation, including one for the training of workers with young children in remote areas of the Rocky Mountain states, another for educational and community development purposes in Alaska, and another – based at the University of Hawaii – for the interconnection of 15 Pacific universities.

Although television is the only medium that actually requires satellite transmission to be received beyond the horizon, satellite channels are being increasingly used for telephone calls and newspaper copy.

PROFESSIONAL TRAINING AND ASSOCIATIONS

Formal journalism training in the United States was first offered in universities such as Illinois (1904), Wisconsin (1905), Missouri (1908) and Columbia (1912). By 1972, there were 41 691 journalism students enrolled in 166 schools and departments of journalism, exclusive of enrolments in courses at several hundred junior and community colleges. The larger schools offer graduate-level training leading to master's and doctor's degrees and a range of specializations in mass communication fields. Most have media facilities of their own, including newspapers and broadcasting stations, and are subscribers to the main news services. Much journalistic training, however, is still given on the job, supplemented by in-service and refresher courses such as those offered by the American Press Institute, the Washington Journalism Center and other professional and academic institutions.

In a nation-wide survey of 223 four-year colleges and universities providing courses in radio and television in 1971–2, 180 reported that broadcasting was offered as a major subject leading to a degree – with a total of 12 162 students enrolled. In 26 of the universities, 251 students were enrolled in doctoral-degree programmes in broadcast communications. Most of these colleges and universities are equipped with their own radio and/or (educational) television stations, closed-circuit television, etc.

The motion picture has become an established subject of study in higher education in the United States; 301 colleges and universities offer 1669 undergraduate and graduate courses to 4231 students majoring in film studies, and 889 faculty members teach the subject. Included in these figures are training opportunities for film professionals, which are available to degree level in 54 universities and colleges and to other recognized professional standards in a further 168 institutions.

The American Film Institute, established under the National Foundation of the Arts and Humanities Act of 1965 to promote film training and education, production, publications and archives, has a library of 5000 film titles. Other archives include those of the University of California Theatre Arts Library (20 000 stills and 1044 scripts) and the Museum of Modern Art, New York (4500 film titles).

The largest national professional association for journalists is the American Newspaper Guild, which has over 30 000 members in its affiliated local guilds. It was founded in 1934 to serve the vocational interests of its members, improve their conditions of work and raise the standards of journalism. The National Press Club, founded in 1908, has some 5000 members, and the American Society of Newspaper Editors (1922) around 740 members. The largest grouping of newspaper publishers is the American Newspaper Publishers' Association (ANPA) founded in 1887 and now representing over 1000 newspaper members; it has a Foundation which sponsors research and encourages professional training. Various branches of the press have their own associations, such as the Magazine Publishers' Association (111 publishers of some 400 magazines), the Periodical Publishers' Association of America (110 members) and the Educational Press Association of America (740 members). In addition to these, there are numerous other press associations, guilds and groups at national, state and local levels.

In broadcasting, the National Association of Broadcasters (founded 1923) – whose membership of over 4000 includes about 50% of the country's radio stations and 86% of its television stations – has adopted self-regulation codes to which its (voluntary) members subscribe. Broadcasting professionals have some 150 associations and societies to promote their interests and standards, as well as about 50 guilds and unions representing technical employees and, also, performers. Some, like the Radio Television News Directors' Association, have adopted their own professional codes of ethics. Representing both institutions and individuals, the National Association of Educational Broadcasters (founded 1925) has 190 educational radio station members and 135 educational television station members, as well as 5000 individuals and 100 schools operating closed-circuit television systems.

A number of associations overlap several media fields, such as the Association of Motion Picture and TV Producers (incorporated 1924) which has 22 major producer members. The most influential body in the film industry, however, is the Motion Picture Producers' Association which represents the nine major producing companies and sets general principles governing feature-film content, operates a rating code and deals with copyright, advertising, legal and financial problems affecting the industry. The Motion Picture Export Association of America represents the interests of these companies abroad. An Independent Motion Picture Producers' Association (founded 1932) has nine members.

Other associations whose memberships cover both broadcast and film media include guilds of actors and artists, directors, writers, composers, etc., as well as engineers, theatrical employees and technicians. Film distributors and exhibitors and cinema owners are organized at national, state and regional levels, while experimental film-makers have set up cooperative distribution centres for their productions. Public interest in films as an art is expressed through film societies, exemplified by the 1500 groups (mostly on college campuses) affiliated to the American Federation of Film Societies.

VIRGIN ISLANDS (UK)

Population	11 000
Area	153 sq. km.

PRESS

Newspapers	Non-dailies 1
Total circulation	Non-dailies 2000
Copies per 1000 people	Non-dailies 182

RADIO

Transmitters	Medium-wave 2
Total receivers	9000 estimated in use
Receivers per 1000 people	818

FILM

Cinemas	Fixed 1
Total seating capacity	328
Seats per 1000 people	30
Total annual attendance	55 000
Annual visits per capita	5

PRESS

A weekly newspaper, a tourist magazine circulating about 2000 copies and an Education Department report are published on the island of Tortola where the bulk of the population live.

RADIO

A commercial station operated by Virgin Islands Broadcasting, with two medium-wave transmitters (10 and 1kW), reaches 80% of the population. Weekly programmes totalling around 30 hours consist of music and drama (105 hours), news and information (12 hours), light entertainment (7 hours), broadcasts for special audiences (5 hours), cultural programmes (3½ hours) and education (3 hours), in addition to advertising.

No receiver licence fee is payable.

FILM

The islands' one cinema is in Roadtown, Tortola. About 60 features are imported annually from the USA, and 50 documentaries from the USA (30) and the UK (20).

VIRGIN ISLANDS (USA)

Population	65 000
Area	344 sq. km.

PRESS

Newspapers	Dailies 3, Non-dailies 2
Total circulation	Dailies 14 000, Non-dailies 11 300
Copies per 1000 people	Dailies 215, Non-dailies 174

RADIO

Transmitters	Medium-wave 3, VHF–FM 1
Total receivers	75 000 estimated in use
Receivers per 1000 people	1154

TELEVISION

Transmitters	2
Receivers	32 000 estimated in use
Receivers per 1000 people	492

FILM

Cinemas	Fixed 5
Total seating capacity	2700
Seats per 1000 people	42
Total annual attendance	800 000
Annual visits per capita	12

PRESS

Daily newspapers are published in English: two in the capital, Charlotte Amalie, on the island of St Thomas, and one in Christiansted, on St Croix. An English-language weekly on St Croix has a free distribution of 8000 copies, and an English/Spanish weekly has a paid circulation of 3300 in all the Virgin Islands and about 500 in Puerto Rico.

NEWS AGENCIES

Both AP and UPI have reporters. News media also get their news by staff reporters, official releases from the Governor's public relations department and press conferences given by the Governor. Broadcasting stations receive AP's wire service.

RADIO

The island of St Thomas has two privately owned broadcasting stations: the Thousand Islands Corporation and WSTI, operating medium-wave transmitters of 1kW and 0.25kW respectively. On the island of St Croix, there are two privately owned broadcasting stations: the VI Broadcasting Corporation with one 5kW medium-wave transmitter, and HRH, with one FM transmitter.

All stations are commercial concerns, deriving their revenue from advertising. All broadcast in English for between 16 and 20 hours a day and provide full radio coverage for the islands.

TELEVISION

There are two privately owned, commercially operated television stations: Island Tele-radio, on St Thomas, and the Quality Telecasting Corporation, St Croix – each on the air for about 50 hours a week. Their programmes are all in English; some are in colour. Both have cable systems with 1000 and 500 subscribers respectively.

FILM

Some 700 feature films are imported annually, as well as newsreels and documentaries, primarily from the USA. All US films are in English, and most have Spanish subtitles. Other films are sometimes dubbed in English, but are usually in the original language with English subtitles. In addition to fixed cinemas, there is one drive-in accommodating 500 cars. The Education and Health Departments sponsor a number of educational film shows in schools.

PART FOUR

SOUTH AMERICA

Argentina
Bolivia
Chile
Columbia
Ecuador
Falkland Islands
French Guiana

Guyana
Paraguay
Peru
Surinam
Uruguay
Venezuela

ARGENTINA

Population	23 552 000
Area	2 776 889 sq. km.

PRESS

Newspapers	Dailies 180, Non-dailies 63
Total circulation	Dailies 4 250 000
Copies per 1000 people	Dailies 180

RADIO

Transmitters	Long/medium-wave 118, Short-wave 16, VHF–FM 13
Total receivers	10 000 000 estimated in use
Receivers per 1000 people	424

TELEVISION

Transmitters	59
Receivers	4 500 000 estimated in use
Receivers per 1000 people	191

FILM

Cinemas	Fixed 1637
Total seating capacity	733 100
Seats per 1000 people	31
Total annual attendance	53 900 000
Annual visits per capita	2

PRESS

Daily newspapers are published in all 24 provincial capitals (several with two or three dailies) and some 60 other towns. The federal capital, Buenos Aires, alone has some 20 dailies with an overall circulation of 2.5 million copies, the two largest being popular evening and morning papers with circulations of 482 000 (491 000 on Sundays) and 415 000 (532 000 on Sundays) respectively, while a third publishes two editions of 333 000 and 282 000 copies daily. All three have national as well as city readerships, as have the capital's two internationally known dailies, founded in 1869 and 1870, both of which also circulate more than 200 000 copies per issue. In addition to its Spanish-language press, Buenos Aires also has dailies in English, German, Italian and French. A number of the larger-city dailies also put out Sunday editions. Though overall daily circulations have increased by about 40%, the actual number of dailies published is 50 fewer than ten years earlier. The non-daily press includes 36 papers appearing weekly and 23 more frequently (a few are in foreign languages).

Of a reported total of 1360 periodicals, the 50 largest have a combined circulation of about 6 million copies per issue. Among the highest circulations are those of two broadcasting and film magazines (over 200 000 copies each) and a women's weekly (160 000 copies). Main subject categories are trade and communications (176 titles), commercial organization and administration (144 titles), agriculture (134 titles), arts and architecture (130 titles), recreation and sports (122 titles), law and administration (115 titles),etc.

NEWS AGENCIES

Telenoticiosa Americana (Telam), the government-operated wire service founded in 1945, has headquarters in Buenos Aires, several other bureaux in Argentina and one in Montevideo (Uruguay). It issues a daily bulletin to 78 domestic subscribers (newspapers and broadcasting stations).

Noticias Argentinas, founded in 1973, is a consortium owned by 57 newspapers. It distributes national and local news and photos.

Smaller, privately owned, agencies include Agencia Noticiosa Saporiti (ANS), which was founded in 1900, Servicio Informativo Continental (SIC), founded in 1959, and Centro de Información y Documentación (CID), founded in 1965.

The Agencia Latinoamericana de Información (Latin), an agency founded in 1969 to serve the Latin American countries, also has its headquarters in Buenos Aires.

Foreign agencies with bureaux or representatives in Buenos Aires are AFP, ANSA, AP, DPA, Efe, Inter Press Service (Italy), Reuters and UPI.

RADIO

Radio stations, located in all parts of the country and covering at least 75% of the population, are owned and operated by the State, private interests, provincial and municipal authorities or universities.

Radio Nacional's 21 medium-wave, 4 short-wave and 2 FM stations, operated by the Ministry of Works' Ente de Radiodifusión y Televisión (ERT), broadcast national and regional programmes for up to 18 hours a day, while the second government system of 36 commercial stations, operated by the Dirección General de Emisoras Comerciales, broadcasts on both medium and short waves.

The private stations, of which there are 52, are grouped in a single association. All have medium-wave transmitters and a few FM transmitters as well. Several are on the air for 24 hours a day.

The three provincial, five municipal and several university stations are financed partly by subsidies from public funds and partly from their own commercial advertising revenue.

In a typical week in 1972, radio broadcasting time for all stations totalled 15 820 hours (all but 29 hours of which represented domestically produced programmes) consisting of the following categories: light entertainment (9798 hours), news and information (3148 hours), advertising (2408 hours), education (202 hours), arts, letters and sciences (165 hours), broadcasts for special audiences (34 hours) and for ethnic minorities (15 hours).

The number of radio receivers in use (for which no licence fee is payable) has almost trebled in ten years.

External broadcasting is conducted by Radio Nacional, with programmes beamed: to Europe, north Africa and the Near East in Spanish, German, Italian and French; to North, central and South America in Spanish, Portuguese and English; and to Asia in Japanese.

TELEVISION

Television broadcasting (625 lines) began in November 1951. There are now 31 stations (with 28 repeaters) all commercially operated, under the ownership of private enterprise (23 stations), the national government (1 station), provincial governments (3 stations), universities and municipal authorities (3 stations). About 66% of the population are covered by existing stations. General supervision of all stations is exercised by the Ministry of the Interior.

Buenos Aires has four stations with an average daily transmitting time of 15 hours. One, a state-owned station founded in 1951, operates relays in Mar del Plata, Rosario, Santa Fe and Chivilcoy and broadcasts for 11 hours a day, thus covering a larger potential audience than any other.

Cordoba's three stations include one operated by the National University, broadcasting for 12 hours daily. San Miguel de Tucuman also has a university station. The cities of Mendoza, Bahia Blanca, Mar del Plata and Rosario each have two privately owned stations. Stations operated by provincial governments are located in Rio Gallego (Santa Cruz) and in Rio Grande and Ushuaia (both in the national territory of Tierra del Fuego). Average transmitting time for provincial stations is about 8 hours a day.

All stations carry commercial advertising, now limited (by legislation introduced in 1973) to 10 minutes per hour.

Programmes totalling 2363 hours a week for all stations include light entertainment (1309 hours), advertising (378 hours), news and information (328 hours), broadcasts for special audiences (115 hours), education (131 hours, including 51 hours broadcasts to schools), arts, letters and sciences (89 hours) and broadcasts for ethnic minorities (12 hours). Approximately 70% of all programmes broadcast are of domestic origin, produced in Buenos Aires. Imported programmes (750 hours a week) come mainly from the USA, with a few hours from European and other Latin American countries.

Broadcasts to primary schools under the auspices of the National Council of Education have been carried for 30 minutes daily on several channels in the capital and the provinces since 1966 and were received in 1971 by 150 receivers in official schools and 80 in private schools. Similarly, secondary teaching, educational training and permanent education courses for adults are carried by television. Closed-circuit television is extensively used in the National University of Buenos Aires and several other university establishments. Stations are not yet carrying colour programmes but the SECAM system has been adopted in principle.

No licence fee is payable for television receivers.

FILM

Commercial film production in 1972 amounted to 28 features and 40 short films (33 documentaries, 4 educational and 3 entertainment). In addition, a number of experimental films are made by film schools, clubs, etc.

Imports for the same year, totalling 397 features, came from the USA (237), Italy (59), France (39), the UK (18), Spain (10), the Federal Republic of Germany (9), Switzerland (6), Japan (5) and other countries (14). Documentaries were imported from the USA (12), the USSR (5), Italy (4) and France, Japan and Yugoslavia (1 each). All foreign films are released with subtitles.

Of the total number of cinemas, over 300 are in the Buenos Aires area where practically a third of the population live. These include seven drive-ins (with overall accommodation for 4550 vehicles and annual attendances of 1.4 million persons). There are also 38 mobile cinemas. Over 1200 cinemas have closed down in the last ten years.

The Instituto Nacional de Cinematografía (a government agency) administers legislation affecting the industry, classifies films for public exhibition, awards subsidies to producers of 'meritorious' films, etc.

SPACE COMMUNICATIONS

An Atlantic Intelsat earth station at Balcarce, 350km south of Buenos Aires, was opened in 1969. It is operated by the national telecommunications service (ENTEL).

PROFESSIONAL TRAINING AND ASSOCIATIONS

Training in journalism is offered in 19 schools, of which 9 are in Buenos Aires, including those of the Instituto Grafotécnico (since 1934), the Public Opinion Institute, the Faculty of Information Sciences of the Museo Social University, the Institute of Information Sciences and the Catholic Institute of Social Studies. Schools and institutes in other centres include one at the National University of La Plata (school founded in 1934), the D. F. Sarmiento Institute in Mar del Plata, higher schools of journalism in Mendoza, Rosario (two schools) and Concordia (two schools); and the Institute of Communication Science, D. F. Sarmiento University, in San Juan. Courses may be from three to five years in length; eight of the schools have entrance requirements below university-entrance level.

Cinematographic studies form part of the curricula of universities in Cordoba and Santa Fé (both with four-year degree courses) and Mendoza, while a private university in Buenos Aires awards a professional qualification in television.

Professional associations include associations of newspaper publishers, magazine publishers, the technical press, journalists, specialized journalists, private broadcasting stations, television broadcasters, film producers, directors, actors, distributors, exhibitors, clubs, etc.

BOLIVIA

Population	5 190 000
Area	1 098 581 sq. km.

PRESS

Newspapers	Dailies 16, Non-dailies 13*
Total circulation	Dailies 169 000
Copies per 1000 people	Dailies 33, Non-dailies 15

RADIO

Transmitters†	Long/medium-wave 70, Short-wave 48, VHF–FM 15
Total receivers	1 350 000 estimated in use
Receivers per 1000 people	260

TELEVISION

Transmitters	1
Receivers	11 000 estimated in use
Receivers per 1000 people	2

FILM

Cinemas	Fixed 120‡
Total seating capacity	66 000
Seats per 1000 people	13
Total annual attendance	3 200 000
Annual visits per capita	0.6

*In 1963   †In 1968   ‡In 1964

PRESS

The capital, La Paz, has 3 morning and 3 evening dailies, the largest of which prints 60 000 copies per issue. Together they represent 70% of the country's daily newspaper circulation. Three of these also have Sunday editions. Other towns with daily newspapers are Cochabamba (3), Santa Cruz (5), Oruro and Potosi. All dailies are published in Spanish and are read almost entirely by town dwellers. The same applies to the non-daily papers which appear at weekly (9 titles) or less frequent intervals (4 titles). Over 60% of the population are either Quechua or Aymará-speaking Indians who, because of the language problem, illiteracy or their remoteness from publishing centres, are practically untouched by the press.

Periodicals other than newspapers, including a number of technical and specialized publications, appear mostly in La Paz, with a few in Santa Cruz, Sucre and Oruro. The total circulation per issue for 18 titles is about 55 000 copies.

NEWS AGENCIES

There is no national agency, and newspapers rely on their own correspondents for domestic news. UPI has an office at La Paz, and AP, DPA, AFP and TASS are also represented.

RADIO

Radio broadcasting is state controlled, technical supervision being exercised by the Dirección General de Comunicaciones, which is also responsible for granting operating licences to private stations.

Of the 80 stations affiliated to the Asociación Boliviana de Radiodifusoras, one is government-owned and financed, partly by state funds and partly by advertising. This is Radio Illimani, which has 1 medium-wave transmitter (20kW) on the air for 130 hours a week, 3 short-wave transmitters (10 and 20kW) and 2 FM transmitters, all at La Paz. Several stations or networks belong to religious organizations; the largest is La Cruz del Sur, with 1 medium-wave, 1 FM and 2 short-wave transmitters, operated and supported by the Canadian Baptist Foreign Mission Board, and broadcasting musical, educational and cultural as well as religious programmes for about 120 hours a week. All other stations rely on advertising and sponsored programmes for their income. Some, notably those operated by universities and those with their own 'radio schools', such as Radioemisoras Bolivia and the Escuelas Radiofónicas San Gabriel, San Rafael, Fides, El Condor, etc., broadcast literacy courses and educational programmes for both adult groups and schools. Most programmes are in Spanish, with some in Quechua and a few in English and German.

No licence fee is payable for radio receivers.

TELEVISION

Television broadcasting began in 1969 when the Government established the Empresa Nacional de Televisión Boliviana with one transmitter (625 lines) located in La Paz. One of its main objects is to broadcast literacy and fundamental education programmes which, in 1971, represented 13% of the total programme time. Other components were entertainment (63%) and news and information (24%), much of which is imported from the USA, Mexico and Argentina. Televisión Boliviana is at present on the air for 24½ hours a week. Part of its revenue is derived from commercial advertising.

FILM

Short films and documentaries are produced, but no long films. All feature films exhibited are imported, mostly from the USA and also from Latin American and European countries. Films are shown in commercial cinemas in the towns and also in cinemas operated by mining enterprises for their employees. Educational and cultural film shows are organized by government departments and by foreign diplomatic and information services.

PROFESSIONAL TRAINING AND ASSOCIATIONS

A three-year course in journalism has been offered (since 1968) at the Universidad Católica Boliviana, in La Paz, and at a school of journalism in Santa Cruz.

Professional associations include two journalists' associations, an association of radio stations and another for broadcasting personnel, and a film chamber (for distributors, exhibitors, etc.).

BRAZIL

Population	98 850 000
Area	8 511 965 sq. km.

PRESS
Newspapers	Dailies 261, Non-dailies 730
Total circulation	Dailies 3 498 000
Copies per 1000 people	Dailies 35

RADIO
Transmitters	Long/medium-wave 866, Short-wave 79, VHF–FM 49
Total receivers	5 700 000 estimated in use
Receivers per 1000 people	58

TELEVISION
Transmitters	50
Receivers	6 500 000 estimated in use
Receivers per 1000 people	66

FILM
Cinemas	Fixed 3194
Total seating capacity	1 911 200
Seats per 1000 people	19
Total annual attendance	240 000 000
Annual visits per capita	2

PRESS

Daily newspapers (227 morning and 30 evening) are published in some 95 towns, almost half the total national daily circulation being accounted for by the papers of Rio de Janeiro (907 000) and São Paulo (615 000). Ten of Rio's 14 dailies appear in the morning, seven have circulations ranging between 70 000 and 150 000, one deals with sports, one is published in English (all others are in Portuguese). and the majority have Sunday editions with rather higher circulations than on week days. The Rio press also circulates in other main towns in Brazil and abroad. São Paulo has some 20 dailies, mostly morning papers, the three largest of which have individual circulations of between 50 000 and 110 000 copies. One morning daily is published in German and another in Japanese. Other towns with over seven dailies are Porto Alegre (10), Belo Horizonte (7), Recife (7), Curitiba (9) and Fortaleza (8). In Brasilia, the new federal capital, there is one daily with a circulation of 15 000 (20 000 on Sundays); it is published by one of the country's large mass media enterprises which owns 30 other newspapers, as well as magazines and broadcasting stations.

The number of daily newspaper titles has dropped by about 30 over the last ten years with a corresponding drop of 450 000 in overall circulation figures.

In 1971, the non-daily general interest and specialized press included 550 titles published weekly or more frequently, including week-end editions of dailies. Periodicals number around 700, the largest group being general readership magazines (97 titles), women's and home magazines (25 titles), recreation and sports (41 titles), religion and theology (83 titles) and medicine and health (30 titles).

Portuguese is the official and universally used language and the language of the press, except for 2 dailies, 10 non-dailies and 19 periodicals published in Spanish, English, German and Japanese, either with or without accompanying Portuguese text.

National newsprint consumption (273 300 metric tons in 1970) exceeds production (124 400 metric tons). Imports are subject to federal government quota controls.

NEWS AGENCIES

The Agência Nacional (AN), founded in 1946 and based in Rio de Janeiro, is a government agency supplying official news and cultural information received through federal, state and local authorities and public and private enterprises.

The Agência Meridional founded in 1931 is the oldest Brazilian agency and has its headquarters in Rio de Janeiro and offices in Brasilia and São Paulo, with a permanent staff of 55 persons (all within the country). It issues a daily bulletin of 13 400 words of national and local news in Portuguese, along with features, photos and audio-radio services to its subscribers consisting of 34 newspapers, 23 radio stations and 14 television stations. Transmission of news is effected by leased telex and private-wire circuits, press radio and air mail.

Another private agency, the Agência J. B. Serviços de Imprensa, founded in 1966, has its head office in Rio de Janeiro and employs 28 permanent staff. It receives the foreign services of the *New York Times, Los Angeles Times* and *The Economist* (London). Its own services, supplied to 28 newspapers, 5 news agencies and several magazines, include 30 000 words a day of national and local news in Portuguese, plus features, photos and occasional radio services.

Transpress (TRP), a private agency founded in 1958, has headquarters in Rio de Janeiro and branches in the principal cities and some minor towns, it has 38 permanent employees, of whom 21 are editorial staff. TRP issues 25 000 words in Portuguese and 3000 in Spanish daily to 58 subscribers in Brazil and to Efe in Spain. It receives DPA and ANSA services.

Other domestic agencies include Argus Press (1937) and Asapress (1942), with head offices in Rio de Janeiro, and Orbe-Press.

Foreign services received in Brazil by press, radio, television and agencies include UPI, AFP, ANSA, AP and Efe, while Reuters serves seven newspapers. All these are represented in the country, as also are DPA, Jiji, Kyodo, Novosti and TASS.

RADIO

Under the central control of the federal Ministry of Communications, radio and television broadcasting is conducted either by government stations or by private enterprises operating under government concession or licence.

Government radio stations are financed by subsidies from the state budget, except for a number of commercial stations — formerly under private ownership but since acquired by the state (notably the Radio Nacional do Rio de Janeiro and Radio Maná networks) — which continue to function on the same basis and with the same status as private commercial enterprises. The commercial stations receive their revenue from advertising and sponsored programmes. A third category of broadcasting, those operated by public foundations, by the Catholic Church or by other Christian missions, etc., are financed by their sponsoring organizations or by private donations and subscriptions.

The government-owned stations operate 54 transmitters (31 medium-wave, 18 short-wave and 5 FM), compared with 940 transmitters (835 medium-wave, 61 short-wave and 44 FM) operated by some 390 private organizations and enterprises. Programmes, totalling 90 369 hours a week, consist of light entertainment (47 862 hours), advertising (17 575 hours), news and information (13 262 hours), broadcasts for special audiences (7845 hours), arts, letters and sciences (3418 hours) and broadcasts for ethnic minorities (407 hours). Educational programmes (accounted for in several of the above categories) are broadcast by government stations, notably one in Brasilia and three in the state of Guanabara (including one owned by the Ministry of Education), and by private foundations and missions. The government-sponsored programmes are mainly academic and are relayed or transmitted by short wave throughout the country, while Catholic organizations (operating over 140 transmitters) and other Christian missions concentrate on programmes of the 'radio school' type, directed largely towards rural audiences. A number of specialized foundations furnish programme material, equipment and guidance to their own or other educational networks.

Commercial broadcasting is often highly competitive (Recife, for example, has 13 commercial radio stations), and many stations belong to powerful media groups.

About 68 are affiliated to a national broadcasters' association, the Associação Brasileira de Emissoras de Rádio e Televisão (ABERT). Advertising may occupy up to 15 minutes in every hour. All stations are required to broadcast a daily government information programme.

No licence fees are payable for radio receivers, the total number of which has increased by almost 1 million over the last ten years. Over 76% of all receivers are found in villages in the interior of this vast country where radio is the main, and often the sole, source of information and education.

TELEVISION

Regular television broadcasts began in São Paulo in 1950 and in Rio de Janeiro in 1951 under private enterprise. Now, under the same federal administration as radio broadcasting, Brazil has 4 government stations (financed by the State subsidy), 4 commercial networks, with 26 originating stations, and 20 independent stations, internetwork liaisons being effected by the official telecommunications network (EMBRATEL) or by air transport of tapes and films. Non-governmental stations are affiliated to the broadcasters' association (ABERT).

Programmes, of which 75% are nationally produced, were broadcast for 3137 hours a week in 1970, consisting of news and information (1294 hours), light entertainment (512 hours), broadcasts for special audiences (491 hours), advertising (471 hours), arts, letters and sciences (291 hours) and broadcasts for ethnic minorities (78 hours). (In 1971, the total broadcasting time had increased to 4000 hours a week.) Among these categories are literacy programmes, and primary, secondary and university educational programmes broadcast mainly by government or specialized educational stations, such as that operated by Recife University since 1968, the commercial station in São Paulo, bought by the Government in 1969, and a similar station acquired with government aid in Porto Alegre. Their work is aided by various audio-visual institutes and foundations including, notably, a federal government foundation set up to coordinate the development and programming of educational television through-out the country. Popular programmes, like those produced and transmitted by Catholic organizations and viewed by group audiences in churches and shopping areas, have been particularly successful. The number of receivers in use has more than doubled in five years, but, because of the cost of receivers and the absence of electric power in many areas, television is still almost exclusively an urban phenomenon.

The definition system used is 525 lines, and the PAL system was adopted for the first colour broadcasts in 1972.

No licence fee is charged.

FILM

Brazilian film production averages between 50 and 60 long films a year, though the number of releases rose to 72 in 1970, as well as short educational and documentary films and newsreels.

The industry is promoted by the government enterprise EMBRAFILME, established in 1969 to encourage the production (through loans and grants) and export of Brazilian films, and by the Instituto Nacional do Cinéma (INC) set up in 1966 with responsibility for the internal regulation of imports, distribution, exhibition, licensing, film supplies, etc. INC requires, for example, that one Brazilian feature be shown for every eight foreign programmes in cinemas and that every programme include locally produced newsreel and short films.

Brazil imports about 700 features a year. These productions, along with Brazilian feature films, are shown in 2567 35mm and 627 16mm fixed cinemas. Annual attendances, which dropped from almost 317 million in 1960 to 235 million in 1967, have again shown a slight improvement in the last few years.

SPACE COMMUNICATIONS

Brazil's Atlantic Intelsat earth station at Tangua (opened in February 1969) in the state of Rio de Janeiro is linked to all radio and television stations using the national telecommunications network through the EMBRATEL television centre near the city of Rio de Janeiro. A study is being made of the possibilities of broadcasting educational television programmes via satellite.

PROFESSIONAL TRAINING AND ASSOCIATIONS

Four-year courses in journalism are available in 24 university faculties and schools (12 of these courses have been established since 1960). In 1968, there were 1942 students of journalism (1073 male and 869 female), enrolled in 18 institutions. Diplomas in journalism awarded in 11 institutions in 1967 totalled 272 (awarded to 154 male and 118 female graduates). About 10 other institutions conduct research programmes in communications.

Broadcasting training opportunities include courses for radio technicians at the Lutheran Evangelical radio centre at Porto Alegre and training for television and educational television personnel in various state schools, in the São Paulo Regional Centre for Educational Research, in the Guanabara Institute of Education, in universities in São Paulo and São Luis, and the television station operated by Recife University.

Press associations include a national association of journalists, various state associations of newspaper and periodical proprietors and a confederation of workers in communications and publicity. The Associacão Brasileira de Emmissoras de Rádio e Televisão (ABERT) groups together most radio and television stations. Film professions are served by the Associacão Brasileira de Cinematografía and the Sindicato Nacional de la Industria Cinematográfica (producers), by associations of film technicians and artists (State of São Paulo), and by distributors and exhibitors in several states.

CHILE

Population	8 992 000
Area	756 945 sq. km.

PRESS
Newspapers	Dailies 46

RADIO
Transmitters	Long/medium-wave 156, Short-wave 32, VHF–FM 41
Total receivers	1 400 000 estimated in use
Receivers per 1000 people	156

TELEVISION

Transmitters	25
Receivers	500 000 estimated in use
Receivers per 1000 people	56

FILM

Cinemas	Fixed 360
Total seating capacity	245 749
Seats per 1000 people	27
Total annual attendance	44 619 000
Annual visists per capita	5

PRESS

In 1971, the capital Santiago, which with its surrounding area accounts for a quarter of the country's population, had 10 dailies printing from 25 000 to 130 000 copies per issue and together totalling more than half the national daily circulation.

Altogether, over 20 towns had daily newspapers. Valparaiso had four, and Antofagasta and Concepción three each, but the majority had only one or two circulating no more than a few thousand copies. Several of the larger dailies published Sunday editions with considerably higher circulations. Some 200 separate weekly and other non-daily newspapers mostly served local readerships. All dailies and most other newspapers were published in Spanish, the national language and the first language of most of the population.

Two main publishing concerns controlled a number of the larger urban papers while a third group, in which the government acquired a controlling interest in 1971, was the country's leading magazine and periodical publisher.

Chile's pulp and paper industry produced 122 000 metric tons of newsprint in 1970, which was sufficient to supply national needs (50 000 metric tons) and to export to other Latin American countries.

NEWS AGENCIES

The Agencia Noticiosa Prensa, Radio y Cine (PYRC), founded in 1945 and the oldest of the four national agencies, distributed a daily national news service, plus a foreign news summary supplied on request to provincial subscribers.

The Agencia Noticiosa Corporación de Periodistas (COPER), founded in 1948, distributed national news mainly to Santiago broadcasting stations and provincial daily newspapers.

The Agencia Informative Orbe, a private company founded in 1952 and employing a permanent editorial staff in Santiago and the provinces, along with many part-time correspondents, distributed a domestic news service to several newspapers and 10 broadcasting stations. This service was also taken by government agencies and private enterprises.

The Agencia Orbe Latinoamericana, founded in 1956 and also privately run, dealt mainly in foreign news. It had representatives in a number of Latin American counties and exchanged news with the Agencia Informative Orbe in Chile and with other Latin American agencies, mainly in Brazil, Colombia,

Guatemala and Uruguay. More than 20 subscribers received its domestic and foreign news services.

All these agencies had headquarters in Santiago and correspondents throughout the country.

Foreign agencies represented in Chile in 1971 included AFP, AP, UPI, Reuters and ANSA, all of which had permanent offices in Santiago, and DPA, TASS and PRELA.

RADIO

Radio broadcasting came under the technical supervision of the government's telecommunications service. The majority of the country's 145 broadcasting organizations were affiliated to the Asociación de Radiodifusoras de Chile, four were affiliated to Radiodifusoras Australes and 17 had no affiliation. Most were privately owned, by universities, cooperatives or commercial enterprises, but the government operated 11 medium-wave, 4 short-wave and 3 FM transmitters. In all, over 220 transmitters, located throughout the country from Africa in the tropics to Punta Arenas on the Straits of Magellan, provide at least some radio coverage for most areas of this 2500-mile long territory. In addition, by agreement between the Ministry of the Interior and the Radio-Club de Chile, a network of 14 amateur stations could be linked to the public broadcasting networks within 10 minutes in case of national emergency.

Educational and cultural programmes were broadcast by university and technical university stations at Concepción, Copiapó, Antofagasta, Santiago, Valdivia, Temuco, La Serena, Valparaiso and Punta Arenas, while broadcasting to schools was supervised by the Ministry of Education.

TELEVISION

Under the terms of a new law drafted in 1971, all matters concerning television broadcasting at national level, including programme organization, electoral broadcasts and advertising time, were dealt with by a 15-member National Television Council within the Ministry of Education.

Chile's first television broadcasts were made in August 1959 by the Universidad Católica which now has transmitters in both Santiago and Valparaiso. Shortly afterwards, the Universidad de Chile also established a television station, with one transmitter in Santiago. Both these stations were commercially operated and derived their revenue from advertising and sponsored entertainment programmes occupying about 40% of their broadcasting time, the remainder being devoted to cultural and educational programmes at university, teacher-training and secondary-school levels and to broadcasts for adult groups, teleclubs, etc. Each station broadcast for 56 hours a week.

In August 1969, a government network, Televisión Nacional de Chile, began broadcasting and rapidly extended its potential coverage to most of the population, from the Peruvian border in the north to Tierra del Fuego in the south. By early 1971, 19 of its proposed 25 transmitters were in operation. Programmes of national interest were broadcast for 70 hours a week.

In addition to public television broadcasting, a number of universities and some schools have made use of closed-circuit television for teaching purposes. In the city of Concepción, there was a closed-circuit television station operated by a commercial radio station.

The definition system used is 525 lines.

FILM

A government service (CORFO), responsible for the encouragement of film production, owned Chile Films, the only Chilean studio and processing laboratory, where films (mainly documentary) were produced for the State Information Department and other ministries. There are also several commercial producers in the country.

In recent years, about 500 feature films were imported annually, mostly from the USA. Of the 20 or so importers and distributors, eight mainly supplied television stations.

In 1971, apart from 35mm commercial cinemas, there were 150 16mm houses in small towns. In addition, some 300 non-commercial 16mm units operated in churches, schools and community groups throughout the country. The Ministry of Education maintained a film library.

SPACE COMMUNICATIONS

Chile has an Atlantic Intelsat earth station, opened in July 1968, at Longovilo (about 120km south-west of Santiago), operated by the Empresa Nacional de Telecomunicaciones.

PROFESSIONAL TRAINING AND ASSOCIATIONS

Schools of journalism and of communication studies provided professional training courses at two universities in Santiago and at the universities of Valparaiso and Concepción. The latter had 140 students enrolled in its journalism and communication courses in 1970. The Organization of American States holds training courses and seminars for educational television personnel at its regional training and research centres in Latin America, one of which is located in Chile.

In 1971, associations for media professions included the National Press Association (newspaper publishers), journalists' associations in most large towns and a foreign correspondents' association in Santiago. Most radio stations belonged to the main broadcasting association, while the film industry had associations of producers, cinema operators, film importers and distributors, and film critics (with radio and theatre critics), all based in Santiago.

COLUMBIA

Population	22 490 000
Area	1 138 914 sq. km.

PRESS
Newspapers	Dailies 36, Non-dailies 16
Total circulation	Dailies 2 369 400, Non-dailies 218 000
Copies per 1000 people	Dailies 105, Non-dailies 10

RADIO
Transmitters	Long/medium-wave 188, Short-wave 43
Total receivers	2 917 000 estimated in use
Receivers per 1000 people	130

TELEVISION
Transmitters	18
Receivers	1 200 000 estimated in use
Receivers per 1000 people	53

FILM
Cinemas	Fixed 378
Total seating capacity	291 757
Seats per 1000 people	13
Total annual attendance	65 401 800
Annual visits per capita	3

PRESS

While circulation figures for Columbia's press have increased by 66% over the last ten years, the number of daily newspapers has dropped from 44 to 29. Of these, the five main dailies (some with special weekly numbers) published in the capital, Bogotá, account for about half the country's overall circulation figure. Dating from 1911 and 1887, Bogotá's two largest papers have circulations of 185 000 (rising to 380 000 on Monday) and 225 000 (235 000 on Monday) respectively.

Separated by high mountain ranges, the provincial centres of Colombia tend to have a well-developed local press. These include particularly the industrial city of Medellín, with five dailies, the largest circulating over 65 800 copies, and Cali, in the rich Cauca valley, with three dailies ranging from 53 000 to 78 000 copies. Influential dailies also appear in major towns such as Barranquilla, Bucaramanga, Cartagena and Manizales. Some papers have distinct political orientations, and all devote a large proportion of space (about 70% on an average) to local and national affairs. It is estimated that about 50% of the population, mostly town dwellers, are reached by the press.

One weekly paper published by a private organization which also operates the popular educational broadcasting station, Radio Sutatenza, serves a widespread readership, both urban and rural, with agricultural, economic and cultural news and information, as well as with details of its educational radio programmes.

Periodicals other than newspapers number about 300 and have a total circulation of over 850 000 copies, the largest subject categories being legal, administrative and social welfare (57 titles), general and current affairs (44 titles) and economics and political sciences (31 titles).

Columbia produces practically all the newsprint required by the national press.

NEWS AGENCIES

Ultra Prensa (UP), a private agency with an editorial staff of eight at its headquarters in Bogotá, and correspondents in Barranquilla, Medellín, Cali, Cartagena and Bucamaranga, provides a daily service of about 2500 words in national news in Spanish. News received from correspondents is transmitted by telex, radio and teleprinter to the agency's four main subscribers. UP has no foreign correspondents.

Other agencies include Columbia Press, founded in 1955, with several bureaux and permanent correspondents in the country; Teleprensa (TP), founded in 1957, with correspondents in Columbia and abroad; Servicio Nacional de Prensa (SP), founded in 1958, with bureaux in several Columbian cities; and Interpress, founded in 1960. All of these, based in Bogotá, supply news to the press, radio and television. The main centres in Columbia are linked by telex.

Foreign news is supplied by UPI and AFP (for press, radio and television), Efe, Novosti and TASS (press and radio) and Reuters (press). AP, UPI and AFP have bureaux in Bogotá – UPI and AFP in other towns as well. TASS, also is, represented in Columbia.

RADIO

Among Columbia's many radio stations, there is one government network, Radio Nacional de Colombia, operated by the Instituto Nacional de Radio y Televisión (Inravisión) at Bogotá. With medium-wave stations at Bogotá (100kW), Cali (50kW) and Manizales (10kW) and short-wave stations of 25 and 50kW at Bogotá, Radio Nacional is on the air for 168 hours a week, broadcasting cultural and scientific programmes (96 hours), educational programmes (21 hours, including 6 hours for schools and 10 hours of adult courses), programmes for children and youth (14 hours), news and information (12 hours, including 4 hours of sports), serials (12 hours), musical and dramatic programmes (7 hours), religious broadcasts (4 hours) and language courses (2 hours). These include 85 hours originating in Columbia, of which 51 hours are live broadcasts. Senate and Congress debates are rebroadcast during parliamentary sessions.

All other stations are independently operated, the majority being financed by advertising and sponsored programmes. In addition to various smaller groups and broadcasting associations, there are three main commercial networks: Caracol, Bogotá, grouping 58 stations; Todelar, Cali, with 63 stations; and Radio Cadena Nacional (RCN), Medellín, with 41 stations.

It is estimated that for 80% of the population of Columbia the radio is the main regular source of news. Some networks, like RCN, carry a high proportion of newcasts and documentary programmes. A similar informative function is fulfilled in a number of provincial centres by stations such as La Voz de Medellín, La Voz de Barranquilla and La Voz de Santa Marta.

The educational and cultural potential of radio broadcasting in such a country is further exemplified by an independent non-profit-making association, Acción Cultural Popular, officially recognized by Church and state, which from small beginnings as a 'radio school', in 1947, has now become the nation-wide network, known as Radio Sutatenza, broadcasting from four regional centres with well-equipped studios and laboratories and operating 6 medium-wave transmitters (10, 120 and 250kW), 5 short-wave transmitters (10, 25 and 50kW) and 1 FM transmitter. The stations are on the air every day from 03.55 to 23.00 hours, broadcasting a variety of graded courses, particularly in the early morning and the evening, for rural adult listeners, and cultural, recreational and news programmes during the day. Radio Sutatenza's educational broadcasts are received by over 200 000 adult members of more than 23 000 'radio schools' in 1100 towns and villages. Supplementary help and guidance is provided by 20 regional cultural centres and 580 radio-school centres in local communities.

No radio licence fee is payable in Colombia. The number of receivers has increased by almost a million over the last ten years.

TELEVISION

Television broadcasting, which began in 1954, is state controlled and is administered by the Instituto Nacional de Radio y Televisión (Inravisión) in Bogota.

There are two services, a national service — general and educational with programmes operated by Inravisión with a network of 17 powerful transmitter and repeater stations covering most populated areas — and an official commercial service — Telebogota — which can be received by viewers in central Columbia. About 84% of the population live in areas with television coverage. The definition system used is 525 lines.

The national sevice is well equipped, with modern studios and a developing relay network constantly bringing television coverage to more of the country's mountain-shadowed areas, and is one the air for 115 hours a week, broadcasting dramatic and serial programmes (47 hours), news and information (31 hours, including sports), educational and cultural programmes (16 hours), music, dance and comedy (9 hours), games and contests (8½ hours), literary and artistic programmes (2½ hours), and women's sessions (30 minutes).

About 34% of programmes are imported. The majority of the feature films, serials and children's programmes shown (about 50 hours a week) come from the USA. An agreement has also been signed for import of Mexican programmes. Other programmes are locally produced.

Inravisión's educational television broadcasts, first introduced in 1964, now reach half a million listener students in schools and 'telecentros' throughout the country, under the supervision of some 10 500 teachers and instructors. In addition to day-school and domestic, cultural and recreational programmes, there are regular evening courses for adults in literacy and all basic school subjects.

A regional pilot centre in Bogotá, sponsored by the Organization of American States, produces experimental educational television programmes (at primary-school level) for the organization's 17 member countries.

Telebogota, the commercial service, with one 2.5kW transmitter, is on the air for 5 hours daily.

FILM

There is no regular industrial production of long films though studio and laboratory facilities are available, principally in Bogotá. Several features and coproductions (mainly with Mexico) have been made in recent years, some of them being adaptations of Columbian literary works. The Ministry of Education, which also maintains an educational and cultural film library and mobile projection units, has a production unit which makes 16mm and 35mm educational films for use in schools and community centres. Inravisión has its own laboratories and produces newsfilms and documentaries, mainly for television presentation. Advertising films, for both cinema and television exhibition, are almost all produced in Columbia.

Feature films are imported, mainly from the USA, Mexico, Italy, the USSR, Argentina and the UK. In 1970, documentaries were imported from the USA, the Netherlands, the UK, the Federal Republic of Germany, Italy, Japan, Peru and Sweden.

SPACE COMMUNICATIONS

An Atlantic Intelsat earth station, opened in 1970 for transmission and reception of satellite radio and television broadcasts, at Choconta, 80km north-west of Bogotá, is owned and operated by the Empresa Nacional de Telecomunicaciones.

PROFESSIONAL TRAINING AND ASSOCIATIONS

Training in journalism is offered in Bogotá, at schools of communication sciences at two private universities, and at a school of journalism in a third university; and in Medellín at the schools of communication sciences of the Universidad de Antioquia and a private university, and at the universities in Cali and Barranquilla. These are all diploma courses for which candidates must possess university-entrance qualifications and also pass a competitive entrance examination.

Broadcasting and audio-visual personnel are trained by Acción Cultural Popular (Radio Sutatenza) which holds courses for rural-community radio educators; by the Pontificia Universidad Javeriana in Bogotá, which has a four-year course for producers and directors of audio-visual education programmes; and by the Organization of American States which organizes five-month training courses and one-month seminars at its regional training and research centres in Argentina, Chile, Columbia and Mexico for primary-school heads and inspectors concerned with educational television in Latin America.

National associations exist for both newspaper owners and journalists. Press workers in most large towns may join professional associations or unions, while editorial staff of Bogotá newspapers have their own association.

Radio-station owners and operators and radio and television stations belong to several associations and federations. There is an association of film distributors in Bogotá.

ECUADOR

Population	6 510 000
Area	283 561 sq. km.

PRESS

Newspapers	Dailies 22, Non-dailies 17
Total circulation	Dailies 283 300, Non-dailies 19 200
Copies per 1000 people	Dailies 43, Non-dailies 3

RADIO

Transmitters	Long/medium-wave 329, Short-wave 5, VHF—FM 2
Total receivers	1 700 000 estimated in use
Receivers per 1000 people	261

TELEVISION

Transmitters	14
Receivers	150 000 estimated in use
Receivers per 1000 people	23

FILM

Cinemas	Fixed 164
Total seating capacity	114 600
Seats per 1000 people	18
Total annual attendance	22 500 000
Annual visits per capita	3

PRESS

Quito, the capital, and Guayaquil, the largest city, with five and four daily newspapers respectively (some with large Sunday editions), account for the bulk of the country's newspaper circulation and readership. One Quito daily and one from Guayaquil are circulated throughout the country.

Non-dailies are also published in the main towns. Other periodicals number 39 with a combined circulation of 280 000 copies per issue. All newspapers and periodicals are in Spanish, which is the official language and the main urban language. In rural areas, where considerably more than half the population live, the most common, and often the only, language spoken is Quechua.

The mass media are required by the government to participate actively in the national literacy and adult-education campaign launched in 1944. Daily newspapers must devote a half-page a week, and non-dailies and other periodicals 1½ pages per issue, to promotion of the campaign's objectives.

NEWS AGENCIES

There is no national news agency. A local agency, Agencia Ecuatoriana de Prensa, has its head office in Guayaquil; another, Producciones del Ecuador, is based in Quito.

UPI, AP, AFP and DPA supply news to Ecuadorian newspapers, radio and television; Efe to newspapers and radio, and ANSA and TASS to newspapers only. AFP has a correspondent in Quito, while AP and TASS have bureaux in Guayaquil.

RADIO

Of Ecuador's 336 radio stations, 16 are publicly owned. The remainder are under private ownership and, apart from a few cultural and Christian mission stations, are commercially operated. Broadcasting ranges from 1 or 2 hours daily, for small local stations, to the almost uninterrupted services of the more powerful transmitters in heavily populated areas; 14 stations are on the air for 24 hours a day.

Educational broadcasts figure in all programmes, ranging from the daily 15-minute adult-education programmes required, by law, of all stations, to radio schools like that conducted by the Escuelas Radiofónicas Populares in the highland city of Riobamba.

Two commercial stations, Radio de la Casa de Cultura (Quito) and Radio Nacional del Ecuador (Guayaquil), with medium-wave and short-wave transmitters, broadcast cultural programmes which are received both in Ecuador and abroad.

The most powerful network in Ecuador is the non-commercial La Voz de Los Andes, with medium-wave (30kW) and short-wave transmitters (100kW) based in Quito and owned and operated by the World Radio Missionary Fellowship. Its home service of religious and cultural programmes in Spanish (21 hours a day) is broadcast on four different wave bands. International services on six different wave bands are on the air for 59 hours a day in English, Spanish, Russian, German, Japanese, Portuguese, Romanian, Quechua, French, Hungarian and Scandinavian languages, and are beamed to North and South America, Europe, Australia and New Zealand, Japan, the Caribbean and Jamaica, Siberia, south-east Asia, the Mediterranean and the south Pacific.

No licence fee for radio receivers is payable. The total number of receivers in use has increased tenfold since 1960.

TELEVISION

Television broadcasting in Ecuador, which dates from 1959, now reaches about 1 million of the population in and around five major towns. With the exception of one missionary station, all networks are commercially owned and operated.

The four principal organizations are Telecuador, with stations in Guayaquil and Quito, broadcasting for 13 hours and 7 hours a day respectively; the World Radio Missionary Fellowship's station in Quito, La Ventana de Los Andes, broadcasting religious and cultural programmes for 4 hours 45 minutes a day; Telesistema del Ecuador, with stations in Guayaquil, broadcasting for 8½ hours daily and in Cuenca, Ambato and Manta, each on the air for 5 hours a day; and the Corporación Ecuatoriana de Televisión, Guayaquil, broadcasting for 12 hours a day. Two other stations are based in Quito, and one each in Guayaquil and Cuenca.

About 73% of programmes are imported, the largest number from the USA.

All stations are required to devote at least 5 minutes a day to literacy programmes.
The definition system used is 525 lines.
No licence fee for receivers is payable.

FILM
Feature films exhibited are almost all imported, mainly from the USA, but also from Mexico, Argentina and various European countries. Such films must be passed for exhibition in each province by the provincial censorship board.

The 15 main importing and distributing companies are based in Quito and Guayaquil, 42 of the cinemas in these two cities being operated by three distributing circuits.

Ecuador's annual commercial cinema attendance figures have increased by 50% over the last five years. There are also some 70 16mm projection units in the country, either commercially operated or belonging to educational and cultural institutions or the information services of diplomatic missions.

PROFESSIONAL TRAINING AND ASSOCIATIONS
Schools of information sciences (established in 1945) at the Central University in Quito and the University of Guayaquil offer four-year courses in journalism which have been attended by 200 students. Of the 15 graduates from the Quito School, 10 have been women.

Founded in 1958 with UNESCO assistance, the Centro Internacional de Estudios Superiores de Periodismo para América Latina (CIESPAL), located in Quito, organizes two-month international information-sciences courses every year, for Latin American directors and professors of schools of journalism and for university-trained journalists with six years' continuous professional experience.

Ecuador has two national journalists' associations with headquarters in Quito and Guayaquil respectively.

Licensed radio stations may belong to an association which, in turn, is a member of the Inter-American Association of Broadcasters.

FALKLAND ISLANDS

Population	2000
Area	11 961 sq. km.

PRESS

Newspapers	Non-dailies 2
Total circulation	Non-dailies 1400
Copies per 1000 people	Non-dailies 700

RADIO

Transmitters	Long/medium-wave 1, Short-wave 1
Total receivers	Licensed 1100
Receivers per 1000 people	550

FILM

Cinemas	Fixed 2
Total seating capacity	500
Seats per 1000 people	250
Total annual attendance	20 000
Annual visits per capita	10

PRESS

There is no daily press. The official government gazette and one other journal appear monthly in the only town, Stanley, on East Falkland.

RADIO

Radio broadcasting is carried out by the Falkland Islands Broadcasting Service, financed by direct government subsidy. With one medium-wave (5kW) transmitter and one short-wave (0.5kW), its station is on the air for 38 hours a week, broadcasting news (including BBC (UK) relays), entertainment programmes and official announcements.

A licence fee is payable for receivers, either wireless or served by a wired distribution system (with 387 subscribers in 1970).

TELEVISION

There is no television.

FILM

There is no local film production. Imported films, mainly from the USA and UK, are shown in the two 16mm cinemas in Stanley and on West Falkland.

FRENCH GUIANA

Population	51 000
Area	91 000 sq. km.

PRESS

Newspapers	Dailies 1, Non-dailies 2
Total circulation	Dailies 2000, Non-dailies 2000
Copies per 1000 people	Dailies 39, Non-dailies 39

RADIO

Transmitters	Long/medium-wave 2, Short-wave 2, VHF–FM 2
Total receivers	20 000 estimated in use
Receivers per 1000 people	392

TELEVISION

Transmitters	2
Receivers	Licences 2 240
Receivers per 1000 people	44

FILM

Cinemas	Fixed 9
Total seating capacity	3400
Seats per 1000 people	66
Total annual attendance	700 000
Annual visits per capita	14

PRESS

One daily and two weekly newspapers are published, in French, in the capital, Cayenne.

NEWS AGENCIES

There is no local agency. Foreign news is received by radio teleprinter from AFP, which also has a permanent correspondent in Cayenne.

RADIO

The Cayenne station of the Office de Radiodiffusion-Télévision Française (ORTF), financed by receiver licence fees, French government subsidies and advertising revenue, broadcasts a home service in French, with medium-wave transmitters at Cayenne (4kW) and St Laurent du Maroni (0.5kW), short-wave transmitters at Cayenne (4 and 1kW) and FM transmitters at Cayenne and Kourou, together covering 95% of the population. Weekly programmes of both locally originated material and material supplied by ORTF from Paris total 70 hours, including light entertainment (39 hours), news and information (14 hours), broadcasts for special audiences (6 hours) and cultural programmes (5 hours).

TELEVISION
ORTF's transmitters (625 lines) in Cayenne and Kourou are on the air for 23
hours a week, broadcasting light entertainment (12 hours), news and information
(6 hours), broadcasts for special audiences (3 hours) and cultural programmes (2
hours). ORTF programmes, for the most part supplied from France, account for
90% of the total, the remainder being imported from non-French sources.

FILM
Mainly French, and some foreign, films are shown in the commercial (35mm and
16mm) cinemas.

GUYANA

Population	784 000
Area	214 969 sq. km.

PRESS

Newspapers	Dailies 4, Non-dailies 6
Total circulation	Dailies 82 000, Non-dailies 29 000
Copies per 1000 people	Dailies 104, Non-dailies 37

RADIO

Transmitters	Medium-wave 4, Short-wave 3, VHF–FM 1
Total receivers	100 000 estimated in use
Receivers per 1000 people	127

FILM

Cinemas	Fixed 50
Total seating capacity	375 000
Seats per 1000 people	48
Total annual attendance	9 200 000
Annual visits per capita	12

PRESS
Dailies are published in English, in the capital, Georgetown. The non-daily press
is mainly weekly, and includes the Sunday edition of a daily newspaper, and
another Sunday paper associated with the government party.
    Periodicals total 6 titles (2 military, 2 technical, 1 commercial and 1
historical) with a combined circulation of 13 600 copies. In addition, the
Ministry of Information issues a weekly gazette and a weekly current affairs

bulletin, while a business firm prints 10 000 copies of its house journal. A parish magazine circulates 2000 copies.

NEWS AGENCIES
There is no national agency. Several papers receive world news from Reuters, and one from ADN.
AFP has a correspondent in Georgetown.

RADIO
Radio broadcasting is conducted by a government service and a privately owned commercial station, both with full national coverage.

The Guyana Broadcasting Service (GBS), established after the government's purchase of a private station in 1968, became a public corporation in 1972. With medium- and short-wave and FM transmitters, it is on the air for 136 hours a week. Programmes include light entertainment (53 hours), news and information (43 hours), broadcasts for special audiences (12 hours), education (4 hours), etc. All programmes are domestically produced except for daily relays of BBC (UK) news and sports programmes.

The Guyana Broadcasting Company (Radio Demerara), a subsidiary of a British firm, Rediffusion, also using medium- and short-wave transmitters, broadcasts for over 100 hours weekly.

A radio licence fee is payable but the actual number of receivers in use is considerably in excess of the number of licences (60 000).

FILM
Occasional short films are produced but there is no regular production. Foreign films, imported on a rental basis, are shown in fixed cinemas, as well as in the drive-in (accommodating 385 cars) which recorded an annual attendance of 645 600 in 1972. Non-commercial showings by ten mobile units were attended by 480 000 people in 1972.

PARAGUAY

Population	2 470 000
Area	406 752 sq. km.

PRESS

Newspapers	Dailies 4
Total circulation	Dailies 75 000
Copies per 1000 people	Dailies 30

RADIO

Transmitters	Long/medium-wave 23, Short-wave 8, VHF—FM 6
Total receivers	175 000 estimated in use
Receivers per 1000 people	71

TELEVISION

Transmitters	1
Receivers	51 000 estimated in use
Receivers per 1000 people	20

FILMS

Cinemas	Fixed 61*

*In the city of Asunción.

PRESS

Though there have been as many as 11 or 12 daily newspapers published at the same time in recent years, there are now only three dailies in the capital, Asunción, and one other in Encarnación. Asunción papers are also read in other main towns. The capital's largest, and oldest, daily (established in 1925) has a week day circulation of 30 000 copies. The non-daily press includes two Sunday editions of dailies and several weeklies.

All newspapers are in Spanish, the official language, though some 50% of the population speak only Guaraní.

About 20 periodicals are published, dealing mainly with technical subjects, education and current affairs.

NEWS AGENCIES

There is no national agency. The local press is supplied with domestic news through its own correspondents and reporters. Foreign news is received from ANSA and Efe, both of which have bureaux in Asunción. UPI also has an office in the capital.

RADIO

General supervision of broadcasting is exercised by the National Telecommunications Administration. There is one government-owned non-commercial radio station, Radio Nacional, with 1 medium-wave transmitter (100kW), 2 short-wave transmitters (100 and 3kW) and 2 FM transmitters, all in Asunción. Another station, also government-owned but commercially operated, with 1 medium-wave (25kW) transmitter and 1 short-wave (5kW) transmitter, is located in Encarnación. About 20 other stations, including one in each of the eight main provincial towns, are privately owned and commercially operated. The majority broadcast for 12 to 16 hours a day. Languages used are Spanish and Guaraní.

No receiver licence fee is payable.

TELEVISION

Asunción has one commercial television station, covering the area around the capital, which began operating in September 1965. It is on the air for 65 hours a week, broadcasting entertainment programmes (73% of the total broadcasting time), news (14%) and educational and cultural programmes (13%), a high proportion of these being imported from the USA and from other Latin American countries.

FILM
There is no local film production. Feature films are imported from the USA and from Latin American and European countries. The majority of the country's covered cinemas are in the capital. There are outdoor cinemas in other towns, and rural areas are served by mobile projection units.

PROFESSIONAL TRAINING AND ASSOCIATIONS
The Institute of Journalism, established in 1965 at the Universidad Nacional, Asunción, offers a three-year course and research facilities. The Department of Communication Science (founded 1966) at the Universidad Católica, also in Asunción, has a four-year programme.

There is a press association in Asunción. Private radio-station owners have their own association.

PERU

Population	14 460 000
Area	1 285 216 sq. km.

PRESS
Newspapers	Dailies 56, Non-dailies 320*

RADIO
Transmitters	Long/medium-wave 187, Short-wave 106, VHF–FM 11
Total receivers	2 000 000 estimated in use
Receivers per 1000 people	138

TELEVISION
Transmitters	19
Receivers	410 000 estimated in use
Receivers per 1000 people	28

FILM
Cinemas	Fixed 276

*In 1968.

PRESS
Lima, the capital, accounts for over half the national daily circulation, with 12 dailies, some of which have nation-wide readerships. The highest circulation (149 000) is recorded by a tabloid with both morning and afternoon editions (this paper was nationalized in 1970 when a new press law was adopted); five others circulate between 90 000 and 134 000 copies per issue (two of the largest have been jointly run as a cooperative since 1970). Several dailies have Sunday editions with higher circulations. Apart from a few larger papers in Trujillo, Arequipa, Chimbote, Huancayo and Piura, the provincial dailies appearing in over 30 towns rarely reach circulations of over 10 000. Two dailies are published in Chinese and one in Japanese.

Non-daily newspapers (some weekly but the majority less frequent) are published, like the dailies, in Spanish. Exceptions are a few foreign-language journals serving the English, German and Chinese-speaking communities in the larger towns. About half the population are Indians, speaking mainly Quechua and Aymará. Only the small number who are literate in Spanish are reached by the press.

There were 11 general readership periodicals reported in 1971, but, in addition to these, specialized journals are published, dealing principally with education, political science, sociology, sports and recreations, agriculture and medicine.

NEWS AGENCIES
There is no national agency. Newspapers depend largely on their own correspondents and on the official government radio news bulletin for domestic news.

The Centro de Información Católica and Noticias Aliadas both gather and supply religious and other news to subscribers in Peru and other Latin American countries. The foreign news services of AP, AFP, Reuters and UPI are received by the main newspapers. All these agencies, plus ANSA, Jiji and TASS, have bureaux in Lima.

RADIO
Both radio and television broadcasting are regulated by the General Tele-communications Law promulgated in 1971. All telecommunications facilities are controlled by the state, which owns some broadcasting stations and has an interest in other associated stations (a 51% interest, for television, 25% for radio). The Oficina Nacional de Información (ONI) is the department responsible for government broadcasting stations and the part-government, part-private Empresa Nacional de Telecomunicaciones (ENTEL–Peru) is responsible for the associated stations.

Of the 230 stations operating, the most powerful are those of the government network Radio Nacional (13 stations) which operates on both medium and short waves, broadcasting news, information, entertainment and educational programmes on its foreign services in English, French, Spanish, German and Japanese beamed to Europe, North America and the Far East. Radio Nacional derives its revenue from taxes on imported receivers, registration fees paid by private stations and advertising.

Other stations (8) are operated by educational, cultural or religious organizations or by commercial enterprises, often in association with newspaper publishing houses. At least 60% of programme material and 100% of advertising programmes are required to be of national origin. Medium-wave stations cover over 62% of the population.

No licence fee is payable for radio receivers.

TELEVISION
The country's first telecasts were made by the Ministry of Education's station at Lima in January 1958. It is now the country's most powerful station and broadcasts mainly educational and cultural programmes, as does the privately owned station operated by the University of Lima. Other stations in Lima and Teledos (now state owned) and four commercial associated stations (mixed state and private ownership). Three of the latter have repeater station in other parts of the country. The only station outside Lima is Televisora Continental, at Arequipa (with one relay station at Tacna).

Total broadcasting time for the Lima stations is 390 hours a week, consisting, on average, of films, serials and direct broadcasts (44%), advertising (37%), cultural and educational programmes (8%), sports (6%) and information (5%). Educational television centres in Lima and other parts of the country produce programmes and organize groups of school-age and adult learners, in cooperation with educational authorities, religious organizations and local teleclubs. Regular educational programmes are being broadcast initially in Lima, Arequipa and Tacna for up to 6 hours a day.

Imported programmes come from the USA, Argentina, Mexico, the UK and Federal Republic of Germany. Coproductions are made with Peruvian, Mexican and Venezuelan television organizations.

FILM
Some documentary films are produced by the two main documentary studios, for government departments, private interests or television stations. Newsreels and advertising films are also produced.

Films commercially exhibited are imported from the USA, other Latin American countries, European countries and Japan. Affected by the extension of television, the number of cinemas and cinema attendances has declined markedly in recent years. Commercial cinemas are all 35mm, but a large number of 16mm projection units are used throughout the country, for cultural and information showings and for private exhibition of imported feature films which are distributed in 16mm versions. There is one drive-in cinema accommodating 100 cars.

SPACE COMMUNICATIONS
Peru has an Atlantic Intelsat earth station, opened in 1969, at Lurin in the outskirts of Lima.

PROFESSIONAL TRAINING AND ASSOCIATIONS
The country's first schools of journalism were established in the Catholic and San Marcos Universities at Lima in 1945 and 1947 respectively, followed by another at the University of Trujillo and then by various other university institutes, schools, etc., in the main towns. Diplomas and professional working

qualifications for all journalists in Peru are granted by a central official body, the College of Journalists, at Lima, established by law in 1971. Training for educational broadcasting is provided by the Asociación Latinoamericana de Teleducación founded in Lima in 1970.

Professional associations include several unions of journalists, associations of broadcasting stations, film distributors and exhibitors, etc.

SURINAM

| Population | 406 000 |
| Area | 163 265 sq. km. |

PRESS

Newspapers	Dailies 3, Non-dailies 2
Total circulation	Dailies 20 000, Non-dailies 2000
Copies per 1000 people	Dailies 49, Non-dailies 5

RADIO

Transmitters	Long/medium-wave 4, VHF–FM 1
Total receivers	100 000 estimated in use
Receivers per 1000 people	246

TELEVISION

Transmitters	1
Receivers	32 000 estimated in use
Receivers per 1000 people	79

FILM

Cinemas	Fixed 26
Total annual attendance	1 700 000
Annual visits per capita	4

PRESS

Two dailies in Dutch, the official language, and a small Chinese-language daily are published in the capital, Paramaribo.

The non-daily and periodical press consists of two newspapers – one published twice weekly by the government, and the other weekly – and a Catholic weekly journal, with a combined circulation of about 4000 copies.

NEWS AGENCIES

The Surinam branch of ANP issues daily bulletins in Dutch and English.

RADIO

The Stichtung Radio Omroep Suriname, the government-owned Surinam Broadcasting Corporation financed by government subsidy and commercial advertising, operating a 50kW medium-wave transmitter and an FM transmitter at Paramaribo, broadcasts for 18 hours daily in Dutch, Hindi, Indonesian and English.

Radio Paramaribo and Radio Apinte, both privately owned commercial stations each with one 10kW medium-wave transmitter, also broadcast for 18 hours daily, in the same languages plus Chinese and the Surinamese vernacular. Two other private stations, with 1kW medium-wave transmitters, operate from Paramaribo and the second largest town, Nieuw Nickerie.

TELEVISION

Television broadcasting began in 1968. The government service, Surinaamse Televisie Stichting (STVS), partly financed by advertising, now operates a main transmitter (525 lines) at Paramaribo, with relay stations at Moengo and Brokopondo, west and south of the capital. Programmes (including colour), mainly imported from the USA, the Netherlands and the Federal Republic of Germany, are broadcast for about 30 hours a week.

FILM

All films shown in commercial cinemas are imported. Government departments organize educational showings.

URUGUAY

Population	2 960 000
Area	177 508 sq. km.

PRESS
Newspapers	Dailies 29
Total circulation	Dailies 795 000
Copies per 1000 people	Dailies 269

RADIO
Transmitters	Long/medium-wave 79, Short-wave 16, VHF–FM 4
Total receivers	1 500 000 estimated in use
Receivers per 1000 people	507

TELEVISION
Transmitters	17
Receivers	300 000 estimated in use
Receivers per 1000 people	101

FILM

Cinemas	Fixed 180
Total seating capacity	124 700
Seats per 1000 people	42

PRESS

The 15 dailies published in the capital, Montevideo (the three largest with circulations of 170 000, 120 000 and 90 000 copies per issue respectively), account for over 90% of the country's total daily circulation. Most of these papers have political-party affiliations and are read in all parts of the country. Other dailies published in provincial centres, such as Salto (three dailies), Paysandú (two dailies), Rocha, Rivera, Mercedes, Florida, Colonia, Punta del Este, etc., concentrate on local news.

The non-daily press includes many provincial twice-weeklies and weeklies, often associated for group purchasing of materials, etc. One English-language weekly appears in Montevideo.

Some 300 periodicals, mostly monthlies, are published, the majority in Montevideo.

NEWS AGENCIES

Since the disappearance of the Agencia Nacional de Informaciones in 1967, there has been no national agency. The press and broadcasting stations receive foreign news from AP, UPI, AFP, Reuters and ANSA, all of which have their main Latin American bureaux in Montevideo, and also from DPA, TASS, PRELA and Interpress.

RADIO

Broadcasting, which is under the control of the Dirección Nacional de Communicaciones, is partly public owned and partly private. The government service, the Servicio Oficial de Difusión Radio Eléctrica (SODRE), with three medium-wave transmitters (6, 10 and 12kW) and four short-wave transmitters (0.5 and 10kW), broadcasts school and general educational and cultural radio programmes for 15 hours a day. Most of the other radio stations are privately owned and commercially operated; 22 are based in Montevideo, and the others in various provincial centres so that no part of the country is without radio coverage. Some are on the air round the clock, the majority for 15 hours or more daily.

Total broadcasting time for all stations amounts to almost 11 000 hours a week, over 75% of which is locally produced. Programmes consist mainly of light entertainment (25%), news and information (20%), advertising (16%), arts, letters and science (11%), broadcasts for special audiences (11%), education (10%) and broadcasts for ethnic minorities (5%). All programmes are in Spanish.

No licence fee is payable for receiving sets.

TELEVISION

The country's first television station, SAETA, began commercial operation in December 1956 in Montevideo. The capital now has four commercial stations, each broadcasting for about 15 hours a day, in addition to the government-owned service, SODRE, which has a second station in the provincial city of Melo. SODRE stations, also operated on a commercial basis, are on the air for up to 18 hours a day, carrying a higher proportion of educational and cultural programmes. Other commercial stations operate in 11 provincial capitals (Artigas, Melo, Colonia, Maldonado, Paysandú, Fray Bentos, Rivera, Rocha, Salto, Tacuarembó and Treinta y Tres), thus bringing potential television coverage by one station, at least, to around 90% of the population.

Programmes, totalling 740 hours a week, consist of light entertainment (24%), news and information (19%), advertising (16%), broadcasts for special audiences (13%), cultural broadcasts (12%), education (10%) and broadcasts for ethnic minorities (5%). A large proportion of programmes (between 40 and 60%) are imported, principally from the USA, from Argentina, and to a lesser extent from the UK, France and Italy.

The definition system used is 525 lines.

FILM

Feature films are produced only occasionally, but government departments, private companies and a university film institute have a steady output of educational and scientific films.

In the capital, there is a government film library – which also has projection facilities – and three film clubs; 17 other film clubs are found in provincial centres. Films exhibited in the commercial cinemas throughout the country are imported mainly from the USA, Mexico, Argentina, Spain, the UK, France, Italy, other European countries and the USSR.

SPACE COMMUNICATIONS

Uruguay has no satellite earth station of its own but has access to Argentina's Atlantic Intelsat facilities.

PROFESSIONAL ASSOCIATIONS

There is a journalists' association in Montevideo, and another grouping together provincial newsmen, an association of newspaper owners and editors and a union of graphic arts and printing workers. Radio and television organizations include a national broadcasters' association, which groups station owners, an association for programme staff and a national association (with provincial branches) of educational television personnel. Film producers and technicians have their own national association, while most of the country's film distributors and exhibitors are members of a trade centre.

VENEZUELA

Population	10 970 000
Area	912 050 sq. km.

PRESS

Newspaper	Dailies 42, Non-dailies 21
Total circulation	Dailies 997 660
Copies per 1000 people	Dailies 91

RADIO

Transmitters	Long/medium-wave 132, Short-wave 87, VHF–FM 16
Total receivers	2 000 000 estimated in use
Receivers per 1000 people	182

TELEVISION

Transmitters	37
Receivers	980 000 estimated in use
Receivers per 1000 people	89

FILM

Cinemas	Fixed 429
Total seating capacity	544 400
Seats per 1000 people	49
Total annual attendance	37 700 000
Annual visits per capita	3

PRESS

With three exceptions, Venezuela's daily newspapers are morning editions. Both the number of dailies and their total circulation have increased since 1960 when there were 29 titles circulating 646 000 copies. Ten dailies are published in Caracas, the capital, the largest being two afternoon tabloids under the same ownership, circulating over 100 000 copies, and a morning daily with a weekday circulation of 97 000, rising to 126 000 on Saturdays. One Caracas paper is published in English. Altogether, the capital accounts for over half the country's daily newspaper circulation.

The busy port of Maracaibo, with three dailies (one in Spanish and English circulating 62 000 copies) is the main publishing centre outside Caracas. Nineteen other provincial towns have one or more dailies each, few exceeding 15 000 copies per issue.

Based mainly in Caracas, the non-daily periodical press consists of over 300 titles, including a number of weekly magazines with circulations ranging from 40 000 to 165 000 copies, which are distributed throughout the country.

NEWS AGENCIES

The national agency, Prensa Venezolana (PEVE), founded in 1940, has its head office in Caracas, and correspondents in all the country's main towns. It deals only with collection and distribution of national news.

Foreign news is supplied to Venezuelan newspapers and broadcasting organizations by AP, UPI, Reuters, TASS, AFP, AMEX, Efe and Latin.

RADIO

The government network, Radio Nacional de Venezuela, attached to the Central Office of Information under the direct control of the President of the Republic's Office, broadcasts mainly educational, cultural and informative programmes via 8 medium-wave transmitters (1, 10 and 50kW), 10 short-wave transmitters (up to 50kW) and 2 FM transmitters located in 11 different towns. Radio Nacional broadcasts are received throughout the national territory and in foreign countries (in Spanish, English and French).

The national Office of Adult Education, in conjunction with a private group, operates Escuelas Radiofónicas, a network of three short-wave transmitters of 1 and 10kW in Caracas and San Fernando de Apure, broadcasting educational programmes.

All other stations (approximately 140) are commercially operated and are affiliated to a central assoociation of the Venezuelan radio and television industry. All are required, by government decree, to broadcast a quota of cultural programmes and certain programmes of national interest.

Broadcasting hours vary considerably: four stations are on the air 24 hours a day, a further 60 for 18 hours a day or more, with another large group averaging around 12 hours a day. Advertising occupies over 50% of programme time, followed by light entertainment, news and sports broadcasts.

TELEVISION

Television was introduced in Venezuela in 1952 by the government network Televisora Nacional (TVN–5), under the direct control of the Office of the President of the Republic, which now broadcasts for 49 hours a week from its transmitter in Caracas, covering the metropolitan and surrounding area inhabited by over 1 million people. TVN–5 broadcasts a 60-minute news programme, with a special international news service, daily. Other programmes are popular, cultural and scientific broadcasts, children's (including pre-school and school) programmes, drama, music (including special broadcasts for young musicians) and study programmes at university and teacher-training level.

Commercial television is the main source of entertainment and information for a large proportion of the population. There are private stations with main transmitters in Caracas and repeaters in other main population centres – Radio Caracas with 13 repeaters (including one in Curaçao, Netherlands Antilles), broadcasting for 18 hours a day, Venevision with 10 repeaters, broadcasting for 9 hours a day, Cadena Venezolana (equipped for colour), with 8 repeaters, and Teletrece. Other commercial stations in Valencia and Maracaibo were inactive at the time of writing.

Programmes of Caracas stations are approximately 50% imported (feature films, serials, cartoons, documentaries and advertising), mainly from the USA,

20% nationally produced and 30% live advertising. All stations are required to broadcast certain cultural programmes and programmes of national interest.

Television receivers, including 25 000 colour sets, are found mainly in the Caracas metropolitan area (66%), the Caribbean coast (22%) and parts of the interior (12%). The definition system used is 625 lines.

No licence is required for television receivers.

FILM

Venzuela produces, on average, two or three feature films yearly, including occasional coproductions with the USA and Mexico, several weekly newsreels, a quantity of advertising film and an annual average of about 20 16mm documentaries and educational short films. Films for government requirements are produced under contract by private companies. Studio and laboratory facilities are sufficient to handle a much larger output, and the government is seeking to stimulate production, particularly through its recently established Consultative Committee for the Development of the Film Industry.

Imports for 1970 included 200 feature films, from the Federal Republic of Germany, Mexico and the USA, and 100 35mm documentaries. There are no import quotas but licences are required for various types of film, processed, partly processed and unprocessed.

The number of commercial cinemas has dropped by more than 300 over the last ten years. Drive-ins have increased in number from 3 to 20 with total accommodation for 4000 cars. In addition, films are shown by mobile units, notably those of the Instituto Nacional de Cultura y Bellas Artes (INCIBA), which takes programmes of 16mm films, slides, recorded music and talks on cultural and current affairs to outlying communities as part of its pilot cultural programme.

SPACE COMMUNICATIONS

Radio and television programmes broadcast via Atlantic Intelsat satellite are received and transmitted by an earth station at Camatagua, 150km from Caracas, serving all Venezuelan television stations and those of the Netherlands Antilles. A second, non-standard station near Caracas is approved for reception of television and associated audio signals only.

PROFESSIONAL TRAINING AND ASSOCIATIONS

Diploma courses of four years' duration for journalists are offered by the communications schools of three universities: the Universidad Católica 'Andrés Bello', Caracas, with a current enrolment of 280 students having passed an entrance examination, and a total of 175 graduates in six separate years; the Universidad Central de Venezuela, Caracas, admitting students having passed the baccalaureate examination; and the Universidad del Zulia, Maracaibo.

The Ministry of Education's Audio-visual Centre in Caracas trains monitors for the pilot cultural plans of the Instituto Nacional de Cultura y Bellas Artes (see under Film).

Professional associations include a national journalists' association with branches throughout the country. In 1973, under the terms of a new law on the professional practices of journalism, an official 'Colegio Nacional de Periodistas' was established, to which all journalists will be affiliated. There is a national press and typographical workers' union, and an association of film workers and critics. Radio and television personnel have a single union, and there is one association for broadcasting-station owners. In addition to the National Chamber of Film-makers' Associations, there is an association of exhibitors, grouping together most of the country's cinema operators, and another of distributors.

PART FIVE

ASIA

Afghanistan
Bahrain
Bangladesh
Bhutan
Brunei
Burma
China (People's Republic of)
Cyprus
Hong Kong
India
Indonesia
Iran
Iraq
Israel
Japan
Jordan
Khmer Republic
Korea (Republic of)
Korea (Democratic People's Republic of)
Kuwait
Laos
Lebanon

Macau
Malaysia (Federation of)
Maldives
Mongolia
Nepal
Oman
Pakistan
Philippines
Portuguese Timor
Qatar
Saudi Arabia
Sikkim
Singapore
Sri Lanka
Syria
Thailand
United Arab Emirates
Vietnam (Republic of)
Vietnam (Democratic Republic of)
Yemen (Arab Republic of)
Yemen (People's Democratic
Republic of)

AFGHANISTAN

Population	17 480 000
Area	647 497 sq. km.

PRESS

Newspapers	Dailies 18, Non-dailies 2
Total circulation	Dailies 101 000, Non-dailies 7500
Copies per 1000 people	Dailies 6, Non-dailies 0.4

RADIO

Transmitters	Long/medium-wave 2, Short-wave 4, VHF—FM 1
Total receivers	108 000 estimated in use
Receivers per 1000 people	6

FILM

Cinemas	Fixed 24
Total seating capacity	12 000
Seats per 1000 people	0.6
Total annual attendance	19 200 000
Annual visits per capita	1

PRESS

With one exception, all dailies are evening papers, 6 appearing in the official national language, Pushtu, 10 in both Pushtu and Dari (a form of Persian widely used in Afghanistan), 1 in Dari and 1 in English. The majority are government owned. The capital, Kabul, has 7 dailies, the two largest of which, published in both Pushtu and Dari, circulate over 20 000 copies each. Dailies, mostly with small circulations, are also published in ten provincial capitals. The non-dailies appear in Pushtu and Dari (5000 copies) and Dari alone (2500 copies).

With approximately the same language distribution, periodicals total 24 titles with a combined circulation of around 30 000 copies, the majority being published by government ministries and academic bodies and institutions. Main subject categories are education (6 titles with a combined circulation of 38 000 copies), general interest (2 titles, 7500 copies), law, administration, etc. (3 titles, 6500 copies), political science (2 titles, 5000 copies), literature, religion, etc.

NEWS AGENCIES

The Bakhtar News Agency, founded in 1939–40 under the Ministry of Information and Culture, is the national agency and the main source of news for both press and radio. Home news is gathered by about 16 reporters in Kabul, and by staff correspondents and stringers in the provinces who telephone their stories to Kabul.

The main foreign agencies supplying international news are Reuters, AP and DPA, but the services of TASS, Tanjug, Hsinhua, CTK and AFP are also received. Stories are translated into Dari in Kabul, for transmission to the agency's subscribers, which receive around 6000 words daily. AFP, DPA and TASS have representatives in Kabul.

RADIO
Radio Afghanistan, government owned and operated under the supervision of the Ministry of Information and Culture, with medium-wave transmitters (20 and 100kW) and short-wave transmitters (10, 50 and 100kW), broadcasts its main home service in Pushtu and Dari, with a second early-afternoon programme in other nationally used languages: Turko-Afghan (45 minutes) and Uzbek and Baluchi (15 minutes each). Broadcasting hours total 132 hours a week, consisting of cultural programmes (65 hours), broadcasts to ethnic minorities (26 hours), news and information (23 hours), light entertainment (7 hours), education (5 hours), advertising (3 hours) and broadcasts for special audiences (2 hours), almost all being nationally produced.

The foreign service is on the air for about 35 hours a week in Pushtu (10½ hours), Urdu (7 hours), English (7 hours), Dari, German and Russian (3½ hours each).

No radio licence fee is payable.

FILM
Film production is under government auspices; 1 feature and 14 documentaries were made in 1971.

About 200 features, including some 16mm, are imported annually: from India (96 titles in 1971), Iran (40), the USA (25), the USSR (20), Pakistan (9), France, Italy and other countries. They are shown in field cinemas in the main towns or by mobile units (of which there are two in constant operation).

PROFESSIONAL TRAINING AND ASSOCIATIONS
A four-year journalism course was instituted at Kabul University in 1963. Technical training in communications is available at the Polytechnic Institute, Kabul, which was opened in 1967.

There is a journalists' association in Kabul. A book publishing institute was opened in 1966 under the joint sponsorship of the government press, the Bakhtar News Agency and leading newspapers.

BAHRAIN

Population	220 000
Area	598 sq. km.

PRESS

Newspapers	Non-dailies 3
Total circulation	Non-dailies 4500
Copies per 1000 people	Non-dailies 29

RADIO

Transmitters	Long/medium-wave 3
Total receivers	75 000 estimated in use
Receivers per 1000 people	341

TELEVISION

Receivers	13 000 estimated in use
Receivers per 1000 people	59

FILM

Cinemas	Fixed 9
Total seating capacity	9845
Seats per 1000 people	45
Total annual attendance	1 358 790
Annual visits per capita	6

PRESS

There are no daily newspapers, but two weekly newspapers in Arabic, and one in English, serve the Bahraini population and the European community.

Some 16 periodicals are published in Arabic (9 titles, with a combined circulation of 17 775 copies), Arabic and English (3 titles, 11 500 copies) and English alone (4 titles, 4000 copies). The majority are for general readership (including 2 radio magazines, one published by the Ministry of Information); 5 titles deal with commerce and industry, 2 with sociological subjects and 1 with education.

NEWS AGENCIES

There is no national agency.

RADIO

The government-owned Bahrain Broadcasting Station operates two 2kW medium-wave transmitters which are on the air for 55 hours a week, broadcasting, in Arabic, light entertainment (37 hours), news and information (11 hours), programmes on arts, letters and science (5 hours), education (3 hours) and broadcasts for special audiences (3 hours). Programmes are almost entirely of national origin.

The Bahrain Petroleum Company also has two 0.1kW medium-wave transmitters broadcasting daily programmes in English, with periods of uninterrupted
light music.
No licence fee is payable.

TELEVISION
Though there is no local service, television broadcasts are received from the
nearby station operated by the Arabian American Oil Company at Dharan in
Saudi Arabia.

FILM
In addition to the fixed cinemas, there is one mobile projection unit. Imported
feature films totalled 330 in 1971, coming from the USA (173), Egypt (42),
India (39), Italy (26), the UK (25), India, the USSR, Lebanon and France.

SPACE COMMUNICATIONS
Bahrain's Indian Ocean Intelsat earth station came into operation in July 1969.

BANGLADESH

Population	60 670 000
Area	142 776 sq. km.

PRESS	
Newspapers	Dailies 25

RADIO	
Transmitters	Long/medium-wave 7, Short-wave 4, VHF—FM 5

TELEVISION	
Transmitters	1

PRESS
The capital, Dacca, has 16 dailies (11 in Bengali and 5 in English), the largest of
which circulates some 30 000 copies per issue. Daily papers appear also in
Chittagong (6 in Bengali and 2 in English) and Bogra (1 in Bengali).
    Weekly and fortnightly papers, almost all in Bengali, are published in Dacca,
Chittagong, Bogra, Comilla, Dinajpur, Faridpur, Jessore, Khulna, Mymensingh,
Pabra and Sylhet. Periodicals, for which exact data are not available, are
published mainly in Bengali with some titles in English.
    Annual newsprint production is around 47 000 tons.

NEWS AGENCIES

The national agency, founded in 1972, is the Bangladesh Sangbad Sangasta or Bangladesh News Agency (BNA), with headquarters in Dacca. Other agencies are Bangladesh Press International (BPI), Eastern News Agency (ENA) and United Press of Bangladesh (UPB), all formed since January 1972.

RADIO

The government broadcasting service, Radio Bangladesh, operates 7 medium-wave transmitters in Dacca (5 and 100kW), Chittagong (10kW), Rangpur (10kW), Rajshahi (10kW), Khulna (10kW) and Sylhet (2kW), 4 short-wave transmitters (including two of 100kW) in Dacca and 5 FM transmitters in Dacca (two), Rajshahi, Chittagong and Sylhet.

A home service is broadcast on medium waves from Dacca and regional stations for 13 hours daily and on short waves from Dacca for 8 hours a day. Bengali and English are the languages of transmission.

A foreign service, on short waves, is broadcast in Bengali (3 hours a day), English (1¾ hours) and Nepali, Hindi and Urdu (30 minutes each).

TELEVISION

Television programmes were first broadcast from Dacca in 1964. The Bangladesh Television Corporation, formed in 1971, with a main transmitter in Dacca, now covers the areas around Dacca, Comilla, Tangail, Mymensingh and Faridpur.

FILM

There is no local production of films. While no exact information is available about cinemas, it is estimated that there are around 100 fixed cinemas in the country, showing films imported mainly from India.

BHUTAN

Population	854 000
Area	47 000 sq. km.

PRESS
Newspapers	Non-dailies 3
Total circulation	Non-dailies 1620
Copies per 1000 people	Non-dailies 2

FILM
Cinemas	Fixed 3
Total seating capacity	1500
Seats per 1000 people	2
Total annual attendance	183 700
Annual visits per capita	0.2

PRESS
A fortnightly official bulletin is published in the capital, Thimphu, in three separate language editions, Dzongka (the official language), Nepali and English, each with a circulation of 500 copies.

RADIO
There is no radio station in Bhutan, but broadcasts from other countries are received. An annual licence fee is payable for radio receivers.

FILM
In addition to the three cinema halls, there is one mobile 16mm projection unit. About 50 feature films and 20 documentaries are imported each year from India.

BRUNEI

Population	140 000
Area	5765 sq. km.

PRESS

Newspapers	Non-dailies 3
Total circulation	Non-dailies 30 500
Copies per 1000 people	Non-dailies 218

RADIO

Transmitters	Long/medium-wave 4, Short-wave 2, VHF–FM 2
Total receivers	15 500 estimated in use
Receivers per 1000 people	111

TELEVISION

Receivers	3000 estimated in use
Receivers per 1000 people	21

FILM

Cinemas	Fixed 8
Total seating capacity	8390
Seats per 1000 people	60
Total annual attendance	2 629 500
Annual visits per capita	19

PRESS

Although Brunei's only daily newspaper ceased to appear in 1969, both Chinese and English-language dailies from neighbouring Sarawak, as well as overseas papers, circulate in the Sultanate.

There are three weeklies: one in English, published in Kuala Belait and circulating 26 000 copies, one in romanized Malay and Chinese (3500 copies) distributed free of charge by the Department of Broadcasting and Information in Brunei Town and one in Chinese (1000 copies). A twice-monthly radio magazine (multilingual) circulates 1600 copies and an annual publication circulates 2500 copies. A large oil company which employs a tenth of the working population also circulates, free of charge, a weekly news bulletin in English, romanized Malay and Chinese.

NEWS AGENCIES

A radio news service is received from Reuters in Singapore.

RADIO

Radio Brunei, a government network operated by the Brunei Broadcasting Service (BBS), with medium-wave transmitters at Tutong (10 and 20kW), Berakas (10kW) and Kuala Belait (0.6kW), broadcasts mainly in Malay (13 hours a day), English (6½ hours), Chinese (5 hours) and Ghurkhali (1 hour) plus a few minutes daily in Iban and Dusun, covering 95% of the population.

Of Radio Brunei's 180 hours of programmes a week, over 80% are of national origin. Main programme categories are light entertainment (92 hours), news and information (29 hours), broadcasts for special audiences (11 hours), cultural programmes (5 hours), education (3 hours) and broadcasts for ethnic minorities (30 minutes). BBS radio reporters take their microphones into villages every Friday for two-way discussions on community problems.

No receiver licence fee is payable. Low-cost receivers are made available, by the government, on easy terms, for poorer families.

TELEVISION

There is no local television service, but there are 3000 receivers in use in the coastal areas, where reception is possible from Sabah (Malaysia).

FILM

During 1969–72, 1 entertainment film, 8 documentaries and 1 instructional film were produced by the Department of Broadcasting and Information and the Department of Lands. Three of these films were coproduced with Malaysian film units.

Imported films, mainly from the USA and the UK, are exhibited in 8 fixed cinemas in the main towns, in 1 outdoor cinema open for less than six months in the year, and by 8 itinerant 16mm units which travel throughout the sultanate, serving millions of rural spectators.

BURMA

Population	27 584 000
Area	678 033 sq. km.

PRESS	
Newspapers	Dailies 8, Non-dailies 133
Total circulation	Dailies 230 000, Non-dailies 1 285 680
Copies per 1000 people	Dailies 8, Non-dailies 47

RADIO	
Transmitters	Long/medium-wave 4, Short-wave 4
Total receivers	400 000 (licences)
Licences per 1000 people	14

FILM	
Cinemas	Fixed 452
Total seating capacity	364 800
Seats per 1000 people	13
Total annual attendance	218 000 000
Annual visits per capita	8

PRESS

Most of the country's daily newspapers appear in the capital, Rangoon. Of these, three in Burmese, all controlled by the Ministry of Information and Culture, have circulations ranging from 40 000 to 70 000 copies per issue. The two English-language dailies carry a large proportion of international news, as does one of the Burmese-language papers. Other papers devote most of their space to national affairs.

Other general interest newspapers are published at Mandalay and Moulmein and in smaller centres and include some in Chinese, Tamil and Urdu. All dailies have Sunday editions with popular features which raise their circulations considerably above their weekday levels. But circulation figures are far from representing actual readerships since papers are read aloud in community groups, and copies are passed from hand to hand.

Periodicals numbering some 600 titles with a combined circulation of over 3 million copies per issue include 166 religious journals, 124 dealing with the arts and architecture, 73 with linguistics, 53 with philosophy, 47 with medicine, 33 with history, 28 with ethnography, 21 with recreation, 21 with politics and 14 illustrated general readership magazines, as well as legal, educational, literary and domestic-science publications. Some of these are government sponsored.

Some newsprint is domestically produced.

NEWS AGENCIES

The national agency is the News Agency of Burma (NAB), founded in 1963, which provides both national and international news services. NAB has no foreign correspondents, its international news being obtained from TASS, UPI, AP, Reuters, AFP and Hsinhua. This makes up 90% of its daily bulletin containing over 100 items, 430 000 copies of which are distributed to all newspapers and many other subscribers.

RADIO
The government-owned Burma Broadcasting Service broadcasts a home service in Burmese (mainly) and English for 111 hours a week with a further 23 hours a week of parallel programmes in various indigenous languages, including Shan, Karen, Kayah, Kachin and Chin. Programmes include news and information (24 hours a week), folklore and popular music (59 hours) and a range of educational and cultural programmes for schools and for occupational, vocational, library and other adult listening groups (5 hours).

FILM
With a total production in 1972 of 43 feature films and 49 short films (including 14 entertainment and 27 instructional), the Burmese film industry is active and receives goverment support through the national film council.

Feature films imported in 1972 totalled 38, coming from the USA and the UK (18), Italy, France and the Federal Republic of Germany (9), Japan (5), the USSR (3), India and Pakistan (2), Yugoslavia and Hungary (1). About 180 16mm documentaries were imported mainly from the USA and the UK (99) and the USSR (62). The sole importer of films is the Ministry of Information's Motion Picture Agency of Burma.

In addition to the fixed commercial cinemas, there are 45 mobile units in continuous operation serving an additional 39.5 million spectators a year.

PROFESSIONAL TRAINING AND ASSOCIATIONS
Seven-month courses in journalism are available at the School of Journalism founded in 1967 by the Ministry of Information in Rangoon.

There are professional associations for journalists, for stage and screen directors, artists, operators and technicians, and for film distributors and exhibitors.

CHINA (People's Republic of)

Population	787 180 000
Area	9 561 000 sq. km.

RADIO

Total receivers	15 000 000 estimated in use
Receivers per 1000 people	19

430 per 1000 in USSR   1695 per 1000 in U.S.

TELEVISION

Receivers	600 000 estimated in use
Receivers per 1000 people	0.7

PRESS

The daily press in the People's Republic was reported to consist of 1908 titles in 1966 (more recent statistics are not available). Newspapers could be classified as national and regional and local.

The national papers (of which there were 28 in 1960) are published by, or under, the direct supervision of the Central Committee of the Chinese Communist Party. The most important is the six-page official party organ published in Peking since 1948 and now circulating a total of 3.4 million copies seven days a week, largely by subscription (1.5 million of these in Peking and the rest in nine other cities where satellite editions are published using facsimiles or stereotyped mats). Of its 1000 employees, about 160 are writers, based either in Peking or on regional or local assignments. The type for each edition is set by 140 printers and is confined mainly to some 2000 of the possible range of over 6000 Chinese characters in use (proposals for romanization of the script have yet to be implemented). Apart from the special feature pages prepared from material gathered by reporters, domestic news is supplied by the national news agency, Hsinhua, which also provides the bulk of the foreign news published, though the paper also has its own foreign correspondents.

Another major daily is published by the People's Liberation Army, and another (with a circulation of 600 000) by the All-China Labour Unions Federation, both of these being based in Peking. Some semiweekly and weekly papers could also be included in the national press. The regional newspapers are published by the regional bureaux of central committees of the mass organizations or by provincial, regional or municipal party committees. Most of the provincial papers also have rural editions appearing daily or twice weekly and these, along with the newspapers or bulletins of educational institutions, administrations, industrial undertakings, etc., constitute the local press.

Each of the main types can be further subdivided into publications for distinct groups or classes (party members, officials, educators, unionists, industrial workers, women, youth, etc.). In 1966, there were also 15 major newspapers published in non-Chinese languages (Tibetan, Mongolian, Uighur, Kazakh, Yi, Korean, etc.) for large minority groups. This differentiation of newspapers according to social groups, and the organization of publishing patterns to fit in with administrative and territorial divisions, have done much to spread the news flow more evenly throughout the population.

Around 1960, the reported circulation figures per issue for 1455 dailies were some 20.9 million copies, a total which would have given an average of about 27 copies per 1000 inhabitants, although it would not have represented the full impact of the press since reading groups, mobile reading teams, etc., considerably augment the numbers of readers/listeners per copy. Furthermore, wall (poster) or blackboard newspapers were, and are, an important adjunct to the conventional press in towns, villages, schools, industrial establishments, etc.

Periodical publishing, which is closely related to the newspaper publishing structure, also shows the same national, provincial and local distribution pattern. Of a reported total of some 500 titles before 1966 (with a combined circulation of over 12 million), about 40% were national, the most important being the fortnightly (or monthly) official publication of the Central Committee of the Chinese Communist Party. Subject content, except in the case of a few general interest publications, was usually limited to a single field and designed for a particular readership. Among academic publications, for example, there were some 60 journals dealing with science and technology, and issued by the Chinese Academy of Science or its various related institutes. Minority groups were catered for by over 20 titles in non-Chinese languages used within the People's Republic, while a fair number were published in European, Asian and African languages for distribution abroad. Subscriptions and deliveries were handled largely by the Ministry of Post and Telecommunications.

The language of the press is the official 'national language' based on the Chinese of Peking. Although there are wide variations in pronunciation of the spoken language, the ideographic written form is uniform throughout the country. Its accessibility to a wider range of readers is being increased by language-reform measures.

Newsprint production in the People's Republic is reported to have increased from 2.1 million metric tons in 1960 to 2.5 million tons in 1970.

NEWS AGENCIES

The principal source of domestic news, and the sole source of foreign news, is the state-owned Hsinhua (or New China) News Agency, founded in 1937, which is closely connected with the Ministries of Education and Culture and operated by the Central Committee of the Chinese Communist Party. With headquarters in Peking, regional bureaux in Peking, Shanghai, Shenyang, Wuhan, Sian, Chungking and Tsinan, and numerous sub-offices throughout the country, Hsinhua's full-time employees include some 1300 persons in Peking and over 400 in the main city and provincial bureaux, in addition to a national network of many thousands of part-time correspondents. It also employs 200 persons in more than 40 countries outside China. Its main foreign bureaux are in Geneva, London, Paris, Hong Kong and at the United Nations in New York.

In 1973, Hsinhua was receiving, by agreement, the foreign services of AP, UPI, Reuters, AFP and Kyodo.

The agency's daily Chinese-language radio service provides 32 000 words of national and local news and 30 000 words of foreign news, for the use of newspapers and broadcasting stations. Special services for provincial newspapers and local newspapers amount to 35 000 and 10 000 words respectively. A world-wide English-language service of 12 000 words, and a Russian-language service of 10 000 words, are also transmitted.

In addition, Hsinhua is the publisher of a special four-page reference news journal circulating 6 million copies daily, which is not on sale to the public since it is designed exclusively for officials and government offices and agencies in all administration centres throughout the country.

The main world agencies are represented by permanent correspondents in Peking.

RADIO

The state-owned Central People's Broadcasting Station (Radio Peking) broadcasts four home-service programmes, principally in Chinese, ranging from 15 to 19 hours a day, plus a local Peking programme of 5½ hours a day, on medium and short waves. Home-service programmes are relayed by over 100 medium- and short-wave local and provincial stations which in turn feed a network of thousands of small stations and rediffusion systems reaching all parts of the country through either individual or collective receivers or wired loudspeakers. In the absence of a standard form of spoken Chinese throughout the country, a number of dialects are used. In addition, a number of powerful stations with similar subsidiary networks broadcast to national minorities in their own languages (Tibetan, Kazakh, Korean and Uighur).

Programmes consist of a large amount of news and information and educational broadcasts, often paralleling material published in the press, as well as music, theatre and other cultural programmes, sports, etc.

The People's Liberation Army is also reported to broadcast a home service on medium and short wave in the Fukien area.

External broadcasting is carried out by Radio Peking, with both medium- and short-wave (up to 240kW) transmitters in China and a relay station at Tirana (Albania). From just over 1000 hours in 1966, Radio Peking's weekly external broadcasting time had risen to 1584 hours in 1972 (a total surpassed only by the USSR and the USA). Programmes in Chinese and in foreign languages, including English, French, German, Spanish and Albanian, are beamed to nine different areas in all continents.

RELATIONS BROKEN OFF. — RADIO SERVICE RELAY NOT AVAILABLE

The number of receivers (including loudspeakers linked to rediffusion networks) rose from 6 million in 1966 to 15 million in 1972. Radio and television transmitting and receiving equipment is nationally produced.

TELEVISION

The first television broadcasts were made in 1958 from Peking, where the Central People's Broadcasting System is now established, exercising control over all television broadcasting throughout the country. Peking now has two programmes, one of which is relayed by a transmitter at Tangshan, while Shanghai (relayed from Hangchow, Soochow and Wuhsi), Tientsin, Harbin, Shenyang, Changchun, Canton, Sian, Taiyan, Hofei, Nanking and Wuhan each have one. There are a dozen experimental stations also in operation, so that all provinces except Tibet now reportedly have at least one television station. Stations are on the air for about 3 hours a night or less. Composition of programmes is approximately: literature and art (40%), documentaries (30%), news (20%) and children's programmes (10%). In 1973, the Central Broadcasting Bureau reached an agreement with the American Broadcasting Company (USA) for an exchange of newsfilm documenting and sports programmes.

A 'TV University' programme broadcast in the main television transmitting cities from 1960 onwards, for 4 hours a week, offered study courses leading to both secondary and university diplomas. (The Peking 'TV University' reported an enrolment of 35 000 students in 1962.)

The television-set count, which was 70 000 in 1966, had risen to a total variously reported as being between 100 000 and 600 000 receivers in 1972.

FILM

The Ministry of Culture's Film Administration Bureau has two main divisions –

one concerned with film production and processing, and the other with distribution and exhibition – both of which are represented at provincial and municipal levels.

Production in 1964, from the seven major and numerous smaller studios, totalled 480 feature films, 3000 newsreels, 1400 scientific films and over 200 cartoons, many of which are shown on television. No figures are available for years later than 1964, but it is reported that film production has since been greatly reduced.

The largest audiences are reached by mobile projection teams that travel from village to village in every administrative area of the country. In 1964, there were 12 000 such teams, in addition to 4000 film clubs and over 2000 fixed cinemas.

SPACE COMMUNICATIONS
Although the People's Republic is not a member of Intelsat, there are Pacific Intelsat earth stations at Peking and Shanghai, opened in 1972 and 1973 respectively, and an Indian Ocean station was due to come into operation in 1974.

PROFESSIONAL TRAINING
In 1957, three universities were known to offer courses in journalism: the School of Journalism within the Department of Languages at Peking University (a five-year course), the People's University, Peking (a three-year orientation course for working journalists and a four-year course for prospective journalists) and Fu Tan University, Shanghai (a five-year training course).

The Peking Institute of Filmology, founded in 1959, trains film directors and producers.

CYPRUS

Population	650 000
Area	9251 sq. km.

PRESS

Newspapers	Dailies 12, Non-dailies 21
Total circulation	Dailies 80 000, Non-dailies 137 000
Copies per 1000 people	Dailies 123, Non-dailies 211

RADIO

Transmitters	Long/medium-wave 4*
Total receivers	170 509 licensed
Licences per 1000 people	262

TELEVISION

Transmitters	5
Receivers	66 114 (licences)
Licences per 1000 people	102

FILM

Cinemas	Fixed 150
Total seating capacity	88 000
Seats per 1000 people	135
Total annual attendance	6 000 000†
Annual visits per capita	9†

*Not including foreign relay and British Forces stations.
†For all cinemas in 1971.

PRESS

All daily newspapers are published in the capital, Nicosia, and all but one are morning papers. Nine are in Greek, 2 in Turkish and 1 in English. Most are privately owned, and a number have clear political orientations. Several also have weekend (usually Monday) editions. There are 21 weeklies and other non-dailies published in Greek (no figures are available for Turkish non-dailies).

There are 36 periodicals published in Greek (with a combined circulation of 114 copies, in 1972), some others in Turkish and 1 in English (8000 copies). Main subject categories are general readership (20 titles, 51 750 copies), literature (5 titles, 10 000 copies), education (4 titles, 3000 copies), etc. In addition, a children's magazine circulates 15 000 copies.

NEWS AGENCIES

Cyprus has no national news agency. Reuter's world service is received by all dailies and weeklies and the national radio and television stations; one daily and one weekly also receive the AP world service. Both these agencies have offices in Nicosia, as have AFP, TASS and other agencies.

RADIO

The Cyprus Broadcasting Corporation (CyBC) set up, by law, in 1952, is responsible for 'operating, by sound or television, a public broadcasting service'. Its board of governors is appointed by the Council of Ministers. Its revenue comes from government funds, licence fees and some advertising.

CyBC's radio programmes are broadcast on two channels. The first, with medium-wave transmitters of 20kW (Nicosia), 2kW (Paphos) and 0.5 (Limassol), is on the air for 18 hours daily, in Greek (including morning broadcasts to schools). The second, with a 20kW medium-wave transmitter at Nicosia, broadcasts in Turkish for 6½ hours daily, in English for 3½ hours and in Armenian for 1 hour on Sundays and Wednesdays. It also carries a classical-music programme for 3 hours daily with announcements in Greek, and, for 3 hours daily, an international programme mainly of pop music with announcements in English, Arabic and French. Programmes on both channels, totalling 242 hours a week, include light entertainment (151 hours), cultural and scientific programmes (36 hours), news and information (26 hours), broadcasts for special audiences (20 hours), education (6 hours) and advertising (3 hours). Less than 10% of these programmes are imported.

Broadcasts cover the whole country. Of the 170 509 licences current at the end of 1972, 22 043 were for car radios.

The British Forces Broadcasting Service operates two medium-wave and four FM transmitters broadcasting non-commercial programmes in English, for about 110 hours a week for the information and entertainment of forces personnel and their families.

The BBC (UK) has a 100kW transmitter in Cyprus which relays, on medium and short waves, its Arabic, Persian and world services.

Radio Monte Carlo (Monaco) also has a relay station (20kW) in Cyprus, relaying programmes on medium waves in French and Arabic for 12¼ hours daily.

TELEVISION

CyBC's television service began in 1957 with a pilot service covering a small radius round Nicosia. It now broadcasts simultaneously on three channels from transmitters on Mts Olympus and Sina Oros, with three relay stations, covering the whole island. Programmes, consisting of about 48% locally produced material are broadcast for 34½ hours a week, including long films and series (12½ hours), news and information (9 hours), advertising (4½ hours), cultural programmes (3 hours), light entertainment (3 hours), broadcasts for special audiences (2 hours) and education (1½ hours). School television programmes are broadcast in the mornings during school terms.

A separate licence fee is payable for television receivers.

FILM

One feature film was completed in 1973 and one instructional short film. The only locally based producer is the film section of the Public Information Department which works in cooperation with government ministries.

Feature films totalling 681 were imported in 1972: from Turkey (170), the UK (142), the USA (127), Greece (104), Italy (70), France (22), the Federal Republic of Germany (18), the USSR (8) and other countries (20). In addition to the 150 year-round fixed cinemas, there are 180 open-air projection places, often served by mobile units, where some 97 000 seats are available during the summer.

Interest in the cinema is fostered by the Cyprus Broadcasting Corporation, which runs a film club and conducts various competitions. A well-stocked library of 16mm and 35mm films and filmstrips is maintained by the Information Department's film section, whose mobile units exhibit educational, agricultural and health films to schools, clubs and village audiences.

PROFESSIONAL TRAINING AND ASSOCIATIONS

There are no schools of journalism in Cyprus. Local papers train their own editorial staff. The Cyprus Union of Journalists is studying the question of a professional code of ethics for journalists.

HONG KONG

| Population | 4 089 000 |
| Area | 1034 sq. km. |

PRESS

Newspapers	Dailies 81, Non-dailies 36
Total circulation	Dailies 1 500 000*
Copies per 1000 people	Dailies 367*

RADIO

Transmitters	Long/medium wave 7, VHF–FM 2
Total receivers	725 000† estimated in use
Receivers per 1000 people	177

TELEVISION

Transmitters	1‡
Receivers	690 000 estimated in use
Receivers per 1000 people	169

FILM

Cinemas	Fixed 97
Total seating capacity	118 355
Seats per 1000 people	29
Total annual attendance	71 279 000
Annual visits per capita	17

*Approximate estimation.
†Including wired receivers.
‡Not including HK–TVB's 9 wireless relay stations or RTV's 2 wired networks.

PRESS

With 75 Chinese-language and 5 English-language and bilingual dailies, Hong Kong publishes more daily newspaper titles per head of population than any other territory in the world and more Chinese-language papers than any other territory outside China itself. The 2 largest papers circulate almost 200 000 copies each per issue, 2 others exceed 100 000 copies (each of these 4 devoting 50 to 60% of space to advertising), a dozen more exceed 50 000, while a further 20 circulate between 25 000 and 50 000. The 4 English-language papers have circulations between 25 000 and 40 000 copies. Three major Chinese dailies have air-mail editions for mailing to overseas Chinese communities, and 1 English paper also has a weekly air-mail supplement. Most of the larger papers carry a fair proportion of international and domestic news and are increasingly reflecting public attitudes and reactions to local issues. Some 40 dailies, together circulating 40 000 copies, carry little news and are almost entirely devoted to entertainment.

Papers are sold very cheaply despite the high labour costs involved in the manual typesetting of Chinese characters (a mechanized typesetting system, using about 4000 characters is currently being developed by the Chinese Language Press Institute in collaboration with the Department of Communications of the Hong Kong Baptist College).

The non-daily press consists of 27 titles in Chinese and 9 in English, two of the latter being Sunday editions of dailies.

Over 200 periodicals are published, including 137 in Chinese, 55 in English, 10 bilingual Chinese/English and 2 in Japanese, the majority being monthlies. Of 105 reported titles with a combined circulation of 85 000 copies, the main subject categories are art, architecture, etc. (14 titles, 13 000 copies), entertainment and sports (13 titles, 9600 copies), technology, industry, etc. (12 titles, 8000 copies), religion (10 titles, 3600 copies) and literature (8 titles, 7800 copies); 3 medical journals circulate 6900 copies, 2 educational journals 7300 copies and 1 natural science journal 6000 copies. Among the many publications not included in these figures are locally produced editions of foreign periodicals such as, for example, the Asian English and Chinese editions of an American monthly digest circulating 310 000 and 230 000 copies respectively. Other categories not included are young people's magazines (36 titles, 20 500 copies), comics (9 titles, 39 500 copies) and school magazines (14 titles, 76 000 copies).

NEWS AGENCIES

Three privately owned agencies provide services mainly to the Chinese-language press. They are the Hsin Yah News Agency, the International News Service and the United Newspaper Agency. The latter, for example, has 17 correspondents in Hong Kong and serves 11 newspapers with 12 000 words of local news daily.

The Pan Asia Newspaper Alliance, founded in 1949, has head offices in Hong Kong and Tokyo, as well as branch offices in six other Asian cities. It issues a local news service in English, a Morse radio service and features. The Chinese Language Press Institute, in cooperation with the Press Foundation of Asia, issues a weekly background service in Chinese for its members. There are also half a dozen specialized feature agencies and services.

The government information services' news division issues a daily bulletin, as well as features, photos and film, to the press and broadcasting organizations. Its weekly news digest is distributed to thousands of overseas Chinese.

Most of the larger papers, however, depend on their own correspondents for local news and on overseas agencies for news of foreign and international affairs. UPI and Reuters both serve one television station, the government information services and (respectively) 27 and 21 newspapers; AP services are received by 23 newspapers and one television station, AFP by 10 newspapers, and Hsinhua by an unstated number.

AFP, Antara, AP, DPA, Jiji, Kyodo, Reuters and UPI have bureaux in Hong Kong, and other agencies and foreign newspapers are represented by staff and part-time correspondents.

RADIO

Of Hong Kong's three radio stations, one is government owned and two privately owned. Radio Hong Kong (RHK), a government department, entirely financed from public funds, broadcasts separate Chinese (both Cantonese and standard

Chinese) and English programmes for 142 and 185 hours a week respectively on medium-wave and FM transmitters (20 and 50kW), with emphasis on information and public affairs. English programmes include some BBC (UK) news relays.

The Hong Kong Commercial Broadcasting Co Ltd operates 2 medium-wave transmitters (10kW each) for its two Cantonese services, each broadcasting 120 hours a week, and 1 medium-wave transmitter (10kW) for its English service (133 hours a week), 80% of programmes consisting of light entertainment and 11% of news and information.

Rediffusion (Hong Kong) Ltd, a subsidiary of a UK-based organization, operates two simultaneous, wired sound networks, carrying its own originated material and relays of Radio Hong Kong, BBC and other organizations, 64% of its programmes being light entertainment and 12% news and information. Rediffusion has 31 842 subscribers.

Main content categories of Chinese and English programmes respectively are light entertainment (86 and 83 hours), news and information (38 and 33½ hours), light entertainment (61 and 5 hours), broadcasts for special audiences (7½ and 5 hours) and education (6 and 3½ hours). RHK also produces (but does not transmit) television programmes on public affairs to be carried by Hong Kong television stations.

No licence fee is payable for radio receivers.

The British Forces Broadcasting Service (Hong Kong) operates a 2kW medium-wave transmitter broadcasting non-commercial programmes in Gurkhali for Gurkha forces stationed in the area.

TELEVISION

Both of Hong Kong's television stations are privately owned. The first, Rediffusion (Hong Kong) Ltd (RTV), began operating a wired service in 1957. It now has a two-channel wired service (405 lines), one in Chinese, the other in English, providing a total viewing time of 193 hours a week. It serves more than 100 000 subscribers in Hong Kong island, Kowloon and the New Territories.

Television Broadcasts Ltd (HK–TVB), partly owned by the USA and the UK media interests, began its service in 1967 and now has two simultaneous Chinese and English wireless services (625 lines and PAL-system colour) on the air for a total of 173 hours a week. In addition to its main transmitters, HK–TVB has nine auxilliaries which give almost complete coverage to both urban and rural Hong Kong.

Programmes for all stations, totalling 366 hours a week, include entertainment (117½ hours), cultural and scientific broadcasts (81 hours), education (56½ hours), news and information (51 hours), broadcasts for special audiences (40 hours) and advertising (14 hours). Educational programmes include 50 hours a week of school broadcasts produced by the government's educational television division and carried on both networks. Public affairs programmes produced by the television unit of Radio Hong Kong are also carried by both networks.

Imported programmes account for about 30% of broadcasting time on Chinese channels and 40% on English-language channels. Of this imported material, 83% comes from the USA, and 12% from the UK, the largest components being series and long films. Programmes are also received from Australia, Japan, Canada and Italy.

No licence fee is payable for (wireless) television receivers. Television coverage extends to 92% of the population, while 79.6% of households have television sets capable of receiving either or both stations.

FILM

Once producing Cantonese feature films almost exclusively, numbering as many as 500 a year in the sixties, Hong Kong has now switched entirely to Mandarin Chinese, with an annual production of 133 features and six documentaries in 1972, one studio alone producing about 50 features. Documentaries and newsreels are also produced by the government information services.

Imported features, in the same year, totalled 483, coming mainly from the USA (149), Italy (67), the UK (56), India (36), France (24) and other countries (151). Both the number of cinemas and annual attendance figures have increased over the last ten years, cinemas by over 30% from 73 in 1961, and attendances by 6% from 65 million in the same year.

SPACE COMMUNICATIONS

Hong Kong has two antennae at its earth station, one opened in 1969 working with the Pacific Intelsat satellite, and the other, opened in 1971, working with the Indian Ocean satellite. The station, owned by Cable and Wireless, has a specially equipped telecine studio which can be used by news agencies for colour-film transmission.

PROFESSIONAL TRAINING AND ASSOCIATIONS

The New Asia College of the Chinese University of Hong Kong offers a two-year BSc course for third-year undergraduates at its Department of Journalism (founded in 1965). Total enrolment in the course is over 50 students. A four-year diploma course at post-secondary level is offered at the Hong Kong Baptist College's Department of Communication, founded in 1968, which has a total course enrolment of about 250 students. In both courses, Chinese is the principal language, but much material is also taught in English.

Professional organizations of the press include the Hong Kong Journalists' Association, with over 300 members; the Newspaper Society (founded in 1954), with 19 members and three associate member newspapers (both Chinese and English); and the Hong Kong Chinese Press Association. There is also a foreign correspondent club. The Chinese Language Press Institute (now with 92 member newspapers) was set up in 1968 to promote the interests and standards (including training) of both journalists and technical staff.

Broadcasting stations belong to both the Asian Broadcasting Union and the Commonwealth Broadcasting Conference. Motion-picture workers and exhibitors each have their own associations.

INDIA

Population	563 490 000
Area	3 268 090 sq. km.

PRESS	
Newspapers	Dailies 821, Non-dailies 4102
Total circulation	Dailies 9 096 000*, Non-dailies 5 771 000†

RADIO	
Transmitters	Medium-wave 105, Short-wave 32
Total receivers	11 746 600 licences
Licences per 1000 people	21

TELEVISION	
Transmitters	2
Receivers	56 868 (licences)
Licences per 1000 people	0.1

FILM	
Cinemas	Fixed 4716
Total seating capacity	3 066 000
Seats per 1000 people	5
Total annual attendance	3 430 000 000
Annual visits per capita	6

*For 534 titles.
†For 2064 titles.

PRESS

Publishing a larger number of daily newspapers than any other country in Asia and the third highest number in the world (after the USA and the Federal Republic of Germany), the Indian press covers a range of languages and a cultural diversity unparalleled anywhere except in the USSR. Over the past ten years, the number of daily titles and their combined circulations have doubled and the growth of the non-daily press has been even more striking.

Of the 20 or so languages in which daily newspapers are published. Hindi has the highest number of titles (222), followed by Urdu (102), Tamil (97), English (78), Marathi (77), Malayalam (60), Gujarati (43), Kannada (39), Punjabi (18), Telegu (17), Bengali (15), Oriya (7), Sindhi (4), Assamese (2), Sanskrit (1) and several others. There are also 24 bilingual and 4 multilingual dailies.

In terms of overall circulation — though complete figures are not available for all papers — English-language dailies head the list (2 219 000 copies per issue for 59 of the 78 titles published), followed by Hindi (1 516 000 copies for 146 titles), Marathi and Tamil (each with over 900 000 copies), Gujarati and Bengali (each with over 600 000 copies), Urdu and Kannada (each with over 300 000 copies), etc. The largest circulations for one-city titles are those of 2 Bengali dailies published in Calcutta (231 000 and 161 000 copies), a Malayalam daily published in Kottayam (178 000 copies) and 2 English-language dailies published in Madras and Bombay respectively (150 000 and 147 000 copies). Fourteen other papers in Marathi, Hindi, English, Malayalam and Tamil also exceed 100 000 copies per issue. Some 25 groups publish multi-city dailies, papers with individual editions in several different cities. These include a seven-city English-language title with a combined circulation of over 400 000, a six-city Tamil title with over 300 000 copies, 2 Hindi titles published in four and five cities respectively, and a number of other two-city titles. An important Madras daily now transmits facsimile pages for its associated editions in Coimbatore and Bangalore. But while a few papers, particularly the larger English and Hindu-language dailies, are widely circulated, there is really no national press to span the country's great geographical distances and its cultural and liguistic diversity.

Using a wider range of languages, and with Hindi showing a clear majority in both numbers and circulation figures, the non-daily press has 1729 Hindi titles, 543 Urdu, 445 English, 247 Bengali, etc., and almost 700 bilingual and multilingual titles. Over half the non-dailies appear weekly (2825 titles).

Periodicals published in 1971 numbered around 11 000 in 52 languages. The highest individual circulations were recorded by a Tamil literary and cultural weekly (336 800 copies), a dozen illustrated weeklies and women's, film, religious and medical journals, etc. (each with over 100 000 copies), in Tamil, Hindi, Malayalam, Telegu and Gujarati. The largest subject categories are general and current affairs (over 4000 titles), literary and cultural studies, and religion and philosophy (each over 1000 titles), then commerce, medicine, social welfare, film (over 300 titles), labour, education, law, agriculture, engineering (over 200 titles). Central and state government publications totalled almost 400 titles.

Over 100 newspapers (including nine dailies) and magazines, circulating over 1 million copies, are published in India by about 30 foreign diplomatic missions.

Financial and technical difficulties make the existence of many smaller papers and periodicals precarious. Between 300 and 400 titles cease publication every year, to be replaced, however, by over 1000 new ones. At the same time, more and more papers are associated in common-ownership groups which already account for 57% of the total national daily circulation and up to 90% or more of the daily circulation in some of the larger state capitals. Apart from English, only Bengali, Tamil and Hindi of the main scripts used can be adapted for linotype machines, and even in these languages a large proportion of papers are manually composed. No type face has yet been developed for Urdu, and all texts must be handwritten by calligraphers for lithographic reproduction.

Perhaps the greatest material problem is the shortage of newsprint, the bulk of which must be imported at the expense of foreign-currency reserves. For the year ended May 1970, around 200 000 metric tons were allocated to the press (180 000 metric tons for daily newspapers) under the official newsprint allocation policy. Of this total, about 40 000 metric tons are accounted for by domestic production at Nepa, the country's only functioning mill. Plans to increase Nepa's capacity to 75 000 metric tons a year, and to set up new mills in Kerala (75 000 metric tons) and Madhya Pradesh (45 000 metric tons), are being implemented under government supervision. Official allocation policy, while allowing for the growth of all newspapers, is particularly helpful to new and independently owned smaller and medium-size papers, which are granted larger imported newsprint quotas, import licence fee exemptions, etc.

NEWS AGENCIES

Some 30 domestic news agencies are reported as serving daily and other newspapers in India. Of the three leading agencies, by far the largest is the Press Trust of India (PTI), with headquarters in Bombay. Founded in 1949, the Press Trust of India took over the outlets of Reuters and the Associated Press of India. PTI is a cooperative enterprise owned by the Indian newspapers. It maintains 57 bureaux in India, with 188 staff correspondents plus 250 stringers throughout the country. Abroad it has offices in Colombo, Kathmandu and Tokyo, and maintains staff or, in a few cases, part-time correspondents in Cairo, Nairobi, Johannesburg, Belgrade, Moscow, Georgetown (Guyana), New York (covering also the United Nations), Rangoon and Kuala Lumpur. One correspondent is also assigned to AFP in Paris and covers all important international conferences in western Europe. PTI has a direct teleprinter line to Colombo, and a beam service to Tokyo and Kathmandu.

It puts out daily, in English, 75 000 words on national affairs when parliament is in session, which is about six months in the year (otherwise, 50 000 words), and 35 000 words on foreign affairs, plus 15 000 words on regional news distributed to the four main regions of India.

PTI sells its news service to Reuters and the Press Trust of Sri Lanka (Newstrust) and owns distribution rights for the Reuter, AFP and UPI services in India. It has exchange agreements with Kyodo News Service, News Agency of Burma and Orient Press (Korea). All-India Radio and 198 newspapers subscribe to the PTI service.

The United News of India (UNI), founded in 1961, with headquarters in New Delhi, is also cooperatively owned by Indian newspapers. It provides a comprehensive national and international news service to about 200 subscribers through 40 offices linked by more than 20 000km of leased teleprinter lines passing through all Indian states. Its subscribers include all the leading newspapers of India published in 15 different languages, and the state-owned radio network.

News is fed daily into the UNI network by 273 full-time and part-time journalists in all the state capitals and in over 100 other news centres in India. UNI's foreign news comes through AP, DPA, Tanjug, ANSA and Jiji. The agency also has staffers or stringers at Colombo, Kathmandu and Gangtok (Sikkim).

UNI's Mailer News and Background Department issues, each week, feature, agricultural and other services designed for the periodical press.

Hindustan Samachar, with its head office in New Delhi, is run by a cooperative society of its own workers. It provides news in 10 Indian languages besides a service in English, and is particularly valuable to newspapers published in regional languages. Its subscribers now total 104 newspapers, which receive an average daily output of 14 000 words of national news. Hindustan Samachar has 17 offices and 10 sub-offices within the country and 2 abroad, in Kathmandu and Gangtok, and has plans to open additional news bureaux in India and to establish correspondents in Sri Lanka, Burma, Singapore, east Africa, Mauritius, Japan, Afghanistan, Pakistan and some other neighbouring countries.

Samachar Bharati, founded in 1961, is an independent multilingual agency serving smaller newspapers in the various states with news in Hindi, Marathi and Gujarati.

A news-cum-feature agency, the Indian News and Feature Alliance (INFA) was set up in New Delhi in 1959 to meet the special needs of the regional press, for specialized news and features. It was the first agency in India to offer a daily service carrying signed articles on topical subjects written by well-known and informed commentators, publicists and news analysts, which could be published by its newspaper subscribers in the various regions on a predetermined date and with exclusive regional rights.

The India Press Agency (IPA) was founded in New Delhi in February 1957. It is essentially a special-correspondent service, specializing in background and interpretative news coverage and exclusive spot news, mainly confined to domestic events, together with special international reports from selected world capitals.

The Eastern India News Agency, Calcutta, came into being in 1960 and changed hands in 1962. It specializes in news from eastern and north-eastern India, including Sikkim, Bhutan, Nepal, the North East Frontier Agency and other border areas. Besides its correspondents all over India, the agency maintains bureaux in New Delhi, Cuttack and Shillong.

One of 12 main purely feature agencies used by the daily press is News Features of India (NFI), Bombay, founded by a group of young writers and journalists in 1953 and run on a cooperative basis, serving national, provincial and suburban newspapers and periodicals with specialized news and features. NFI now has over 50 newspapers and periodicals in all parts of the country subscribing to its services. A network of its own correspondents in almost all state capitals provides leading newspapers with telegraphic service twice daily. Its features include special weekly articles, a newsletter on national and international affairs, literary and political write-ups, cinematic material, short stories and photographs, including colour transparencies.

The press also uses the news services of All-India Radio.

The main sources of foreign news for the Indian press are Reuters, AFP, AP, UPI and TASS. Radio and television are served via the national agencies PTI, UNI, Hindustan Samachar and Samachar Bharati, which supply foreign news received from Reuters, AFP, UPI, Kyodo, AP, Jiji, ANSA and Tanjug.

RADIO

All-India Radio (AIR), the only broadcasting organization in the country, is controlled by the Ministry of Information and Broadcasting and financed by an annual grant voted by parliament, by receiver licence fees and (since 1967) by advertising revenue. Since 1952, when India's first five-year plan was introduced, AIR's equipment has been increased from 44 transmitters with a combined power of 370kW reaching just over 20% of the population, to 137 transmitters totalling 5544kW giving medium-wave coverage to 78% and short-wave coverage to practically 100% of the population.

The north, west, south and east regional home services, with headquarters in Delhi, Bombay, Madras and Calcutta, respectively, broadcast principally in Hindi, English, Gujarati, Marathi, Tamil, Telegu, Urdu, Bengali and Malayalam, but also in 51 local languages and 82 tribal dialects. Radio Kashmir with stations at

Srinagar and Jammu, has a separate network. Each of these services – in addition to a national programme (consisting largely of news bulletins) from Delhi – carries its own main regional programme supplemented by the programmes of individual stations within the network which cater for more localized needs and interests. A combined total of some 4780 hours of broadcasting time per week is distributed approximately as follows: cultural programmes (1500 hours), light entertainment (1110 hours), news and information (1080 hours), broadcasts for special audiences (856 hours), advertising (87 hours), broadcasts for ethnic minorities (74 hours) and education (69 hours). The educational broadcasts include those transmitted from 30 centres for classroom reception in 20 000 primary and secondary schools equipped with their own radio sets; and special series for adult and university students (including support courses for three university correspondence courses) and industrial workers. Special audiences include women, young people (there is even one channel carrying only youth programmes), followers of various religions and a great range of village groups, notably those participating in the 25 800 radio rural forums operating so successfully in all parts of India. Collective listening is common in the villages where there are now some 77 500 community receivers.

Parallel to the regional services is a self-contained All-India popular entertainment service, known as Vividh Bharati, broadcast from 30 centres throughout the country for a total of around 2500 hours a week, and carrying popular music, light features and (from 18 of the 30 centres) commercial advertising.

In ten years, the number of radio receivers in use has increased fivefold. The demand for receiving sets is met by domestic production.

AIR first began its external broadcasts in October 1939. Today the external services are on the air round the clock in 24 languages, with a total of over 50 hours' daily programme time.

In addition to its Urdu and Bengali programmes, which are administratively part of the external services, AIR beams foreign broadcasts to Indians overseas in south-east Asia (in Hindi and Tamil) and east Africa (in Hindi, Gujarati, Konkani and Swahili); its eastern service to Nepal (in Nepali), Bhutan and Sikkim (in Tibetan), Burma (in Burmese), Thailand (in Thai), China (in Cantonese and Kuoyu) and Indonesia (in Indonesian); its western service to Afghanistan (in Pushtu and Dari), Iran (in Persian) and west Asia (in Arabic and French); and its general overseas service in English to east and south-east Asia, north-east Asia, Australia and New Zealand, the UK and western Europe, east Africa, and west and north Africa. Other languages being introduced are Korean, Cambodian, Vietnamese, Malay, Russian and Lao.

AIR also exports a considerable volume of recorded programmes to the broadcasting services of other countries.

TELEVISION

Beginning with an experimental service in September 1959, All-India Radio maintained a television service of two 1-hour programmes a week for some years, broadcast from a transmitter in New Delhi and covering a radius of 18km around the capital. The Delhi transmitter's effective radius has now been increased to 60km, and the programme time to 25 hours a week for the general programme, plus 12½ hours for schools. The general programme's weekly content, in Hindi and English, includes news and information (10 hours), broadcasts for special audiences (4 hours), light entertainment (2 hours) and cultural programmes (1 hour), the remainder consisting of feature films and answers to listeners' letters. In-school instructional programmes from the Delhi Television Centre are broadcast six days a week, reaching over 200 000 pupils in 411 schools. Programmes for farmers – broadcast three times a week – are received by 80 farm teleclubs, as well as other individual and group viewers. Over 90% of the programmes shown are nationally produced. The remainder are imported, or received under AIR's exchange agreements with 10 national broadcasting systems or through cultural agreements between the Government of India and nine other governments.

A new television station at Bombay began broadcasting late in 1972 and others are scheduled to come into operation in Srinagar, Calcutta, Madras and Lucknow (with relays at Amritsar, Poona, Kanpur, Durgapur, Asansol and Mussoorie) in the course of the current five-year plan. AIR's future television plans maintain the present strong educational emphasis and include a pilot project for the transmission of school programmes via satellite, to begin in 1975.

The definition system used is 625 lines. A licence fee is payable for television receivers, schools and teleclubs being required to pay only a third of the full amount. Licences issued in 1971 more than doubled the previous year's total. Indian industry supplies the bulk of the receivers sold.

FILM

India has one of the largest film industries in the world. In 1971, the total number of nationally-produced feature films approved by the censor amounted to 433 (132 in colour) as against 396 (82) in 1970 and 324 in 1960. Of the total, 118 were in Hindi, 83 in Telegu, 73 in Tamil, 52 in Malayalam, 33 in Kannada, 30 in Bengali, 23 in Marathi and others in Gujarati, Assamese, Tulu, Punjabi, English, Bhojpuri, Maithili, Chattosgarhi, Sindhi, Oriya and Konkani. Madras and Bombay are the country's largest production centres, with Calcutta in third place. Together, they have some 250 producing companies and over 60 studios, mostly under private commercial ownership. A factory at Ootacumund in south India makes a large variety of raw film, supplying the bulk of the country's monochrome requirements.

Some 2340 short films were approved for release in 1971, a number of them produced by government units including the Ministry of Information's film division which makes about 150 documentaries annually in 13 languages, as well as a weekly newsreel in 13 languages. The division also prepares over 40 000 prints a year for commercial and non-commercial distribution and other institutions. There are also many private producers of documentary, educational and instructional shorts.

In addition to the training and promotional activities undertaken through such establishments as the Film Institute, the University Film Council, etc., the government encourages the industry by special legislation, such as that requiring 2000 ft of Indian film to be exhibited at every showing in commercial cinemas, and by financial grants and loans (through the Film Finance Corporation), prizes and other awards for quality productions.

Imports for 1971 were 125 features: from the USA (86), Italy (12), the

USSR (9), Japan (6), France (6), the UK (4) and two other countries. The 225 documentaries imported came from the USA (118), the USSR (51), the UK (12), Italy (10), France (7), Japan (3), etc.

Films are exhibited in fixed cinemas in cities and towns and also by the 2575 commercial (35mm) mobile projection units constantly serving rural circuits throughout the country. Hundreds more (mainly 16mm) are operated by the central and state governments, showing government-produced films free of charge to audiences of up to 3000 or 4000 persons a time, totalling some 60 million spectators a year.

SPACE COMMUNICATIONS

An earth station working with the Indian Ocean Intelsat system was opened at Arvi near Poona (Maharashtra State) in February 1971 and future plans include another, at Doowala near Dehra Dun, to be operational in 1975.

Also in 1975, a one-year instructional television experiment is scheduled to begin in India, using a geosynchronous ATS-F satellite to retransmit educational programmes from a ground station at Ahmedabad to some 5000 villages in various parts of the country. Programmes are to be received either directly from the satellite by antennas in village schools or centres or indirectly via conventional VHF transmission from three redistributing earth stations at Delhi, Bombay and Srinagar.

PROFESSIONAL TRAINING AND ASSOCIATIONS

Training for the press is promoted by the Indian Association for Education in Journalism. Diploma and degree courses in journalism are available at 12 universities: Bangalore, Bihar and Calcutta (three-year BA course with journalism); Calcutta (two-year MA and diploma courses); Gauhati, Gujarat and Madras (one-year diploma courses); Mysore (two-year MA courses); Nagpur and Osmania (one-year BJ courses); Poona and Punjab (one-year diploma courses).

Private institutions with communications courses include St Xavier's College (Bombay), the Bombay College of Journalism, the Bharatiya Vidya Bhawan Rajendra Prasad College of Mass Communications (Bombay) which since 1967, with its branches in New Delhi, Madras, Trivandrum, Bangalore, Guntur and Ahmedabad, has offered a course in audio-visual communications (film, radio and television), the Institute of Journalism (New Delhi), and the New Delhi Polytechnic for Women.

The Press Institute of India, New Delhi, organizes in-service training for newspaper personnel, as do some of the major press enterprises.

The Indian Institute of Mass Communication's eight-month post-graduate diploma courses at New Delhi, started in 1969, are for Indian graduates with two years' practical experience or for sponsored foreign entrants. This institute, founded in 1965 under the Ministry of Information and Broadcasting, also conducts communications research, and trains government information specialists in all media.

All-India Radio's staff training scheme in New Delhi, in addition to seminars for its own producers, staff artists, etc., includes special one-week courses on radio in education.

Established by the Ministry of Information and Broadcasting in 1961, the Film Institute of India, in Poona, conducts three-year courses for film-makers – in writing, directing, photography and sound – and two-year courses in editing and acting, as well as a range of refresher courses. The institute also includes television training as from 1973.

Madras also has an institute of film technology.

Bodies concerned with the promotion and functioning of the media and the interests of media professionals include several established by government action, such as the Press Council of India, which has the two objectives of preserving press freedom and improving the standards of newspapers in India; the Film Institute of India, the National Film Archive of India (1964), the Children's Film Society (1955), the Indian Motion Pictures Export Corporation and the Indian Institute of Mass Communication.

The main associations of the press are the All-India Newspaper Editors' Conference, the Indian and Eastern Newspaper Society, the Indian Federation of Working Journalists (all based in New Delhi), the Indian Languages Newspapers' Association and the Press Owners' Association (both in Bombay) and the Southern India Journalists' Federation (Madras).

Associations in the film industry, on both national and regional levels group together producers, technicians, performers, film journalists, exporters, importers, distributors, exhibitors, etc. There is a federation of film societies of India.

INDONESIA

Population	121 198 000
Area	1 904 345 sq. km

PRESS

Newspapers	Dailies 120
Total circulation	1 200 000
Copies per 1000 people	10

RADIO

Transmitters	Medium-wave 2, Short-wave/tropical-wave 137, VHF–FM 1
Total receivers	13 796 277 estimated in use
Receivers per 1000 people	114

TELEVISION

Transmitters	12
Receivers	208 968 estimated in use
Receivers per 1000 people	2

FILM

Cinemas	Fixed 490

PRESS

The concentration of newspapers in a small number of cities characterizes the structure of the press in Indonesia – the largest and most populous country in south-east Asia. This is particularly marked on the island of Java where Djakarta, capital of the republic, alone has 24 dailies accounting for about half the total national newspaper circulation. All of these are published in Bahasa Indonesia (the national language, spoken by most persons under 40 years of age), with the exception of 2 in English and 1 in Chinese. Also in Java, Surabaya has 9 dailies, and Bandung, Jogjakarta and Semarang have 4 each. In Sumatra, Medan, the capital of the northern province, has 12 dailies, while in Sulawesi (Celebes), Menado and Makassar have respectively 15 and 5 dailies with a total circulation of some 65 000 copies. A few of these papers have twelve or eight pages and circulation figures running into several tens of thousands but the majority are four-page publications circulating only a few thousand copies

A similar pattern is observed for the periodical press. Weeklies and other magazines number about 360 titles in all, with a total weekly circulation of over 3 million, of which Sunday and weekly newspapers account for approximately 1.5 million copies.

Newspaper readers are to be found mostly among urban populations representing about 20% of the total population. Press (and other media) coverage for the remaining 80% living in rural areas is severely hampered by material shortages, especially of printing plant and paper, and by the geographical configuration of this archipelago of 3000 islands stretching over 3000 miles of ocean.

The government is currently attempting to relieve paper shortages by encouraging the pulp and paper industry, through the development budget.

NEWS AGENCIES

The national agency is Antara (Lembaga Kantorberita Nasional Antara) founded in 1937 and government controlled since 1962, when it was merged with Jajasan Persbiro Indonesia. It comes under the direct control of the President of the republic through a governing council consisting of several cabinet ministers and representatives of newspapers and journalists.

Antara's main domestic bureaux, in addition to its head office in Djakarta, are located in nine provincial capitals on the islands of Java, Sumatra, Sulawesi, Kalimantan (Borneo), Moluccas and West Irian. Abroad, it has bureaux in Kuala Lumpur, Hong Kong, Tokyo, Bonn, The Hague and Beirut, and correspondents in Cairo, Belgrade, East Berlin, Moscow, Manila, Washington and Canberra.

It has exchange agreements with the following foreign agencies: Reuters AFP, AP, TASS, DPA, Kyodo, NCNA, KCNA and VP, of which the first four have bureaux in Djakarta.

Antara provides news, feature and photo services with a daily output of 50 000 words of local news in Indonesian and 20 000 words in foreign news in English for the newspaper and periodical press, as well as special services for government departments, the national broadcasting organizations and diplomatic missions. Bulletins appear twice daily in Indonesian and English, and contain both news and comment; press reviews, in the same languages, are issued weekly. Also available are an English-language financial and economic news service and a scientific reports series in Indonesian.

The Jajasan Pena News Agency (JP), founded in Djakarta in 1969 by a Muslim newspaper publishers' association, issues a news bulletin twice daily. Other private agencies exist and also a special news service for the armed forces.

RADIO

Radio Republik Indonesia (RRI), a government service under the Department of Information, operates 138 transmitters with studios in 45 towns throughout the country. Of these Djakarta has a large new studio centre and operates 18 transmitters including 2 of 120kW, 2 of 100kW and 4 of 50kW in the short-wave and tropical wave bands, 2 (recently established) medium-wave transmitters and 1 FM transmitter.

Two national programmes broadcast from Djakarta are on the air for 124 hours a week and include light entertainment (32 hours), news and information (21 hours), broadcasts for young people (13 hours), educational programmes (6 hours) and advertising (5 hours), as well as programmes for religious and other special community groups.

Regional stations, situated in the main centres, and local or provincial stations (of which there are over 100) are equipped to relay the news and special broadcasts of the national programmes but, for the most part, they originate their own programmes. A successful series, begun in 1969 and now transmitted by 34 stations with a total programme time of about 170 hours a week, comprises broadcasts to farms – these are widely followed by rural listeners, including 275 organized listening groups.

An Air Force radio station with 3 short-wave transmitters in Djakarta is on the air for 7 hours a day. In addition, there are over 500 small commercial and 'amateur' stations broadcasting (usually only within a very small radius) in the more densely populated areas.

The country's external broadcasting service, Voice of Indonesia, operates 5 short-wave transmitters (100 and 120kW) near Djakarta. Programmes (news, features, traditional music, etc.) totalling 13¼ hours a day in English, Indonesian, Chinese, Arabic, French, Malay, Hindi and Urdu are beamed to 17 target areas in Asia, the Pacific, the Americas, Africa, the Middle East and Europe.

TELEVISION

Televisi Republik Indonesia (TVRI) is a government-controlled service with 5 main and 7 relay transmitters giving coverage to the island of Java (stations at Djakarta, Jogjakarta, Bandung and Samarang), to north Sumatra (Medan), to south Sumatra (Palembang) and south Sulawesi (Ujung Padang). Factors limiting the extension of television services, apart from the size of the country, are the many mountainous areas and the absence of electricity supplies outside towns and major villages.

TVRI is on the air for 5 or 6 hours a day with largely commercial-type and some educational programmes including French, English and Indonesian language teaching. Most programme material is relayed from Djakarta to other stations by TVRI's network of microwave repeaters and translators on Java, or sent out as video tapes to other areas. With the completion of new studio facilities at Medan, Palembang and Surbaya, in addition to those existing at Djakarta and Jogjakarta, more programmes will be originated locally.

The definition system used is 625 lines.

FILM

With an annual production of 14 feature films and five short entertainment films in 1969–70, the Indonesian film industry, based in Djakarta, is growing steadily, thanks in some measure to government support and protection. The Department of Information has a special fund to assist film makers, and it sets annual production targets (eg 30 films to be produced in 1971). Also in 1971, imports are to be restricted to 600 titles (200 each from Europe and Asia, 150 from the American continent, and 50 others).

Foreign feature films shown in 1970, totalling 617, were imported: from the USA (156), Hong Kong (103), Italy (95), India (68), Japan (30), France (27), the Federal Republic of Germany (26) and other countries (112). The number of fixed cinemas has dropped from 680 to 490 over the last few years. Total annual attendances are variously reported, ranging from 21 million upwards.

SPACE COMMUNICATIONS

An earth station at Djatilujur in western Java capable of receiving telephone, telegraph and television transmissions through Indian Ocean Intelsat system was opened in 1969. A second station, linking Indonesia with the Pacific Intelsat system, was scheduled for completion at the same site, in 1974.

PROFESSIONAL TRAINING AND ASSOCIATIONS

Courses in journalism are offered in the appropriate faculties of seven universities, private and public, in Djakarta, Bandung, Jogjakarta, Samarang and Makassar and at three other private colleges. Broadcasting personnel are mostly trained on the job, though there is a school in Djakarta for technical television staff, and an extensive training scheme to be set up under international auspices will train senior telecommunications technicians.

There are associations of journalists, newspaper publishers and film producers, exporters, importers and distributors, all in Djakarta.

IRAN

Population	30 480 000
Area	1 648 000 sq. km.

PRESS

Newspapers	Dailies 39, Non-dailies 78
Total circulation	Dailies 750 000, Non-dailies 150 000
Copies per 1000 people	Dailies 25, Non-dailies 5

RADIO

Transmitters	Long/medium-wave 28, Short-wave 6, VHF—FM 4
Total receivers	7 000 000 estimated in use
Receivers per 1000 people	230

TELEVISION

Transmitters	70
Receivers	1 000 000 estimated in use
Receivers per 1000 people	33

FILM

Cinemas	Fixed 437
Total seating capacity	282 000
Seats per 1000 people	9
Total annual attendance	28 120 000
Annual visits per capita	0.9

PRESS

The country's dailies are published in Persian (34 titles), English (4), and French (1). The capital, Tehran, has 20 of these. The publishers of the two leading dailies, circulating 200 000 and 100 000 copies per issue respectively, each also publish associated foreign-language dailies, as well as various other periodicals. Only one other Tehran daily circulates more than 20 000 copies. Isfahan, Tabriz, Meshed, Shiraz and Ahwaz also have daily newspapers. Non-dailies, which include two bilingual German/Arabic papers, are published in Tehran and some 30 provincial towns.

Most newspapers are privately owned and depend largely on advertising revenue, much of which comes from government sources. Under the terms of the Press Law of 1955, modified in 1963, those papers whose circulation figures drop below 3000 copies per issue may have their licences withdrawn.

Periodicals total over 200 titles circulating 650 000 copies per issue. Highest circulations are recorded by a women's weekly (150 000 copies), a satirical weekly (65 000), a young people's weekly (65 000) and a sports weekly (50 000). Main subject categories are literature (28 titles), medicine (18), arts and literature (13), political science (12), agriculture (11), history, law and young people's journals (8 each), education, trade and communications, and business management (5 each), etc. Also included in the total are 39 business house organs and 19 school magazines.

NEWS AGENCIES

The official national agency is the Pars News Agency, founded in 1938 and operated by the Ministry of Information's General Department of Publications and Broadcasting, in Tehran. It receives Reuters, UPI, AP, AFP, DPA and TASS services and is the main source of foreign news for the Iranian press (though some of the larger publishers also subscribe, themselves, to international agency services) and for the country's radio and television stations. Both radio and printed news bulletins are issued in Persian and foreign languages.

Another agency is the International Press Agency of Iran, also based in Tehran.

AFP, ANSA, AP, Reuters, TASS and UPI have bureaux in Tehran.

RADIO

The government authority responsible for broadcasting is the General Department of Publications and Broadcasting, but actual production and transmission operations are carried out by National Iranian Radio and Television (NIRTV), an administratively independent body directed by an interministerial board.

Iran's first radio station began broadcasting in Tehran in 1940. There is now a home service bringing programmes within reach of 80% of the population. Radio Iran, the first of the three home-service programmes is a national programme in Persian broadcast for 24 hours a day by medium-wave (100 and 500kW) and short-wave (100 and 250kW) transmitters from Tehran and Kamalabad. The second programme, Radio Tehran, with one medium-wave transmitter (100kW), is on the air for 18 hours a day in Persian. Short programmes are also broadcast in English, French, German and Russian. The third programme (FM, stereo), serving the capital, broadcasts only music for 3 hours daily.

The 13 regional stations (in Abadan, Ahwaz, Gorgan, Isfahan, Kerman, Kermanshah, Meshed, Resht, Rezaiyeh, Samandaj, Shiraz, Tabriz and Zahidan), most of which broadcast for around 18 hours a day on medium waves, originate their own programmes and also relay those of Radio Tehran. Languages used besides Persian include Arabic, Turkmen, Kurdish, Azerbaijani, Assyrian, Armenian, Baluchi and Urdu.

Broadcasting time for all government stations, including the foreign service, adds up to some 300 hours a week, 238 of which are accounted for by nationally produced programmes. Principal programme categories are light entertainment (114 hours), cultural and scientific programmes (82 hours, 50% of which is European and Persian classical music), broadcasts for special audiences (46 hours), news and information (45 hours) and education (5 hours).

The foreign service, with short-wave transmitters in Tehran (100kW) and Kamalabad (250kW), broadcasts daily 30-minute programmes beamed to Europe in Russian, Turkish, Arabic, German, French and English and a 1-hour programme for Iranians abroad.

There are also two private stations both on the air for 20 hours daily: the National Iranian Oil Company, with a 10kW medium-wave transmitter in Abadan, broadcasting in Persian (including relays of Radio Tehran), and the United States Air Force's 1kW medium-wave transmitter in Tehran.

No licence fee is payable for radio receivers.

TELEVISION

The first television stations operating in Iran were established under private ownership in 1958, in Tehran, and in 1959 at Abadan. All television broadcasting (except for one station) is now carried out by NIRTV with two channels in Tehran and nine provincial stations (at Abadan, Ahwaz, Bandar Abass, Isfahan, Kerman, Kermanshah, Meshed, Resht and Tabriz) potentially covering 80% of the population. From mid-1971 to mid-1973, the number of receivers in use doubled, but the actual number of viewers is even more augmented by the fact that, in addition to their own families, almost all set owners regularly invite from one to seven or more friends into their homes to watch programmes (according to a 1970 inquiry). In addition, receivers are often placed in cultural and community centres.

Broadcasting time totals over 97 hours a week, about 70% of which is accounted for by imported programmes. Main categories are long films and series (40 hours, almost all imported), news and information (19½ hours), cultural and scientific programmes (12 hours), light entertainment (14 hours), broadcasts for special audiences (7 hours), education (7 hours) and advertising and announcements (3 hours).

No licence fee is payable for television receivers. Sets are manufactured and assembled in Iran. The definition system used is 625 lines.

The United States Air Force has a television station in Tehran.

FILM
In 1972, 90 long films were produced. Production of non-commercial short films totalled 148 in 1971 (1 entertainment, 130 documentary and 17 instructional). Many documentaries and educational films are produced by government units or with state aid.

Government encouragement to the industry, through the Ministry of Arts and Culture, also includes technical assistance for Iranian film producers, prizes for the best films and performers, distribution of films for showing in schools, factories and cultural centres and the organization of mobile-unit showings in rural areas. The ministry is also responsible for general supervision of film production, releases, imports, etc. On average a ratio of 35 to 40% of Iranian films to 60 to 65% of imported films holds for films exhibited in the country's cinemas.

The development of film clubs is fostered, as also is amateur film-making, the productions of amateurs, university film clubs, etc., being broadcast on television.

Imports for the year 1972 included 289 features: from the USA (135), Italy (65), France (21), the UK (20), India (13), Turkey (4) and other countries (31). In 1971, 767 documentaries were imported from the USA, the UK, Japan, the Federal Republic of Germany, Canada, France, the USSR, Bulgaria and other countries.

About 50% of fixed cinemas are in the 14 towns with populations of over 100 000, including Tehran which has an average of one cinema seat per 30 inhabitants. Another 25% are in towns with between 25 000 and 100 000 habitants. In addition to the 437 fixed cinemas, which record 22 million admissions a year, there are 45 seasonal cinemas (with a combined capacity of 25 000 seats), 102 mobile units (with an annual attendance of about 6 million) and one drive-in accommodating 236 cars and recording an annual attendance of 150 000.

SPACE COMMUNICATIONS
An Atlantic Intelsat earth station at Asadabad, about 350km west of Tehran, was opened in October 1969. An Indian Ocean Intelsat station at the same location is expected to come into operation late in 1973.

PROFESSIONAL TRAINING AND ASSOCIATIONS
The Institute of Communication Research, originally sponsored in 1964 by one

of the main press groups as the Institute of Journalism and now recognized by the University of Tehran, offers a four-year course in journalism, cinematography and photography, public relations and translation. A College of Television and Cinema associated with the National Radio and Television Organization in Tehran conducts a two-year professional training course.

There are two main press associations, with memberships of about 40 and 20 newspapers and journals respectively. There is also an association of journalists and reporters and a national Iranian film syndicate.

IRAQ

Population	10 070 000
Area	434 924 sq. km.

PRESS	
Newspapers	Dailies 7, Non-dailies 15

RADIO	
Transmitters	Long/medium-wave 7, Short-wave 14
Total receivers	1 700 000 estimated in use
Receivers per 1000 people	169

TELEVISION	
Transmitters	5
Receivers	250 000 estimated in use
Receivers per 1000 people	25

FILM	
Cinemas	Fixed 24
Total annual attendance	8 095 700
Annual visits per capita	0.8

PRESS

Following the enactment of new press legislation in the late sixties, the number of daily newspapers was reduced from some 16 titles to 7 in 1972. Of these, 4 are in Arabic, 2 in Kurdish and 1 in English, all published in Baghdad except for one of the Kurdish papers which appears in the north of the country. Circulations range up to around 50 000 copies per issue. The daily press comes under the jurisdiction of a special government publishing service. The state-sponsored publishing house is itself the publisher of an Arabic and an English daily, as well as 4 weeklies in Arabic, Kurdish and Turkman.

The non-daily press includes a number of twice-weekly, weekly and fortnightly general interest newspapers – some with special emphases or representing community groups – published mainly in Baghdad and also in Mosul, Sulaimaniya, Samarra and Basra. The majority are in Arabic, but French, Turkman and Kurdish are also used.

In addition to a government gazette and periodicals published by various ministries, political, economic and cultural journals appear, usually monthly, and there is a fortnightly broadcasting magazine issued by the official radio, television and cinema establishment.

NEWS AGENCIES

The government-owned Iraqi News Agency (INA), founded in November 1959, with headquarters in Baghdad and five bureaux abroad, employs 230 full-time staff in the country and 20 abroad.

Overseas news is received from AP, Reuters, AFP, TASS, Tanjug, CTK, DPA, ADN, MENA, SANA, APS and Anatolia, and the agency has exchange agreements for both news and photos with Reuters, Tanjug, CTK, ADN, MENA and SANA.

On average, INA issues 3000 words of local and national news daily in Arabic and 4000 words of international news in English. Its subscribers in the country include 4 newspapers, 1 radio and 4 television stations. Transmissions are effected by radio teletype.

ADN, AFP, AP, DPA, Hsinhua, MENA, Reuters, TASS and Novosti are represented in Baghdad.

RADIO

All broadcasting is controlled by the official Iraqi Broadcasting and Television Organization which is financed by government funds. Sound broadcasting began in 1936 and now covers the entire national territory with two programmes broadcast via medium-wave transmitters of 20, 100 and 150kW and short-wave transmitters of 50, 100 and 250kW located near Baghdad, at Salman Pak and Abu Ghuraib. Further medium-wave stations are being built at Basra (two 600kW transmitters) and Kirkuk (two 120kW transmitters).

The home-service programme and 'The Voice of the Masses' use mainly Arabic but also Kurdish and Turkman. Together they are on the air for about 150 hours a week, broadcasting light entertainment (104 hours), news and information (16½ hours), programmes for special audiences (10½ hours), cultural programmes (8¾ hours), education (1¾ hours) and advertising (1¾ hours). All programmes are of national origin.

The foreign service, using both medium and short waves, is on the air for 7½ hours a day, broadcasting 50- or 60-minute programmes in Turkish, Persian, Hebrew, Urdu, English, French, German and Russian, beamed either to the Near and Middle East or to Europe.

No licence fee is payable for radio receivers.

TELEVISION

A public television service from Baghdad was in operation as early as 1956. The government-owned Baghdad Television now has a main station at Baghdad and local stations at Kirkuk, Mosul and Basra. Two additional stations are being built to serve the provincial areas of Muthanna and Maisan, and a microwave link from Baghdad to Kirkuk and from Baghdad to Basra, with a further connection to Amara, is also planned. Between 50 and 60% of the population are within receiving distance of television programmes.

Weekly broadcasting time amounts to about 50 hours and, depending on the station, includes broadcasts for special audiences (13 hours), cultural programmes (11 hours), light entertainment (9 hours), news and information (9 hours), education (7 hours) and advertising (1½ hours). Programmes for upper secondary schools, produced by the Ministry of Education, are broadcast for 1½ hours on school days for eight months of the year.

Almost half the material broadcast is locally produced. Imported programmes come principally from Egypt, Lebanon, Algeria, the UK, the USSR, the German Democratic Republic and France. Programmes are in Arabic except for those of the Kirkuk stations which produce 50% in Kurdish. The definition system is 625 lines.

No receiver licence fee is payable.

FILM

Both the Baghdad Television and Cinema Establishment and the official Cinema and Theatre Administration produce about 12 short films each year. One feature film (coproduced with the German Democratic Republic) was made in 1971. A fortnightly newsreel is also produced.

Imported feature films from Egypt, Italy, the UK, France, the USSR, the German Democratic Republic and other countries are shown in Baghdad, Basra, Mosul and Kirkuk. Imports in 1971 totalled 250 features, as well as some 300 documentaries (including 123 from the USSR).

PROFESSIONAL TRAINING AND ASSOCIATIONS

The Department of Journalism at the University of Baghdad offers a four-year degree course established in 1964. There were 16 graduates in 1970.

A union of journalists was founded in 1959.

ISRAEL

Population	2 998 000
Area	20 700 sq. km.

PRESS

Newspapers	Dailies 24, Non-dailies 101
Total circulation	Dailies 550 000
Copies per 1000 people	Dailies 183

RADIO

Transmitters	Long/Medium-wave 20, Short-wave 12, VHF—FM 15
Total receivers	660 000 estimated in use
Receivers per 1000 people	220

TELEVISION

Transmitters	21
Receivers	356 000 estimated in use
Receivers per 1000 people	119

FILM

Cinemas	Fixed 252
Total seating capacity	177 000
Seats per 1000 people	59
Total annual attendance	32 288 700
Annual visits per capita	11

PRESS

Daily newspapers are published in Tel Aviv (20 titles) and Jerusalem (4 titles), mainly in Hebrew (12 titles) but also in Yiddish, English, Arabic, Hungarian, French, Polish, Bulgarian, Romanian and German. All consider themselves national, not local. Evening dailies have the largest circulations (the 2 largest circulate around 200 000 and 150 000 copies on week days), although morning papers are considered more influential. Morning papers contain 6—16 pages (weekdays); evening papers, 24—32 pages (weekdays). The size of the Friday issues is more than doubled by weekend supplements and circulations increase by up to 50 000 copies. No papers appear on Saturday.

Few dailies are self-supporting. Advertising income is considerable, but unevenly distributed. In consequence, most newspapers are subsidized by political parties, religious groups or public funds.

All the dailies receive the services of Reuters, UPI, AFP, the Jewish Telegraphic Agency (JTA) and ITIM, and a few receive AP bulletins as well. Nevertheless, most of them, including the small ones, maintain part-time correspondents in the major capitals and at the United Nations.

The non-daily press is mainly in Hebrew (or Hebrew plus one or more other languages); 9 titles appear in English, 6 in Arabic and 12 in various other languages.

There are also approximately 360 other periodicals, including more than 70 government publications. Among them are illustrated, technical, commercial, literary, political and art magazines.

National newsprint consumption amounts to around 31 000 metric tons annually of which some 9400 metric tons are accounted for by domestic production.

NEWS AGENCIES

ITIM, the cooperatively owned and operated news agency of the Associated Israeli Press, founded in 1950, is Israel's largest and only truly national agency.

Its headquarters are in Tel Aviv, and there are permanent bureaux at Jerusalem, Lod Airport and Haifa. Abroad, ITIM maintains no bureaux of its own. When special reports are needed, it turns to the respective national news agencies with whom it has standing exchange arrangements. Apart from editors, translators and other staff, ITIM has some 40 correspondents.

For home consumption, the agency distributes daily to its 18 newspaper subscribers and to 3 radio and TV stations, some 12 000 words of national news, some 14 000 words selected from world news items supplied by AFP and UPI, some 4000 words of news from the Jewish world, received from the Jewish Telegraphic Agency (JTA) in New York and London, and some 3000 words of radio-monitored Middle Eastern news. This brings the average daily total to 33 000, all in Hebrew, flowing over two parallel networks of Hebrew teleprinters. At the same time, ITIM distributes the full original English versions of UPI and JTA news and the full original French version of AFP news to anyone interested, mainly foreign-language newspapers, the radio and TV and some embassies. In addition, special services of economic news are supplied to banks, importers, exporters, etc., via six more teleprinter networks, of which one is in French and the rest in English. ITIM has exchange arrangements with news agencies in over 40 countries which receive a weekly 1800 word English-language air-mail bulletin of Israeli news, as well as special releases.

The Israel News Agency (INA), with headquarters in Tel Aviv, is a public company whose main shareholders are the Jewish Telegraphic Agencies in New York and London. It has special correspondents in London, New York and Washington.

Practically all the local dailies and the Israel Broadcasting Authority take its daily service of some 8000 words in Hebrew and English, mainly incorporating material received from New York and London.

Reuters, UPI, AFP, AP, ANSA and DPA have bureaux in Tel Aviv. All agencies have correspondents in Jerusalem.

RADIO

The Israel Broadcasting Authority, an autonomous public body distinct from the Government of Israel, was established by the Broadcasting Authority Law of 1965, and assumed responsibility in that year for the Israel Broadcasting Service. In 1968, the law was amended to include television broadcasts as well. The authority derives its revenue from receiver licences, advertising, services to government agencies and from state funds.

The radio service broadcasts three home programmes from Broadcasting House in Jerusalem and studios in Tel Aviv and Haifa, each of which is on the air for up to 19 hours a day, using medium-wave transmitters (600kW), short-wave transmitters (up to 300kW) and FM transmitters (including stereo), located throughout the country. The main national programme, Network A, from Jerusalem is in Hebrew. Network B, also from Jerusalem is a light programme with commercial advertising broadcast in Hebrew and (for 2 hours a day) special programmes for new immigrants in easy Hebrew, Yiddish, Ladino, Moghrabi, Romanian, Russian and Hungarian. Network D, with programmes in Arabic for over 14 hours daily, also carries some programmes in English and French. Weekly programmes total 398 hours, including broadcasts for ethnic minorities

(110 hours), broadcasts for special audiences (99 hours), light entertainment (78 hours), arts, letters and science (54 hours), news and information (44½ hours), advertising (8½ hours) and education (5 hours). Four times a week, special programmes are broadcast to primary schools by arrangement with the Ministry of Education and Culture.

Network C is operated by the external services division and broadcasts short-wave programmes in 10 languages for 6½ hours daily, beamed to audiences in Latin America, south and west Africa and Europe, as well as medium-wave transmissions to the Middle East in three languages in addition to Hebrew. The authority also regularly distributes recorded programmes to stations in over 70 countries.

The Israel Defence Forces also have five medium-wave transmitters. There are no privately owned stations.

The annual licence fee may cover several receivers.

TELEVISION

After a series of experimental telecasts in 1968, the Israel Broadcasting Authority started regular television broadcasting on 25 May 1969. Programmes are now broadcast daily from three main transmitters and a number of low-power satellite transmitters throughout the country. Programmes are mainly in Hebrew, but also in Arabic (for 1½ hours daily), often with subtitles in the other language.

Total broadcasting time is 62 hours a week consisting of educational broadcasts (30 hours), broadcasts for ethnic minorities (10 hours), news and information (7 hours), broadcasts for special audiences (6½ hours) and arts, letters and science (3 hours). Domestic production accounts for about 40 hours a week; 95% of imported programme material comes from the USA and the UK. Reuters, UPI, AP and AFP news services are used. The broadcasts to schools, numbering 76 a week in 1971, are prepared by a special Instructional Television Centre under the Ministry of Education and Culture and service some 1300 schools with 550 000 pupils. The definition system used is 625 lines.

An annual licence fee is payable.

FILM

In 1971, feature-film production amounted to 15 titles. The country now has two colour laboratories. A number of shorts and television films are also produced by local and foreign companies, the Instructional Television Centre alone being responsible for 250 short films in one year, and the government film service for 30 more. The main producers' association now has 33 full members.

Government encouragement to the industry takes the form of tax facilities, advances and loans, training scholarships and financial aid to young directors and producers, and is administered by the Israel Film Office within the Ministry of Commerce and Industry.

Imports for 1971 included 443 features, coming from the USA (123), the Arab countries (120), Italy (61), Greece (11), France (30), the UK (16), India (15), the Federal Republic of Germany (11), Scandinavian countries (6) and others. The number of operating cinemas has markedly declined since the introduction of television, as have annual ticket sales (from 51 million admissions in the peak year 1966 to just over 32 million in 1971–2). A government fund established in 1970 provides loans for the improvement of cinemas and services.

SPACE COMMUNICATIONS
A government-owned Atlantic Intelsat earth station at Emeq Ha'ela, west of Jerusalem, came into operation on 26 May 1972.

PROFESSIONAL TRAINING AND ASSOCIATIONS
The Communications Institute at the Hebrew University of Jerusalem, founded in 1966, offers a two-year MA course in journalism, with a full enrolment of about 50 students in both years, and also a one-year post-graduate diploma course in communications, for which internships are available for media professionals. The American College in Jerusalem is also introducing courses in journalism and film making. Educational television training is available at Bar Ilan University.

The National Union of Israel Journalists and the Israel Press Council (founded by the National Union) have professional rules and a code of ethics, respectively. There is also a new association of daily-newspaper publishers and a daily-newspaper editors' committee.

JAPAN

Population	105 611 000
Area	372 077 sq. km.

PRESS

Newspapers	Dailies 172, Non-dailies 800*
Total circulation	Dailies 55 845 000
Copies per 1000 people	Dailies 529

RADIO

Transmitters	Long/medium-wave 474, Short-wave 19, VHF–FM 396
Total receivers	46 600 000 estimated in use
Receivers per 1000 people	441†

TELEVISION

Transmitters	4991
Receivers	24 200 000 ‡ estimated in use
Receivers per 1000 people	229‡

FILM

Cinemas	Fixed 2673
Total seating capacity	1 249 000
Seats per 1000 people	12
Total annual attendance	187 000 000
Annual visits per capita	2

*Approx.
†Wireless receivers only.
‡Subscribers' contracts.

PRESS

Japan's daily press consists of 45 morning, 21 evening and 51 'set' newspapers (ie separate morning and evening papers sold as one for a single subscription). Counting each set as two papers, each with its own circulation, Japan has the third largest daily newspaper circulation in the world, after the USSR and the USA.

Of around 60 cities in which daily newspapers are published, Tokyo is the most important, with 23 general interest dailies (12 of which are the morning and evening papers of 6 'set' dailies; 7 are single dailies; and 4 English-language, single dailies). Tokyo also has 6 sports dailies and 5 other specialized dailies, one of which is in English. Three great Tokyo-based newspaper concerns (the 'Big Three') dominate the national publishing scene. In addition to their 'set' dailies published in the capital with a combined circulation of 14.6 million, they also have satellite papers in other cities (Osaka, Nagoya, Sapporo, Kitakynshu, Takaoka), totalling a further 12.3 million copies a day. Delays in communication between the central and satellite presses are overcome by the radio transmission of facsimile pages from Tokyo. Next in importance to Tokyo, Osaka has 5 'set' dailies, 5 evening and 2 morning dailies (one in English) and 4 sports dailies. Sapporo has 6 'set' dailies and 2 sports dailies, while Nagoya has 3 'set' dailies, 2 single and 2 sports dailies. Other large cities have up to 7 dailies but the majority have 1 or 2. One of Okinawa's 6 dailies appears in English and the United States Armed Forces also have their own English-language daily.

Overall daily circulation figures for the country have increased by some 15 million copies over the last ten years, largely accounted for by morning papers. Some 90% of Japanese newspapers are sold by subscription and are home-delivered through a country-wide set-up of over 200 000 separately owned agencies. Some distribution operations for larger papers are now being computerized.

News (spot news 11% plus features 39%) accounts for 50% of space in Japanese newspapers, with growing attention being given to local news even in the national press, which often has special local news pages inserted into its area editions. Readers' opinions are increasingly solicited, and letters to the editor take up 1.8% of space. Editorial matter accounts for 1%. The growth of newspaper advertising (now representing 45% of total daily space), despite the competition of television, is largely responsible for the increased size of newspapers – the national papers consist usually of 16 pages in the morning and 8 in the evening.

Newspaper type is set in vertical lines reading from the righthand corner of the column, the column rules being horizontal. The characters used are those of the simplified list of 1850 *kanji* (Chinese characters) adopted by the official language reform of 1946 and supplemented by the use of syllabic symbols. Because of this multiplicity of characters, mechanical typesetting is an extremely difficult problem to which solutions are gradually being developed by the use of computer-controlled phototypesetters. Up to ten years ago, all Japanese newspapers were printed by the letterpress process. Now there are some dailies using offset, and others plan to do so, particularly because of the growing use of colour printing (though the transfer will not be easy for the large-circulation papers which have made enormous investments in high-speed rotary presses). Most of the offset newspapers print from plates made from films of proof prints produced from pages set in hot-metal type, but a number of satellite printing plants of the major press concerns (12 newspapers publishing in 28 localities) are now using plates made directly from film transmitted in facsimile form from their head offices. A further extension of this technique, still experimental, is the development of equipment to transmit facsimile newspaper pages to the homes of television viewers either by UHF carriers or by coaxial cable.

The non-daily press, totalling some 800 titles in the sixties includes Sunday editions of almost all dailies plus a number of local papers.

Over 5700 periodical titles are published, among which weekly journals have a total circulation of 640 million copies. Individual circulations of around 1 million copies are recorded for several magazines. Among monthlies are cultural journals with circulations of up to 700 000.

With a total production of 1 968 137 metric tons in 1971, Japan is the world's third largest producer of newsprint. Consumption for the same year was 1 925 893 metric tons.

NEWS AGENCIES

Kyodo Tsushin (Kyodo News Service), established in 1945, is the largest and most important news agency in Japan. With headquarters in Tokyo, it has 51 permanent bureaux within the country as well as 24 bureaux abroad, in Washington, New York, London, Moscow, Paris, Bonn, Geneva, New Delhi, Singapore, Djakarta, Hong Kong, Seoul, etc. A cooperative, whose membership includes the principal newspapers of Japan, exclusive of the 'Big Three' which rely on their own correspondents for national news, Kyodo supplies a wide variety of services to its 66 member newspapers, 14 other newspapers and 46 radio and television companies. The 'Big Three' subscribe to its foreign service. It distributes daily some 220 000 letters in Japanese and 35 000 words in English.

Of the 80 newspaper subscribers, some 65 take the ideographic teletype service, the others taking facsimile casts equivalent to 40 000 lines. Other services include features, photos, short-wave broadcasts for domestic subscribers, a 13-hour daily English-language news service and a Japanese-language facsimile service for ocean-going ships. Kyodo has a large monitoring station at Noda, Chiba prefecture, where the daily newscast intake averages 700 000 words.

Kyodo has exchange agreements and subscriptions with AP, UPI, TASS, Reuters and 28 other news agencies, and receives news from Hsinhua.

The Jiji Press, also founded in 1945 and also a cooperative with headquarters in Tokyo, has 62 bureaux in Japan and 31 abroad, including offices in Hong Kong, Bangkok, London, New Delhi, Bonn, Washington and New York. It maintains 54 staff correspondents abroad. Its average daily distribution in facsimile cast is 400 000 Japanese letters (roughly 18 500 English words) on national news for domestic use, the equivalent of 12 000 words for overseas Chinese use, 30 000 English words for domestic and overseas use and 4000 Spanish words for middle and South American use. Jiji also supplies market-quotation services and maintains research services for international affairs, public opinion and market research. It exchanges news with and subscribes to AFP, Reuters, UPI and Antara.

Other agencies include Sun Telephoto (founded 1952) and Radio Press (founded 1945). Radio Press supplies news, but principally features, to 94 clients. Its principal sources of daily news are government-operated short-wave stations throughout the world, monitored in five languages. Another service monitoring Radio Moscow broadcasts supplies news of the Soviet Union.

Kyodo Television's newsfilm agency has its head office in Tokyo, as does the Net-Asahi newsfilm agency. Both were founded in 1958.

Reuters, AFP, TASS, AP and UPI maintain bureaux in Tokyo. The Tokyo AP office is the relay point for all Asian and Philippine news, which is assembled in Tokyo and channelled to New York. Almost all news agencies maintain bureaux or correspondents in Tokyo, where there are 105 accredited news-agency correspondents, 82 newspaper correspondents, 19 radio correspondents and 4 television correspondents.

RADIO

Broadcasting is conducted by two systems: the government service, Nippon Hoso Kyokai (NHK) or Japan Broadcasting Corporation, which derives its revenue from the monthly subscription fees which must be paid for all television (but not radio) receivers; and the privately owned commercial stations grouped within the National Association of Broadcasters (NAB), which are financed from advertising revenue.

NHK operates three national radio networks, broadcasting almost exclusively in Japanese. The first, with 170 medium-wave transmitters, is on the air for 133 hours a week, broadcasting 43% news, 30% cultural, 26% entertainment and 1% educational programmes. The second network, with 141 medium-wave trans-mitters broadcasting for 130 hours a week, carries 80% educational programmes, while the third, with over 300 FM transmitters (the majority providing stereo programmes), broadcasts for 126 hours carrying 50% cultural, 29% educational, 11% news and 10% educational programmes. Both second and third networks broadcast for 18½ hours a day. Cultural and educational broadcasts include programmes for primary and secondary schools, and special programmes for correspondence courses for high-school and university students. Over 99.5% of all schools are equipped with receivers. There is no advertising on NHK radio.

The commercial stations are owned by 50 companies (35 of which also operate television stations) and are equipped with 160 medium-wave trans-mitters, 6 short-wave transmitters and 5 FM transmitters. They are on the air for from 18 to 24 hours a day, broadcasting 50.2% music, 18.5% cultural programmes, 13.2% news, 9.9% entertainment, 5.5% educational programmes,

1.5% sports, 0.9% advertising, etc. A Christian mission station in Okinawa, with 3 medium-wave transmitters, broadcasts in English and Japanese.

Domestic broadcasting services cover 99.7% of the national territory.

The Far East Network of the United States Armed Forces Radio and Television Service has medium-wave transmitters (up to 50kW and one of 10kW) in seven localities, and short-wave stations (up to 10kW) in Tokyo; it is on the air for 24 hours a day.

NHK's overseas broadcasting service, Radio Japan, conducts a regional short-wave service beamed to nine areas throughout the world, and broadcasts for 23 hours a day in 23 languages. Its general overseas service, consisting mainly of news and commentaries in English and Japanese, is on the air for 14 hours a day, giving a total of 37 overseas broadcasting hours a day. Programmes consist of 42.6% news, 19.9% commentary, 30.3% information, 5.3% music, 1.3% sports and 0.6% entertainment and are compiled by NHK with the advice of an expert Overseas Broadcast Programme Deliberation Council.

The Voice of America (USA) has 1 medium-wave (1000kW) and 3 short-wave (one 100kW and two 35kW) transmitters in Okinawa, relaying programmes to Far East listeners.

TELEVISION

Regular television broadcasts were first made in 1953 by the publicly owned Japan Broadcasting Corporation (NHK) and by the privately owned commercial concern, Nippon Television Network (NTV). Since then, both public and private stations have developed side by side and it is estimated that 97% of Japanese households are now covered by television (525-line definition). Tokyo has 8 channels, Osaka 6, Fukuoka and Nagoya 5 and Sapporo 4.

NHK provides two services, each carried by over 1500 transmitters and each of the air for 126 hours a week covering 23.8 million subscribing households. The general service broadcasts cultural programmes (46 hours a week), news (40 hours), entertainment (28 hours) and education (12 hours), but no advertising. The educational service devoted 106 hours a week to specifically educational programmes, and 20 hours to other cultural broadcasts. The educational service's programmes are at four school levels, and were utilized (in 1970) by 88% of the nursery schools, 90% of the primary schools, and 37% and 29% respectively of the junior and senior high schools which have television sets. In addition, a correspondence high-school course, college courses, special education programmes and language and vocational courses are broadcast. NHK exchanges television programmes with 40 countries, including exchanges through the Asian, European and other broadcasting unions. Its imports (less than 5% of the total) come mainly from the USA (50%), the UK (20%), Australia, France, Italy and the Federal Republic of Germany.

Some 1250 commercial stations (472 VHF and 778 UHF) are operated by 85 companies. Most of these stations are grouped contractually for purposes of programme provision (Japanese law prevents multiple station ownership by one company) in four big networks (FUJI, NET, NTV and TBS), all based in Tokyo, which have a number of 'key' stations through which local stations are supplied. Commercial stations also have links with other national and local media interests, particularly the press. Their programmes, which are broadcast for 14 to 20 hours a day, consist of 48% entertainment, 28% cultural programmes, 11.2%

news, 8.7% educational programmes, 3% sports and 0.5% commercial advertising. The Broadcasting Law (1950) requires commercial stations to devote 30% of ordinary television programmes to cultural and educational broadcasts. One station operated by the Japanese Science Foundation in Tokyo broadcasts mainly educational programmes.

Between 80 and 90% of programmes are in colour (NTSC system) and approximately half the receiver subscriptions are for colour receivers. The actual number of receivers in use is greatly in excess of subscriptions since these may cover more than one set.

Cable or community-antenna television (CATV), a recent development in urban, high-density housing and new town areas, is governed by a law effective from 1 January 1973 which obliges all CATV facilities to retransmit simultaneously all wireless-television programmes broadcast in their operating areas and allows them to rebroadcast freely signals from distant stations with the prior approval of the originating station. CATV facilities with more than 500 subscriber terminals (of which there are about 300 in operation) require approval to operate from the Minister of Posts and Telecommunications.

The United States Armed Forces Radio and Television Service has transmitters in Misawa and Okinawa.

FILM

Japan has been one of the world's leading feature-film producers. Production rose from 549 feature titles in 1960 to 893 in 1965 and has gradually declined to 390 in 1972. About half of these are made by five major producing companies, and the remainder by independent producers. Some 1450 short films, including 856 documentaries, 541 instructional and 57 entertainment, were produced in 1972. There are about 190 companies producing educational and industrial documentaries.

Of the 283 feature films imported in 1972, 138 came from the USA, 33 from France, 31 from the UK, 30 from Italy, 27 from the Federal Republic of Germany, 9 from the USSR, 6 from Sweden and 9 from seven other countries.

Annual cinema attendance, which totalled 1014 million in 1960, had declined to little more than a sixth of that figure in 1972. Over the same period, the number of cinemas (7200 in 1960) dropped by more than 60%. About 60% of all cinemas show Japanese films and 24% imported films, while the remainder present both Japanese and foreign films. The usual programme consists of two features and one newsreel.

SPACE COMMUNICATIONS

The organization authorized by the government to carry out international telecommunications operations via Intelsat satellite is the Kokusai Denshin Denwa Company (KDD). KDD has already broadcast television programmes via satellite without radio in Japan and world television broadcasts via Pacific Ocean, Indian Ocean and Atlantic Ocean Intelsat satellites. Japan's earth stations for these satellites are at Ibaraki near Tokyo (opened in 1967, 1968 and 1971) and at Yamaguchi near Hiroshima (opened in 1968). NHK and the four main commercial television companies formed the Japan Satellite News Pool (JSNP) in 1969 to share satellite relay costs.

PROFESSIONAL TRAINING AND ASSOCIATIONS
Media training, for which entrants must have completed 12 years of primary and
secondary education, is provided in the institutes of journalism of Tokyo and
Keio Universities (non-degree courses), in the departments of broadcasting, of
journalism and of literary arts, at Nihon University the departments or faculties
of mass communication (Tokai University), sociology (Tokyo University), arts
and literature (Seijo University), literature (Waseda University) and political
science and economics (Meiji University), all these being four-year degree
courses. A two-year post-graduate course is offered at the International Christian
University (Department of Audio-Visual Education). Of a total enrolment of
4780 students in 1970, some 650 were women.

The Nihon Shinbun Kyokai (NSK) or Japan Newspaper Publishers' and
Editors' Association, founded in 1946, groups together 110 newspapers, 8 news
agencies and 48 broadcasting enterprises which subscribe to its canons of
journalism. There are also associations of provincial and regional and specialized
newspapers, and press clubs for national and foreign journalists.

All commercial radio and television stations belong to the National
Association of Commercial Broadcasters in Japan (NAB) which has its own
recommended codes of ethics for the media, while the Motion Picture Producers'
Association of Japan also has a self-regulatory code of ethics. Associations also
exist for film directors, writers, engineers and exhibitors.

JORDAN

Population	2 470 000
Area	97 740 sq. km.

PRESS
Newspapers	Dailies 4, Non-dailies 7
Total circulation	Dailies 58 000, Non-dailies 48 000
Copies per 1000 people	Dailies 23, Non-dailies 19

RADIO
Transmitters	Long/medium-wave 3, Short-wave 4, VHF–FM 2
Total receivers	521 000 estimated in use
Receivers per 1000 people	211

TELEVISION
Transmitters	4
Receivers	105 000 estimated in use
Receivers per 1000 people	42

FILM

Cinemas	Fixed 39
Total seating capacity	22 000
Seats per 1000 people	9
Total annual attendance	2 000 000*
Annual visits per capita	0.8*

*In 1970.

PRESS

All dailies are published in the capital, Amman, in Arabic. The largest is an independent daily (circulation 15 000) founded in 1934. Another is government controlled and a third is published by a company with a minority government shareholding.

The main political weekly circulates from 12 000 to 15 000 copies, and a weekly official gazette circulates 8000 copies.

The periodical press in 1973 included 23 titles with a combined circulation of 81 500 copies per issue. Main subject categories are law (4 titles, 10 500 copies), political science (3 titles, 15 000 copies), religion (3 titles, 5000 copies), literature (2 titles, 7000 copies), agriculture (2 titles, 4000 copies), arts and architecture (2 titles, 4000 copies), military science (1 title, 12 000 copies), education (1 title, 12 000 copies), etc. Most are in Arabic, but some professional journals are bilingual Arabic and English. Periodicals from Lebanon, Kuwait and Egypt also have appreciable readerships in Jordan.

NEWS AGENCIES

The Jordan News Agency (JNA), founded in 1969, is government owned, with headquarters in Amman and a bureau in Beirut. Permanent staff number 20 in Jordan and four abroad. JNA receives the overseas services of Reuters, AFP, AP, UPI, MENA and TASS. It supplies three newspapers and one radio station with news, including 5000 words of national and local news daily, in Arabic, as well as features and photos. News transmission is effected by public telecommunication services and telex.

The Jordanian press and broadcasting services also receive news from MENA, Reuters, AP, UPI, AFP, DPA and TASS.

RADIO

The Broadcasting Service of the Hashemite Kingdom of Jordan, under the Ministry of Communications, is financed directly from the government budget and is responsible for all radio broadcasting in the country. It broadcasts a home service with two 100kW medium-wave transmitters, and a foreign service using short-wave transmitters of up to 100kW, all in Amman. Some 98% of the population is covered by radio.

Radio Jordan broadcasts 168 hours a week, including 136 hours in Arabic, 28 hours in English and 4 hours of school and sponsored commercial programmes. Programmes include light entertainment (85 hours), news and information (38 hours), broadcasts to special audiences (27 hours), cultural programmes (13 hours), education (3 hours) and advertising (3 hours).

The foreign service is on the air for 4 hours a day in English, 1 hour in Spanish and 30 minutes each in Hebrew and French.

No licence fee is required for radio receivers.

TELEVISION

The government-owned Jordan Television Corporation, financed directly from the government budget, began operating in 1968. It now broadcasts two programmes with two main transmitters and two repeaters, potentially reaching over 85% of the population. Programmes in mid-1973 totalled over 60 hours a week and consist of films and serials (30 hours, mostly imported), news and information (13 hours), light entertainment (8½ hours), cultural and scientific programmes (4½ hours), broadcasts for special audiences (4 hours) and advertising (2 hours). During school terms, educational programmes, mainly for adults, are broadcast on three days a week, in the early morning and at midday. Programme material is imported from many countries and the corporation has regular exchange arrangements with the BBC (UK), ORTF (France) and with other Arab television organizations. The definition system used is 625 lines.

An annual licence fee is payable for television receivers.

FILM

One feature was produced in 1972. All films shown in cinemas are imported. Annual cinema attendances dropped by almost 2 million from 1960 to 1970. Amman has 15 fixed cinemas, Irbid and Zarka 4 each and the remainder are in smaller towns. There are 3 mobile units.

SPACE COMMUNICATIONS

An Atlantic Intelsat earth station at Baqa came into service in December 1971.

KHMER REPUBLIC

Population	6 701 000
Area	181 035 sq. km.

PRESS

Newspapers	Dailies 3

RADIO

Transmitters	Long/medium-wave 2, Short-wave 2, VHF—FM 1
Total receivers	100 000 estimated in use
Receivers per 1000 people	15

TELEVISION

Transmitters	2
Receivers	50 000 estimated in use
Receivers per 1000 people	7

FILM

Cinemas	Fixed 59
Total seating capacity	28 800
Seats per 1000 people	4
Total annual attendance	20 000 000
Anual visits per capita	3

PRESS

Daily newspapers, which totalled 26 circulating 145 000 copies in 1968, were all published in the capital Phnom Penh, in Khmer (21 titles), French (3 titles), Chinese and Vietnamese (1 title each). In 1970, only three dailies were published. The non-daily press, consisting principally of 15 weeklies in 1968, had approximately the same language coverage. Periodicals, mainly specialized, were published in Phnom Penh.

Newsprint production was 1000 metric tons a year.

NEWS AGENCIES

The Agence Khmère de Presse (AKP), set up by the Government in 1950, had a head office in Phnom Penh and branch offices in the provinces. It had an exchange agreement with Reuters and subscribes to the services of AFP, whose premises it shared. AKP and TASS had a free reciprocal news exchange agreement. With a daily output of 5000 words of national and foreign news in French, AKP served several newspapers, 1 radio station and 1 television station.

Foreign agencies represented in the republic included Tanjug, Hsinhua, ADN, Agence Vietnamienne d'Information and VP.

RADIO

Radiodiffusion Nationale Khmère (RNK), with two medium-wave (20 and 120kW) and two short-wave transmitters (15 and 50kW), operated by the Ministry of Information, broadcasts a national programme, mainly in Khmer, for 116 hours a week and an international service in Khmer, English, French, Lao, Vietnamese, Chinese and Thai for over 90 hours a week.

TELEVISION

The first experimental telecasts were made under governmental auspices in the capital in 1962. RNK now broadcasts (on 525 lines) for 3 hours a day, five days a week, with a main transmitter and one relay at Bokor extending coverage to an area south of the capital.

FILM

Local film production, which included as many as 72 feature films a year up to 1960, has now declined to a few documentaries. Films exhibited in public cinemas are imported from the People's Republic of China, India, the USA, the UK, the USSR and Japan. Government-sponsored mobile unit circuits show educational and cultural films.

KOREA (Republic of)

Population	31 920 000
Area	98 477 sq. km.

PRESS

Newspapers	Dailies 42, Non-dailies 105
Total circulation	Dailies 4 400 000, Non-dailies 2 764 000
Copies per 1000 people	Dailies 138, Non-dailies 86

RADIO

Transmitters	Long/medium-wave 70, Short-wave 6, VHF- FM 47
Total receivers	4 100 000 estimated in use
Receivers per 1000 people	128

TELEVISION

Transmitters	39
Receivers	905 363 licences
Receivers per 1000 people	28

FILM

Cinemas	Fixed 793
Total seating capacity	473 110
Seats per 1000 people	15
Total annual attendance	131 370 000
Annual visits per capita	4

PRESS

Daily newspapers are published in the capital, Seoul (12 titles), and in 17 provincial cities, 4 of which (Taegu, Chonju, Chunchon and Inchon) have 3 dailies each. The Seoul dailies, for the most part nationally distributed, account for almost half the country's total circulation. The leading paper is an independent evening paper circulating over 500 000 copies; six others circulate over 100 000 copies each. Two papers are printed in English and one in Chinese.

The majority of papers consist of four pages, with illustrations and are printed in the Korean (Hangul) script but with many borrowed Chinese words printed in Chinese characters in the text, a fact which makes reading difficult even for readers with secondary education. A recent decision (1967) limits the number of Chinese characters to be used in newspapers to 2000.

Over 800 periodicals are published, with a total circulation of 2 530 000 copies per issue. Most are in Korean, though there are about 20 published in English and 1 in Chinese. Sports, pastimes and general entertainment journals command the highest circulations (43 titles circulating 272 000 copies) but they are closely followed by educational (30 titles, 195 000 copies) and political and economic publications (38 titles, 155 000 copies).

Domestic newsprint production (101 700 metric tons in 1970) almost covers the country's requirements (108 300 metric tons in 1970).

NEWS AGENCIES

The Hapdong News Agency, a privately owned organization founded in 1945, has its headquarters in Seoul. 6 bureaux in provincial centres and 2 bureaux abroad, in the USA and Japan. Hapdong has 124 permanent staff members within the republic, 2 abroad and 38 part-time correspondents. Overseas news services received include AFP, DPA, and Kyodo; the agency has news exchange agreements with Kyodo and DPA. Services provided by Hapdong to its own subscribers include 90 000 words a day of national and local news in Korean and 200 000 words of foreign news in English, as well as features and photos. These are received by 38 newspapers, 5 main and 21 local radio stations and 4 television stations. English teletype and audio-radio news services are also available for organizations and agencies. Transmission of news is effected by public telecommunication services.

Orient Press (OP), also privately owned, has headquarters in Seoul, 10 provincial bureaux, 3 foreign bureaux (in the USA, Japan and the Republic of Vietnam), a permanent staff of 117 persons at home and 3 abroad and 35 part-time correspondents. It receives the overseas news services of UPI, ANSA, VP, Antara, PTI and has news exchange agreements with Kyodo, Antara and VP. Orient Press subscribers, which include 37 newspapers, 5 main and 21 local radio stations and 4 television stations, receive a national and local news service in Korean of 85 000 words a day and a foreign news service in English of 200 000 words a day.

The third large agency in the republic is the Donghwa News Agency founded in 1956, also privately owned and based in Seoul. With a permanent staff of 219 at home and 3 abroad and 45 part-time domestic and 2 part time foreign correspondents, it maintains 21 permanent bureaux in provincial centres and 3 abroad, in the USA, Japan and the Republic of Vietnam. Donghwa receives AP and Reuters overseas news services, the New York Times News Service, and the AP–Dow Jones Economic Report and has exchange agreements with the three. With a daily output of 90 000 words in Korean on national and local news and 24 000 in English on foreign news, plus features and photos, it serves 39 newspapers, 5 main and 21 local radio stations and 4 television stations, along with other subscribers.

The Sisa News Agency, Sanop News Agency, Economic News Service and Trade News Service also have their head offices in Seoul.

AP, UPI, AFP and Reuters are represented in Seoul and include most of the daily press and 26 radio and 4 television stations among their subscribers.

RADIO

The government-owned Korean Broadcasting System (KBS) comes under the direct control of the Ministry of Public Information. With 22 medium-wave transmitters (including one of 500kW and two of 100kW), it broadcasts on two national networks, potentially reaching 93% of the population, the second network having a higher proportion of educational programmes. Main programme categories making up the weekly total of 266 hours of broadcasting time are light entertainment (67 hours), news and information (64 hours), cultural programmes (46 hours) and education (41 hours including 15 hours for schools and 18 hours adult education). Most programmes are nationally produced and recorded.

KBS also has an international network consisting of three stations at Seoul, Sewon and Taegu, broadcasting via short-wave transmitters of 1, 5, 10 and 50kW to 11 areas throughout Europe, Asia and the Americas, in English, French, Japanese, Russian, Spanish, Chinese and Vietnamese for 19 hours a day.

Other non-commercial broadcasting organizations include stations operated by Christian organizations transmitting religious, cultural and educational programmes: the Christian Broadcasting System with five stations throughout the country; the Evangelical Alliance Mission, with a 50kW medium-wave transmitter at Seoul; and the Far East Broadcasting Company, which is erecting a 250kW medium-wave station on Cheju Island. The Korean Army Radio Station broadcasts a home service from Seoul.

There are three commercial networks: Dong-A, Tong-Yang, and the Hankuk Munhwa Broadcasting Corporation, the latter incorporating 19 separate stations transmitting entertainment and educational programmes.

The American Forces Korea network broadcasts from 19 stations throughout the country.

Over 500 000 receivers are connected to a wired rediffusion service. Radio audiences have greatly increased in recent years partly because of lower prices for receivers, which are now manufactured locally, and partly because of the spread of group listening.

TELEVISION

The Korean Broadcasting System (KBS), the government broadcasting service, has a television station in Seoul, operating a main transmitter (525 lines) with 11 low-power repeaters throughout the country. It is on the air for 36 hours a week, of which only 10 hours are accounted for by imported programmes, broadcasting light entertainment (34 hours), news and information (27 hours), cultural programmes (7 hours), educational programmes (6 hours), etc. Revenue is derived from government subsidies and licence fees for receivers.

The Tong-Yang Broadcasting Company, a large group with other media interests, operating stations in Seoul and Pusan and the Hankuk Munhwa Broadcasting Corporation, with stations in Seoul and six other large towns are on the air for about 10 hours a day The American Forces Korea network has nine principal stations and four rebroadcast translators. Imported programmes make up about 40% of the total for all stations.

The number of television receivers in use has almost doubled since 1968. Approximately 40% of the population live in areas with television coverage.

FILM
Feature-film production has trebled since 1960. A total of 207 35mm features, a single, long 16mm documentary and 202 short films (mostly documentary and instructional) were made in 1971, mainly by commercial organizations. The National Film Centre, which serves government departments, accounted for 6 of the short films produced, plus some newsreels. Five coproductions were made with companies in other Far Eastern countries including Hong Kong (3 films).

Features imported in 1971 totalled 70, of which 39 came from the USA, while 7 documentaries were also imported (5 from the USA). Films are frequently shown in public halls, schools, outdoor cinemas, etc., in addition to commercial cinemas, and a large public is reached by the government's 118 mobile units.

SPACE COMMUNICATIONS
The republic's Pacific Intelsat earth station at Kum San came into operation in 1970.

PROFESSIONAL TRAINING AND ASSOCIATIONS
Journalism training is offered at BA level at Hanyang, Choongang, Ewha (Women's), Korea, Kyunghee, Sukang and Sungkunkwan Universities, and at MA level at the Graduate School of Mass Communication, Seoul National University. Over 1000 students have graduated from these courses.

The Korean Press Ethics Commission, consisting of 11 members, of whom five are newspapermen, applies the code of ethics adopted by the Korean Newspaper Editors' Association to safeguard the interests of both the press and the public.

Professional associations in the media include associations of newspaper owners, editors, journalists, women journalists, copy editors, news agencies, radio and television personnel, film producers, technicians, distributors, etc.

KOREA
(Democratic People's Republic of)

Population	14 281 000
Area	120 538 sq. km.

PRESS
Newspapers   Dailies 6, Non-dailies 30*
RADIO
Transmitters   Long/medium-wave 7, Short-wave 12

TELEVISION
Transmitters   1

*Approx.

PRESS

Daily newspapers, published in the capital, Pyongyang, are issued by the central government, government departments and party organizations. The largest, the organ of the Korean Workers' Party, circulates about 300 000 copies. The main dailies circulate throughout the country and usually carry provincial and local news sections. There is little advertising. Other newspapers are published every two days, twice weekly or weekly, both in the capital and in provincial centres. Many news-sheets are issued by industrial enterprises.

The periodical press is large and includes popular magazines, a fair number of scientific and technological journals and others concerned with social and political affairs, literature and the arts. Some are produced in foreign languages for readers abroad (Russian, Chinese, English, French and Japanese), but the majority are in Korean.

The fact that Korean is the sole national language, together with the gradual elimination of the Chinese characters which were formerly mixed with the phonetic Korean alphabet, has accelerated literacy and made the press more widely accessible.

NEWS AGENCIES

Chung Yang Tong Shin (Chung Yang), or the Korean Central News Agency (KCNA), is the national agency. founded in 1949. From its headquarters in Pyongyang it issues a daily news bulletin in Korean, periodical bulletins in English and Russian and a national yearbook. Chung Yang is the sole distributor of news to the national press. It exchanges news services with TASS, Hsinhua and the press of neighbouring socialist countries, and receives the bulletin of the Japanese agency, Kyodo.

RADIO

The Korean Central Broadcasting Committee (DPRK) broadcasts from 7 medium-wave and 12 short-wave stations to listeners at home and abroad. The home service's two programmes, broadcast on both medium and short waves from Pyongyang and regional stations, are on the air for 19 and 21 hours a day respectively. Programmes are largely relayed from Pyongyang and consist of news and current affairs, weather reports, music, drama, literary recitations and light entertainment. Special broadcasts include twice-daily workers' sessions and regular broadcasts of family messages for listeners in the Republic of Korea.

Programmes are exchanged with the USSR, the People's Republic of China and other east European and Asian countries.

Most domestic broadcasts are received via a wired distribution network which extends to almost all towns and villages in the country, reaching about a million homes and community listening points.

Foreign-service broadcasts, on medium and short waves, are beamed to six areas in the Near and Middle East, Africa, Europe, south-east Asia, the Far East, Japan and Latin America, in English (6½ hours a day), Chinese (3 hours), French, Spanish, Russian and Japanese (2 hours), Arabic (1 hour) and Korean (3 hours).

TELEVISION
It is reported that regular telecasts are made from a transmitter in Pyongyang.

FILM
The film industry is largely controlled by the films bureau of the Ministry of Culture. Features and documentaries, in black and white and colour, are produced by the Korean Art Film Studio, the Documentary Film Studio, the Scientific Film Studio and others (about 140 films were produced in 1967). Imported films come mainly from the People's Republic of China and the USSR. Films draw large audiences both to fixed cinemas and to showings by the mobile units which cover rural areas.

PROFESSIONAL ASSOCIATIONS
Media professionals belong to unions such as the Korean Writers' Union and the Korean Film Workers' Union.

KUWAIT

Population	910 000
Area	16 000 sq. km.

PRESS

Newspapers	Dailies 6, Non-dailies 11
Total circulation	Dailies 40 000, Non-dailies 50 000
Copies per 1000 people	Dailies 44, Non dailies 55

RADIO

Transmitters	Long/medium-wave 8, Short-wave 5, VHF—FM 1
Total receivers	400 000 estimated in use
Receivers per 1000 people	439

TELEVISION

Transmitters	7
Receivers	150 000 estimated in use
Receivers per 1000 people	165

FILM

Cinemas	Fixed 7
Total seating capacity	12 000
Seats per 1000 people	13
Total annual attendance	3 945 000
Annual visits per capita	4

PRESS

The daily press consists of four Arabic-language papers with a combined circulation of 25 000 copies and two English-language papers (15 000 copies), the largest of the Arabic and English dailies being published from the same address.

Non-daily newspapers are all in Arabic.

Subject categories of the 21 periodical titles (total circulation 262 000 copies) include general interest journals (6 titles, 193 000 copies), social and political sciences (4 titles, 18 000 copies) and literature, religion and education. The Ministry of Information publishes a weekly official gazette and a fortnightly illustrated magazine.

Kuwaiti papers are also circulated in other Arab countries.

NEWS AGENCIES

There is no national agency, but studies are being made with a view to establishing one. UP, AP, Reuters and MENA serve the local press and radio. AFP and TASS services are also received by the radio station. The television receives UPI, Visnews, DPA, MENA and E-TE-S services.

MENA and TASS have bureaux in Kuwait.

RADIO

The government-owned Kuwait Broadcasting Service. financed from the budget of the Ministry of Guidance and Information, is responsible for all radio and television broadcasting in Kuwait.

The radio service, with medium-wave transmitters of 100 and 750kW and short-wave transmitters of 250kW, broadcasts an Arabic-language programme for over 129 hours a week, consisting of light entertainment (97 hours), broadcasts for special audiences (14 hours), news (13 hours), education (1½ hours) and cultural broadcasts (4 hours). In addition, there are 5 hours a day in English.

Both Arabic and English-language programmes are received throughout the national territory and are also beamed to five areas in the Gulf area, north Africa, the Middle East, south Asia and Europe.

No licence fee is payable for radio receivers.

TELEVISION

Television of Kuwait, under the same government service as radio, with 5 main and 2 auxiliary transmitters and 1 experimental transmitter. now covers not only all Kuwait, but parts of southern Iraq, Saudi Arabia and other Gulf states.

Programmes totalling about 38 hours a week include light entertainment (25 hours), news (8½ hours), broadcasts for special audiences (4 hours), cultural and educational programmes (1 hour) plus some advertising. A little over 60% of programmes are nationally produced. Imported programmes come mainly from Egypt, the UK and the USA, and regular exchanges are carried out with other Arab countries. In addition, experimental school television broadcasts are being carried out for several hours a day for selected secondary schools, as a preliminary to a large-scale educational television and audio-visual system.

The definition system used is 625 lines. The introduction of colour is planned.

No licence is required for television receivers.

FILM
Film production by local companies (of which there are four, all recently established) is encouraged by the government but, so far, the main producer is the cinema section of Kuwait Television whose output for 1969 consisted of 10 titles dealing with education, health, industry, agriculture and social affairs. In 1971, three long documentaries were produced.

Feature films shown in the seven fixed and some open-air cinemas are all imported. In 1971, 246 features were imported: from the USA (101), India (56), other Arab countries (43), Italy (26), etc. In the same year, 29 documentaries were imported: from the UK (13), the USA (13) and the USSR (3).

SPACE COMMUNICATIONS
Kuwait's earth station at Umm al-Aish, linked to the Indian Ocean Intelsat system, came into service in October 1969. A further, Atlantic Intelsat, station was due to be in operation at the end of 1974.

LAOS

Population	110 000
Area	236 800 sq. km.

PRESS	
Newspapers	Dailies 6
Total circulation	Dailies 8000
Copies per 1000 people	2

RADIO	
Transmitters	Long/medium-wave 4, Short-wave 5
Total receivers	100 000
Receivers per 1000 people	32

FILM

Cinemas	Fixed 16
Total seating capacity	8200
Seats per 1000 people	3
Total annual attendance	1 000 000
Annual visits per capita	0.3

PRESS

Daily newspapers are printed (or, in most cases, duplicated) in the administrative capital, Vientiane, with the exception of one published in the southern town of Pakse, and are distributed almost entirely in the more densely populated areas along the Mekong valley which marks the frontier with Thailand. One paper is published in Chinese, the rest in Lao (some with occasional extra editions in French). News – local, national and foreign – accounts for about 50% of space in newspapers; editorial matter 10%; and advertising 35%.

About 10 other periodical publications in French and Lao have a total circulation of around 10 000 copies.

NEWS AGENCIES

Founded in 1950, the national news agency, Lao Press. is controlled by the Ministry of Information. It has four bureaux in the country with a permanent staff of 20 persons, in addition to 7 part-time correspondents. Foreign news is received under exchange agreements from UPI, AFP and Reuters.

Lao Press subscribers, which include 8 newspapers and 3 civil and 6 military radio stations within the country, receive the agency's daily bulletin of 20 typed pages of local and national news in Laotian and French, and a similar quantity of foreign news. Other services include features and photographs. Transmission is effected by air mail and by audio-radio service at dictation speed.

UPI, AFP, Reuters, Novosti and Time–Life Magazines have bureaux in Vientiane, while other world and national agencies, newspapers and broadcasting systems have correspondents in Laos.

RADIO

Radiodiffusion Nationale Lao, the government-owned and operated broadcasting service, has a 10kW medium-wave transmitter and a 25kW short-wave transmitter in Vientiane and regional medium-wave transmitters in the royal capital, Luang Prabang, and in Pakse. Revenue is derived from a state budget allocation and from commercial advertising.

A home service is broadcast in Lao, French and Vietnamese (with some local programmes in Meo and other tribal languages) for 94 hours a week, main programme categories being news and information (34 hours), light entertainment (32 hours), cultural programmes (9 hours), educational programmes (8 hours), broadcasts for ethnic minorities (6½ hours), programmes for special audiences (2½ hours) and advertising (1¾ hours). Reception is good along the Mekong plains and valley areas where most of the population live but uncertain in the mountainous areas in the north and east.

Military stations and the Voix du Pathet-Lao also broadcast on medium and short waves in Lao, French and Vietnamese, to both domestic and external listeners. Owing to the practice of village group listening, to both national and foreign broadcasts, radio audiences are much larger than the number of receivers in use suggests.

TELEVISION
Laos has no television service but viewers near the Thai border can receive broadcasts from transmitters in Thailand.

FILM
News and other films are produced from time to time by government information services and private operators. A government-sponsored film association endeavours to encourage domestic film-making. Feature and documentary films shown in the few cinemas (mainly in Vientiane and the provincial capitals) are all imported.

PROFESSIONAL ASSOCIATIONS
There is an association for journalists and one for the cinema.

LEBANON

Population	2 873 000
Area	10 400 sq. km.

PRESS
Newspapers	Dailies 52, Non-dailies 46

RADIO
Transmitters	Long/medium-wave 2, Short-wave 1, VHF–FM 3
Total receivers	605 000 estimated in use
Receivers per 1000 people	210

TELEVISION
Transmitters	8
Receivers	325 000 estimated in use
Receivers per 1000 people	113

FILM
Cinemas	Fixed 170
Total seating capacity	86 640
Seats per 1000 people	30
Total annual attendance	49 700 000
Annual visits per capita	17

PRESS

The daily press, based almost entirely in the capital, Beirut, consists of 43 Arabic-language papers, 4 French, 4 Armenian and 1 English. The 2 largest dailies circulate around 50 000 and 35 000 copies per issue, 4 others exceed 20 000 copies and 6 others (including two in French) circulate between 10 000 and 20 000. Most of the remaining papers, some with very small circulations, represent various political, religious and other interests. Under the terms of a press law of 1948, revised in 1962, papers whose circulations remain below a minimum of 1500 for a given period may have their licences withdrawn. The same law guarantees certain press freedoms. A few Lebanese papers circulate throughout the Middle East.

Weekly general interest papers include several published in association with leading dailies, the largest circulating 117 000, and 4 more between 30 000 and 57 000. An illustrated weekly news magazine circulates 20 000 of its 28 500 copies outside Lebanon. Several other Lebanese papers and periodicals have readerships extending throughout the Middle East. Periodicals number over 320 titles including general interest journals (93 titles), sociology (66 titles), religion (27 titles), arts and literature (25 titles), home economy (24 titles) and education (18 titles).

NEWS AGENCIES

The official national agency, Wakalat Al Anbaa Al-Wataniyah or National News Agency (NNA), founded in 1964 as a department of the Ministry of Information, has its headquarters in Beirut, branches in Tripoli, Saida and Zahleh, and foreign bureaux in Cairo and Paris. Of its 102 employees, 50 are staff editors. NNA supplies local and national news to some 600 subscribers including most of the press and broadcasting stations. It issues two daily Arabic-language bulletins, a local press digest and daily radio bulletins totalling 30 000 words in Arabic and 20 000 each in English and French.

Foreign news is received from UPI, AP, AFP, Reuters, TASS, ADP and MENA.

There are 26 other agencies in the country (16 with purely local coverage) and 2 press-clipping services.

Some newspapers subscribe individually to the international services of Reuters, AP, UPI, AFP, TASS, MENA, ADN, CTK and Tanjug, all of which are represented in Beirut. DPA and the INA (Baghdad) also have offices there.

RADIO

The Lebanese Broadcasting Station, founded in 1937, comes under the jurisdiction of the Ministry of Information. With medium-wave and short-wave transmitters (up to 100kW) and three FM transmitters, all at Amchitt, north of Beirut, it broadcasts two home-service programmes, the first in Arabic, and the second in French, English and Armenian. Both can be received in all parts of the country. The FM stations transmit mainly music.

Programmes, totalling 702 hours a week, include light entertainment (605 hours), news and information (33 hours), cultural and scientific programmes (10 hours), broadcasts for special audiences (9 hours) and education (2½ hours). There is no advertising. All programmes are of national origin.

The foreign service's 100kW transmitter broadcasts a 2¼ hour African service in English, Arabic and French, 2½ hours in Portuguese, Arabic and Spanish beamed to South America, and 2½ hours in Spanish, French and Arabic beamed to Europe and North America.

During the last ten years, radio-set ownership has increased sixfold.

No licence fee is payable for radio receivers.

TELEVISION

Of the two commercial television companies operating in Lebanon, the oldest is the Compagnie Libanaise de Télévision (CLT), founded in 1959. It now has two transmitters in Beirut and two relay transmitters, one in the mountains south of Beirut, the other near Tripoli.

Its two programmes, one Arabic and the other French and English, are on the air for about 60 hours a week and include light entertainment (28 hours), news and information (12½ hours), arts, letters and science (5½ hours), education (4½ hours), broadcasts to ethnic minorities (3½ hours) and advertising (up to 6 minutes in every hour). About 40% of these programmes are of national origin. Colour programmes (SECAM system) are broadcast for about 10 hours a week.

Télé-Orient, also a commercial company, began broadcasting in 1962. With two transmitters in Beirut and relays at Mt Knaisse and Tripoli, it also broadcasts two programmes, one in Arabic and one in French and English, which include light entertainment (19½ hours), advertising (12 hours) and news (8 hours). It has also adopted the SECAM colour system.

Both companies use the 625-line definition system and both import over 50% of their programmes, particularly from France and the USA.

No licence fee is payable for television receivers.

FILM

Lebanon has five film studios. The national production for the year 1970–1 totalled 6 features and 5 short documentaries. Official responsibility for the industry is exercised by the National Centre for Film and Television within the Ministry of the Interior.

Imported features in the same year numbered 441, coming from the USA (158), Italy (75), Egypt (62), the UK (52), France (52), Turkey (21) and the USSR (21). The number of cinemas (mostly in Beirut, several each in Tripoli, Saida and Zahleh, and the rest in smaller towns) has changed little over the last ten years though the seating accommodation available has dropped by about 15%. A few mobile units serve the remoter towns and villages. There are also two drive-in cinemas.

SPACE COMMUNICATIONS

An Intelsat earth station at Arbaniyah, originally limked to the Atlantic system, but now operating with the Indian Ocean Satellite, was opened in January 1971.

PROFESSIONAL TRAINING AND ASSOCIATIONS

Training in journalism is offered at the Institute of Journalism and Mass Communications founded in 1969 within the University of Lebanon, and a new department of mass communications providing a three-year degree course in all media is to be established at the American University of Beirut.

The Lebanese Press Syndicate is a journalists' association founded in 1911. There is also an association of newspaper publishers, a motion-picture association, and associations of cinema operators and technicians.

MACAU

Population	321 000
Area	16 sq. km.

PRESS

Newspapers	Dailies 6

RADIO

Transmitters	Long/medium-wave 3, VHF–FM 2
Total receivers	60 000 estimated in use
Receivers per 1000 people	187

FILM

Cinemas	Fixed 12
Total seating capacity	12 600
Seats per 1000 people	39

PRESS

Two Portuguese-language dailies are sold mainly by subscription, while four published in Chinese are on sale in the streets.

Non-dailies and periodicals include a twice-weekly general interest paper a weekly official bulletin and a few religious papers, all in Portuguese, as well as Chinese-language publications, some of the latter designed for tourists (of whom there are said to be over 3 million yearly. mainly from Hong Kong).

NEWS AGENCIES

There is no national agency. Reuters, AP, UPI, AFP and Antara are represented in Macau.

RADIO

The government-owned radio station, Emissora de Radiodifusao de Macau, with two medium-wave transmitters (10 and 25kW) and one FM transmitter. broadcasts a home service for 10 hours a day, 6 hours in Portuguese and 4 hours in Chinese (Cantonese).

A private commercial station, Emissora Vila Verde, with one medium-wave transmitter (10kW) and one FM transmitter, is on the air for 17 hours a day, broadcasting in Chinese only.

TELEVISION

There is no local television service but programmes from a Hong Kong station can be received clearly in Macau.

FILM

Imported films are shown in Macau's 12 cinemas.

MALAYSIA (Federation of)

Population	12 324 000
Area	332 633 sq. km.

PRESS

Newspapers	Dailies 40, Non-dailies 20
Total circulation	Dailies 950 000, Non-dailies 216 000
Copies per 1000 people	Dailies 77, Non-dailies 17

RADIO

Transmitters	Long/medium-wave 33, Short-wave 25, VHF- FM 3
Total receivers	2 000 000* estimated in use
Receivers per 1000 people	162

TELEVISION

Transmitters	18
Receivers	300 000 estimated in use
Receivers per 1000 people	24

FILM

Cinemas	Fixed 550
Total seating capacity	385 000
Seats per 1000 people	31
Total annual attendance	90 000 000
Anual visits per capita	7

*Including 500 000 wired receivers.

PRESS

West Malaysia, consisting of the 11 peninsular states of Malaya, has 22 daily newspapers, 14 of which (4 in Malay, 4 in Chinese, 3 in English, 2 in Punjabi and 1 in Tamil) are published in the capital, Kuala Lumpur. Of these, the most widely distributed is an English-language paper with a circulation of 210 000, rising to 250 000 on Sundays. Next in importance are the Malay papers, 4 of which have circulations of over 50 000. The largest Chinese daily, published in Penang, circulates 32 000 copies. The port of Penang has 7 dailies (3 in Chinese, 2 in English, 1 in Tamil and 1 in Malay), while Ipoh has 1 in Chinese. The non-daily press consists mainly of weeklies, in the same range of languages, with a global circulation of around a million copies.

Sabah, in the north of Borneo, has 9 dailies with a total circulation of 58 000, 6 being published in the capital, Kota Kinabalu (formerly known as Jesselton), and the others in Sandakan and Tawau. Two are in English or English and Malay, the remainder in Chinese.

Sarawak, also on Borneo, is served by 7 Chinese and 2 English-language dailies, totalling 54 000 copies daily. Seven are published in the capital, Kuching, while the river port of Sibu has 2 and the oil town of Miri, 1. Most of these papers are also circulated in the neighbouring territory of Brunei. A few weekly and monthly papers, including some free government publications, appear in Malay, Iban (Sea Dayak) and English.

Periodicals other than newspapers published in the whole of the federation number over 700 (among these are 136 school magazines and 74 business house organs). Main subject categories are legal and administrative (142 titles), general interest (100 titles), agriculture (57 titles), religion (45 titles), sociology (26 titles), political science (19 titles), recreation (17 titles), trade and communications (14 titles), technology (13 titles), arts and architecture (12 titles), geography (11 titles), literature (10 titles), medicine (8 titles), education and sciences (7 titles each), business management and history (6 titles each), etc. Periodicals appear not only in the main languages used by the newspaper press but in a number of the tribal languages as well, including Iban (6 titles) and Jawi (2 titles). Imported periodicals, particularly in English and Chinese, together circulate several hundred thousand copies per issue.

NEWS AGENCIES

The national agency, Pertubohan Berita Nasional Malaysia (Bernama), founded in 1967, actually began operations in May 1968. Its headquarters are in Kuala Lumpur and it has domestic bureaux in Penang and Ipoh (west Malaysia), and in Kota Kinabalu (Sabah) and Kuching (Sarawak), the latter bureau having a two-way teleprinter link with Kuala Lumpur. There are also seven correspondents in the states of west Malaysia. Bernama, which has only one foreign bureau (in Djakarta), supplies west Malaysia with mostly national and local news, its daily wordage being 12 000 in Malay and 12 000 in English. With 90 subscribers (including Reuters, AP and AFP), it serves all the media throughout the federation, as well as government, educational, industrial and diplomatic users. News is exchanged with 10 other Asian news agencies.

The information department of the Ministry of Information and Broadcasting also provides material for the printed media, including press releases and photos, and publishes its own weekly tabloid.

Malaysian newspapers, radio and television are supplies with overseas news by AP, UPI, AFP and Reuters, all of which have bureaux in the capital and correspondents in the main towns. Twenty-one other agencies, newspapers and broadcasting organizations maintain correspondents in Malaysia.

RADIO

Broadcasting is a government monopoly conducted by the Ministry of Information and Broadcasting and financed by an annual government allocation. Revenue is derived from licence fees, commercial advertising and sponsored programmes. Radio Malaysia headquarters are in Kuala Lumpur, coordinating the three networks of west Malaysia, Sabah and Sarawak, which potentially cover 80% of the population.

A household receiver licence fee is payable (there were 456 307 licences current at the end of 1972).

The west Malaysian component of Radio Malaysia, consisting of eight stations with 37 medium-wave and short-wave transmitters totalling 955kW, broadcasts its programmes in separate Malay, English, Chinese and Indian-language segments, the national (Malay) service being on the air 24 hours a day (168 hours a week), and the others for 100, 101 and 92 hours a week respectively. The regional stations, which are linked to one another and to Kuala Lumpur by a microwave system, broadcast both the national programmes and programmes of their own origination. The national programme includes light entertainment (85 hours a week), news and information (34 hours), broadcasts for special audiences (17 hours), education (16 hours), cultural and scientific programmes (12 hours) and advertising (4 hours). All of this is nationally produced.

Educational broadcasting is conducted jointly by Radio Malaysia and the Ministry of Education and is directed to schools, with morning and afternoon programmes on four days a week in each of the language segments.

Radio Malaysia Sabah, with short- and medium-wave transmitters, rebroadcasts national programmes received by short wave from Kuala Lumpur and also originates its own programmes, particularly in the local languages. Its total of 126 broadcasting hours a week consist of 65% entertainment, 31% news and information and 4% education. Languages used are Malay (54¾ hours), English (25¾ hours), Chinese (18 hours), Kadazan (16¼ hours), Murut (5¼ hours), Indonesian (2 hours) and Bajan (1¾ hours).

Radio Malaysia Sarawak has 18 medium- and short-wave transmitters and is on the air for 342 hours a week, broadcasting seven separate language services, in Malay (73½ hours), English (44 hours), Chinese (47 hours), Iban (42 hours), Bidayuh (56 hours), Kayan/Kenyah (7 hours) and Melanau (1 hour). In addition, the Malay Forces and English Forces Services are on the air for 14 hours and 1 hour respectively, and the schools broadcasting service (in Malay, English, Tamil and Chinese) for 19½ hours spread over four weekdays. A further 37½ hours are devoted to special programmes in Bahasa Malaysia, the standardized form of Malay which has been adopted as the official language of the federation.

Radio Malaysia's overseas service, the Voice of Malaysia, broadcasts daily programmes in Indonesian (7 hours), English (2½ hours) and Mandarin Chinese (2 hours), beamed to northern and eastern Asia, southern Asia and Indonesia.

A privately operated wire rediffusion service is available in Kuala Lumpur, Penang and Ipoh. The three separate networks each carry two programmes, consisting of relays of Radio Malaysia or the BBC (UK) or the service's own or recorded programmes. Subscribers numbered 29 000 in 1969.

Other radio stations in the federation are the BBC's Far Eastern station at Johore Bahru relaying programmes in 12 languages to Asia, and a Royal Australian Air Force station at Butterworth.

TELEVISION

The Malaysian television service is operated by the Ministry of Information and Broadcasting's Television Department. Network I, established in 1963, with its main station in Kuala Lumpur (100/20kW video/audio power) and regional stations at Johore Bahru, Taiping, Penang, Ipoh, Malacca, Batu Pahat and Kluang, is on the air for 9 hours a day. Network II, with stations in the same eight towns, broadcasts for 4 hours a day.

Programmes for both networks, totalling over 84 hours a week in 1973, consist of cultural and scientific broadcasts (27 hours), news and information (25 hours), light entertainment (16 hours), broadcasts for special audiences (10 hours), advertising (5 hours) and education (3 hours). Programmes, which are presented in Malay, English, Chinese and Tamil, are about 55% of national origin and 45% imported (from the USA, the UK, the Federal Republic of Germany, Australia, France, Japan and Indonesia); or they are received on an exchange basis from Asian and Pacific countries through the Asian Broadcasting Union (ABU), of which Malaysia is a member. In Sabah, a pilot television service is in operation, covering most of the west-coast areas, and other densely populated areas are to be covered by the end of 1971.

The definition system used is 625 lines. In all, about 15% of the population is covered by existing transmitters.

A joint radio–television licence fee is payable.

FILM

In 1972, eight feature films were produced by independent producers. Film Negara Malaysia is the film department of the Ministry of Information and Broadcasting, responsible for servicing government departments, training cinema personnel and providing up-to-date cinematographic equipment, studios and laboratories – both for its own use and for hiring to private film-making individuals and enterprises – and for maintaining a film library. The department's own annual production amounts to around 60 short films (35mm and 16mm) in both major and local languages. About half the total are educational or instructional. Many of these films are used by the Ministry's mobile field information units (114 vehicles and 24 boats in 1969), which visit the remoter parts of the federation with lectures, film shows and community information programmes.

A large number of features are imported yearly. In 1972, 754 were imported: from the USA (160), Hong Kong (160), India (122), Italy (58), the UK (50), Indonesia (32), the Federal Republic of Germany (30) and other countries (142). In the same year, 117 documentaries were imported: from the UK (75), the USA (24), Hong Kong (9), the Federal Republic of Germany (2), Japan (1), the USSR (1) and other countries (7).

Annual cinema attendance has increased by about 50% for commercial cinemas, over the last decade. In addition, however, there are a further 300 non-commercial mobile units drawing annual audiences totalling more than 46 million. Of the total number of cinemas, 61 are in Sarawak and 23 in Sabah.

SPACE COMMUNICATIONS

The government Indian Ocean Intelsat earth station at Kuantan on the east coast of the peninsula was completed in April 1970.

PROFESSIONAL TRAINING AND ASSOCIATIONS

Journalists are trained at courses and seminars organized by the South East Asia Press Centre (Press Institute of Malaysia) in Kuala Lumpur. Also in Kuala Lumpur, the National Broadcasting Training Centre conducts courses for both national broadcasting personnel and trainees from other Asian countries. Penang University has a communications programme, as has the Mara Institute of Technology.

Professional associations include a national union of journalists, a press club, a public relations institute and associations of women journalists, science writers, newspaper publishers and film renters and exhibitors.

MALDIVES

Population	110 000
Area	298 sq. km.

PRESS

Newspapers	Dailies 1
Total circulation	Dailies 155
Copies per 1000 people	Dailies 1

RADIO

Transmitters	Long/medium-wave 1, Short-wave 4
Total receivers	2000 estimated in use
Receivers per 1000 people	18

FILM

Cinemas	Fixed 2
Total seating capacity	823
Seats per 1000 people	7
Total annual attendance	147 230
Annual visits per capita	1

PRESS

One daily newspaper, circulating 155 copies per issue, is published on the capital island, Malé, where about 10% of the population live.

Four periodicals circulate a total of 1150 copies.

RADIO

The government-owned radio station Radio Maldives, in Malé, operates one medium-wave transmitter (7kW) and four short-wave transmitters (up to 30kW) which can be received in India, Pakistan and Sri Lanka, as well as in the 200 inhabited islands of the Maldives.

The home service is on the air for 16½ hours daily in the Maldivian language, 4 hours of this time being transmitted on short waves for Maldivians abroad. The home service also relays a BBC (UK) news bulletin daily. In addition, Radio Maldives operates a 2½ hour daily English-language commercial service, broadcast on short waves for overseas listeners. Programmes consist mainly of light entertainment (60%), advertising (27%), news and information (9%) and broadcasts for special audiences, including educational (4%). Daily news bulletins from Radio Peking, Radio Australia and the BBC are also relayed by one of the short-wave transmitters.

A licence fee is payable for radio receivers.

A military station, Radio Gan, jointly operated by the British and United States Air Force, in the Addu Atoll, broadcasts daily on medium waves in English for 18 hours.

FILM

The 60 feature films shown in 1970 came from the USA (37) and India (23).

MONGOLIA

Population	1 283 000
Area	1 565 000 sq. km.

PRESS

Newspapers	Dailies 1, Non-dailies 30
Total circulation	Dailies 100 000
Copies per 1000 people	Dailies 78

RADIO

Transmitters	Long-wave 2, Short-wave 20
Total receivers	170 000* estimated in use
Receivers per 1000 people	132

TELEVISION

Transmitters	1
Receivers	27 000 estimated in use
Receivers per 1000 people	21

FILM

Cinemas	Fixed 60

*Including 70 000 wired loudspeakers.

PRESS

The national daily, founded in 1920, is the official organ of the Central Committee of the Mongolian People's Revolutionary Party, published six times a week (not Mondays) in the capital, Ulan Bator, where there are also about 10 other newspapers appearing once, twice, three or four times a week, all published by official bodies and in most cases addressed to particular readerships (youth, trade unions, military, cultural workers, etc.). There are also twice-weekly and weekly newspapers in the other administrative city, Darhan, and in the 18 provinces. With the exception of a provincial bi-weekly in Kazakh and the foreign-language bulletins of the national news agency, all papers are published in Mongolian.

About 30 periodicals covering political, cultural and technical subjects are published in Ulan Bator, where the State Publishing Committee and the Department for the Supervision of the Press and Literature are based. The Ministry of Foreign Trade publishes an annual in English and Russian.

NEWS AGENCIES

The national government-owned agency, Mongol Tsahilgaan Medeeniy Agentlag (Montsame), established in 1957 under the State Committee for Information, Radio and Television, supplies the press and broadcasting services with home and foreign news. Montsame has a radio-teletype service in Russian and issues a twice-weekly newspaper in Russian, weekly news bulletins in English, French and Chinese, as well as its national news magazine published monthly in Russian and every two months in English.

TASS has a representative in Ulan Bator.

RADIO

All broadcasting comes under the authority of the State Committee for Information, Radio and Television. Ulan Bator Radio is equipped with long-wave (60 and 150kW) and short-wave transmitters (up to 50kW) in the capital, in Olgiy and perhaps in other centres. It broadcasts two home-service programmes for 16 and 3 hours a day respectively, in Mongolian. These programmes are also distributed by wired relay systems in larger population centres.

The foreign service broadcasts for about 20 hours a week in Mongolian, Kazakh, English, Russian and standard Chinese.

TELEVISION

The television service, which began regular operations in 1967, now broadcasts for 30 hours (6 days) a week from its new centre in Ulan Bator to the area surrounding the capital and (by relay) to the town of Darhan 200km to the north. Programmes include locally originated material, imported films and relays of programmes from the USSR, via Molniya satellite, received by an Orbita earth station near the Mongolian frontier.

FILM

Film production is reported to average 10 feature films annually plus some newsreels. Films are imported mainly from the USSR and eastern European countries and occasionally from western Europe and the USA. In addition to fixed cinemas, there are over 400 touring film projection teams which visit small towns and rural areas.

PROFESSIONAL TRAINING AND ASSOCIATIONS

Journalistic training is available at the University of Ulan Bator.

The Mongolian Union of Journalists, founded in 1965, has some 300 members.

NEPAL

Population	11 470 000
Area	140 797 sq. km.

PRESS	
Newspapers	Dailies 30, Non-dailies 41
Total circulation	Dailies 39 000, Non-dailies 4 400
Copies per 1000 people	Dailies 3, Non-dailies 0.3

RADIO	
Transmitters	Long/medium-wave 2, Short-wave 2
Total receivers	70 000 estimated in use
Receivers per 1000 people	6

FILM	
Cinemas	Fixed 10

PRESS

Most of the country's newspapers are published in the capital, Kathmandu, and the surrounding valley, where the population density is greatest. Others appear in towns along the south-eastern border or in more isolated localities. Circulations are often precariously small and localized because of communication difficulties in this mountainous country, limited literacy and the variety of languages spoken. Kathmandu has some 20 dailies — mainly in the national language, Nepali, but also in Newari, English and Hindi — as well as the major share of the non-daily and periodical press.

Some 90 periodicals are reported, with a total circulation of 92 000 copies.

NEWS AGENCIES

Founded in 1962 with government and press support, the national agency, Rastriya Sambad Samiti (RSS), is an autonomous company with a 60% state shareholding. In addition to its headquarters staff in Kathmandu, it has correspondents in the various administrative zones who keep it supplied with local and national news.

Foreign news is received regularly through AFP (English-language service), AP, PTI and Hsinhua. RSS issues daily services of home and foreign news to the national daily and weekly press and broadcasting services.

Foreign news services represented in Kathmandu include AFP, Reuters, DPA, TASS, Hsinhua, the main Indian agencies and leading Indian and other newspapers.

RADIO

Radio Nepal, founded in 1951, is operated by the government's Department of Broadcasting. With two medium-wave (0.25 and 10kW) and two short-wave transmitters (5 and 100kW), it broadcasts a home service for 8 hours a day and an external service for 30 minutes a day on four days a week, in Nepali, English, Newari and Hindi.

An annual licence fee is payable for radio receivers.

FILM

The Ministry of Information's film unit produces documentary films, particularly for use in government information programmes. A recently formed national film board, under government auspices and representing various community interests, promotes and regulates the industry and is also responsible for some documentary production.

Kathmandu has four cinemas and a number of district centres have one each. The feature films shown are imported, mostly from India, but also from the USA and the UK.

PROFESSIONAL ASSOCIATIONS

The Nepal Journalists' Association has its headquarters in Kathmandu, as do associations grouping together film exhibitors and distributors. A press council was established in 1972.

OMAN

Population	680 000
Area	212 457 sq. km.

RADIO	
Transmitters	Long/medium-wave 2

PRESS

One weekly newspaper, in Arabic, is published in the capital, Muscat.

RADIO

Radio Oman, founded in 1970, broadcasts for 7 hours a day in Arabic.

The eastern relay station of the BBC (UK), on the island of Masirah, with two 750kW medium-wave transmitters, relays the BBC's Arabic, Hindi, Urdu and world services.

PAKISTAN

Population	56 040 000
Area	801 408 sq. km.

PRESS	
Newspapers	Dailies 98, Non-dailies 436

RADIO	
Transmitters	Long/medium-wave 10, Short-wave 12
Total receivers	1 033 000 estimated in use
Receivers per 1000 people	18

TELEVISION	
Transmitters	7
Receivers	129 000 licences
Licences per 1000 people	2

FILM	
Cinemas	Fixed 578
Total seating capacity	300 000
Seats per 1000 people	5
Total annual attendance	18 373 000
Annual visits per capita	0.3

PRESS

Daily newspapers, mainly in Urdu (70 titles) and English (22 titles), are published in 16 towns and cities, of which Karachi, Lahore, Hyderabad, Lyallpur, Peshawar, Rawalpindi (with Islamabad) and Quetta all have five or more separate titles or editions (several leading papers publish simultaneous editions in two or more cities).

The largest city, Karachi, has over 20 dailies, about half of them in Urdu, including the country's leading paper with simultaneous Karachi (180 000 copies), Rawalpindi (65 000 copies) and Quetta editions (the Rawalpindi edition also serves the new administrative capital, Islamabad). Karachi's main English-language dailies, one of which also has a Gujarati edition, circulate between 15 000 and 50 000 copies. Next in order is Lahore, with 17 dailies. Its largest Urdu papers circulating 130 000 copies and 40 000 copies, respectively, also have simultaneous editions in other cities, the first in Karachi, Quetta and Peshawar, the second in Multan, while the leading English paper (40 000 copies) is published in Rawalpindi as well.

The non-daily press consists mainly of weeklies in Urdu, though there are 30 titles in English and a number in local languages such as Gujarati, Pushto, Sindhi, Punjabi and Baluchi.

A total of 468 periodical titles is reported, the majority appearing monthly, with a language distribution similar to that of the daily press.

NEWS AGENCIES

The Associated Press of Pakistan (APP), founded in 1949 and government controlled since 1961, has metropolitan bureaux in Karachi (head office), Rawalpindi and Lahore and seven regional bureaux, employing 257 full-time and 15 part-time staff. It has no foreign bureaux but has 2 full-time correspondents abroad, in London and Kathmandu. Foreign services received include Reuters, Hsinhua, UPI, TASS and Kyodo, and news is exchanged with the two latter and with Antara, Anatolia, NAB, Bernama, RSS, Agerpress, GNA and Pars. With a daily output of 30 000 words of national and local news and 20 000 words of foreign news, all in English, 20 features and eight air-mail letters a week, photos and a special video-television service, APP serves the press, broadcasting services, government departments, diplomatic missions, the university and commercial interests. Radio teletype is used for broadcasts to Moscow, Peking and Tokyo and teleprinter for the press, radio and television.

Pakistan Press International (PPI), a joint-stock company with four of its 11 directors elected from clients in the mass media, was founded in 1956. Karachi is the headquarters, and there are other permanent bureaux in Hyderabad, Lahore, Rawalpindi, Peshawar and Quetta, employing 200 full-time and 60 part-time staff. AP, AFP and DPA services are received and the agency also has exchange arrangements with Bernama, ATA, PAP, MTI, AN (Brazil), Tatrapress, Tanjug, BTA, Novosti, KCNA, INA, CTK, Jiji and ANSA.

With an average daily output of 150 000 words of national and local news and 150 000 words of foreign news, all in English, PPI serves 55 newspapers, the Pakistan Broadcasting Corporation and 3 television stations. Its other services include features (40 to 50 a month) and photos (300 a month). Transmission is by leased telegraph network.

A third agency, United Press of Pakistan (UPP), founded in 1949, specializes in national news.

Major foreign agencies with correspondents in Pakistan include Reuters, APA, UPI, AFP, TASS and Hsinhua. Several large foreign newspapers also have stringers in Pakistan.

RADIO

The Pakistan Broadcasting Corporation, an autonomous statutory body set up in 1973 under a government-appointed board of governors, supersedes the former government department, Radio Pakistan, as the official radio broadcasting service.

With medium- and short-wave transmitters of up to 100kW in power, stations located at Islamabad/Rawalpindi, Karachi, Lahore, Multan, Peshawar, Hyderabad and Quetta broadcast home-service programmes for a total of over 800 hours a week, consisting of broadcasts for ethnic minorities (254 hours), news and information (158 hours), light entertainment (150 hours), advertising (88 hours), broadcasts for special audiences (85 hours), arts, letters and science (37 hours) and education (30 hours). In addition, special broadcasts to schools are on the air for 15 minutes daily from all stations during school terms. While Urdu is the main language used, programmes are also broadcast in English, Punjabi, Pushto, Sindhi, Baluchi and other languages according to local requirements.

The corporation's short-wave broadcasts are widely received and it is expected that, by 1975, reliable medium-wave coverage will be extended to all parts of the country, when a second programme is to be introduced to bring instructional broadcasts on health and hygiene, farming methods, etc., to rural areas.

External broadcasts, totalling about 80 hours a week, under the call-sign Radio Pakistan, with a general overseas service in English, and other programmes in 16 languages including Arabic, Bengali, Burmese, Dari and Turki, French, Gujarati, Hindi, Indonesian, Nepali, Persian, Swahili, Turkish and Urdu, are beamed towards Asia, Africa, the Middle East and Europe.

TELEVISION

Public television services began in 1964. The Pakistan Television Corporation, a public company with the government as majority shareholder, now operates stations at Rawalpindi/Islamabad, Karachi and Lahore, covering 38% of the population (but there are plans for 2 new stations to be opened at Peshawar and Quetta by the end of 1973 plus a projected network of 10 rebroadcasting stations and 4 translators to link distant areas to the main stations). Revenue is derived from receiver licences (since 1970), state subventions and commercial advertising.

Each of the main stations originates its own programmes which total 105 hours a week (5 to 6 hours daily) and consist of light entertainment (31 hours), news and information (29 hours), broadcasts for special audiences (17 hours), advertising (13 hours), arts, letters and science (11 hours), broadcasts for ethnic minorities (2 hours) and education (1½ hours). Nationally produced material amounts to about 86 hours of broadcasting time a week. Imported programmes come mainly from the USA and the Federal Republic of Germany.

Newsfilm, on both national and international subjects, is supplied through the Asian Television Service, a subsidiary of the corporation established in conjunction with a West German film-production agency, and from other countries including the People's Republic of China.

The definition system used is 525 lines. Television sets are installed in restaurants, clubs, city parks, etc., and the government is considering a scheme to provide receivers for communal viewing in rural areas.

FILM

In 1972, film production amounted to 88 features (21 in colour) in five languages (Urdu, Sindhi, Gujarati, Pushto and Punjabi). Some 40 documentaries and 42 newsreels were also produced, mainly by the Department of Films and Publications and the Information Department of the Government of Pakistan and the Education Department of the Punjab.

Imports totalled 175 features in 1973, coming mainly from the USA, France, Japan, Italy, the Federal Republic of Germany and the UK. Among the large city cinemas there are 10 equipped for 70mm projection and one drive-in with accommodation for 1000 cars and seats for 100 persons. Over 40 mobile units show films in the open air, drawing annual attendances of 500 000.

SPACE COMMUNICATIONS

Pakistan's Indian Ocean Intelsat earth station near Karachi came into operation in 1971.

PROFESSIONAL TRAINING AND ASSOCIATIONS

The University of the Punjab, Lahore, first offered a one-year evening course for a diploma in journalism in 1941; this has now expanded to a three-year BA (Hon) course. In addition, it has a two-year MA course with an enrolment of about 35 students. The University of Karachi's one-year diploma course and two-year MA courses (both requiring a BA degree for admission) have enrolments of over 200 students each.

Central Information Service probationers are trained in communications science and public relations at a government training institute in Islamabad.

The Pakistan Press Institute has a school of press photography.

The main press organizations are the All-Pakistan Newspaper Society (newspaper owners), the Council of Pakistan Newspaper Editors and the Pakistan Federal Union of Journalists, each of which has its professional statutes. There are also local journalists' unions and press clubs in the larger cities. Film producers, distributors and exhibitors have their own associations.

PHILIPPINES

Population	39 040 000
Area	300 000 sq. km.

PRESS

Newspapers	Dailies 19, Non-dailies 143
Total circulation	Dailies 650,000, Non-dailies 1 028 735
Copies per 1000 people	Dailies 17, Non-dailies 26

RADIO

Transmitters	Long/medium-wave 289, Short-wave 38
Total receivers	1 633 400 estimated in use
Receivers per 1000 people	42

TELEVISION

Transmitters	15
Receivers	450 000 estimated in use
Receivers per 1000 people	11

FILM

Cinemas	Fixed 951

PRESS

Although English is the mother tongue of relatively few Philippinos, it is, with Tagalog, the country's most widely used second language and by far the most important language of the daily press. Manila, the capital, has 16 dailies, nine of which are printed in English, one circulating 186 000 copies and seven others ranging between 50 000 copies and 75 000 copies. Manila also has 4 dailies in Chinese (with circulations of between 10 000 and 15 000), 2 in Tagalog (circulating 20 000 and 8000 copies respectively) and 1 in Spanish (21 000 copies). Other dailies are published in Cebu City, either in English or in English and Cebuano. A number of Manila dailies are grouped under the ownership of a few large publishing concerns, mainly family enterprises, some of which also own magazines and radio and television stations.

Periodical publications, including the 143 non-daily newspapers total about 1000 with an overall circulation of some 6 million copies. Of these, several general readership weeklies circulate up to 170 000 copies per issue. The largest weeklies are published in Tagalog but, in general, English is again the most widely used language, often in bilingual publications along with Tagalog, Vivasan, Spanish, Pangasinam, Ilocano, Bicolano, Cebuano, Chinese, etc.

The country's newsprint consumption (70 200 metric tons in 1970) has doubled over the last ten years. A newly opened pulp- and paper-mill on the east coast of Mindanao, which started newsprint production in 1972, is beginning to relieve the import burden.

NEWS AGENCIES

The Philippine News Service (PNS), founded in 1949, has a main office in Manila and 190 correspondents throughout the country, but no representatives abroad. PNS issues about 100 items a day dealing with national government affairs, provincial news, etc., as well as news photos. All newspapers, and all but one of the broadcasting networks, receive the PNS service.

The National News Service, founded in Manila in 1955, has 84 correspondents throughout the country and part-time abroad in New York, Washington, London and Tokyo. It issues a daily bulletin of national news, a features service and some foreign news; these are received by 10 radio and 4 television stations.

The Wireless News Agency, Manila, founded in 1961, which subscribes to AP, supplies 15 provincial newspapers and 44 provincial radio stations with a daily 5000-word service of national and foreign news.

Philippine Press International was founded in 1962. It subscribes to Reuters and issues a daily English-language news service to the local press.

Foreign agencies with bureaux in Manila include AP, UPI, Antara, Reuters and TASS.

RADIO

Responsibility for the regulation of radio broadcasting is exercised by the Radio Control Office of the government Department of Public Works and Communications. Broadcasting is carried out by over 70 different organizations and associations, public and private, operating 333 stations in all.

In an archipelago of more than 7000 mountainous islands, stretching over 1200 miles of ocean, good-quality radio coverage is difficult to maintain.

Nevertheless, a high proportion of households have receivers, particularly in the major areas of population concentration (the islands of Luzon, the Visayas and Mindanao); the greater Manila area (which includes the capital Quezon City and is served by 46 stations) has over 83% of households with receivers.

Of the 100 or so languages and dialects spoken in the Philippines, the most used in broadcasting is English – the medium of instruction in most schools and the common business language. Pilipino, the national language which is a standardized version of Tagalog, is almost equally widely used especially in the greater Manila area. Many stations broadcast in 2, 3 or 4 other dialects as well.

The largest government network is that operated by the Philippine Broadcasting Service (PBS), under the direct authority of the Office of the President with three medium-wave and 13 short-wave stations, giving special emphasis to news, health, education and general welfare programmes. The National Teachers' College and the National Civil Defence Administration also receive state subsidies for their radio stations, the latter augmenting its revenue from commercial advertising as well.

Commercial stations are the most numerous. They are either independent or affiliated to networks, often in conjunction with other media enterprises (91 belong to networks which may supply them with between 20 and 90% of their programme material). The majority are on the air for more than 16 hours a day, broadcasting music, news, drama, comedy and special events. Some also carry agricultural, vocational and educational programmes.

A third category of stations are those (25 in all) operated by religious bodies or groups and largely supported by subscriptions, donations, etc. All broadcast, in addition to religious programmes, news, music, agricultural information and educational and community-development programmes.

Educational and instructional broadcasting is carried out at various levels. One programme, in operation since 1959, is conducted by the Bureau of Public Schools' radio–TV education unit jointly with PBS (nine stations), which provides the technical facilities and personnel, and 15 private stations in various parts of the country. A total of 22 broadcasts a week reach some 48 000 classes in primary schools. Stations belonging to educational institutions, like the University of the Philippines, or the Mindanao colleges, broadcast live and taped lectures supplemented by printed study material (particularly for advanced training of serving teachers) and augmented by end-of-term examinations. Agricultural instruction is offered through the well-established Farmers' School of the Air programmes broadcast by public and private stations with the cooperation of government agencies.

Programmes for overseas listeners are broadcast by the short-wave transmitters of PBS and of several private religious networks including those of the National Council of Churches (one 10kW transmitter) beamed to Burma, China and India; Radio Veritas (50kW) beamed to Siberia, Thailand, Indonesia and Vietnam: and the Far East Broadcasting Company (1, 5 and 10kW) in 46 languages and dialects beamed to seven areas in Asia, the Pacific and the USSR.

The Voice of America owns and operates a 1000kW transmitter at Poro in the north of Luzon, and 20 other transmitters including several of 250kW on the same island. VOA broadcasts round the clock, in English and the languages of Asia and the Middle East.

TELEVISION

Responsibility for television, as for radio broadcasting, rests with the government's Radio Control Office. Television was first introduced in 1953 in Manila. There are now 21 stations, 7 of which are in the greater Manila area and the remainder in the provinces: 3 in north and south Luzon (Baguio, Batangas and Naga City), 7 in the Visayas (Cebu, Bacolod and neighbouring areas) and 4 in Mindanao (Davao and Cagayan de Oro).

Languages used by six of the metropolitan area stations are English and/or Pilipino. Provincial stations use additional languages: Cebuano and Ilongo in the Visayas and Mindanao, and Bicolano in southern Luzon.

The majority of stations are independent with respect to administration and programme policies, while seven belong to networks which provide some common programme material. Programmes are mainly general entertainment, news, panel discussions and broadcasts of special events. Educational programmes are prepared by the Centre for Educational Television (CETV) at Ateneo University, Manila, and are shown either on closed circuits in two local schools, or through a commercial channel (linked by microwave with CETV) to 51 elementary and high schools, reaching over 20 000 pupils in 1968–9. Broadcasting hours, governed by the type of licence issued to the station, exceed 19 hours a day for two provincial stations; 13 other stations are on the air for between 10 and 19 hours daily.

All television is on 525 lines. Three Manila stations broadcast in colour (NTSC system); colour receivers in use total about 6000.

FILM

With 194 feature films produced by 45 companies in 1970 (compared with 112 features in 1960), as well as a number of documentary, travel and other short films, the Philippine film industry is largely in the hands of small independent producers. Processing is carried out in local laboratories or sent to Japan (especially for colour films).

Imports, totalling about 550 features and 100 documentaries in 1970, came mainly from the USA and European countries.

Film going is increasingly popular in the Philippines, where city cinemas may open as early as 07.00 hours and run continuously till midnight. Annual attendances have increased from 14.8 million in 1960 to over 22 million. In addition, mobile projection units operated by government agencies tour the rural villages and draw audiences from many miles around to see documentary, educational and instructional films shown as part of the national community-development effort.

SPACE COMMUNICATIONS

The Philippines has two earth stations under joint government/private ownership at Tanay, near Manila. The first, receiving Pacific Intelsat transmissions was opened in April 1968 and the second (Indian Ocean Intelsat) in 1971.

PROFESSIONAL TRAINING AND ASSOCIATIONS

Media training is offered in institutes and schools of mass communication and journalism at the Universities of the Philippines (Quezon City), Santo Tomas (Manila), Silliman (Negros Island), at the Philippine Press Institute and the

Lyceum of the Philippines (Manila) and at the Ateneo Graduate School and Siena College (Quezon City).

Technical training for government telecommunications engineers is provided by the Telecommunications Training Institute at Valenzuela, Bulucan, at which 23 group courses were held in 1968–9, with 431 graduates.

Professional associations include a journalists' newspaper guild, a press club, an overseas press club, associations of film producers and distributors, and the non-profit-making Film Society of the Philippines, formed to promote the artistic appreciation and creation of films.

PORTUGUESE TIMOR

Population	614 000
Area	14 925 sq. km.

PRESS	
Newspapers	Non-dailies 2

RADIO	
Transmitters	Short-wave 1
Total receivers	13 000 estimated in use
Receivers per 1000 people	21

FILM	
Cinemas	Fixed 1
Total seating capacity	600
Seats per 1000 people	0.9
Total annual attendance	40 000
Annual visits per capita	0.06

PRESS

The press consists of a weekly newspaper (circulating 600 copies) and a weekly official bulletin. There is also a bi-monthly Catholic missionary journal. All are published in Portuguese in the capital, Dili.

NEWS AGENCY

The Portuguese news agency Lusitania has a correspondent in Dili.

RADIO

Emissora de Radiodifusao de Timor Portugues, owned and operated by the territorial administration, with one 10kW short-wave transmitter, is on the air for nearly 60 hours a week, broadcasting in Portuguese except for a daily 10-minute broadcast in the local language, Teum, and two 30-minute broadcasts a week in Chinese.

FILM

All films exhibited in the cinema at Dili are imported.

QATAR

Population	81 000
Area	22 014 sq. km.

PRESS	
Newspapers	Non-dailies 2
Total circulation	Non-dailies 1500
Copies per 1000 people	Non-dailies 18

RADIO	
Transmitters	Long/medium-wave 2, Short-wave 2
Total receivers	35 000 estimated in use
Receivers per 1000 people	432

TELEVISION	
Transmitters	2
Receivers	30 000 estimated in use
Receivers per 1000 people	370

FILM	
Cinemas	Fixed 2
Total seating capacity	3300
Seats per 1000 people	41
Total annual attendance	500 000
Annual visits per capita	6

PRESS

Two weekly newspapers are published in Arabic. The government Department of Information also publishes a monthly magazine. All publications appear in the capital, Doha.

NEWS AGENCIES
There is no national agency. The press and broadcasting stations receive the services of Reuters, MENA, DPA and AFP.

RADIO
The Qatar Broadcasting Service (radio and television) is a service of the Ministry of Information.

Radio Qatar, established in 1968, operates two medium-wave transmitters (10 and 50kW) and two short-wave transmitters (each of 100kW) located at Doha and covering the whole of the national territory.

Programmes totalling 104 hours a week include light entertainment (60 hours), news and information (15 hours), broadcasts for special audiences (14 hours), broadcasts for ethnic minorities (7 hours), arts, letters and sciences (7 hours) and education (1¼ hours). All programmes are in Arabic except for 1 hour daily in English. Radio frequencies are allocated by a Gulf-area frequency assignment committee.

No licence fee is payable for radio receivers.

TELEVISION
The Qatar Television Service began operating in 1970. With two transmitters at Doha, it not only covers the national territory but can also be received (since 1972) in much of the Gulf area and in part of southern Iran.

Programmes are broadcast in Arabic for 36 hours a week and include light entertainment (27 hours), news and information (5 hours), broadcasts for special audiences (2 hours) and education (1½ hours). Of these, 28 hours are imported, mainly from the USA, the UK, Egypt, Jordan, Kuwait, Iraq, France and the Federal Republic of Germany. The definition system used is 625 lines.

No licence fee is payable for television receivers.

FILM
The television service has a film unit which produces some documentaries. Films exhibited in the two fixed cinemas are all imported.

SAUDI ARABIA

Population	7 965 000
Area	2 149 690 sq. km.

PRESS

Newspapers	Dailies 5, Non-dailies 5
Total circulation	Dailies 55 000, Non-dailies 38 000
Copies per 1000 people	Dailies 7, Non-dailies 5

RADIO

Transmitters	Long/medium-wave 4, Short-wave 4, VHF—FM 3
Total receivers	250 000 estimated in use
Receivers per 1000 people	31

TELEVISION

Transmitters	6
Receivers	150 000 estimated in use
Receivers per 1000 people	19

PRESS

Daily newspapers are published in Jeddah (three papers circulating respectively 20 000, 10 000 and 3500 copies) and Mecca and Riyadh (each circulating 10 000 copies). All are in Arabic, and all are published by officially approved – though independent – press organizations, as required under the terms of the Press Law of 1964.

The largest weekly, circulating 22 000 copies, is the Ministry of Information's English-language news bulletin issued from Jeddah. The four leading Arabic weeklies total 16 000 copies per issue. One of them, a government gazette, originally established in 1924 as a private weekly in Mecca, is the country's oldest newspaper.

The periodical press consists of 10 titles (total circulation 43 000 copies), the main subject categories being business (4 titles, totalling 16 000 copies), general interest (2 titles, 9000 copies), religion (2 titles, 8000 copies), literature and entertainment. Some of these, in both Arabic and English, are published by the Arabian American Oil Company (Aramco).

NEWS AGENCIES

There is no national agency. Foreign agencies whose services are received in the country are UP, AP, AFP, MENA and Reuters. An English-language newsletter is issued daily by Saudi newspapers and the broadcasting service.

RADIO

The Saudi Arabian Broadcasting Service, a department of the Ministry of Information and financed from its budget, has three medium-wave radio transmitters at Riyadh (1200kW), Jeddah (50kW) and Damman (100kW) and four short-wave transmitters (100 and 50kW) at Riyadh and Jeddah, giving country-wide reception. It broadcasts a general Arabic programme, a second programme, also in Arabic, beamed to Europe, north Africa and North America, and a foreign service, beamed to five world areas, in Arabic, English, French, Indonesian, Persian, Swahili and Urdu. These programmes together total 822 hours a week.

Aramco Radio, a private station serving Aramco employees, broadcasts three programmes of continuous music (rock, pop and classical) via medium-wave and FM (stereo) transmitters.

No licence fee is payable for radio receivers.

TELEVISION

The Saudi Arabian Government Television Service which began test transmissions in 1965, now has five transmitters at Riyadh, Jeddah, Medina, Damman and Qassim broadcasting for over 38 hours a week. Main programme categories are light entertainment (13 hours), news (11 hours), broadcasts to special audiences (8 hours), cultural programmes (3 hours), education (2½ hours) and advertising (27 minutes). Of these, 20 hours are of domestic production. The definition system used is 625 lines.

No receiver licence is payable.

Aramco Television, a privately operated non-commercial station at Dhahran, broadcasts for 4 or 5 hours a day (525-line definition).

FILM

The television service of the Ministry of Information has a film unit which produces films for television. Official authorization is not given for commercial public exhibition of films. All showings are therefore organized privately or on a non-profit-making basis.

SPACE COMMUNICATIONS

An Atlantic Intelsat earth station, at Tais near Jeddah, and an Indian Ocean Intelsat station, near Riyadh, are scheduled to come into service in 1975.

SIKKIM

Population	200 000
Area	7107 sq. km.

PRESS	
Newspapers	Non-dailies 1

PRESS

A fortnightly newspaper is published in the capital, Gangtok, in the national language, Sikkimese (other languages widely spoken in the country are Nepalese and, to a lesser extent, Epcha).

Sikkim has no postal service or public broadcasting services.

SINGAPORE

Population	2 150 000
Area	581 sq. km.

PRESS	
Newspapers	Dailies 10, Non-dailies 11*
Total circulation	Dailies 414 696, Non-dailies 400 000
Copies per 1000 peopl⌐	Dailies 193, Non-dailies 186

RADIO	
Transmitters	Long/medium-wave 5, Short-wave 7, VHF–FM 4
Total receivers	279 000† licences
Licences per 1000 people	130†

TELEVISION	
Transmitters	2
Receivers	204 847 licences
Licences per 1000 people	95

FILM	
Cinemas	Fixed 75
Total seating capacity	62 916
Seats per 1000 people	29
Total annual attendance	37 369 700
Annual visits per capita	17

*Including Sunday editions of dailies.
†Not including wired receivers.

PRESS

The daily press consists of 4 titles in Chinese, together totalling 200 000 copies per issue, 2 in English totalling over 100 000 copies, 1 in romanized Malay with 20 000 copies, 3 in Tamil and 1 in Malayalam. Sunday editions of 9 of the dailies (with somewhat higher than weekday circulation figures), 2 English weeklies and 1 Punjabi twice-weekly make up the non-daily general interest press.

Periodicals total over 1000 titles: 464 in English, 98 in Chinese, 38 in Malay, 15 in Tamil and 271 multilingual. Main subject categories are religion (118 titles), political science (91 titles), education (81 titles), sociology (79 titles), general readership (74 titles), recreation (59 titles), geography (58 titles), trade and communications (48 titles), business management (45 titles), art and architecture (43 titles), medicine (42 titles), technology (39 titles), law (29 titles), literature (24 titles), etc. With these are included 122 school magazines and 39 business house organs.

NEWS AGENCIES

There is no national news agency. Newspapers receive local news from their own reporting staffs and foreign news from the numerous foreign news agencies and organizations represented in Singapore, including Reuters—AAP, UPI, AP, Kyodo, PANA and TASS. Radio and television services use Reuters, UPI and Kyodo only.

Subscribers also receive feature and photo services from most of the agencies while some also provide special audio-radio and video-television services. Means of transmission used include leased networks, microwave, radio-teletype and radio-photo systems, as well as public telecommunication services.

The total of over 60 foreign correspondents in Singapore includes those of the agencies mentioned, of Tanjug, and of various newspapers and broadcasting organizations.

RADIO

The Department of Broadcasting of the Ministry of Culture operates the radio and television services of the republic, revenue for which is derived from radio and television receiver licences and from advertising.

Domestic radio broadcasts cover the entire population and are also received by audiences of millions in neighbouring countries. Operating 5 medium-wave transmitters (four 20kW and one 100kW), 7 short-wave transmitters (from 7.5 to 50kW) and 4 FM transmitters, Radio Singapore broadcasts Malay, Chinese and Tamil-language services, each for 133 hours a week, an English-language service for 126 hours a week, a multilingual (Malay, Chinese, Tamil and English) service for 8 hours a day and a stereo FM service in English and Chinese, also for 8 hours a day. The English-language programmes consist mainly of light entertainment (78 hours a week), news and information (23 hours), cultural programmes (12 hours), programmes for special audiences (9 hours) and advertising (1 hour).

A commercial station, Rediffusion (Singapore), operates four simultaneous wired networks serving 60 000 subscribers; broadcasts are of its own pro-grammes (mainly in six Chinese dialects and in English, Malay and Tamil), relays of Radio Singapore news, and transcriptions from other stations including the BBC (UK).

The British Forces Broadcasting Service, Singapore, a non-commercial station operated by the UK Ministry of Defence, broadcasts information and enter-tainment programmes for over 80 hours a week for military forces stationed locally.

TELEVISION

Television Singapore, which began broadcasting in February 1963, now broadcasts on two channels (625 lines) in all four official languages (Malay, Chinese, Tamil and English), covering the entire population (and also clearly received in neighbouring countries).

Programmes, of both the national and the educational television service, total around 133 hours a week and consist of light entertainment (54 hours), education (28 hours), news and information (23 hours), broadcasts for special audiences (11 hours), arts letters and science (9 hours) and advertising (7 hours).

The educational television service, whose programmes are provided by the Ministry of Education, was introduced in 1967 for secondary schools and extended in 1971 to cater for primary schools and pre-university students. Programmes are broadcast in the mornings, in all four official languages (with repeats in the afternoons), on the transmitter of the second channel. All schools are equipped with television receivers.

Television Singapore imports a little less than 50% of its programmes, mainly from the USA and the UK, and also from the Federal Republic of Germany, Hong Kong and Australia. It also has some exchanges with member countries of the Asian Broadcasting Union. All programmes broadcast are originally made or dubbed in one of the four official languages and are often subtitled in the others.

A licence fee covers both radio and television receivers installed at the same address.

FILM

No feature film production is reported for 1972, although annual production had averaged around five titles in preceding years, most of these in Malay, the remainder in Chinese.

Films exhibited in the 75 fixed covered cinemas (36 of which are air-conditioned) and one drive-in accommodating 900 cars and with annual admissions of 646 500 persons are mainly imported. Imported features totalled 773 in 1972, coming from the USA (166), Hong Kong (137), the UK (111), India (108), Italy (51), Indonesia and Malaysia (together 38) and other countries (150).

In 1972, 36 documentaries were imported from France (15), the USSR (9), the Federal Republic of Germany (7), Korea (3) and Japan (2).

Two large distribution circuits control the majority of the cinemas in Singapore and Malaysia, so that many films imported into Singapore are for exhibition in both countries. The Ministry of Culture arranges frequent. local film showings outside the urban area.

SPACE COMMUNICATIONS

An Indian Ocean Intelsat earth station at Sentosa came into operation in 1971.

PROFESSIONAL TRAINING AND ASSOCIATIONS

The fundamentals of journalism and news reporting are included in the arts curriculum of Nanyang University, and training and research in the mass media are carried out at the Asian Mass Communications Research and Information Centre, established in 1971. The Singapore Government's telecommunications centre (with training facilities for 200 persons) trains engineering, technical and operations staff for its broadcasting and telecommunications services.

The Singapore National Union of Journalists has its own code of ethics. Other press associations include a press club and an association for foreign correspondents.

SRI LANKA

Population	12 760 000
Area	65 610 sq. km.

PRESS

Newspapers	Dailies 17, Non-dailies 17
Total circulation	Dailies 612 000, Non-dailies 1 058 000
Copies per 1000 people	Dailies 48, Non-dailies 83

RADIO

Transmitters	Long/medium-wave 9, Short-wave 12, VHF—FM 8
Total receivers	846 000
Receivers per 1000 people	66

FILM

Cinemas	Fixed 303
Total seating capacity	128 544
Seats per 1000 people	10
Total annual attendance	98 135 800
Annual visits per capita	8

PRESS

The daily press – 10 morning and 7 evening newspapers – is entirely based in the capital, Colombo, though most papers have a much wider readership, in one or other of the three main publishing languages: Sinhalese, with 5 newspapers circulating a total of 374 568 copies daily, Tamil, with 6 newspapers (111 675 copies) and English, 6 newspapers (12 588 copies).

Non-daily general interest newspapers, mostly weekend or weekly papers, are also published in Colombo; 9 in Sinhalese, 5 in Tamil and 3 in English. In addition, there are many periodical publications dealing with political, cultural or religious affairs, women's and children's interests, industry and commerce, annual surveys, etc.

NEWS AGENCIES

The national agency is the Press Trust of Ceylon (Sri Lanka) Ltd (Newstrust), a private company founded in 1951 and dealing only in foreign news, which it receives from Reuters (London) and the Press Trust of India. It distributes 35 000 words a day, in English, to its 12 subscribers in Sri Lanka (11 newspapers belonging to the four main groups and government radio stations). Newstrust has its permanent bureau in Colombo with a staff of 15, but employs no local or foreign correspondents.

Most of the world's leading agencies have either permanent or part-time correspondents in Colombo.

RADIO

The Sri Lanka (Ceylon) Broadcasting Corporation, formerly Radio Ceylon, was established as a public corporation under the Ministry of Information in 1967. In addition to government subsidies, it is financed by listeners' licence fees and commercial advertising revenue. There were 466 000 licences in 1972 (each licence may cover more than one receiver).

The corporation operates 9 medium-wave transmitters (including three of 50kW), 8 FM transmitters (totalling 2kW) at various points on the island, and 12 short-wave transmitters (including three of 100kW) all at Ekala.

The national service has three language programmes, in Sinhalese (74 hours a week), Tamil (72 hours) and English (45 hours) which, with the alternative light programme in Sinhala – Radio Sandhaya (31 hours) – brings the total broadcasting time to 222 hours a week. Main programme categories are: light entertainment (75 hours), broadcasts for special audiences (59 hours), artistic and cultural (37 hours), news and information (17 hours), educational (15 hours), broadcasts for ethnic minorities (7 hours) and advertising (7 hours). A highly successful innovation is the education programme, replacing the former day-time schools service, which is broadcast nightly for 1¾ hours and is designed not only to supplement school curricula but to prepare secondary-level students for recognized examinations.

The commercial service consists of a domestic network which is on the air 192 hours a week in Sinhalese (79 hours), English (69 hours) and Tamil (44 hours), and an overseas service beamed to south-east Asia and broadcasting in Hindi (52 hours), English (46 hours) and Tamil (18 hours a week).

A commercial rediffusion company under government contract and with government participation operates a four-channel wired network rebroadcasting the national service programmes in Sinhala, Tamil, English and Hindi to over 22 250 subscribers (in 1969) in Colombo and district, and the inland city of Kandy.

The Voice of America has a station in Colombo with four 35kW short-wave transmitters broadcasting VOA programmes in English, Urdu and Hindi.

TELEVISION
There is no television but preliminary planning for its introduction is under way.

FILM
Local film companies produced 25 feature films and 8 short films in 1971. Apart from its weekly newsreel, the government film unit's annual production of 53 short films in 1970 included 49 educational and instructional titles.

A national film institute, set up under government auspices in 1970, deals with film imports and distribution. the operation of a government film studio for local producers and the production of educational, cultural and children's films.

Annual imports in 1971 included 198 feature films from the USA (107), India (55), the UK (14), Italy (10), France (6) and the USSR (4). Annual cinema attendances have more than trebled over the last ten years. In addition, non-commercial exhibition of educational and cultural films, mainly by mobile units, attracts large audiences.

SPACE COMMUNICATIONS
An Indian Ocean Intelsat earth station is planned to be built at Mirigama in 1974.

PROFESSIONAL TRAINING AND ASSOCIATIONS

The Broadcasting Corporation has a newly opened training institute in Colombo with facilities for training in all broadcasting techniques.

In February 1973, the Sri Lanka Press Council Bill was passed, instituting a seven-member press council including the director of information and one representative each of working journalists and newspaper owners. Its objects include ensuring press freedom promoting professional standards and ethics, improving the recruitment, training and welfare of journalists, press research and professional advice to the Government.

SYRIA

Population	6 660 000
Area	185 180 sq. km.

PRESS

Newspapers	Dailies 5, Non-dailies 12
Total circulation	Dailies 60 000
Copies per 1000 people	Dailies 9

RADIO

Transmitters	Long/medium-wave 8, Short-wave 3
Total receivers	2 500 000 estimated in use
Receivers per 1000 people	375

TELEVISION

Transmitters	7
Receivers	150 000 estimated in use
Receivers per 1000 people	22

FILM

Cinemas	Fixed 70

PRESS

The largest dailies (two morning papers each circulating about 20 000 copies) appear in the capital, Damascus. The other papers, based in Damascus, Aleppo and Hama range from 2000 to 10 000 in circulation. The press is largely owned by political or other organizations, trade unions, etc.

Non-daily newspapers are published in the two main cities and in Hama, Homs and Latakia. Almost all are in Arabic, although there is a weekly press digest in English and a fortnightly press review in French. About 70% of the national territory is regularly served by either the national or the local press.

Periodicals number 35 titles and include 13 general readership, 4 literary, 3 recreational, 3 military, 2 religious, 2 legal, 2 educational, 2 medical, 2 architectural, 1 agricultural and 1 commercial. The majority are in Arabic; a few appear in English, French or Spanish.

NEWS AGENCIES

The national agency is the government-owned Syrian Arab News Agency (SANA) founded in 1965. It has headquarters in Damascus and offices in the main towns of Syria, as well as offices abroad in Beirut, Baghdad, Amman, Cairo, Sana'a, Algiers, Tripoli, Paris, Moscow and Prague. SANA issues 59 000 words daily in Arabic and 3000 words in English to its subscribers.

Foreign agencies represented in Damascus include ANSA, UPI, DPA, Reuters and TASS.

RADIO

The national broadcasting service, responsible under the Ministry of Information, for both radio and television, was established in 1945 and is financed directly from the state budget.

The radio home service, with medium-wave transmitters 10, 60, 100, 300 and 600kW at Damascus, Aleppo, Deir-ez-Zor, Sabburah, Homs and Tartus, and short-wave transmitters of 20 and 50kW, is on the air for 140 hours a week in Arabic, French, English, Turkish, German, Hebrew and Russian, serving the whole of the national territory. Programmes consist of light entertainment (64 hours a week), news and information (35½ hours), broadcasts to special audiences (19 hours), education (12½ hours) and arts, letters and science (9 hours), almost entirely of national origin.

A foreign service is broadcast for 35 hours a week in German, French and English (to Europe), and Arabic and Spanish (to central and South America).

No licence fee is payable for radio receivers.

TELEVISION

Television broadcasting, also under government auspices, began in 1960 with stations at Damascus, Aleppo and Homs. To these, further stations have been added at Slenfe and Sarankhiyah to provide potential television coverage for 75% of the population. Programmes, broadcast for 54½ hours a week, consist of education (29 hours), news and information (12½ hours), broadcasts to special audiences (4 hours), light entertainment (3 hours), advertising (2¾ hours) and arts, letters and science (2½ hours). In addition to locally produced material, programmes are imported from Arab countries, France, the German Democratic Republic and other countries.

The definition system used is 625 lines. Television receivers are assembled in the country.

An annual licence fee is payable for receivers.

FILM

Some documentary and instructional (mostly agricultural) films are produced. Feature films are imported mainly from the USA, Egypt, France, the UK, India and Italy. In addition to the fixed cinemas, there are a dozen mobile projection units and an number of open-air summer cinemas.

PROFESSIONAL TRAINING AND ASSOCIATIONS

A communications institute in Damascus, founded in 1970, had an initial enrolment of 57 students (including three women). It offers a two-year certificate course open to candidates of university-entrance level who pass an entrance examination. The Ministry of Information also conducts short courses for practising journalists.

A newly established press association in Damascus is studying projects for the professional advancement of journalists. There are two associations of cinema owners and three associations of cinema technicians and employees.

THAILAND

Population	35 335 000
Area	514 000 sq. km.

PRESS

Newspapers	Dailies 35, Non-dailies 32
Total circulation	Dailies 849 000, Non-dailies 250 000
Copies per 1000 people	Dailies 24, Non-dailies 7

RADIO

Transmitters	Long/medium-wave 108, Short-wave 26
	VHF–FM 10
Total receivers	3 000 000 estimated in us
Receivers per 1000 people	85

TELEVISION

Transmitters	30
Receivers	350 000 estimated in use
Receivers per 1000 people	10

FILM

Cinemas	Fixed 392
Total seating capacity	422 216
Seats per 1000 people	12

PRESS

Daily newspapers are published in the Thai language (19 titles), Chinese (11 titles) and English (5 titles). With the exception of a Thai daily published in the northern town of Chiengmai, all are based in Bangkok, the capital, a number of them being linked by common ownership. Thai-language papers have the largest circulations, two exceeding 100 000 copies per issue.

The non-daily press is strongest in the metropolitan area of Bangkok and the nearby city of Thon Buri, but a number of papers serve the provincial areas as well. To avoid competition with the nationally distributed Bangkok dailies, the provincial press concentrates strongly on local news and topics.

In the absence of reasonably priced mechanical typesetting machinery, large staffs of typesetters must be employed to set the complex Thai script by hand, thus raising newspaper costs to almost luxury level. Publishers attempt to recoup this outlay by devoting a large proportion of space to advertising.

Over 300 periodicals are published in the three main languages. Many of them are directed towards popular readerships and carry news and articles on films, sport, women's interests, etc.

NEWS AGENCIES
Thailand has no national agency but the government has a news service to which most papers subscribe. A free daily bulletin in Thai and English distributed by the government's Public Relations Department also supplies newspapers and broadcasting stations with domestic news only. Additional local and international news is available through the correspondents of foreign agencies represented in the country.

AP, UPI, AFP, Reuters and TASS, which have bureaux in Bangkok, and provincial correspondents, offer daily news services. In all, 22 foreign news agencies, 3 radio and 8 television news services and 3 photographic agencies, are represented in Thailand, along with 22 correspondents of overseas journals.

RADIO
Public broadcasting is conducted by governmental and semi-governmental organizations, including the Public Relations Department, the armed forces, the police, the Post and Telegraph Office, universities and the Minstry of Education. Income is derived from government subsidies and commercial advertising.

The Thai National Broadcasting Station, under the direction of the Public Relations Department, operates 23 medium-wave transmitters (with a combined power of 643.5kW), 7 short-wave transmitters (totalling 145kW) and local FM transmitters. Its home service, in Thai, is on the air for 166 hours a week, of which 124 hours are filled by nationally produced programme material. Light entertainment occupies 74 hours a week, news and information 25 hours, educational broadcasts 15 hours, broadcasts for ethnic minorities 15 hours (in Mong, Yao, Meo, Karen, Muser, Lesor and Egor), programmes for special audiences (women, young people, etc.) 6½ hours and cultural programmes 3½ hours.

Overseas services of the Thai National Broadcasting Station are beamed to neighbouring countries, North America and Europe and are broadcast for 38½ hours a week in Chinese, Malay, Cambodian, Laotian, French and English. The home service in Thai is also relayed on short-wave overseas services.

The Ministry of Education's station with a 1kW medium-wave transmitter in Bangkok is on the air for 3 hours a day, in Thai and English, broadcasting educational programmes, news and foreign-language courses, for the general public, and (for an additional 5½ hours a day during school holidays) special vacation broadcasts for students.

A semi-governmental company which also operates a television station broadcasts four radio programmes including some stereo transmissions and one daily 24-hour service. Some of these programmes are also relayed by the local stations belonging to a government Public Relations Department network. Over 100 other stations are operated by various government departments, some of them on an experimental basis.

A 1000kW medium-wave transmitter, the Voice of Free Asia, at Ban Pachi, broadcasts locally produced programmes in Thai and English, and Voice of America programmes in English, Laotian, Cambodian and Bengali.

The United States Air Force also has a network of seven medium-wave and two FM transmitters in Thailand.

No licence fee is payable for radio receivers.

TELEVISION

The first television station was opened in 1955 by the Thai Television Company, a commercial company with government participation. In addition to its main transmitter in Bangkok, the station now has relay transmitters at Khonkaen, Lampang and Haadyai and is on the air for 68 hours a week, broadcasting light entertainment (29 hours), educational programmes (11½ hours), news and information (10 hours), commercial advertising (5½ hours) and various other cultural, instructive and special programmes. Colour telecasts (PAL system) began in March 1970.

The Army Television Station, opened in 1958, has a similar governmental/commercial basis, receiving its income from state subventions and commercial advertisements. Operating a main transmitter in Bangkok, with a relay station at Saraburi, it is on the air for 37 hours a week and carries news, entertainment, educational and special (women's and children's) programmes. Colour telecasts were introduced in 1968.

In 1961, the Public Relations Department opened a network of three regional stations in Chiengmai, Haadyai and Khonkaen, to cover the main population centres in the north, north-east and southern peninsular regions. These broadcast for 4 hours a day; colour is being introduced as from 1970.

Programmes are imported from the USA, the UK, Japan, the Federal Republic of Germany, France, Australia, India, Hong Kong and the Philippines, and exchanges are carried out with members of the Asian Broadcasting Union. All stations transmit on 525 lines.

No licence fee is payable for receivers.

FILM

Thailand has an active film industry with an annual production of about 27 35mm and 231 16mm entertainment films (in 1970), in addition to some documentary and short films mostly made or commissioned by the Ministries of Education, Health and Agriculture and the Public Relations Department.

Imports for 1971 totalled 465 entertainment films, principally from Italy (130), the USA (120), India (40), Japan (30), France (30), Indonesia (10) and the Philippines (5). Some are shown in the original language version, others are subtitled in Thai and Chinese. Newsreels are mainly imported from the USA.

A committee set up by the government to study the film industry has recommended the establishment of a film institute, encouragement of national production and the adoption of a film act governing the industry.

Bangkok alone has 66 cinemas, most of them well equipped, and there are 35mm cinemas in other cities as well. There are 173 16mm cinemas throughout the country.

SPACE COMMUNICATIONS

Thailand is a member of Intelsat and has two earth stations equipped to receive and transmit broadcasts via both the Pacific and Indian Ocean Intelsat systems. The stations, opened in 1968 and 1970 respectively, are at Srivacha, south-east of Bangkok.

PROFESSIONAL TRAINING AND ASSOCIATIONS

Four-year journalism courses leading to a bachelor's degree are offered at the Department of Mass Communication at Chulalongkorn University, Bangkok (with 455 graduates since the course was established in 1964); at the Faculty of Humanities, Chiengmai University (with 47 graduates since the course was established in 1964) and at the Department of Journalism and Mass Communications, Thammasat University, Bangkok (with 314 graduates since the course was established in 1954). All candidates must pass an entrance examination.

The government's Public Relations School has a six-month diploma training course for government officials, 850 of whom have been trained since the school opened in 1961.

Professional associations include a national and several regional journalists' associations, the Radio Society of Thailand, founded under government patronage, for radiocommunications personnel, and a motion-picture exhibitor's association.

UNITED ARAB EMIRATES

Population	200 000
Area	83 600 sq. km.

PRESS
Newspapers   Non-dailies 2

RADIO
Transmitters	Long/medium-wave 6, Short-wave 5, VHF FM 1
Total receivers	35 000 estimated in use
Receivers per 1000 people	175

TELEVISION
Transmitters   2
Receivers   15 000 estimated in use
Receivers per 1000 people   75

PRESS
There are no daily newspapers. Abu Dhabi has a weekly news publication issued in English by the Department of Information and Tourism, and a monthly commercial review in Arabic. In Dubai, the municipality has a fortnightly Arabic journal, and there is a monthly official gazette in both Arabic and English. Both Sharjah and Ras al Khaimah have monthly publications in Arabic.

RADIO
The Voice of the Arab Emirates, a government station, with 1 medium-wave (50kW) transmitter, 4 short-wave transmitters (120kW) and 1 FM transmitter, broadcasts a home service from Abu Dhabi for 17½ hours a day in Arabic and English (2 hours daily).

Radio Dubai, also government owned, with 2 medium-wave transmitters (10 and 50kW) and 1 short-wave transmitter (10kW), is on the air in Arabic for over 20 hours a day and in English for 13 hours a day.

Radio Ras al Khaimah, also government owned, operates 1 medium-wave transmitter (10kW).

Sharjah's 50kW medium-wave station covers a large area of the Gulf coast with Arabic-language broadcasts. A second station in Sharjah, the Forces Radio Station, broadcasts in English. Both these stations carry commercial advertising.

TELEVISON
The United Arab Emirates Television Service has transmitters (625 lines) at Abu Dhabi and Al Ain broadcasting for 6 hours daily. In addition, western parts of the territory can receive the programmes of the Qatar Television Service.

VIETNAM (Republic of)

Population   18 810 000
Area   173 809 sq. km.

PRESS
Newspapers   Dailies 56, Non-dailies 32*
Total circulation Dailies 95 000, Non-dailies 250 000*
Copies per 1000 people Dailies 5

RADIO

Transmitters	Long/medium-wave 14, Short-wave 6, VHF- FM 2
Total receivers	6 000 000 estimated in use
Receivers per 1000 people	319

TELEVISION

Transmitters	4
Receivers	500 000 estimated in use
Receivers per 1000 people	26

FILM

Cinemas	Fixed 143
Total seating capacity	91 000
Seats per 1000 people	5
Total annual attendance	25 500 000
Annual visits per capita	1

*Weeklies only.

PRESS

Evening newspapers number 44 as against 10 morning editions. Of the total, 40 are printed in Vietnamese, 12 in Chinese, 3 in English and 1 in French. Most appear in the capital, Saigon, from which news published in the provincial papers is often reproduced. Newspapers are often read several times over, readers hiring them for an hour or two and returning them to the newsvendor.

Periodicals number about 120, practically all in Vietnamese, the principal categories being religion, political and economic sciences, and topics for women and young people.

To overcome price and foreign-exchange difficulties which restrict the availability of newsprint, the Economics and Finance Ministry subsidizes the establishment of local paper-mills.

NEWS AGENCIES

The national agency, founded in 1951, is Vietnam Press (VP), a financially autonomous organization under government control. In addition to its head office in Saigon, it has 41 provincial offices in the country, with a total permanent staff of 201 persons, plus 60 part-time correspondents. Foreign bureaux are maintained in Paris and Djakarta, and correspondents in Tokyo and Stockholm.

Services totalling 75 000 words a day of local news in Vietnamese, French and English, and a similar amount of foreign news in the same languages plus Chinese, are supplied to 59 newspapers and 4 radio and 2 television stations. Other subscribers incude government services, educational and cultural centres, business firms and diplomatic missions in Saigon and abroad.

News is received from AFP, AP, UPI and Reuters and also, through exchange agreements, from other Asian agencies, including Kyodo, Orient Press, Hapdong, Antara, JP, Lao Press and AKP.

Apart from its duplicated bulletins, VP transmits (and receives) news by telex and radio teletype.

Five private agenices monitoring foreign news broadcasts and handling local news, features, pictures and translations also have offices in Saigon.

RADIO

The Office National de Radiodiffusion du Viêt-Nam, which comes under the control of the Ministry of Information, operates 14 medium-wave, 6 short-wave and 2 FM transmitters, with a total power of 651kW, broadcasting from Saigon and eight regional stations.

The home service in Vietnamese is on the air for 24 hours a day, and the Vietnamese Forces programme for 18 hours a day, including an all-night service. The regional programmes, all in Vietnamese, are also broadcast throughout the night. Other language services are in French, English, Chinese, Thai and Cambodian.

Programmes, almost all nationally produced, consist of light entertainment (29%), news and information (26%), broadcasts for special audiences (20%), education (15%), cultural and scientific programmes (3%), advertising, etc.

The Voice of America's 50kW short-wave transmitter at Hué is on the air for 4 hours a day in Vietnamese.

No licence fee is payable for receivers. A large part of the domestic demand for radio receivers is met by an assembly plant near Saigon.

TELEVISION

The National Television Service, based at Hué and operating four transmitters covering 78% of the population, broadcasts 42 hours a week, including news and information (21 hours), light entertainment (10 hours) and cultural and educational broadcasts (2 hours each). An experimental programme of school broadcasts is at present being conducted by the Ministry of Education with a view to permanent establishment.

The definition system used is 625 lines.

FILM

National production of long films in 1971 included 18 feature and 92 short films. The Centre National Cinématographique in Saigon produces a weekly newsreel for local and foreign exhibition, as well as numerous documentaries.

Feature films imported in 1971 totalled 354; 71 came from Italy, 40 from the USA and 16 from India. In addition to the exhibition of films in public cinemas, there are frequent showings of educational and instructional films organized in schools and for adult groups by the government information services. Educational and documentary films are also shown by French and United States information services.

PROFESSIONAL TRAINING

University courses in journalism are offered at Saigon and Dalat.

VIETNAM (Democratic Republic of)

Population	21 154 000
Area	158 750 sq. km.

PRESS

Newspapers	Dailies 50*

RADIO

Total receivers	510 000† estimated in use
Receivers per 1000 people	24†

*Approximately.
†Wireless only.

PRESS

The largest of the three main dailies published in the capital, Hanoi is the official organ of the leading political party, with a reported circulation of 100 000 copies per issue. The others are the workers' party organ. circulating 30 000 copies, and a governmental paper (25 000 copies) carrying official announcements and national and international news but no editorials. There are also many regional and local daily newspapers and bulletins (between 40 and 50).

The non-daily papers, published twice weekly and weekly by local party organizations throughout the country, are mainly concerned with local conditions and events, but rural readers also see the Hanoi and main provincial papers which are regularly posted on village notice-boards. A special peasant-agricultural newspaper, circulating over 20 000 copies per issue, is published twice weekly in Hanoi.

Periodicals – largely based in Hanoi, though smaller journals are produced in the provinces – are mostly published under official auspices. They include special publications for various readerships (youth, women, military personnel) as well as literary, cultural, professional and technical journals. A leading political monthly publishes 50 000 copies per issue. In addition to the Vietnamese-language press, there are several officially produced journals with editions addressed to foreign readerships in English, French, Spanish and Russian.

NEWS AGENCIES

The official wire service is the Vietnam Thong Tin Xa, or Vietnam News Agency (VNA), founded in 1946 and government owned and operated. In addition to its Hanoi headquarters, it has offices in Paris, Peiping and Vientiane. News is received from Hsinhua and TASS and from the agency's own correspondents at home and abroad. Teletype links are maintained from Hanoi with Moscow and with Peiping. VNA supplies the domestic press and radio with both national and international news and also issues more than 40 000 words daily in its international radio-teletype services to Europe and south-east Asia.

The Liberation News Agency (LNA), established by the party front organization, also supplies news to the domestic and foreign press.

CTK, Novosti and TASS have bureaux in Hanoi.

RADIO

The official broadcasting organization is the Voice of Vietnam which comes under the control of the Council of Ministers. From Hanoi it broadcasts on medium-wave and short-wave frequencies with transmission power of up to 100kW. There are also regional short-wave stations in Tay Bac and Viet Bac.

Two home-service programmes are broadcast in Vietnamese for 18 hours and 3 hours a day respectively, while a third is broadcast in minority languages for about 5 hours a day.

In addition to individual radio receivers, there are a number of wired relay systems serving villages, farms, factories, schools, hospitals, etc., thus reaching several million listeners.

The Voice of Vietnam's foreign service broadcasts daily in English (8½ hours), Khmer (3 hours), French and Laotian (2½ hours each), Indonesian, Japanese, Korean and Thai (2 hours each), Vietnamese (1¾ hours), and Cantonese and standard Chinese (1½ hours each).

TELEVISION

There is no regular public television service, though an announcement was published on 7 September 1971, concerning the establishment of a station.

FILM

The government-sponsored film industry produces documentaries, newsreels and some features, but the majority of films projected are imported from the USSR, the People's Republic of China and other countries.

Most showings are by mobile projection units of which there are several hundred in operation catering to overall annual audiences of many millions. No recent figures are available but, in 1963, fixed cinemas numbered about 50 and outdoor cinemas 11.

PROFESSIONAL TRAINING AND ASSOCIATIONS

Training courses are organized by the national journalists' association. A film school founded in 1958 in Hanoi offered two-year courses in script writing, photography, acting and other technical skills.

YEMEN (Arab Republic of)

Population	6 060 000
Area	195 000 sq. km.

PRESS

Newspapers	Dailies 3, Non-dailies 1

RADIO

Transmitters	Long/medium-wave 3, Short-wave 2
Total receivers	250 000 estimated in use
Receivers per 1000 people	41

PRESS
Two daily newspapers are published in the capital, Sana'a, and one in Taiz where a fortnightly political and social affairs newspaper is also published. All are in Arabic. An officially sponsored printing and publishing company in the capital produces a number of periodical publications.

NEWS AGENCIES
The Saba News Agency, founded in 1970, has its headquarters in Sana'a. MENA and TASS have offices in Sana'a.

RADIO
The government station, Radio Sana'a, with 3 medium-wave transmitters (two of 10kW and one of 60kW) and 2 short-wave transmitters (5 and 25kW), broadcasts a home service in Arabic for about 14 hours daily

FILM
Imported feature films are shown in fixed and mobile cinemas.

PROFESSIONAL TRAINING
There is a radio-telecommunications college in the republic.

YEMEN (People's Democratic Republic of)

Population	1 510 000
Area	287 683 sq. km.

PRESS

Newspapers	Dailies 4, Non-dailies 5
Total circulation	Dailies 29 000
Copies per 1000 people	Dailies 19

RADIO

Transmitters	Long/medium-wave 2, Short-wave 1
Total receivers	80 000 estimated in use
Receivers per 1000 people	53

TELEVISION

Transmitters	5
Receivers	25 000 estimated in use
Receivers per 1000 people	16

PRESS

All daily newspapers are published in Arabic in the capital, Aden, with circulations ranging from 1500 to 10 000 copies per issue. Two are sponsored by the government through the Ministry of Information.

Non-daily general interest papers include the Sunday edition of the largest daily and one other weekly in Arabic, two weeklies in English and a bilingual monthly newspaper for the armed forces. With the exception of a weekly published in Mukalla, all non-dailies are based in Aden.

The broadcasting service publishes a weekly magazine, the Ministry of Information a cultural monthly (2500 copies) and there is another independent monthly; all are in Arabic. An oil-company magazine appears in English and Arabic.

NEWS AGENCIES

The Aden News Agency has its head office in the capital. Services of major foreign agencies are received.

RADIO

The government broadcasting service, financed from state funds and commercial advertising, is responsible for all radio and television broadcasting.

Radio programmes are broadcast from Aden for 76 hours a week in Arabic on medium waves (one 50kW transmitter) and short waves (one 7.5kW transmitter).

TELEVISION

The first telecasts from Aden were made in 1964. With stations at Al-Airahr, Al-Bargh and Ga'ar, plus two low-power satellites, the government television service now broadcasts for 4½ hours daily in the evenings. In addition, special programmes are broadcast to schools for 2½ hours weekly. The definition system used is 625 lines.

FILM

Most of the country's cinemas are in Aden, which has 9 fixed cinemas – 6 showing mainly Arabic-language films, 2 mainly Western and 1 Indian films.

PART SIX

EUROPE

Albania
Andorra
Austria
Belgium
Bulgaria
Czechoslovakia
Denmark
Faeroe Islands
Finland
France
German Democratic Republic
Germany (Federal Republic of) and West Berlin
Gibraltar
Greece
Holy See
Hungary
Iceland
Ireland

Italy
Liechtenstein
Luxembourg
Malta
Monaco
Netherlands
Norway
Poland
Portugal
Romania
San Marino
Spain
Sweden
Switzerland
Turkey
United Kingdom
Yugoslavia

ALBANIA

Population	2 230 000
Area	28 748 sq. km.

PRESS
Newspapers	Dailies 2, Non-dailies 10
Total circulation	Dailies 130 000, Non-dailies 140 000
Copies per 1000 people	Dailies 58, Non-dailies 63

RADIO
Transmitters	Long/medium-wave 11, Short-wave 8
Total receivers	170 000 estimated in use
Receivers per 1000 people	76

TELEVISION
Transmitters	1
Receivers	3000 estimated in use
Receivers per 1000 people	1

FILM
Cinemas	Fixed 93
Total seating capacity	23 700
Seats per 1000 people	11
Total annual attendance	8 400 000*
Annual visits per capita	4

*For fixed and mobile cinemas.

PRESS

The two dailies, both organs of political parties, with circulations of 100 000 and 30 000 copies respectively, are published in the capital, Tirana, as are several twice-weekly and weekly papers. Other non-dailies and periodicals are published in district centres, mostly under the auspices of ministries, trade unions, the state university, etc. Periodicals total around 50 titles including some in Arabic, Chinese, English, French, Italian and Russian.

NEWS AGENCIES

The government-controlled Albanian Telegraph Agency (ATA· Agjensia Telegrafike Shqijetare), founded in 1945, is the sole distributor of domestic and foreign news. ATA has close relations with Hsinhua and also has arrangements for foreign news with other agencies. With headquarters in Tirana, ATA also has branches in district centres. Foreign agencies represented in Tirana include BTA and Hsinhua.

RADIO
The Radiodifuzion i Television e Shqipërisë, established in 1944, is the state radio and broadcasting system. It broadcasts a home service for 18½ hours a day on medium and short waves with transmitters of 50, 100, 240 and 500kW in Tirana. In addition, the service is relayed by wire in the Tirana area and to factories, mines and clubs throughout the country. Local stations in Kukës, Shkodër, Korçe and Gjirokastër, all operating medium-wave transmitters, are on the air for about 6 hours daily.

Radio Tirana's overseas programmes are broadcast for 487 hours a week in 17 languages (Albanian, Arabic, Bulgarian, Czech, English, French, German, Greek, Hungarian, Indonesian, Italian, Polish, Portuguese, Romanian, Russian, Serbo-Croat and Spanish) and are beamed to all parts of the world. Radio Tirana also relays Radio Peking's external service at various hours of the day in Czech, Polish, Italian, Serbo-Croat and Turkish.

TELEVISION
Television programmes, first broadcast in 1961 from Tirana's experimental transmitter (625 lines), are now on the air for 3 hours a day, three days a week.

FILM
The film industry is nationalized, and a few films are produced. Imported films are shown in the 93 fixed cinemas (seating 23 700 persons) and by 69 mobile projection units.

PROFESSIONAL TRAINING AND ASSOCIATIONS
There is a union of Albanian journalists and a union of writers and artists, both of which publish professional periodicals.

ANDORRA

Population	20 000
Area	453 sq. km.

RADIO
Transmitters	Long/medium-wave 1, Short-wave 1, VHF—FM 2
Total receivers	7500 (licences)
Licences per 1000 people	375

TELEVISION
Receivers	1900 estimated in use
Receivers per 1000 people	95
Licences per 1000 people	375

FILM

Cinemas	Fixed 7
Total seating capacity	2900
Seats per 1000 people	145
Total annual attendance	300 000
Annual visits per capita	15

PRESS

No newspapers are published in Andorra, a small principality between the French and Spanish frontiers under the joint sovereignty of the President of the French Republic and the Spanish Bishop of Urgel. French and Spanish and other foreign newspapers are the main printed sources of foreign news. One locally produced periodical circulating 5000 copies per issue appears twice monthly in French, Spanish and Catalan. Six other periodicals and one sports annual are published in Catalan or Catalan and Spanish.

RADIO

Andorra has two privately owned radio stations, Radio Andorra and Sud Radio, both of which derive their revenue from advertising. Radio Andorra, with a medium-wave transmitter of 300kW and a short-wave transmitter of 25kW is on the air for 21 hours a day, broadcasting in French, Spanish and English to France and Spain during the day (the station has headquarters in Toulouse and Barcelona) and, by short-wave relay, to the rest of Europe from 21.00 to 24.00 hours.

Sud Radio, formerly known as Radio des Vallées d'Andorre, has headquarters in Andorra and offices in France (Paris and Toulouse). With one 300kW medium-wave transmitter, soon to be augmented by another of 600kW, and one FM transmitter, Sud Radio broadcasts for 147 hours a week to listeners in the principality and in the south of France. Programmes consist mainly of light entertainment (78 hours a week), broadcasts for women (24 hours) and young people (15 hours), news and information (13 hours), advertising (10 hours), classical music, theatre and literature (5 hours), educational programmes for children (2 hours) and religious broadcasts (1¼ hours).

TELEVISION

Andorra has no television station of its own but reception conditions are good for French television Channels 1 and II and Channel 1 of the Spanish television system.

No licence is required for television receivers.

FILM

There is no local film production. Andorra imports about 700 long feature films each year, about 150 of which are of French origin. The remainder is composed of American films with soundtracks dubbed in Spanish, and Spanish films. The few documentary films imported are French.

AUSTRIA

Population	7 490 000
Area	83 849 sq. km.

PRESS

Newspapers	Dailies 31, Non-dailies 125
Total circulation	Dailies 2 460 000*
Copies per 1000 people	Dailies 328*

RADIO

Transmitters	Long/medium-wave 142, Short-wave 2, VHF–FM 222
Total receivers	2 153 556 licences
Licences per 1000 people	287

TELEVISION

Transmitters	322
Receivers	1 695 378 licences
Licences per 1000 people	226

FILM

Cinemas	Fixed 835
Total seating capacity	276 500
Seats per 1000 people	37
Total annual attendance	28 500 000
Annual visits per capita	4

*Copies printed.

PRESS

Austria has one of the world's oldest continuously published daily newspapers, founded in 1703. The main press centre today is Vienna, with nine dailies with a combined circulation of 1 759 000. Newspapers are also published in Graz, Salzburg, Innsbruck and smaller provincial towns, most papers devoting a considerable proportion of space to foreign news.

In 1972, a total of 2624 periodicals were published, 72 in 14 minority and foreign languages. Of this total, 946 were issued 8 to 12 times a year, 611 either quarterly or twice yearly, 384 from 5 to 7 times a year, 32 once a year or less and the remainder more often than monthly. The total number of copies printed was 2.3 million.

Austria is an important producer of newsprint, only about half of which is required for domestic consumption. Exports for 1970 amounted to 91 131 metric tons.

NEWS AGENCIES

The national news agency is the Austria Presse Agentur (APA), a cooperative jointly owned by daily newspapers and the Austrian broadcasting service. It has its headquarters in Vienna and bureaux in Salzburg, Linz, Graz, Innsbruck, Klagenfurt and Eisenstadt, employing 143 correspondents and 160 part-time correspondents in the principal European countries and in the USA, Australia and Canada.

APA distributes daily an average of approximately 40 000 words in German, fairly evenly divided between national and international news, to 24 newspapers and to the national radio and television stations. Other services offered include features, photos, telephone news bulletins (7 bulletins daily) and a video-television service for private subscribers. In addition to government departments, political and community organizations, APA has about 450 private subscribers for its commercial services. Transmission of news is largely effected through leased networks.

APA receives AP and Kyodo news services and has exchange arrangements with Reuters, AFP, TASS and other European national news agencies, and with the News Agency of the Associated Israel Press (ITEM).

Reuters, UP, AFP, AP and TASS maintain bureaux in Vienna, while several other agencies are represented by correspondents.

RADIO

Osterreichischer Rundfunk (ORF), a state-owned corporation, is the national radio and television broadcasting organization, financed by licence fees, commercial advertising revenues and (for short-wave radio broadcasting only) government subventions.

There are three national radio programmes, the home and regional programmes being broadcast on medium-wave and FM transmitters and the third (all stereo) on FM only, giving radio coverage to over 90% of the population. The total weekly broadcasting time for national services is 688 hours, including light entertainment (275 hours), news and information (144 hours), arts, literature and science (137 hours), advertising (58 hours), broadcasts for special audiences (39 hours), education (15 hours) and broadcasts to ethnic minorities (8 hours).

In addition, the external short-wave service, with 100kW transmitters, broadcasts programmes in English, French, Spanish and German beamed to Europe, north and South Africa, the Middle East, the Americas, Asia and Australia.

The production of radio receivers in Austria meets the country's needs.

TELEVISION

Regular television programmes were first broadcast in Austria in 1956. Like radio, the television service is operated by ORF. With a complex network of powerful stations and auxiliaries, it potentially covers 85% of the population of this mountainous country.

Two programmes are broadcast (the second being on the air for 4 hours five evenings a week) totalling 87½ hours a week including 45 hours of local origin. Classified by content, programmes consist of news and information, sports, etc. (29 hours a week), light entertainment (19 hours), cultural programmes (16 hours), educational (10 hours), broadcasts for special audiences (7 hours), advertising (2½ hours) and language and other courses (1 hour). Special morning programmes are broadcast for schools (4½ hours) and for shift workers.

Television programmes are exchanged on a regular basis with the European Broadcasting Union (for newsreels), and with the Federal Republic of Germany and Switzerland (other programmess).

FILM

With annual totals of 7 35mm features, including 4 coproduction (1970) and 14 short documentaries in 1972, Austrian film production is on a rising trend after a decade averaging only 3 or 4 features a year – though it is still far from the feature production of the fifties, which fluctuated between 20 and 37 films a year. This improvement is due partly to government encouragement to the industry, in the form of financial aid and an annual documentary prize, partly also to the growing demand for documentaries for television showing.

Instructional and educational films are produced by a specialized centre run by the Ministry of Education, with separate departments for school and university films, which also maintains an extensive library of films and projection equipment for loan or rental. Various other institutions in Austria are concerned with the production and promotion of educational and scientific films.

In 1972, 432 feature films were imported: from the USA (132), the Federal Republic of Germany (128), Italy (56), France (37), the UK (30), the USSR (7), Japan (5) and other countries. A few documentary films were also imported. Annual cinema attendances have decreased over a decade from 106.5 million in 1960 to less than a third of that number in 1971. Over the same period, the number of cinemas has dropped from 1244 to 835. The country's one drive-in can accommodate over 1000 cars. There are 35 mobile projection units in operation.

PROFESSIONAL TRAINING AND ASSOCIATIONS

There are no formal schools of journalism in Austria, but journalists and other media personnel can receive training either on the job or by taking the four-year PhD courses available at the mass communication research institutes at the Universities of Vienna and Salzburg. In 1969, 25 students graduated from these courses.

Internal press control, particularly with regard to professional ethics, is exercised through the Austrian Press Council, on which newspaper publishers and journalists are equally represented.

There is an association of publishers of periodicals, another of newspaper publishers, and seven different associations of journalists. Branches of the film industry and professions are represented by five associations.

BELGIUM

Population	9 726 000
Area	30 513 sq. km.

PRESS

Newspapers	Dailies 55, Non-dailies 107
Total circulation	Dailies 2 450 000*

RADIO

Transmitters	Long/medium-wave 8, Short-wave 5, VHF–FM 17
Total receivers	3 560 000 licences
Licences per 1000 people	366

TELEVISION

Transmitters	27†
Receivers	2 289 000 licences
Licences per 1000 people	235

FILM

Cinemas	Fixed 740
Total seating capacity	400 000
Seats per 1000 people	41
Total annual attendance	31 567 000
Annual visits per capita	3

*For 45 titles only.
†Including 10 auxiliary transmitters.

PRESS

There are 45 main daily newspapers in Belgium, 14 of which together publish more than 40 additional regional editions, some of the latter being considered separate publications for statistical purposes. Of the main papers, 11 are published in Brussels, 9 in Antwerp, 4 in Ghent, 3 each in Charleroi, Liège and Verviers, and the remainder in eight other centres.

Two other factors characterize the daily press in Belgium: its division into two main language groups and the extension of various forms of cooperation among press enterprises. The Walloon (French-language) press accounts for 29 of the main daily titles, with an aggregate circulation of some 1.25 million copies, and the Flemish (Dutch) press 16 titles with an almost equal circulation total of 1.2 million copies. One German-language newspaper circulating 15 000 copies is also published in the frontier-region town of Eupen. Three of the Flemish dailies and 1 published in French have circulations exceeding 200 000 copies; 4 other dailies circulate over 100 000 copies each.

Concentration is most marked in the Flemish press where four companies publish 12 of the principal dailies, representing a total circulation of around 1 million copies. In the French-language press, 25 dailies circulating about 1.1 million copies are published by 12 separate enterprises in which one or other of seven financial groups has a controlling interest. Cooperation within these various forms of association may extend from the pooling of technical, distribution or advertisement services to formal editorial links and, even, joint publication of whole news, editorial or feature sections.

A daily official gazette (bilingual) and 7 specialized dailies, all in French, are also published in Brussels. There are 107 non-daily general interest papers, 16 financial journals, 81 agricultural journals and 17 dealing with the arts and literature. Two illustrated Sunday papers circulate 309 000 and 230 000 copies respectively.

A total of 4952 periodicals, including the non-daily newspapers, consists of 2570 titles in French, 1695 in Dutch, 85 in English and 42 in German. Main subject categories are technology, crafts, etc. (759 titles), political and economic sciences (585 titles), law, administration and social welfare (500) and general interest periodicals (452). Highest periodical circulation figures are recorded for a women's magazine circulating 1 160 000 copies of its French edition in France and a combined total of 400 000 copies of its French and Flemish editions in Belgium. Other high circulations include several women's magazines (one circulating over 277 000 for both its language editions), a family magazine (177 000) and a radio–television weekly (160 000).

Of the total annual consumption of newsprint (179 700 metric tons) for Belgium and Luxembourg combined in 1970, domestic production accounted for 95 000 metric tons.

NEWS AGENCIES

The national agency, Agence Belga (Agence Télégraphique Belge de Presse, or Agentschap Belga), founded in 1920 as a private joint-stock company and now 80% owned by the Belgian newspapers, is an entirely independent body administered as a cooperative.

With headquarters in Brussels, Agence Belga has branch offices in Antwerp and 106 permanent correspondents and 242 part-time correspondents throughout the country, but it no longer maintains offices abroad. It distributes a full range of both Belgian and foreign news, including economic, sports and photographic services. The foreign-news service is based mainly on the world services of AFP and DPA, both of which are represented in Belgium by Belga. Other agencies, such as ANP, Efe and AZP act as correspondents and supply news to Agence Belga. News is exchanged with all of these agencies.

Belga's daily average output in French and Flemish is 10 000 words of national and local news and over 27 000 words of foreign news, plus 5000 words on national and foreign sports news. Subscribers to these services include 23 daily newspaper publishers and national and commercial radio and television stations, as well as the Belgian Parliament, government departments, industrial and banking firms, embassies and one large hotel.

News transmission is effected by teleprinter with full-time leased cable circuit and radio, telex, telephone, etc.

Brussels is also the headquarters of another agency, the Centre d'Information de Presse (CIP), a Catholic organization created in 1934, which distributes national and international religious news in both French and Flemish. CIP has exchange agreements with other national news agencies and with NCNS. Its services are used by over 17 newspapers and the national radio and television organizations.

A third agency is Inbel, founded in 1942 as part of the government's Institut Belge d'Information et de Documentation.

RADIO

Radio and television broadcasting in Belgium is carried out by Radio-diffusion-Télévision Belge/Belgische Radio en Televisie (RTB/BRT), a public organization established by law in May 1960. It consists of three autonomous institutes responsible respectively for French-language broadcasts, Flemish broadcasts, and the Institute of Common Services which is also responsible for German-language and foreign broadcasting. Financial resources are derived mainly from receiver licence fees, government subventions and taxes on recordings. There is no commercial advertising.

Each domestic-language network consists of three programmes broadcast on medium-wave transmitters of up to 150kW in power and 17 FM stations and relays: a first (national) programme of wide audience appeal; a second (regional) programme carrying frequent news bulletins and continuous light entertainment, linked with the regional stations; and a third programme broadcasting more classical music. A German-language programme is broadcast by an FM transmitter located near Liège. A total weekly broadcasting time of 425 hours includes cultural programmes (111 hours), news and information (102 hours), light entertainment (94 hours), broadcasts to special audiences (83 hours) and to ethnic minorities (30 hours) and broadcasts to schools (4 hours). All programmes can be received in all parts of the country.

The international service, with 100kW short-wave transmitters, is on the air almost continuously, broadcasting in French, Dutch, English and a number of African languages to five areas in Africa, North and South America, Europe and the Far East. Much of the programme material is relayed from RTB/BRT domestic stations.

While there is no commercial radio in Belgium, broadcasts from commercial stations in adjacent countries are readily received, particularly Radio Luxembourg (which has studios and offices in Brussels) and Europe No. 1, based in Saarbrücken.

TELEVISION

Television broadcasts began in 1953. The RTB/BRT French and Flemish institutes are responsible for their respective television programmes, each broadcasting two programmes on 19 principal and 10 auxiliary transmitters. About 40 hours a week are now broadcast in colour (PAL system) on 625 lines. Television broadcasts cover 98% of the population.

Total broadcasting time of 100 hours a week in 1971 consisted of news and information (31 hours), programmes for special audiences (22 hours), educational programmes (20 hours), light entertainment (13 hours), cultural programmes (9½ hours) and advertising (4½ hours). School television programmes in both languages are designed for various age groups and cover a wide range of subjects, including zoology, geography, languages and literature. Both institutes send out printed schedules and other materials to assist schools in planning and utilizing the programmes to the best advantage.

Imported programmes and exchanges through Eurovision account for 26% of RTB and 39% of BRT transmissions. The European Broadcasting Union's technical and engineering offices are in Brussels, and Belgian stations serve as important links in the Eurovision network. RTB/BRT also exchanges programmes on a smaller scale through Intervision and Mondovision.

Private interests operating under licence distribute television programmes by cable to some 200 000 subscribers in a dozen localities. In addition to the 2 national programmes, programmes of 2 Dutch, 2 French, 3 German and 1 Luxembourg networks are relayed.

FILM

By 1970, the film industry, which receives various forms of state encouragement, had increased its annual production of feature films from an average of 5 around the year 1960, to a total of 12, of which 4 were coproductions. Short-film production totalled 78 titles, some of these being produced by the Ministries of Education and Agriculture, the Institut National de Cinématographie Scientifique and the Université Libre de Bruxelles. Imported feature films total about 360 a year.

Total annual cinema attendance has dropped over the last ten years from some 80 million to around 31.5 million, while the number of commercial cinemas has halved. Of the total number, about 20 are 16mm cinemas and there is one drive-in.

PROFESSIONAL TRAINING AND ASSOCIATIONS

At university level, the Université Libre de Bruxelles offers a two-year course leading to a 'licence' in journalism, as does the University of Ghent which also awards a doctorate in information sciences, while the Catholic University of Louvain has a four-year 'licence' course in social communication. The Institut des Hautes Études des Communications Sociales (Tournai) and the journalism section of the Katholieke Vlaamse Hogeschool voor Vrouwen (Antwerp) also have four-year diploma courses. Evening courses are available in Brussels at the Institut pour Journalistes de Belgique, while on-the-job training, for a year, may be taken at the Institut Belge d'Information et de Documentation.

Film and television training is offered at the University of Louvain, the National School of Architecture (Brussels), the Institut des Hautes Études des Communications Sociales (Tournai) and at specialized technical institutes in Brussels. The Solvay Institute attached to the Université Libre de Bruxelles carries out research into the educational and cultural implications of films.

The Institut Belge d'Information et de Documentation (INBEL) provides training for information officers from many countries.

Professional associations for the press in Belgium include 7 for publishers, 17 for journalists and 1 for foreign correspondents. The film industry has 2 general professional associations, 2 for producers, 2 for cinema technicians, 2 for writers and performers, 2 for distributors and 1 for exhibitors. Radio programme personnel and radio journalists each have their own association while there is a single organization for film and television technicians and programme personnel.

BULGARIA

Population	8 580 000
Area	110 912 sq. km.

PRESS

Newspapers	Dailies 13, Non-dailies 33
Total circulation	Dailies 1 765 000, Non-dailies 919 700
Copies per 1000 people	Dailies 206, Non-dailies 107

RADIO

Transmitters	Long/medium-wave 12, Short-wave 4, VHF–FM 10
Total receivers	2 301 462 licences
Licences per 1000 people	268

TELEVISION

Transmitters	118
Receivers	1 285 848 licences
Receivers per 1000 people	150

FILM

Cinemas	Fixed 3106
Total seating capacity	707 100
Seats per 1000 people	82
Total annual attendance	110 217 600
Annual visits per capita	13

PRESS

Eight of Bulgaria's daily newspapers are published in the capital, Sofia. The most important are the organ of the Communist Party (circulation 650 000), the Fatherland Front daily (circulation 150 000) and the youth newspaper (circulation 170 000). Non-dailies include 23 appearing two or three times weekly. Weeklies include 1 paper in Armenian and 1 in Greek.

Some 1700 magazines and other periodicals are published in Bulgaria, with a total circulation of over 8 million copies. Most publications show a steady increase in circulation. A number of periodicals are also published in foreign languages – Russian, English, Turkish, Greek and Armenian. Some foreign-language magazines are exported. There is no private ownership of publications.

Main subject categories are political sciences (144 titles circulating 1 073 000 copies per issue), technology (226 titles, 568 970 copies), medicine (116 titles, 407 300 copies), general readership (84 titles, 216 600 copies), agriculture, etc. (72 titles, 481 200 copies), administration and communications (62 titles, 175 000 copies), natural sciences (55 titles, 80 900 copies), arts and architecture (49 titles, 280 700 copies), education (42 titles, 327 700 copies), etc. In addition, 15 periodicals for young people circulate 1 440 000 copies per issue.

NEWS AGENCIES

The national news agency is the state agency Bulgarska Telegrafitscheka Agentzia (BTA) founded in 1898.

BTA has 20 correspondents in the principal departmental centres of the country and 20 foreign correspondents in Algiers, Athens, Belgrade, Berlin, Beirut, Bonn, Bucharest, Budapest, Cairo, Havana, London, Moscow (2), New York, Paris, Peking, Prague, Rome, Tokyo and Warsaw. The BTA staff numbers 485 persons.

The daily output of BTA is 15 000 words on national and regional affairs, in Bulgarian and 100 000 words on international affairs in Russian, English, French, German, Spanish, etc. BTA also issues 4 articles daily for the use of local newspapers, 2 on home affairs and 2 on international affairs. It receives 24 000 photos a year from other countries and sends an equal number abroad. BTA has exchange agreements with 35 foreign agencies including TASS, AFP, Reuters, AP, UPI, CTK, DPA, Tanjug, MENA, PRELA, etc.

Besides daily bulletins intended for newspapers, radio, television and the state public institutions, BTA publishes 4 weekly bulletins – on foreign affairs, on literature, art and culture, on science and technology and an illustrated bulletin of general interest.

Sofia-Press Agency (Sofiapres), founded in 1967 by the Union of Bulgarian Writers, the Union of Bulgarian Journalists and the Union of Bulgarian Artists, is an autonomous body preparing articles and films about Bulgaria for the foreign press, radio and television and publishing houses. It publishes books, pamphlets, magazines, journals, bulletins, articles in English, French, Italian, German, Russian, Spanish, Czech, Arabic, Esperanto, and newspapers in English and German.

Permanent bureaux are maintained in Sofia, Varna, Plovdiv, Burgas, Turnovo, and 2 abroad in Moscow and Vienna. The agency staff consists of 425 persons working in Bulgaria and 5 abroad.

Sofia press has exchange agreements with Novosti, PAI, Pragopress, Budapresse, PRELA, Orbe-Press, Kimon and THA.

RADIO

The Committee for Television and Radio of the Council of Ministers of the People's Republic of Bulgaria operates 12 medium-wave transmitters (up to 250kW), 4 short-wave transmitters (up to 120kW) and 10 FM transmitters. Revenue is derived from licence fees, a state subsidy, tape-recording services and sales from the committee's official radio and television journal.

There are two home-service programmes in Bulgaria, the first broadcasting for 20 hours daily and the second for 16 hours daily.

The foreign service's programmes in Bulgarian, Arabic, English, Esperanto, French, German, Greek, Italian, Serbo-Croat, Spanish and Turkish are beamed to European countries, Africa and North and South America.

Radio 'Rodina', operated by the Slav Committee of the Union of Bulgarian Writers and the Union of Bulgarian Journalists, broadcasts daily from 12.00 to 23.00 hours, its programmes being for Bulgarians living abroad. It is financed by the sponsoring organizations.

TELEVISION

Bulgarian Television, which is also run by the Committee for Television and Radio of the Council of Ministers, began operating experimentally in 1954, and regularly in 1959. Programmes are broadcast from Sofia, Botev Peak, Slantcher Birag, Vidan Peak, Kirdjali, Varna and Petrohan.

The television broadcasting time is 6 hours a day. The programme distribution is as follows: news and politics 27%, cultural programmes 16% (literature 3%, music 5%, variety 4.5%, plays 3.5%, films 16%, programmes for children and youth 15%, educational programmes 12.5%, sport 6.5%, Intervision programmes 6% and advertising 1%.

Bulgarian Television is a member of Intervision and regularly exchanges programmes with Soviet Television and the television of the socialist countries, the Arab States and a considerable number of western countries. It uses material supplied by UPI, Visnews and Eurovision (through Intervision).

The definition system used is 625 lines. Colour television, introduced in 1972, uses the SECAM system.

An annual licence fee is payable.

FILM

The film industry in Bulgaria is nationalized. The production, distribution, import and export of all films are controlled by Bulgarian Cinematography.

Bulgaria produces all types of films. The national production of long films increased from 1 in 1950 to 11 in 1960 and to 22 (including 17 features) in 1972. Some 370 short films of all kinds (documentary, instructional, entertainment and cartoons) were produced in 1972, plus a number of newsreels.

Import totals for 1972 were 150 long films and 310 documentaries. The long films were imported from the USSR (46), Czechoslovakia (14), the German Democratic Republic (11), Hungary, Poland and Yugoslavia (9 each), Romania (6), the Democratic Republic of Korea (2), and the Democratic Republic of Vietnam, Cuba and Mongolia (1 each). Documentaries were imported mainly from the USSR (162), Poland (44) and Czechoslovakia (26).

PROFESSIONAL TRAINING AND ASSOCIATIONS

A four-year course at the Department of Journalism, Faculty of Letters, Sofia University, has a present enrolment of 895 students at all levels. There is a research institute of cinematography and radio in Sofia, founded in 1953. The Union of Bulgarian Journalists has its own statutes.

CZECHOSLOVAKIA

Population	14 500 000
Area	127 869 sq. km.

PRESS

Newspapers	Dailies 27, Non-dailies 105
Total circulation	Dailies 4 059 100, Non-dailies 852 000
Copies per 1000 people	Dailies 280, Non-dailies 59

RADIO

Transmitters	Long/medium-wave 55, Short-wave 32, VHF–FM 32
Total receivers	3 858 000 licences
Receivers per 1000 people	266

TELEVISION

Transmitters	680
Receivers	3 305 441 licences
Licences per 1000 people	228

FILM

Cinemas	Fixed 3469
Total seating capacity	992 765
Seats per 1000 people	68
Total annual attendance	98 362 000
Annual visits per capita	7

PRESS

Of the daily newspapers, 9 are published in Czech in Prague and 9 (1 in Hungarian and 8 in Slovak) in Bratislava. More than 1300 other periodicals, apart from newspapers, are also published, with a total circulation of over 20 million copies. In addition, factories and firms often produce their own daily or weekly news-sheets, dealing mainly with local issues.

The most influential and widely read newspapers are the Prague dailies. The principal daily, the organ of the Communist Party of Czechoslovakia, produced both in Prague and Bratislava, has a nation-wide circulation of over 900 000 copies. The leading provincial daily, the organ of the Slovak Communist Party, appears in Bratislava with a circulation of 270 000. Other important dailies are organs of trade unions, both Czech and Slovak, and of the People's Party and the Socialist Party. In all, 16 dailies and 65 non-dailies are published in Czech and 10 dailies and 30 non-dailies in Slovak.

General readership periodicals – including several women's magazines – number 232, circulating over 4 million copies per issue. Other important subject categories are entertainment and sports (55 titles, 2.5 million copies), arts and architecture (47 titles, 1.5 million copies), agriculture, etc. (57 titles, over 1 million copies), technology (74 titles, 723 000 copies), natural sciences (60 titles, 110 000 copies), commerce (56 titles, 304 000 copies), and medicine (55 titles, 215 000 copies). In addition, 33 young people's periodicals circulate almost 2.7 million copies per issue, 231 business house journals (internal) circulate 1.2 million copies, and 3 illustrated humorous magazines circulate 790 000 copies.

NEWS AGENCIES
The governmental news agency Československá Tisková Kancelář (CTK) founded in 1918, with headquarters in Prague, distributes news to the press, radio and television of the country. It derives its revenue from a state subsidy and from subscriptions from newspapers, radio and television stations.

CTK has 14 permanent bureaux within the country and 30 abroad. Staff, including permanent correspondents, number more than 1 600 persons.

CTK daily news service includes over 40 000 words in Czech and over 40 000 words in Slovak, 18 000 in English, 10 000 in French, 10 000 in Spanish and 8000 in Russian. Besides, the agency publishes bulletins in English, French, Spanish, Russian, German, Czech and Slovak, averaging together over 200 000 words on a daily basis.

CTK has over 50 agreements with foreign news agencies, papers, etc., for the purchase, sale or exchange of news and photos, in particular with TASS, PAP, BTA, MTI, ADN, DPA, AFP, ANSA, Reuters, UPI and AP.

Pragopress, CTK's feature service, supplies information about Czechoslovakia to the foreign press and publishing houses, on a commercial basis.

Tatrapress (the Slovak Cultural and Tourist News Agency), situated in Bratislava, distributes material about Slovakia abroad.

RADIO
The state-owned Czechoslovak Radio's total broadcasting time is 675 hours a week, including light entertainment (164 hours), arts, letters and science (128 hours), information and news (75 hours), programmes for special audiences (52 hours), education (49 hours), programmes for ethnic minorities (49 hours), advertising (4 hours) and other programmes (153 hours).

The foreign service, using 120 and 200kW short-wave transmitters, is broadcast daily to Europe (18 hours), Africa (2 hours), south Asia (1½ hours), the Far East and Australia (2 hours) and to Latin America (2½ hours) and North America (2 hours), in English, French, German, Italian, Spanish, Arabic, Portuguese, Czech and Slovak.

TELEVISION
Experimental broadcasts were initiated from Prague in 1953, and regular programmes in 1954. The state-owned Czechoslovak Television now operates 17 principal and 663 auxiliary transmitters which cover 100% of the population.

Of 76 hours a week total broadcasting time, 32 hours are devoted to information, 24 hours to arts, letters and sciences, 15 hours to advertising and announcements, 8 hours to light entertainment and 5 hours to films.

An annual licence fee is payable.

Czechoslovak Television, a member of Intervision, imports television programmes from countries of eastern Europe, as well as from the USA, the UK, the Federal Republic of Germany, France, Belgium, Italy, Switzerland Denmark and Finland. Television programmes are regularly exchanged with socialist countries.

The definition system used is 625 lines. Experimental colour transmissions, using the SECAM system, are being carried out. Television equipment and receivers are locally produced.

FILM

The Czechoslovak film industry is nationalized. In 1972, 36 feature films and 13 full-length documentaries were produced. Czechoslovakia produces yearly more than 1200 short films; a total of 1214 in 1972 included 840 entertainment films, 86 documentaries and 288 instructional films.

Four long films were coproduced, 2 with the USSR and 2 with the German Democratic Republic.

Imports in 1972 totalled 142 long and 106 short films: from the USSR (28 long and 39 short), the German Democratic Republic (17 and 4), France (14 and 2), Poland (13 and 19), the USA (13 and 1), Italy (10 long), Hungary (9 and 10), Bulgaria (7 and 3) and other countries (31 and 28). Of the total number of cinemas, 1387 are equipped for 16mm projectors. There are 16 mobile 16mm units as well.

PROFESSIONAL TRAINING AND ASSOCIATIONS

The Faculty of Social Sciences and Journalism of the University Charles of Prague has an enrolment of over 1200 students. Over 140 students follow the five-year course of studies in journalism at the Comenius University, Bratislava. There are three professional associations: the Union of Czech Journalists (3000 members), the Union of Slovak Journalists (1300 members) and the Journalists' Centre of Czechoslovakia (4200 members).

DENMARK

| Population | 4 966 000 |
| Area | 43 069 sq. km. |

PRESS	
Newspapers	Dailies 53
Total circulation	Dailies 1 808 000*
Copies per 1000 people	Dailies 364*

RADIO	
Transmitters	Long/medium-wave 6, Short-wave 1, VHF–FM 24
Total receivers	1 636 000† licences
Licences per 1000 people	329†

TELEVISION

Transmitters	25‡
Receivers	1 411 000† (licences)
Licences per 1000 people	284†

FILM

Cinemas	Fixed 350
Total seating capacity	138 200
Seats per 1000 people	28
Total annual attendance	21 022 000
Annual visits per capita	4

*Copies printed.
†Including combined radio and television licences.
‡Including 17 auxiliary transmitters.

PRESS

Denmark has a large number of daily newspapers, with a very high readership rate. In spite of rising production costs and the trend towards fewer but larger papers, circulation figures have slightly increased (in 1960, there were 86 dailies circulating 1 617 000 copies).

Copenhagen, the capital, has 9 dailies (5 with Sunday editions), of which the largest, founded in 1749, circulates some 175 000 copies on weekdays and 335 000 on Sundays. Four others have circulations in excess of 100 000. Of the provincial dailies, 2 published in Aarhus circulate over 60 000 copies each while 10 others have circulations between 20 000 and 46 000. Most of the important papers depend on financial support from organizations, or income from other activities. Thirty general interest non-dailies have a combined circulation of 2 882 000 copies; these include 14 Sunday newspapers totalling 1 294 000 copies.

The periodical press, with almost 5000 titles, is largely based in Copenhagen. The main subject categories are literature (1538 titles), history (435), technology, industry and trade (312), natural sciences (261), economic and political sciences (219) and law, public administration and social services (212). Illustrated magazines, a number of which belong to four large publishing concerns, have circulations of up to 370 000, the highest figures being recorded by family, women's and radio and television journals.

The provincial press exercises considerable influence on political affairs. Generally, these newspapers consist of 6–8 pages and give good coverage to national and international news. The cartoon is a particularly notable feature of Danish newspapers, and comments with effective satire on the news and politics of the day.

A cooperative distribution organization owned and controlled by leading Copenhagen newspapers handles almost all newspaper distribution in the country, serving 7000 news-stands and nearly 4 million subscribers yearly.

NEWS AGENCIES

The principal agency in Denmark is the Ritzaus Bureau (RB), with headquarters in Copenhagen. Its daily output for 58 newspapers and one radio and television station averages 50 000 words in Danish, 20 000 of which are devoted to world news. RB has exchange agreements with AFP and Reuters, as well as with STT-FNB, DPA and other European agencies.

The major political parties also possess their own news agencies and, in addition, there are a number of small, mainly specialized agencies.

AFP, AP, Reuters, UPI and TASS maintain bureaux in Copenhagen. A duplex circuit, inaugurated by AP in 1961, links Denmark, Norway and Sweden, permitting the AP bureau in each country to file directly into the European trunk wire without impeding reception of incoming news.

RADIO

Danmarks Radio, a public corporation, has the monopoly of sound and television broadcasting. It is governed by a radio council of 19 members, 10 of whom are appointed by parliament to represent listeners and viewers. Its revenue is derived entirely from licence fees; there is no advertising.

The three domestic programmes and the regional radio programmes are broadcast from 1 long-wave transmitter (150kW), 5 medium-wave and 30 FM transmitters. The total number of broadcasting hours per week is 245, 153 of which are devoted to light entertainment, 62 to news bulletins, public affairs, sports, etc., 25 to programmes for special audiences, and 5 to educational programmes.

The Voice of Denmark, operating a 50kW short-wave transmitter has carried out regular broadcasts to foreign countries since 1948, with daily programmes in Danish, Spanish and English beamed to Greenland, the Far East, Asia, Africa and North and South America.

TELEVISION

A regular television service has been operated since 1954 by Danmarks Radio, on the same basis as sound radio; its revenue comes from licence fees, and there is no advertising. It operates eight principal and 22 auxiliary transmitters. The broadcasting time of 38 hours a week includes news, public affairs, sports, etc. (14 hours), cultural and scientific programmes (9 hours), broadcasts for special audiences (6 hours), light entertainment (4 hours), educational programmes (2 hours) and broadcasts for ethnic minorities (2 hours). Television programmes are imported from many countries, and programmes are exchanged on a regular basis with all the Nordic countries and member countries of the European Broadcasting Union. Programmes in colour (PAL system) are broadcast for 16 hours a week.

FILM

The Danish film industry produced 18 feature films in 1972. Production facilities, particularly those of the five principal studios, are both modern and extensive. Government encouragement of the industry is given through the Danish Government Film Foundation, financed by a 15% tax on all cinema tickets, which allocates grants and guarantees loans for the production of Danish films, maintains a film school and offers various forms of general assistance.

A total of 270 feature films imported in 1972 came from the USA (130), the UK (40), France (20), Italy (25) and the Federal Republic of Germany (15).

Annual cinema attendance has halved over the last ten years, and the number of cinemas has dropped by about 100. The country's one drive-in accommodates 900 cars, and there are 10 mobile cinema units serving about 342 000 spectators annually.

SPACE COMMUNICATIONS
Denmark is linked to the Atlantic Intelsat system through the common Scandinavian earth station at Tanum (Sweden). Danmarks Radio is responsible for the country's satellite broadcasting activities.

PROFESSIONAL TRAINING AND ASSOCIATIONS
Education in journalism is provided at the Danish School of Journalism at Aarhus, offering a 2½-year course at upper-secondary level, a 6½-month course at lower-secondary level, and a three-month course open to journalists from other Nordic countries. For the press, there are 16 associations, of which 7 are for publishers, 4 for editors, 5 for journalists (including 1 for radio) and 1 foreign press association. Film associations number 8, for producers, cinema technicians, writers, performers, distributors and exhibitors. Sound and vision broadcasters also have an association.

FAEROE ISLANDS

Population	41 000
Area	1399 sq. km.

PRESS

Newspapers	Non-dailies 7
Total circulation	Non-dailies 20 000
Copies per 1000 people	Non-dailies 488

RADIO

Transmitters	Long/medium-wave 1, VHF–FM 3
Total receivers	15 000 estimated in use
Receivers per 1000 people	366

FILM

Cinemas	Fixed 9
Total seating capacity	1292
Seats per 1000 people	31
Total annual attendance	272 675
Annual visits per capita	7

PRESS
There are no daily newspapers. All non-dailies are published in the capital, Thorshavn, except for one provincial weekly. There are 41 other periodical publications in Faeroese circulating 85 800 copies, and one in Danish circulating 500 copies.

NEWS AGENCIES
There is no national news agency. Journalists correspond with Ritzau, Reuters, AP, TT, NTB and DPA and with some Scandinavian newspapers.

RADIO
The government broadcasting organization, Utvarp Foeroya, financed from receiver licence fees, operates one medium-wave transmitter (5kW) and three FM transmitters. Programmes, in Faeroese, are broadcast for 33 hours a week and consist of light entertainment (18 hours), news and information (8 hours) and programmes for special audiences (7 hours).
    A receiver licence fee is payable.

FILM
Documentaries are produced by the government from time to time. A total of 269 feature films were imported in 1970; from the USA (194), the UK (22), Denmark (20), France (17), Italy (7), the Federal Republic of Germany (5) and Sweden (4).

PROFESSIONAL ASSOCIATIONS
An association, founded in 1952, with a membership of 14, groups together journalists, editors and radio personnel.

FINLAND

Population	4 630 000
Area	337 009 sq. km.

PRESS

Newspapers	Dailies 60, Non-dailies 173
Total circulation	Dailies 1 970 000
Copies per 1000 people	Dailies 425

RADIO

Transmitters	Long/medium-wave 13, Short-wave 5, VHF–FM 79
Receivers	1 895 869 licences
Licences per 1000 people	409

TELEVISION

Transmitters	70
Receivers	1 182 957 licences
Licences per 1000 people	255

FILM

Cinemas	Fixed 318
Total seating capacity	97 000
Seats per 1000 people	21
Total annual attendance	10 000 000
Annual visits per capita	2

PRESS

Of Finland's dailies, 52 are in Finnish and 8 in Swedish, the latter all published in towns on the west and southern coasts. Helsinki, the capital, has 10 dailies including 2 in Swedish. Other important publishing centres are Tampere, Turku and Vaasa, each of which has 2 dailies in Finnish and 1 in Swedish.

With the exception of an independent daily published in Helsinki and circulating 260 000 copies per issue, circulation figures range from a few thousand for small provincial papers to 95 000 and 90 000 respectively for the leading dailies in Tampere and Turku. But the provincial press is growing, and the last ten years have seen some of the larger provincial dailies double their circulations while the big Helsinki morning papers have shown little or no variation, despite the fact that they are now widely available on the day of publication, even in remote parts of the country.

Annual subscriptions account for 90% of newspaper sales in Finland, and only 2 of the 4 main afternoon papers have reasonably large single-copy sales.

There are 139 non-dailies appearing weekly and 63 more frequently. Of these, 17 are published in Swedish. Periodicals number 2029 of which 138 are in Swedish and 134 bilingual Finnish/Swedish. Several of the popular weeklies have circulations in excess of 200 000 copies.

One of Europe's largest newsprint producers, Finland exports over 90% of its output.

NEWS AGENCIES

The national news agency in Finland is Suomen Tietotoimisto-Finska Notisbyrån (STT-FNB), founded in 1887. It is owned cooperatively by some of the leading newspapers and the state radio and television corporation; its headquarters are in Helsinki and it has eight permanent bureaux in other parts of Finland, as well as the branches in Brussels and Moscow in conjunction with the other Scandinavian news agencies. The only national agency distributing international news, STT-FNB averages 11 000 words daily on national affairs and 9000 on foreign affairs. Subscribers to this service, which is distributed in Finnish and Swedish, include 63 newspapers, the state radio and television station and six telephone associations.

Exchange arrangements exist with Reuters, AFP, DPA, TASS, TT, NTB and RB. In addition, there is a limited exchange service with ADN, Tanjug and other

European national agencies. The main facilities used for the transmission of news are public telecommunications services, permanently leased networks and the Scanplex system between Helsinki and the Hague (Netherlands) in cooperation with the other Scandinavian agencies.

Other Finnish domestic news agencies are Tyovaën Sanomalehtien Tieto-toimisto, founded in 1920, Taloudellineor Tietotoimisto, founded in 1947 and specializing in economic affairs, and Uutiskeskus/Maaseutulehtien Liitto, owned by an association of 14 newspapers.

RADIO

The radio organization, Yleisradio, is a state monopoly which is also responsible for the national television service. Radio broadcasting is financed from receiver licence fees. There is no advertising.

Yleisradio's 1 long-wave, 12 medium-wave, 1 short-wave and 79 FM transmitters equip the two country-wide Finnish-language networks and a third regional network for the Swedish-speaking coastal areas of the country. Each of these networks is on the air for about 18 hours a day and, during the day-time, they transmit partly the same programme. Regional programmes, divided into 16 regional units, and accounting for about 10% of total transmission time are broadcast on the Swedish network and one of the Finnish networks. Main programme categories are news and information (37% of total time), light entertainment (31%), cultural and scientific broadcasts (20%), programmes for special audiences (8%) and education (2.3%). School broadcasting amounts to nearly 10 hours a week, of both original and repeat transmissions. Almost half are language courses. About 90% of the country's schools have receiving sets.

The foreign service, with short-wave transmitters of up to 100kW at Pori, is beamed to Europe and North and South America in Finnish, Swedish and English. Of the 2300 hours of foreign broadcasts every year, about 400 hours are specially produced, the remainder consisting of national programmes.

Most of the radio receivers in use are of Finnish manufacture. Practically every household has a radio set, and about 90% of these are FM receivers.

TELEVISION

The Finnish television service is operated through Yleisradio, the state monopoly, which derives revenue from television licence fees and a limited amount of advertising. In addition to the national network, which practically covers the country, there is a second channel now reaching 65% of the population and scheduled to provide full national coverage by the mid-seventies. The two networks consist of 40 main stations and 30 auxiliary transmitters.

The combined programme time for the two television channels exceeds 70 hours per week. Approximately 60% of all programmes are of national origin; of these some 10% are in Swedish (the Swedish programmes are transmitted over the second network). Main programme categories are news and information (42%), cultural and scientific programmes (32%), entertainment (11%), broadcasts for special audiences (7%) and education (7%). School programmes are broadcast for 5 hours a week, about 70% of the schools having television receivers.

About 20% of the total programme time is bought by a private commercial company, Mainos-TV-Reklam, that rents Yleisradio's studios and channels and uses them for commercial television, broadcasting entertainment programmes and advertising, but no news. The company is not licensed but operates as a subsidary production unit to Yleisradio.

Imported programmes account for about 46% of programme time, of which 40% is of USA origin, 30% from the UK and 10% from socialist countries.

Finland is a member of both Eurovision (EBU) and Intervision (OIRT). Besides the daily exchange of news material, Finland transmitted over 250 hours of programmes from Eurovision countries in 1970; about half were of Scandinavian origin (Nordivision), and 10 hours were of Intervision production. Finland's own contribution to Nordivision amounted to nearly 70 hours, to other Eurovision countries about 15 hours and to Intervision countries almost 30 hours.

All stations use the 625-line definition. Television sets are owned by more than 80% of Finnish households. The majority of sets used are manufactured in Finland. There is some broadcasting in colour.

FILM

During the last decade, the country's annual film production averaged around 11.4 new domestic feature films and some 150 short films. Figures for 1972 were 8 features and 161 short films completed by about 30 independent producers. No newsreel films have been produced since 1964.

From 1961 to 1970, approximately 300 feature films were projected annually, 96% of which were foreign. Of the 333 feature films exceeding 1000m in length, and the 339 of less than 1000m, released in 1972, some 126 long and 156 short films came from the USA; other sources were the UK (24 and 25), the USSR (25 and 19), Italy (25 and 17), the Federal Republic of Germany (18 and 5), Sweden (11 and 7), the German Democratic Republic (5 and 6) and other countries (75 and 80).

In 1969, the Finnish Film Foundation was established by the Ministry of Education and three central film organizations. The purpose of the foundation is to give subsidies and loans for domestic film production, to encourage the export of Finnish films to organize Finland's participation at international film festivals and to import foreign films of high artistic value, and children's films, and to assist educational research. The foundation receives 4% of cinema ticket sales.

The development of educational films, once widespread, has ceased since school television programmes began during the sixties. The production of children's films is on the decline. Annual attendance in cinemas has decreased from 28 million in 1960, to little more than a third of that number. There are five mobile projection units.

SPACE COMMUNICATIONS

Finland owns a quarter of the joint ground station at Tanum (Sweden) that has been in service since August 1971 for the reception of Intelsat and Eurovision signals for Denmark, Finland, Norway and Sweden.

PROFESSIONAL TRAINING AND ASSOCIATIONS

Training courses in journalism are provided at the University of Helsinki, the University of Tampere and the Swedish School of Social Work and Local

Administration (Tampere) where candidates, graduated from high school and/or holding a college matriculation examination, may complete a course of study ranging from 2 to 4 years.

Film and television professionals are trained at the Finnish Institute of Industrial Arts, Helsinki (about 10 students a year graduate from its four-year course in camera art).

Professional press associations include 5 associations of publishers, 10 associations of journalists (including the Union of Journalists in Finland whose code of ethics is observed by other professional groups) and 1 foreign correspondents' association. There are 8 film associations, grouping together producers, technicians, performers, writers, distributors and exhibitors, and 4 associations of broadcasting personnel.

The Council for Mass Media, founded in 1969 at the instigation of interests including the Newspaper Publishers' Association, the Periodical Publishers' Association, the Local Newspaper Publishers' Association, the Union of Finnish Periodical Journalists, the Union of Radio and Television Journalists and the Union of Journalists in Finland, is supported by the national broadcasting organization and the commercial-television firm, Mainos. Its chairman, two members representing the fields of publishing, broadcasting and journalism, and four lay members, hear complaints concerning material published or broadcast by the mass media, methods of information gathering, and the freedom of the press and broadcasting.

FRANCE

Population	51 720 000
Area	547 026 sq. km.

PRESS

Newspapers	Dailies 106, Non-dailies 934
Total circulation	Dailies 12 066 800, Non-dailies 26 429 400
Copies per 1000 people	Dailies 233, Non-dailies 511

RADIO

Transmitters	Long/medium-wave 55, Short-wave 21, VHF—FM 218
Total receivers	16 160 000 (licences)
Receivers per 1000 people	312

TELEVISION

Transmitters	1961*
Receivers	12 600 000 (licences)
Receivers per 1000 people	244

FILM

Cinemas†	Fixed 4237
Total seating capacity	2 012 017
Seats per 1000 people	39
Total annual attendance	174 900 000
Annual visits per capita	3

*Not including certain low-power repeaters serving small audiences.
†Figures refer only to 35mm cinemas.

PRESS

Of France's 80 morning and 26 evening general interest daily newspapers, 12 (including one in English) are published in Paris, printing a total of 4.3 million copies. The remainder appear in over 60 provincial and regional centres throughout the country, including Marseille with 4 and Bastia, Lille and Saint-Étienne with 3 each. Six dailies circulating 187 000 copies appear in languages other than French.

Over the last ten years, while overall printing and circulation figures for dailies have shown a slight increase, the actual number of titles has decreased by about 20, either because papers have gone out of business or because they have been absorbed by other publishing concerns. Concentration of ownership has also affected about 25 other dailies which continue publication under changed ownership or control. In certain areas, cooperative arrangements for group publication of classified advertisements and common use of production and distribution facilities have created further links which may eventually affect the editorial independence of the papers concerned.

Increases in printing and circulation figures have been most notable in the regional and provincial press which now includes 13 dailies printing over 200 000 copies per issue, 1 of these with over 650 000 copies and 4 more with over 400 000.

One Paris daily prints over 1.2 million copies (in 5 or 6 editions) and 3 others print 890 000, 530 000 and 470 000 copies per issue respectively. Among those with increased circulations are the 2 papers devoting most space to national and world affairs, one of these having more than doubled its circulation in the past ten years. Increases have also been recorded by a Catholic daily, the official organ of a political party and 2 popular morning papers.

Some of the larger dailies have their own correspondents abroad and one has an agreement with leading English, Italian and Federal German dailies for the exchange of feature material and the joint preparation and publication of special articles and supplements of European interest.

Paris also has 5 specialized dailies: 2 leading with economic affairs plus some general news, 2 sporting and 1 medical.

The non-daily newspaper press includes 20 titles published two or three times a week and 480 weeklies, most of these serving smaller communities with local news; 184 non-dailies circulating 773 500 copies appear in languages other than French.

For periodicals, in contrast to the daily press, the last decade has been one of continuing expansion. Circulation figures in 1970 for a recorded total of 10 532 titles amounted to almost 164 million copies, headed by the 3800 general readership periodicals circulating over 31 million copies per issue. Among the 21 women's magazines, 10 titles circulated over 500 000 copies each, while 2 of the 5 journals carrying weekly radio and television programmes each topped 2 million. Religious and theological journals (715 titles) together circulated more than 7.3 million copies, and those dealing with law, public administration and social welfare (948 titles) circulated 17 million copies. In addition to these, there were also 3764 school, parish, children's and house magazines circulating 34.2 million copies per issue.

NEWS AGENCIES

Paris is the headquarters of the Agence France-Presse (AFP), established in 1944 in succession to the Agence Havas (founded in 1835) and other smaller, wartime agencies. AFP is both a world news agency and a French national agency and operates as an autonomous public body under statutes laid down by law in 1957. It is governed by an administrative council composed of 8 representatives of the daily newspapers, 2 representatives of radio and television broadcasting (ORTF), 3 persons representing the public service as users of the agency and 2 members of the agency itself, including a professional journalist.

AFP, which has 17 bureaux located in the main French towns and 92 foreign branches, employs a total of 1126 permanent staff in France and 822 abroad, in addition to its part-time correspondents (1060 at home and 357 abroad). News is received under subscription or exchange agreements from agencies based in 46 different countries.

The agency's own daily output of French and foreign news includes 394 000 words in French, 72 000 in English, 35 000 in German, 45 000 in Spanish, 20 000 in Arabic and 30 000 in Portuguese. Other services offered are features, photographs and audio-radio bulletins. Direct subscribers to these services include 379 newspapers and 154 radio and television stations. Indirectly, AFP's general service is received by 12 400 foreign newspapers and radio and television stations subscribing through 61 national agencies. Various services are also supplied to 590 diplomatic, governmental and industrial and commercial subscribers.

AFP's international cable network works 24 hours per day, linking Paris with the principal provincial and European centres. The English service on this network covers London, Copenhagen, Oslo, Helsinki, Stockholm and Moscow; a German service goes to Sarrebruck, Bonn, Dusseldorf and Berlin, while the French service, divided into five channels, links Paris with Berne, Milan, Rome, Madrid, Lisbon, Brussels, The Hague, Luxembourg, Prague and Budapest. AFP's transatlantic cable links Paris with New York, Washington and Montreal; the African cable links Paris with Rabat, Tunis and Algiers.

In its South and central American services, operating since 1950, AFP transmits news for 18 hours a day with six telex services in Spanish covering Brazil, Argentina and Uruguay, and central America via Fort de France. The Far East receives a service in English for 20 hours per day.

Private agencies include the photo and feature agency, Paris Internationale Presse (PIP), founded in 1886; the specialized news and feature agency Agence Parisienne de Presse (APP) founded in 1949; the Agence Centrale Parisienne de

Presse (ACP), founded in 1951, which works with Reuters, Maghreb Arabe Press and the Algerian Press Service; the Agence Coopérative Interrégionale de Presse (ACIP); and a number of photo agencies such as the Agence d'Illustrations pour la Presse (AGIP), founded in 1935, which has permanent offices throughout the world.

AP, Reuters, UPI, TASS, Kyodo and Hsinhua maintain bureaux in Paris, and almost all other news agencies and leading foreign newspapers and magazines are represented by correspondents. Many foreign photo agencies have offices in Paris, including Keystone Photographic Agency.

RADIO

The Office de Radiodiffusion-Télévision Française (ORTF) is a government-sponsored organization set up under public ownership to provide a national radio and television broadcasting service meeting the public's needs for information, culture, education and entertainment. It is governed by an administrative council, the members of which represent the state, viewers and listeners, professional organizations and ORTF staff. The Director-General, who is also chairman of the council, is appointed by the government. Revenue is derived from receiver licence fees, subventions and some commercial advertising (on television only).

The domestic radio broadcasting service, covering 99% of the population, consists of three main networks, of which the largest is France-Inter (with its alternative programme Inter-variétés). Operating high-powered long-wave and short-wave transmitters, at Issoudun, along with over 100 other medium-wave and FM transmitters, France-Inter is on the air for 24 hours a day, broadcasting news, information and entertainment programmes designed for the general listening public. Its programmes are relayed by the regional stations – Île de France (Paris and Rouen), Bordeaux, Clermont, Grenoble, Lille, Limoges, Lyon, Marseille, Montpellier, Nancy, Nice, Radio Armorique (Rennes), Strasbourg and Toulouse, operating medium-wave transmitters of up to 300kW – all of which also originate programme material of their own.

The other two networks reach more limited and specialized audiences. France-Culture, operating 17 FM transmitters and occasionally relayed by regional stations, is on the air for 17 hours a day. Its programmes, some of which are experimental, cover the arts, literature and contemporary problems. France-Musique, with 70 FM transmitters equipped for stereophony, broadcasts music and related spoken programmes, also for 17 hours daily.

Educational broadcasts include programmes for schools (four afternoons a week) on France-Inter's FM transmitters, and France-Culture, adult education on the regional networks and Radio Sorbonne's direct or recorded broadcasts of university lectures on its own 10kW medium-wave transmitter. Most of these programmes are produced by educational authorities by special agreement with ORTF.

Total broadcasting time on domestic radio stations averages 500 to 600 hours a week, comprising (in 1971) arts, letters and science (215 hours), light entertainment (182 hours), education (111 hours), news and information, sports, etc. (81 hours), broadcasts for special audiences (7 hours) and (non-brand) advertising (35 minutes)

ORTF conducts regular exchanges of radio programmes with other countries, either through bilateral agreements, the international broadcasting unions of the Communauté Radiophonique des Programmes de Langue Française. About 2000 hours of ORTF recorded programmes (news, light entertainment and music) are broadcast by stations in 50 countries, plus about 25 hours' direct relays. Foreign programmes broadcast by ORTF in 1970 totalled 614 hours of direct relays and 628 hours of recorded material, the latter coming from 32 countries including the Federal Republic of Germany (131 hours), Belgium (74 hours), the USSR (73 hours), Switzerland (55 hours) and Italy (30 hours).

The overseas broadcasting service, largely subsidized by the Ministry of Foreign Affairs and governed by an interministerial committee responsible for general policy, broadcasts about 200 programme hours a week beamed to Europe, Africa, north Africa and the Middle East, south-east Asia, the Far East and Latin America. French-language programmes are either relayed from France-Inter or especially produced for the overseas services; others are in foreign languages, including Arabic, Czech, English, Greek, Hungarian, Kabyle, Polish, Portuguese, Romanian, Russian, Serbo-Croat, Slovakian and Yiddish. The overseas service has 5 short-wave transmitters (four of 100kW and one of 4kW) at Allouis and 16 short-wave transmitters (100kW) at Issoudun.

Five commercial radio stations based on the periphery of the French national territory (one each in the Federal Republic of Germany, Luxembourg and Monaco and 2 in Andorra) broadcast commercially sponsored French-language programmes for up to 22 hours a day, designed specifically for listeners in France. The French-language programmes of both the Swiss and Belgian national broadcasting services are also clearly received in many parts of the country.

An annual licence fee is payable for radio, or radio and television combined, exemption being granted to certain categories of persons and institutions.

TELEVISION

Television is operated by the Office de Radiodiffusion-Télévision Française (ORTF) on the same basis as radio broadcasting. Regular telecasts in France date from 1935. There are now three national channels covering 98%, 95% and (initially) 26% respectively of the population· Channel I (819 lines), with 66 main transmitters and 1380 low-power relay stations· Channel II (625 lines), with 97 main transmitters and 710 low-power relay stations· and Channel III (625 lines), with 6 main transmitters (when the channel began operating in 1973). Colour (SECAM system) was introduced in 1967 and is now carried on Channels II and III.

Total broadcasting time for Channels I and II averaged about 108 hours a week in 1972, including news and information and sports (42%), films and cinema programmes (15%), light entertainment (10%), documentaries (9%), youth programmes (5%), drama and theatre (4.5%), music (3%) and religious services (2.5%). These figures do not include school and adult educational programmes supplied by various educational bodies, which average 15 hours a week, or commercial advertising for which seven 15-minute periods a day are allowed in programme schedules. Channel III broadcasts for 27 hours a week.

The exchange of television programmes with other countries is carried out as for radio, either by bilateral agreement or as part of the exchange programmes of international broadcasting unions, principally the European Broadcasting Union

(Eurovision). In 1972, over 94 hours of ORTF broadcasts were transmitted direct on Eurovision. During the same year, 312 programmes received as direct broadcasts from abroad were retransmitted on French television, the principal originating countries being Italy, Japan, Mexico and the UK.

Television film exports exceeded 10 000 antenna hours in 1972. These included 2000 hours of newsreels exported to 76 different countries, along with information and cultural programmes exported to 90 and 27 countries respectively. About 65% of French television-programme exports go to African countries, 15% to the Middle East, 7% to Latin America, 5% to the Far East, 4% to western Europe and 1% to eastern Europe.

Feature films broadcast on French television in 1972 totalled 370 titles, of which 179 were French, 131 from the USA and 60 from other countries.

Studies are being carried out under ORTF auspices to consider the local distribution of television programmes by cable, possibly in cooperation with the local press and other community interests.

FILM

The production of feature films rose to 169 in 1972 (71 entirely French, 49 with majority French participation and 49 with majority foreign participation). Of these, 166 were in colour including four for wide screen. Commercial short films produced numbered about 350. Foreign films imported in 1971 included 331 features (139 dubbed in French and 113 in original versions) and 118 short films (of which 35 were dubbed).

The total annual attendance figure for standard cinemas — 354.6 million in 1960 — had declined to less than 50% of that figure by 1971. Over the same period, the number of standard cinemas dropped from 5800 to 4237. These figures do not include (substandard) projection points which, from a total of 11 000 with an annual attendance of 18 million persons in 1960, dropped to only 2480 in 1971 with an annual attendance of 2 million persons. In 1971, there were also six drive-in cinemas with a total capacity of 6448 cars.

Government encouragement for the film industry in France is the province of the Centre National de la Cinématographie (CNC) which comes under the authority of the Ministry of Cultural Affairs. Its functions include the preparation of draft legislation concerning the industry, the coordination and rationalization of the industry's operations, the verification of film-financing estimates and returns, the allocation and administration of state aid to producers, the promotion and development of the non-commercial film sector, the organization of professional training facilities and the maintenance of film archives. Recent policy trends have included the establishment of an experimental and research group to identify and encourage new creative talent, improved cooperation between cinema and television, the promotion and distribution of films for children, adoption of a socially relevant policy for the establishment of cinemas in populous zones, further promotion of experimental and art films and the establishment of film clubs.

SPACE COMMUNICATIONS

France has a satellite earth station at Pleumeur-Bodou in Brittany, operated by the Ministry of Posts and Telecommunications. The two antennae at Pleumeur-

Bodou receive and transmit television broadcasts via Atlantic Intelsat satellite. A further Atlantic Intelsat earth station was opened in the French overseas department of Martinique in 1971.

PROFESSIONAL TRAINING AND ASSOCIATIONS

France is relatively well provided with training facilities for journalists. The Centre de Formation des Journalistes (Paris), founded in 1945, offers advanced two-year diploma courses, for which the total enrolment in 1970 was 110 students, of whom 60 graduated in that year. The École Supérieure de Journalisme (Lille), founded in 1924, offers a three-year course at university ('licence') level, from which 40 of a total enrolment of 152 students graduated in 1970. The Centre Universitaire d'Enseignement du Journalisme, at Strasbourg, awards a professional diploma in journalism, as well as academic degrees. The International Centre for Higher Studies in Journalism, founded in 1956 under UNESCO auspices and also at the University of Strasbourg, offers training for teachers of journalism, and refresher courses for both teachers and practising journalists from any country. Other universities with 'licence'-level journalism courses are Bordeaux and Tours, while university institutes at Paris, Bordeaux, Dijon and Toulouse offer research and training in various communication fields. The Institut Français de Presse is a teaching, research and documentation centre for the mass media, attached (since 1971) to the University of Paris and awarding diplomas and 'licence' and doctorate degrees in information sciences. A private school of journalism founded in 1899 in Paris, offering a two to three-year diploma course, has an annual intake of 300 students.

Radio and television training is provided by ORTF at its own Paris centre, and by four other centres in the Paris area. There are two main film training instututions, both in Paris: the Lycée Technique Cinématographique et de Photographie, under the Ministry of Education, offers technical training while the Institut des Hautes Etudes Cinématographiques, with more emphasis on the artistic and cultural approach, is jointly financed from a public fund, the Ministry of Cultural Affairs' budget and ORTF.

Professional association include organizations of publishers of national, regional and specialized newspapers and periodicals, journalists (grouped in two major federations), radio and television journalists, technicians and engineers and other broadcasting personnel, film-makers and cinema technicians.

GERMAN DEMOCRATIC REPUBLIC

Population	17 040 000
Area	107 771 sq. km.

PRESS

Newspapers	Dailies 40, Non-dailies 612*
Total circulation	Dailies 7 235 710, Non-dailies 1 970 000
Copies per 1000 people	Dailies 425, Non-dailies 116

RADIO

Transmitters	Long/medium-wave 35, Short-wave 10, VHF—FM 61
Total receivers	6 050 000 (licences)
Licences per 1000 people	355

TELEVISION

Transmitters	455
Receivers	4 820 000 (licences)
Receivers per 1000 people	283

FILM

Cinemas	Fixed 1197
Total seating capacity	354 964
Seats per 1000 people	21
Total annual attendance	81 500 000
Annual visits per capita	5

*Newspapers issued in factories only.

PRESS

Over a quarter of the total circulation of the daily press is accounted for by 9 Berlin dailies, 2 of which, published by the Socialist Unity Party (which controls the majority of the country's newspapers), circulate 800 000 and 500 000 copies respectively. Dailies are also published in 18 provincial centres: 3 (in Halle, Leipzig and Magdeburg) with individual circulations of over 300 000 copies, 4 more with over 200 000 copies (in Dresden, Erfurt, Rostock and Potsdam) and the remainder circulating fewer than 85 000 copies per issue. German is the language used by all the dailies except 1 (5000 copies per issue) published in the Sorb language in Bautzen (Saxony) to serve the Sorb minority in the area. All newspapers are owned by political organizations, trade unions, cultural associations, party committees, youth organizations, etc., and this is also the case with the periodical press.

The majority of non-daily newspapers are issued in factories, etc. The periodical press totals over 500 titles, with a combined circulation of 15.6 million copies per issue. More than half the monthlies together circulate 9.5 million copies. The principal subject categories are politics and society (100 titles circulating 2 807 000 copies), education (71 titles, 4 737 100 copies), health and welfare (56 titles, 613 600 copies), economics and industrial technology (100 titles, 1 758 000 copies), agriculture, etc. (37 titles, 857 400 copies), fashion and style of living (13 titles, 2 403 000 copies), sports and recreation (17 titles 1 184 000 copies) and culture (31 titles, 622 800 copies). In addition, 14 titles for young people circulate 3.9 million copies.

A state-owned publishing organization comprises publishing houses, printing offices, paper-mills, book-stores, distributing and import—export agencies, as well as film-distribution circuits, cinemas and theatres.

Newsprint production in 1971 totalled 96 800 metric tons and domestic consumption 83 400 metric tons.

NEWS AGENCIES

The national news agency is the Allgemeiner Deutscher Nachrichtendienst (ADN), founded in 1946 as a limited corporation and state owned since 1953, has headquarters in Berlin and 14 regional branches in the country. ADN also has branches in about 30 foreign countries, and correspondents in 10 other major foreign cities. A total permanent staff of over 1000 persons includes some with editorial responsibilities. News is received by contract from 65 foreign agencies, under exchange agreements.

ADN distributes daily services of 75 000 words in German, 7750 in English, 6500 in Spanish and 5000 each in French and Arabic; and weekly newsletters of 2000 words each in Russian and Greek and 1250 in Swedish, as well as special telephoto, feature and bulletin services. Since the agency has the sole distribution rights for all news by word and image in the country, its domestic subscribers include the whole of the press and the broadcasting media which are served by a full-time cable-teleprinter circuit and rotaprint service. Foreign subscribers are also served by full-time cable teleprinter, as well as by radio teleprinter and air-mail newsletters. Foreign agencies represented in the Democratic Republic include AGP, Agerpress, BTA, CTK, Hsinhua, INA, MENA, MTI, PAI, PAP, PRELA, Reuters, SANA, Tanjug and TASS.

RADIO

Radio broadcasting is controlled by the 12-member State Broadcasting Committee of the Council of Ministers.

The domestic radio service consists of four separate programmes. The national programme (Stimme DDR) is on the air for 24 hours a day, broadcasting on 1 long-wave transmitter (200/1000kW) in Berlin, 4 medium-wave transmitters (250kW) in Berlin, Burg, Schmerin and Suhl, 2 short-wave transmitters (5kW) in Berlin and 10 FM transmitters serving the larger population centres throughout the country. Radio DDR I, a 24-hour information and entertainment service with 12 medium-wave transmitters of up to 250kW and 9 FM transmitters throughout the country, also covers the entire population. Radio DDR II, with 13 FM transmitters in main population centres, is on the air for 14 hours a day, broadcasting a high proportion of current affairs programmes and also relaying DDR I programmes. Berlin is also served by Berliner Rundfunk, with 6 medium-wave transmitters (including one of 500kW) and 2 FM transmitters. Berliner Rundfunk programmes are also broadcast by the FM transmitters of nine other cities. All programmes are in German, with the exception of some special broadcasts on Radio DDR in Sorb, catering for the Sorb minority near the cities of Cottbus and Bautzen.

Radio Berlin International is the national external broadcasting organization and is equipped with 1 medium-wave transmitter (500kW) and 25 short-wave transmitters (5, 50, 100 and 250kW). Its European service is broadcast in English, French, Swedish, Danish and Italian for 7½ hours daily, while the overseas service, on the air for 34½ hours a day in eight languages (Arabic, English, French, German, Hindi, Portuguese, Spanish and Swahili), is beamed to eight areas in the Near East, Africa, Asia and the Americas.

Radio Volga, the station of the Soviet Armed Forces in Germany, operates a 200kW transmitter at Burg, broadcasting for 18 hours a day, of which 16 hours are relayed from Radio Moscow.

The number of radio receivers produced in the German Democratic Republic in 1970 totalled 807 000.

TELEVISION

The national television service, which began operating in December 1952, is financed by state funds and by licence revenue. It is controlled by the State Television Committee of the Council of Ministers and has a governing board consisting of a director of programmes, a chief commentator and six other members responsible for various programme fields.

Since 1969, two parallel programmes have been broadcast. The first, with 19 main transmitters and an extensive network of translators covering the entire country, is on the air for about 90 hours a week; the second, with main transmitters in nine cities and a smaller number of translators, reaching 75% of the population, is on the air for about 26 hours a week, of which about 8 hours are in colour (SECAM system).

Average weekly programmes include feature and documentary films (33 hours), news, current affairs and politics (23 hours), sports (13½ hours), announcements (11 hours), light entertainment (10 hours), economic, scientific and educational programmes (9½ hours), children's and youth broadcasts (9 hours), cultural and dramatic programmes (8 hours), agriculture (1½ hours) and informative advertising on community affairs and services (1½ hours). Some night programmes are repeated for shift workers in the day-time. During the school year, language courses are broadcast for about 5 hours a week and, in addition, there are 3 hours a week of Russian-language programmes in the evenings. About 32% of programmes are imported, the majority from the USSR.

DDR Television is a member of Intervision and (indirectly, since 1960) of Eurovision. Intervision programmes are received from seven other member countries and include sports, news and cultural broadcasts. In 1970, DDR Television supplied 23% of the programmes rebroadcast through Intervision, and eight programmes carried by Eurovision. The definition system used in 625 lines.

About 80% of households are equipped with television, the number of receivers having increased by more than 250% over the last ten years. Domestic production of sets is around 400 000 a year.

A combined radio and television licence fee is payable.

FILM

All film production is carried out by the state-owned organization Deutsche

Film AG (DEFA), under the Ministry of Culture, with its studios in Berlin. In 1972, 17 feature and short films were produced. Of these, seven were made in cooperation with Czechoslovakia, Poland, the USSR, Bulgaria and Romania. Film distribution is handled by a special unit of the national publishing organization. Also in 1972, 128 features were imported· from the USSR (32), other socialist countries (62) and other countries (34), and 40 documentaries from socialist countries.

In 1971, a total of 948 000 showings were given in both fixed cinemas and in the 400 village halls (with an overall seating capacity of 73 000) which are equipped and regularly used for public film projection. Open-air cinemas and showings by mobile units accounted for almost 15 million of the annual total visits. Attendances at all categories of cinema declined over the last decade, from almost 219 million in 1961 to little more than a third of that total.

PROFESSIONAL TRAINING AND ASSOCIATIONS

The first institute for the study of newspapers was set up at the University of Leipzig in 1916 and a chair of journalism was established in 1926. Renamed the Institute for Journalism and Newspaper Study after the Second World War, the institute became an independent faculty of journalism in 1954, and today – with a teaching staff of over 40 – offers four-year full-time and five-year correspondence courses and a wide range of research facilities. Since 1957, its courses have included on-the-job experience alternating with academic instruction. In addition, in Berlin, the Union of Journalists has its own school, as well as its special 'Solidarity School', founded in 1964, to provide training for journalists from developing countries. The University of Halle-Wittenburg has a film school, and there is also an advanced school in Potsdam-Baselburg, for directors, producers and other film personnel.

The Union of Journalists of the German Democratic Republic has regional branches throughout the country. There is also a foreign press association.

GERMANY (Federal Republic of) AND WEST BERLIN

Population	59 600 000
Area	247 973 sq. km.

PRESS

Newspapers	Dailies 1093, Non-dailies 93
Total circulation	Dailies 19 701 000, Non-dailies 4 918 000
Copies per 1000 people	Dailies 330, Non-dailies 82

RADIO
Transmitters	Long/medium-wave 52, Short-wave 21, VHF—FM 240
Total receivers	20 289 571 licences
Receivers per 1000 people	340

TELEVISION
Transmitters	958
Receivers	27 100 000 estimated in use
Receivers per 1000 people	455

FILM
Cinemas	Fixed 3171
Total seating capacity	1 279 861
Seats per 1000 people	21
Total annual attendance	149 800 000
Annual visits per capita	2

PRESS

The press in the Federal Republic of Germany is essentially regional and local, almost any town of any size having its own daily newspaper. Over 40 cities publish one or more dailies with circulation figures exceeding 100 000. This decentralization is one of the reasons for the large number of daily newspaper titles, but about half are subsidiary editions (with different mastheads, local news and advertising sections) of main papers published in larger centres.

The largest publishing centre is the city of Hamburg which accounts for more than a quarter of the national daily newspaper circulation. Two of its 4 dailies (a tabloid circulating 4.8 million copies and a more traditionally styled journal circulating 250 000 copies, both owned by the country's largest publishing concern), along with the leading Munich and Frankfurt dailies, can be considered as having national readerships. West Berlin, with a population of just over 2 million, has 5 dailies circulating a total of some 800 000 copies per issue.

Many newspapers still depend largely on subscriptions for their sales but the more popular papers are almost all bought at news-stands.

A number of dailies publish special Saturday issues; some may amount to 120 pages, of broadsheet size, much of the space being accounted for by advertising. Apart from these, there are few weekly newspapers (as distinct from magazines), the only 2 with national readerships being published in Hamburg, again by the country's largest publishing group (with circulation figures of 2 million and 340 000 respectively).

The weekly periodical press (other than newspapers) continues to flourish, and the estimated total of over 10 000 titles includes a dozen circulating over 2 million copies each: 8 mass-readership illustrateds, 2 women's magazines and 2 carrying television and radio programmes (1 selling 3.8 million copies per issue); the best-known weekly news magazine has a circulation of 900 000.

Concentration of press ownership — 40% of the country's daily newspaper circulation is accounted for by one enterprise and 70% of the periodical circulation by four large groups — has led to protective action by both the government and the industry, eg there are state credits for the modernization of newspaper plants, and cooperative arrangements for news-gathering and advertising services among smaller publishers.

Newsprint production in 1970 totalled 408 000 metric tons and consumption 1 077 300 metric tons.

NEWS AGENCIES

The Deutsche Presse-Agentur (DPA), founded as a private company in 1949, is the main news agency and one of the largest in Europe. With headquarters in Hamburg, it has 3100 correspondents at home and abroad, 39 bureaux in the Federal Republic and 52 bureaux in other countries.

DPA transmits daily about 100 000 words on national affairs in German and about 70 000 words on foreign affairs in German, English, French and Spanish. Subscribers to its news, features and photo services include radio and television stations and 1200 newspapers, as well as more than 100 agencies, broadcasting organizations and large newspapers abroad. DPA has exchange agreements with 52 international and national news agencies. It operates its own television information service, E-TE-S, which supplies newsfilm to both national and foreign stations.

The Vereinigte Wirtschaftsdienste (VWD), also founded in 1949, has headquarters in Frankfurt. It is a limited company jointly owned by DPA, Reuters and a holding company which represents the country's leading economic federations. VWD has a permanent staff of 300 (including correspondents), plus 50 part-time correspondents in the federal republic and 30 permanent staff members abroad. It supplies commercial services to some 5000 subscribers, including all newspapers and broadcasting stations in the country. Its services include 19 daily financial, commodity and general economic teleprinter services and three financial wireless services to private subscribers, market quotations by teleprinter daily to private subscribers, newspapers and radio stations, a daily foreign-trade paper, a weekly foreign-trade magazine and 25 daily bulletins of specified economic news. The daily output in German is approximately 40 000 words of national and local news and approximately 60 000 of foreign news. Its main facilities for news transmission are a leased teleprinter network, a leased wireless transmitter, telephone, mail and a public-telex network. VWD receives the overseas news services of Reuters, and exchanges news with Reuters, APA and ANP.

The Katholische Nachrichten-Agentur (KNA), a member of the International Federation of Catholic News Agencies, founded in 1952, with headquarters in Bonn and offices in six other German cities and in Rome, has 290 correspondents within the country and 60 abroad. It issues some 8000 words daily of domestic and foreign (special Vatican) news, in German, to more than 540 publications and broadcasting stations and some 3200 individual subscribers.

The Evangelischer Pressedienst (EPD), founded in 1908 and owned by the Protestant Press Association, has 25 correspondents in the country and 6 abroad, 21 part-time correspondents in Germany and 8 abroad. Overseas news is received through RNS. Its average daily output of national news in German is 6500 words. Subscribers include 137 newspapers, 13 radio stations, 10 television stations, Church offices and organizations and governmental and educational authorities concerned with Church affairs. EPD uses a leased wireless network, telex and newsletters for its transmission of news.

Other smaller or more specialized agencies include Dimitag (DMT), in Bonn, providing a domestic news service in German; its sister agency, Presseplan, which serves foreign subscribers in English, French, Spanish and Arabic; and Nordpress Verlag, in Hamburg and Bonn, providing news, features and photos especially on international affairs.

Foreign and world agencies represented in the federal republic include AFP, ANSA, Antara, AP, BTA, CTK, Jiji, Kyodo, MENA, Reuters, TASS and UPI.

RADIO

Broadcasting is coordinated by the Arbeitsgemeinschaft der öffentlich-rechtlichen Rundfunkanstalten der Bundesrepublik Deutschland (ARD) – a federal consortium founded in 1950 to safeguard the collective interests of member organizations and deal with common programme, legal, technical and management questions. Its members are the nine *Land* public broadcasting corporations: Bayerische Rundfunk (BR) in Munich, Hessischer Rundfunk (HR) in Frankfurt, Norddeutscher Rundfunk (NDR) in Hamburg. Süddeutscher Rundfunk (SDR) in Stuttgart, Südwestfunk (SWF) in Baden-Baden, Sender Freies Berlin (SFB), Radio Bremen (RB), Saarländischer Rundfunk (SR) in Saarbrücken, Westdeutscher Rundfunk (WDR) in Cologne; and the two federal public broadcasting corporations: Deutsche Welle (DW) in Cologne and Deutschlandfunk (DLF) in Cologne-Marienburg.

The nine *Land* broadcasting corporations were established by Act of Parliament or inter-state treaty of the *Länder* to provide a radio and television service to all areas of the federal republic, while the two federal broadcasting organizations were instituted by Federal Act of Parliament, to carry out radio broadcasts chiefly to areas outside the federal republic. They are all autonomous with regard to internal administration, statutes (in most cases) and budget, and each is responsible for its own programming. The *Länder* corporations finance their operations mainly from receiver licence fees and, to some extent, from advertising, while the federal organizations are largely financed out of federal government funds.

Each *Land* corporation broadcasts three programmes: the first, on medium waves, FM (including some stereo) and, sometimes, short waves, consisting in most cases of a round-the-clock service of news, information, music and general entertainment; the second (mainly FM), concentrating on classical music with news, cultural and educational programmes; and the third (also FM), largely constituting light music and entertainment with foreign-language programmes for the many immigrant workers employed in the federal republic. Both second and third programmes are used for the schools broadcasts prepared in consultation with the Ministries of Education and the teaching profession.

Programmes are regularly exchanged and relayed among the *Land* networks and with DW and DLF. Exchanges with foreign countries are effected through EBU or under agreements with broadcasting orgânizations. Commercial advertising is broadcast on all *Land* networks except NDR and WDR, for limited periods and at specified times of the day.

Deutschlandfunk (DLF), established by the federal government for the purpose of broadcasting 'to Germany and foreign countries in Europe', operates

1 long-wave (70kW) and 4 medium-wave transmitters (ranging up to 800kW). It broadcasts a German-language informative and cultural programme round the clock, and a series of 30- or 40-minute programmes nightly in each of 14 other European languages, along with German-language courses.

The federal government's short-wave service established specifically to broadcast 'to overseas countries' is Deutsche Welle (DW), which operates 13 transmitters of 100,250 and 500kW in the federal republic, and relay stations in Portugal (Sines) and Rwanda (Kigali), each with two 250kW transmitters. DW programmes are broadcast to 12 areas throughout the world for 27 programme hours a day in German, and over 50 programme hours a day in 32 other languages.

A privately owned commercial station, Europe No. 1, is based in Saarbrücken and has studios in Paris. It broadcasts French-language programmes for 21 hours a day from its 1200kW long-wave transmitter at Felsberg.

Private non-commercial organizations operate the stations Radio Free Europe and Radio Liberty. Radio Free Europe, with headquarters in Munich and operating one 150kW medium-wave and 13 short-wave transmitters in the federal republic and 18 short-wave transmitters of up to 250kW in Portugal, broadcasts programmes in German and in Bulgarian, Czech/Slovakian, Polish, Hungarian and Romanian to six areas in central and eastern Europe. Radio Liberty, also with headquarters in Munich, has 8 short-wave transmitters in the federal republic, 6 in Spain (ranging from 100 to 1000kW), and 3 in the Far East. Its programmes, in six languages, are beamed to different areas in the USSR and to the German Democratic Republic.

The US Government service Voice of America (VOA) operates a relay station in Munich, with 1 long-wave transmitter (1000kW), 1 medium-wave transmitter (300kW) and 4 short-wave transmitters (10kW), broadcasting for over 50 hours a day in English, French. Russian, Slovene. Hungarian, Czech and Polish to European areas. The station also serves as European correspondent for VOA, gathering material for headquarters at the United States Information Agency in Washington, where broadcast programmes are originated. Another organization also related to the United States Information Agency is RIAS-Berlin (Rundfunk im Amerikanischen Sektor Berlins) which operates medium-wave (up to 300kW), short-wave (100kW) and FM transmitters, broadcasting two German-language programmes round the clock. The British Broadcasting Corporation (BBC) has a relay station in West Berlin, with 1 medium-wave and 1 FM transmitter, for its external-service broadcasts in Europe.

Military stations providing broadcasting services for foreign forces stationed in the federal republic are located at Frankfurt, Cologne and Berlin.

TELEVISION

Television broadcasting in the federal republic is carried out by the *Land* broadcasting organizations grouped within ARD (as described above, under Radio) and by the public organization Zweites Deutsches Fernsehen (ZDF).

The ARD first programme, which dates from the television agreement of March 1963 when the *Land* broadcasting organizations undertook to operate a joint ARD community-television network, is received throughout the national territory. It consists of a weekday afternoon programme, an evening programme and a weekend programme (from Saturday evening to Sunday evening), broadcast through the transmitters of the nine *Land* organizations linked by the communication circuits of the Federal Post Office. Into this programme are slotted eight regional programmes of up to 2 hours a day, broadcast by the individual *Land* organizations (NDR and RB jointly) usually in the early evening (and including a limited amount of commercial advertising). The costs of the first-channel community and regional programmes are met by the *Land* organizations from licence fees and advertising revenues.

The second channel is operated by ZDF, established jointly in 1961 by all the *Länder* and financed out of their licence fees (30%) and advertising revenue. Administratively autonomous, though subject to government legal supervision, ZDF is governed by a council on which all the *Land* organizations are represented. It broadcasts a continuous late-afternoon and evening programme, plus an afternoon programme on Saturdays and morning and afternoon programmes on Sunday, as an alternative to the first channel, its purpose being to present 'an objective account of world affairs and a comprehensive picture of the German reality'. Both these programmes are supplemented by a joint ARD–ZDF morning programme from 10.00 to about 13.00 hours

Since 1964, third programmes have also been broadcast by the *Land* organizations (separately or jointly), using the transmitters of the Federal Post Office. These vary from one organization to another, but generally consist of about 3 hours in the evenings (longer at weekends) and morning programmes for schools and high schools. Evening broadcasts also include educational programmes such as the successful TV vocational high school, 'Telekolleg', begun in 1967.

At the end of 1972, the number of combined radio and television licences was 18 063 882, though the actual number of receivers in use is considerably higher (one licence may cover more than one receiver). Colour broadcasts (PAL system), introduced in August 1967, are now seen on all three channels and constitute the majority of programmes on the first and second. Over 2 million colour receivers are in use in the country.

Cable transmission of national television programmes and, in some localities, those of neighbouring countries, is highly developed and over 2 million viewers are thus served.

A United States Armed Forces television station also broadcasts from seven regional transmitters.

FILM

From 72 titles in 1961, long-film production rose to 129 in 1970, dropping again to 94 in 1972. Of these, 9 were documentaries. There were 28 coproductions with France/Italy (10), Italy (7), France (3), Spain/Italy (3), Austria (7) and other countries (4). Short films produced in 1972 totalled 167.

Imports of feature films in 1972 totalled 290: from the USA (102), Italy (52), the UK (35), France/Italy (25), France (21), Japan (8), Austria (5), Spain (5) and other countries (37). Short films imported in 1970 totalled 99: from Italy (14), the USA (12), the UK (8), France (4), Denmark (2), France/Italy (1), Japan (1) and other countries (59).

The number of annual cinema attendances has dropped to only a quarter of the 1960 total of 609 million, while the number of cinemas has halved since 1960. Drive-in cinemas have increased to 19, and there are 41 mobile units.

SPACE COMMUNICATIONS

The federal republic is a member of Intelsat and has an earth station at Raisting, with three antennae: the first, in operation since 1965, is now used for Indian Ocean Intelsat transmissions and the other two, in operation since 1969 and 1972 respectively, are used for Atlantic Intelsat transmissions.

PROFESSIONAL TRAINING AND ASSOCIATIONS

Opportunities for communications training are numerous in the federal republic and West Berlin. Courses in journalism and other communications fields are available at professional and research levels at the Universities of Munster, Munich, Gottingen, Nuremburg, Mainz, the Ruhr, Fribourg, Hamburg and the Free University of Berlin, and at institutes in Hamburg, Bremen and Dortmund, and schools in Munich, Cologne, Dusseldorf, Hamburg and Berlin. Training for radio and television is also provided at Deutsche Welle's Department of Training for Radio Journalists and at the Schools of Television and Broadcasting in Berlin, Cologne, Munich and Tübingen.

The German Press Council, founded in 1956, is composed of 20 publishers and journalists, 10 appointed by the professional associations of newspaper and magazine publishers and 10 by the German Association of Journalists. Its role is to protect the freedom of the press, to maintain the reputation of the profession and to protect the interests of the press *vis-à-vis* government, parliament and the public. A body for the internal control of magazines was created in 1966 with 4 members representing the big mass-circulation magazines.

Professional associations for the press include 4 for publishers, 1 for editors-in-chief, 10 for journalists including radio journalists, 1 for news agencies and 2 for foreign correspondents. There are 3 organizations for the broadcasting professions, a general association to promote school radio and television broadcasting and a radio section of the Central German Workers' Federation. The cinema world has 13 associations covering producers, technicians. writers and performers, distributors and exhibitors.

GIBRALTAR

Population	27 000
Area	6 sq. km.

PRESS

Newspapers	Dailies 2, Non-dailies 2
Total circulation	Dailies 6100, Non-dailies 4200
Copies per 1000 people	Dailies 226, Non-dailies 155

RADIO

Transmitters	Long/medium-wave 3, VHF–FM 1
Total receivers	3700 licences
Licences per 1000 people	137

TELEVISION

Transmitters	2
Receivers	6528 licences
Licences per 1000 people	242

FILM

Cinemas	Fixed 3
Total seating capacity	2394
Seats per 1000 people	89
Total annual attendance	408 700
Annual visits per capita	15

PRESS

In addition to two English-language dailies, each circulating 3000 copies, there are two non-dailies in both Spanish and English — one weekly (2700 copies) and the other less frequent (1500 copies). Other periodicals include a weekly gazette, a fortnightly broadcasting magazine and a quarterly directory.

NEWS AGENCIES

There is no local news agency. Foreign news is received through the Gemini News Agency and the Observer Foreign News Service.

RADIO

The Gibraltar Broadcasting Corporation is the official body responsible for radio and television broadcasting under government sponsorship. Its revenue is derived from licence fees, government grants and, to a large extent, advertising.

Radio Gibraltar's three medium-wave transmitters, covering the whole territory, are on the air for 112 hours weekly in English and Spanish. Programme time includes light entertainment (53 hours), news and information (32 hours), cultural programmes (14 hours), programmes for special audiences (6 hours), advertisements (3 hours) and education (1 hour). A licence fee is payable for radio receivers, but the number of sets in use is certainly greatly in excess of the number of licences.

The British Forces Broadcasting Service operates one FM transmitter, broadcasting for 10 hours each weekday, 7 hours on Saturdays and over 15 hours on Sundays. Its information and light entertainment programmes are intended for British forces and their families stationed in Gibraltar.

TELEVISION

Gibraltar Television is a commercially operated service under the responsibility of the Gibraltar Broadcasting Corporation. With one main transmitter and one auxiliary transmitter (635 line definition), covering the whole territory, programmes are broadcast for about 33 hours weekly and include cultural and scientific broadcasts (10 hours), news and information (6 hours), light entertainment (5 hours), broadcasts for special audiences (5 hours), advertising (3½ hours) and education (1 hour). Television programmes are imported from the UK and the USA.

An annual licence fee is payable.

FILMS

There is no local film production. Feature films and documentaries exhibited are imported, mainly from the UK and the USA.

GREECE

Population	8 957 000
Area	131 944 sq. km.

PRESS
Newspapers	Dailies 104, Non-dailies 557

RADIO
Transmitters	Long/medium-wave 11, Short-wave 2, VHF–FM 37
Total receivers	2 800 000 estimated in use
Receivers per 1000 people	313

TELEVISION
Transmitters	17*
Receivers	520 000 estimated in use
Receivers per 1000 people	58

FILM
Cinemas	Fixed 1034
Total seating capacity	135 300 000
Annual visits per captia	15

*EIRT stations only.

PRESS

Daily newspapers are published in some 30 towns, on both the mainland and offshore islands, some serving small local readerships only. Athens, the capital, has 12 dailies (as compared with 23 in 1967), 2 with circulations in the region of 100 000 and the remainder considerably smaller. Other towns with several dailies include Piraeus, Salonika, Corinth and Corfu. Almost all dailies appear in the morning. Some of the larger papers have weekend editions. Total circulation figures for the whole country, which had remained at around 1 million copies a day since 1960, dropped by about 30% in 1967 following the institution of official press-control measures. Complete data were not available in 1972, but the 10 largest dailies of Athens and Salonika together circulated an average of 666 000 copies a day.

The language used by the press is the official revival of classical Greek (Katharevousa), as distinguished from the vernacular (Demotiki). Two Athens dailies are published in English and 1 in Armenian.

Non-daily newspapers, including 4 in English 4 in Turkish and 1 in French, are published in over 50 localities. Periodicals total some 850 titles including 120 children's, school and parish magazines. Of the remainder, the principal subject categories are law and related fields (110 titles), agriculture (70), religion and theology (65), industry and technology (60) and medical sciences (40). The 40 largest periodicals had a total annual circulation of 116.4 million copies in 1972.

NEWS AGENCIES

The national agency, founded in 1905, Athens News Agency (ANA; Agence d'Athènes), has its headquarters in the capital, and offices in the main provincial towns. It is represented abroad by correspondents in the world's major capitals. ANA, which is the main supplier of news to the national press, receives news from UPI, AFP, Reuters, DPA and ANSA and has exchange agreements with Reuters and DPA. A few newspapers subscribe to AP services.

RADIO

The National Radio Broadcasting and Television Institute (EIRT) is a state-controlled public body. In its home service, it broadcasts a national programme, from a 150kW medium-wave transmitter in Athens with a 50kW relay transmitter at Zakynthos, which is partly rebroadcast by eight regional stations. The second programme, broadcast from a 50kW transmitter in Athens, is mainly news, light entertainment and advertising, while the third (Athens, 15kW) carries serious music only. A number of FM transmitters (some stereo) broadcast on an experimental basis.

The largest of the private radio stations, at Pyrgos (western Peloponnesus) is on the air for 17 hours a day and, in addition to its Greek programmes broadcasts weekly programmes for tourists in English and German. The 626-hour total weekly broadcasting time for all stations includes light entertainment (273 hours), cultural and scientific programmes (97 hours), news and information (71 hours), broadcasts for special audiences (34 hours) and education (1 hour). Advertising totals 120 hours a week. Foreign-service broadcasts on short waves from Athens, in English, French, German, Greek, Turkish, Serbian, Albanian, Romanian and Bulgarian, are beamed to six areas: Cyprus, Egypt, Turkey and the Balkans, the Near East, western and north-western Europe and the north Atlantic (for seamen).

The Greek Armed Forces Information Service (YENED), with a 20kW medium-wave transmitter and a 5kW short-wave transmitter in Athens, is on the air for about 19 hours a day. It is also relayed by a number of Armed Forces regional stations.

The Voice of America (USA) has powerful short-wave and medium-wave transmitters broadcasting in English, Arabic and Turkish from Rhodes, and in Greek, English, Romanian, Albanian and Serbo-Croat from Thessaloniki.

TELEVISION
EIRT, with 17 transmitters (625 lines) covering much of the country, is on the air for 58 hours a week and includes cultural and scientific programmes (22 hours), news and information (16 hours), light entertainment (12 hours), broadcasts for special audiences (5 hours), advertising (2 hours) and education (1 hour). About two-thirds of the programmes broadcast are imported (many from France) or received through Eurovision exchange agreements.

The Greek Armed Forces Information Service also operates an extensive network of stations.

FILM
Responsibility for the film industry is vested in the Ministry of Industry with regard to national production, and in the cinema department of the Ministry of the Presidency for matters of distribution and censorship and the granting of licences to foreign producers wishing to make films in Greece. Founded by the state-owned Hellenic Industrial Development Bank (ETBA), the General Cinematographic Enterprise is responsible both for the encouragement of private film enterprise and for the actual production and exploitation of films, including the negotiation of coproductions with foreign film-makers using local equipment and resources.

National production in 1972 included 142 feature and 22 short 35mm films and a number of 16mm films made by government departments and by independent producers.

In the same year, 847 imported feature films were released: from Italy (223), the USA (207), the UK (60), the Federal Republic of Germany (54), France (50), the USSR (20), Turkey (20) and other countries (210). Short film imports for 1972 totalled 54. Cinema attendances, both in the fixed establishments and in the 2000 or so outdoor screening places used in the summer, have shown a slight but steady decline over recent years.

SPACE COMMUNICATIONS
Greece has an earth station for Atlantic Intelsat transmissions, opened in April 1970, at Thermopylae.

PROFESSIONAL TRAINING AND ASSOCIATIONS
A school of journalism is to be founded in the near future. Organizations of media professionals include associations grouping together newspaper and periodical journalists, foreign correspondents, newspaper owners, periodical publishers, cinema performers and film distributors and exhibitors.

HOLY SEE

Population	1000
Area	0.44 sq. km.

PRESS

Newspapers	Dailies 1, Non-dailies 7
Total circulation	Dailies 30 000, Non-dailies 75 000

RADIO

Transmitters	Long/medium-wave 3, Short-wave 12, VHF—FM 1

PRESS
The Vatican's daily newspaper, which has a world-wide readership, is published in Italian but with certain texts in other languages, including Latin. A daily news bulletin, for local and world circulation, is produced by the press-room of the Holy See which also organizes press conferences. The non-dailies, read in Italy and abroad, consist of one Sunday paper (30 000 copies) and six other weeklies published in English (11 000 copies), Spanish (10 000 copies), and French, German, Italian and Portuguese (6000 copies each). The State Secretariat publishes a quarterly official journal, which contains the official texts of the Holy See in Latin.

NEWS AGENCIES
The most important news service is the Agenzia Internationale Fides (Fides Service), an autonomous agency which receives a subvention from the Congregation for the Evangelization of the Nations. Fides Service is located in Rome and has 12 permanent members of its staff at home and 50 abroad, while part-time correspondents include missionaries, nunciatures and bishops' conferences in missionary countries. News is exchanged through the Federation of Catholic Agencies. It issues two weekly bulletins in English, French, German and Italian to its 2000 subscribers consisting of newspapers, radio stations, religious congregations and bishops' conferences.

RADIO
The Vatican Radio, owned by the state, has been in existence since February 1931, when Pope Pius XI first addressed the people of the world from the Holy See. Some 430 religious programmes are broadcast weekly in 32 languages: 160 programmes in 16 languages for Europe, 126 programmes in nine languages for western Europe and 76 programmes in five languages for Africa. For listeners in Asia, programmes are broadcast in Arabic, Chinese, Tamil. Hindi, Malayalam and English.

FILMS
No films are produced and no commercial films are shown. The Vatican Film Library, founded in 1959, is now the responsibility of the Pontifical Commission

for Social Communication. Its holdings include major religious films produced throughout the world, and recordings of television programmes relating to the life of the Church.

HUNGARY

Population	10 400 000
Area	93 030 sq. km.

PRESS

Newspapers	Dailies 27, Non-dailies 80
Total circulation	Dailies 2 250 670, Non-dailies 4 278 920
Copies per 1000 people	Dailies 216, Non-dailies 411

RADIO

Transmitters	Long/medium-wave 14, Short-wave 10, VHF–FM 5
Total receivers	2 542 500 licences
Licences per 1000 people	244

TELEVISION

Transmitters	12
Receivers	2 003 950 licences
Licences per 1000 people	193

FILM

Cinemas	Fixed 3755
Total seating capacity	595 239
Seats per 1000 people	57
Total annual attendance	74 700 000
Annual visits per capita	7

PRESS

The six daily newspapers of Budapest, the capital, are distributed throughout the country and represent 67% of the national total circulation. The most important of these is the national organ of the Hungarian Socialist Workers' Party which has a circulation of over 800 000 copies. The provincial daily newspapers have a total circulation of about 500 000 copies. Most of these publications are the organs of political parties, trade unions, youth and social organizations. A very substantial percentage – up to 80% – of newspaper sales are to regular subscribers and the rest are sold through news-stands.

The periodical press of Hungary consists of 760 periodicals. A wide range of specialist periodicals are published by societies, factories, scientific institutions, etc. These appear not only in Hungarian and the languages of national minorities, but in a number of foreign languages as well. There is no private ownership of publications.

NEWS AGENCIES
News reception and dissemination is the monopoly of Magyar Távirati Iroda (MTI). Its Director-General and his deputies are appointed with government approval. Inside the country, MTI has correspondents in 19 county towns. Abroad, it has correspondents in Berlin, Belgrade, Bonn, Bucharest, London, Moscow, Paris, Peking, Prague, Rome, Sofia, Vienna, Warsaw and Washington.

The agency's daily service for the Hungarian press consists of 40 000 words of domestic and foreign news. This service, in English, German and Russian, transmitted by radioteletype and telex to the foreign news agencies with which MTI has agreements, consists of 10 000 words. Besides, MTI prepares, for the foreign press, weekly bulletins in English, Russian, French and German.

MTI has exclusive distribution rights for news received from Reuters, AP, UPI, AFP, DPA, Antara, MEN, APA, TASS, ADN, CTK, Hsinhua, PAP, Agerpress, Tanjug, BTA, and ATA. In addition, it has agreements with 35 other news agencies for exchange of information on request. The photo section of MTI has relations with 65 foreign photo agencies. It receives and transmits photos by telephoto, radiophoto and by mail.

Since 1967, MTI has published a bilingual newspaper in English and German.

RADIO
The state-owned Magyar Radio es Televizio (Hungarian Radio and Television Service) has developed considerably in recent years. It now operates 14 medium-wave transmitters (including one of 300kW), 10 short-wave transmitters (up to 100kW) and 5 FM transmitters (totalling 18kW).

There are two main home-service programmes (Kossuth and Petöfi) in Hungarian, with a number of regional programmes broadcast in Hungarian, German and Serbo-Croat. Total broadcasting time for the home service is 45 hours a day, with the following time distribution: music (62.9%), news and information (19.1%), literary programmes (9.2%) and youth programmes (6.5%). There are also special programmes for those learning Russian, French and English. Numerous programmes are exchanged with European and Asian countries.

The foreign service's programmes in Hungarian, English, German, Greek, Spanish and Turkish are beamed to European countries, the Near East, the Far East, North America and Latin America.

Hungary produces its own studio equipment, receivers and transmitters, and some equipment is exported.

TELEVISION
Television broadcasting, like radio, is controlled by Magyar Radio es Televizio. Transmissions began on a regular basis in 1958. The main transmitters are at Budapest (established 1958), Pécs (1959), Miskolc (1959), Sopron (1959), Szentes (1960), Kékestetö (1960), Tokaj (1960), Kabhégy (1962), Szekszárd

(1963), Ozd (1963), Salgótarján (1965) and Komádi (1968). The most powerful transmitter is at Kabhégy. With the completion of the transmitter at Zalaegerszeg, 90 to 92% of the country will be able to receive television (as compared with 85 to 87% at present). The definition system used is 625 lines.

The total television broadcasting time is around 43 hours a week, devoted to news and information (26.6%), entertainment programmes (17.1%), popular scientific programmes (13.7%), long films (12.8%), sport (11.9%), literary programmes (5.8%), classical music and operas (5.6%), children's programmes (4.4%) and programmes for school (2.1%).

In 1970, Hungarian television transmitted 134 programmes from abroad — 75 from Intervision members and 59 from other countries, while 59 Hungarian programmes were transmitted abroad, 57 in Intervision member countries.

The SECAM colour system is used. Television equipment is locally produced. An annual licence fee is payable.

FILM

The film industry in Hungary is nationalized. Feature-film production has nearly tripled since 1953 when 8 feature films were made. In 1971, 19 long films were produced and 492 short feature films, television films, newsreels, documentaries and other films. Coproductions were made with the USSR (2), Romania and Czechoslovakia (1 each).

Long films imported in 1970 numbered 150, including 31 from the USSR, 25 from the USA, 16 from France, 10 each from Italy and Czechoslovakia and 9 each from Poland and the German Democratic Republic. Annual attendance at cinemas has almost halved over the last ten years. In addition to fixed cinemas there are 63 mobile units.

PROFESSIONAL TRAINING AND ASSOCIATIONS

The Hungarian Centre for Training of Journalists and the International Centre for Training of Journalists run by the International Organization of Journalists are the two schools of journalism for university graduates. The Hungarian Centre, founded in 1958, offers a two-year course. The International Centre for Training of Journalists, in existence since 1964, offers courses varying in duration from 4 to 6 months. There is also, in Budapest, a training course for editors.

Professional training for film producers and directors is available at the Academy for Theatre and Film Art in Budapest.

There is a National Association of Hungarian Journalists. Its ethics committee is working out a code of professional ethics.

ICELAND

Population	214 000
Area	103 000 sq. km.

PRESS

Newspapers	Dailies 5, Non-dailies 49
Total circulation	Dailies 94 000
Copies per 1000 people	Dailies 439

RADIO

Transmitters	Long/medium-wave 15, VHF—FM 14
Total receivers	65 000 licences
Receivers per 1000 people	303

TELEVISION

Transmitters	59
Receivers	44 000 estimated in use
Receivers per 1000 people	206

FILM

Cinemas	Fixed 25
Total seating capacity	9541
Seats per 1000 people	44
Total annual attendance	1 565 000
Annual visits per capita	7

PRESS

All the daily newspapers are published in Reykjavik, the capital, which – with neighbouring towns – accounts for about half the country's population. More distant towns receive the press by internal air mail. Four dailies have Sunday but not Monday editions. The largest circulates 39 000 copies per issue. Of the 200 or so periodicals other than newspapers the main subject categories are general interest (36 titles); law, public administration social welfare, etc. (18 titles), political and economic sciences (13 titles), agriculture, fisheries, etc. (13 titles), technology (12 titles), religion (11 titles), education (10 titles), entertainment (8 titles), etc. Over 30 magazines for young people, and parish magazines, house organs, etc., are published.

NEWS AGENCIES

There is no national news agency in Iceland. The majority of newspapers subscribe to NTB, Reuters and AP, and one receives CTK and Hsinhua services.

RADIO

The Icelandic State Broadcasting Service (Rikisutvarpid) is a government authority deriving its revenue from radio licence fees and a limited amount of advertising. It has the monopoly for the sale and repair of receiving sets.

Domestic broadcasts, reaching 98% of the population, are on the air for over 113 hours a week; nearly half this time is devoted to music and cultural programmes, and the remainder to news bulletins, sports, etc. (18½ hours), programmes for special audiences (15 hours), light entertainment (14 hours), advertising (5 hours) and educational programmes (1 hour).

The United States Armed Forces Radio and Television Service has a medium-wave station in Keflavik, which is on the air for 24 hours a day.

TELEVISION
The Icelandic State Broadcasting Service began television broadcasting in 1966, and now potentially covers 98% of the population with eight main transmitters and 51 low-power repeaters that are on the air for 24 hours a week. There are no broadcasts on Thursdays and the station closes down completely during July. News and sports broadcasts occupy 25% of programme time, documentary films (15%), education (2%) and the remainder is largely entertainment. About 30% of programmes are domestic production. Imports come mainly from the USA (38% of all imports) and the UK (29%).

The United States Armed Forces Radio and Television Service operates a television service from Keflavik, for 72 hours a week.

FILM
There is no local film production and, in 1970, feature films imported totalled 391; from the USA (267), the UK (39), France (30), the Federal Republic of Germany (14), Italy (13), Denmark (10). Sweden (10) and other counties (8). In the same year, 204 short films were imported.

A large number of schools have projectors and give educational film shows. The State Educational Library maintains a collection of educational films which are available free of charge to schools and cultural organizations.

PROFESSIONAL ASSOCIATIONS
Professional associations include an association of journalists and one of broadcasting performers.

IRELAND

Population	3 010 000
Area	70 283 sq. km.

PRESS

Newspapers	Dailies 7, Non-dailies 50
Total circulation	Dailies 702 477, Non-dailies 1 420 761
Copies per 1000 people	Dailies 233, Non-dailies 472

RADIO

Transmitters	Long/medium-wave 3, VHF—FM 9
Total receivers	640 000 licences
Licences per 1000 people	209

TELEVISION

Transmitters	20
Receivers	536 000 licences
Receivers per 1000 people	168

FILM

Total annual attendance	22 000 000*
Annual visits per capita	7

*Estimated.

PRESS

Ireland's daily newspapers are published in the capital, Dublin (3 morning and 2 evening), and in Cork (1 morning and 1 evening). The 4 morning dailies, with circulations ranging from 60 000 to 160 000 copies per issue, are all nationally distributed, as are Dublin's 3 weeklies (2 Sunday papers circulating 407 000 and 321 000 copies respectively, and a sporting weekly). Ownership of all these papers is in the hands of three groups in Dublin and one company in Cork.

Weeklies, which account for 48 of the country's 50 non-daily general interest newspapers, are published in all the county seats as well as in Dublin, Cork and Waterford. But, though this provincial press is highly influential, few papers realize sales of over 15 000 copies.

All daily newspapers, and 48 of the non-dailies, are published in English; the remaining 2 non-dailies (together circulating 15 000 copies) appear in the Irish language. British newspapers are also circulated in Ireland.

Periodical titles and readership figures have more than doubled in recent years, the growth being particularly noticeable with respect to general interest news magazines (including some imported publications) and trade, technical and professional journals. There are now 278 periodicals published in the country, with a total circulation of just over 3.6 million copies per issue. Ten of these are published in the Irish language, and the rest in English — official publications are issued in both languages. By subject categories, religious journals head the list (54 titles circulating 722 826 copies), followed by trade, transport etc. (44 titles, 566 225 copies), general interest magazines (26 titles, 307 853 copies), agriculture (22 titles, 459 332 copies), entertainment and sports (20 titles, 239 317 copies), medicine (15 titles, 192 567 copies), geography and travel (9 titles, 464 000 copies), commerce and communications (9 titles, 195 096 copies), education (9 titles, 46 550 copies), etc.

Domestic newsprint production amounts to about 6000 metric tons a year. and the annual consumption is over 57 000 metric tons, the latter representing an increase of almost 60% over the last ten years.

NEWS AGENCIES

There is no national news agency, the daily press depending on its own sources for domestic news and on the world services of Reuters and AP for international news.

The Irish Features Agency (IFA), with headquarters in Dublin, distributes some domestic and foreign news in the country and exchanges features with some overseas agencies and syndicates.

The government has its own central information agency, the Government Information Bureau, which was founded in 1934 and reorganized and expanded in 1968.

Reuters and AFP maintain correspondents in Dublin.

RADIO

The Irish national broadcasting organization is Radio Telefís Éireann (RTE) a statutory autonomous corporation orginally set up in 1960 as Radio Éireann under the Broadcasting Authority Act (amended in 1966, when the present title was adopted). RTE is financed by licence revenues, operating surpluses and advertising.

RTE radio operates three medium-wave transmitters at Athlone (100kW), Dublin (5kW) and Cork (10kW) and, since 1966, a VHF–FM network at the same sites as the five main television transmitters. Radio services are potentially available to 98% of the population. Regular radio programmes, broadcast in Irish and/or English, are transmitted for approximately 113 hours a week, including light entertainment (41 hours), news and information (31 hours), music, drama, etc. (19 hours), broadcasts to special audiences (8 hours, including 3 hours of religious broadcasts) and adult education (40 minutes). Advertising is limited to a maximum of 10% of total transmission time.

British radio broadcasts are also received throughout the country.

TELEVISION

Irish television, introduced at the end of 1961, is operated by RTE on the same basis as radio.

Five main transmitters totalling 600kW in power are located at Maghera (County Clare), Mullaghanish (County Cork), Truskmore (County Sligo), Kippure (County Dublin) and Mount Leinster (County Carlow). Three of the transmitters operate on 625 lines only while those at Kippure and Truskmore use both 405 and 625 lines. In addition, 15 low-power 'satellite' transposers cover areas of poor reception caused by the irregular configuration of the country. About 75% of homes have television receivers, which constitutes an 83% coverage of the population.

For most of the year, regular television programmes – in Irish and/or English – are on the air for about 55 hours a week, religious services, sports coverage and special events being broadcast additionally outside the regular schedule when necessary.

Programme content, about half of which is produced in Ireland, includes light entertainment, drama, music, etc. (21 hours), news, information, sports, etc. (14½ hours), broadcasts for special audiences (2 hours) and arts, letters and sciences (1 hour 10 minutes). Educational programmes for schools of approximately 7 hours a week are broadcast for about 33 weeks of the year. Adult education on television is being developed and includes early-afternoon programmes on Sundays.

RTE buys imported television programmes mainly from the USA and the UK, and also from France, the Federal Republic of Germany, Italy, Sweden, Australia and Canada. It coproduces programmes with the BBC (UK) and participates in special European Broadcasting Union productions. RTE programmes are available for commercial distribution and are exhibited throughout the world, in Europe especially.

FILM
Ireland produced 6 feature films, 2 short documentary and 2 short educational films in 1972. Imported feature films totalled 331: from the USA (199), the UK (66), France (21), Italy (20), the Federal Republic of Germany (10), Spain (6), the USSR (2) and Canada (2), and 1 each from the Netherlands, Belgium, Denmark, Switzerland, New Zealand, Yugoslavia and South Africa. Seven long and 130 documentary films were also imported from abroad.

Cinema attendaces are estimated to have dropped to barely half the 1960 total of 41.2 million. This decline has been most marked in the urban provincial areas, followed by the rural provincial districts, but least noticed in the Dublin city-centre cinemas where the trend has been towards a greater number of smaller cinemas with a wider range of appeal. The number of commercial cinemas is variously reported as between 200 and 300.

The National Film Institute of Ireland, which produces 35mm and 16mm documentary and sports films, also operates three 16mm mobile units, and maintains Ireland's only educational film library which consists of over 1800 titles. The Irish Film Society organizes showings of film classics and documentaries for the general public.

SPACE COMMUNICATIONS
As a member of the European Broadcasting Union, RTE supports the union's plans for a proposed telecommunication and broadcasting satellite for Europe.

PROFESSIONAL TRAINING AND ASSOCIATIONS
Full-time and part-time courses in journalism are available at the College of Commerce, Dublin, for which the average intake is about 15 students a year. Over the period 1968–70, 40 students completed the 38-week course to obtain a university-level diploma. Mass media studies are included in the courses offered at St Patrick's College, Maynooth, which mainly trains students for the

priesthood. The Catholic Communications Institute at Booterstown gives brief training courses in press, radio and television.

Professional associations for the press include 1 for provincial newspapers, 3 for journalists and 1 printing federation. There are also associations of broadcasting and programme personnel and television actors, a trade union for Irish film producers, and associations of film distributors and exhibitors.

ITALY

Population	54 350 000
Area	301 225 sq. km.

PRESS
Newspapers	Dailies 78, Non-dailies 119
Total circulation	Dailies 7 700 000
Copies per 1000 people	Dailies 142

RADIO
Transmitters	Long/medium-wave 128, Short-wave 10, VHF–FM 1736
Total receivers	12 488 026* licences
Licences per 1000 people	230

TELEVISION
Transmitters	1193
Receivers	10 951 341 licences
Licences per 1000 people	201

FILM
Cinemas	Fixed 10 719
Total annual attendance	555 438 000
Annual visits per capita	10

*Including 283 894 wired receivers.

PRESS

Daily newspapers are published in 34 Italian cities and towns, more than half appearing in five main centres: Rome (15), Milan (10), Genoa (5), Naples (4) and Turin (3). Two Milan dailies top the circulation figures with 860 000 and 497 000 respectively, followed by 1 published in Turin (421 000) and Rome's largest daily (301 000). Radio-transmitted facsimile pages are used to print southern editions (in Rome) of the leading Milan and Turin dailies. Several of the larger papers have Sunday editions with considerably higher circulations than their weekday totals. Three papers are printed in foreign languages (English, German and Slovene), 6 specialize partly, or entirely, in economics and finance, and 4 are sporting papers (two with daily circulations of over 300 000 copies).

During the sixties, concentration of ownership brought about the disappearance of 10 dailies, though overall circulation figures have varied little. Many papers have political or Church affiliations, others are associated with industrial enterprises.

Non-daily newspapers circulated an overall total of 152 million copies in 1972. Other periodicals number about 3000, including 112 in foreign languages and 434 in Italian plus another language with a total annual circulation of 1932 million copies. Of these, illustrated weeklies, particularly women's magazines, have much higher circulations than daily newspapers.

Main subject categories are political science and economy (1267 titles), law, administration, etc. (644 titles), religion and theology (590 titles), general readership (557 titles), medicine (536 titles), technology (432 titles), agriculture (369 titles), recreation (329 titles), commerce and communications (273 titles), arts and architecture (244 titles), sociology (214 titles), education (203 titles), etc. Parish magazines and business house journals number 937 and 330 titles respectively.

Italian newsprint production (311 000 metric tons in 1970) more than covers the country's requirements (1970 consumption was 282 300 metric tons).

NEWS AGENCIES

The most important of the unusually large number of news agencies in Italy is the Agenzia Nazionale Stampa Associata (ANSA), cooperatively owned by Italian newspapers. With headquarters in Rome, ANSA has 14 branches in Italy, 56 correspondents all over the world, and part-time correspondents in Italy and abroad. Its permanent staff totals more than 600 people.

It distributes some 250 000 words daily on national and international affairs, the domestic service being entirely in Italian while the foreign service is also issued in English, French, German, Spanish, Portuguese and Arabic. News is supplied to more than 100 newspaper subscribers in Italy, to Radiotelevisione Italiana and to over 150 foreign newspapers. For transmission of news, ANSA uses a permanently leased cable-teleprinter circuit, telex, telephone or telegraph services. ANSA has exchange agreements with Reuters, AFP, UPI and with at least 21 other agencies.

Agenzia Giornalistica Italia (AGI) is a general news service with headquarters in Rome, and correspondents in all the main Italian cities, as well as many foreign correspondents -- both full-time and part-time -- throughout Europe. AGI transmits news by telex several times a day, supplies national news in English, French, German and Spanish to the foreign press in Italy, and issues a monthly bulletin on Italian regional affairs.

The Associated Catholic Press (ASCA), reorganized in 1970, is located in Rome and transmits news by telex daily to its associated papers; it maintains correspondents in Italy and abroad.

The other agencies mostly distribute more specialized news and information on cultural, economic, social and political issues or on Italian parliamentary and government affairs, for foreign correspondents in Rome. There are also a number of national and international photo agencies. One firm handles all telegraph and radio services for telex exchanges.

Reuters and UPI maintain bureaux in Milan and Rome, while AP and AFP have offices in Rome only.

RADIO

Radiotelevisione Italiana (RAI) is a joint-stock company having an exclusive concession for broadcasting by agreement with the Ministry of Posts and Telecommunications.

RAI's domestic radio service, broadcasting on medium and short waves and FM, is on the air for about 340 hours a week, covering 98% of the national territory. Of the three programmes, the national programme is of general appeal; the second programme consists mainly of entertainment for general audiences; and the third is devoted principally to cultural broadcasts, including a high proportion of music. Programmes, totalling 343 hours a week, consist of light entertainment (67.9%), news and information (15.9%), programmes for special audiences (5%), cultural programmes (4.4%), advertising, announcements, etc. (4.4%), children's programmes (0.6%) and broadcasts for primary and intermediate schools (0.6%).

In addition, regional programmes totalling 158 hours a week are slotted into the second national programme at fixed periods each day. They are designed to respond to regional interests and those of ethnic and linguistic minorities and include broadcasts in Slovene (86 hours a week), German (78 hours) and Ladin (3 hours) for the Trentino/Alto Adige region.

Experimental stereophonic programmes are also broadcast three times a day from Rome, Turin, Milan and Naples.

The external broadcasting service, with 10 short-wave transmitters of up to 100kW, carries programmes in Italian (107 hours a week) and in 26 foreign languages (108 hours) beamed to Europe, the Mediterranean, the Far East, Africa, Latin America and North America. The night programme, 'Notturno dall'Italia', on both short and medium wavelengths in Italian, French, English and German, is intended not only for countries outside Italy, but also for the national territory, after the three national networks have closed down.

TELEVISION

The Italian television service is exclusively operated by Radiotelivisione Italiana by agreement with the Ministry of Posts and Telecommunications. Revenue for both radio and television broadcasting is derived mainly from radio and television licences and from advertising.

There are two channels operating 88 main and 1105 auxiliary transmitters: the national programme, inaugurated in 1954 and covering 98.1% of the population, and the second programme inaugurated in 1961, covering 91% of the population. The two channels, on the air respectively for over 71 hours and 25 hours a week, are independent, the only principle governing programme coordination being that viewers should have a choice of distrinctive types of programme at any given time. Programmes consist of news and information

(36%), entertainment (19%), educational and school broadcasts (17%), broad-casts for special audiences (14%), cultural programmes (4%) and announcements, etc. (10%). All broadcasts are in Italian except for a local programme in German broadcast for 1½ hours daily for the German-speaking minorities in Alto Adige.

The total number of RAI programmes retransmitted abroad and foreign programmes received through Eurovision in 1969 was 2353. Programmes are also imported from OIRT countries, the USA and Japan, and from private commercial producers.

It is estimated that 22 million televiewers watch television in Italy each day for an average of 1 hour and 20 minutes. There are over 60 receivers in use for every 100 families in the country.

FILM

The Italian film industry is among the world's largest. In 1972, 294 feature films (as against 168 in 1960) and 317 short-length films were produced, in addition to an average output of over 600 newsreels a year. The features included 128 coproductions: with France (53), Spain (31), the Federal Republic of Germany (16) and other countries (28).

National film policy is governed by a law passed in 1965 and administered by the Ministry of Tourism and Recreation, the prime object of which is to promote and consolidate the national industry. To encourage artistic and cultural film production, 13% of box-office receipts for recognized quality films goes to producers, and a series of 20 annual prizes (of 40 million lire each) are awarded to films of outstanding artistic or cultural merit. Loans and grants are also available to producers. Cinemas are required to exhibit Italian feature films for at least 25 days every three months, and Italian short films for 45 days every three months.

In 1972, 261 feature films were imported: the USA (139), France (24), the UK (27), Federal Republic of Germany (20), Japan (7), Spain (6), Mexico (6) and other countries (22). In the same year, 73 documentary films were imported: from the USA (21), the UK (21), France (14), the Federal Republic of Germany (8), Belgium (3), the Netherlands (3) and Japan (2). Over the last ten years, while the number of cinemas has risen slightly, total attendances have dropped by almost 20%. There is one drive-in accommodating 980 cars; also, 240 mobile projection units.

SPACE COMMUNICATIONS

In 1962, the company Telespazio was vested with the authority to carry out all research and development in Italy concerning satellite communications. Atlantic Intelsat transmissions have been received at the earth station at Funcio, since 1965, and Indian Ocean Intelsat transmissions since 1970.

PROFESSIONAL TRAINING AND ASSOCIATIONS

Two training courses for journalism are offered at the Faculty of Statistical Sciences at Rome University, and another at a public opinion institute, also in Rome. There is an experimental journalism centre in Milan, and higher institutes of journalism at Palermo and Urbino Universities, and an advanced institute of journalism at the Pro Deo University in Rome, as well as 16 communications research centres throughout the country. Professional training for film and television is available at a state institute in Rome, and film studies can be undertaken at the Universities of Genoa and Urbino, as well as at the Sacred Heart University in Milan.

There are 6 organizations of publishers and editors of the press in Italy, one of these being a professional association for both periodical publishers and journalists. There are 8 other professional associations for journalists and 1 for foreign correspondents. The 18 film organizations include associations for producers (2) and directors, 9 organizations for cinema technicians. writers, performers, distributors and exhibitors, and a single professional association for all categories of staff in sound and vision broadcasting.

LIECHTENSTEIN

| Population | 21 000 |
| Area | 157 sq. km. |

PRESS

Newspapers	Dailies 1, Non-dailies 2
Total circulation	Dailies 5516, Non-dailies 6850
Copies per 1000 people	Dailies 263, Non-dailies 326

RADIO

| Total receivers | 4300 licences |
| Licences per 1000 people | 205 |

TELEVISION

| Receivers | 4000 licences |
| Licences per 1000 people | 190 |

FILM

Cinemas	Fixed 3
Total seating capacity	700
Seats per 1000 people	33
Total annual attendance	90 000
Annual visits per capita	4

PRESS

All newspapers are in German, as are the nine periodicals with a total circulation of about 10 000; Among the many newspapers and periodicals imported from other countries, the Swiss-German press is the most widely represented.

RADIO AND TELEVISION

There is no national broadcasting service. The principality is served by Swiss radio and television, licence fees for which are collected by the Swiss postal authorities. School broadcasts in German are received from Switzerland by establishments with receiving sets.

Radio licences include 600 paid by subscribers to a Swiss wired broadcasting system.

FILM

Feature films and documentaries are imported through Switzerland, mainly from the USA, Italy, the Federal Republic of Germany, France and the UK.

LUXEMBOURG

Population	350 000
Area	2586 sq. km.

PRESS

Newspapers	Dailies 6, Non-dailies 1
Total circulation	Dailies 158 000
Copies per 1000 people	Dailies 451

RADIO

Transmitters	Long/medium-wave 2, Short-wave 2, VHF–FM 3
Total receivers	157 000 licences
Licences per 1000 people	448

TELEVISION

Transmitters	5
Receivers	71 000 licences
Licences per 1000 people	203

FILM

Cinemas	Fixed 37
Total annual attendance	1 500 000
Annual visits per capita	4

PRESS

Of the locally published dailies, 3 appear in German and French, 2 in French only and 1 in Luxemburgish. Newspapers from France, Switzerland and the Benelux countries also circulate freely. Over 80% of daily newspaper sales are by subscriptions.

One non-daily newspaper and 229 other periodicals were accounted for in 1970. The periodicals are often bilingual or trilingual, with articles in German, French and Luxemburgish. The main subject categories are entertainment, pastimes, games and sports (40 titles), religion and theology (21), education (17), law, public administration, social welfare, etc. (17), technological subjects (15), town planning, architecture, plastic arts, music and the mass media (13).

Combined newsprint consumption and production figures for Belgium and Luxembourg are shown under Belgium.

NEWS AGENCIES

Luxembourg has no national news agency. Press, radio and television are catered for by the services of AP, AFP, Belga, DPA, UPI and Reuters, while two leading newspapers have their own correspondents abroad. The Ministry of State publishes a monthly information bulletin.

AFP maintains a bureau in the capital. Newspapers and news agencies of the other Benelux countries and the Federal Republic of Germany are represented by correspondents.

RADIO

Radio Luxembourg is operated by the privately owned Compagnie Luxembourgeoise de Télédiffusion, known as Radio-Télé-Luxembourg, in which French financial interests have a majority shareholding. Its finances are derived entirely from advertising revenues.

Two programmes are broadcast simultaneously on AM – one exclusively in French from a 1100kW long-wave transmitter, and the other in Dutch, English, German and Luxemburgish from 1 medium-wave transmitter (1200kW) and 2 short-wave transmitters totalling 550kW. This second programme is also relayed by 2 FM transmitters (10kW). Both programmes are received in all neighbouring countries and include numerous news bulletins. A third programme on FM, intended mainly for reception within the Grand Duchy, is broadcast from a 10kW transmitter, in Luxemburgish only.

The 430 hours of weekly broadcasting time, over half of which is of national origin, includes light entertainment (309 hours), advertising (43 hours), broadcasts to special audiences (37 hours), news bulletins, commentaries, etc. (23 hours), cultural broadcasts (18 hours) and educational programmes (45 minutes).

Radio receivers are subject to a licence fee, which is retained by the State Treasury.

TELEVISION

Television, like radio, is commercially operated by Radio-Télé-Luxembourg, which made its first telecasts in 1955. Using one main and four auxiliary transmitters, programmes are now on the air for about 40 hours a week and potentially reach 98% of the population of the Grand Duchy, as well as viewers in parts of Belgium and France. Programmes are all in French and consist of light entertainment (26¾ hours a week), news bulletins, commentaries, etc. (4½ hours), programmes for special audiences (3½ hours), advertising (2¾ hours), and language and other courses (1½ hours).

Télé Luxembourg exchanges programmes with other member countries of Eurovision. Programmes are also imported from the USA, and from French-speaking countries. The definition system used is 625 lines.

A receiver licence fee is payable.

FILM

There is no local production of feature films but documentaries of all kinds are produced by Télé Luxembourg. Feature films imported totalled 303 in 1972, coming from the USA (101), France (65), the Federal Republic of Germany (52), Italy (49), the UK (25), Belgium (4), Sweden (2), the USSR (2), Denmark (1) and Hungary (1). A total of 21 documentaries were imported from Italy (8), the USA (7) and France (6).

PROFESSIONAL ASSOCIATIONS

Professional associations include 3 for journalists, 1 for foreign correspondents, 1 for newspaper publishers and 1 for film exhibitors and distributors.

MALTA

Population	325 000
Area	316 sq. km.

PRESS
Newspapers	Dailies 6, Non-dailies 4

RADIO
Transmitters	VHF–FM 1
Total receivers	66 695* licences
Licences per 1000 people	205

TELEVISION
Transmitters	1
Receivers	57 300* licences
Licences per 1000 people	176

FILM
Cinemas	Fixed 40
Total seating capacity	24 847
Seats per 1000 people	76
Total annual attendance	4 495 000
Annual visits per capita	14

*Including 54 648 combined radio and television licences.

PRESS

All but one of the daily newspapers are published in the capital, Valletta, the majority with circulations ranging between 10 000 and 18 000 copies per issue. Three appear in Maltese and 3 in English, with a total annual circulation of 10.5 million copies. Two weeklies are in Maltese and 2 in English, with a total annual circulation of 1.7 million copies.

Other periodicals in 1972 totalled 160 titles, 77 in Maltese, 63 in English and 20 bilingual; most are specialized in content and have a limited circulation. Main subject categories are religion and theology (51 titles), political science (12 titles), commerce and communications (8 titles), technology (6 titles), arts and architecture (5 titles) and education (5 titles). Total annual circulation was around 1.8 million copies.

NEWS AGENCIES

The only news agency is the privately owned Associated News (Malta) Ltd, founded in May 1968. This agency maintains permanent bureaux in London, Tripoli and Benghazi, 10 permanent correspondents in Malta and 3 abroad, and 3 part-time correspondents in Malta and 1 in London. An average of 1400 words in English are distributed in addition to feature, photo and audio-radio services. For transmission of news, Associated News (Malta) Ltd uses telex, air-mail services and international telephone; its subscribers include large newspaper groups in the UK, South Africa, Australia, the Federal Republic of Germany and the USA.

News is also distributed to newspapers and radio and television stations by UPI, Reuters, AGIT, East-West News Agency, AFP, Observer Foreign News Service, ANSA, Financial Times Syndication Service and Visnews.

RADIO

Since September 1961, radio and television broadcasting in the Maltese islands has been controlled and supervised by the Malta Broadcasting Authority, which is also empowered to prescribe and produce programmes. As yet there is no national radio station but a commercial company, Rediffusion (Malta) Ltd, under contract to the Broadcasting Authority. operates a two-channel wired sound network with a combined output of 34 programme hours daily. Over 50 000 loudspeakers are served by the network.

The Maltese-language channel provides entertainment, news, and current affairs programmes, all of which are originated or produced in Rediffusion's own studios. The English-language channel relays programmes broadcast by the world service of the BBC with a number of local substitutions. Weekly programme content for both channels consists of light entertainment (112½ hours), news, information and sports broadcasts (86½ hours), broadcasts to special audiences (20 hours), educational programmes (10½ hours) and cultural broadcasts (9 hours). In addition, commercial advertising is permitted.

The Broadcasting Authority has assumed responsibility for programmes for schools, and its school broadcasting unit – working in close contact with the Ministry of Education – organizes and produces over 200 sound broadcasts annually. Political broadcasting, under the auspices of the Broadcasting Authority, is a regular feature throughout the year.

The British Forces Broadcasting Service operates a VHF transmitter, broadcasting general information, music and entertainment programmes mainly for resident British military personnel stationed in Malta with their families.

TELEVISION

A contract was signed in 1961 between the Malta Broadcasting Authority and the Malta Television Service Ltd. a commercial aerial television service, to provide television on the island for 25 years. The television service was started in 1962 and transmits programmes in Maltese and English.

In 1972, the total television broadcasting time per week was around 34 hours, consisting of light entertainment (13 hours), news bulletins, sports, etc. (10 hours), broadcasts for special audiences (6 hours), cultural programmes (2 hours), advertising (2 hours) and educational broadcasts (1 hour). About 34% of the progamme material is nationally produced, the remainder originating from the UK, Commonwealth countries, the USA and other sources.

School television was started in 1966 and is organized by the Broadcasting Authority in cooperation with the Ministry of Education, the British Council and the Malta Television Service. The programmes are mainly directed towards the senior classes of both private and state secondary schools.

Since 1957, television viewers on the island have been receiving programmes from a station on Monte Mauro in Sicily, which relays broadcasts from Radiotelevisione Italiana. Reception is generally good.

FILM

The government Department of Information has a film section that produces occasional documentaries, otherwise there is no local film production. In 1970, 498 foreign films were imported.

In addition to the year-round cinemas, there are seven (with 8471 seats) open for less than six months which record a total attendance of 46 238. Over the last ten years, commercial cinema attendances have dropped by almost 20%. The Visual Education Centre organizes educational film shows in schools and provides projectors and films for most government schools on the island. It maintains a large library of 35mm and 16mm films and filmstrips which are available to schools, government services and cultural institutions. The film section of the Catholic Institute also has a library of entertainment, documentary and educational films for the use of religious and social institutions.

PROFESSIONAL TRAINING

Short courses for journalists are organized by the local journalists' association.

MONACO

Population	24 000
Area	1 sq. km.

RADIO

Transmitters	Long/medium-wave 2, Short-wave 4, VHF–FM 1
Total receivers	14 000 estimated in use
Receivers per 1000 people	583

TELEVISION

Transmitters	1
Receivers	6300 estimated in use
Receivers per 1000 people	262

FILM

Cinemas	Fixed 2
Total seating capacity	1051
Seats per 1000 people	44
Total annual attendance	117 147
Annual visits per capita	5

PRESS

The principality has no daily press or non-daily newspapers of its own, but special editions of two French newspapers based in Nice are circulated in Monaco. Italian, Swiss, British and American newspapers are also widely read.

The periodical press includes a weekly official government bulletin and a bi-monthly published in English.

RADIO

Radio Monte Carlo is a private commercial corporation, controlled by French financial interests, which derives its entire revenue from advertising. It operates 1 long-wave, 1 medium-wave, 1 FM and 2 short-wave transmitters which are actually located in French national territory and from which two main programmes in French and French/Italian are broadcast throughout the day and evening for a total of 197 hours per week, reaching mainly French audiences. The programme content includes broadcasts to special audiences (90 hours), light entertainment (52 hours), commercial advertising (39 hours) and news bulletins, sports, etc. (16 hours).

Trans World Radio, a Christian broadcasting organization maintained entirely by private contributions, has one of its stations in Monte Carlo. Operating 2 short-wave transmitters of 100kW each, TWR broadcasts Gospel programmes in 35 languages beamed to Europe, north Africa, the Middle East and the Americas. A medium-wave service is also broadcast in 14 languages on different days of the week to Europe and north Africa, and there is an early-morning long-wave programme in French only, on Tuesdays and Sundays.

TELEVISION

Télé Monte Carlo is controlled by the same interests as Radio Monte Carlo and also derives its entire revenue from advertising. Its station, with one transmitter (819 lines) at Mt Agel in France, is on the air for almost over 30 hours a week. All programmes are in French and are received not only in Monaco but by many viewers in France. Most of the programme material broadcast is imported. Télé Monte Carlo is a member of Eurovision.

FILM

There is no local feature-film production. Films exhibited in commercial cinemas are all imported. Educational and documentary film shows are arranged by a specialized studio, for students and general audiences.

NETHERLANDS

Population	13 330 000
Area	40 844 sq. km.

PRESS
Newspapers	Dailies 95, Non-dailies 138
Total circulation	Dailies 4 100 000, Non-dailies 1 055 061
Copies per 1000 people	Dailies 307, Non-dailies 79

RADIO
Transmitters	Long/medium-wave 7, Short-wave 5, VHF–FM 22
Total receivers	4 036 000 licences
Licences per 1000 people	303

TELEVISION
Transmitters	16
Receivers	3 268 007 licences
Licences per 1000 people	245

FILM
Cinemas	Fixed 321
Total seating capacity	187 774
Seats per 1000 people	14
Total annual attendance	25 703 000
Annual visits per capita	2

PRESS

In addition to Amsterdam and Rotterdam, which each have 10 daily newspapers, 53 towns have at least one daily paper, more often than not representing a distinctive political viewpoint. Several papers have subeditions in other towns, included in the above total, and some have editorial links with one another. Eight papers have a nation-wide readership; two of these have circulation figures exceeding 300 000.

Of the non-daily general interest newspapers, 46 appear two or three times weekly, and 92 weekly. Most newspapers devote a high proportion of space to international and foreign news.

Circulation figures totalling 15 million copies for a recorded total of 421 periodicals in 1971 — which does not include many 'underground' or transient publications — are headed by a radio and television magazine (2 966 837 copies), two women's magazines (1 994 522 and 1 088 995) and a trade journal (1 127 225). In the same year, there were 24 mass-circulation periodicals for general readership and 96 for special readership groups, 18 specialized periodicals for children and youth, 33 dealing with religion and philosophy, 306 for trade and professional readerships and 22 house journals, government and other information bulletins, etc.

NEWS AGENCIES

The national agency, Algemeen Nederlands Persbureau (ANP), in operation since 1934, is an independent foundation jointly owned by daily newspaper publishers. It has its headquarters in The Hague, with branches in Amsterdam, Rotterdam, Utrecht and at Schiphol Airport and a picture department in Amsterdam. Permanent personnel number 230, of whom 80 are staff editors. Branches abroad are at Brussels, Djakarta, Curaçao and Surinam. Transmission of news from foreign correspondents is by telex and leased radio teleprinter.

ANP has a daily output of 60 000 words in Dutch and 6000 in English. All Dutch newspapers (54 publishers) are subscribers along with radio and television organizations and a large number of private subscribers receiving the agency's economic services.

News is received, by leased cable-teleprinter circuits and ANP's own radio teleprinter, from six foreign agencies (ANSA, Antara, AP, UPI, DPA and TASS) on contract and from about 20, including Reuters and AFP, on an exchange basis.

A smaller agency is the Katholiek Nederlands Persbureau (KNP), an independent company established in The Hague in 1947 by Catholic daily newspapers. It has a branch in Rome and other correspondents abroad, and issues up to 5000 words a day in Dutch and 500 in English, with occasional features in German or French. News is exchanged with other Catholic agencies.

RADIO

Broadcasting, both radio and television, is carried out by private organizations and groups, licensed by the government via the Ministry of Cultural Affairs Recreation and Social Welfare, and working together through a central body, the Nederlandse Omroep Stichting (NOS). The broadcasting organizations, of which there are seven in NOS at the present time, are associations of listeners and viewers sharing particular cultural, religious or political interests recognized as being of general benefit to the community and having a regular membership of at least 100 000 radio and television licence holders.

Broadcasting time is allocated to each organization according to the size of its membership. 'Aspirant' groups with at least 15 000 members are also allocated broadcasting time over a period of two years with a view to their achieving 100 000 members and the status of recognized organizations. The coordination of the individual programmes of the various organizations and groups, the supervision of jointly sponsored programmes and the management of the studios and common technical services are the responsibility of NOS, as also are the production and transmission of special regional broadcasts to the northern and eastern provinces (2 hours a day) and the southern provinces (1 hour a day). The governing body of NOS consists of 24 members, half of them appointed by the broadcasting organizations, a quarter by certain recognized cultural organizations, and a quarter — plus the chairman — by the Crown.

Total broadcasting time on the three home services, Hilversum I, II and III, is approximately 300 hours a week, almost 70% of which is taken up by the programmes of the individual organizations and groups, and 25% by their joint programmes. The remaining time is allotted to other approved organizations to primary- and secondary-school broadcasts, commercial advertising (limited to 24 minutes a day), etc. Regular exchanges of Dutch-language programmes are carried out with Belgische Radio en Televisie (Belgium).

Short-wave broadcasts beamed to foreign countries and overseas territories are the responsibility of Wereldomroep, the Netherlands World Broadcasting Service. It broadcasts in Dutch, Afrikaans, Arabic, English, French, Indonesian and Spanish, and also produces taped and recorded programmes in some 40 languages for the use of radio stations in over 100 countries.

Transmitting installations are owned and operated by a company whose shares are jointly held by the government (Post Office) and the broadcasting corporations. Seven medium-wave transmitters (from 2.5 to 125kW) and 22 FM transmitters (from 4 to 100kW) broadcast the home and regional programmes while the European and overseas services of Wereldomroep are broadcast from 3 short-wave transmitters (one each of 10 and 50kW and three of 100kW). Relay transmitters for short-wave services are situated in the Netherlands Antilles and Madagascar.

Wire-relay systems for radio (first established in 1926) are run by the Post Office. Three lines distribute the three home radio programmes and a fourth carries mainly programmes from foreign stations. A monthly fee is payable in addition to the ordinary licence.

TELEVISION

The organization and management of television services are as described above for radio broadcasting. Broadcasting time on the two television channels, totalling 63 hours a week, is allocated to the NOS corporations and other authorized organizations as in the case of radio, except that approximately 40% of the total time is devoted to the NOS joint programme. Educational television programmes are provided for primary and secondary schools through the Netherlands School Television Association in collaboration with NOS, and for post-school youth and adult groups by the Television Academy.

As in radio broadcasting, commercial advertisements immediately precede and follow the regular news bulletins, the time limit being 15 minutes a day per transmitting station.

In 1970, as a member of the European Broadcasting Union (EBU), NOS originated 17 Eurovision programmes (4 current affairs, 10 sports, 1 religious, 1 light entertainment and 1 music) and transmitted 245 programmes, totalling 386 hours, through the Eurovision network.

Thirteen transmitters, ranging from 5 to 100kW, ensure television coverage of the whole country. The definition used is 625 lines. Since 1968, both channels broadcast programmes in colour. The Post Office is currently experimenting with high-frequency wire-relay networks for both radio and television programmes.

FILM

The 41 companies which are members of the Netherlands Cinema League (no data are available for the country's 250 other film producers) produced 5 feature films and 74 short films in 1971. A weekly newsreel is produced and many newsfilms are exchanged with other countries.

Various forms of aid and encouragement to the industry are provided by the government, notably a production fund (to which the Netherlands Cinema League also contributes) to foster the production of Dutch feature films, financial aid for independent short-film directors, and the provision of production facilities for Dutch and foreign film-makers at the Cinetone Studios in Amsterdam.

There are no official restrictions governing the import of foreign films, though the Netherlands Cinema League requires its members to show at least 12 non-USA films a year. In 1970, 358 feature films were imported; from the USA (113), the UK (61), Italy (57), France (51), the Federal Republic of Germany (43), Sweden (7), the USSR (6), Japan (5) and other countries (15). Some 400 documentaries were imported in 1970. Cinema attendance figures have halved in the last ten years.

SPACE COMMUNICATION

An earth station, at Burum near Groningen, came into service in 1973 for reception of Atlantic Intelsat transmissions.

PROFESSIONAL TRAINING AND ASSOCIATIONS

A three-year course for journalists is offered by the National School of Journalism, at the University of Utrecht. Other communications courses, including part-time courses, are available at the Institute of Sciences of the Press, Amsterdam, and the Institute for Mass Communications, University of Nijmegen.

The Netherlands Film Academy in Amsterdam and the Academy of Art in Breda provide professional training for film and television writers, technicians, directors and producers, while the Wereldomroep (overseas broadcasting service) has a radio and television training centre for communicators from developing countries.

Professional associations include organizations of publishers of periodicals and daily and other newspapers, associations of newspaper editors, journalists, specialized journalists and foreign correspondents, the Netherlands Cinema

League, the Netherlands Film-makers' Association and an association of cinema technicians.

NORWAY

Population	3 940 000
Area	324 219 sq. km.

PRESS
Newspapers	Dailies 79, Non-dailies 80
Total circulation	Dailies 1 541 000, Non-dailies 327 000
Copies per 1000 people	Dailies 391, Non-dailies 83

RADIO
Transmitters	Long/medium-wave 37, Short-wave 2, VHF–FM 209
Total receivers	1 235 450 licences
Licences per 1000 people	313

TELEVISION
Transmitters	525
Receivers	894 555 licences
Licences per 1000 people	227

FILM
Cinemas	Fixed 450
Total seating capacity	145 000
Seats per 1000 people	37
Total annual attendance	18 870 000
Annual visits per capita	5

PRESS

Because of the geographical configuration of the country, the Norwegian press is typically decentralized with a large number of daily papers and relatively small local readerships.

Of the 12 dailies appearing in Oslo, the capital, only 2 exceed 100 000 in circulation: one has separate morning and evening editions circulating 184 000 and 156 000 copies respectively, the other circulates 100 000 copies on weekdays and 147 000 on Saturdays. Bergen has 4 dailies. There are no Sunday papers. While only 2 newspapers are the official organs of political parties, most have some party connections. Both the daily and non-daily newspapers carry a high proportion of serious feature articles on political, social and cultural subjects.

More than 2500 periodicals are published, of which 334 (concerning which information is available) have a total circulation of 4 132 000. Weekly family-type magazines alone account for about 2 million of this total.

Norway is one of the world's chief newsprint-producing countries and exports over 400 000 metric tons annually.

NEWS AGENCIES

The national news agency is Norsk Telegrambyrå (NTB), which is a limited company with shares held exclusively by the Norwegian newspapers. National news is received at NTB headquarters in Oslo from two permanent correspondents in Bergen and Trondheim and from 120 part-time correspondents throughout the country. NTB maintains permanent correspondents in Brussels, Moscow and New York (with the Danish, Finnish and Swedish agencies), and has a stringer in Reykjavik.

NTB distributes to the Norwegian press and the Broadcasting Corporation a daily average of 13 000 words on national news plus 3000 on sports. International news, which is obtained through Reuters and AFP, through special services of DPA and TASS and through exchange agreements with most European national news agencies — particularly those of Denmark, Finland and Sweden — has an average daily distribution of 10 000 words a day.

NTB also provides a news-photo service, based on the international photo service of UPI and the exchange arrangement between EPU members for foreign pictures. National pictures are collected from some 150 part-time photo correspondents all over Norway, and a staff of photographers at headquarters in Oslo. NTB also has its own photographic-block factory.

AP maintains a bureau in Oslo which distributes news to the Norwegian Broadcasting Corporation and to special press subscribers; AP also reports on Norwegian events. TASS and UPI have permanent correspondents while Reuters, AFP and DPA have part-time correspondents. UPI distributes news to the Norwegian Broadcasting Corporation only.

RADIO

The Norwegian Broadcasting Corporation, Norsk Rikskringkasting (NRK), is an independent public body, subject to parliament only, for approval of its budget. It is self-supporting, all its equipment and operating expenses being met by licence fees and a purchase tax of 17% on the wholesale price of radio and television receivers.

The national radio network, which covers the entire population, is equipped with 8 long-wave transmitters (up to 200kW), 29 medium-wave transmitters (up to 100kW), 181 FM transmitters and 2 short-wave transmitters.

The home service broadcasts a total of 119 hours a week, consisting of news and information (44 hours), cultural broadcasts (46 hours), broadcasts for special audiences (19 hours), light entertainment (13 hours) and educational broadcasts (3 hours). School broadcasts, including language and music lessons, are received by some 2500 educational institutions

The NRK news-room is linked with NTB, AP and UPI news services.

The foreign service operates 100 and 120kW transmitters at Fredrikstad and another at Tromsø, the latter being used to broadcast home-service programmes in Norwegian, English and Spanish to the merchant navy in the north Atlantic. Other programmes are beamed to 14 areas of the world.

TELEVISION

The NRK television service has one programme, broadcast on 625 lines by 42 main and 483 auxiliary transmitters and reaching 94% of the population. Weekly broadcasting time is 45 hours, of which about 57% is nationally produced, the remainder consisting of foreign films and programmes broadcast through Eurovision, Nordvision and Intervision.

Main programme categories include news and information (12 hours a week), light entertainment (11 hours), cultural programmes and films (7 hours), educational broadcasts (4 hours), broadcasts for special audiences (3 hours) and advertising (1 hour).

An automatic transmitter of taped video programme flown in from Norway serves the small mining community of the Svalbard archipelago.

FILM

In 1972, 9 feature films were produced including one coproduction with Sweden. Of the 81 short films produced, 6 were entertainment films, 56 documentaries and 19 instructional. Many films are subsidized by the state. In addition, the government is a shareholder of the principal producing company, which makes all types of films.

The Statens Filmsentral (Government Film Service) coordinates film production by government departments and serves as a central library for films and filmstrips for schools, the merchant navy, voluntary bodies and other organizations. It has a modern laboratory equipped to process 35mm and 16mm films. The Ministry of Agriculture also produces films and filmstrips for use in agricultural schools.

The 336 features imported in 1969 came from the USA (130), the UK (44), France (38), Sweden (26), Germany (14), Denmark (11), Japan (8), Spain (6), Italy (5), Austria (2), Canada (2), the USSR (2), Brazil and Switzerland.

The development of television has affected both film production and cinema attendance in Norway, the latter having decreased from about 35 million in 1960 to only 54% of that figure in 1971. Films are also shown by 20 mobile units, drawing an annual attendance of 472 000 (included in the general total).

SPACE COMMUNICATIONS

Norway shares the Atlantic Intelsat earth station at Tanum in Sweden with the other Scandinavian countries.

PROFESSIONAL TRAINING AND ASSOCIATIONS

One-year courses in journalism are offered at the Norwegian School of Journalism at Oslo. Entrants must have completed their secondary education. Social science students receive mass communication teaching at the Universities of Oslo and Bergen.

There are 10 professional organizations for the press, 5 for publishers, 1 for editors in chief and 4 for journalists, one of which is for radio journalists. Film organizations include 1 for producers, 1 for cinema technicians, 3 for writers and performers, 2 for distributors and 3 for exhibitors. The programme personnel administrative and technical staff employed by the Norwegian Broadcasting Corporation have an association to safeguard their economic and professional interests.

POLAND

Population	32 749 000
Area	312 677 sq. km.

PRESS
Newspapers	Dailies 44, Non-dailies 42
Total circulation	Dailies 7 553 0000, Non-dailies 1 896 000
Copies per 1000 people	Dailies 231, Non-dailies 58

RADIO
Transmitters	Long/medium-wave 30, VHF–FM 21
Total receivers	5 795 000* licences
Licences per 1000 people	177

TELEVISION
Transmitters	52
Receivers	5 199 960 licences
Licences per 1000 people	159

FILM
Cinemas	Fixed 2465
Total seating capacity	576 445
Seats per 1000 people	18
Total annual attendance	114 207 0000
Annual visits per capita	3

*Including wired receivers.

PRESS

Daily newspaper readership is increasing in Poland. Over ten years the total circulation of dailies has risen by 2.5 million copies per issue (the 1960 total was 4.3 million copies per issue for 44 titles). Warsaw is the main publishing centre, with 10 dailies appearing six or seven times a week, including the organs of the three main parties – the Polish United Workers' Party (480 000 copies per issue), the United Peasants' Party (152 000) and the Democratic Party (158 000) — as well as the organ of the Union of Socialist Youth (250 000).

Circulations of up to 400 000 are also recorded for non-party newspapers. The other 33 dailies are published in the 17 provinces, often with distinctive city editions for the main population centres — of these, Lodz, Krakow. Wroclaw, Poznan and Katowice have 3 or more dailies. The country's highest circulating daily is published in Katowice, with over 600 000 copies per weekday issue and 750 000 on Sundays.

Non-dailies include 29 weeklies, 8 appearing more frequently (two, three or four times a week), one of these being German, and 5 less frequently.

By far the largest enterprise in both newspaper and periodical publishing is the United Workers' Party press.

The periodical press, with 3625 titles circulating 29.5 million copies per issue. is mainly published in Warsaw. Apart from Polish, periodicals are published in English (110 titles), German (34 titles), Russian (29 titles), French (26 titles), Spanish (8 titles), Czech (5 titles) and 16 other languages.

Main subject categories are general readership (530 titles circulating 8 562 000 copies per issue), technology (529 titles, 2 219 000 copies), sociology and statistics (247 titles, 945 000 copies), political sciences (238 titles, 2 675 000 copies), agriculture (205 titles, 2 470 000 copies), natural sciences (198 titles, 232 000 copies), education (169 titles. 1 146 000 copies), medicine (144 titles, 842 000 copies), administration (129 titles, 1 132 000 copies), law (112 titles, 1 255 000 copies), religion (79 titles, 419 000 copies) and children and youth (72 titles, 5 102 000 copies). In addition, 156 journals circulating 417 copies are issued by industrial enterprises, etc.

Domestic newsprint production is sufficient for the country's requirements. The 1970 total was 87 900 metric tons.

NEWS AGENCIES

Polska Agencja Prasowa (PAP), founded in 1944, is a government agency with headquarters in Warsaw and branches in 21 foreign cities. In addition to the news supplied by its own correspondents. PAP receives the services of 32 foreign news sources and itself issues 60 000 words a day of domestic and foreign news in Polish, 1200 words in Russian, 1000 words in English and 300 words each in French and Spanish. Among the 5200 subscribers to these daily services or to the special economic-news service also issued, over 2000 are in foreign countries.

The Polska Agencja Interpress (PAI), a cooperative agency has its headquarters in Warsaw and other home offices in Poznan, Gdansk and Katowice as well as branches in 14 foreign countries to which its information services and publications on Polish life and affairs are primarily directed. The latter include foreign-language periodicals and an annual total of about 100 books in 17 different languages. Its various daily news bulletins amount to 4000 words each in English, Russian and German, 3000 words in French, 2000 in Spanish and 2000 in seven other European languages. Special services are also issued to 100 weekly and 120 monthly foreign subscribers, as well as to 80 Polish newspapers and journals.

The Certralna Agencja Fotograficzna (CAF), associated with Interpress, is also based in Warsaw and has branches in Poland and abroad. CAF issues photo information on Polish and foreign affairs to the press and television, amounting to some 372 000 photos annually for the Polish press and 31 000 for foreign journals. The agency works with more than 50 foreign agencies and transmits its photos by radio and, also, by a telephoto circuit linking Warsaw to 16 regional centres and three cities abroad.

The Agencja Robotnicza (AR) issues daily news summaries and articles for the Polish press, radio and television, weekly features and film and television coverage for both Polish and foreign media.

RADIO

Polskie Radio is directed by a broadcasting committee appointed by the government. The committee is responsible for the production and diffusion of programmes, while the transmitters and land-lines are controlled by the Post and Telegraph Service. Revenue is derived from licence fees on radio receivers and from a state subsidy.

Three national programmes are broadcast from Warsaw: the first, from a 500kW long-wave transmitter; the second, from a 150kW medium-wave transmitter; and the third, on FM. The first programme, which is of a popular nature, and also the second, are received throughout the whole national territory. The FM programme, consisting mainly of literary broadcasts and symphonic music, is on the air for 19½ hours a day.

The three national programmes, which are on the air for over 430 hours a week, consist of music (52.7% of total broadcasting time), news and information (24.5%), literary and theatrical presentations (9.9%), broadcasts for children and schools (5.7%), general educational programmes (2%) and advertising (3.7%). Almost all are of national origin.

In addition to relaying the national programmes, 16 regional stations daily originate from 1 to 5 hours of programmes of local interest.

Polskie Radio broadcasts talks for teachers, and daily programmes for the 30 000 schools equipped with receivers. The programmes supplement the school curriculum and are approved by the Ministry of Education. They are provided for all classes in primary and secondary schools.

Educational programmes intended mainly for industrial and agricultural workers and broadcast as the 'University of the Air' have a nation-wide audience. Courses at three different levels concentrate on history, social and natural sciences, literature and agro-biology, as well as Russian, English, French and German-language lessons.

Several thousand wired relay centres transmit programmes to 883 395 loudspeakers and wired receivers installed at state farms agricultural cooperatives, factories, hospitals, clubs and schools. These centres transmit their own broadcasts in addition to relaying the national programmes.

Poland's external broadcasting service, with short-wave transmitters of up to 100kW in power, is on the air for 14 hours a week in Polish and 25 hours a week in English, French, Spanish, Italian, German, Swedish, Danish, Finnish, Arabic and Esperanto.

TELEVISION

Television broadcasting is operated in the same manner as radio broadcasting. Polskie Radio i Telewizja began experimental transmissions in 1952 and regular programmes in 1954. It now broadcasts from 24 main stations and 28 auxiliary transmitters, covering 85% of the national territory. The definition system used is 625 lines and the colour system SECAM.

Two programmes are broadcast for a total of 135 hours a day respectively, consisting of news and information (35%), light entertainment and sports (17%), drama (15%), 10 artistic films a month (14%), programmes for children and youth (14%) and a small amount of advertising. Included in these figures are some 15 hours a week of educational programmes.

In 1971, Polish television carried over 400 school broadcasts (340 for primary and secondary schools, and 63 for agricultural schools) and, as part of the Unesco-assisted 'Television Polytechnic', transmitted from Gdansk, Wroclaw and Katowice, 146 lectures for higher technical-school candidates, 198 lectures for first-year students and 60 lectures for secondary-school teachers (40 in mathematics and 20 in physics).

Programmes supplied by foreign countries through Intervision and Eurovision account for about 50 hours a year. Over 82% of programme material is of national origin. Television equipment is locally produced.

FILMS

The control of production, distribution and exhibition of commercial educational and newsreel films is vested in Film Polski, a government operated agency, under the overall authority of the Central Film Office of the Ministry of Culture and the Arts.

Long-film production amounted to 25 titles in 1972, 4 of which were long documentaries. In the same year, short-film production amounted to 586 titles including 322 instructional films and 98 entertainment films, and 249 films intended specifically for television.

Imported feature films numbered 154 in 1972, coming from the USSR (28), the USA (21), France (18), Czechoslovakia (13), the UK (13), Hungary (13), Romania (9), Yugoslavia (8), Italy (7), Bulgaria (5), the German Democratic Republic (5), Japan (4), Spain (4), the Federal Republic of Germany (4) and other countries (4). Some short and medium-length films were imported for commercial exhibition in 1970.

Films are distributed by an official film-renting centre and (for educational institutions, clubs and cultural centres) by an educational film centre, 'Filmos'. While the total number of cinemas has dropped by about 300 over the last ten years, many former 16mm theatres have been converted to 35mm bringing the 1972 total of 35mm and 16mm cinemas to 1784 and 681 respectively, to which should be added 475 mobile units (235 35mm and 240 16mm). Annual attendances dropped by over 50 million during the ten-year period.

PROFESSIONAL TRAINING AND ASSOCIATIONS

The Institute of Journalism at Warsaw University (established as a faculty in 1952) offers two-year full-time post-graduate diploma courses dealing with press, radio and television, from which 112 students graduated in 1970, while the Silesian University in Katowice has had a two-year post-graduate course in journalism since 1969 (about 80 graduates in 1971).

Mass culture courses at the University of Lodz deal with cinema and television and, in the same town, there is an advanced school for the training of film and television directors, producers and cameramen. Additional training facilities are provided by the Journalism Centre run by the Polish Journalists' Union.

PORTUGAL

Population	9 630 000
Area	92 082 sq. km.

PRESS
Newspapers	Dailies 33, Non-dailies 645
Total circulation	Non-dailies 2 361 000
Copies per 1000 people	Non-dailies 245

RADIO
Transmitters	Long/medium-wave 46, Short-wave 33, VHF–FM 16
Total receivers	1 405 000 licences
Licences per 1000 people	146

TELEVISION
Transmitters	23
Receivers	388 000 licences
Licences per 1000 people	40

FILM
Cinemas	Fixed 485
Total seating capacity	273 300
Seats per 1000 people	28
Total annual attendance	28 000 000
Annual visits per capita	3

PRESS

Of Lisbon's 10 dailies, all of which have nation-wide circulations, the two largest are partly or wholly government owned. One of these circulates 160 000 copies on weekdays and 250 000 on Sundays, and the other nearly 128 000 on weekdays and 131 000 on Sundays. Seven Lisbon dailies and all four dailies published in Oporto have Sunday editions. Provincial and island newspapers have much lower circulations.

The periodical press, including non-daily general interest newspapers, totals over 1200 titles. Highest circulations are recorded for women's and sports magazines and a weekly news magazine.

Portugal produced 800 metric tons of newsprint in 1970, during which year the national consumption amounted to 44 100 metric tons.

NEWS AGENCIES

The Agencia de Noticias e de Informações (ANI), founded in 1947, is a privately owned company with headquarters in Lisbon. ANI maintains branches with full-time correspondents in Rio de Janeiro, Luanda and Lourenço Marques and has stringers in some European capitals and in Brazil, Portuguese Guinea, Mozambique, the USA, Bermuda, Mexico and Canada. It distributes a daily average of 40 000 words in Portuguese, using its own teleprinter circuit for Portugal, and a radio teleprinter, telex, leased cable teleprinter and air mail for its other transmission of news.

Special services are received from UPI, DPA, Efe and ANSA while UPI also provides an economic-news service and stock-exchange, sports and shipping news which is sold by ANI to banks, newspapers, and ship owners and builders.

The Agencia Noticiosa Portuguesa Lusitania, founded in 1944, is a non-profit-making cooperative enterprise located in Lisbon. It distributes a daily service by radio to Portuguese-language newspapers overseas, and also provides the metropolitan press with news from Portuguese-speaking areas abroad.

UPI, DPA, ANSA and Reuters maintain bureaux in Lisbon.

RADIO

Radio broadcasting is operated under both public and private ownership. The state-owned broadcasting organization is the Emissora Nacional de Radiodifusão (ENR) which derives its revenue from licence fees and government subsidies. Its home services are broadcast daily on two networks, Network I (medium and short-wave) for 24 hours and Network II (medium-wave and FM) for 16½ hours.

Regional stations on the adjacent islands (Emissora Nacional do Arquipelago de Madeira, with 1 medium-wave and 1 FM transmitter, and the Emissora Regional dos Açores with 1 short-wave transmitter) relay ENR programmes and also originate their own programmes, consisting mostly of light music and local news and information.

Radio Universidade, under the auspices of the Ministry of Education, broadcasts cultural and informative programmes for 30 minutes each weekday and for nearly 2 hours on Sundays and holidays, on Network II via a medium-wave transmitter of 135kW. This station publishes a monthly bulletin free of charge.

The overseas service of ENR is on the air for over 60 hours a day, transmitting programmes via 9 short-wave transmitters (up to 100kW), in Portuguese and in French, German, Italian, Spanish and Konkani (a dialect spoken around Goa in India), beamed to 14 different areas throughout the world. A medium-wave international service in French, English and German is also broadcast to Europe every evening for 2¼ hours.

A number of private and commercial stations are licensed to broadcast – under the supervision of the government telecommunications services (for technical matters) and the National Secretariat for Information, Popular Culture and Tourism (for programming). These stations include Radio Renascença, a

Catholic organization with stations in Lisbon and Oporto, broadcasting religious programmes for 19 hours a day on 2 medium-wave, 1 short-wave and 13 FM transmitters; Radio Clube Portugues, a cooperative association of commercial radio clubs with their own medium- and short-wave and FM transmitters; Emissores Associados de Lisboa, a commercial association constituting three small independent stations in Lisbon with shared medium-wave and FM transmitters; Emissoras do Norte Reunidos in Oporto, which groups together several small commercial stations; Radio Ribatejo in Santarém, broadcasting for 11½ hours a day in Portuguese, Spanish, French and English; Radio Alto Douro in Oporto; Radio Altitude in Guarda; and Radio Polo Norte in Caramulo.

Deutsche Welle (Federal Republic of Germany) has two relay transmitters of 250kW each, at Sines in Portugal.

TELEVISION

Radiotelevisão Portuguesa (RTP), a private corporation in which the state holds 60% of the shares, derives its revenue from licence fees and advertising. It began broadcasting in Lisbon, in 1956, and now has a network serving over 90% of the continental population. The first programme is on the air for 6½ hours on weekdays, for 8 hours on Sundays in summer and for 11½ hours daily in winter.

Its programmes include news, information and sports (20% of total programme time), broadcasts to schools (19%), films and serials (12%), cultural broadcasts (11%), light music (6%), advertising (5%), serious music (3.5%), etc. The second programme (2½ hours a day) includes music and films.

FILM

Feature-film production amounts to about three films a year. Production of short films totalled 205 titles in 1970. Practically all films exhibited are imported. The 1970 total of 347 came from the USA (147), Italy (64), the UK (46), France (28), France/Italy (17), Spain (9), the Federal Republic of Germany (5), Spain/Italy (5) and the USSR (4).

PROFESSIONAL TRAINING

There is no professional media training as such, but the Technical University of Lisbon offers a one-year course on the sociology of information, and the Institution of New Professions – also in Lisbon – provides regular teaching on the mass media.

ROMANIA

Population	20 470 000
Area	237 500 sq. km.

PRESS

Newspapers	Dailies 57, Non-dailies 19
Total circulation	Dailies 3 537 877, Non-dailies 661 733
Copies per 1000 people	Dailies 173, Non-dailies 32

RADIO

Transmitters	Long/medium wave 21, Short-wave 18, VHF–FM 13
Total receivers	3 106 337 licences
Receivers per 1000 people	152

TELEVISION

Transmitters	111
Receivers	1 703 240 licences
Receivers per 1000 people	83

FILM

Cinemas	Fixed 6244
Total annual attendance	189 238 000
Annual visits per capita	9

PRESS

Though Romania has a well-developed regional press, with newspapers and periodicals appearing in almost all administrative districts, the most influential papers are published in the capital, Bucharest. These include 10 dailies, 5 of which have circulations in excess of 200 000, by far the largest and most important being the official organ of the Central Committee of the Romanian Communist Party, circulating 900 000 copies per issue. Some 40 district centres also have daily papers, with circulations generally ranging between 20 000 and 50 000. Seventeen newspapers, 11 of which are dailies, are published in the languages of the national minorities of Romania, including Hungarian, German, Serbian and Armenian.

There were 637 periodicals published in 1971, with a total circulation of 7 352 000 copies per issue, covering a broad range of subjects: technical, professional, literary, art, health, scientific, medical, statistical, etc. There are also special magazines for women and children.

Domestic production of newsprint totals 58 000 metric tons a year.

NEWS AGENCIES

The national agency is the Agentia Romana de Presa (Agerpres), set up in 1949 as a government department, with headquarters in Bucharest and branches in all regional centres, as well as in 22 foreign countries. It has a total staff of 580 persons, two-thirds of whom have editorial responsibilities. Foreign news is received from 36 agencies by agreement. In addition to its services to the national media in Romanian, Agerpres issues 14 300 words daily in English, 9400 in French, 6550 in Spanish, 13 250 in Russian 2600 in German and a small volume in Arabic. Home news is transmitted to the central office by telex and telephone and from external sources by permanently leased teleprinter circuit and the agency's own RTT equipment. Subscribers are served by leased teleprinter circuits and RTT, as well as by telex and telegraph. Subscribers number over 4000.

Foreign agencies represented in Bucharest include ADN, Novosti, BTA, CTK, INA (Iraq), MTI, Hsinhua, PAP, Tanjug and TASS.

RADIO

Under the official direction of the State Radio and Television Committee Radioteleviziunea Romana operates all radio and television services. It is financed from licence fees, government subsidies and advertising.

Romanian Radio's home service, based in Bucharest, consists of three programmes. The first, a national programme appealing to all sections of the public, is broadcast on 1 long-wave transmitter (1200kW) and 4 medium-wave transmitters (up to 400kW), and on 9 FM transmitters in as many cities, and carries all or part of the 22-hour daily schedule. The second is primarily an educational and cultural programme broadcast for 19 hours a day on medium waves (6 transmitters of up to 100kW) and FM (3 transmitters). The third is devoted largely to music and is broadcast on 9 city FM transmitters for 8 or 9 hours a day.

The six regional stations (at Bucharest, Cluj, Tirgu Mures, Timisoara, Craiova and Iaşi) originate their own programmes and also link up with the national network. In addition to Romanian-language programmes, these stations also broadcast in Hungarian, German and Serbian, with some summer-time programmes in English, Russian and French as well.

Domestic programmes, totalling over 510 hours weekly, consist of cultural and scientific programmes (251 hours), light entertainment (98 hours), news and information (78 hours), broadcasts for ethnic minorities (45 hours), education (37 hours, including 10 hours for schools) and advertising (6 hours).

The foreign service, Radio Bucharest, with two medium-wave transmitters of up to 240kW, is on the air for about 200 hours a week, broadcasting programmes in Arabic, English, French, German, Greek, Iranian, Italian, Portuguese, Romanian, Serbian, Spanish, Turkish and Yiddish, and beamed to Europe, Africa, the Near East, Asia, the Pacific, North America and Latin America.

TELEVISION

Radioteleviziunea Romana's television service began regular operations in 1957. With 18 main transmitters and 93 auxiliary stations, it now broadcasts two programmes covering respectively 84 and 14% of the population (a radius of 50 to 60km around the capital). Programmes, totalling around 60 hours a week, consist of news and information (16 hours), arts, letters and science (13 hours), light entertainment (12 hours), school and pre-school education (6 hours), adult education (5 hours) and broadcasts for ethnic minorities (3 hours, in Hungarian and German).

About 27% of programmes are imported, through Intervision and from other European countries and the USA. In 1970, Romanian television originated 59 hours of Intervision programmes and received 289 hours. Colour television (SECAM system) is shortly to be introduced. The definition system used is 625 lines.

FILM

The state-owned National Film Centre exercises overall responsibilities for the national film industry, including the choice of themes for the production of the three national studios.

Film production averages around 12 to 16 features a year, a number of which are exported. Production in 1971 included 15 features and 185 short films (139 documentary, 28 entertainment and 18 educational). Most of the short films are produced for ministries, government departments, etc. Film imports in 1971 totalled 156 features and 32 documentaries.

The number of cinemas has increased by 3600 over the last decade, and annual attendances by 25 million. Only 559 of the fixed cinemas (seating 217 728 persons) are equipped for the projection of 35mm films. There are five mobile units in operation reaching audiences totalling 366 000 persons a year.

PROFESSIONAL TRAINING AND ASSOCIATIONS

Training courses for journalists are available at the University of Bucharest. The Institute of Theatrical and Film Art in Bucharest, trains cameramen, film directors and other potential film-makers (100 students were enrolled in the film department in 1971–2).

There is a professional association of journalists in Bucharest.

SAN MARINO

Population	19 000
Area	61 sq. km.

PRESS

Newspapers	**Non-dailies 5**
Total circulation	Non-dailies 6000
Copies per 1000 people	Non-dailies 316

RADIO

Total receivers	3723 estimated in use
Receivers per 1000 people	196

TELEVISION

Receivers	2400 estimated in use
Receivers per 1000 people	126

FILM

Cinemas	Fixed 9
Total annual attendance	203 833
Annual visits per capita	11

PRESS

There is no daily press. The non-dailies consist of 3 fortnightly and 2 monthly newspapers all appearing in Italian — 3 of these are the official organs of political parties. Of the other 8 periodicals, with a total circulation of over 24 000 copies, 4 deal with political and economic sciences. In addition, the Italian daily and periodical press is widely read.

NEWS AGENCIES

There is no national news agency. ANSA and some of the larger Italian dailies maintain part-time correspondents in San Marino.

RADIO

There is no local broadcasting service. San Marino is served by the stations of Radiotelevisione Italiana (RAI). This service includes broadcasts to schools.

TELEVISION

The RAI television programmes are adequately received.

FILM

All films and newsreels are imported. In 1970, a total of 366 films originated from the USA (152), Italy (131), the UK (29), France (27), the Federal Republic of Germany (12), Spain (9), Japan (4), Yugoslavia (3) and others (2).

Of the fixed cinemas, two show 16mm films only.The government maintains a small film library; educational and documentary film shows are given by religious organizations which operate 16mm cinemas.

SPAIN

Population	34 360 000
Area	504 750 sq. km.

PRESS

Newspapers	Dailies 115, Non-dailies 121
Total circulation	Dailies 3 396 000, Non-dailies 3 851 000
Copies per 1000 people	Dailies 99, Non-dailies 112

RADIO

Transmitters	Long/medium wave 188, Short-wave 15, VHF—FM 260
Total receivers	7 042 000 licences
Receivers per 1000 people	205

TELEVISION

Transmitters	641
Receivers	5 800 000 estimated in use
Receivers per 1000 people	169

FILM

Cinemas	Fixed 6064
Total seating capacity	4 444 000
Seats per 1000 people	129
Total annual attendance	293 082 000
Annual visits per capita	8

PRESS

Daily newspapers are published in over 60 cities and towns throughout peninsular Spain and the Balearic and Canary Islands. Some of the larger provincial centres have as many as 4 or 5 general interest dailies, while Madrid and Barcelona have 13 and 10 respectively. Most of the towns have 1 or 2 papers with circulations ranging from 3000 to 40 000 copies. This decentralization of the industry is due partly to communications difficulties — same-day delivery of Madrid morning papers is impossible in many areas — and partly to the persistence of long-standing regional loyalties. The state has considerable powers, defined by the Press Law of 1938, with regard to the professional and industrial functioning of the press.

The highest circulation figures reported are those of 1 evening and 2 morning papers in Madrid circulating 225 000, 220 000 and 197 000 copies per issue (the latter also publishing an illustrated colour edition of about 100 pages on Sundays), and 2 morning papers in Barcelona with 217 000 and 180 000 copies per issue. There are 3 English-language dailies. Most devote more space to feature stories than to news reporting.

While there are few Sunday papers or Sunday editions of dailies published, over 30 towns have special Monday papers (almost all entitled *Hoja del Lunes*), often produced as a joint operation by several of the local daily publishers.

The majority of dailies and weeklies are organs of political, religious or commercial institutions or organizations. One group directed by the Falange nationalist movement controls 33 morning and 6 evening dailies, 5 weeklies and 4 magazines. A non-political Catholic movement with a strong social-welfare vocation controls 5 dailies (including 1 in Madrid) and one of the Madrid weeklies.

Periodicals other than newspapers number 4192, with a total circulation of over 34 million copies per issue. General interest magazines account for about 300 titles. The main specialized subject categories are religion and theology (533 titles), technology, etc. (465), law and administration, etc. (405), recreation and sports (387), medical sciences (355), general readership (309 titles), arts and architecture (295 titles), education (170 titles), etc. Seventeen periodicals appear in regional languages of Spain other than Spanish, and about 40 in foreign languages.

Domestic production of newsprint amounted to 111 000 metric tons in 1970.

NEWS AGENCIES

The most important of the news agencies is the Agencia Efe (Efe), an independent company founded in 1938, with headquarters in Madrid, branch offices in Barcelona, Bilbao, Sevilla and Santiago de Compostela and some 750 correspondents in the major towns. Of its 500 permanent employees, about 200 are editorial staff. Foreign branches are maintained in 30 world capitals and major cities. Efe receives the world services of DPA, UPI, AP, AFP and Reuters and issues 190 000 words (including 50 000 words of foreign news) daily in Spanish to its subscribers which include all information media in Spain and 200 daily newspapers, broadcasting stations and magazines in Latin America. For its transmissions Efe uses a leased cable teleprinter, radio teleprinter, telex, telephone, etc.

The Agencia Logos founded in Madrid in 1928 by a Catholic publishing organization has a permanent staff of 36 (17 editorial) and many part-time correspondents at home and in its foreign offices. It issues 45 000 words of national and foreign news daily in Spanish plus features and photos to its subscribers which include over 50 newspapers.

Agencia Mencheta, the oldest Spanish agency, founded in 1882, has its head office in Madrid and correspondents in the main towns. AFP, UPI, Reuters and DPA subscribe to its (mainly sports) services.

Prensa y Radio Español (Pyresa), founded in 1940, belongs to the Falangist organization, Prensa del Movimiento. From its Madrid headquarters, it issues daily domestic and foreign news bulletins to numerous radio and television stations and newspapers. Pyresa has working agreements with other Spanish agencies and obtains its international news from leading foreign agencies.

There are also over 30 smaller news services and agencies in Spain.

Foreign agencies with bureaux in Madrid include AFP, AP, Reuters and UPI. DPA, TASS and other agencies are also represented.

RADIO

All sound and television broadcasting in Spain, whether operated by public organizations or private enterprise, is controlled by the Dirección General de Radiodifusión y Televisión, an agency of the Ministry of Information and Tourism. Apart from the special nation-wide news service of the government network, which is relayed by all stations, the networks are independently operated. Advertising is permitted but is limited to 5 minutes in each hour. Publicly owned stations are financed by state subsidies plus advertising revenue and the proceeds of licences and taxes on the sale of receivers, while the private stations are wholly supported by commercial advertising.

Radio Nacional de España (RNE), the government network of 11 short-wave, 18 medium-wave and 58 FM transmitters throughout the country, covers the whole of peninsular Spain. It broadcasts three home-service programmes: the national programme, on medium waves, provides a general 24-hour service: the second (mainly musical) programme is on the air for 18 hours a day on FM; and the third programme consists of educational broadcasts in the morning (including Spanish for foreigners) and cultural broadcasts from 12.00 hours to midnight every day, also on FM. Some of RNE's musical programmes and language classes are redistributed by telephone circuit to over 20 000 subscribers in Madrid and Barcelona.

Other networks of official organizations include those of the Red de Emisoras del Movimiento (REM), which consists of 16 medium-wave regional stations operated by the Falange movement, and of the Cadena Azul de Radiodifusión (CAR) operated by the Frente de Juventudes. CAR's 17 medium-wave and 28 FM transmitters carry mainly educational programmes, with some news and entertainment, for 13 to 20 hours a day. These include elementary and secondary-level courses for persons living in remote areas.

Average weekly programme content for RNE stations, totalling 185 hours, consists of light entertainment (77 hours), news and information (47 hours), arts, letters and science (35 hours), education (3½ hours), advertising (3 hours) and other programmes (16 hours, including programmes for women and children, religious broadcasts, etc).

About 56% of all broadcast programme material is nationally produced.

The commercial stations broadcast on medium waves (168 transmitters) and FM (213 transmitters) and are mostly affiliated to country-wide or regional networks. The main networks are: the Sociedad Española de Radiodifusión, the country's oldest broadcasting service, which has 15 main stations and 37 associated stations, including two in the Spanish north African territories of Ceuta and Melilla; the Cadena de Ondas Populares Españolas, with 35 stations; the Cadena de Emisoras Sindicales with 17 stations; Radio España, Madrid; and Radio España de Barcelona.

External broadcasting is carried out by RNE which has short-wave transmitters of up to 700kW near Madrid. Programmes totalling 251 hours a week are beamed to five main areas: Europe (in Spanish and eastern European languages), Morocco (in French and Arabic), equatorial Guinea (in Spanish), the USA and Canada (in English) and Latin America (in Spanish).

TELEVISION

Televisión Española (TVE) is a public service with a degree of financial autonomy, operated and controlled by the Dirección General de Radio y Televisión. Its financial resources consist of a state subsidy (10%), advertising revenues (80%) and revenue from programme sales, exploitation of microwave links, etc. (10%). There is no privately owned television in Spain.

The service's first telecasts were carried out in Madrid in 1951 and regular programmes were broadcast in October 1956. TVE now consists of two networks with a complex system of 32 main transmitters and over 600 relays and repeaters capable of providing at least one-channel coverage for practically the whole country. There are good programme-production facilities, especially at the well-equipped centres in Madrid, Barcelona and Las Palmas (Canary Islands).

The first network (625 lines, VHF) with 20 main transmitting stations, including one of 500kW at Navacerrada just north of Madrid, covers 95% of the country, including Ceuta in north Africa, and potentially reaches 98% of the population. It is on the air for at least 74 hours a week. The second network (625 lines, UHF) is on the air for over 26 hours a week, broadcasting from 11 main transmitting stations, of which the most powerful are those at Madrid (1500kW) and Barcelona (300kW), potentially covering about 50% of the country's urban population. Since 1971, the stations of the peninsula and the Canary Islands have been linked by satellite, for about 2 hours a day, through the earth stations at Buitrago (Madrid) and Aguimes (Canary Islands). Other programmes (films and recordings) are dispatched to the Canary Islands by air.

Average weekly programme content for both networks includes light entertainment (38 hours), news and information (28 hours), arts, letters and science (25 hours), programmes for special audiences (13½ hours), advertising (3½ hours) and education (3 hours). Educational broadcasts include regular programmes for primary schools and secondary-level adult-education programmes (supplementing the radio broadcasts already mentioned) which are on the air for 30 minutes three times a week. Other civic and cultural programmes are specially broadcast for community viewing in the 3350 teleclubs run by the Ministry of Information in isolated rural areas. Approximately 80% of programmes are of domestic origin. Imported material comes mainly from the USA, European Broadcasting Union member countries and Latin America. Some 720 Eurovision programmes were transmitted by TVE in 1970.

Some colour programmes (PAL system) are broadcast. Cable distribution of national television, programmes began in Madrid in 1973, and in Barcelona in 1974, and is to be extended to five other towns.

FILM

Feature-film production increased from 73 titles in 1960 to 103 in 1972 (of which 51 were coproductions, with Italy mainly, and with France, the Federal Republic of Germany, Mexico and Portugal). Short-film production amounted to 118 titles in 1972 (25 entertainment, 31 documentary and 59 educational).

There are eight studios in Madrid and two in Barcelona. Annual imports of feature films totalled 398 in 1972, these coming from the USA (120), Italy (87), France (46), the UK (45), Mexico (23), the Federal Republic of Germany and Argentina (5 each), Australia (4) and other countries (27). Documentaries were imported from Canada (3), Hungary (2), Czechoslovakia, Japan, Portugal Romania and Sweden (1 each). Most foreign films are dubbed in Spanish.

There is a national film council with consultative and administrative functions which is responsible for the general organization and development of the film industry. The industry receives government support, in the form of loans and subsidies to producers and protective legislation, through the Ministry of Information and Tourism which also issues import licences, controls cinema admission prices, etc. Distributors are required to show 1 Spanish film for every 4 films from the USA.

Cinema attendances have dropped over ten years by about 25%, though the overall number of cinemas has remained fairly stable. In addition to the fixed cinemas, there are many open-air summer screening places and a number of drive-ins.

SPACE COMMUNICATIONS

Spain operates three Intelsat earth stations: one at Buitrago near Madrid with antennae for Atlantic and Indian Ocean satellites (operating since 1967 and 1970 respectively); another (non-standard) at Maspalomas in the Canary Islands operating since 1967; the the third at Aguimes (1971), also in the Canary Islands and destined to replace Maspalomas, receiving and transmitting Atlantic Intelsat communications.

TVE uses the facilities of Buitrago and Aguimes for the transmission of its television programmes under an agreement with the Compañia Telefónica Nacional de España.

PROFESSIONAL TRAINING AND ASSOCIATIONS

Courses in journalism, open to holders of the *Bachillerato superior* and leading to an official diploma after four years' study, are offered by the Official Schools of Journalism in Madrid and Barcelona, founded in 1941 and 1968 respectively; by schools of journalism at the Universities of La Laguna (Canary Islands), founded in 1964, and Navarra (Pamplona), founded in 1958; and by the School of Journalism of the Church, in Madrid. Graduates of other schools wishing to obtain the official diploma are required to pass a special examination. Broadcasting training and communications research are conducted by the state-financed Escuela Oficial de Radio y Televisión, Madrid. Similarly, practical and theoretical film training is offered at the state-run Escuela Oficial de Cinematografía.

The main professional associations in the mass media are grouped in two national federations: one of press associations, the other of press, radio, television and advertising associations, both in Madrid, where there is also an international press club. Other professional groups include national syndicates of the theatre, film actors, film directors and film producers and a national federation of film clubs.

SWEDEN

Population	8 120 000
Area	449 750 sq. km.

PRESS

Newspapers	Dailies 108, Non-dailies 53
Total circulation	Dailies 4 183 500, Non-dailies 367 400
Copies per 1000 people	Dailies 515, Non-dailies 45

RADIO

Transmitters	Long/medium-wave 34, Short-wave 2, VHF FM 256
Total receivers	2 984 207 estimated in use
Receivers per 1000 people	367

TELEVISION

Transmitters	299
Receivers	2 701 493 licences
Receivers per 1000 people	333

FILM

Cinemas	Fixed 1334
Total annual attendance	26 600 000
Annual visits per capita	3

PRESS

With one of the highest circulation rates in the world, averaging more than 1.5 copies daily per household, the Swedish press is still expanding its readership and, at the same time, concentrating its resources. While some 30 dailies have disappeared from the scene over the last decade, overall circulation figures have increased by about 1 million copies, largely reflecting the growth of the city dailies, particularly the evenîng papers which almost doubled their readership over the ten-year period. Stockholm with 6 dailies (3 with circulations of over 400 000), and Göteborg and Malmö with 4 dailies each – most appearing seven days a week – account for more than half the country's total circulation.

Dailies, and also non-dailies, are published in some 80 cities and provincial centres throughout the country almost all – either directly or indirectly – being associated with political parties.

The growing concentration of press ownership is a matter of concern to the government, which has established a special aid fund for newspapers in economic difficulty, providing subsidies for newsprint, state advertising contracts and bonuses on subscriptions.

Over 4000 magazines and other periodicals are published, the most widely read being the popular weeklies, 40 of which circulate well over 7 million copies per issue. Main subject categories are general readership (298 titles), religion

(241), law (196), political science (170), technology (164), trade and communications (157), education (155), geography and travel (143), recreation (142), agriculture, etc. (140), etc. In addition, there are about 1000 parish bulletins, some 270 school magazines and 240 house organs.

Sweden shares in the general increase in Scandinavian newsprint production. Of its annual output of over 1 million metric tons, more than two-thirds is exported, mainly to Denmark, France, the Federal Republic of Germany and the UK.

NEWS AGENCIES

The only national agency is the cooperative Tidningarnas Telegrambyra (TT), founded in 1921, which has its headquarters in Stockholm, branches in Göteborg, Malmö, Sundsvall and Luleå, and between 400 and 500 local part-time correspondents throughout the country. Abroad, it has bureaux in Brussels, Moscow and New York (together with other Scandinavian agencies). The agency's total permanent staff is 170 persons at home and 3 abroad.

Foreign news is received under exchange agreements with Reuters, AFP, DPA, TASS, FNB-STT, NTB, RB, ANP, ANSA, Belga, APA, ATS, Tanjug, ADN, Agerpres, BTA, CTK, MTI, PAP, Hsinhua and Kyodo.

In addition to its daily services of 25 000 words of national and local news and 11 000 words of foreign news, in Swedish, received by 155 subscribers including 140 newspapers and the national radio and television systems, TT broadcasts a special audio-radio service with five newscasts a day, and provides a telephone news service. A permanent teleprinter network links TT's offices with subscribers, and about 75 newspapers receive daily teletypesetting services. Since 1970, a new data-transmission service (Scanplex) owned by the national news agencies of the Scandinavian countries links these agencies in The Hague with Reuters' European multiplex circuit.

RADIO

Sveriges Radio, the Swedish Broadcasting Corporation, is an independent public service vested with the sole rights of sound radio and television broadcasting in Sweden. Its share capital is owned by community organizations (60%), industry and commerce (20%) and press organizations and individual newspapers (20%). It is governed by a board, six members being government appointees and five representing the shareholders. Apart from educational programmes and external broadcasting, which are financed out of public funds, its activities are financed by receiver licence fees. No commercial advertising is carried. Licences may be combined radio and television or radio only.

The corporation's three national services are on the air for about 350 hours a week, broadcasting light entertainment (146 hours), arts, letters and science (83 hours), news and information (56 hours), broadcasts for special audiences (40 hours), education (14 hours) and broadcasts for ethnic minorities (8 hours), etc. Programme I broadcasts a wide range of light and serious programmes and detailed newscasts; Programme II carries educational programmes in the day-time and serious music at night; while Programme III carries light entertainment round the clock, interspersed with frequent headline news summaries

School broadcasts (about 1400 a year) are conducted in cooperation with the Royal Board of Education, although the actual programmes are the responsibility of Sveriges Radio. Programme information is published in a special magazine for teachers which appears six times a year. Educational broadcasting also includes subject courses for adults and language courses both for the general public and for schools.

The external broadcasting service produces special programmes for both foreign listeners and Swedish people living abroad. Some of these are broadcast from its two 100kW transmitters at Hörby, in English, French, German, Portuguese, Spanish, Russian and Swedish, and are beamed to the Middle and Far East, Africa and North and South America. Others are exported under exchange arrangements for the use of foreign broadcasting systems. Some 400 programmes are thus distributed.

Sveriges Radio has its own foreign correspondents in Beirut, Bonn, Geneva, Hong Kong, London, Moscow, New York, Paris, Rome, Washington and Vienna.

TELEVISION

Experimental telecasts began in Sweden in 1954, regular programmes in 1956, and colour broadcasts (PAL system) in 1970. There are now 107 main and 192 auxiliary transmitters, enabling 99.6% of the population to receive the first programme, and 98.3% the second.

Total programme time is about 100 hours a week (two-thirds of which is on Channel 1), including arts, letters and science (29 hours), light entertainment (23 hours), news and information (20 hours), broadcasts for special audiences (12 hours) and education (8 hours). Apart from a common news service, the two channels are independent of each other.

Considerable provision is made for repeats and regional programmes. About 39% of programme material is imported, 53% of it from western Europe (principally the UK), 13% from other Scandinavian countries. 7% from eastern Europe, etc. Programmes are exchanged on a regular basis through the European Broadcasting Union and the International Radio and Television Organization.

FILM

Sweden's annual film production, severely affected by competition from television, had dropped from 30 feature films in 1957 to only 15 in 1961. But government encouragement, mainly through entertainment-tax relief and the founding of the Swedish Film Institute, has helped to raise annual production to around 19 features in 1971–2 (with a peak figure of 30 in 1968). In addition, 2 coproductions were made with the USSR and the USA.

Financed from a 10% levy on ticket sales, the Swedish Film Institute uses 20% of its income for general support of full-length film production, 18% for awards for features, 2% for awards for short films, 10% to offset losses on quality films, 5% for public relations, 30% for culturally significant activities (archives, film education, research, clubs, etc.) and 15% for loans and guarantees to producers. The institute has its own production centre and makes some short films.

In 1971, Sweden imported 290 feature films, including coproductions, from the USA (119), the UK (40), Italy (13), France/Italy (10), Italy/Spain (15), Denmark (8), Poland (8), France (9) and other countries (68). Annual cinema attendance has declined to little more than half the 1960 total of 50 million, and the number of cinemas has dropped by about 1000.

SPACE COMMUNICATIONS

Sveriges Radio, in cooperation with the Central Telecommunications Administration, is responsible for the development of satellite communications in Sweden. Sweden receives and transmits Atlantic Intelsat broadcasts through its earth station at Tanum (opened in October 1971) which also serves Denmark, Finland and Norway.

PROFESSIONAL TRAINING AND ASSOCIATIONS

Education in journalism is provided at two state colleges, the Journalist-högeskolan in Stockholm and the Journalist-högeskolan in Göteborg, each offering two-year courses at university level and each with a current enrolment of about 230 students. Women graduates slightly outnumber men. Admission of qualified candidates is by aptitude tests. The Dramatiska Institutet, a government training centre for film, theatre, radio and television, began operating in 1970. Also in Stockholm, film training is available at the Swedish Film Institute while communications training is offered at the Mass Communications Institute at Lund.

The Swedish Press Council — or Court of Honour — founded in 1916, was reorganized in 1969. Changes included the appointment to the Court of two representatives of the general public in addition to the three members appointed by the press organizations; newly granted authority to impose administrative fines on offending newspapers; and the appointment of a Press Ombudsman to whom complaints lodged against the press are submitted for settlement, where possible, or referral to the Court.

Professional organizations include 8 publishers' associations, 8 associations for journalists and 1 for foreign correspondents; 3 associations of film producers, one association each for performers, for distributors and for exhibitors; and a joint association of cinema and television workers.

SWITZERLAND

Population	6 320 000
Area	41 288 sq. km.

PRESS

Newspapers	Dailies 98, Non-dailies 173
Total circulation	Dailies 2 466 414, Non-dailies 900 000
Copies per 1000 people	Dailies 390, Non-dailies 142

RADIO

Transmitters	Long/medium-wave 5, Short-wave 9, VHF FM 186
Total receivers	1 958 000 licences
Licences per 1000 people	310

TELEVISION	
Transmitters	446
Receivers	1 535 888 licences
Licences per 1000 people	243

FILM	
Cinemas	Fixed 554
Total seating capacity	204 000
Seats per 1000 people	32
Total annual attendance	29 000 000
Annual visits per capita	5

PRESS

The traditionally independent attitudes of the 25 Swiss cantons, and the division of the country into distinct linguistic areas, largely explains the decentralization of the press in Switzerland and the fact that relatively few papers reach high circulation figures.

Of around 80 towns which have at least one daily newspaper, Zurich is the largest publishing centre, with 7 major German-language dailies totalling over 70 000 copies per issue and including the country's 3 highest individual circulations (276 000, 229 000 and 107 000). Basle and Berne, also German-speaking, have 5 and 4 dailies respectively. The French-language press is centred in Geneva and Lausanne with 5 and 3 major dailies respectively, the highest circulating papers being 2 in Lausanne (87 000 and 61 000) and 2 in Geneva (67 000 and 62 000). Lugano has 4 dailies, all in Italian, none of which exceeds 20 000 copies per issue.

Altogether 72 dailies are published in German, 20 in French and 6 in Italian, but none in the fourth national language, Romansch, which is spoken by less than 1% of the population. Several influential German and French-language dailies have national and international readerships.

The total number of dailies has dropped by 15 titles over the last five years but without a corresponding drop in overall circulation figures.

Non-daily general interest newspapers appear mainly once, twice or thrice weekly, 97 being in German, 57 in French, 15 in Italian and 4 in Romansch. Other periodicals numbered 1429 titles in 1972 (644 of these being in German, 278 in French, 63 in Italian and 444 in other languages), printing altogether 15 million copies per issue. Main subject categories include entertainment and pastimes (216 titles), technology, industry, trades, etc. (204 titles), law, public administration and social welfare (154 titles), medical sciences (116 titles) and farming, forestry and fisheries (111 titles), etc.

Switzerland's newsprint production amounted to 143 000 metric tons in 1970.

NEWS AGENCIES

The most important agency is the Agence Télégraphique Suisse (ATS) which supplies national and foreign news to almost all Swiss newspapers. Founded in 1894, ATS is completely independent of the state and is owned by the newspapers, the Société Suisse de Radiodiffusion, the Association Suisse des Editeurs de Journaux, the Union Romande de Journaux and the Association de la Press Suisse. Its headquarters are in Berne, but bureaux are maintained in Zurich, Geneva, Basle, Lausanne, Lugano, Delémont and Coire.

ATS distributes daily – in German, French and Italian – some 100 000 words, of which about 60 000 are foreign news. Its clients are the press, the radio and television services, public services and private enterprises. In addition, a daily news service by telephone includes eight bulletins in each of the three main national languages.

ATS has exchange agreements with Reuters, AFP, DPA and a certain number of national agencies.

A smaller agency, the Correspondance Politique Suisse (CPS), also has its headquarters in Berne and maintains bureaux in Zurich and Lugano and, also, Vienna.

The Agence Catholique Internationale d'Information (ACII) has its headquarters in Fribourg.

Reuters and UPI maintain bureaux in Geneva and Zurich, while AFP, AP and DPA have their bureaux in Geneva, where TASS has a permanent correspondent. Many other agencies are represented in Switzerland by either bureaux or correspondents.

RADIO

The sole concession for radio and television broadcasting in Switzerland, granted by the Federal Council, is held by the Société Suisse de Radiodiffusion et Télévision (SSR), a public company founded in 1931. It is financed by 70% of the concession receipts (the remaining 30% going to the federal telecommunications services responsible for technical operations and equipment). There is no commercial advertising on Swiss radio.

An annual licence fee is payable for radio and television receivers.

SSR consists of three regional organizations, each representing one of the major linguistic areas (Romansch broadcasts are provided for in the German-language service) and is responsible for ensuring coordination and exchanges among the regions. Broadcasts cover the entire country.

Each of the three regional services broadcasts two domestic radio programmes, the first consisting mainly of information and general entertainment while the second is devoted especially to cultural and musical programmes. Joint programmes for all language services are broadcast for 1½ hours on Saturdays on the first network and for 9 hours during the week, on the second.

The German service, based in Basle and with studios in Basle, Berne and Zurich, broadcasts about 200 hours a week via a powerful medium-wave transmitter (500kW) at Beromünster, and an extensive FM network. The French service, also with a 500kW medium-wave transmitter, at Soltens, and FM transmitters, is on the air for 247 hours a week. It has one studio in Lausanne, at its headquarters, and one in Geneva. The headquarters and studio of the Italian service are at Lugano and its main medium-wave transmitter (150kW) is at Monte Ceneri. It also has a network of FM transmitters, and broadcasts for 192 hours a week.

The weekly programme content for the three networks consists mainly of light entertainment (243 hours), arts, science and culture (186 hours), news and information (105 hours), broadcasts for special community groups (57 hours) and educational broadcasts (4 hours). In addition, a comprehensive programme of school broadcasts in all languages is on the air during school terms.

A six-channel wired broadcasting system, operated by SSR for 24 hours a day, distributes the radio programmes of the three regional services, plus one programme of continuous classical music programme, another of light music and another of relays from the broadcasting systems of neighbouring countries. Subscribers number about 420 000.

European and overseas short-wave services in English, German, French, Italian, Spanish, Portuguese, Arabic and Esperanto are broadcast round the clock by SSR, which operates transmitters of up to 500kW at Beromünster, Schwarzenburg and Sottens. Weekday programmes, including relays of the home services, are mainly information, while more feature-type programmes are broadcast at weekends.

The United Nations Radio operates a 25kW short-wave transmitter at Prangins, near Geneva, while the International Red Cross Committee, also in Geneva, broadcasts via a short-wave transmitter belonging to SSR's overseas service.

TELEVISION

Television broadcasting, also operated by the Société Suisse de Radiodiffusion et Télévision (SSR), in financed from licence fees, advertising revenue and a government loan.

The first Swiss telecasts took place in July 1953 and regular television programmes were broadcast from the beginning of 1958. In 1973, there were three television channels, one for each regional language service (German with Romansch, French and Italian) covering respectively 98.6%, 68% and 57% of the country's population, and broadcasting from 59 main and 387 auxiliary transmitters. Under the Director-General of the SSR, who is responsible for all programmes broadcast, the directors of the three regional services programme their own networks, assisted by a widely representative advisory committee.

The main programmes of the three services are broadcast from Zurich, Geneva and Lugano, along with regional variants from the studios of other stations in the network. Programmes for all services totalling approximately 173 hours a week consist mainly of broadcasts to special audiences (56 hours, mostly for children and youth), news, information and sports (55 hours), light entertainment, serials, etc. (40 hours), scientific, cultural and literary programmes (12 hours), advertising (6 hours) and school and adult education (4 hours). It is estimated that some 70 000 viewers follow the 'Telekolleg' evening educational broadcasts using material supplied by the Bavarian television (Federal Republic of Germany). Commercial advertising is authorized for a maximum of 15 minutes, in three blocks every evening, except on Sundays and public holidays.

The definition system used is 625 lines. Colour (PAL system) was introduced in 1968 and colour programmes are broadcast on all networks.

In some parts of Switzerland, collective transcoders have been installed to allow viewers to receive, also, television broadcasts from France, the Federal Republic of Germany and Austria, the programmes being distributed by cable networks operated either by private interests or by local authorities. Subscribers number over 100 000.

FILM

Switzerland's film production averages 5 features and between 40 and 60 documentaries a year. A weekly newsreel is also produced in the three main official languages. In 1972, 8 features and 6 long documentaries were produced, and 50 short films (30 entertainment and 20 documentary). Two of the features were coproductions with France.

The Federal Department of Internal Affairs, through its film section, offers various forms of encouragement to the industry, including subsidies to film societies and organizations, loans and grants for feature and documentary production, awards for quality productions, and study grants for film-makers and researchers.

In 1972, 453 feature films were imported: from the USA (154), France (73), Italy (91), the Federal Republic of Germany (66), the UK (35) and other countries (34). A total of 245 documentary films were imported: from the USA (47), France (55), the Federal Republic of Germany (30), Italy (9), the UK (8) and other countries (96).

Cinema attendances have decreased by over 25% in the last ten years. The Association Suisse des Offices du Film d'Enseignement deals with the distribution of educational films throughout the 25 cantons and is also responsible for the exchange of such films with foreign countries. Various private non-profit-making institutions concentrate on the distribution of theatrical or cultural types of films which are mainly projected in the afternoons from October to March. La Fédération Suisse de Cinéclubs procures feature films for its 46 clubs with some 7000 members, while the Union Suisse du Film Documentaire distributes cultural films to its 203 sections with about 150 000 members.

Film education for young people is entrusted to various organizations and institutions which are connected with the organization known as 'Jeunesse et Cinéma'. The Swiss Film Library in Lausanne holds 1500 feature films, as well as slides and books on the cinema. There is also a film museum in Zurich.

SPACE COMMUNICATIONS

Switzerland has an Atlantic Intelsat earth station at Leuk (Loèche) which came into service in 1973.

PROFESSIONAL TRAINING AND ASSOCIATIONS

Training for media professionals is offered at Lausanne (by the Association de la Presse Suisse and the Union Romande des Journalistes) and Friburg (at the University's Institute of Journalism), the latter including cinema and television options. The Universities of Berne, Neuchâtel, Geneva, Zurich and Lausanne also have courses on the history of the press, journalism, sociology of the mass media, etc. An international training seminar for directors and producers of educational and school television programmes is organized annually in Basle by the European Broadcasting Union. Courses in film-making are available at the Zurich Art School.

Professional associations include one for newspaper publishers, one for

French-language newspapers, one for the technical and professional press and one for the French-language Catholic press. There are seven associations for journalists, one for the foreign press in Switzerland and for foreign correspondents in their relations with the United Nations. Film organizations include the Chambre Suisse du Cinéma, a film producers' association, a union for cinema technicians, an association for performers, another for film distributors and three organizations for cinema owners in the different linguistic areas. There is also a federation of associations of broadcasting personnel and a union of theatrical, radio and television workers.

TURKEY

Population	37 010 000
Area	780 756 sq. km.

PRESS
Newspapers	Dailies 432, Non-dailies 661

RADIO
Transmitters	Long/medium-wave 14, Short-wave 13, VHF FM 2
Total receivers	4 900 000 estimated in use
Receivers per 1000 people	132

TELEVISION
Transmitters	7
Receivers	200 000 estimated in use
Receivers per 1000 people	5

FILM
Cinemas	Fixed 700*

*In the larger towns only.

PRESS

While the total number of dailies in the country has dropped by about 40 over the last ten years, there has been a steady growth in overall circulation figures, which are now estimated to exceed 2.8 million copies per issue (no exact figures are published).

The city of Istanbul has about 40 dailies, including the country's largest and most influential papers. The 2 largest (circulating over 500 000 and around 370 000 copies per issue) are associated with a group which also owns a number of weekly and monthly papers and operates its own news agency. Two other dailies circulate over 250 000 copies each.

Newspapers are privately owned and the majority are politically independent, though there are several with recognized party links. Apart from a few titles in Armenian, Greek, English and French, all are published in Turkish. Leading Istanbul papers also have editions published simultaneously in Ankara and Izmir. In addition to its same-day issues of Istanbul papers, the capital, Ankara, has around 25 dailies of its own (one of which is an official gazette, several mainly commercial in content, and one an English-language paper). Only 3 Ankara dailies, however, circulate over 15 000 copies. The largest of Izmir's 6 dailies circulates over 60 000 copies. About 40 other towns have between 3 and 10 locally published dailies, mostly with circulations of a few thousand copies.

The large non-daily press tends to be more specialized in content or orientation in the larger cities (Ankara has 2 English-language weeklies), but for the most part it consist of small community weeklies.

Periodicals number over 1300 titles – possibly as many as 2000 – of which the bulk are general interest journals (some 800 titles), other large subject categories being administrative, commercial, technical and professional journals. About 100 periodicals appear in foreign languages, including English (56 titles), French (11 titles) and German (7 titles). Recent years have seen a trend towards ownership concentration in the newspaper and periodical press. but the majority of journals are still independently published. Complete circulation figures are not available but considerable increases in periodical readerships are reported over the last ten years.

Of Turkey's 70 000 metric tons annual consumption of newsprint, around 11 000 metric tons are domestically produced.

NEWS AGENCIES

The official national agency is Anadolu Ajansi (Anatolia), founded in 1920, which is state owned and has its headquarters in Ankara and other offices in Istanbul, Izmir and Adana. It has a permanent staff of 180 plus 517 correspondents throughout the country, but no foreign correspondents. Anatolia receives the foreign services of AP, AFP, DPA, TASS, Tanjug, PARS, APP (Pakistan), INA (Iraq), Agerpress, ANA and BTA, and is in negotiation with Reuters and UPI. With a daily bulletin of 25 000 to 30 000 words of national and local news, and 10 000 to 15 000 words foreign news and an economic-news service, the agency serves 65 newspapers and 130 other subscribers.

Türk Haberler Ajansi (THA), founded in 1950, is a cooperative news agency with its head office in Istanbul and branches in Ankara and Izmir, as well as correspondents throughout the country. It also has permanent correspondents abroad in the UK, the USA, France and the Federal Republic of Germany.

Haber Ajansi, also privately owned, was founded in 1963. It has overseas correspondents in London and Munich.

ANKA Ajansi, a daily news agency based in Ankara, was founded in 1973.

IKA Ajansi, an economic and commercial news agency also based in Ankara, was founded in 1954. It publishes daily bulletins, in both Turkish and English, on economic and commercial affairs and on investment and financial news, plus other bulletins on labour, law and social-insurance affairs and economic and political affairs in Turkish only.

Foreign agencies with bureaux in Ankara are AFP, ANSA, AP, DPA and UPI. Reuters and TASS are also represented.

RADIO

Control of both radio and television broadcasting is vested in the Turkish Radio and Television Corporation (TRT), a state-owned autonomous enterprise financed by receiver licence fees, advertising, etc., and by government funds, TRT's governing board, under a state-appointed director, includes representatives of government, the universities, cultural fields and TRT staff.

A licence fee is payable for receivers (at different rates for cities and villages) but is not applicable to sets classified as portable. Hence the number of radio receivers estimated in use (approaching 5 million) is much higher than the number of licences (3 856 000).

A national programme, on the air for 18 hours a day, is broadcast on medium-wave transmitters from Ankara (1200kW), Erzurum (100kW), Cukurova (300kW), Istanbul (150kW), Izmir (100kW) and Diyabakir (300kW). The second programme, of an entertainment and cultural nature, is broadcast for 7 hours daily by the second (2kW) transmitters of Ankara, Istanbul and Izmir. Regional stations, broadcasting both locally originated programmes and relays of the national network, are located at Kars, Van, Gaziantep, Antalya and Trabzon (all with 2kW medium-wave transmitters) and Diyabakir (1kW short-wave). Together these stations, broadcasting in Turkish, provide effective radio coverage for over 87% of the population.

FM stations broadcasting mainly musical programmes are operated by TRT (Radio Ankara III) and by the State Technical University of Istanbul (which also has a 1kW short-wave transmitter).

TRT programmes, totalling 1455 hours a week, consist of light entertainment (960 hours), news and information (170 hours), education (166 hours), advertising (67 hours), broadcasts for special audiences (49 hours) and arts, letters and science (44 hours).

In addition to TRT's regular school broadcasts, begun in 1963 and carried out in conjunction with the Ministry of Education's educational film—radio—television centre, there are several experimental stations transmitting educational material, at Izmir (for technical-school students) and in the Anatolian towns of Tokat, Turhal and Zile (for secondary schools). Istanbul's University (science faculty) and the School of Technology both have their own short-wave transmitters.

The state Meteorological Service has a short-wave transmitter in Ankara on the air for 10 hours daily, broadcasting music and weather reports.

External broadcasting is carried out by TRT which has short-wave transmitters of 250kW and 100kW at Ankara. The foreign service, on the air for 47 hours a week, is broadcast in Arabic, Bulgarian, English, French, German, Greek, Persian, Pushtu, Romanian, Serbo-Croat and Urdu. In addition, there is a special service, including relays of home-service programmes, broadcast for over 100 hours weekly for Turks living abroad.

The United States Armed Forces Radio and Television Service also operates three short-wave stations at Adana, Diyabakir and Karamursel.

TELEVISION

TRT's first television broadcasts (625 lines) were made on an experimental basis in February 1968. The corporation now has seven stations at Istanbul, Ankara, Eskisehir, Balikesir, Edirne, Izmir and Kirikkale, covering about 50% of the population (with a further 11 stations projected in current development plans).

Stations are on the air for five days a week, totalling 17 hours of programme time, 13 hours of which are accounted for by domestic production. Main programme categories are news and information (6 hours), broadcasts for special audiences (5 hours), education (2 hours), arts, letters and science (2 hours) and light entertainment (1 hour). One-hour programmes for primary schools, broadcast on one morning and one afternoon per week, are prepared in cooperation with the Ministry of Education's educational film--radio--television centre at Ankara.

Television broadcasts from Bulgaria, Romania, Cyprus, Lebanon, the USSR, Iran, Iraq and Syria can be received in the adjacent parts of Turkey.

As with radio, licence fees (differing for cities and villages) are not payable for portable receivers. There are thus some 212 000 licensed receivers as against an estimated 300 000 in actual use (March 1973). Some receivers are produced or assembled in the country but many are imported, often personally by returning emigrant workers.

FILM

In recent years, some 200 to 250 feature films and a number of short films have been produced annually by private firms based in Istanbul. This production is almost entirely destined for the domestic market. Documentaries and instructional short films are produced by the Ministry of Education's educational film—radio—television centre at Ankara, primarily for school use, community-development activities and the ministry's school television programmes. Between 350 and 400 feature films are imported annually, mainly from the USA, France and Italy.

The total number of fixed cinemas is reported at 700, in cities and main towns, as well as café-garden village cinemas run by local operators, giving frequent showings of Turkish and foreign (dubbed) films during the summer. There are well over 1000 such open-air cinemas, as well as some mobile projection units. A film club in Istanbul has a large membership and organizes weekly showings of classic and *avant garde* films.

SPACE COMMUNICATIONS

An Atlantic Intelsat earth station was opened near Ankara in 1972.

PROFESSIONAL TRAINING AND ASSOCIATIONS

Training in journalism is available at five schools. Ankara has a school of journalism and communications, founded in 1965 within the university, and another school of journalism founded in 1967, offering four-year and three-year courses respectively, with respective total enrolments of around 150 and 900 students. Istanbul University has an institute of journalism, founded in 1950, and offering a three-year diploma course with a total enrolment of around 400 students. A higher school of journalism also in Istanbul, has a total of enrolment of over 1000 students attending its three-year course. Izmir's higher school of journalism, founded in 1968, has some 470 students attending its three-year diploma course.

Media organizations, such as the Press Institute, also offer training courses, and the TRT arranges for the training of its own broadcasters, producers directors and technicians.

Major newspaper publishers are grouped in one association, periodical publishers in another. Besides a journalists' association founded in 1946 (2000 members), the Union of Journalists of Turkey founded in 1952 (800 members) and the Turkish Press Institute, there are local and regional associations and unions throughout the country. In all, there are 2300 professional journalists in Turkey, 900 of whom are in Istanbul and more than 500 in Ankara. There are also associations of film producers and of film distributors and cinema operators.

UNITED KINGDOM

Population	55 790 000
Area	244 044 sq. km.

PRESS

Newspapers	Dailies 109, Non-dailies 1163
Total circulation	Dailies 24 356 000, Non-dailies 37 459 000
Copies per 1000 people	Dailies 437, Non-dailies 671

RADIO

Transmitters	Long/medium-wave 78, Short-wave 66, VHF–FM 252
Total receivers	39 000 000 estimated in use
Receivers per 1000 people	699

TELEVISION

Transmitters	314
Receivers	16 658 000 licences
Licences per 1000 people	299

FILM

Cinemas	Fixed 1482
Total seating capacity	1 381 261
Seats per 1000 people	25
Total annual attendance	176 000 000
Annual visits per capita	3

PRESS

The daily press is characterized by the dominance of 9 nationally distributed morning papers which, with an aggregate circulation of 14.3 million copies. account for 60% of the total number of daily newspapers sold throughout the country. All are published in London, but several have additional special editions printed in Manchester for the north of England, one has a special Scottish edition printed in Glasgow and another is produced in Northern Ireland. The 2 largest circulate 4.4 million and 3.6 million copies per issue respectively and 3 others exceed the million mark. London also has 2 evening dailies together circulating 1.2 million copies per issue. While the majority have a generally identifiable political outlook, all but one are without political-party ties. The remaining 98 regional dailies, of which only 12 appear in the morning, are published in over 50 cities and towns in England: 6 in Scotland (12 titles), 4 in Wales, 3 in Northern Ireland and 2 in the Channel Islands. The largest is a Glasgow morning paper with 531 000 copies. Other cities with dailies circulating over 300 000 copies are Manchester, Birmingham and Liverpool while Wolverhampton, Leeds, Newcastle and Belfast all have dailies circulating over 200 000.

In recent years, the total number of dailies has dropped somewhat (most of the changes having occurred in the regional press), as has the total circulation – by almost 3 million (mostly accounted for by the London morning and evening papers).

Sunday newspapers command the highest readerships. Of the 7 nationally distributed Sunday papers, one has a circulation of 6 million, another 4.6 million, 2 more over 4 million and another over 1.4 million copies. Together, these 7 circulate over 22 million copies every week, representing 60% of the country's non-daily newspaper circulation. The 3 larger (in terms of number of pages) and more expensive of the national Sundays are read for their international and national news coverage and background articles, literary and artistic sections. Two have colour supplements, while the third is associated with a national daily which issues a colour supplement with its Friday edition. The other Sunday papers are designed principally to entertain. Despite the links between some of them and daily newspapers, the Sunday newspapers are separate entities and not simply Sunday editions of those dailies. In addition, there are Sunday newspapers published in other parts of England (3) and in Scotland (2) and Northern Ireland (1).

Other non-daily newspapers, some published twice weekly but most weekly, include 149 weeklies published in the districts of Greater London, 640 local newspapers in other parts of England, 146 in Scotland, about 50 in Wales including some all-Welsh and some bilingual Welsh/English, 42 in Northern Ireland and 5 in the Isle of Man. These carry mostly regional and local news and advertising, with little reference to national political issues. About 30 specialized newspapers, mainly religious, are published and also (not classified or counted here) over 100 free-distribution papers reaching some 3 million readers. The number of non-daily titles has decreased by about 100 and the total circulation by about 3 million since 1960.

Periodicals (apart from newspapers) for 'general and specialized' and 'trade, technical and professional' readerships number 4260, many of which have considerable circulations abroad, as well as at home. The majority are published in London.

After the two journals with the exclusive right to publish, respectively, BBC and IBA weekly broadcasting programmes, each circulating over 3 million copies, the highest circulations are commanded by 4 women's and general mass-circulation magazines each selling from 1 to over 2 million copies weekly; 8 others, mostly general readership illustrateds. exceed the 250 000 mark. Among the 6 influential weekly journals of opinion, 2 circulate over 100 000 copies.

Trade, technical and professional journals, ranging from weeklies to quarterlies, deal with over 500 subjects, some of which are becoming increasingly highly specialized (eg there are 150 journals catering for the engineering industry. 64 dealing with electronics, 28 with computers and data processing and 17 with nucleonics). This increasing specialization and subject coverage, together with the growth of foreign-language publishing, information services to readers, etc., has made this branch one of the most important in British publishing. Some 600 official, industrial and commercial house journals are published by organizations and firms for their employees and/or clients.

The concentration of newspaper and periodical press ownership in the UK, though partly due to economic pressures, is mainly the result of the continuing amalgamation of enterprises. Six major corporations with interests in the whole field of publishing and communications, including independent television programme companies, dominate the national scene. followed more or less closely by a number of metropolitan and regional groups. Even in local newspaper publishing, amalgamation has become more frequent, though many private companies still survive.

Concern with this trend is expressed in legislation such as the Monopolies and Mergers Act, 1965 (which provides that the transfer of newspaper assets involving circulations of over 500 000 copies shall be void unless written consent is obtained from the appropriate government authority) and the Television Act, 1963 (regulating the activities of newspaper interests in independent-television programme companies). On the economic side, the press itself has instituted training and organization measures to increase the operating efficiency and commercial viability of enterprises. Certain newspapers, including several of national and regional importance, seeking to preserve their established character and editorial independence, to avoid death duties, to ensure the ploughing-back of profits, etc., have vested the ownership of their enterprises in trusts which are bound to safeguard their particular interests.

Newsprint consumption in the UK amounts to over 1.6 million metric tons a year (27.7kg *per capita* of population), of which about a third is supplied by British paper-mills; of the remainder, two-thirds is imported from Canada and one-third from Scandinavia. Problems of supply and increasing cost are presenting difficulties and reducing the size of some papers.

NEWS AGENCIES

London is the headquarters of the world news agency Reuters, founded in Aix-la-Chapelle in 1850 and transferred to the British capital in 1851. The agency is now owned by the newspapers of the UK, Australia and New Zealand, through the Newspaper Publishers' Association, the Press Association (both UK), the Australian Associated Press and the New Zealand Press Association. One of these joint owners, the Press Association, supplies Reuters with a complete daily service of UK home news. Reuters has about 1000 correspondents in 180 countries and territories, as well as links with 77 national or private news agencies, giving access to coverage by many thousands of local reporters.

The average daily output thus received in London is 500 000 words, covering news and economic service reports, transmitted over 615 610 miles of leased cable and 19 leased inward radio circuits. Regionalized news services are arranged according to the needs of the recipients in the UK and eight main overseas regions, and are transmitted to 124 countries over leased cables and 31 outward leased radio circuits. Distribution is made, either directly or through national news agencies, to 6600 daily newspapers with a combined circulation of some 300 million, as well as to radio and television networks which serve almost 650 million receiving sets.

Since May 1968, Reuters has used a computerized message-handling system known as Automatic Data Exchange (ADX) to increase the speed of handling and distributing news. It also has a Stockmaster computer network for its economic service in order to obtain the latest market prices.

The Press Association (PA) is a British national news agency founded in 1868 by newspaper members and cooperatively owned by the principal UK newspapers outside London, and by those of the Republic of Ireland. This agency provides a comprehensive service of home news, including general and parliamentary news, legal reports and all branches of financial, commercial and sporting news to London and regional newspapers, to the broadcasting organizations and to 60 other news agencies. It also supplies its members in the regions with Reuters and Associated Press world news. London and the regional papers receive a daily picture service through its photographic department while its Special Service Department provides reports of local or special interest to daily and weekly trade papers and periodicals.

The Exchange Telegraph Company (EXTEL) is an independent news agency founded in 1872. It is a public company, forming part of the EXTEL group, with over 1000 shareholders. This agency supplies financial, commercial and sports news to newspapers and broadcasting organizations. Horse-racing news services are also provided by teleprinter and telephone to subscribers in London and the provinces from offices in all important cities and towns.

Associated Press Ltd is the British operating company of the Associated Press of America, and supplies a world-wide overseas news service to the British press and broadcasting organizations.

There are also some 70 British, Commonwealth and foreign news agencies and services with offices in the UK, specializing in such newspaper and periodical requirements as parliamentary, commercial and sports news, photographs, etc.

Visnews, founded in 1957 and jointly owned by the BBC, Reuters and the Australian, Canadian and New Zealand national broadcasting corporations, supplies newsfilm to 140 television organizations in more than 80 countries, and its services are also syndicated from New York, San Francisco and Seattle (USA) and Hong Kong, Singapore and Sydney (Australia).

Independent Television News, a private company, is half-owner with UPI (USA) of the newsfilm agency UPITN which supplies a daily service from London, New York and other centres to more than 100 television stations in various countries.

RADIO

Sound radio and, since 1936, television broadcasting services, are provided by the British Broadcasting Corporation (BBC), an autonomous non-profit making public corporation established in 1927 by royal charter. Since 1955, television services have also been provided through an autonomous commercial organization, the Independent Television Authority (ITA), established by the Television Act of 1954; since 1973, the authority has also been responsible for the operation, through a number of independent companies, of local radio broadcasting stations and has changed its name to the Independent Broadcasting Authority (IBA). The BBC's domestic services are financed almost entirely from a government grant voted by parliament and derived from licences, the cost of which is fixed by parliament; it cannot obtain income from commercial advertising. The IBA and the broadcasting services of the constituent companies which operate under the IBA for defined geographical areas are financed by revenue from commercial advertising inserted between (not during) programmes within time limits laid down by the IBA. No receiver fee is payable in respect of IBA services. The IBA is required to remit a part of its revenue to the national exchequer. Both BBC and IBA cover the cost of constructing and running their broadcasting services.

Overseas radio broadcasting services, by the BBC only, are financed by an annual grant voted by parliament on the Foreign Office budget. Parliament may decide to which countries, in which languages and for how many hours overseas broadcasting shall be conducted, but the BBC is alone responsible for the content of the programmes. Both the BBC and IBA exchange television programmes with, and sell them to, television companies in other countries as they wish.

Licences to operate broadcasting services which lay down terms and conditions covering frequency allocations, number and times of broadcasting hours, etc., are granted by parliament. The current licences to the BBC and IBA run until 1976.

The BBC is governed by a board of governors of 12 members, appointed by the Queen, normally for a term of five years. It determines and controls the basic policies and practices of the BBC; they are executed by a Director-General appointed by the board of governors, and a staff appointed by him. The chairman, deputy-chairman and 9 members of the IBA are appointed by the Minister of Posts and Telecommunications. They are responsible for selecting commercially operated independent broadcasting companies, each of which is granted the licence to diffuse programmes for a defined geographical area or certain days of the week; programmes initiated by one company are sometimes diffused by several, or all of them. The IBA is also responsible for approving programme plans and controlling the distribution and content of advertising. Both organizations have established regular and local councils to advise them; the BBC is required by its charter to do so for Scotland and Wales.

Both the BBC and the IBA are required to present annual reports to parliament, to which the Minister of Posts and Telecommunications is responsible for broad policy questions (though he is not responsible to it for the day-to-day operations of either organization).

The BBC's domestic radio services are provided by four national channels and by local stations (of which 21 were in operation in 1972, and it is expected that there will eventually be 40). There are also services for the national regions of Scotland, Wales and Northern Ireland. For each local radio station, there is a local radio council.

Radio 1 broadcasts on medium-wave and, occasionally, on the FM transmitters of Radio 2 and carries a continuous programme of popular music. Radio 2's light entertainment programmes include music, serials, sports and women's programmes. These two channels, with estimated audiences of 5 million or more, also carry hourly news summaries and a special daily service of road-transport information. Radio 3 incorporates the former evening Third Programme of plays, talks and special interest broadcasts, which continues to draw audiences of 1 to 2 million but now concentrates particularly on classical music, with frequent stereophonic broadcasts. Its programmes also include news bulletins, religious broadcasts, study courses and Saturday sports commentaries. Radio 4 provides the principal news and information services of the BBC (to which over 10 million listeners tune in during the day), with parliamentary reports, political broadcasts and a wide range of music (especially in the evening) and plays. It carries all broadcasts to schools, some Open University courses and the bulk of religious broadcasts, and also accommodates the alternative regional programmes in its daily timetable.

In addition to the extensive FM network which permits Radios 2, 3 and 4 to offer high-quality reception in many areas, Radio 2 has one long-wave transmitter, serving practically the whole of the British Isles, and four medium-wave transmitters in Scotland; Radio 3 has one central, medium-wave transmitter with 17 auxiliaries serving local areas, while Radio 4 operates 29 medium-wave transmitters including those of the regional services.

Programmes on the four national channels together consist principally of light entertainment and music (42.9%), serious music (21.2%), talks (9.7%), news and outside broadcasts (9.1%), drama (4.8%), educational broadcasts (3.6%), programmes for special minorities (3.1%), features (2.2%) and religious broadcasts (1.8%).

Educational broadcasting includes 119 series of weekly broadcasts for schools, used systematically by about 32 000 schools in the UK; 39 series of further education courses for adult listeners, on business, industry, science and technology, family and community questions, languages and the arts; and Open University courses (in conjunction with television, correspondence and study-centre tuition). Guides, handbooks and audio-visual materials are published by the BBC.

The new local radio stations have their own FM transmitters, at present potentially covering 74% of the population in England, to which will be added some medium-wave transmitters as the regional services' facilities are redeployed. Local stations are designed to carry a full range of locally originated programmes of interest to the communities and groups served, in addition to some relays of national services.

The first two commercial radio stations under the IBA were set up in London in 1973. One was largely devoted to news, and the other to light music and pop. Each company is independent and has its own directors; some commercial radio companies are linked with newspaper and publishing interests.

From 1962–3, the number of domestic radio receiver licences in the UK increased by over 3 million, bringing the total to 18.2 million. Of these,

2 279 017 were for radio receivers only, the remainder being combined radio and television licences. However, since licences covered more than one receiver, the total number of sets in use was much higher. Some 184 000 radio receivers are connected to wired redistribution networks.

The external radio services broadcast over 700 hours a week in English and 39 other languages, via 70 transmitters (mostly short-wave), of which 44 are located in the UK and 26 at overseas relay bases.

The world service broadcasts in English for 24 hours a day, with news, live coverage of important events, and programmes of all kinds including English by radio, and replies to listeners' correspondence. The European services include the German, south-east and central European, Finnish and Yugoslav services and the Hebrew unit (supplying material to the Israel Broadcasting Authority for retransmission) and carry mainly news, topical talks, English lessons and listeners' correspondence, as well as some local coproductions. The overseas services (African, Arabic, Eastern, Far Eastern and Latin American) are broadcast directly or by BBC relay stations, rebroadcast by national services or supplied in recorded form for use by local stations. In addition, through the overseas regional services, direct or transcribed programmes are exchanged by broadcasters throughout the English-speaking world.

TELEVISION

Television broadcasting in the UK was first publically demonstrated in 1926. In 1932, the BBC began running a few regular experimental transmissions which eventually became a public high-definition service with a daily 2-hour programme in 1936. There are two channels operated by the BBC and, since 1955, a third operated by ITA (now IBA). The government is to decide shortly when to allow a fourth channel and for which purposes it shall be used, and whether to give it to the BBC, the IBA or another body to be created.

At the end of 1972, the BBC operated 83 main and 179 auxiliary transmitters, and the IBA 37 VHF and 26 UHF main and 10 VHF and 8 UHF auxiliary transmitters.

The services on the two BBC channels are planned to provide viewers with a choice of programme subject or style of treatment at a number of programme junctions each evening. BBC 1, which uses the 405-line system on VHF for black and white transmissions and the 625-line system on VHF for colour, is potentially available (in black and white) to 99% of the population in Britain, while BBC 2, using the 625-line system on VHF for both black and white and colour, potentially reaches some 75% of the population.

BBC 1, with programmes planned to appeal to a wide range of tastes and interests, is on the air for about 82 hours a week (72% in colour), while BBC 2, with evening broadcasts which also cater for more specialized programme needs, averages about 42 hours a week, almost all in colour. Programme content on a yearly average for the two BBC networks includes news, documentary and information programmes (31%), feature films and series (15.5%), outside broadcasts (14%), light entertainment and family programmes (13.5%), educational broadcasts (11.1%), drama (8%), religious programmes (2.2%), music (1.6%), etc.

Over 11 000 screen hours of BBC television programmes are sold yearly to some 80 countries in addition to educational and documentary programmes on 16mm film and footage from the Television Film Library.

There are 15 independent television companies chosen by the IBA, each for a separate geographical area (with two for London, one for weekdays and the other for weekends), which produce programmes and diffuse them by transmitters owned by the authority. Within limits set by the IBA, programmes initiated and produced by one company are transmitted by other companies; this is especially so for news and sports programmes.

IBA's network of 405-line VHF transmitters potentially provided 98% of the population of the UK with black and white television coverage. It is being superseded by a VHF network diffusing 625-line colour/black and white pictures, of which 26 main stations and 18 local relays are already in service, reaching over 80% of the population.

The average weekly composition of IBA programmes is plays, drama and serials (20%), news, documentaries, features and outside broadcasts (18%), entertainment and music (14%), sport (13%), feature films (12%), education and school programmes (10%, including repeats) and religion (3%). National and international news programmes are provided by a non-profit-making company jointly owned by all the regional programme companies. Advertising is limited to 6 minutes in an hour averaged over the day.

Educational television in Britain includes: (a) broadcasts to schools provided since 1957 by both BBC and IBA networks, each bringing over 30 primary and secondary-level series to over 25 000 schools every week during school terms, (b) further and adult education programmes, usually in series of weekly or fortnightly broadcasts occupying between 3 and 4 hours a week on both BBC and ITV, (c) the Open University courses leading to a degree, which began on BBC 1 and 2 in January 1971 with about 4 hours a week, increasing to some 12 hours a week in 1972; 40 000 students are now enrolled. In these three fields, coordination with related radio programmes and inter-network consultation between BBC and IBA are provided for, as well as the publication and distribution of supporting printed and other course aids.

Both the BBC and the IBA are members of the European Broadcasting Union and participate in EBU (and other) international programme exchanges, including satellite links. Programmes are imported from various countries, principally from the USA.

From 12.5 million television receivers in 1962, the total for the UK increased by 25% over the next ten years, bringing the ratio of receivers per 1000 inhabitants from 211 to 299. This total includes 1.4 million households receiving television programmes via cable networks, for which restricted experimental licences have been granted to private companies in the London area and four provincial centres. Since colour broadcasts (PAL system) began in 1967, the number of licences for colour receivers has increased yearly to reach over 1.3 million in 1972.

FILM

British-made feature films continue to draw the largest cinema audiences in the UK, five of the country's top six box-office successes in 1970 being national productions. Full-length feature films registered in 1972 with the Board of

Trade, which, through its films branch, is responsible for the commercial and industrial aspects of the film industry in Britain, totalled 89, as compared with 79 in 1960. However, against these encouraging figures must be set the fact that over half the features produced in recent years have been either fully or partly financed from USA sources and, also, that if medium length features and short films are taken into consideration (production of the latter having dropped from 315 to 108 titles since 1960) the industry is not really gaining ground.

One restricting influence on short-film production by independent film-makers is the priority given by the larger chains to films of their own production for screening in the cinemas under their control. On the other hand, the wider use of visual aids in education and training, information and publicity is a continuing stimulus to both private and officially sponsored film production. On behalf of government departments and services, the Central Office of Information commissions many films from private companies belonging to the Association of Specialized Film Producers and from television organizations, including the BBC. The British film industry's facilities include 16 main studios and 10 major processing laboratories.

Direct government encouragement to the industry consists of: (a) a regulation requiring that 30% of first feature films shown are British made, (b) a levy on cinema admission which goes towards British production costs, and (c) aid from the National Film Finance Corporation for the production of export films. In addition, the British Film Institute, founded in 1933, receives an annual government grant 'to encourage the development of the art of the film, to promote its use as a record of contemporary life and manners and to foster public appreciation and study of it from these points of view'. These objects were extended in 1961 'to foster study and appreciation of films for television and television programmes generally and to encourage the best use of television'.

The institute's activities fall broadly into three main divisions. A national film archive is maintained to acquire and preserve important films. An education department provides lecturers and other services to societies, schools and colleges running film courses. In London (where the National Film Theatre is located) and, increasingly, in the provinces, the institute assists the maintenance of cinemas devoted to showing films of high quality.

Imports of full-length feature films increased over the ten-year period from 227 to 297 in 1972; sources were mainly the USA (155), France (31), Italy (29), the Federal Republic of Germany (10), France/Italy (5), Sweden (5), Spain (5), Switzerland (5), Japan (1.8%) and other countries (52). The 61 shorter entertainment films imported came from the USA (24), the Federal Republic of Germany (8), France (7), Italy (6) and other countries (16).

In ten years, the number of cinemas has halved while annual attendances have dropped by over 60%, from 502 million to 193 million, reducing the number of annual visits *per capita* from 9.5 to 3.3. At the same time, ownership of cinemas has been concentrated so that now the chains owned by two major companies constitute almost half the cinemas in the country. Among successful innovations, especially in the larger towns, are the installation of automatic projection units and the building of several smaller studio-cinemas in place of one large cinema. Cinema-goers are now younger than they were – 75% of admissions in recent years are estimated to have been of persons under 35 years of age.

Film societies are found throughout the country, 600 of these with 120 000 members being grouped in the British Federation of Film Societies. Such societies, along with schools and other institutions, draw on the resources of film libraries like those of the British Film Institute, the Central Office of Information, the Children's Film Foundation, the Educational Foundation for Visual Aids, etc.

SPACE COMMUNICATIONS

The UK is a member of Intelsat and has an earth station at Goonhilly Downs in the south of England, with three antennae (in operation since 1962, 1968 and 1972) for Indian Ocean and Atlantic Intelsat satellite transmissions. A further station in Hong Kong has antennae (in operation since 1969 and 1971) for the Pacific and Indian Ocean satellites while a non-standard Atlantic Intelsat station on Ascension Island has been in operation since 1967.

The UK Post Office Corporation provides the facilities for the exchange of programmes between broadcasting organizations via satellite as and when required.

PROFESSIONAL TRAINING AND ASSOCIATIONS

The Printing and Publishing Industry Training Board, which includes employers, employees and educational interests, in consultation with the National Council for the Training of Journalists (NCTJ), deals with the training of British journalists and also training in the printing, publishing and professional-photography industries. One-year pre-entry journalism courses and eight-week block release courses for apprentices are offered by nine technical colleges in the country. Entry requirements are secondary-level education.

A management course sponsored by the Newspaper Publishers' Association and the Newspaper Society is held at Warwick University, and a one-year post-graduate course in journalism at the University College of South Wales, in Cardiff. Sussex University has a Department of Press Studies. Short courses in management are also run by the Newspaper Society in conjunction with the University of Aston, Birmingham.

Opportunities for further training and travel for British and commonwealth media professionals are offered by the Commonwealth Press Union, the Thomson Foundation and the Commonwealth Secretariat. The Universities of Leicester, Leeds, Birmingham, Essex and Keele and the London School of Economics conduct communications studies and research.

The government's Centre for Educational Development Overseas (CEDO) conducts continuing training courses, both in the UK and abroad, for key personnel in educational broadcasting from developing countries, while the BBC trains broadcasting and engineering staff both for its own requirements and in answer to those of overseas radio and television organizations.

In addition to the newly established National Film School's two-year course in London, film training courses of 1, 2 or 3 years are offered at eight colleges of art and technology throughout the country

The Press Council in the UK consists of an independent chairman, 20 professional members nominated by the Newspaper Publishers' Association, the Newspaper Society, the Periodical Publishers' Association, the Scottish Daily Newspaper Society, the Scottish Newspaper Proprietors' Association, the Guild of British Newspaper Editors, the National Union of Journalists and the Institute of Journalists and five members of the general public. Its objects include the preservation of the established freedom of the British press, the maintenance of the highest professional and commercial standards and the consideration and appropriate treatment of complaints about the conduct of the press. There are 18 other professional press associations in the UK.

Broadcasting staff, radio and television writers, screen and television writers, actors, producers, engineers, technicians, cinema producers and film-makers, art directors, artists, distributors, renters and exhibitors all have associations for the promotion of their professional interests. Public societies for the development of the media, and for information, research, training and appreciation include the British Film Institute, the British Institute of Recorded Sound and the Television Society.

YUGOSLAVIA

Population	20 770 000
Area	255 804 sq. km.

PRESS

Newspapers	Dailies 25, Non-dailies 1493
Total circulation	Dailies 1 853 000, Non-dailies 6 630 000
Copies per 1000 people	Dailies 89, Non-dailies 319

RADIO

Transmitters	Long/medium-wave 293, Short-wave 7, VHF—FM 163
Total receivers	5 000 000 estimated in use
Receivers per 1000 people	241

TELEVISION

Transmitters	348
Receivers	2 500 000 estimated in use
Receivers per 1000 people	120

FILM

Cinemas	Fixed 1393
Total seating capacity	479 950
Seats per 1000 people	23
Total annual attendance	83 484 000
Annual visits per capita	4

PRESS

Daily newspapers are published in all the republics of Yugoslavia – Bosnia-Hercegovina, Croatia, Macedonia, Montenegro, Serbia and Slovenia – as well as in the autonomous regions, Kosovo and Vojvodina. The majority (17 titles) of the dailies, accounting for 1.5 million copies daily, appear in Serbo-Croat, 3 (with 193 000 copies) in Slovene, 2 in Macedonian and 1 each in the 3 largest minority languages: Hungarian, Italian and Albanian. Most of these dailies are published by different branches of the Socialist Alliance of the Working People of Yugoslavia, which, although not a political party, is the largest political organization in the federal republic.

The most influential newspaper in Yugoslavia is the organ of the Socialist Alliance of Working People, with a circulation of 34 000. The largest daily accounts for 264 000 of the total circulation.

A few non-dailies are published several times a week, 129 weekly and 1353 less frequently. The majority (116 titles, together circulating over 5 million copies per issue) appear in Serbo-Croat, 215 titles (931 000 copies) in Slovene, 81 titles (211 000 copies) in Macedonian and 81 titles in the following minority languages: Albanian, Bulgarian, Czech, Hungarian, Italian, Romanian, Russian and Turkish. The official publication of the Communist League of Yugoslavia, a weekly with a country-wide circulation of 216 000, is the most widely read non-daily newspaper.

Periodicals number 1436 printing a total of 10.5 million copies per issue. Among them are 984 titles in Serbo-Croat, 263 in Slovene, 59 in Macedonian and 130 in other languages; these include publications in the minority languages already mentioned, and separate or multilingual editions, in English, French, German, Spanish.

Main subject categories are political science (208 titles, together printing a total of 815 000 copies per issue), education (117 titles, 789 000 copies), technology (108 titles, 300 000 copies), medicine (101 titles, 277 000 copies), religion (85 titles, 645 000 copies), arts and architecture (81 titles, 529 000 copies), law and public welfare (75 titles, 171 000 copies), comics and humour (73 titles, 4 158 000 copies), general readership (71 titles, 271 000 copies), magazines for young people (62 titles, 695 000 copies), school journals (56 titles, 187 000 copies), agriculture, etc. (55 titles, 250 000 copies), trade and communications (28 titles, 94 000 copies), military sciences (26 titles, 277 000 copies), etc. In addition, there are 121 journals circulating within business enterprises, with a total of 212 000 copies per issue.

Around 75 000 metric tons of newsprint a year are produced in the country.

NEWS AGENCIES

Telegrafska Agencija Nova Jugoslavija (Tanjug), founded in 1943, is the national news agency with headquarters in Belgrade and nine bureaux in the most important cities of the republic. It has 16 permanent correspondents within the country. Abroad, it maintains 30 bureaux and 30 permanent correspondents, 17 of them in Europe, 4 in Asia, 4 in Africa, 4 in America and 1 in Australia, plus 12 part-time correspondents in various countries,

Tanjug issues 35 000 words daily in Serbo-Croat, on national and foreign affairs, to 21 newspapers, 7 radio stations and 6 television stations; also a 7000-word daily service to foreign countries in several languages. It supplies feature, economic and photographic services (50 telephotos a day). Tanjug transmits 80 news bulletins in French and English for 7 hours a day, by radio teleprinter, to Europe and the Middle East, and also transmits 11 daily bulletins 13 hours a day to some Asian, African and American countries.

Tanjug has exchange agreements with 56 other news agencies, including AFP, AP, TASS and Reuters, and furnishes technical assistance to news agencies in Ghana, Guinea, Mali, Indonesia, the Arab Republic of Egypt and some other countries.

RADIO

The state-owned Jugoslovenska Radio-Televizija (JRT) is the national broadcasting organization, coordinating the activities of the eight regional services with a network of medium-wave, short-wave and FM transmitters, covering 90% of the country.

Home-service broadcasting is carried out by regional broadcasting authorities in Belgrade, Ljubljana, Novi Sad, Pristina, Sarajevo, Skopje, Titograd and Zagreb. Some of these have a number of separate programmes so that all national minorities are served by local stations broadcasting programmes in their own languages. For example, Radio Novi Sad and Radio Pristina, using 100kW medium-wave transmitters, broadcast daily programmes in Albanian, Hungarian, Romanian, Slovene and Turkish, while Radio Koper's programmes include some in Italian.

Belgrade also has another metropolitan station with two programmes: the first broadcasting non-stop entertainment and commercials, and the second light and folk music plus news.

Programmes exceeding 5000 hours broadcast weekly in 1972 by all stations included light entertainment (3487 hours), news and information (714 hours), cultural programmes (512 hours), advertising (423 hours), education (255 hours), etc.

The number of domestic radio receivers in use has trebled over the last ten years, about 75% of the increase being accounted for by rural areas. There were 3 555 715 licences current at the end of 1972 (one licence covers all sets in the same household). There are now more receivers in use than there are households.

The foreign service is broadcast from Belgrade and Skopje in Albanian, Arabic, Bulgarian, English, French, German, Greek, Russian and Spanish. It also includes relays of some home-service programmes for Yugoslavs living abroad.

TELEVISION

Television, like radio broadcasting, is operated by Jugoslovenska Radio-Televizija (JRT). Revenue is derived from government subventions, licence fees and advertising.

There are six regional services based in Belgrade, Ljubljana, Sarajevo, Skopje, Titograd and Zagreb, with a complex system of 46 main transmitters (625 lines) and 302 auxiliary stations and low-power repeaters which bring television programmes within reach of over 87% of the population. Colour (PAL system) on UHF is soon to be introduced.

The total of 220 hours weekly programme time, consisting mainly of the joint JRT programme on all stations plus regional alternatives, includes cultural programmes (85 hours, including 17 hours of long films and 21 hours series), news and information (65 hours), advertising (27 hours), light entertainment (20 hours), education (19 hours), etc. Imported programmes average about 11 hours a week.

Yugoslavia imports television programmes through EBU (Eurovision) and OIRT (Intervision) with which it has exchange agreements. Apart from these, the main source of imported programmes is the USA.

FILM

The film industry is nationalized, and all film production and distribution enterprises are grouped in a central organization, Jugoslavijafilm, which handles export and import operations for its members and represents Yugoslavia abroad. Thanks to financial assistance from government cultural funds, the number of film makers has trebled in the last ten years and artistic standards have improved considerably.

In 1972, 26 long films (24 features and 2 documentaries) were produced, including 5 coproductions (2 with the Federal Republic of Germany, the others with Italy, Romania and the USSR). The year's total of 522 short films included 267 documentaries, 187 economic-promotion films, 39 cartoons. 33 instructional films and 16 entertainment films.

During the same year, imported long films numbered 244: from the USA (57), Italy (51), France (33), the UK (18), the USSR (18), Poland (9), the Federal Republic of Germany (8), Japan (8), Spain (8) and Albania, Bulgaria, Canada, Czechoslovakia, Hungary, Mexico, the German Democratic Republic, Romania, Sweden and Turkey. Short films imported totalled 27.

Annual cinema attendance has decreased by over a third in the last ten years, but attempts are being made to check the decline, by revised admission prices, the use of mobile projection units (142 mobile units drew audiences totalling 2.3 million in 1972), the establishment of special film 'theatres', etc. Over 70% of cinema audiences are in urban areas (which account for only 15% of the country's total population). There are 31 seasonal cinemas open only in summer. An important influence in the popularization of the cinema is the Yugoslav Central Film Archive in Belgrade.

SPACE COMMUNICATIONS

An Atlantic Intelsat earth station at Ivanjica, south of Belgrade, was due to come into service in 1974.

PROFESSIONAL TRAINING AND ASSOCIATIONS

The Faculties of Political Sciences at Belgrade and Zagreb Universities and the Ljubljana School of Political Sciences all have chairs of journalism. Shorter training courses for journalists – of 3 to 9 months' duration – are available at the Yugoslav Institute of Journalism in Belgrade.

Savez Novinara Jugoslavije (Federation of Yugoslav Journalists) adopted in 1965 a 'code of Yugoslav journalism' setting out ethical and political professional standards for journalists.

Film training institutes include the Film Radio and Television Academy in Belgrade and the Zagreb School of Animated Cartoons.

PART SEVEN

OCEANIA

American Samoa
Australia
British Solomon Islands
Cook Islands
Fiji
French Polynesia
Gilbert and Ellice Islands
Guam
Nauru
New Caledonia

New Hebrides
New Zealand
Niue
Norfolk Islands
Pacific Islands
Papua New Guinea
Tokelau Islands
Tonga
Western Samoa

AMERICAN SAMOA

Population	29 000
Area	197 sq. km.

PRESS

Newspapers	Dailies 1, Non-dailies 2
Total circulation	Dailies 3000, Non-dailies 7500
Copies per 1000 people	Dailies 103, Non-dailies 259

RADIO

Transmitters	Long/medium-wave 1
Total receivers	1000 estimated in use
Receivers per 1000 people	34

TELEVISION

Transmitters	6
Receivers	2000 estimated in use
Receivers per 1000 people	69

FILM

Cinemas	Fixed 5
Total seating capacity	1800
Seats per 1000 people	62
Total annual attendance	300 000
Annual visits per capita	10

PRESS

The daily bulletin appears in English and the two non-dailies bilingually, in English and Samoan.

NEWS AGENCIES

The Office of Samoan Information (OSI), which functions as a news agency, maintains a six-man bureau at Pago Pago, the main island centre. A government agency, it exchanges news with UPI and serves as correspondent for UPI, AP and newspapers and magazines.

OSI supplies 3000 words of domestic news and 5000 of foreign news daily, in English and Samoan, to the news bulletin, radio station and television station. Features, photos and audio-radio services are also provided. Leased teletype services are used for local transmission and cable, radiotelephone and air mail for overseas communication.

RADIO

The radio station, which was operated by OSI until June 1973, is now privately owned and commercially operated. Radio Samoa has a 10kW transmitter in Pago Pago which broadcasts in English and Samoan for 133 hours a week. This includes over 50% light entertainment, plus cultural and news programmes (news is received from UPI and CBS in the USA) and, as from 1973, advertising. The station gives 100% territorial coverage.

TELEVISION
The Education Department operates all six transmitters during the day for education. Two channels are used at night for general programmes. The station, which gives complete coverage of all islands, broadcasts 260 hours a week, including education (202 hours), news (15 hours), programmes for special audiences (25 hours) and light entertainment (14 hours). Telecasts are in English and Samoan. Some 70% of the material is local, the rest comes from the USA.

FILM
The Education Department produces educational films and, on occasion, a news documentary. Some 400 feature films are imported annually, mostly from the USA, the UK, Japan, Italy and Australia. About 150 short films are also shown.

AUSTRALIA

Population	12 552 000
Area	7 686 810 sq. km.

PRESS
Newspapers	Dailies 58, Non-dailies 502
Total circulation	Dailies 4 028 000
Copies per 1000 people	Dailies 321

RADIO
Transmitters	Medium-wave 191, Short-wave 21
Total receivers	2 758 000 estimated in use
Receivers per 1000 people	220

TELEVISION
Transmitters	199
Receivers	2 939 000 estimated in use
Receivers per 1000 people	234

FILM

Cinemas	Fixed 1100*
Total seating capacity	800 000*
Seats per 1000 people	64
Total annual attendance	36 000 000
Annual visits per capita	3

*Including drive-ins.

PRESS

With 16 metropolitan dailies (published in the federal capital, Canberra, and the six state capitals), one of which is a national paper based in Sydney but also printing facsimile-transmitted editions in Melbourne and Brisbane (total circulation about 130 000 copies), and around 40 provincial dailies, the Australian daily press shows little change in overall figures over the last decade (in 1962, there were 58 dailies circulating just over 4 million copies).

Sydney, with 4 general interest dailies (individual circulations ranging between 297 000 and 354 000 copies per issue) plus a smaller financial daily, and Melbourne, with its 3 large dailies (190 000, 501 000 and 648 000 copies respectively), account for about 70% of the national daily circulation. The ratio of advertising to total content is over 60%, and some weekend editions of the larger dailies may have as many as 80 out of 112 pages consisting of classified advertisements alone.

Non-daily newspapers include 9 metropolitan Sunday or Saturday papers (of which Sydney has 3 with circulations of 541 000, 577 000 and 657 000), around 380 provincial papers appearing once, twice or thrice weekly, and over 100 suburban papers (some distributed free). There are over 40 foreign-language papers catering for the immigrant element in the population, in 17 languages including Greek (13 titles with over 175 000 copies per issue), Italian (5 titles, 97 000 copies), Maltese (3 titles, 37 000 copies), Polish (3 titles, 14 800 copies), Hungarian (3 titles, 14 600 copies), etc.

Press ownership is becoming increasingly concentrated, three major groups and two smaller ones controlling most of the metropolitan dailies, as well as other newspapers, periodicals, broadcasting stations and recording companies.

The periodical press consists of 1230 titles, with 3 women's weeklies (360 000, 500 000 and 820 000 copies per issue), 2 television magazines (284 000 and 458 000 copies) and the Australian edition of an American monthly digest (715 000 copies) topping the circulation lists. Main subject categories are technology, industry, etc. (177 titles), entertainment and sports (142 titles), law, administration and welfare (108 titles), political science and economy (97 titles), trade, communications and transport (86 titles), general (74 titles), medicine and health (71 titles), etc.

Of a total annual newsprint consumption of 448 500 metric tons. domestic production accounted for 173 300 metric tons in 1970.

NEWS AGENCIES

The major national agency, the Australian Associated Press (AAP), established in

1935, is a newspaper cooperative which has been a partner of Reuters since 1946. With headquarters in Sydney, AAP is linked by cable with London and New York while, through Asia, a team of AAP– Reuters correspondents provides coverage for Australia and London. AAP receives, in addition to the Reuters service, those of AP and UPI and also has access to the world cover of *The Times* (London) and the *New York Times*. It has its own staff in London and receives dispatches from AAP–Reuters correspondents in many parts of the world.

Over 200 000 words of foreign news only are distributed daily in English by teleprinter and other means to almost all newspapers and to radio and television stations throughout the country. AAP also has a feature service. It distributes Australian news abroad through Reuters.

Australian United Press (AUP), with offices in Sydney, Melbourne and Canberra, and correspondents throughout Australia, was founded in 1932 when smaller agencies merged. It gathers and distributes domestic news within Australia and also distributes AAP foreign news to newspapers published outside metropolitan areas. It is a company whose shareholders are its subscriber newspapers.

Most Australian papers, however, have large reporting staffs and rely more on them than on agency sources for their national and local news. A number of the larger newspapers also have their own overseas representatives for exclusive or feature reporting. Since many of the commercial radio and television stations are affiliated to newspaper groups, they draw on the same news sources.

One of the main newspaper publishing groups, News Ltd, receives foreign news through AFP's English-language service.

The Australian Broadcasting Commission (ABC) has its own news service supplied by its own correspondents and provides national (non-commercial) radio and television stations with domestic and overseas news including news on film. Overseas newsfilm is received from Visnews.

Foreign agencies with bureaux in Sydney are ANSA, AP, Hsinhua, NZPA and UPI. Also represented are DPA, Jiji, Reuters, TASS, Antara and Kyodo.

RADIO

The radio broadcasting and television system in Australia is comprised of two distinct and independent services provided by the government and private enterprise respectively.

The government (or national) services are operated by the Australian Broadcasting Commission (ABC) and are financed by the Federal Government under the authority of the Broadcasting and Television Act 1942–71. Commercial radio and television stations are operated under licences from the Postmaster-General by companies dependent on advertising for their revenue.

The Australian Broadcasting Control Board is responsible for the overall planning of the radio and television services, the determination of technical standards and for ensuring that the programmes of commercial stations are adequate and comprehensive. It also fixes hours of service of stations and determines the extent to which advertisements may be broadcast by commercial stations. Subject to the direction of the Postmaster-General, the board has power to determine the site, operating power and frequencies of radio and television stations.

Separate or combined radio and television receiver licence fees are payable.

Combined licences are issued free to blind persons and schools. In 1972, some 2 758 000 radio licences were issued (including combined licences), with 8 million radio sets in use. In the same year, there were 2 939 000 television licences (again, including combined licences), representing as many sets in use.

The national radio service, equipped with 72 medium-wave and six short-wave transmitters, is broadcast over three networks which are on the air for an average of 18 hours a day. Two of these are metropolitan networks, with a total of 16 stations in the federal and state capitals, and in the large town of Newcastle in New South Wales, which operate powerful medium-wave transmitters of up to 50kW and, also, some short-wave transmitters. The third is a regional network with stations in 58 other centres, originating their own material as well as relaying programmes (by high-quality transmission lines) from the metropolitan stations. The five ABC stations in Papua and New Guinea are also part of the national service.

The proportion of time allotted to the various types of programme by ABC in 1970 was: entertainment 29.9%, classical music 25%, news 9.2%, spoken word 7.5%, drama and features 4.1%, education 3.4%, parliament 3.4%, religious 2.9%, rural 2.4%, children's programmes 1.9% and presentation 3.3%. The ABC has its own news service with correspondents in every regional centre and reporters in many overseas countries, concentrating particularly on south-east Asia. ABC's daily school broadcasts are received by 10 335 schools (90% of the national total). Regular educational programmes are also broadcast for adults.

The commercial stations are operated under licence granted initially for five years and renewable yearly, for a fixed fee, in addition to which an amount rising from 1 to 4% of gross advertising revenue is payable on the results of the preceding year's activities. Of the total of 118 stations, 25 are metropolitan, and the remainder country stations.

All use medium-wave transmitters, up to 5kW in power, and are on the air for periods ranging from 12 to 24 hours a day. Their revenue is derived principally from the sale of advertising time. Most have financial links with commercial networks, the two largest of which have 18 and 15 member radio stations respectively. Over 60 stations are linked in some way with newspapers or publishing concerns, most of which have television interests as well. Three leading press groups alone have associations with 38 radio stations. A few privately owned stations are operated by Church bodies, and one by the University of Adelaide. Average programme content for metropolitan commercial radio stations includes (approximately): entertainment (60.9%, of which over 50% is light and popular music), advertisements (14.7%), news (9.9%), sport (6.2%), religious, social and political topics (5%), family and children (2%), etc.

External broadcasting is conducted by ABC, whose overseas service - Radio Australia - operates 7 short-wave transmitters (four of 100kW and three of 50kW) at Shepparton, 3 at Lyndhurst (10kW), 3 at Darwin (250kW) and 2 (10kW) at Perth. It is on the air for an average of 113 hours a week, broadcasting programmes in English, French, Thai, Vietnamese, Mandarin, Cantonese, Japanese and Indonesian, beamed to eight target areas in Asia, the Pacific, Europe, the Americas and Africa. Programmes include news, current affairs, talks, music, drama, sport and English-language courses. In addition, Radio Australia's transcription service supplies 230 programmes on tape to 60 separate organizations in 28 countries each week.

Australian firms produce sufficient transmitters and receivers to meet local needs, and some are also exported — mainly to neighbouring countries.

TELEVISION

The country's first national television station began regular transmission in Sydney, in November 1956. By the end of 1972, there were 53 national stations (with 42 translator stations) operated by ABC, six (in the state capitals) being classified as metropolitan, and the remainder regional. Programmes on national stations, averaging about 90 hours a week, include (approximately): drama (28.6%), public interest (15.9%), education (18.3%), sports (9.3%), variety (7.2%), news (6.5%), special arts and aesthetics (6.0%), religious broadcasts (1.4%), rural (1%), musical performances (0.9%) and presentation (4.9%). Educational programmes are broadcast for almost the whole school day to both primary and secondary schools, some 6000 schools being equipped to receive these broadcasts. Pre-school and adult-education programmes are also broadcast.

Commercial television also began operation in 1956. Stations are licensed under the same system as commercial radio stations (except for a difference in fees) and similarly derive their income from the sale of advertising time. The majority are associated with larger media-ownership groups, over 60 having links with newspaper publishers. There are now 48 stations (including 3 in each of the state capitals of Sydney, Melbourne, Brisbane and Adelaide, 2 in Perth and 1 in Hobart) with a further 48 translators. In addition, 8 repeater stations are licensed to transmit only programmes recorded on magnetic tape (by arrangement, these stations transmit recorded programmes supplied by ABC).

Programmes consist mainly of drama and light entertainment with approximately 6% of total transmission time given to news and weather reports and around 15% to advertising. Educational programmes account for 0.4% of transmission time. Licensees of commercial stations are required to ensure that a minimum of programme matter televised is of Australian origin (a requirement that does not apply to non-metropolitan stations which have not completed three years of operation).

There is a two-way traffic in television programmes (though no regular exchange systems) between Australia and the UK, the Netherlands, New Zealand and other countries. Most imported programmes come from the USA and the UK. In 1970, 9311 films and converted video tapes for television use (equalling 5848 hours screening time) were submitted to the Film Censorship Board.

It is estimated that television services are available to about 98% of the population of Australia. Over 80% of households have a television receiver. A 625-line definition system is in use. Colour television (PAL system) is expected to be introduced about 1975. Existing legislation restricts the use of community-antenna television systems to areas of inadequate television reception.

FILM

Feature-film production (including coproductions) rose from an annual average of only a few titles to 16 in the year 1971—2. In addition, over 100 35mm and many more 16mm documentaries, newsreels and other short films were produced, a number by the Australian Commonwealth Film Unit, the official government production and distribution agency. The unit produces around 50 films a year, some of which are released commercially abroad but the majority are information and educational films for non-theatrical showing.

The Australian Film Development Corporation, established by Act of Parliament in 1970, administers a fund to provide loans and assistance to film and television producers, and further encouragement for film making is offered by the Experimental Film and TV Fund of the Australian Council for the arts.

A national film board advises government departments on the production, acquisition and use of films for government use at home and abroad. Australian production facilities are used by overseas producers for feature and other coproductions. An experimental film making cooperative also rents and screens imported *avant garde* films.

In 1970, 549 feature films were passed for public showing, including productions from the USA (167), the UK (88), Italy (73), Greece (46), France (36), the USSR (34), Japan (25), Czechoslovakia (12), Sweden (11) and Yugoslavia (9). The number of cinema theatres in operation declined noticeably between the mid-fifties and the early sixties, as did overall attendances (in 1956, 1774 cinemas recorded a gross annual attendance of 137 million). Since 1962 (when there were 1317 cinemas) the decline has been much less marked. Surveys show that film audiences are largely in the 16 to 34 age group. Almost 25% of cinemas are drive-ins.

SPACE COMMUNICATIONS

The Overseas Telecommunications Commission (Australia), the national authority responsible for Australia's overseas telecommunications services, operates Pacific Intelsat earth stations at Moree (New South Wales) and Carnavon (Western Australia), opened in 1968 and 1969 respectively, and an Indian Ocean Intelsat station at Ceduna (South Australia) opened in 1969.

PROFESSIONAL TRAINING AND ASSOCIATIONS

The Universities of Melbourne and Brisbane offer diploma courses in journalism. Most journalists, however, are trained on the job. Summer seminars for working journalists are organized by the Australian Journalists' Association and an on-the-job training scheme for Asian student journalists is operated under the Colombo Plan. The Australian Broadcasting Commission's news service, which is the largest single employer of journalists in Australia, has its own broadcasting-journalism training courses. Closed-circuit television is used in most teachers' colleges, mainly as an educational aid, but some courses are given in the use of television as a medium of instruction. A national film and television school was established at MacQuarie University, Sydney, in 1973.

The Australian Journalists' Association, founded in 1910, has some 7600 members who subscribe to its code of ethics. An Australian Newspapers Council founded in 1958, has a membership of 13 metropolitan dailies and Sunday papers. Other papers are grouped in the Provincial Press Association and state country press associations.

Commercial broadcasters and commercial television stations each have their own national federations, while film associations include a producers' association, a recently formed Australian Film Council (of professional film makers) and various organizations of distributors, exhibitors, theatre managers. employees, etc.

BRITISH SOLOMON ISLANDS

Population	170 000
Area	29 785 sq. km.

PRESS	
Newspapers	Non-dailies 5
Total circulation	Non-dailies 6400
Copies per 1000 people	Non-dailies 38

RADIO	
Transmitters	Long/medium-wave 1, Short-wave 2
Total receivers	12 000 estimated in use
Receivers per 1000 people	70

FILM	
Cinemas	Fixed 1
Total seating capacity	600
Seats per 1000 people	3
Total annual attendance	100 000
Annual visits per capita	0.6

PRESS

There are no daily newspapers in this territory of many islands scattered over a vast area of ocean. The five non-daily news publications include a fortnightly official bulletin published in Honiara, and mission news leaflets. The three periodicals published deal with education (300 copies per issue), agriculture (3500 copies) and radio broadcasting (3800 copies).

RADIO

The Solomon Islands Broadcasting Service established in 1962 at Honiara, the capital, on Guadalcanal, is government owned and financed by government subsidy, advertising revenue and UK grants-in-aid. With one medium-wave and two short-wave transmitters (all 5kW), the service is on the air for 80 hours a week in English and pidgin English, broadcasting light entertainment (35½ hours), educational programmes (17½ hours), news and information (17 hours. including relays of BBC (UK) and Australian Broadcasting Commission news), arts, letters and science (4 hours), broadcasts for special audiences (4 hours) and advertising (2 hours).

Of the educational programmes, 12½ hours a week are special broadcasts for schools, 320 of which, on various islands, are equipped with radio receivers. About 75% of programmes are locally produced.

FILM

All films shown in the one fixed cinema and by mobile units are imported. Of an annual total of 152 features, 91 came from the USA and 61 from the UK.

The Chief Education Officer maintains a film library and is responsible for film distribution; 16mm films are shown in schools and are used for training purposes.

COOK ISLANDS

Population	25 000
Area	234 sq. km.

PRESS

Newspapers	Dailies 1
Total circulation	Dailies 750
Copies per 1000 people	Dailies 30

RADIO

Transmitters	Long/medium-wave 1, Short-wave 1
Total receivers	2500 estimated in use
Receivers per 1000 people	100

FILM

Cinemas	Fixed 12
Total seating capacity	5000
Seats per 1000 people	200
Total annual attendance	300 000
Annual visits per capita	12

PRESS

A bilingual English/Maori daily paper is published in Rarotonga. There are also 21 periodicals with a total circulation of 21 000.

News is received by radio from the New Zealand Press Association.

RADIO

The government-owned Cook Islands Newspaper and Broadcasting Corporation, financed by government subvention, advertising and receiver licence revenue, operates one medium-wave transmitter (10kW) and one short-wave transmitter (1kW) which cover the 12 permanently inhabited islands.

The 68 hours of weekly programme time consists of light entertainment (41 hours), news and information (22 hours including relays of Radio New Zealand), educational broadcasts (2½ hours) and broadcasts for special audiences

(2½ hours). Programmes include 38 hours a week of local origin and are presented in English and Maori.

FILM

Films are imported mainly from the USA and the UK.

FIJI

Population	540 000
Area	18 272 sq. km.

PRESS
Newspapers	Dailies 1, Non-dailies 8
Total circulation	Dailies 16 000
Copies per 1000 people	Dailies 30

RADIO
Transmitters	Long/medium-wave 10, VHF−FM 2
Total receivers	53 000 estimated in use
Receivers per 1000 people	98

FILM
Cinemas	Fixed 35
Total seating capacity	17 470
Seats per 1000 people	32
Total annual attendance	4 175 444
Annual visits per capita	8

PRESS

Fiji's only daily, published in English at Suva, the capital, was founded in 1869. The same firm also publishes weeklies in Hindi and Fijian (Indians now outnumber Fijians in the population).

There are 5 weekly Hindi newspapers and 2 in Fijian, 1 English/Fijian tri-weekly, a fortnightly magazine published by the Alliance Party, a monthly review and a monthly women's magazine. Two Hindi newspapers are published at Lautoka and 1 in Nadi. All the rest are published at Suva. The languages used in these publications are Fijian, Hindi and English.

NEWS AGENCIES

The Government Public Relations Office supplies news of government affairs to all news media. The daily newspaper receives world news from the AAP−Reuter services in Australia.

RADIO

The Fiji Broadcasting Commission, an independent statutory body established in 1954, is equipped with 10 medium-wave transmitters (up to 5kW) and FM transmitters in Suva and Lautoka.

Programmes are broadcast in English for 110 hours a week, in Hindustani (54½ hours a week) and in Fijian (38 hours a week). They include news bulletins, BBC (UK) relays and transcriptions, as well as commercial advertising. Schools broadcasts are transmitted for 4½ hours a week.

FILM

Most of the features shown are of USA, UK or Indian origin. Newsreels are also imported from the USA and the UK. There are 24 35mm and 11 16mm fixed cinemas.

The Education Department maintains a film library and lends films free of charge to schools, organizations and clubs. It has a mobile unit for educational film shows in schools and villages. The government's Public Relations Office and certain commercial companies have mobile film units which organize film shows of general interest for audiences in rural areas.

FRENCH POLYNESIA

Population	121 000
Area	4000 sq. km.

PRESS
Newspapers	Dailies 4

RADIO
Transmitters	Long/medium-wave 1, Short-wave 4
Total receivers	62 000 estimated in use
Receivers per 1000 people	512

TELEVISION
Transmitters	4
Receivers	12 000 estimated in use
Receivers per 1000 people	99

FILM
Cinemas	Fixed 10
Total seating capacity	4000
Seats per 1000 people	33

PRESS

Three French-language dailies and one English-language daily are published in Papeete, the capital of Tahiti. There are also 10 periodicals (in French, Tahitian and English) with a total circulation of 10 700 copies.

NEWS AGENCIES

There is no local agency. AFP maintains a correspondent in Papeete who supplies news to the local mass media.

RADIO

Radio Tahiti, a regional station of the Office de Radiodiffusion-Télévision Française (ORTF) financed by government subsidies and advertising revenue, operates 1 medium-wave transmitter of 20kW and 4 short-wave transmitters (including 1 experimental) of 4 and 20kW which are on the air for 63 hours a week, over 70% of programmes being of local origin Languages used are French and Tahitian.

No receiver licence fee is payable.

TELEVISION

The television service, also a regional unit of ORTF, broadcasts for 24½ hours a week from four transmitters, bringing 30% of the population within reception range. Some 60% of programmes are received from ORTF in Paris.

Receivers are not licensed.

FILM

One short entertainment film was produced in 1970. Features are imported mainly from France and the USA and are shown in 10 fixed cinemas, five of these being in Tahiti and the rest in Moorea and outlying islands. In Tahiti, there is a drive-in cinema which accommodates 424 cars and has an annual attendance of 200 000 persons. There are also several mobile cinema units.

GILBERT AND ELLICE ISLANDS

Population	57 000
Area	886 sq. km.

PRESS

Newspapers	Non-dailies 3
Total circulation	Non-dailies 2800
Copies per 1000 people	Non-dailies 49

RADIO

Transmitters	Long/medium-wave 2
Total receivers	8000 estimated in use
Receivers per 1000 people	140

FILM

Cinemas	Fixed 2
Total seating capacity	1600
Seats per 1000 people	28
Total annual attendance	200 000*
Annual visits per capita	3

*For fixed and mobile cinemas.

PRESS

Three weekly bulletins carrying domestic and world news are published by the government (on Tarawa Island) in the English, Gilbertese and Ellice languages. There are also four church periodicals with a total circulation of 7000 which carry some general news.

RADIO

The Gilbert and Ellice Broadcasting Service (Radio Tarawa), a government department financed by government subsidy and advertising revenue, operates two 10kW medium-wave transmitters which are on the air for 41 hours a week, broadcasting in the English, Gilbertese and Ellice languages and reaching 98% of the population.

Programmes consist mainly of arts, letters and sciences (16 hours a week), light entertainment (12 hours), news and information (8½ hours), broadcasts for special audiences (2 hours), advertising (1 hour 10 minutes) and education (1 hour). Programmes, 70% of which are locally originated, also include BBC (UK) transcriptions.

FILM

A short entertainment film was made in 1970. All films are imported, mostly of USA and UK origin, and are shown by two fixed 16mm cinemas and five mobile units. The Government Information Office occasionally shows documentary and educational films.

GUAM

Population	100 000
Area	549 sq. km.

PRESS

Newspapers	Dailies 2, Non-dailies 7
Total circulation	Dailies 17 000
Copies per 1000 people	Dailies 170

RADIO

Transmitters	Long/medium-wave 1
Total receivers	100 000 estimated in use
Receivers per 1000 people	1000

TELEVISION

Transmitters	2
Receivers	42 000 estimated in use
Receivers per 1000 people	420

FILM

Cinemas	Fixed 25
Total seating capacity	8500
Seats per 1000 people	85
Total annual attendance	500 000
Annual visits per capita	5

PRESS

One morning and 1 evening paper appear in English, which is the official language. Of the 7 non-dailies, 5 are published in English and 2 in Chamorro, the most widely used native language. One of the Sunday papers circulates 14 800 copies. There are 14 other periodicals (13 in English, 1 in Chamorro) with a total circulation of 28 000.

NEWS AGENCIES

AP and UPI maintain correspondents on the island. The dailies receive the services of both these agencies, as well as syndicated news features from the USA.

RADIO

Radio Guam, which is privately owned and derives revenue from advertising, broadcasts 125 hours a week — in English, Chamorro, Tagalog, Illocano and Visayan — with one 10kW medium-wave transmitter. Music programmes and hourly news bulletins predominate. Eighteen hours a week are locally produced.

TELEVISION

Guam Television, under the same private ownership as Radio Guam, also derives its revenue from commercial advertising. It broadcasts, in colour, for 15 hours a day, on one main channel from Agaña, with translators on five channels to ensure complete coverage of Guam.

An educational station, KGTF Television – also based in Agaña – broadcasts child, youth and adult educational and cultural programmes.

No licence fee is payable for receivers.

FILM
All films shown by the 26 fixed cinemas, one drive-in (250 cars) and 32 mobile units are imported, mainly from the USA and the Philippines.

SPACE COMMUNICATIONS
A Pacific Intelsat earth station was opened at Pulantat in December 1969.

NAURU

Population	7000
Area	21 sq. km.

PRESS	
Newspapers	Non-dailies 1
Total circulation	Non-dailies 950
Copies per 1000 people	Non-dailies 136

RADIO	
Transmitters	Long/medium-wave 1

FILM	
Cinemas	Fixed 3
Total seating capacity	1000
Seats per 1000 people	143

PRESS
There is one weekly newspaper.

RADIO
The government-owned Nauru Broadcasting Service, with one medium-wave transmitter (0.13kW), is the main source of news and covers the entire population. Programmes are broadcast in Nauruan and English for 42 hours a week and include relays of Radio Australia.

No licence fee is payable.

FILM
The three fixed cinemas show about 300 imported feature films a year mostly received through Australia and Hong Kong.

NEW CALEDONIA

Population	107 000
Area	19 000 sq. km.

PRESS

Newspapers	Dailies 1, Non-dailies 10
Total circulation	Dailies 7000, Non-dailies 7500
Copies per 1000 people	Dailies 65, Non-dailies 70

RADIO

Transmitters	Long/medium-wave 2, Short-wave 2
Total receivers	17 000 estimated in use
Receivers per 1000 people	159

TELEVISION

Transmitters	6*
Receivers	800 estimated in use
Receivers per 1000 people	7

FILM

Cinemas	Fixed 4
Total seating capacity	3000
Seats per 1000 people	28
Total annual attendance	700 000
Annual visits per capita	6

*Including 4 auxiliary transmitters.

PRESS

The daily morning paper and the non-dailies (three of which appear twice weekly) are published in French only, in the capital, Nouméa. There are five other periodicals with a total circulation of 4500.

NEWS AGENCIES

There is no local agency. AFP has a correspondent in Nouméa, who supplies overseas news to the local mass media.

RADIO

Radio Nouméa, a regional station of the Office de Radiodiffusion-Télévision Française (ORTF), operates one medium-wave transmitter (20kW) and three short-wave transmitters (up to 20kW). Programme time, totalling 67 hours a week, includes arts and letters (19 hours), advertising (18 hours), light entertainment (17 hours), news (10 hours) and education (1 hour). A large proportion of programme material comes from ORTF in Paris.

Receivers are not licensed, but the station is financed to a large extent from advertising revenue in addition to government subsidies.

TELEVISION

The television service, also a regional unit of ORTF, operates main transmitters and four auxiliaries giving a population coverage of 58%. Broadcasts total 25 hours a week, including light entertainment (10 hours), news (9 hours), arts and letters (4 hours) and advertising (2 hours). ORTF programmes are imported from Paris.

Receivers are not licensed.

FILM

There is no local production. Some 300 features and 50 short films are imported yearly, mostly from France and the USA. Two drive-ins, which together accommodate 1500 cars, attract more than half the total annual audiences. There are two mobile units.

NEW HEBRIDES

Population	84 000
Area	14 763 sq. km.

PRESS
Newspapers	Non-dailies 5
Total circulation	Non-dailies 5700
Copies per 1000 people	Non-dailies 68

RADIO
Transmitters	Long/medium-wave 1, Short-wave 1
Total receivers	9000 estimated in use
Receivers per 1000 people	107

FILM
Cinemas	Fixed 5
Total seating capacity	3000
Seats per 1000 people	36
Total annual attendance	200 000*
Annual vistis per capita	2*

*For fixed and mobile cinemas.

PRESS
There is no daily press. Non-daily papers (which include 3 officially sponsored English news bulletins) are published in French (1 weekly with 1500 copies), in Bislama or pidgin English (2 with 800 copies), in English and Bislama (1 with 2800 copies) and in English and French (1 with 600 copies). Periodicals include 6 in English and 2 in French, as well as a number of mission and school news-sheets in English or French.

RADIO
The New Hebrides Broadcasting Service, in which the British and French services of the Anglo-French Condominium Administration share equally, operates Radio Vila with one 2kW short-wave transmitter and one 1kW medium-wave transmitter, broadcasting for 22½ hours a week and covering 95% of the population. Programmes, in English, French and pidgin English, consist of light entertainment (12 hours), news and information (8½ hours), broadcasts for special audiences (45 minutes), cultural broadcasts (30 minutes), education (30 minutes, in pidgin English only) and advertising (15 minutes). Imported programmes account for 6 hours a week.

There is no licensing system: some broadcasting revenue is derived from advertising.

FILM
No films are produced; 350 features are imported annually, mainly from the USA, France, the UK and Australia. These are shown in five fixed cinemas and by three mobile 16mm units. Annual attendance for all cinemas totals 200 000.

NEW ZEALAND

Population	2 910 000
Area	268 675 sq. km.

PRESS

Newspapers	Dailies 40, Non-dailies 103
Total circulation	Dailies 1 067 000
Copies per 1000 people	Dailies 367

RADIO

Transmitters	Long/medium-wave 56, Short-wave 2
Total receivers	2 050 000 estimated in use
Receivers per 1000 people	704

TELEVISION

Transmitters	7*
Receivers	726 032 estimated in use
Receivers per 1000 people	249

FILM

Cinemas	239
Total seating capacity	143 969
Seats per 1000 people	49

*Main transmitters.

PRESS

The country's largest dailies, accounting for over 70% of the total daily circulation, are the morning and evening papers of the four main city centres: Auckland (2 dailies circulating 223 000 and 135 000 copies respectively), Wellington (2 dailies, one with 78 000 copies on weekdays rising to 100 000 on Sundays, and the other with 95 000 copies), Christchurch (2 dailies with 68 500 and 67 000 copies) and Dunedin (2 dailies with 41 000 and 30 000 copies). While only one of these major dailies has a separate Sunday edition, most have special magazine-type weekly (usually Saturday) supplements. Of the remaining dailies published in 31 smaller cities and towns, 3 have circulations of between 20 000 and 50 000 copies, and a further dozen between 10 000 and 20 000. Most are independently owned papers, over 75% having been founded before the turn of the century. Publishing groups, including overseas interests, have financial interests in a few of the larger papers.

Over the last ten years (during which time the population has increased by 16%), the number of dailies published has decreased by 2 while the overall circulation has increased by around 10%, though the ratio of copies per 1000 inhabitants has dropped from 406 to 367.

Non-dailies, with a total circulation estimated at above 1.5 million copies per issue, include 25 papers appearing two or three times a week and 55 weeklies, 4 of the latter (including the Sunday edition of a Wellington daily and 2 other Sunday papers) having nation-wide readerships.

More than 1500 periodicals are published (502 of them monthly), printing a total of 32 million copies a year (circulation figures per issue are not available). Besides 350 school magazines and papers and 150 parish magazines, they include 170 titles dealing with law, public administration, etc., 150 dealing with agriculture, fisheries, etc., another 150 dealing with technology, 130 dealing with religion and theology, 120 on sports and entertainments, 110 on architecture, arts, etc., and 100 general readership journals. All are in English, except a few publications partly or entirely in Maori. Newspapers and journals from Australia, the UK and the USA are imported, to the value of some $NZ 4 million annually. Highest circulations are recorded for the New Zealand Broadcasting Corporation's weekly journal carrying radio and television programmes (133 000 copies per issue), and for several women's magazines.

Newsprint production is of the order of 211 000 metric tons annually, about 50% of which is exported.

NEWS AGENCIES

The main source of both national and foreign news for the country's newspapers and broadcasting stations is the New Zealand Press Association (NZPA), a cooperative owned by New Zealand newspapers, and itself (like AAP, of Australia), a co-owner of Reuters (UK). NZPA has its headquarters in Wellington and branch offices in Melbourne (Australia) and London. It receives Reuter's world service and other overseas news from AP and UPI, as well as from its own correspondents.

RADIO

The New Zealand Broadcasting Corporation (NZBC), a statutory public body set up by Act of Parliament in 1961, is at present responsible for all television and sound broadcasting in the country, except for a certain number of recently established privately owned radio stations. A three-member Broadcasting Authority, set up in 1969, allots warrants to broadcast to both NZBC and private operators, regulates overall programme balance. in consultation with the NZBC, and monitors programme standards, accuracy and impartiality of news, etc.

A proposed new structure, adopted in 1973, is to replace the NZBC by three separate corporations (TV-1, TV-2 and Radio New Zealand), and the Broadcasting Authority by a Broadcasting Council of New Zealand, the latter with additional responsibilities — among which will be overall financing and the operation of common services including a central broadcast-news service.

Public radio broadcasting began in 1926 and a government commercial service was added in 1936, both services combining in 1943 to form what is now the NZBC. NZBC's national programme, of general interest, is broadcast over a national non-commercial network of medium-wave transmitting stations based in Wellington (100kW) with other main stations in Auckland, Christchurch and Dunedin (20kW each) all of which are on the air for 24 hours a day, and is also carried by 11 other regional stations broadcasting, for 17 hours a day, a combination of relays and their own locally originated programmes. (During parliamentary sessions, the main Wellington station braodcasts the debates from the House of Representatives, and its programmes are taken over by a standby station.) A second link of 4 stations in the four main centres broadcast mainly concert-type evening programmes with some theatre and spoken programmes. All programmes are in English, with some bulletins in Maori.

NZBC's commercial stations, located in 30 city and smaller centres, serve local communities with frequent news bulletins, light entertainment and advertising, for 17 or 18 hours daily. In addition, 5 privately owned stations in Auckland (2 stations), Hamilton, Whakatane and Dunedin, also carry popular music, news and advertising (a further 2 private stations are planned).

Despite mountainous terrain in many parts of the country, it is estimated that more than 98% of the population are covered by at least one radio station.

Overall programme output of NZBC stations consists of 5860 hours a week (all but 500 hours of which are domestically produced), the main content categories being light entertainment (3707 hours), news and information (713 hours), broadcasts for special audiences (450 hours, including 322 women's and 85 religious programmes), arts, letters and science (397 hours), advertising (380 hours) and education (215 hours, including 111 for adults and 73 for schools).

Private stations broadcast some 830 hours a week (over 600 hours of which are imported programmes), consisting mainly of entertainment (654 hours), news and information (84 hours) and advertising (57 hours).

Since 1971, no licence fee has been payable for radio receivers. Production of radio sets in New Zealand amounted to 117 600 units in 1971, and television sets to 49 000.

External broadcasting is carried out by Radio New Zealand, with two 7.5kW short-wave transmitters in Wellington. Programmes, including relays of home services, are beamed to the Pacific Islands, Australia and south-east Asia for 36 hours a week, plus a 30-minute programme on Sundays for scientific personnel in Antarctica. All broadcasts are in English, except for weekly or fortnightly 30-minute broadcasts in Samoan, Rarotongan and Niuean.

TELEVISION

Following experimental broadcasts from Auckland in 1959, a regular television service (625 lines) was established in June 1960. By 1973, 83% of the country's households had television receivers, and 93% of the population were within reach of one of NZBC's national network of 450 television transmitters (potential coverage rises to 99% if the 350 repeaters of less than 0.5kW owned by viewers' societies, individuals or NZBC are considered).

At present, a single common programme – to be converted to colour (PAL system) in late 1973 – is broadcast by all stations from 14.00 to 19.20 hours local time, after which, parallel programmes are broadcast in each of the four main viewing areas, from Auckland, Wellington, Christchurch and Dunedin. Of the 65 hours of weekly programme time, about 49 hours are accounted for by imported material, including 20 hours of series, 15 hours of long films and 8 hours of children's programmes – 60% of imports come from the USA and most of the rest from the UK.

A typical week's programming consists of light entertainment (32 hours), news and information (19 hours), broadcasts for special audiences (8½ hours, including 5 for children), education (2 hours), advertising (40 minutes) and arts, letters and science (30 minutes). Commercial advertising is broadcast on four days a week with no more than three breaks (6 minutes) in an hour. A pilot scheme for introducing an educational television service, beginning with broadcasts for primary schools, is under consideration.

Under the proposed new structure for broadcasting in New Zealand (see under Radio), a second network (also colour) run by a second independent public corporation will be introduced in October 1974 with the same mixture of commercial and non-commercial programming, though not on the same days of the week as the first channel, to avoid simultaneous programmes competing for the same audience.

FILM

No feature films have been produced in recent years. The country's two production studios, one government-owned and one private. make about 20 short films a year (16 entertainment and 3 documentaries were made in 1972).

Annual imports of feature films totalled 323 in 1972, coming from the USA (140), the UK (54), Italy (24), Greece (22), India (17), France (16), Mexico (9), the Federal Republic of Germany (9) and others (32). In the same year, short films were imported from the USA (6) and the UK (3), and Mexico, the Federal Republic of Germany, Canada and Australia (1 each).

Cinemas, which numbered 545 in 1961, with 40.6 million paid admissions annually, now total barely half that number (215 35mm plus 24 16mm cinemas), with annual attendances (in 1969) of only 14.3 million. Closures have been largely in rural areas where both the programmes of fixed cinemas and weekly showings by itinerant operators have been discontinued. There are 13 cinemas equipped for the exhibition of 70mm films. A film industry board represents exhibitors, distributors and government departments. Both distributors and exhibitors must be licensed under the terms of the Cinematograph Films Act, 1961, which is administered by the Department of Internal Affairs.

Films are also shown in film clubs and societies, in most of the larger towns, and in schools and other educational organizations. The National Film Library — a branch of the Department of Education — holds over 8000 titles. and issues up to 7500 reels weekly on loan. mostly to schools and colleges.

SPACE COMMUNICATIONS

A Pacific Intelsat earth station, owned and operated by the New Zealand Post Office, was opened at Warkworth, north of Auckland, in July 1971.

PROFESSIONAL TRAINING AND ASSOCIATIONS

The University of Canterbury, Christchurch, has had a one-year (professionally oriented) post-graduate diploma course in journalism since 1969. Mass communications courses at second- and third-year level are in the BA (political science) syllabus at Victoria University, Wellington, while the University of Otago, Dunedin, offers some mass media studies in the Departments of Education, Anthropology and Political Science.

Press organizations include a newspaper publishers' association (founded in 1898, and now with 45 members) and a national journalists' association — both of which jointly set up a press council in 1972, to deal with complaints about the press and to strive to maintain press freedom. Film organizations include national associations of distributors, and exhibitors, and a federation of (licensed) projectionists.

NIUE

Population	5000
Area	259 sq. km.

PRESS

Newspapers	Non-dailies 1
Total circulation	Non-dailies 800
Copies per 1000 people	Non-dailies 160

RADIO

Transmitters	Long/medium-wave 1
Total receivers	800 estimated in use
Receivers per 1000 people	160

FILM

Cinemas	Fixed 1
Total seating capacity	120
Total annual attendance	6000
Seats per 1000 people	24
Annual visits per capita	1

PRESS

A weekly official bulletin published in English and Nuiean prints 800 copies per issue.

RADIO

The Niue Government operates one medium wave transmitter (0.25kW) which is on the air for 25 hours a week in English and Niuean, broadcasting light entertainment (18 hours), news and information (6 hours), educational programmes (30 minutes), etc. Population coverage is practically 100%.

No receiver licence fees are charged, all broadcasting expenses being met from public funds.

FILM

A few feature films and about 70 shorts are imported, mostly from the USA and the UK, and are shown in the island's one fixed cinema or by a mobile projection unit.

NORFOLK ISLAND

Population	2000
Area	36 sq. km.

PRESS	
Newspapers	Non-dailies 1
Total circulation	Non-dailies 850
Copies per 1000 people	Non-dailies 425

RADIO	
Transmitters	Long/medium-wave 1
Total receivers	1050 estimated in use
Receivers per 1000 people	525

FILM	
Cinemas	Fixed 1
Total seating capacity	100
Total annual attendance	8000
Seats per 1000 people	50
Annual visits per capita	4

PRESS

A weekly newspaper in English circulates 850 copies.

RADIO

The Norfolk Island Broadcasting Service, owned by the administration and under the technical direction of the Australian Post Office, operates one medium-wave transmitter (0.05kW) and is on the air for 16½ hours a week in English, broadcasting educational programmes (7½ hours), broadcasts for special audiences (4½ hours), news (4¼ hours) and advertising (20 minutes). Territorial coverage is 100%.

There is no receiver licensing system. Some 500 receivers are in use.

FILM

The island's one fixed 16mm cinema records an annual attendance of 8000, many of whom are tourist visitors.

PACIFIC ISLANDS

Population	107 000
Area	1779 sq. km.

PRESS

Newspapers	Non-dailies 6
Total circulation	Non-dailies 4400
Copies per 1000 people	Non-dailies 41

RADIO

Transmitters	Long/medium-wave 6
Total receivers	48 000 estimated in use
Receivers per 1000 people	449

TELEVISION

Transmitters	3
Receivers	3000 estimated in use
Receivers per 1000 people	28

FILM

Cinemas	Fixed 19
Total seating capacity	4500
Total annual attendance	461 000
Seats per 1000 people	42
Annual visits per capita	4

PRESS

Six non-dailies make up the press in this United Nations trust territory, consisting of the widely scattered Caroline, Mariana and Marshall Islands, administered by the USA. Two papers appear two or three times a week in English/Ponapean and English/Trukese respectively: 3 appear weekly in English only, English/Marshallese and English/Palapauan respectively: and 1 appears twice monthly in English/Yapese. Another periodical of 9000 circulation is published two or three times monthly.

NEWS AGENCIES

Founded by the Trust Territory Government in 1968, the Micronesian News Service (MNS) serves 3 newspapers, 6 radio stations and 1 television station from its bureau at Saipan (Marianas). Some 2000 words of domestic news are supplied daily, in English, by radio teletype and air mail. Features and photos are occasionally provided. UPI serves a radio and a television station.

RADIO

Six publicly owned, medium-wave transmitters (1kW each) give 85% population coverage. Frequencies are assigned by the Federal Communications Commission (USA). Broadcasts, which total 756 hours a week, include light entertainment (576 hours), news and other information (115 hours), programmes for special audiences (50 hours) and education (12 hours). Some 48 000 radio receivers are in use.

There is no licensing system for radio or television.

TELEVISION

Three public transmitters in Saipan, with a total power of 0.15kW, give 10% population coverage. Broadcasts, which total 33 hours a week, include news and information (14 hours), light entertainment (13 hours), education (3 hours) and programmes for special audiences (2 hours). Of the weekly total, 4 hours are of local origin.

FILM

All films shown are imported, mainly from the USA.

PAPUA NEW GUINEA

Population	2 481 000
Area	461 691 sq. km.

PRESS

Newspapers	Dailies 1, Non-dailies 1
Total circulation	Dailies 14 000, Non-dailies 4500
Copies per 1000 people	Dailies 6, Non-dailies 2

RADIO

Transmitters	Long/medium-wave 2, Short-wave 20
Total receivers	100 000 estimated in use
Receivers per 1000 people	40

FILM

Cinemas	Fixed 13
Total seating capacity	7305
Seats per 1000 people	3

PRESS

A daily newspaper in English and a weekly in pidgin English are published in Port Moresby, the administrative centre of this former United Nations trust territory which attained independent status in 1973.

Periodicals total 88 titles with a combined circulation of 339 500 copies. Subject categories include general information (29 titles circulating 84 000 copies, including a Department of Information fortnightly in English and pidgin English circulating over 14 000 copies), education (10 titles, 165 700 copies), religion (14 titles, 45 800 copies), entertainment (4 titles, 15 700 copies), sociology (19 titles, 8000 copies), agriculture and medical sciences. The majority appear in English, a number in the two linguae francae, pidgin English and Police Motu, and others in various vernaculars.

RADIO

General responsibility for broadcasting is exercised by the Department of Information and Extension Services but actual broadcasting operations are conducted both by the Administration of Papua and New Guinea and by the Australian Broadcasting Commission (ABC). These two were merged into the Papua New Guinea Broadcasting Commission on 30 November 1973.

The Administration, with short-wave transmitters at Port Moresby, Rabaul, Daru, Wewak and Milne Bay (each 10kW), Goroka, Mount Hagen, Keita-Bougainville, Madang and Lae (each 2kW) and Kerema (0.25kW), broadcasts especially to local indigenous audiences both in the vehicular languages (English, pidgin English and Police Motu) and in 15 vernaculars (Tolai, Toaripi, Orokolo, Kerowo, Kiwai, Gogodala, Gahuku, Kafe, Enga, Medlpa, Mid-Wahgi, Wedau, Susu, Dobu and Misima), potentially reaching some 1 380 000 listeners in their own languages. Programmes include agricultural and general educational broadcasts, technical information, news, etc., of local and specialized interest, as well as relays from the central station in Port Moresby which consist mainly of news and information read slowly in English, and other programmes in pidgin English. Broadcasting times vary from 2 to 9 hours daily.

ABC operates a national network consisting of 1 medium-wave and 2 short-wave transmitters at Port Moresby broadcasting for 18 hours a day, 1 medium-wave transmitter at Rabaul broadcasting for over 14 hours a day and 1 short-wave transmitter each at Goroka, Lae and Madang broadcasting for 18 hours a day. The medium-wave stations are both 2kW, and the short-wave 10kW. ABC programmes, with their wide coverage, consist largely of information and entertainment-type programmes presented in English, pidgin English, Police Motu and Kuanua.

Programme categories for all stations, based on a 130-hour broadcasting week, include light entertainment (65½ hours), news and information (32 hours), education (11 hours), broadcasts for special audiences (10½ hours), arts, letters and science (8 hours) and advertising (3½ hours). About 95% of the population are potentially covered by radio services.

No licence fee is payable for receivers.

FILM

Film production consists of short documentaries (13 titles in 1969). Imported films are shown in 13 fixed cinemas, one drive-in (with accommodation for 420 cars and an annual attendance of 188 000 persons) and 23 mobile units.

TOKELAU ISLANDS

Population	2000
Area	10 sq. km.

RADIO

Radio is the only communications medium in the group (apart from imported printed matter). There are no local transmitters but broadcasts from Apia, Western Samoa, are readily received. Schools are equipped with receivers in order to benefit from the Western Samoa Education Department's daily educational broadcasts.

TONGA

Population	90 000
Area	699 sq. km.

PRESS
Newspapers	Non-dailies 2
Total circulation	Non-dailies 3800
Copies per 1000 people	Non-dailies 42

RADIO
Transmitters	Long/medium-wave 2
Total receivers	Licences 9000
Receivers per 1000 people	10

FILM
Cinemas	Fixed 5
Total seating capacity	3600
Seats per 1000 people	40

PRESS

An illustrated weekly is published under government sponsorship at Nukualofa, capital of the islands. Three thousand copies appear in Tongan and 800 in English (42 copies per 1000 of the population). Other periodicals are published by Church missions. There is no news agency.

RADIO

The government-sponsored Tonga Broadcasting Commission operates two medium-wave transmitters (10kW each) which give complete territorial coverage. Revenue is derived from advertising and from broadcasting personal messages.

The commission broadcasts for 60 hours a week. Programmes, which are in Tongan and English, with some Fijian and Samoan, include light entertainment (33 hours), news and information (12 hours), advertising (6 hours), educational broadcasts (5 hours), broadcasts for special audiences (5 hours) and broadcasts for ethnic minorities (2 hours). About half the programmes are of domestic origin.

TELEVISION

There is no television.

FILM

Feature films are imported, mainly from the USA and the UK. In addition to the five fixed cinemas, there are six mobile projection units. Projectors from fixed cinemas are also used periodically to show entertainment and documentary films in the villages.

WESTERN SAMOA

Population	143 000
Area	2842 sq. km.

PRESS

Newspapers	Non-dailies 3
Total circulation	Non-dailies 50 000
Copies per 1000 people	Non-dailies 350

RADIO

Transmitters	Long/medium-wave 1
Total receivers	32 000 estimated in use
Receivers per 1000 people	244

TELEVISION

Receivers	75 estimated in use
Receivers per 1000 people	0.5

FILM

Cinemas	Fixed 13
Total seating capacity	4500
Seats per 1000 people	31
Total annual attendance	471 000
Annual visits per capita	3

PRESS

There are no daily newspapers, but one weekly circulates 8000 copies and two other non-dailies with a combined circulation of 42 500 copies appear less frequently, giving a ratio of 350 copies of non-daily papers per 1000 inhabitants. All three papers are bilingual in English and Samoan, these being the two official languages. One is a government publication (fortnightly) issued free.

NEWS AGENCIES

There is no local agency. The New Zealand Press Association has a part-time correspondent at Apia, the capital, through whom the press is supplied with overseas news.

RADIO

The government-controlled Samoa Broadcasting Service, with a 10kW medium-wave transmitter at Apia, is on the air for 105 hours a week in Samoan and English, broadcasting news and information (36 hours), light entertainment (26 hours), educational programmes (14 hours), programmes for special audiences (14 hours), advertising (10 hours) and cultural programmes (6 hours). About 12 hours a week are of local origin.

A receiver licensing system is in force but there are many unlicensed sets in use. The estimated total is 32 000 (244 sets per 1000 inhabitants).

TELEVISION

Although there is no local television service, 60% of the population are within receiving range of transmitters in neighbouring American Samoa which broadcast 80% educational programmes.

FILM

All films shown are imported, mainly from the USA and the UK. Three fixed cinemas are equipped for 35mm and nine for 16m projection and, along with a drive-in accommodating 200 cars, record a total annual attendance of 471 000. There is also a mobile projection unit.

PART EIGHT

USSR

Union of Soviet Socialist Republics

UNION OF SOVIET SOCIALIST REPUBLICS

Population	245 090 000
Area	22 402 200 sq. km.

PRESS

Newspapers	Dailies 639, Non-dailies 8055
Total circulation	Dailies 81 633 000, Non-dailies 59 083 000
Copies per 1000 people	Dailies 333, Non-dailies 241

RADIO

Transmitters	3034
Total receivers	105 300 000
Receivers per 1000 people	430

TELEVISION

Transmitters	1466
Receivers	45 400 000
Receivers per 1000 people	185

FILM

Cinemas	Fixed 147 200
Total annual attendance	4 569 000 000*
Annual visits per capita	19*

*For both fixed and mobile cinemas.

PRESS

Although Russian is the official language throughout the Soviet Union, it is at the same time only the second language for many of the country's inhabitants who live outside the RSFSR (capital, Moscow). Each of the 14 other union republics has its own official language, and the newspapers published by official bodies are printed both in that language and in Russian. The majority, however, are printed in the most widely used language. Newspapers, including many published at factories, collective farms, state farms, state institutions and higher educational establishments, appear in 57 languages of the USSR, including those of nationalities which did not have a written language before the revolution (Chuvash, Nogai, Kalmuck, etc.).

The daily press has shown a rapid development in recent years. In 1970, 608 morning daily and 31 evening daily papers were published (as against 444 and 13 respectively in 1960), with a total print run per issue of 81.6 million copies in 1970 (as against 39.4 million in 1960). The 3 largest dailies are the official organs of the Central Committee of the Communist Party (circulating 9 million copies per issue), of the Supreme Soviet (8.4 million copies) and of the Central Committee of the Young Communist League (7.7 million copies). Special editions of the main Moscow papers are also printed in district publishing houses using matrices flown direct from Moscow

A total of 8694 daily and non-daily newspapers of all types were published in 1970; among these were 3739 newspapers appearing twice or thrice weekly. Daily and other newspapers are also published in the republics, areas, regions and districts, and about 100 are published in the autonomous republics and areas. Local newspapers and journals are printed in small towns and rural centres. The main languages of publication are Russian, Ukrainian, Byelorussian, Kazakh, Uzbek, Georgian, Lettish, Moldavian, Lithuanian, Azerbaijan, Armenian, Kirghiz, Tajik, Turkmen, Estonian, Bashkir, Tartar, Udmurt, Chuvash, Yakut and Mari; newspapers and journals are also published in other languages of the USSR and in nine foreign languages.

The press is regarded as the tribune of the people. For example, newspapers carry many reports by industrial or agricultural correspondents assessing or criticizing the achievements of industrial and agricultural undertakings, etc. Numerous letters from readers are also published.

A feature of the periodical press continues to be the increasing number of weekly magazines for women, designed particularly for women agricultural and industrial workers. One of the country's major newspapers publishes an illustrated Sunday magazine (founded in 1960) containing stories, articles on various amateur activities, home management, etc. The total number of copies of periodicals printed in the Soviet Union has increased considerably since around 1960, when 4121 titles were published with a total annual circulation of 872.4 million copies. By 1970, there were 5969 periodicals printing a total of 2675 million copies annually. These include 1204 magazines printing 1995.3 million copies a year, 62 leaflets with 31.9 million copies a year, 2307 scientific journals with 65.8 million copies a year and 2396 bulletins with 582 million copies a year.

Soviet periodicals are published in many languages. In 1970, 4913 periodicals were published in Russian and 915 in other languages of the USSR; 141 publications appeared in a total of 23 foreign languages, including German, English, Arabic, Chinese, French, Hindi, Hungarian, Japanese, Urdu and Serbo-Croat.

National newsprint production amounted to 1 150 000 metric tons in 1970, of which 247 700 metric tons were exported.

NEWS AGENCIES

The central news agency of the Soviet Union, Telegrafnoie Agentsvo Sovetskovo Soyuza (TASS), comes under the direction of the Council of Ministers of the USSR. The managing board consists of a Director-General nominated by the Council of Ministers, his four deputies, the editors-in-chief of the six principal departments and the head of the communications control office.

The main departments of the head office in Moscow are foreign news, home news, home news for abroad, foreign news broadcasts, home news broadcasts and photo news. There is also a sports news department, an observer's group, a reference department, a communications control office, an international relations department and a general management department. There are about 2000 people on the permanent staff.

TASS has its own correspondents in Moscow and in all regional and provincial centres and major industrial and cultural centres throughout the RSFSR. It has branch offices in Leningrad, Vladivostock, Khabarovsk, Novosibirsk, Irkutsk and Rostov-on-Don which gather news for the agency and relay news from Moscow to nearby towns.

In the union republics, the telegraph agencies of the Ukraine, Byelorrussia, Uzbekistan, Kazakhstan, Georgia, Azerbaijan, Lithuania, Moldavia, Latvia, Kirghizia, Tadshikistan, Armenia, Turkmenistan and Estonia act as joint TASS correspondents. The total number of TASS correspondents in the Soviet Union, including correspondents of the republic agencies, is more than 500.

The agency's network of foreign correspondents has increased in recent years. It now has 100 departments and correspondence points abroad, employing 180 correspondents. The most important department, in the capitals of the socialist countries and in New York, Washington, London, Paris, Bonn, Stockholm, Helsinki and Cairo, are linked with headquarters in Moscow by a two-way, round-the-clock teleprinter service.

TASS receives information from the agencies of all the socialist countries and from AFP, Reuters, AP and UPI, Kyodo and Jiji, DPA and other national agencies in 50 countries. All the world agencies, the agencies of the socialist countries, and agencies and information services throughout Europe, Asia, Africa and Latin America receive information from TASS. Teleprinter links – leased duplex cable lines or one-way radio-teleprinter channels – are used for the exchange of information.

TASS's photo service in the USSR, including the photo services in the republics, employs 370 correspondents. Urgent photos from Moscow are transmitted to all the capitals of the union republics, to the large towns of the Russian Federation and to destinations abroad by cable links and by radio. Up to 150 items of Soviet and foreign photo news are sent out for the press every day.

TASS has about 10 000 subscribers among which are 3700 newspapers, 50 radio and 83 television stations. About 300 foreign subscribers (70 agencies, 100 newspapers and a number of radio and television companies) receive the full TASS service direct from the agency. Subscribers receive up to 120 000 words daily of general news in Russian, English, French, German, Spanish and Arabic, and also, through the various public information agencies, in the languages of all the union republics. Sports, scientific, technical, economic and commercial information and articles are also supplied on request. News services are transmitted by teleprinter, by direct line and by radio, and also by post in the form of bulletins.

TASS is financially self-supporting, its sole source of revenue being the payments it receives for its services, the rates for which are fixed by agreement between the agency and its subscribers, both in the Soviet Union and abroad.

The Soviet Union's second agency, Novosti (APN), was founded in 1961 by the Union of Journalists of the USSR, the Union of Writers of the USSR, the Union of Soviet Societies for Friendship and Cultural Relations with Foreign Countries and the USSR Society for the Dissemination of Political and Scientific Knowledge. Its headquarters are in Moscow and it has 40 domestic branch offices, as well as bureaux and representatives in many foreign countries.

Novosti's services, for which it draws on the talents of more than 7000 eminent writers and public figures, both in the Soviet Union and abroad, include a daily press bulletin, nine specialized bulletins, features commentaries, interviews, talks, items, essays, reports, photographs, radio and television programmes and other material dealing with political, economic, social and cultural affairs in the USSR and reflecting Soviet public opinion on major world issues. Other material is designed to inform Soviet readers of life and conditions in other countries. Printed books and albums, colour slides and other publications are produced by the agency, either alone or in collaboration with publishing houses abroad.

Subscribers and users of Novosti material in 110 countries include over 100 national and international agencies, 120 publishing houses, more than 100 broadcasting organizations and more than 7000 foreign newspapers and journals published in 65 languages. Radio-telegraphic and telex communications are maintained with 150 localities in 80 countries.

RADIO

All broacasting in the USSR, both radio and television, is state operated. Both to further the development of broadcasting and to place it under centralized management, an edict of the Presidium of the Supreme Soviet was issued on 12 July 1971, transforming the Radio and Television Committee of the USSR Council of Ministers into a Union Republic State Committee of the USSR Council of Ministers (Article 70). The chairman of the State Television and Radio Committee of the USSR Council of Ministers thus becomes a member of the Government of the USSR.

No dues are levied for the use of television and radio receivers, the expenses of the State Television and Radio Committee of the USSR Council of Ministers being met by a subsidy from the state budget and by income from announcements and information services, the sale of television and radio programmes, public concerts, etc.

Radio and television broadcasts are made from Moscow, the capitals of all the union and autonomous republics, and from territory and district centres. Local responsibility for broadcasts is vested in television and radio committees, of which there are 14 in the union republics and some 140 in the autonomous republics and their districts and in other territories and districts. operating 10 main area, 200 municipal and 2824 regional radio broadcasting offices. Of the Soviet Union's 105.3 million radio receivers (at the end of 1972), some 52 million are linked to 32 400 wired redistribution networks. Efforts are being made to extend both wired and wireless radio coverage, particularly in rural districts.

The Central Radio Service from Moscow broadcasts seven programmes, all in Russian, via radio stations using long, medium, short and ultra-short waves (FM), the total listening time being 990 hours a week.

The first programme is broadcast on a nation-wide network and is relayed for 20 hours a day by all local radio stations and retransmission networks. Information programmes cover national, foreign and international affairs, including news bulletins, talks and commentaries, broadcasts entitled 'International diary', 'International observers at a round table', 'In the vanguard of world progress', 'The earth and its people' (a daily radio journal dealing with agricultural production and featuring scientists, agronomists and animal specialists), programmes for young people and literary, musical and children's broadcasts.

The second is a 24-hour programme known as 'Mayak' (The Beacon) broadcasting 48 news bulletins a day covering home and foreign affairs and, for the rest of the time, music and light entertainment.

The third programme, on the air for 17 hours daily is of a general educational character, including literature and music, and is designed to attract the widest possible audiences. The bulk of the programme material consists of stage productions; drama and music; portraits of authors, playwrights, composers and actors; studio concerts and direct transmissions from concert halls.

The fourth (FM) programme is a music, literature and drama programme designed to promote knowledge and aesthetic appreciation of the best works and performances in those fields. It is on the air for 8 hours daily (13 hours on Saturdays and Sundays).

The fifth programme is a 24-hour sociopolitical, news and music programme intended for Soviet citizens working abroad and includes transmissions beamed to Soviet fishermen and seamen.

The sixth and seventh programmes, designed for listeners in the eastern regions (Far East, Siberia, central Asia and Kazakhstan), are mainly repeats of the first programme, scheduled to allow for time-zone differences.

Cultural and educational programmes occupy a high proportion of broadcasting time. These include the regular festivals of the musical collectives of the All-Union Radio and Television Service, musical evenings of the union republics, radio festivals devoted to the literature and arts of the autonomous republics, and the comprehensive cycles of broadcasts on both radio and television collectively known under the title 'the Lenin University of the millions'. The latter are for listeners studying the fundamentals of politics, history, political economy and philosophy.

The Central Radio Service's weekly programme consists of news broadcasts (13.2%), sociopolitical, economic, scientific, cultural and sports broadcasts (15.5%), plays and literature (9%), broadcasts for children and young people (13.7%), music (39.1%) and other broadcasts (8.5%).

There are broadcasting stations in various republics, territories and regions, as well as in factories and collective and state farms. These operate their own local systems, under the supervision of local television and radio committees, relaying Russian-language programmes from Moscow in addition to their own locally originated programmes in one or other of the 67 national languages of the USSR.

Broadcasts to foreign countries are carried out by the state station, Radio Moscow, which is on the air in 64 foreign languages for a total of 178 hours a day. Its programmes are beamed to Europe, Africa, the Middle East, south and south-east Asia, the Far East, Latin America, and (in English) to Europe, Africa, Australia and New Zealand, south-east Asia and North America. Stations in 10 union republics also broadcast for foreign listeners, for a total of 210 hours a week, in 10 national and 10 foreign languages.

Another radio station — Peace and Progress — operated by Soviet public organizations, broadcasts to Europe, Asia, Australia, Africa, the Near and Middle East and Latin America in 14 languages and dialects.

Radio programmes are at present exchanged with 79 countries. These exchanges are mostly carried out under intergovernmental agreements, cultural and scientific cooperation arrangements and various broadcasting agreements and working protocols. At present, the State Television and Radio Committee of the USSR Council of Ministers has 39 long-term agreements with foreign radio and television organizations, and the USSR is a member of the International Radio and Television Organization.

In addition to recorded programmes, including many musical works, foreign radio organizations regularly receive teletyped copies of political, economic and cultural news-broacast items arranged in systematic order and translated into the appropriate languages. At their request, some of these organizations get same-day wired comments, statements and reports on major domestic and foreign-policy events in the USSR and on the economic, scientific and cultural progress of the Soviet people. The State Television and Radio Committee also produces some programmes in conjunction with foreign broadcasting organizations. Some of these exchanges and coproductions are associated with reciprocal visits of journalists and other broadcasting personnel under the auspices of the State Committee.

TELEVISION

Television, like radio broadcasting, is state operated. It is also controlled by the State Television and Radio Committee of the USSR Council of Ministers. The first telecasts in the Soviet Union were made in 1931 and stations began operating regularly in Moscow and Leningrad in 1938. A third station, in Kiev, was commissioned in 1951.

At the end of 1972, the Soviet Union had around 300 main stations and over 1100 relay stations, all using 625-line definition and transmitting either the programmes of the Central Television Service or locally originated material. Over the last ten years, the number of studios producing their own programmes has increased from 60 to 127. The largest and most advanced installation is the new Ostankino television centre, the first section of which was opened in 1967 on the fiftieth anniversary of the Soviet State. It is designed as a single complex equipped for all phases of programme production and transmission.

The Central Television Service in Moscow broadcasts five programmes which are on the air for a total of almost 33 hours a day.

The first programme, planned for multinational and international viewing, is transmitted by means of both cable and radio-relay links to almost all parts of European USSR and to parts of central Asia and certain districts in Siberia. Broadcasting information, sociopolitical, cultural and educational programmes it is on the air for an average of 10 hours 10 minutes a day. News and journalistic broadcasts deal with all important social and political events at home and abroad and include on-the-spot reports, statements by scientists. leading government officials and prominent persons in industry. reports from agencies and correspondents, radio and cable relays, and national and international newsreel and filmed material including daily exchanges with Intervision member countries and exchanges under agreements with foreign broadcasting organizations.

Regular first-programme features include 'Time', a daily broadcast on current events in the Soviet Union; the twice-weekly television round table, 'Current economic affairs'; a popular science series entitled 'Health'; the weekly 'Cine-travellers' club'; the arts programmes, 'Talks on literature', 'Theatrical encounters'. 'Masters of the cinema', 'Teletheatre', 'TV cinema', 'Musical kaleidoscope', 'Musical kiosk'; an hour-long Saturday broadcast, twice a month, entitled 'Television atlas of the peoples of the USSR', and the monthly Intervision journal 'Progress' showing the latest achievements in science and technology in the USSR and other countries. There are also numerous sports broadcasts and special programmes for workers in agriculture and for children, youth and women.

The second programme, on the air for 5¾ hours a day, serves Moscow and the surrounding area. Among its large variety of information and feature programmes are 'Moscow News', 'Moscow and Muscovites', 'Youth on the air' and cultural and instructive broadcasts such as 'Round the museums and exhibitions' and 'Objective'.

The third and fourth programmes are educational. The third, on the air for regular morning and afternoon periods, five days a week, is related to secondary-school and university curricula and to the professional requirements of specialists in the national economy, public health and education; while the fourth, broadcast in the afternoon and early evening, could be described as a cultural and scientific university for the millions. Both of these, like the second programme, can be received in and around Moscow

Finally, the Central Television Service has a special programme for the remoter parts of the Soviet Union which is transmitted via satellite through the Orbita network and phased to take account of the different time zones. Orbita receiver stations have been built in 37 towns in the north, in Siberia, and in the Far Eastern and central Asian regions and in several Molnya 1 communication satellites have already been launched.

The international exchange of radio and television programmes (already referred to under Radio) is effected through Intervision and under various types of agreements. Over the past few years, foreign broadcasting organizations have received thousands of newsreel items from the Soviet Union and a great many television programmes, films and recordings. In 1970, the year of his jubilee, much of this material was devoted to the life and achievements of Vladimir Ilich Lenin.

Regular broadcasts in colour (SECAM system) began in October 1967, and in the following year, the USSR Council of Ministers enacted a decree whereby all parts of the Soviet Union receiving black and white television broadcasts would also be able to receive reliable high-quality colour broadcasts by 1975. At present, a colour programme – broadcast as part of the Central Television Service's first programme – is transmitted from Moscow to 64 towns in the Soviet Union. In addition, Kiev and Tbilisi have their own colour-television services. The problem of transmitting colour programmes via satellite is being studied.

FILM

The film industry in the Soviet Union is nationalized, and responsibility for the development of the cinema is vested in the Cinematography Committee of the USSR Council of Ministers, formed in 1963. The committee controls all the country's film studios producing films for commercial hire or for use by various ministries and government departments. Film studios, each financially autonomous, have been set up in all the union republics. The country has 39 studios in all, the biggest being 'Mosfilm', the M. Gorky studio (Moscow), 'Lenfilm' (Leningrad), the A. P. Dovzhenko studio (Kiev) and 'Gruziya-film' (Tbilisi).

In 1972, 234 long films were produced, consisting of 134 entertainment films (7 in 70mm versions), 36 documentary, news and popular-science films and 64 entertainment films for television. Of the long films, 4 were coproductions with Czechoslovakia (2), Yugoslavia, the German Democratic Republic and Bulgaria; 40% of long films are produced in colour. Short-film production totalled 1263 titles, of which 515 were commissioned documentary, news and popular-science films, 396 documentary and news, 138 educational, 133 general audience popular-science and 81 acted films and animated cartoons.

Most films are released in Russian and dubbed in the languages of the USSR; those produced in the various languages of the Soviet republics are dubbed in Russian. The first stereophonic wide-screen films were made in the 'Mosfilm' studio in 1956. All films projected in cinemas are available for showing on television.

Films imported in 1972 for first-run commercial showing included 92 long films from the following countries: the Democratic Republic of Korea (12% of the total), the German Democratic Republic (9.8%), Czechoslovakia (8.8%), Bulgaria, Poland and Romania (7.6% each), France (6.5%), Egypt, Italy and Yugoslavia (5.4%) and other countries (23.9%). The five documentaries imported were from Chile, France, the Federal Republic of Germany, India and the UK.

The USSR is one of the few countries where the development of television has not been to the detriment of the cinema industry. Over the last ten years or so, the number of cinemas, which stood at 90 500 in 1961, has increased by over 60%, and the annual number of spectators (3957 million in 1962), by 15%. In addition to the 147 400 fixed cinemas (over 130 000 of which are in rural areas), there are 8900 mobile projection units.

SPACE COMMUNICATIONS

The USSR has made considerable progress in the use of communication satellites in the mass media. The Molniya series of communication satellites are used to relay from Moscow to other parts of the USSR both black and white and colour television programmes, as well as radio broadcasts, telegraphic messages, meteorological charts and newspaper-page facsimilies through about 30 ground stations in the Orbita space communication network which was put into service on 7 November 1967 – the date of the fiftieth anniversary of the October revolution.

A successful experiment in colour-television transmission was carried out in November 1965 by means of the Molniya 1 satellite linking Moscow and Paris. Through the Molniya–Orbita network, which is in operation for 16 to 20 hours a day, even remote villages in Siberia and the Soviet Far East are able to see programmes from Moscow.

An international system of communications via satellites, with its corresponding international organization, known as Intersputnik, was set up from Moscow on 15 November 1971. With its headquarters in Moscow, the organization consists of the following member countries: Bulgaria, Cuba, Czechoslovakia, the German Democratic Republic, Hungary, Mongolia, Poland, Romania and the USSR.

The system is being established in three stages: (a) experimental work, up to the end of 1973, on members' earth stations using satellite channels provided by the USSR; (b) use of communication channels on members' satellites under lease, (c) commercial operation, when this is considered economically advisable, using the space segment owned by Intersputnik or rented from its members.

Intersputnik is to cooperate with the International Telecommunications Union and other international organizations with regard to technical operations and international regulations. There will be a governing board representing member countries and a permanent executive and administrative body headed by a Director-General.

PROFESSIONAL TRAINING AND ASSOCIATIONS

Training in journalism consists of (a) degree courses at universities, (b) in-service training of working journalists, through seminars, lectures, etc., essentially within the framework of the Union of Journalists of the USSR, (c) opportunities for further professional qualifications through courses organized by the Union of Journalists and university faculties of journalism.

At tbe beginning of the 1969–70 academic year, 14 300 persons were studying journalism in the USSR, some 2000 having graduated in 1969. There are faculties and departments of journalism at the Universities of Moscow, Leningrad, Sverdlovsk, Irkutsk, Vladivostock, Kazan, Rostov and Voronezh (for the RSFSR); Kiev and Lvov (for the Ukraine); and Vilnus, Riga, Tartu, Minsk, Kishinev, Tblisi, Erevan, Baku, Tashkent, Alma-Ata, Dushanbe and Frunze. In addition, journalism is taught by the Faculty of International Journalism of the Moscow Institute of International Relations. The journalism faculties of some of the larger universities, such as Moscow and Kiev, have special sections for the training of journalists for radio and television.

Apart from passing an entrance examination, candidates must have completed their secondary education and have a natural aptitude for journalism as shown by actual contributions to the printed or broadcast media.

The degree course in journalism lasts 5 (for full-time students) or 6 years (for night-school and correspondence students) and includes a good grounding in Russian and foreign literature, social sciences (in particular the theory of scientific communism) and in Russian and foreign languages. On graduation a standard diploma is awarded.

Most film production specialists are trained at the All-Union State Institute of Cinematography (VGIK), Moscow, and at the Leningrad Institute of Cinematographic Engineering (LIKI). These institutes give technical, literary, artistic and linguistic training. Courses of study last from 4 to 6 years, and the instructors include many well-known film producers and historians of the Soviet film industry.

The professional association for working journalists employed in the mass media is the USSR Union of Journalists, a voluntary public organization whose main activities are raising professional standards, the training and further training of journalists practical studies, the exchange of experience, and assistance for periodicals, radio and television stations, etc. To this end, the union has commissions and sections for the various branches of journalism for professional problems and for relations with foreign colleagues. It issues publications on journalism, and manuals and textbooks for industrial and rural correspondents.

and organizes professional evenings, exhibitions, competitions, seminars, opportunities for the exchange of experiences, etc. It is a member of the International Organization of Journalists.

The 53 000 union members are admitted on an individual basis. The union's highest body is the All-Union Congress. Between congresses, business is managed by a board, while the day-to-day ideological and practical work is the responsibility of the Board's secretariat. The union has regional and provincial branches throughout the Soviet Union, as well as affiliated local unions in the individual republics. Its operations are financed by entrance fees and yearly dues and by its publishing revenues.

APPENDICES

INDEX OF NEWS AGENCIES

By-line	Name of agency	Date of foundation	Headquarters	Country
AA	Agence d'Athènes see ANA			
AA	Anadolu Ajansi see Anatolia			
AANS	Argus African News Service	1957	Salisbury	Rhodesia
AAP	Australian Associated Press	1935	Sydney	Australia
ACAP	Agence Camerounaise de Presse	1960	Yaoundé	Cameroon
ACI	Agence Congolaise d'Information	1962	Brazzaville	People's Republic of the Congo
ACII	Agence Catholique Internationale d'Information	1919	Fribourg	Switzerland
ACIP	Agence Coopérative Interrégionale de Presse	1960	Paris	France
ACP	Agence Centrale Parisienne de Presse	1951	Paris	France
	Aden News Agency		Aden	People's Democratic Republic of Yemen
ADN	Allgemeiner Deutscher Nachrichtendienst	1946	Berlin	German Democratic Republic
ADP	Agence Dahoméenne de Presse	1961	Cotonou	Dahomey
AFP	Agence France-Presse	1944	Paris	France
	Agencia Ecuatoriana de Prensa		Guayaquil	Ecuador
	Agencia Información Centroamericana		Guatemala City	Guatemala

By-line	Name of agency	Date of foundation	Headquarters	Country
	Agencia Informativa Orbe	1952	Santiago	Chile
	Agencia J. B. Serviços de Imprensa	1966	Rio de Janeiro	Brazil
	Agencia Meridional	1931	Rio de Janeiro	Brazil
	Agencia Orbe Latinoamericana	1956	Santiago	Chile
	Agence Vietnamienne d'Information *see* AVI			
Agerpress	Agentia Romana de Presa	1949	Bucharest	Romania
AGI	*see* AGIT			
AGIP	Agence d'Illustrations pour la Presse	1935	Paris	France
AGIT	Agenzia Giornalistica Italia	1950	Rome	Italy
AGP	Agence Gabonaise de Presse	1961	Libreville	Gabon
AIP	Agence Ivoirienne de Presse	1961	Abidjan	Ivory Coast
AKP	Agence Khmère de Presse	1950	Phnom-Penh	Khmer Republic
AMEX	Agencia Mexicana de Noticias	1968	Mexico City	Mexico
AMP	Agence Madagascar Presse	1962	Tananarive	Malagasy Republic
AN	Agencia Nacional	1946	Rio de Janeiro	Brazil
ANA	Athens News Agency (Agence d'Athènes)	1905	Athens	Greece
Anatolia	Anadolu Ajansi	1920	Ankara	Turkey
ANI	Agencia de Noticias e de Informaçoes	1947	Lisboa	Portugal
ANIM	Agence Nationale d'Information du Mali	1961	Bamako	Mali
ANKA	ANKA Ajansi	1973	Ankara	Turkey
ANP	Algemeen Nederlands Persbureau	1934	The Hague	Netherlands
ANS	Agencia Noticiosa Saporiti	1900	Buenos Aires	Argentina

ANSA	Agenzia Nazionale Stampa Associata	1945	Rome	Italy
Antara	Lembaga Kantoberita Nasional Antara	1937	Djakarta	Indonesia
AP	Associated Press	1848	New York	USA
AP Ltd	Associated Press Ltd	1939	London	UK
APA	Austria Presse Agentur	1946	Vienna	Austria
APN	see Novosti			
APP	Agence Parisienne de Presse	1949	Paris	France
APP	Associated Press of Pakistan	1949	Karachi	Pakistan
APS	Agence de Presse Sénégalaise	1959	Dakar	Senegal
APS	Algérie Presse Service	1961	Algiers	Algeria
APV	Agence de Presse Voltaïque	1963	Ouagadougou	Upper Volta
AR	Agencja Robotnicza		Warsaw	Poland
	Argus Press	1937	Rio de Janeiro	Brazil
	Asapress	1942	Rio de Janeiro	Brazil
ASCA	Associated Catholic Press	1970	Rome	Italy
	Associated News (Malta) Ltd	1968	Valletta	Malta
ATA	Albanian Telegraph Agency	1945	Tirana	Albania
ATP	Agence Tchadienne de Presse	1964	Fort-Lamy	Chad
ATS	Agence Télégraphique Suisse	1894	Berne	Switzerland
AUP	Australian United Press	1932	Sydney	Australia
AVI	Agence Vietnamienne d'Informations	1945	Hanoi	Democratic Republic of Vietnam
AZAP	Agence Zaïre Presse	1960	Kinshasa	Zaire
Bakhtar	Bakhtar News Agency	1939–40	Kabul	Afghanistan
Belga	Agence Belga	1920	Brussels	Belgium
Bernama	Pertubohan Berita Nasional Malaysia	1967	Kuala Lumpur	Malaysia
BNA	Bangladesh News Agency	1972	Dacca	Bangladesh
BPI	Bangladesh Press International	1972	Dacca	Bangladesh
BTA	Bulgarska Telegrafitscheka Agentzia	1898	Sofia	Bulgaria
	Budapresse			Hungary

By-line	Name of agency	Date of foundation	Headquarters	Country
CAF	Centralna Agencja Fotograficzna	1950	Warsaw	Poland
CBS–News	Columbia Broadcasting System's news-film service		New York	USA
	Centro de Información Católico		Lima	Peru
CETEKA	see CTK			
Chung Yang	see KCNA			
CID	Centro de Información y Documentación	1965	Buenos Aires	Argentina
CIP	Centre d'Information de Presse	1934	Brussels	Belgium
	Colombia Press	1955	Bogota	Colombia
COPER	Agencia Noticiosa Corporación de Periodistas	1948	Santiago	Chile
CP	Canadian Press	1917	Toronto	Canada
CPS	Correspondance Politique Suisse	1917	Berne	Switzerland
CTK	Československá Tisková Kancelář	1918	Prague	Czechoslovakia
DIA	Documentation and Information for and about Africa	1956	Kinshasa	Zaire
DMT	Dimitag	1938	Bonn	Federal Republic of Germany
Donghwa	Donghwa News Agency	1956	Seoul	Republic of Korea
DPA	Deutsche Presse-Agentur	1949	Hamburg	Federal Republic of Germany
DPA–E– TE–S	DPA's television newsfilm service			
	East–West News Agency		Rome	Italy
	Eastern India News Agency	1960	Calcutta	India

Efe	Economic News Agency	1949	Seoul	Republic of Korea
	Agencia Efe	1938	Madrid	Spain
ENA	Eastern News Agency	1972	Dacca	Bangladesh
ENA	Ethiopian News Agency	1941	Addis Ababa	Ethiopia
EPD	Evangelischer Pressedienst	1908	Frankfurt	Federal Republic of Germany
E–TE–S	see DPA–E–TE–S			
EXTEL	Exchange Telegraph Company	1872	London	UK
Fides	Agencia Internazionale Fides	1927	Rome	Italy
	Gemini News Service		London	UK
GNA	Ghana News Agency	1957	Accra	Ghana
HA	Haber Ajansi	1963	Istanbul	Turkey
	Hapdong News Agency	1945	Seoul	Republic of Korea
	Hindustan Samachar	1948	New Delhi	India
Hsinhua	Hsinhua (New China) News Agency	1937	Peking	China
	Hsin Ya News Agency		Hong Kong	Hong Kong
IANA	Inter-African News Agency	1964	Salisbury	southern Rhodesia
IFA	Irish Features Agency		Dublin	Ireland
IKA	IKA Ajansi	1954	Ankara	Turkey
INA	Iraqi News Agency	1959	Baghdad	Irak
INA	Israel News Agency	1923	Tel Aviv	Israel
Inbel	Institut Belge d'Information et de Documentation	1942	Brussels	Belgium
INFA	Indian News and Feature Alliance	1959	New Delhi	India
	Informex	1960	Mexico City	Mexico
	Inter Prensa		Buenos Aires	Argentina
	Inter Press Service		Rome	Italy
	International News Service			Hong Kong
	International Press Agency of Iran	1960	Tehran	Iran
	Interpress		Bogota	Colombia

By-line	Name of agency	Date of foundation	Headquarters	Country
Interpress	Polska Agencja Interpress *see* PAI			
IPA	Indian Press Agency	1957	New Delhi	India
ITIM	Itonut Israel Meougnedet	1950	Tel Aviv	Israel
Jiji	Jiji Press	1945	Tokyo	Japan
JNA	Jordan News Agency	1969	Amman	Jordan
JP	Jajasan Pena News Agency	1969	Djarkarta	Indonesia
JTA	Jewish Telegraphic Agency	1919	New York and London	USA, UK
KCNA	Korean Central News Agency (Chung Yang Tong Shin)	1949	Pyongyang	Democratic Republic of Korea
	Keystone Photographic Agency	1920	New York, London, Paris	USA, UK, France
–	Kimon	–	–	Cyprus
KNA	Katholische Nachrichten-Agentur	1952	Bonn	Federal Republic of Germany
KNA	Kenya News Agency	1963	Nairobi	Kenya
KNP	Katholiek Nederlandsch Persbureau	1947	The Hague	Netherlands
Kyodo	Kyodo Tsushin (Kyodo News Service)	1945	Tokyo	Japan
	Lao Press	1950	Vientiane	Laos
Latin	Agencia Latinoamericana de Información	1969	Buenos Aires	Argentina
LNA	Liberation News Agency		Hanoi	Democratic Republic of Vietnam
LNA	Libyan News Agency	1965	Tripoli	Libyan Arab Republic
Logos	Agencia Logos	1928	Madrid	Spain
Lusitania	Agencia Noticiosa Portuguesa Lusitania	1944	Lisbon	Portugal

MANA	Malawi News Agency	Blantyre	1966	Malawi
MAP	Mahgreb Arabe Presse	Rabat	1959	Morocco
MENA	Middle East News Agency	Cairo	1955	Arab Republic of Egypt
Mencheta	Agencia Mencheta	Madrid	1882	Spain
MNS	Micronesian News Service	Saipan	1968	Pacific Islands
Montsame	Mongol Tsahilgaan Medeeniy Agentlag	Ulan Bator	1957	Mongolia
MTI	Magyar Tavirati Iroda	Budapest	1881	Hungary
NAB	News Agency of Burma	Rangoon	1963	Burma
	National News Service	Manila	1955	Philippines
NCNA	New China News Agency *see* Hsinhua			
NCNS	National Catholic News Service	Washington	1930	USA
Newstrust	Press Trust of Sri Lanka Ltd	Colombo	1951	Sri Lanka
NFI	News Features of India	Bombay	1953	India
NNA	National News Agency (Wakalat Al Anbaa Al-Wataniyah)	Beirut	1964	Lebanon
Nordpress	Nordpress Verlag	Hamburg	1948	Federal Republic of Germany
	Noticias Aliadas			Peru
	Noticias Argentinas	Buenos Aires	1973	Argentina
	Notimex	Mexico City	1968	Mexico
Novosti	Agenstvo Pečati Novosti (APN)	Moscow	1961	USSR
NTB	Norsk Telegrambyrå	Oslo	1967	Norway
NZPA	New Zealand Press Association	Wellington	1879	New Zealand
OP	Orient Press	Seoul	1952	Republic of Korea
	Orbe Press	–		Brazil
OSI	Office of Samoan Information	Pago Pago		American Samoa
PA	Press Association	London	1868	UK
PAI	Polska Agencja Interpress	Warsaw	1966	Poland

By-line	Name of agency	Date of foundation	Headquarters	Country
PANA	Pan Asia Newspaper Alliance	1949	Hong Kong and Tokyo	Hong Kong and Japan
Pananews	*see* PANA			
PAP	Polska Agencja Prasowa	1944	Warsaw	Poland
Pars	Pars News Agency	1938	Tehran	Iran
PEVE	Prensa Venezolana	1940	Caracas	Venezuela
	Philippine Press International	1962	Manila	Philippines
PIP	Paris Internationale Presse	1886	Paris	France
PNS	Philippine News Service	1949	Manila	Philippines
PPI	Pakistan Press International	1956	Karachi	Pakistan
	Pragopress (feature service of CTK)		Prague	Czechoslovakia
PRELA	Prensa Latina, Agencia Informativa Latino-americana	1959	Havana	Cuba
	Presseplan		Bonn	Federal Republic of Germany
Presorient	*see* OP			
	Producciones del Ecuador		Quito	Ecuador
PRYC	Agencia Noticiosa Prensa, Radio y Cine	1945	Santiago	Chile
PTI	Press Trust of India	1949	Bombay	India
Pyresa	Prensa y Radio Español	1940	Madrid	Spain
–	Radio Press	1945	Tokyo	Japan
RB	Ritzaus Bureau	1866	Copenhagen	Denmark
Reuters	Reuters	1850	London	UK
Ritzau	*see* RB			

Abbreviation	Full name	City	Year	Country
RNS	Religious News Service	New York	1962	USA
RSS	Rastriya Sambad Samiti	Kathmandu	1970	Nepal
	Saba News Agency	Sana'a	1961	Arab Republic of Yemen
	Samachar Bharati			India
SANA	Syrian Arab News Agency	Damascus	1965	Syria
	Sanop News Agency	Seoul		Republic of Korea
SAPA	South African Press Association	Johannesburg	1938	South Africa
	Sisa News Agency	Seoul		Republic of Korea
SIC	Servicio Informativo Continental	Buenos Aires	1959	Argentina
Sofiapres	Sofia Press Agency	Sofia	1967	Bulgaria
SONNA	Somalia National News Agency	Mogadishu	1964	Somalia
SP	Servicio Nacional de Prensa	Bogota	1958	Colombia
STT–FNB	Suomen Tietotoimisto–Finska Notisbyrån	Helsinki	1887	Finland
SUNA	Sudan National News Agency	Khartoum	1955	Sudan
	Sun Telephoto	Tokyo		Japan
	Taloudellineor Tietotoimisto	Helsinki	1947	Finland
Tanjug	Telegrafska Agencija Nova Jugoslavija	Belgrade	1943	Yugoslavia
TAP	Tunis–Afrique–Presse	Tunis	1961	Tunisia
TASS	Telegrafnoie Agentzvo Sovetskovo Soyuza	Moscow	1925	USSR
Tatrapress	Slovak Cultural and Tourist News Agency	Bratislava	1968	Czechoslovakia
Telam	Telenoticiosa Americana	Buenos Aires	1945	Argentina
THA	Türk Haberler Ajansi	Istanbul	1950	Turkey
TP	Teleprensa	Bogota	1957	Colombia
	Trade News Service	Seoul		Republic of Korea
TRP	Transpress	Rio de Janeiro	1958	Brazil
TT	Tidningarnas Telegrambyrå	Stockholm	1921	Sweden
	Työväen Sanomalehtien Tietotoimisto	Helsinki	1920	Finland
UNI	United News of India	New Delhi	1961	India

By-line	Name of agency	Date of foundation	Headquarters	Country
	United Newspaper Agency			Hong Kong
UP	United Press International of Canada		Montreal	Canada
	Ultra Prensa		Bogota	Colombia
UPB	United Press of Bangladesh	1972	Dacca	Bangladesh
UPI	United Press International	1958	New York City	USA
UPITN	United Press International Television News (newsfilm service)		New York and London	USA and UK
UPP	United Press of Pakistan	1949	Karachi	Pakistan
	Uutiskeskus/Maaseutulehtien Liitto		Helsinki	Finland
	Vietnam Thong Tin Xa *see* VNA			
	Visnews (newsfilm service)	1957	London	UK
VNA	Vietnam News Agency	1946	Hanoi	Democratic Republic of Vietnam
VP	Vietnam Press	1951	Saigon	Republic of Vietnam
VWD	Vereinigte Wirtschaftsdienste	1949	Frankfurt	Federal Republic of Germany
	Wakalat Al Anbaa Al-Wataniyah *see* NNA			
	Wireless News Agency	1961	Manila	Philippines
ZANA	Zambia News Agency	1969	Lusaka	Zambia

BIBLIOGRAPHY

In addition to the reference works and periodicals listed below, source material consulted in the preparation of this book included reports and surveys dealing with communications media in individual countries, issued by official services, media organizations, etc.

GENERAL

Advertising and Press Annual of Africa, 1972, National Publishing Company, Cape Town (Annual)

Africa Contemporary Record, Annual Survey and Documents, 1971–2, Collings, London (Annual)

African Recorder. A Fortnightly Record of African Events with Index, United India Press, New Delhi, 1970– (Loose-leaf)

Africa, 71/72, Jeaune Afrique Paris (Annual)

Annuaire de la Presse et de la Publicité, SJEM Edition de l'Annuaire de la Presse, Paris

Art of the Cinema in Ten European Countries, Council of Europe, Council for Cultural Cooperation, Strasbourg, 1967

Asian Recorder. A Weekly Digest of Asian Events with Index, United Indian Press, New Delhi 1972– (Loose-leaf)

Ayer Directory of Publications, 1972, Ayer Press, Philadelphia (Annual)

BBC Handbook, 1973, British Broadcasting Corporation, London (Annual)

Broadcasting Yearbook, 1972, Broadcasting Publications, Washington, DC, (Annual)

Editor and Publisher International Yearbook, Editor and Publisher Co., New York (Annual)

Education for Journalism in Latin America, Institute of International Education, Council on Higher Education in the American Republics, New York, 1970

Emery, W. B. *National and International Systems of Broadcasting. Their History, Operation and Control*, Michigan State University Press, East Lansing, 1969

Europa Year-Book, 1973, A World Survey, Europa, London (Annual)

Film Daily Yearbook of Motion Pictures, 1971, Quigley, New York (Annual)

Fundación Konrad Adenauer, Instituto de Solidaridad Internacional ISI. *Problemas de la teleducación latinoamericana (IV Seminario latinoamericano para directores de teleducación, Septiembre 1970*, Mexico, 1970

—— *Sociología y pedagogía de teleducación (IV Seminario latinoamericano para profesores de teleducación, Marzo–Abril 1970)*, Lima, 1970

—— III *Seminario latinoamericano para directivos de teleducación (Junio–Julio 1969)*, Lima, 1969

García Jimenez, J. *Televisión educativa para América Latina*, Instituto Latinoamericano de la Comunicación Educativa, ILCE, Mexico, 1970

Hachten, W. A. *Muffled Drums. The News Media in Africa*, Iowa State University Press, Iowa, 1971

Handbook of News Agencies, International Organization of Journalists, Prague 1969– (Loose-leaf)

Handbuch der Weltpresse, Münster Universität, Institut für Publizistik, 1970, 2 vols

Hennebelle, G. *Les Cinémas africains en 1972*, Société Africaine d'Édition. Dakar, Paris, 1972

How to listen to the World, 1972, Hvidovre (Denmark), World Radio–TV Handbook, 1971

Internationales Handbuch für Rundfunk und Fernsehen, 1971/72, Hamburg University, Hans-Bredow Institut für Rundfunk und Fernsehen, 1972

International Motion Picture Almanac, 1972, Quigley, New York (Annual)

International Television Almanac, 1972, Quigley, New York (annual)

Keesing's Contemporary Archives. Weekly diary of World Events, Keesing's, Bristol 1972– (Loose-leaf)

Lent, John A. *The Asian Newspapers' Reluctant Revolution*, Iowa State University Press, Iowa, 1971

Merrill, J. C., Bryan, C. R. and Alisky, M. *The Foreign Press, a Survey of the World's Journalism*, Louisiana State University Press, Baton Rouge, 1970

Newspaper Press Directory, 1973, Benn, London (Annual)

Paulu, B. *Radio and Television Broadcasting on the European Continent*, University of Minnesota Press, Minneapolis, 1967

Sadoul, G. *Histoire du Cinéma mondial, des Origines à nos Jours*, Flammarion, Paris 1968

South American Handbook, 1972, Trade and Travel, London (Annual)

Statesman's Year-Book, Macmillan, London (Annual)

Szalai, A. *The United Nations and the News Media*, Unitar (United Nations Institute for Training and Research), New York, 1972

Television Factbook, 1970–1, Television Digest, Washington, DC (Annual)

Television. New Broadcasting Techniques and Cultural Development, Council of Europe, Committee for Out-of-School Education and Cultural Development, Strasbourg 1972 (Series including the following titles: *Programme Distribution in the Present-Day World; Satellite Broadcasting in Europe; Audiovision for Information and Entertainment; Evolution of the Public Television Networks; New Techniques for the Dissemination of Culture)*

Ulrich's International Periodicals Directory, Bowker, New York, 15th edition, 1973–74

Willing's Press Guide 1973, Skinner, Croydon (Annual)

World of Learning, Europa, London (Annual)

World Radio–TV Handbook 1973, Hvidovre (Denmark) (Annual)

PERIODICALS

ABU Newsletter, Asian Broadcasting Union, Sydney (Monthly)

Actualité radiophonique et télévisuelle dans le monde, Office de Radiodiffusion-Télévision Française, Direction des Affaires Extérieures et de la Coopération, Paris (Monthly)

Broadcasting, Broadcasting Publications Inc., Washington (Weekly)

Campaign (incorporating *World's Press News*), Haymarket Publishing, London (Weekly)

Carta Informativa del CREFAL, Centro de Educación fundamental para el Desarrollo de la Comunidad en América Latina, Pátzcuaro (Bi-monthly)

Combroad, Commonwealth Broadcasting Conference Secretariat, London (Quarterly)

La Correspondance de Presse, Bérard-Quelin, Paris (Daily)

Democratic Journalist, International Organization of Journalists, Prague (Monthly)

EBU Review, Administrative Office of the European Broadcasting Union, Geneva (Bi-monthly)

Editor and Publisher, Editor and Publisher Co., New York (Weekly)

Educational Broadcasting International, Centre for Educational Development Overseas, Stevenage, Herts (Quarterly)

Fiej − Bulletin, Fédération internationale des Éditeurs de Journaux et Publications, Paris (Quarterly)

Gazette. International Journal for Mass Communication Studies, Uitgeversmaatschappij Kluwer BV, Deventer (Netherlands) (Quarterly)

IFJ Information, International Federation of Journalists, Brussels (Quarterly)

Interstages, Institut Belge d'Information et de Documentation, Brussels (Monthly)

IPI Report, International Press Institute, Zurich (Monthly)

Journalism Quarterly, Association for Education in Journalism, Iowa City

Journal of Broadcasting, Association for Professional Broadcasting Education, Los Angeles (Quarterly)

Movie/TV Marketing, Tokyo (Monthly)

OIRT Information, International Broadcasting and Television Organization, Prague (Monthly)

Presse Actualité, Paris (Monthly)

Radio Télévision OIRT, Organisation Internationale de Radiodiffusion et Télévision, Prague (Bi-monthly)

Revue internationale du Cinéma, Office Catholique International du Cinéma, Paris (Monthly)

Rundfunk und Fernsehen, Hans Bredow-Institut, Hamburg (Quarterly)

Telecommunication Journal, International Telecommunication Union, Geneva (Monthly)

Television Quarterly, National Academy of Television Arts and Sciences, Syracuse, NY (Quarterly)

UNESCO PUBLICATIONS

A Guide to Satellite Communication, Paris, 1972 (Reports and papers on mass communication)

Bhatt, B. P., Krishnamoorthy, P. V., Marathey. R. and Bourgeois, M. *Radio Broadcasting Serves Rural Development. I Radio Rural Forums spread throughout India. II Training for rural broadcasting in Africa*, Paris, 1965 (Reports and papers on mass communication)

Broadcasting from Space, Paris, 1970 (Reports and papers on mass communication)

Codding, G. A. *Broadcasting without Barriers*, Paris, 1959

Communication in the Space Age. The Use of Satellites by the Mass Media, Paris, 1968

Copyright Bulletin. Review of Information, Paris (Quarterly)

Developing Information Media in Africa. Press, Radio, Film, Television, Paris, 1962 (Reports and papers on mass communication)

Developing Mass Media in Asia. Papers of Unesco Meeting at Bangkok (January 1960), Paris, 1960 (Reports and papers on mass communication)

Essais sur les Mass Media et la Culture, Paris, 1971

Hopkinson, P. *The Role of Film in Development*, Paris, 1971 (Reports and papers on mass communication)

Jongbloed, H. J. L. (Ed.) *Film Production by International Co-operation*, Paris, 1962 (Reports and papers on mass communication)

Léglise, P. *Methods of Encouraging the Production and Distribution of Short Films for Theatrical Use*, Paris, 1962 (Reports and papers on mass communication)

Lewis, S. *Principles of Cultural Co-operation*, Paris, 1971 (Reports and papers on mass communication)

Maddison, J. *Radio and Television in Literacy. A Survey of the Use of the Broadcasting Media in Combating Illiteracy among Adults*, Paris, 1971 (Reports and papers on mass communication)

Mass Media in Society. The Need of Research, Paris, 1970 (Reports and papers on mass communication)

Mass Media in the Developing Countries. A Unesco report to the United Nations, Paris, 1961 (Reports and papers on mass communication)

Mathur, J. C. and Neurath, P. *An Indian Experiment in Farm Radio Forums*, Paris, 1959 (Press, film and radio in the world today)

News Agencies. Their Structure and Operation, Paris, 1953

Professional Associations in the Mass Media. Handbook of Press, Film, Radio, Television Organizations, Paris, 1959

Professional Training for Mass Communication, Paris, 1965 (Reports and papers on mass communication)

Radio and Television in the Service of Education and Development in Asia, Paris, 1967 (Reports and papers on mass communication)

Schramm, W. *Communication Satellites for Education, Science and Culture*, Paris, 1968 (Reports and papers on mass communication)

—— *Mass Media and National Development. The Role of Information in the Developing Countries*, Paris, 1964

Social Education through Television. An All-India Radio–Unesco Pilot Project, Paris, 1963 (Reports and papers on mass communication)

Space Communication and the Mass Media. A Unesco report of the 1963 space communications conference. Paris, 1963 (Reports and papers on mass communication)

Statistics of Newspapers and other Periodicals, Paris, 1959 (Statistical reports and studies)

Studies and Documents on Cultural Policies, Paris, 1969– (22 Individual-country titles published by mid-1973)

Szapiro, J. *The Newspaperman's United Nations. A Guide for Journalists about the United Nations and Specialized Agencies*, Paris, 1961

Television for Higher Technical Education of the Employed. A First Report on a Pilot Project in Poland, Paris, 1969 (Reports and papers on mass communication)

Training of journalists. A World-Wide Survey on the Training of Personnel for the Mass Media, Paris, 1958 (Press, film and radio in the world today)

Unesco Chronicle, Paris (Monthly)

Unesco Courier, Paris (Monthly)

Unesco Statistical Yearbook, Paris (Annual)

Waniewicz, I. *Broadcasting for Adult Education. A Guidebook to World-Wide Experience*, Paris, 1972

World Communications. Press, Radio, Television, Film, Paris, 1966, fourth (revised) edition

World Film Directory. Agencies Concerned with Educational, Scientific and Cultural Films, Paris, 1962 (Reports and papers on mass communication)